T0331689

Handbook of Research on Network Forensics and Analysis Techniques

Gulshan Shrivastava
National Institute of Technology Patna, India

Prabhat Kumar
National Institute of Technology Patna, India

B. B. Gupta
National Institute of Technology Kurukshetra, India

Suman Bala
Orange Labs, France

Nilanjan Dey
Techno India College of Technology, India

A volume in the Advances in Information Security,
Privacy, and Ethics (AISPE) Book Series

Published in the United States of America by
IGI Global
Information Science Reference (an imprint of IGI Global)
701 E. Chocolate Avenue
Hershey PA, USA 17033
Tel: 717-533-8845
Fax: 717-533-8661
E-mail: cust@igi-global.com
Web site: http://www.igi-global.com

Library of Congress Cataloging-in-Publication Data

Names: Shrivastava, Gulshan, 1987- editor.
Title: Handbook of research on network forensics and analysis techniques /
  Gulshan Shrivastava, [and four others], editors.
Description: Hershey, PA : Information Science Reference, [2018]
Identifiers: LCCN 2017028583l ISBN 9781522541004 (hardcover) l ISBN
  9781522541011 (ebook)
Subjects: LCSH: Computer crimes--Investigation. l Computer networks--Security
  measures.
Classification: LCC HV8079.C65 H364 2018 l DDC 363.25/968--dc23 LC record available at https://lccn.loc.
gov/2017028583

This book is published in the IGI Global book series Advances in Information Security, Privacy, and Ethics (AISPE) (ISSN: 1948-9730; eISSN: 1948-9749)

British Cataloguing in Publication Data
A Cataloguing in Publication record for this book is available from the British Library.

For electronic access to this publication, please contact: eresources@igi-global.com.

Advances in Information Security, Privacy, and Ethics (AISPE) Book Series

Manish Gupta
State University of New York, USA

ISSN:1948-9730
EISSN:1948-9749

MISSION

As digital technologies become more pervasive in everyday life and the Internet is utilized in ever increasing ways by both private and public entities, concern over digital threats becomes more prevalent.

The **Advances in Information Security, Privacy, & Ethics (AISPE) Book Series** provides cutting-edge research on the protection and misuse of information and technology across various industries and settings. Comprised of scholarly research on topics such as identity management, cryptography, system security, authentication, and data protection, this book series is ideal for reference by IT professionals, academicians, and upper-level students.

COVERAGE

- Tracking Cookies
- IT Risk
- Risk Management
- Security Information Management
- Global Privacy Concerns
- Cyberethics
- Security Classifications
- Internet Governance
- Technoethics
- Device Fingerprinting

IGI Global is currently accepting manuscripts for publication within this series. To submit a proposal for a volume in this series, please contact our Acquisition Editors at Acquisitions@igi-global.com or visit: http://www.igi-global.com/publish/.

Titles in this Series

For a list of additional titles in this series, please visit: www.igi-global.com/book-series

Critical Research on Scalability and Security Issues in Virtual Cloud Environments
Shadi Aljawarneh (Jordan University of Science and Technology, Jordan) and Manisha Malhotra (Chandigarh University, India)
Information Science Reference • copyright 2018 • 341pp • H/C (ISBN: 9781522530299) • US $225.00 (our price)

The Morality of Weapons Design and Development Emerging Research and Opportunities
John Forge (University of Sydney, Australia)
Information Science Reference • copyright 2018 • 216pp • H/C (ISBN: 9781522539841) • US $175.00 (our price)

Advanced Cloud Computing Security Techniques and Applications
Ihssan Alkadi (Independent Researcher, USA)
Information Science Reference • copyright 2018 • 350pp • H/C (ISBN: 9781522525066) • US $225.00 (our price)

Algorithmic Strategies for Solving Complex Problems in Cryptography
Kannan Balasubramanian (Mepco Schlenk Engineering College, India) and M. Rajakani (Mepco Schlenk Engineering College, India)
Information Science Reference • copyright 2018 • 302pp • H/C (ISBN: 9781522529156) • US $245.00 (our price)

Information Technology Risk Management and Compliance in Modern Organizations
Manish Gupta (State University of New York, Buffalo, USA) Raj Sharman (State University of New York, Buffalo, USA) John Walp (M&T Bank Corporation, USA) and Pavankumar Mulgund (State University of New York, Buffalo, USA)
Business Science Reference • copyright 2018 • 360pp • H/C (ISBN: 9781522526049) • US $225.00 (our price)

Detecting and Mitigating Robotic Cyber Security Risks
Raghavendra Kumar (LNCT Group of College, India) Prasant Kumar Pattnaik (KIIT University, India) and Priyanka Pandey (LNCT Group of College, India)
Information Science Reference • copyright 2017 • 384pp • H/C (ISBN: 9781522521549) • US $210.00 (our price)

Advanced Image-Based Spam Detection and Filtering Techniques
Sunita Vikrant Dhavale (Defense Institute of Advanced Technology (DIAT), Pune, India)
Information Science Reference • copyright 2017 • 213pp • H/C (ISBN: 9781683180135) • US $175.00 (our price)

701 East Chocolate Avenue, Hershey, PA 17033, USA
Tel: 717-533-8845 x100 • Fax: 717-533-8661
E-Mail: cust@igi-global.com • www.igi-global.com

Dedicated to our friends and families for their constant support during the course of this book.

Editorial Advisory Board

List of Contributors

Table of Contents

Section 1
Security in Network, Social IoT and VANET, Denial of Service Attack

Section 2
Cyber Crime and Cyber Forensics

Section 3
Security and Privacy in Big Data Analytics and Machine Learning, Biometrics, Audio Watermarking, and Cryptocurrency

Detailed Table of Contents

Section 1
Security in Network, Social IoT and VANET, Denial of Service Attack

This chapter describes how as world is switching from wired communication to wireless communication, the need of a wireless sensor network (WSN) is increasing. WSNs became very popular due to its wide applications. A WSN is a network of small-in-size sensor nodes which are densely deployed for monitoring a chosen environment. In WSNs, each sensor node detects data and sends it to the base station. These sensor nodes have four basic duties, consisting of sensing, computation, transmission and power. Due to the small size, these sensor nodes are more constrained in terms of computational energy and storage resources. Energy awareness is also an essential design issue for routing protocols in WSNs. The focus of this chapter is to provide an overview of WSNs. In addition, this chapter describes the components of WSNs, its challenges and the classifications of WSNs. This chapter compares the results of LEACH, SEP and TEEN protocols.

This chapter describes how with the rapid increase of internet users, more people have access to global information and communication technology. As a result of which, the issues of using the internet as a global platform for the enabling of smart objects and machines to coordinate, communicate, compute and calculate, gradually emerge. In Mobile Ad-hoc Networks (MANETs) the individual nodes are self-reconfigurable according to the changes of the network topology. Joint effort between portable hubs is more critical because they face major challenges such as powerlessness to work safely while protecting its assets and performing secure steering among hubs. With the existence of malicious nodes, one of the principal challenges in MANETs is to outline powerful security arrangement that can shield MANETs from various routing attacks. This chapter highlights major attacks and control mechanism in MANETs with an intention that it will open directions for researchers to explore more in the field of network security. At the end of this chapter, basic security mechanisms and issues related to emergence of IoT from Mobile networks has been highlighted.

Chapter 3

Day by day technologies for mobile computing growing rapidly and its network security changed according to their need. The attacker always trying to learn some new techniques to break those security walls of the wireless network. To prevent our network from attacker various defense techniques are used. Firewalls and encryption are used to prevent our network from malware but it is not sufficient for protecting the networks. Many researchers implement new architecture and techniques or mechanism that protect and detect malicious node and their activity over the network that is intrusion detection system (IDS). IDS provides security wall and it provides network security as well as it has continuously monitored and taken appropriate action against the threat. In this Chapter, we are trying to explain some network attack that is resolved or detect through intrusion detection system by exploiting the technology or information that available across different layers of the protocol stack in order to improve the accuracy of detection.

Chapter 4

This chapter describes how security is an important aspect in today's digital world. Every day technology grows with new advancements in various areas, especially in the development of web-based applications. All most all of the web applications are on the internet, hence there is a large probability of attacks on those applications and threads. This makes security necessary while developing any web application. Lots of techniques have been developed for mitigating and defending against threats to the web based applications over the internet. This chapter overviews the important region of web application security, by sequencing the current strategies into a major picture to further the future research and advancement. Firstly, this chapter explains the major problem and obstacles that makes efforts unsuccessful for developing secure web applications. Next, this chapter distinguishes three basic security properties that a web application should possess: validation, integrity, accuracy and portray the comparing vulnerabilities that damage these properties alongside the assault vectors that contain these vulnerabilities.

Chapter 5

Rohit Anand, G.B.Pant Engineering College, India
Akash Sinha, National Institute of Technology Patna, India
Abhishek Bhardwaj, G.B.Pant Engineering College, India
Aswin Sreeraj, G.B.Pant Engineering College, India

This chapter deals with the security flaws of social network of things. The network of things (NoT) is a dynamic structure that is basically an interface of real world and virtual world having capabilities of collection and sharing data over a shared network. The social network of things (SNoT) is a versatile way of connecting virtual and real world. Like any other device connected to internet, objects in SNoT are also vulnerable to the various security and privacy attacks. Generally, to secure Social Network of Things in which human intervention is absent, data capturing devices must be avoided. Types of security attacks that are huge threats to NoT as well as SNoT will be discussed in the chapter. The huge collection of information without necessary security measures allows an intruder to misuse the personal data of owner. Different types of attacks with reference to the different layers are also discussed in detail. The best possible potential solutions for the security of devices in SNoT will be considered.

Chapter 6

Mannat Jot Singh Aneja, Thapar University, India
Tarunpreet Bhatia, Thapar University, India
Gaurav Sharma, Université libre de Bruxelles, Belgium
Gulshan Shrivastava, National Institute of Technology Patna, India

This chapter describes how Vehicular Ad hoc Networks (VANETs) are classes of ad hoc networks that provides communication among various vehicles and roadside units. VANETs being decentralized are susceptible to many security attacks. A flooding attack is one of the major security threats to the VANET environment. This chapter proposes a hybrid Intrusion Detection System which improves accuracy and other performance metrics using Artificial Neural Networks as a classification engine and a genetic algorithm as an optimization engine for feature subset selection. These performance metrics have been calculated in two scenarios, namely misuse and anomaly. Various performance metrics are calculated and compared with other researchers' work. The results obtained indicate a high accuracy and precision and negligible false alarm rate. These performance metrics are used to evaluate the intrusion system and compare with other existing algorithms. The classifier works well for multiple malicious nodes. Apart from machine learning techniques, the effect of the network parameters like throughput and packet delivery ratio is observed.

Chapter 7

Prachi, The NorthCap University, India

This chapter describes how with Botnets becoming more and more the leading cyber threat on the web nowadays, they also serve as the key platform for carrying out large-scale distributed attacks. Although a substantial amount of research in the fields of botnet detection and analysis, bot-masters inculcate new techniques to make them more sophisticated, destructive and hard to detect with the help of code encryption and obfuscation. This chapter proposes a new model to detect botnet behavior on the basis of traffic analysis and machine learning techniques. Traffic analysis behavior does not depend upon payload analysis so the proposed technique is immune to code encryption and other evasion techniques generally used by bot-masters. This chapter analyzes the benchmark datasets as well as real-time generated traffic to determine the feasibility of botnet detection using traffic flow analysis. Experimental results clearly indicate that a proposed model is able to classify the network traffic as a botnet or as normal traffic with a high accuracy and low false-positive rates.

Chapter 8
Arushi Arora, Indira Gandhi Delhi Technical University for Women, India
Sumit Kumar Yadav, Indira Gandhi Delhi Technical University for Women, India
Kavita Sharma, National Institute of Technology, Kurukshetra, India

This chapter describes how the consequence and hazards showcased by Denial of Service attacks have resulted in the surge of research studies, commercial software and innovative cogitations. Of the DoS attacks, the incursion of its variant DDoS can be quite severe. A botnet, on the other hand, is a group of hijacked devices that are connected by internet. These botnet servers are used to perform DDoS attacks effectively. In this chapter, the authors attempt to provide an insight into DoS attacks and botnets, focusing on their analysis and mitigation. They also propose a defense mechanism to mitigate our system from botnet DDoS attacks. This is achieved by using a through access list based configuration. The artful engineering of malware is a weapon used for online crime and the ideas behind it are profit-motivated. The last section of the chapter provides an understanding of the WannaCry Ransomware Attack which locked computers in more than 150 countries.

Section 2
Cyber Crime and Cyber Forensics

Chapter 9
Gulshan Shrivastava, National Institute of Technology Patna, India
Kavita Sharma, National Institute of Technology, Kurukshetra, India
Manju Khari, Advanced Institute of Advanced Communication Technologies and Research, India
Syeda Erfana Zohora, Taif University, Saudi Arabia

This chapter describes cyber forensics, also known as computer forensics, which is a subdivision of digital forensic science, relating to evidence detection in computers and digital storage media. The purpose of cyber forensics is the forensically-sound investigation of digital media with the intent to: identify, preserve, recover, analyze, present facts, and opinions; concerning the digital information. Even though it is generally allied with the analysis of cyber-based crimes, computer forensics may also be used in civil proceedings. Evidence composed from cyber forensic analysis is typically subjected to similar procedures and performs as supplementary digital evidence. With these advancements, it was desired that cyber forensics be to protect users and remain citizen-centric. This chapter shows that there is additional research needed to understand the implications of cyber forensic research to improve detection of cyber crimes.

    Saurabh Ranjan Srivastava, Malviya National Institute of Technology, India
    Sachin Dube, Malviya National Institute of Technology, India

This chapter describes how with growing reliance of modern society over internet and web-based services in every nook and corner of our daily lives, the threats of disruption and damage to these services has also evolved at a parallel rate. One of these threats having a potential of severe and life-threatening devastations is 'Cyberterrorism.' Contrasting to non-lethal terms such as 'internet vandalism' and 'hacktivism,' cyberterrorism encompasses a daunting reach to destruction to the fabric of our modern society. Because of its nature, despite its rapid growth, contrary to conventional terror attacks, cyberterrorism still seems distant from creating a direct threat to civilian life and society. Due to this distance, there is a lack of attention and focus on counter mechanisms against cyberterrorism. By applying effective techniques and keeping our eyes open, establishments can go a long way to avert cyberterror attacks and also recover quickly in the occurrence of an attack. The conclusion of this chapter is that additional research is needed to identify the areas in which personal and professional functions on the internet are still vulnerable.

    Aarthee R., VIT University, India
    Ezhilmaran D., VIT University, India

This chapter describes how cybercrime, likewise called computer crime, is any illicit activity that includes a PC or system associated gadget. While numerous magnificent items have been produced to secure our information correspondence frameworks, these items must be upgraded significantly more. What is additionally required more are the individuals who know how to explore PC network security episodes and the individuals who have both investigative gifts and specialized knowledge of how the internet truly functions. This allows for an investigative structure which can withstand attack, alongside information of how the internet functions and the instruments to examine cybercrime apparatus to tell the who, where, what, when, why, and how. Cybercrime apparatus make our work substantially more productive.

    Diana Berbecaru, Politecnico di Torino, Italy

Computer forensic is the practice of collecting, analyzing, and reporting digital evidence in a way that is legally admissible in open court. Network forensics, an offset of computer forensic, is mainly concerned with the monitoring and analysis of network traffic, both local and WAN/internet, in order to identify security incidents and to investigate fraud or network misuse. In this chapter, the authors discuss challenges in creating high-speed network forensic tools and propose NetTrack, a tamper-proof device aimed to produce evidences with probative value via digital signatures for the network traffic. Since digitally signing each IP packet is not efficient, the authors used a specific technique exploiting the Merkle trees to create digital signatures for flows and multicasts and implemented it by using an optimized algorithm for Merkle tree traversal to save space and time. Through experiments, the authors show NetTrack signing is fast as it can produce digital evidence within a short time.

Chapter 13

Asha Joseph, VIT University, India
K. John Singh, VIT University, India

This chapter is about an ongoing implementation of a digital forensic framework that could be used with standalone systems as well as in distributed environments, including cloud systems. It is oriented towards combining concepts of cyber forensics and security frameworks in operating systems. The framework consists of kernel mechanisms for data and event monitoring. The system monitoring is done in kernel mode by various kernel modules and forensic model mapping is done in user mode using the data collected by those kernel modules. Further, the authors propose a crime model mapping mechanism that makes use of rule sets that are derived from common cyber/digital crime patterns. The decision-making algorithm can be easily extended from a node in a computing cluster, to a cloud. The authors discuss the challenges to digital forensics in distributed environment and cloud extensions and provide some case studies where the proposed framework is applied.

Chapter 14

Kavisankar Leelasankar, Hindustan Institute of Technology and Science, India
Chellappan C., GKM College of Engineering and Technology, India
Sivasankar P., National Institute of Technical Teachers Training and Research, India

The success of computer forensics lies in the complete analysis of the evidence that is available. This is done by not only analyzing the evidence which is available but also searching for new concrete evidence. The evidence is obtained through the logs of the data during the cyberattack. When performing analysis of the cyberattack especially the botnet attacks, there are many challenges. First and the foremost is that it hides the identity of the mastermind, the botmaster. It issues the command to be executed using its subordinate, the command and control (C&C). The traceback of C&C itself is a complex task. Secondly, it victimizes the innocent compromised device zombies. This chapter discusses the analysis done in both proactive and reactive ways to resolve these challenges. The chapter ends by discussing the analysis to find the real mastermind to protect the innocent compromised system and to protect the victim system/organization affected by the botnet cyberattack.

Section 3
Security and Privacy in Big Data Analytics and Machine Learning, Biometrics, Audio Watermarking, and Cryptocurrency

Chapter 15

Ramgopal Kashyap, Sagar Institute of Science and Technology, India
Albert D. Piersson, University of Cape Coast, Ghana

The motivation behind this chapter is to highlight the qualities, security issue, advantages, and disadvantages of big data. In the recent researches, the issue and challenges are due to the exponential growth of social media data and other images and videos. Big data security threats are rising, which is affecting the data heterogeneity adaptability and privacy preservation analytics. Big data analytics helps cyber security, but no new application can be envisioned without delivering new types of information, working on data-driven calculations and expending determined measure of information. This chapter demonstrates how innate attributes of big data are protected.

Chapter 16

In order to scrutinize or evaluate an extremely high quantity of an ever-present and diversified nature of data, new technologies are developed. With the application of these technologies, called big data technologies, to the constantly developing various internal as well as external sources of data, concealed correlations between data can be identified, and promising strategies can be developed, which is necessary for economic growth and new innovations. This chapter deals with the analysis of the real-time uses of big data to both individual persons and the society too, while concentrating on seven important areas of key usage: big data for business optimization and customer analytics, big data and healthcare, big data and science, big data and finance, big data as enablers of openness and efficiency in government, big data and the emerging energy distribution systems, and big data security.

Chapter 17

In this information era, big data is revolutionizing business. The data are generated by each and every user from servers, terminals, smart phones, appliances, satellites, and a range of other sensors on vehicles: military, agriculture, and the like. Anything the end users does online can be traced, stored, and analyzed. It is also possible to analyze from various diverse sources such as social media postings, credit card or e-cash purchases, internet searches, mobile phone locations, etc. Users are willing to provide their private information, linked to their real-life identities, in exchange for faster or better digital services. But, the companies yet may not have the fundamental rights of the user from a security perspective. More risks are associated with big data security. The main purpose of this chapter is to explore the security concerns and privacy issues in big data environments.

Big data has great commercial importance to major businesses, but security and privacy challenges are also daunting this storage, processing, and communication. Big data encapsulate organizations' most important and sensitive data with multi-level complex implementation. The challenge for any organization is securing access to the data while allowing end user to extract valuable insights. Unregulated access privileges to the big data leads to loss or theft of valuable and sensitive. Privilege escalation leads to insider threats. Also, the computing architecture of big data is not focusing on session recording; therefore, it is becoming a challenge to identify potential security issues and to take remedial and mitigation mechanisms. Therefore, various big data security issues and their defense mechanisms are discussed in this chapter.

Chapter 19

Hemalatha Jeyaprakash, Thiagarajar College of Engineering, India
KavithaDevi M. K., Thiagarajar College of Engineering, India
Geetha S., VIT University, India

In recent years, steganalyzers are intelligently detecting the stego images with high detection rate using high dimensional cover representation. And so the steganographers are working towards this issue to protect the cover element dependency and to protect the detection of hiding secret messages. Any steganalysis algorithm may achieve its success in two ways: 1) extracting the most sensitive features to expose the footprints of message hiding; 2) designing or building an effective classifier engine to favorably detect the stego images through learning all the stego sensitive features. In this chapter, the authors improve the stego anomaly detection using the second approach. This chapter presents a comparative review of application of the machine learning tools for steganalysis problem and recommends the best classifier that produces a superior detection rate.

Chapter 20

Rohit Anand, G. B. Pant Engineering College, India
Gulshan Shrivastava, National Institute of Technology Patna, India
Sachin Gupta, Vivekananda Institute of Professional Studies, India
Sheng-Lung Peng, National Dong Hwa University, Taiwan
Nidhi Sindhwani, Amity School of Engineering and Technology, India

Digital signal watermarking is an indiscernible and safe transmission of freehold data through host signal that includes immersing into and extrication from the actual host. Some algorithms have been investigated for the strong and secure embedding and extraction of watermarks within the host audio files but they do not yet yield good results in compression and re-sampling. In this chapter, an excellent method is suggested for the compressed wave files that uses random carrier to immerse the watermark in the sequence of an audio signal. The watermark is embedded lucently in audio stream after adaptive differential pulse code modulation (ADPCM) before quantization. The proposed scheme has been implemented and its parameters are compared with the finest auditory watermarking method known. A tool has been used to measure the parameters to produce the results and tabular values. The larger PSNR and smaller BER prove that the suggested scheme is robust.

Chapter 21

Feroz Ahmad Ahmad, Galgotias University, India
Prashant Kumar, GCET Noida, India
Gulshan Shrivastava, National Institute of Technology Patna, India
Med Salim Bouhlel, Sfax University, Tunisia

In this chapter, a digital decentralized cryptocurrency system where transactions are secured by cryptography and are independent of any centralized third party is discussed. The different characteristics of bitcoins and how transactions occur between two bitcoin users along with some facts and examples are also discussed. The rapid internet development facilitates cyber-attacks to all type of online transactions and also to bitcoin network transactions. Some security issues are also discussed in the chapter along with the cyber-crimes and their punishments.

Among various biometric indicators, hand-based biometrics has been widely used and deployed for last two decades. Hand-based biometrics are very popular because of their higher acceptance among the population because of their ease of use, high performance, less expensive, etc. This chapter presents a new hand-based biometric known as finger-knuckle-print (FKP) for a person authentication system. FKP are the images obtained from the one's fingers phalangeal joints and are characterized by internal skin pattern. Like other biometrics discrimination ability, FKP also has the capability of high discrimination. The proposed system consists of four modules: image acquisition, extraction of ROI, selection and extraction of features, and their matching. New features based on information theory are proposed for matching. The performance of the proposed system is evaluated using experiment performed on a database of 7920 images from 660 different fingers. The efficacy of the proposed system is evaluated in terms of matching rate and compromising results are obtained.

Preface

INTRODUCTION

In today's digital world, elevations in various fields mostly in the development of web-based applications are expanding. Almost all these applications are working on the internet, thus there is a maximum possibility of attackers to attack. Therefore, network security is important while working on any application. Many new techniques are developing for mitigating and developing threats to web-based applications over the Internet. The foremost methods of network security and analysis including cybercrime, big data security, and cryptocurrency are used.

Network security when merged with forensic computing leads to a term known as "network forensics" which is a type of digital forensics which aims at the analysis of network traffic of a system for collection of information affecting to the legal evidence related to various security contravention and detection of the intruder.

The inquiry of network that is executed by the network forensic employs the dynamic information characteristic of a system, which turns rapidly with time; hence, it is an important task. The attacker tries to steal the remarkable information from the communication that takes place in the network. The analysis of Network forensic deals with identifying all such endangered operation along with the legitimate law imposition that will be activated after that.

Network Forensic has emerged from a comparatively uncertain tradecraft to an important part of many investigations. Their tools are now used on a regular basis by examiners and analysts within local, state and Federal law implementation; inside the military and other government organizations; and inside the private "e-Discovery" industry. Evolution in forensic research, tools, and process over the past decade have been very triumphant and many in leadership positions now depend on these tools on an efficient base frequently without discerning it. Moreover, there seems to be an extensive belief, strengthen on by depiction in the popular media, those advanced tools, and accomplished practitioners can withdraw actionable information from practically any device that a government, private agency, or even an accomplished individual might encounter. The computer forensic analysis field is as rapidly altering as other security fields. Thus, it became the matter of discussion. Accordingly, these tasks and tools will be the focus of this book.

The major tasks to be performed for implementing network forensics are Network Security, Security in Social IoT and VANET, Denial of Service Attack, Cyber Crime, Cyber Forensic, Big Data Analytics and Machine Learning, Biometric, Audio Watermarking, and Cryptocurrency. These tasks help in securing different types of data used in different fields. In addition, it works over different types of network (i.e., MANET, VANET) and technologies (i.e., SNoT, IoT).

OBJECTIVE OF THE BOOK

This book deliberates the foremost methods of network security and analysis including cybercrime, big data security, and cryptocurrency. Network security when combined with forensic computing gives rise to a term known as network forensics which is nothing but a type of digital forensics which aims at the analysis of network traffic of a system for collection of information pertaining to the legal evidence related to various security breaches and intrusion detection. The network investigations that are performed by it utilize the dynamic information characteristic of a system, which changes rapidly with time; hence, it is a crucial task. The intruder tries to steal the significant information from the communication that takes place in the network. Network forensic analysis deals with identifying all such vulnerable operation along with the legal law enforcement that will be triggered after that. Example: analyzing the chat sessions. Several tools are available for performing network forensics like Wireshark. Another category of network forensics is Wireless forensics that deals with the wireless traffic and its transmission. The use of Voice-over-IP (VoIP) technology plays a crucial role in this.

ORGANIZATION OF THE BOOK

The book consists of 22 chapters that are organized into three sections as shown below. The first section of the book encloses eight chapters that introduced the Network Security, Security in Social IoT and VANET, Denial of Service Attack. The second section contains six chapters concerning Cyber Crime and Cyber Forensic. The third section introduces security and privacy issues in Big Data, Machine Learning for the Security of Big Data, Biometric, Audio Watermarking and Cryptocurrency. A brief description of each of the chapters follows:

Section 1: Security in Network, Social IoT and VANET, Denial of Service Attack

Chapter 1

This chapter describes as world switching from wired communication to wireless communication; the need of wireless sensor network (WSN) is increasing. WSN became very popular due to its wide applications. WSN is a network of small size sensor nodes which are densely deployed for monitoring the environment. In WSN, sensor nodes sense the data and send the data to base station. These sensor nodes consist sensing, computation, transmission, and power as four basic elements. Sensor nodes are more constrained in its computational energy and storage resources. Energy awareness is an essential design issue for routing protocols in WSN. The focus of this chapter is to provide an overview of WSNs. In addition, this chapter describes the components of WSNs, its challenges, and classification of WSN. This chapter compares the results of LEACH, SEP and TEEN protocols.

Chapter 2

This chapter describes a methodical study and survey on various attacks and controls in mobile ad-hoc networks. With the fast increment of web clients, more individuals approach worldwide information and communication innovation, because of which the issues of utilizing the web as a worldwide stage and empowering the keen questions and machines to coordinate, discuss, process and ascertain step-by-step develops. In Mobile Ad-hoc Networks (MANETs) the hubs are self-reconfigurable as per the difference in arranging topology. Joint exertion between versatile center points is more basic because of the way that they confront significant difficulties, for example, frailty to work securely while ensuring its advantages and performing secure controlling among center points. In the presence of vindictive hubs, one of the guideline challenges in MANET is to layout intense security game plan that can shield MANET from different steering assaults. Any assault in directing stage irritates the general communication and the entire framework can be weakened. In this manner, security assumes an imperative part of MANET. This part features real assaults and control instrument in MANET with an intention that it will open headings for specialists to investigate more in the field of system security. Toward the finish of this part, fundamental security components and issues identified with rising of IoT from Mobile systems have been featured. This article presents a detailed study on the vulnerability in the wireless network, discusses goals of computer security, various security issues in MANET protocols, types of attacks in MANET such as Blackhole attack, Cache poisoning attack, routing table poisoning attack and some more, congestion control related security issues in detailed with the special highlight on valuable contribution in these areas. It also describes in details about the controls in Mobile Ad-hoc networks against security attacks, Intrusion Detection System and at last, special attention has been focused on IoT. This article has been presented with the intention that it will encourage new researchers to conduct new findings in this magnificent area of computer security.

Chapter 3

This chapter states that the technologies increase day-by-day and same as network security change according to their needs but same as attacker always try to break the security with new techniques of the wireless network. Here author represents the intrusion detection system based on cross-layer. IDS has detected the new unknown intrusion in the different layer with their different prevention technique. The cross-layer detection detects the attack at the same layer. In this chapter author also discussed honeypot and their different type's attacks, and also discussed various types of attack in MANET with their structure and unstructured categories of ad hoc network.

Chapter 4

This chapter states that security is an important aspect of today's digital world. Everyday technology has grown with new advancement in various areas especially in the development of web-based applications. All most all the web applications are on the internet, hence the maximum probability of attacks and threads. Therefore, security is necessary while developing any web application. Lots of techniques are developing for mitigating and defending against threats to the web-based applications over the internet. This chapter overviews, the important region of web application security, with sequencing the current strategies into a major picture to the future research and advancement. Firstly, explain the major problem and obstacle that makes the efforts unsuccessful for developing the secure web application. At this point now, distinguishing three basic security properties that a web application should possess are validation, integrity, accuracy and portray the comparing vulnerabilities that damage these properties alongside the assault vectors that endeavor these vulnerabilities.

Chapter 5

This chapter reviews the different kinds of threats related to security within the Social Network of things have been overviewed. In SNoT, the different devices actively interact with 'Social Things'. Many susceptibilities already exist in NoT, but some new susceptibilities have to be addressed. This chapter has also highlighted some remedies to increase the SNoT security. Some reliable models have suggested and a comprehensive security solution will be generated in the near future for this technology.

Chapter 6

This chapter states vehicular ad-hoc networks (VANETs) belong to wireless ad hoc networks, which do not have a fixed centralized structure. Due to this vulnerability, they are exposed to various security threats. As security is one of the most critical parts of wireless networks, there is a need to give major attention to these defects; the most common of them is RREQ Flooding attack. This chapter uses Artificial Neural Networks as a classifier to detect the attack and later uses an optimization technique in terms of genetic algorithms to reduce the feature subset selection. Firstly, the flooding attack was launched using NS-2 to study the seriousness and effect of this attack in terms of throughput of the network and packet delivery ratio. This chapter detects the flooding attack under two different detection conditions- misuse and anomaly. The accuracy to determine with multiple malicious nodes was recorded as 99%. Also in terms of features reduction, this chapter is able to reduce the features to 18. In addition, the false positive rate is reduced to the remarkable level as compared with existing approaches.

Chapter 7

This chapter presents a real-world botnet detection model that possesses high accuracy and a lesser number of false positives in a small period of time with the help of network flow characteristics. Authors in this chapter used existing datasets as well as created own real-world botnet and normal traffic for training and testing purpose of the proposed model. In order to extract important features out of network traffic, softflowd and nfdump are used for flow collector and exporter purposes respectively. In this chapter, results were analyzed using various machine-learning algorithms such as Random Tree, REP Tree and Support Vector Machine. The author also applied feature reduction/extraction technique in order to retrieve the important subset of features out of the entire feature set because it helps to achieve the more accurate result within lesser time by eliminating the irrelevant set of features. The author concluded from results that Random Tree performed best among all three algorithms in terms of Detection Rate, Accuracy, and False Positive Rate.

Chapter 8

This chapter concludes and presents the past decades have witnessed a number of hazardous DDoS attacks like the Mirai botnet attack which disrupted services in the US and Europe. The cause of these attacks varies from monetary benefits to political unrest. By the time some DDoS solutions are suggested after reporting the attack, the damage is already done. If the mitigation starts too late, the firewall state table may be submerged, effecting reboots, or a state of lockup, intensifies the DDoS attack from the attacker's outlook. The service is no longer available to legal users. A better knowledge of these attacks, threat detection techniques and some effective precautionary measures play an important role to prevent severe damages and ensure security in the network. Hence, in this chapter, the authors analyzed various aspects of DDoS attacks and botnets including their attack types and features, architecture and defensive techniques. A methodology to mitigate networks from DDoS attacks was also proposed. In the technique, it was observed that in a network, the bulk of malicious DDoS traffic could be effectively filtered out using proper configuration and filtering rules on the routers, efficiently eliminating the bogus traffic. In addition, prioritizing of packets to pass through the network and reach the destination does not deny services to the clients. The chapter is concluded with a case study on the recent WannaCry Ransomware attack providing further future research directions.

Section 2: Cyber Crime and Cyber Forensics

Chapter 9

This chapter reviews the recent literature of cyber forensic and explains the role of the computer, cyber forensics in India. This chapter also discussed the loophole of cyber law in India. It shows the comparison between Indian system and U.S. and European court systems.

Chapter 10

This chapter starts by defining cyberattack as an attack on resources and services in cyberspace. Its comparison with conventional terrorism is discussed ahead. The body of the chapter initiates with discussing the various mechanisms of cyber attacks and categorizing them into 3 major categories: physical, electronic and network attacks.

The further author elaborates the definitions, types, and details of cyber attacks, cybercrimes, and cyberterrorism. A comparative contrast among these terms is also presented in this section. After this, various possible instances of cyber-terror attacks on resources and services are discussed. Here cases of email, social media, health and emergency services, military communication, government and corporate servers and internet of things (IoT) are stated. In next section, countries and groups acting as major players in cyberterrorism and their roles with impact are discussed. Here author also present the prominent tools in use for cyberterror attacks. The factors of inclination of terror groups towards cyberterrorism are mentioned in next section. Later techniques for prevention of cyberterrorist attacks are stated. They are further elaborated on validation and verification methods of prevention. Major precautions and practices to combat such an attack are discussed here. Finally, the chapter concludes with a case study of Stuxnet program as an example of a cyberterror attack.

Chapter 11

This chapter presents Cyber forensics, which is expanding its importance for the law application community for a number of reasons, none of which is that computers and the network represent the fastest emerging technology tools that are used by criminals and the trend will continue for the predictable future. To overcome these problems, in this chapter author classify the crimes and detailed about different types of tools and its functions. So the author has to do is first understand the importance of cybercrime and want to improve the cybercrime tools to avoid the problems in the future. In addition to the provisions, in some directions for further research, author study has made three major contributions to the chapter on cyber kit tool development. Firstly, it deals with the different types of computer crimes. Computers are the main reason for a criminal action. When the individual is the main target of cybercrime, the computer can be considered as the tool rather than the target. Secondly, it deals with the different types of cybercrimes. This is not an exhaustive list by any means but will give a comprehensive idea of the loopholes in network and security systems. Finally, author deal with the important tools used for the cybercrime. The Forensic specialist's scrutinizing computer crimes needs a set of dedicated tools as well as the use of very peculiar techniques. Although, depending on the type of computing device and the kind of digital evidence, investigations may choose one tool or another. This chapter work in these areas is relatively new and the related literature is still limited.

Chapter 12

This chapter focuses mainly on the creation of the evidence by digitally signing the time-stamped packets, by exploiting a technique (named tree chaining technique) for digitally signing the IP packet flow based on the use of Merkle trees. Moreover, the author has implemented an optimized algorithm (namely the Log-Log algorithm) to traverse the Merkle trees in order to balance the time and space costs in creating the digital evidence with NetTrack. Experiments performed with NetTrack on different platforms show that NetTrack can deliver the digital evidence to external applications within a reasonable amount of time, e.g. Within 10 seconds.

Chapter 13

This chapter addresses glance over the contemporary literature in computer forensics domain. The major challenges in this domain are described and a framework that is currently in our research is introduced. This framework has components that are parts of the Operating System – the "All Seeing Eye" of any computing platform – to proactively monitor and identify cyber-crime models in real time. Such a monitoring is not possible using tools that work as regular applications. The proposed framework makes use of kernel mode components to monitor virtually all activities of all processes in the system and a user mode application component analyses and maps these activities to known threat models. The implementation of such a framework on standalone hosts as well as virtualized distributed systems - including computing clusters and cloud systems are also discussed with case studies that are relevant in real life.

Chapter 14

This chapter addresses one of the most challenging tasks of the botnet network forensics analysis is that the identity of the botnet hidden master, Traceback to command and control is also very difficult, since the attack is from the compromised zombies, these compromised zombies are the unaware public who get victimized for the crime they haven't done. The ultimate target of the forensics expects is to find the real origin of the attack the master-mind the botmaster. A proper computer forensics investigation is required here to provide the concrete evidence. This chapter discussed the existing works related to botnet attack and the forensics method to find the real origin of the attack. It not only finds evidence that the botnet attack has taken place. It also finds the evidence that the botnet attack has taken place especially using compromised zombies. It also collects the evidence to justify that the compromised zombies are not the real source of the attack. It identifies and collects the evidence that, the Command and Control (C&C) work under the control of the botmaster. The forensic analysis does not stop with this it also finds evidence to identify the real origin of the attack the botmaster, with the help of special marking scheme the mastermind botmaster is identified. The real origin of the attack is identified with concrete evidence then the effect of the botnet could be mitigated very easily.

Section 3: Security and Privacy in Big Data Analytics and Machine Learning, Biometrics, Audio Watermarking, and Cryptocurrency

Chapter 15

This chapter discusses, in particular, the four key components of Big Data: Is our Big Data exact, Is our Big Data secure, Is our Big Data accessible constantly, Does our Big Data scale? The ordering and making of huge valuable Data is an extensively expensive process and requires loads of supposition and extensive building assets to make an in-depth and top-notch set of information streams. Now around 75% of Fortune 500 organizations based on cloud-based arrangements, and the IDC says that around 80% of new plug endeavor applications will be transferred on cloud stages. Given these numbers; Author needs to address the 4 factors above in a particular setting utilizing a cloud-based advanced advertising innovation stage for your Big Data needs. Thus, your innovation ought to have the capacity to track billions of watchwords and pages, vast volumes of area particular information and social signs to give you the privilege investigation. Huge Data requires innovative assets and venture. To augment ROI from these ventures, make sure that your Big Data sources give all of you the information that issues to you and that your sources are credible. Protect Big Data no matter what and have this information readily available dependably. Be set up to get to and dissect significantly more prominent volumes of information when Big Data gets considerably greater; that day isn't too far away, so the best time to begin is present!

Chapter 16

This chapter reviews the big data and cyber security both opportunity and risk for most businesses. The field of cyber security is very similar to big data, which is a defined term used to descript a very large amount of data set that are mined and analyzed to detect patterns and behavioral trends. It is generally described as being dense in variety, velocity, and volume. Considering a cyber security view, big data has escorted in new possibilities in terms of analytics and security solutions to protect data from future cyber attacks. Big data has come up with new possibilities for cyber security and has given opportunities to cyber criminals to access the huge quantity of sensitive and personal information through the use of advanced technologies. This Chapter focused Big Data Analytics from knowledge representation techniques and Challenges to Cyber Security approaches.

Chapter 17

This chapter presents an analysis Big data deal with the large volume of business data hence, most of the industries implementing the big data mechanism to store, process and analyze the petabytes of data to take the business decisions in order to retain and improve the customer relations. As the big data field grows up, there should be an essential effort has to be taken to store confidential and private information of the users in a big data store. Proper security infrastructure has to build and deployed mandatorily on the Big data functional areas. To improve the security and privacy of Big data there is a need for the continual development of the security infrastructure. Security policies and laws need to be regularized in order to ensure the security of big data store. Antivirus software developers need to generously swap over information about current Big Data security threats, and the industry heads often work together to cope up with new malicious software attacks. Big data analytics infrastructure can also use intrusion detection services that analyze system and environment behavior in order to spot possible malicious activity. The trust-based environment should be established for any kind of big data systems while considering the security and privacy of Big Data systems. In addition, there is a need for key management; authentication methods and access control are the areas that require further research in this domain.

Chapter 18

This chapter elaborates various security and privacy issues and factors that affect the Big Data storage, processing and communication such as multiple infrastructure tiers used for both data storage and computing, non-scalability of existing authentication, access control, and encryption schemes, lack of scalable real-time monitoring systems, and lack scalable security analytics. This chapter also presented, various privacy preserving techniques in the big data applications perspective, such as data management, where data classification can avoid phishing and breaching attacks, data discovery can prevent data ex-filtration, data metering and Role Based Access Control for identity and access management, Application level cryptography, Transparent Encryption, Data Redaction or Data Masking for Data Privacy and Protection, Apache Knox Gateway for Data Protection in Transit, Lightweight Directory Access Protocol to prevent Sniffing attack, Apache Falcon, Cloudera Navigator, Zettaset Orchestrator for auditing purpose, SELinux policy for Mandatory Access Control. Therefore Big Data organizations need to employ three key security controls: Preventive, Detective and Administrative for securing Big data life cycle. In addition, various encryption techniques for preserving the privacy of sensitive data, such as searchable, Order Preserving Encryption Scheme and Homomorphic Encryption are presented in this chapter. In future, to provide highly secure Big Data environment it is recommendable to implement application security rather than device security, isolating devices and servers having sensitive data, applying reactive and proactive protection mechanisms, regular auditing, analyzing logs, and updating attack information across the organizations can help for better organization of data.

Chapter 19

This chapter explores the steganalyzers were working on the high dimensional features it is in urgent need, to find the best machine learning tool to learn such a high dimensional features. As per author, support vector machine is the best machine-learning tool but it slows down when learning large training samples and huge dimensional set features. Hence, in this chapter, the author is given the best machine-learning tool to learn the different feature vectors used by different steganalysers to detect the stego images. In addition, it is expecting that deep learning is an emerging tool and it can automatically extract the features by learning and it predicts the stego images more promisingly. In the future, deep learning holds a standard place in all the research areas such as image vision, pattern recognition, steganalysis, recommender systems etc.

Chapter 20

This chapter takes philosophical orientation, debates the audio watermarking technique discussed in this chapter provide negligible Bit Error Rate and high value of Peak Signal to Noise Ratio (PSNR) for watermark embedding, and recovery in case of the different kinds of compressed .wav files. In addition, the signal quality has not been degraded so much. The suggested technique is more reliable and robust compared with the existing technique.

Chapter 21

This chapter identifies the existing challenges in Bitcoin cryptocurrency was discussed where each transaction is secured by using cryptographic algorithms and there is no need of the third party for completing the transactions. Initially, the author has addressed so many questions concerned with bitcoin like the difference between bitcoin and other available currencies, who created it? Who prints it? etc. Later in this chapter author discussed, the various characteristics of bitcoins as well as the author have demonstrated that how transaction took place in the context of bitcoin. For better understanding, the author considered few examples and facts, each example presented by some easy to read figures. Eventually, security issues were discussed along with cyber-crimes and their punishments.

Chapter 22

This chapter proposed a biometric recognition system using Finger Knuckle Print (FKP), a new biometric trait. FKP based biometrics has the advantage over other biometrics because of its properties like good discrimination capability, small image size and thus template (feature), easy to capture or use etc. Recently information theory based features extraction functions have gained popularity in the extraction of image features. The main contribution of this chapter is to propose four information theory based features, which, may be utilized in biometrics-based person authentication systems. Experiments have been performed on the FKP dataset containing 7960 images, designed and created by Hong Kong Polytechnic University using a device designed by them. Matching accuracy of 92% using the proposed feature on FKP dataset prove that these attributes have the capacity to obtain the market for the fingerprint-based authentication system. Experimental results also indicate that information theory based feature functions have the capability to transform rich contents of the image into feature extraction with high accuracy and efficiency. This is also obvious that the Gaussian feature $\sum_1^k h(k) \times g(k) \times e^{-(g(k)/n^a)}$ has the most prejudiced ability and improved performance as compared to other proposed features. Future directions are to exploit more information theoretic features to enhance the matching accuracy of finger knuckle print-based biometrics person authentication systems.

Gulshan Shrivastava
National Institute of Technology Patna, India

Prabhat Kumar
National Institute of Technology Patna, India

B. B. Gupta
National Institute of Technology Kurukshetra, India

Suman Bala
Orange Labs, France

Nilanjan Dey
Techno India College of Technology, India

Acknowledgment

Amateurs hack systems, professionals hack people. — Bruce Schneier

The editors would like to acknowledge the help of all the people involved in this project and, more specifically, to the authors and reviewers that took part in the review process. Without their support, this book would not have become a reality.

First, the editors would like to thank each one of the authors for their contributions. Our sincere gratitude goes to the chapter's authors who contributed their time and expertise to this book. We believe that the team of authors provides the perfect blend of knowledge and skills that went into authorizing this book. We thank each of the authors for developing their time, patience, perseverance and effort towards this book.

Second, special thanks to the publisher team, who showed the editors, ropes to start and continue.

Third, the editors wish to acknowledge the valuable contributions of the reviewers regarding the improvement of quality, coherence, and content presentation of chapters. Most of the authors also served as referees; we highly appreciate their double task.

The editors would like to express their gratitude to all the people support, share, talked things over, read, wrote, offered comments, allowed us to quote their remarks and assisted in editing, proofreading, and design; through the book journey.

Section 1
Security in Network, Social IoT and VANET, Denial of Service Attack

Chapter 1
Wireless Sensor Networks:
A Technical Survey

Sonam
Ambedkar Institute of Advanced Communication Technologies and Research, India

Manju Khari
Ambedkar Institute of Advanced Communication Technologies and Research, India

ABSTRACT

This chapter describes how as world is switching from wired communication to wireless communication, the need of a wireless sensor network (WSN) is increasing. WSNs became very popular due to its wide applications. A WSN is a network of small-in-size sensor nodes which are densely deployed for monitoring a chosen environment. In WSNs, each sensor node detects data and sends it to the base station. These sensor nodes have four basic duties, consisting of sensing, computation, transmission and power. Due to the small size, these sensor nodes are more constrained in terms of computational energy and storage resources. Energy awareness is also an essential design issue for routing protocols in WSNs. The focus of this chapter is to provide an overview of WSNs. In addition, this chapter describes the components of WSNs, its challenges and the classifications of WSNs. This chapter compares the results of LEACH, SEP and TEEN protocols.

INTRODUCTION

In the start of the computer era, a single computer is operated as stand-alone system. Earlier there was no way to connect to other computers. So, whenever there is a need of transferring a file to other system a storage medium was required for example, floppy disk. Organizations can much more efficient & productive manner if they found the ability to share information in overall organization. Computer networks provide the solution for almost every organization. For the setup of a network, every organization has two options. One is a completely wired network, which uses networking wires to connect computers, the other is a wireless network, which uses RFs (Radio Frequencies) to connect computer. Wireless Networks are providing mobile communication in between the organization node. Rather than this lots of organizations are using a combination of both wireless and wired networks (Rathee et al., 2016). The

DOI: 10.4018/978-1-5225-4100-4.ch001

use of wireless sensor networks (WSNs) is increasing day by day as it has low power radios and better sensing capability. WSNs are used in many applications such as smart transportation, health monitoring, battlefield surveillance, weather forecasting, Internet of Things (IoT), etc. WSNs are a set of many sensor nodes. The sensor nodes sense the data, e.g. temperature, humidity, etc., from the environment and then process the data. This processed data is aggregated by the sensor nodes and transferred to the Base Station (BS).

Architecture of WSN

In recent years the implementation and design of WSNs have become a popular research area. The area of WSN is a fast-growing field in the scientific world. WSN consists many small sensor nodes to monitor the environment activities like temperature, pressure, fire etc. Sensor nodes in WSN have limited power so many routing techniques focus mainly on power conservation.

WSN is an application specific technology like temperature sensor nodes only measure temperature and pressure sensor nodes measure pressure. Wireless sensor networks consist of network of sensor nodes which are actually deployed randomly in the field and left unattended. Sensor nodes of the network since the environment and send the data to the base station which store all the measured parameters and provide the parameters to the end user.

Sensor nodes are the small devices also known as motes. In the market, there are many motes available like NOW, Dot etc. Sensor nodes have transceivers to gather information from its environment. Sensor nodes have some constraints such as battery power, communication range, computation capacity and memory. The sensor nodes die slowly due to the energy constraint which makes the network less dense. WSNs can be deployed in harsh environment thus it makes many sensor nodes faulty or inoperable so WSNs need to be fault-tolerant. The network topology of WSN is continuously changing so it is difficult to replace faulty sensor nodes by new sensor nodes. The implementation of energy efficient routing protocols for WSN is the appropriate solution to solve this problem.

In Figure 1, the architecture of WSN is shown. The area where sensor nodes are deployed form a WSN. Sensor nodes are generally scattered in a sensor field and these sensor nodes sense the environment to gather data and after that it transmit the sensed data to base station (BS)/sink node. The user can access the sensed data via internet or satellite.

Types of WSN

WSNs are mainly two types: Structured WSN and Unstructured WSN.

1. **Structured WSN:** Structured WSN is a network in which sensor nodes are actually deployed in a pre-planned manner. The sensor nodes are placed at the specific position, which helps in providing full coverage. WSNs are used in many everyday life activities and services which includes tracking and monitoring of events in various areas. Some of its applications are military, disaster management, patient monitoring in healthcare sectors etc. In this network, the network maintenance is low because of deployment of few distributed nodes in the sensor field.

2. **Unstructured WSN:** Unstructured WSN is a network of many sensor nodes, which are organized randomly in the sensor fields. Due to the random deployment of sensor nodes, there are uncovered areas left in unstructured WSN. In the unstructured network, the network maintenance that includes

Figure 1. WSN architecture

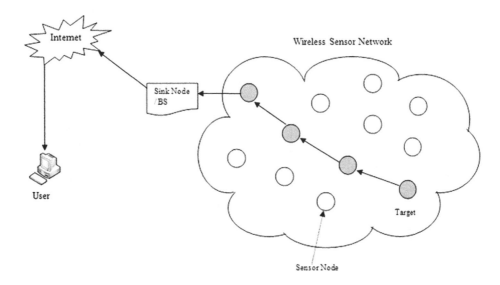

failure detection and connection management is difficult as the network is left unattended to perform the respective reporting and monitoring functions. These networks are less scalable than structured networks (Sharma, Bala, Bansal, & Shrivastava, 2017).

Components of WSN

Sensor Nodes

Many small sensor nodes form a WSN. A sensor node is small devices, which gathers data, process the data and then passes it on to another node in the network via wireless communication. It is also known as motes. Name of some wireless sensor nodes are. NOW, WiSense, FireFly, etc. Sensor nodes are used to collect the parameters like sound, temperature, pressure, humidity, vibration and it collect the changes in health parameter of a person. A sensor node has four basic components i.e. sensing unit, the processing unit, transmission unit and power unit (Figure 2).

The main parts of a sensor node are the radio transceiver, microprocessor, microcontroller, A/D converter, sensor, and battery. A brief description of components of sensor nodes is given below:

- **Radio Transceiver:** Wireless communication among sensor nodes is supported by radio transceiver. It is basically a transmission medium which can be radio frequency, infrared rays etc. Radio transceiver comprises of a short-range radio which has a low data rate and single channel. Basically, radio transceiver function in four different modes: idle mode, standby mode, transmit mode and receive mode.
- **Microprocessor:** The functionality of other components of the sensor node is controlled by the microprocessor. It executes the signal processing algorithms for the collected sensor data (Mishra, Singhadia, & Pandey, 2014). There are four modes in which microprocessor works to save energy: (1) off, (2) sleep, (3) idle and (4) active. The CPU and most internal peripherals are turned off in

Figure 2. Sensor node structure

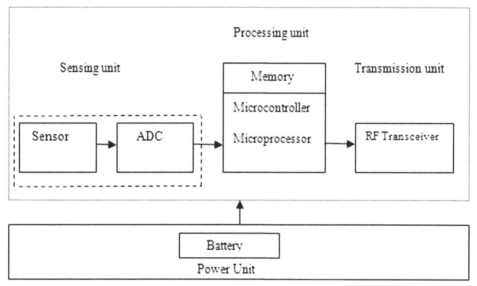

sleep mode and they can only be activated by some external events. In idle mode, the CPU is still inactive, but other peripherals are active. CPU and all peripherals are active in the active mode.

- **Memory:** A sensor node consists memory in the form of the chip to store data in it. Memory requirements are application dependent. Basically, flash memories are used to store data which are less expensive and have large storage capacity.
- **Sensor:** Sensor nodes convert physical phenomena into electrical signals. There are many types of sensors e.g. thermal sensors, electromagnetic sensors, mechanical sensors, etc. It measures environmental factors like temperature, light intensity, sound etc. The energy consumption within on or off state of the sensor node can be measured by time.
- **Analog to Digital Converter:** It converts an analog signal to digital signal so that it is easily readable.
- **Battery:** A sensor node has battery which supplies power to all components of sensor node. Lifetime of the network depends upon the lifetime of sensor nodes and the lifetime of the sensor nodes depends upon its battery. Sensor nodes are cheaper, light in weight and smaller in size. Battery replacement of sensor nodes is not possible in the network because the sensor nodes are deployed in the unattended environment. So, the energy efficient routing protocols for WSN are designed.

Base Station (Central Gateway)

A base station is also called central gateway or sink node. A base station consists of a processor, USB interface board, antenna and radio board. A WSN has at least one base station. All sensor nodes transmit the sensed data to the base station for processing and decision-making. The base station has high computational energy and processing capability. Usually, base stations are considered as static in nature but in some cases, they are mobile to gather the data from the sensor nodes.

Cluster Head

Data fusion and data aggregation functions are performed by cluster head in WSN. In a cluster, all sensing nodes participate to become a cluster head. The cluster node assumed to be highly reliable, high energy and more secure.

Relay Node

Relay node is used to enhance the network reliability. It is usually a midway node, which can be used to connect with its adjacent node. A field device does not have control equipment. The speed of node processor is around 8 MHz.

WSN ORGANIZATION

Before deploying WSN in any application, it is very important to understand the architecture of WSN. There are five layers of sensor network along with three cross planes as shown in Figure 3. The three cross planes are:

- **Power Management Plane:** Sensor nodes use energy for sensing, processing, transmission and reception process. The power management plane balances the level of power of sensor nodes. It also helps to increase the efficiency of the sensor network.
- **Mobility Management Plane:** The movement of sensor nodes can be detected by using this plane. Sensor nodes can keep track of neighbour nodes and power levels. When topology changes the mobility, management plane maintains the connectivity of the network.
- **Task Management Plane:** This plane helps in scheduling the sensing tasks to a given area.

WSN can be organized as a five-layered architecture. Five-layered architecture is explained below (Singh, Kumar, & Singh, 2017):

- **Physical Layer:** The main functions of this layer are frequency selection, signal modulation, and data encryption.
- **Data Link Layer:** This layer took the responsibility of multiplexing of data streams, data frame detection, Medium Access Control (MAC) and error control.
- **Network Layer:** The main function of this layer is routing. This layer route the data packets sensed by sensor nodes to the sink node.
- **Transport Layer:** The transport layer maintains the flow of data between nodes. End-to-end delivery of the data between sink node and sensor nodes is the prime responsibility of the transport layer.
- **Application Layer:** SMP i.e. Sensor Management Protocol in application layer is used to make the software and hardware of lower layers transparent to end user.

Figure 3. Architecture of WSN

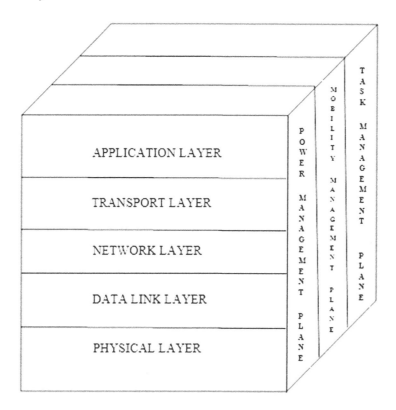

CHARACTERISTICS OF WSN

WSN has many characteristics as follows:

1. **Network Topology:** WSN has dynamic network topology. Node failure, energy depletion, channel fading, addition or removal of nodes is the reasons for changing the topology of a sensor network.
2. **Energy-Constrained:** Sensor nodes are deployed in WSN which are highly limited in energy and computation. The power unit of a sensor node is a very important component of the node as all the activities are supported by the power unit. Redundant activities should be reduced to save power of sensor nodes.
3. **Fault Tolerance:** Fault tolerance is the ability to maintain sensor network functionalities without any disruption due to sensor node failures. In WSN, If sensor nodes are dead or fail to work then there is a requirement to have the capability to reconfigure itself without the human being interference.
4. **Self-Configurable:** In WSN, sensor nodes are deployed randomly. Sensor nodes once deployed in the network, nodes have to configure autonomously themselves into a communication network.
5. **Application-Specific:** WSNs are application-dependent. For the different type of application, we have to design different sensor network.
6. **Scalability:** WSNs can be scalable with the sense that new nodes are added to the network which can expand the network also, failed nodes can be replaced. These does not incur overhead on the network so WSNs are scalable to network size.

7. **Local Computation:** In WSN, sensor nodes collect the data from neighboring nodes and then allow raw data to be buffered then processes it and transmitted to the base station. This helps in reducing the number of transmissions which save energy. This functionality is commonly known as data aggregation.

8. **Multihop:** In WSN, direct communication is limited between sensor nodes because of distance, energy consumption, obstacles etc. So, transmitted packets have to hop from one node to another node to reach the endpoint.

9. **Data-Centric:** In WSN, all nodes have equal importance. In WSN, sensor nodes have no global IDs as only data matters instead of addressing a specific sensor node.

APPLICATION OF WSN

- **Healthcare:** Sensor networks are also widely used in the healthcare area. WSN are constructed in some modern hospital to monitor patients, doctors and to control the drug administration in hospital. Small and lightweight sensor nodes attached to each patient to monitor the patient's physiological parameters for example heartbeat, blood pressure etc.

- **Military Application:** WSNs have the wide range of military applications example nuclear, biological and chemical attack detection, reconnaissance of opposing forces, battlefield surveillance etc. Self-organization, fault tolerance and security of the network should be required in the context of the battlefield.

- **Environmental Monitoring:** Environmental monitoring application can be used for animal tracking, forest surveillance, flood detection, and weather forecasting. In this application, sensor nodes monitor environment like temperature, pressure, humidity etc. In case of fire, sensor nodes can send an alarm to indicate the status of the fire.

- **Law Enforcement:** WSNs can be used for law enforcement. Without depending upon the public cellular network WSN help to the officers to access to the main database so that we can trace the criminal easily. It is installed around areas of high crime rate to capture the sounds of gunshots. The sensors can then trigger the camera to zoom in on the shooter and alert the law enforcement authority.

- **Transportation:** WSNs can be deployed in traffic control system to detect the high-speed vehicles and to broadcast traffic information and allowing travellers to avoid congested roads. The sensor networks are usually found in vehicles to monitor the pressure especially that carry heavy load like train, trucks etc.

- **Agriculture:** WSNs can be helpful to monitor moisture level, temperature and soil conditions. WSNs can also be used to monitor the storage conditions of crops. WSNs can be used to track cattle's location and their health by attaching a sensor node with cattle.

- **Intelligent Buildings:** Intelligent building technologies help to increase user comfort and to reduce energy consumption. Sensors can be used in buildings for detecting and controlling of fire and smoke and to reduce energy wastage by proper humidity, air conditioning control and to monitor the vibration in the building that can damage the building.

- **Space Exploration:** Many space agencies spend billions into space exploration projects. WSN can be used to explore other planets and asteroids.

CLASSIFICATION OF WSN PROTOCOLS

WSN routing protocols can be categorized based on modes of function, participation style of the node and network structure. Classification of WSN is shown in Figure 4.

Mode of Function-Based WSN Routing Protocols

On the basis of mode of function, routing protocols can be classified into three types:

- **Proactive:** These protocols are also called table-driven routing protocols since every node maintains routing information to every other node in the network. Every node generates a routing table to find the path to the destination node. Every sensor node updates their routing table whenever the network topology changes. These protocols are not suitable for large networks.
- **Reactive:** Reactive protocols are also known as On-Demand routing protocols or source initiated routing. In this routing protocol sensor nodes searches for route on-demand i.e., whenever a node wants to transmit data it searches path to the destination node and establishes the connection.
- **Hybrid:** It is a combination of reactive and pro-active routing protocols.

Participation Style of the Nodes Based WSN Routing Protocols

- **Direct Communication Based Routing Protocols:** Indirect communication-based WSN routing protocols, sensed data is directly sent to the base station/sink node. In these types of protocols, there is no need of multi-hopping.
- **Flat Routing Protocols:** All the sensor nodes play the similar role in this routing protocol. All sensor nodes communicate in an ad-hoc mode and they send the data to the base station/sink node by multi-hop routing. If a distant node tries to reach the sink node it needs to find an optimal path.

Figure 4. Classification of WSN routing protocols

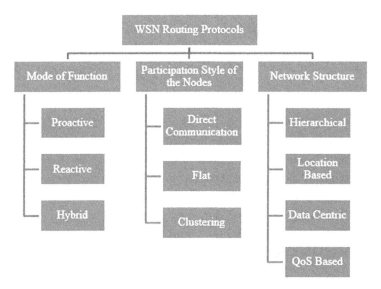

In WSN applications, large number of sensor nodes is deployed randomly so it is not possible to assign the global identifiers (IDs) to each sensor node. It is hard to select a specific set of sensor nodes to be queried due to lack of global IDs. Therefore, data is transmitted from sensor nodes within the deployment region with the significant redundancy. This consideration has led to data-centric routing. In data-centric routing, the base station sends queries to sensor nodes of the certain region and waits for data from the sensor nodes located in the selected region.

- **Clustering Based Routing Protocols:** In these protocols, the areas are categorised into a number of the small clusters. In every cluster, a cluster head is selected which directly communicates with the base station. These types of protocols provide scalability and energy efficient communication to the network.

Network Structure Base WSN Routing Protocols

- **Hierarchical Routing Protocols:** In these protocols, network nodes are organized into small clusters and then a cluster head is selected from every cluster based on some parameters. Cluster head gathers data from all normal nodes and sends the data to other cluster heads. In WSN, the clusters are formed and various special tasks i.e. data aggregation, fusion are assigned to them, to make the sensor network more energy efficient. It increases the overall system scalability, lifetime, and energy efficiency, example: LEACH (Low Energy Adaptive Clustering Hierarchy) (Sharma & Gupta, 2016).
- **Location-Based Routing Protocols:** In these protocols, the information of location of the sensor nodes is specified and can be obtained from GPS i.e. Global Positioning System signals or by finding the coordinate of the neighbouring node. An optimal path can be formed by the help of location information of sensor nodes, which helps to improve the performance. Like IP- addresses WSN does not have this kind of addressing scheme so the information of location are utilized in routing data in energy efficient way.
- **Data-Centric Routing Protocol:** These protocols are query-based protocols and these protocols depend upon the naming of the preferred data, thus it eliminates many redundant transmissions. SPIN (Sensor Protocol for Information via Negotiation) is an example of the data-centric protocol. The base station sends queries to the normal nodes for data and waits for the reply from the nodes to further process data. Depending upon the query sensor nodes gather the specific data from the areas of the interest and this information is required to transmit to the BS and therefore reduces the number of transmission.
- **QoS Based Routing Protocol:** It is important to consider QoS metricssuch as reliability, delay, bandwidth etc. to minimize the energy consumption.The sensor network balances between data quality and energy consumption during transmission of data between sensor nodes and sink node. Sequential Assignment Routing (SAR) and Stateless Protocol for End-to-End Delay (SPEED) are examples of QoS based routing protocol.

SECURITY IN WSN

There are many issues in WSN and security is an important and challenging issue in WSN. Due to the hostile environment of network, conventional techniques of security used in the traditional networks can't be applied for WSN. WSNs are vulnerable to various types of attacks like an adversary can simply eavesdrop the traffic, impersonate one of the nodes of the network also intentionally provides the misleading information to various other nodes. The security is critical for sensor networks as sensor nodes are deployed in the field randomly and then left unattended. Attackers can easily harm WSN as WSN uses wireless communication. WSN is the network of small sensor nodes so enforcing security in WSN is too complex. The security goals of WSN are confidentiality, integrity, authentication, availability, survivability, efficiency, freshness and scalability.

Because of its transmission nature, WSN is prone to attacks along with resource restriction on sensor nodes and deployment of uncontrolled environments. In WSN, False node insertion, malicious data, routing attack are some possible threats among the sensor nodes. Various crypto mechanisms such as symmetric and asymmetric methods are proposed to ensure security services in the WSN. Security can be achieved by encryption and authentication methods in WSN.

Security Services

1. **Confidentiality:** Node information kept secret from unauthorized users but authorized users see it.
2. **Integrity:** It gives assurance to the receiver node that message is not being modified during transmission.
3. **Device Authentication:** Device authentication meant that it provides the validation of the device's identity.
4. **Message Authentication:** Information source is correct or not decided by message authentication.
5. **Non-Repudiation:** Non-repudiation prevents denial of a commitment done in the past.
6. **Availability:** Sensor nodes must be available all the time, which prevents the disruptions in the service due to power outages, node failure, and system upgrades. The denial-of-service attack can be prevented by ensuring availability.
7. **Data Freshness:** Data freshness service ensures that messages are in correct order and have not been reused.
8. **Survivability:** Even if the node is compromised then also the lifetime of the sensor node must be extended.
9. **Access Control:** Access control is the restriction of access to resources.
10. **Revocation:** Refusal of certification or authorization.

The attacks are mainly divided into two types: Host Based attacks and Network Based attacks.

The Host Based attacks are divided into three categories listed below:

1. **User Compromise:** It involves the compromising of the WSNs users for example, cheating the users by revealing the credentials such as passwords and keys about the sensor nodes. Various types of attacks are not possible in WSN as no human operators are required unless user considers the base stations to store keys.
2. **Hardware Compromise:** In these attacks, attackers usually try to extract program code and keys stored within the sensor nodes by tampering the hardware. The attacker might also try to inject malicious code into the tampered sensor node.

3. **Software Compromise:** In these types of attack, the attacker attempts to break the software on the sensor nodes. Applications running on a sensor node and operating system are more vulnerable to attacks like buffer overflows. Therefore, secure coding can help from attacks.

Network Based attacks can be categorized into two ways which are Layer specific compromises and Protocol specific compromises. An attack consists following operations:

1. **Interrupting Messages:** Availability service can be threatened by this operation. The main motive of this is to launch DoS i.e. Denial-of-service attacks also called as radio jamming. This attack is to interrupt the reception of receivers by emitting the radio signals directed towards more receivers.
2. **Intercepting Messages:** It operates commonly at the application layer. Message confidentiality service can be threatened by this operation. In this operation, an attacker can snoop the information carried in the messages. Key management is one of the essential techniques against cryptanalysis.
3. **Modifying Existing Messages:** It operates is commonly at network and application layer. The integrity of Message can be threatened by this method. In this method, attacker tries to confuse or mislead the sender and receiver, for example corrupting the routing control packets, which waste the energy more erroneous routing. Key management is an essential technique against cryptanalysis.
4. **Fabricating False Messages:** It threatens the authenticity of message service. In this operation, the attacker attempts to distort the parties involved in communication protocol by reporting false sensor readings or by propagating bogus routing error. It can also enable DoS attack by flooding bogus messages in the network.
5. **Replaying Existing Messages:** Message freshness service can be threatened by replaying existing messages. Man-in-the-middle attacks use this operation, which can violate confidentiality, integrity, authenticity and service availability. Time-aware cryptographic protocols can be used for preventing this type of attack.

CHALLENGES

-   **Limited Energy Capacity:** Sensors have limited battery power. In WSN, it is difficult to replace batteries of sensor nodes. Therefore, routing protocols designed for sensor network should be energy efficient to extend the lifetime of the network.
-   **Hardware and Software Issues:** A sensor network is formed by deploying many small sized sensor nodes. Cheap sensors are preferred for forming the sensor network. Software in WSN should be hardware independent. Software in WSN must be light and less energy consuming.
-   **Unreliable Wireless Communication:** In WSN, sensor nodes communicate via wireless medium, which is noisy and susceptible to errors. The topology of a network changes frequently due to sensor nodes addition, deletion, and node failures etc. Hence, the routing paths should be considered as dynamics of the network topology due to its limited energy and mobile sensors to maintain specific application requirements in relation to its connectivity coverage.
-   **Heterogeneity:** Heterogeneous WSN all sensor nodes are not identical and have different functionalities for example clusters in which sensor nodes select a cluster head (CII) and send the data

to the CH, which has more energy than other nodes. When two different sensor networks need to exchange information with each other, then homogeneity arises. Across different systems, unified communication interface is required to enable efficient exchange of information.

- **Node Failures:** In WSN, sensor nodes may fail to work properly or die frequently. There is a requirement of fault tolerance to maintain sensor network functionalities without any disruption.
- **QoS (Quality of Service):** Sensor networks provide QoS service to its users. WSN is used for real-time applications so it is very important for the sensor network to provide good quality of services.
- **Security:** WSN has hostile environment so security is a challenging issue. Attackers may insert the malicious node in the network, intercept data, modify node hardware etc. (Saini & Khari, 2011). Enforcing security in WSN is very complex.

PROTOCOLS

There are many routing protocols are designed for WSN. To facilitate the efficient working and increasing lifetime of network, energy efficient routing protocols are designed for WSN. LEACH, SEP, and TEEN are some energy efficient routing protocols.

LEACH

LEACH stands for Low Energy Adaptive Clustering Hierarchy, which is a hierarchical routing protocol that designed to increase the lifetime of the network. It was proposed by Heinzelman, Vhandrakasan, and Balakrishnan in 2000. It is an energy-efficient protocol. In this protocol, nodes form small clusters and a cluster head is selected within each cluster. All sensor nodes send the data to cluster head and then cluster head compress the collected data and send it to the base station through which the user can access the data (Miglani, Bhatia, Sharma, & Shrivastava, 2017).

Two phases of LEACH are:

1. **Set-Up Phase:** Three main fundamental steps of this phase are cluster setup, cluster head advertisement and transmission schedule creation.
2. **Steady Phase:** This phase has three steps: data aggregation, compression, and transmission of data to base station.

If the random number 'r' is less than the threshold value T (n) then the node will be selected as a cluster head. A sensor node chooses a random number between 0 and 1. The threshold value can be calculated using the equation (1). Let a threshold value be T (n),

$$T (n) = p/1\text{-}p \times (r \bmod p\text{-}1) \tag{1}$$

where p is cluster head probability

TEEN

Threshold Sensitive Energy Efficient Sensor Network Protocol is used for real-time applications in which data must be sent within certain time period. In this protocol, sensor nodes sense the environment continuously. In this protocol cluster heads of each cluster sends a hard threshold (HT) to other non-cluster head nodes within the cluster; it is called attribute for the sensed data. Cluster head will also send the soft threshold (ST), which can change the sensed attribute and also trigger the particular node to turn on its transmitter and sending of data will start. Hence hard threshold is used to make the less frequent data transmission of the sensed data and data transmission start when the sensed attribute is within the range. Following conditions must be true to transmit the data by nodes in the current cluster period:

1. The current value of the sensed attribute is greater than the HT.
2. The current value of the sensed attribute differs from the sensed value (SV) by an amount equal to or greater than the ST.

When sensor node transmits data, SV is fixed equal to the current value of sensed attribute. HT attempts to reduce the number of transmissions by allowing the nodes to transmit only when the sensed attribute is in the range of interest. The ST reduces the number of transmissions by removing all the transmissions, which might have otherwise occurred when there is little or no change in the sensed attribute once the HT.

SEP

Stable Election Protocol is an enhanced version of LEACH. SEP is a heterogeneous-aware protocol. In SEP, the cluster head (CH) selected randomly on the basis of probability of each node. Sensor nodes continuously sense the data and transmit it to their associated CH and CH transmit that data to the base station (BS). In this protocol, few of the sensor nodes having high energy known as advanced nodes and other nodes, which has low energy known as normal nodes. As advanced nodes have high energy so, advanced nodes have more chance to become cluster head as compared to the normal nodes. The selection of CH probabilities of sensor nodes is weighted by initial energy of each sensor node in WSN.

Let, n is the total number of sensor nodes in the sensor network and m is the fraction of the total number of nodes n, which are deployed with α times more energy than the other nodes.

Energy per normal node = E0

Optimal probability of each node to become CH = Popt

Number of advanced nodes = m x n   (2)

Energy per advanced node = E0 (1 + α)   (3)

Normal nodes = (1-m) x n (4)

Probability of normal nodes to become CHs, Pnor= Popt/ (1+m.α) (5)

Probability of advanced nodes to become CHs, Padv= Popt (1+ α) / (1+m.α) (6)

SIMULATION

MATLAB (2011 b) is used as a simulator for implementation and comparison of the performance of LEACH, SEP, and TEEN protocols on the basis of energy consumption, the lifetime of the sensor network. Performance attributes used in MATLAB simulations are as follows:

1. Number of dead nodes during each round.
2. The average energy of each node during each round.

The various parameter values taken for experiments are shown in Table 1.

RESULTS

Figure 5 plots the graph of the average energy of each node during each round of LEACH, SEP and TEEN protocols respectively. LEACH protocol is shown as the red curve, SEP protocol is shown as the green curve, and TEEN protocol is shown as the blue curve. LEACH protocol shows parabolic nature which represents that average energy of each node decreases rapidly as the number of round increases. SEP protocol shows linear nature at starting and at the end, it shows a little parabolic nature. TEEN

Table 1. Network parameters

Parameters	Value
Network Area	100×100 m^2
Location of Sink	150,50
n (Number of Nodes)	200
Eo (Initial energy)	0.3 J
Popt	0.1
M	0.2
A	1
ETX (Transmitter energy per node)	50 nJ/bit
ERX (Receiver energy per mode)	50 nJ/bit
EDA (Aggregate Energy)	5 Nj
rmax (Rounds)	1000

Figure 5. Average energy of each node during each round

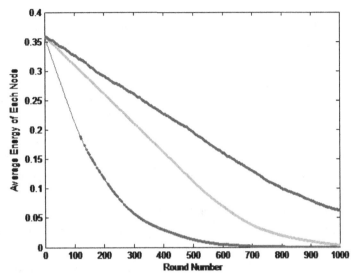

For a more accurate representation see the electronic version.

protocol shows almost linear nature from start to end. But for the small network, SEP and TEEN show same nature at the end. Hence, SEP and TEEN both protocol is almost similar in performance for the small network than LEACH protocol.

As shown in the Figure 6 the graph of nodes dead during each round. The graph shows that at end of 1000 rounds,199 nodes died when LEACH protocol was used,180 nodes died when SEP was used and 119 nodes died when the TEEN protocol was used. The teen protocol has better performance as sensor nodes die later and less as compared to LEACH and SEP protocol.

Figure 6. Nodes dead during each round

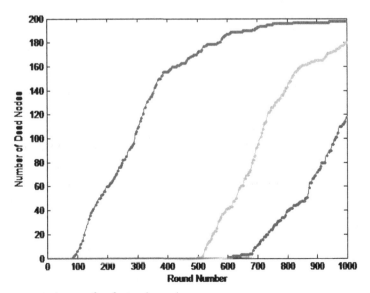

For a more accurate representation see the electronic version.

RELATED WORK

In Rathee, Sing, and Nandini (2016), authors described WSN's architecture, challenges, applications, and classification of various protocols concerning it. This paper provides overview of various security protocols to make WSN a secure network.

In Arora, Sharma, and Sachdeva (2016), authors attempted to enhance the proficiency and different parameters by utilizing improved protocol over existing protocol. Author assessed the execution of TEEN protocols in various node densities as far as throughput, PDR (Packet Delivery Ratio) and delay.

In Kahn, Rakesh, Bansal, and Chaudhary (2015), authors analyzed protocols with respect to the performance metrics and further created a generalized view. In Kahn, Rakesh, Bansal, and Chaudhary (2015), authors provided the comparative study of three of Wireless Sensor Network's Protocols, LEACH, PEGASIS, and TEEN.

In Sharma, Sethi and Bhattacharya (2015), authors provided a brief introduction about the WSN including the widely adopted architecture of WSN and the wireless sensor node. It also focused on critical issues of WSN that includes energy per packet, lower energy consumption, average packet delay, energy spent per round, packet size, distance, time until the first node dies. It focused on hierarchical routing protocols that is based on network structure scheme and explains how neural networks are helpful in providing energy efficiency to wireless sensor networks.

In Aswale and Ghorpade (2015), authors provided a survey on the routing metrics which are chosen as its criteria to categorize state of the art of QoS (Quality of Service) WMSNs (Wireless Multimedia Sensor Networks) routing techniques. In this paper, author discussed about open issues and future research directions to develop efficient routing protocols to guarantee QoS.

In Dhawan and Warauch (2014), authors reviewed the taxonomy of WSN routing protocols and issues in LEACH protocol along with disadvantages. The author provided detail of some improved versions of LEACH and compared some features of LEACH protocol variants.

In Mishra, SInghadia, and Pandey (2014), authors proposed a new protocol Energy Level Bases Stable Election Protocol (ELBSEP) in WSN. The author analyzed and compared the results of protocols like LEACH, SEP, ESEP, TEEN, and TSEP with ELBSEP. The simulation result showed that performance and throughput of ELBSEP give the effective energy efficiency as well as more network lifetime compared to other protocols.

In Singh, Dua, and Mathur (2012), a survey is provided regarding the architecture design issues, classification of protocols, and also an overview on ns-2 simulator tool.

In Singh, Sing, and Singh (2010), author provided a survey of WSN routing protocols by taking into account several classification criteria including location information, network layering, data centricity, path redundancy, network dynamics, QoS requirements, network heterogeneity etc. and discussed a few example protocols for each of these categories and compared their strengths and limitations.

In Yick, Mukherjee, and Ghosal (2008), authors classified the problems into three categories: First, communication protocol stacks and network services, Secondly, internal platform and underlying operating system and lastly provisioning and deployment. In this author compares different proposed designs, protocols, algorithms, services etc.

CONCLUSION

In this chapter, we discussed WSNs, its types, applications, and challenges. This chapter also provides the comparison results of the three routing protocols that are LEACH, SEP, and TEEN respectively. The performance of these routing protocols is measured on some performance parameters like network lifetime and the number of dead nodes. Based on study and results analysis lifetime of the sensor network using TEEN protocol is better than LEACH and SEP and whereas SEP is better than LEACH. So, the overall TEEN is best routing protocol with respect to lifetime and energy consumption of the sensor network.

REFERENCES

Arora, V. K., Sharma, V., & Sachdeva, M. (2016). A survey on LEACH and other's routing protocols in wireless sensor network. *Optik-International Journal for Light and Electron Optics*, *127*(16), 6590–6600. doi:10.1016/j.ijleo.2016.04.041

Aswale, S., & Ghorpade, V. R. (2015). Survey of QoS routing protocols in wireless multimedia sensor networks. *Journal of Computer Networks and communications*, 7.

Dhawan, H., & Waraich, S. (2014). A comparative study on LEACH routing protocol and its variants in wireless sensor networks: a survey. *International Journal of Computers and Applications*, *95*(8).

Khan, A. R., Rakesh, N., Bansal, A., & Chaudhary, D. K. (2015, December). Comparative study of WSN Protocols (LEACH, PEGASIS, and TEEN). In *Proceedings of the 2015 Third International Conference on Image Information Processing (ICIIP)* (pp. 422-427). IEEE.

Miglani, A., Bhatia, T., Sharma, G., & Shrivastava, G. (2017). An energy efficient and trust aware framework for secure routing in LEACH for wireless sensor networks. scalable computing. *Practice and Experience*, *18*(3), 207–218.

Mishra, Y., Singhadia, A., & Pandey, R. (2014). Energy Level Based Stable Election Protocol in Wireless Sensor Network. *International Journal of Engineering Trends and Technology*, *17*(1), 32–38. doi:10.14445/22315381/IJETT-V17P206

Rathee, A., Singh, R., & Nandini, A. (2016). Wireless Sensor Network-Challenges and Possibilities. *International Journal of Computers and Applications*, *140*(2).

Saini, R., & Khari, M. (2011). Defining malicious behaviour of a node and its defensive methods in ad hoc network. *International Journal of Computers and Applications*, *20*(4), 18–21. doi:10.5120/2422-3251

Sharma, K., Bala, S., Bansal, H., & Shrivastava, G. (2017). Introduction to the special issue on secure solutions for network in scalable computing. *Scalable Computing, Practice and Experience*, *18*(3), iii–iv.

Sharma, K., & Gupta, B. B. (2016). Multi-layer defense against malware attacks on smartphone wi-fi access channel. *Procedia Computer Science*, *78*, 19–25. doi:10.1016/j.procs.2016.02.005

Sharma, S., Sethi, D., & Bhattacharya, P. P. (2015). *Wireless Sensor Network Structural Design and Protocols: A Survey*. Communications on Applied Electronics.

Singh, N., Dua, R., & Mathur, V. (2012). Wireless sensor networks: Architecture, protocols, simulator tool. *International Journal (Toronto, Ont.)*, *2*(5), 229–233.

Singh, S. K., Kumar, P., & Singh, J. P. (2017). Localization in Wireless Sensor Networks Using Soft Computing Approach. *International Journal of Information Security and Privacy*, *11*(3), 42–53. doi:10.4018/IJISP.2017070104

Singh, S. K., Singh, M. P., & Singh, D. K. (2010). A survey of energy-efficient hierarchical cluster-based routing in wireless sensor networks. *International Journal of Advanced Networking and Application*, *2*(02), 570–580.

Yick, J., Mukherjee, B., & Ghosal, D. (2008). Wireless sensor network survey. *Computer Networks*, *52*(12), 2292–2330. doi:10.1016/j.comnet.2008.04.002

KEY TERMS AND DEFINITIONS

Denial of Service: DoS is a type of attack on a network that is designed to disrupt the services of a host connected to the internet.

Heterogeneity: Heterogeneity is the state of being different in character or content.

Quality of Service: QoS: is the measurement of the overall performance of a service, such as a computer network.

Wireless Sensor Network: WSN is a network of small size sensor nodes which are densely deployed for monitoring the environment.

Chapter 2
Network Security:
Attacks and Control in MANET

Mamata Rath
C.V.Raman College of Engineering, India

Jhum Swain
Siksha 'O' Anusandhan University, India

Bibudhendu Pati
C.V.Raman College of Engineering, India

Binod Kumar Pattanayak
Siksha 'O' Anusandhan University, India

ABSTRACT

This chapter describes how with the rapid increase of internet users, more people have access to global information and communication technology. As a result of which, the issues of using the internet as a global platform for the enabling of smart objects and machines to coordinate, communicate, compute and calculate, gradually emerge. In Mobile Ad-hoc Networks (MANETs) the individual nodes are self-reconfigurable according to the changes of the network topology. Joint effort between portable hubs is more critical because they face major challenges such as powerlessness to work safely while protecting its assets and performing secure steering among hubs. With the existence of malicious nodes, one of the principal challenges in MANETs is to outline powerful security arrangement that can shield MANETs from various routing attacks. This chapter highlights major attacks and control mechanism in MANETs with an intention that it will open directions for researchers to explore more in the field of network security. At the end of this chapter, basic security mechanisms and issues related to emergence of IoT from Mobile networks has been highlighted.

DOI: 10.4018/978-1-5225-4100-4.ch002

INTRODUCTION

As MANET is a core technology emerged in the new generation, the basic security challenges include seamless communication with reliability in the network. In a wireless network without any infrastructure where there is no base station and access point, the chance of vulnerability is more. The mobile devices are free to move in any direction still maintaining connectivity with other mobile nodes. Due to this special quality of MANET, the design of MANET protocol with high-security features in very much essential. Again, due to dynamic change in topology, the network change takes place dynamically and so the network is decentralized and more vulnerable than the wired based network in many aspects.

In a special network called MANET, electronic devices and gadgets such as tablets, PCs, mobile phones, machines with specially appointed correspondence capacity are connected together to make a system. MANET is a self-organizing structure of flexible switches related hosts associated with secluded connections. The routers move randomly and compose themselves accordingly; along these lines, the systems remote topology may change quickly and capriciously (Huang et al., 2014). In MANETs (Madan Mohan et al., 2013), each node acts as the router and because of dynamic changing topology the accessibility of hubs is not generally ensured (Ling et al., 2012). It likewise does not ensure that the way between any two hubs would be free of pernicious hubs. The remote connection between hubs is exceptionally vulnerable to connection assaults such as passive eavesdropping, active interfering, etc. (Sridhar et al., 2013). Due to inflexibility in the infrastructure of MANET, it affects the security feature whenever any kind of extreme computation is done to perform encryption. So due to this problem, it is important to build a secured connection which can provide the high-security solution to provide secured services like authentication, confidentiality, integrity, non-repudiation, and availability. So here security is provided in each and every layer (Madan Mohan et al., 2013).

SECURITY MECHANISM IN MOBILE AD-HOC NETWORKS

Mobile Ad-hoc Networks have been well appreciated in recent years due to its fantastic features such as self-configurable workstations called nodes and they themselves can do their own maintenance (Jain et al., 2014). There are many open security issues in this special network such as its open architecture of network, its shared medium, the problem of resource constraints, and changeable network topology. In the network layer of the network model various attacks takes place during routing of the packets from one mobile device to other. There are some forwarding attacks, which leave the routing tables alone, but change the delivery of packets. Due to any weakness of the design of the underlying protocol, many attacks happen because of which there is denial of service to authenticated devices and many other type of problems take place (Choudhury et al., 2015). In the data link layer, various attacks take place due to any lacuna in Wireless Encryption Protocol. Similarly, another type of attack called Denial of Service (DoS) takes place (Dolk et al., 2017) in which the attacker prevents the communication between the network and a particular node member by isolating it from the group (Mejri et al., 2017). There are many novel contributions to develop secured protocols to prevent such attack in the network (Rath et al., 2016). The basic objective of security implementation in Mobile Ad-hoc networks is to keep sustainable connectivity over multi-hop wireless channels (Umamaheswari et al., 2015) to provide link-level security solutions and security mechanism provision at the network level (Paramasivan et al., 2015).

Normally in a MANET, two approaches are used for data transmission between source and destination such as proactive and reactive. While designing security solution for MANET, care should be taken to check the effect of network performance with increasing overhead due to complex logic used in security solution (Nakhaee et al., 2011). There has to be a balance level as per simulation result and then only final implementation should be carried out. There are some routing attacks (Yu et al., 2009) in the network layer by intruders, which steal data from the routing tables of the nodes remotely. In forwarding attack, the intruder or the attacker alters the destination address of the packets so that information from the communication channels is diverted towards the hacker computer instead of the destination. The Specific attack mechanism and their incorporation fully depend on the underlying protocol design (Forouzan, 2006). In message authentication, technique to secure the communication, one-way hash function based on shared key is used. To achieve more security, the data must be sent along with the MAC address of the system (Safan et al., 2014). The MAC address of the sender must be verified by the receiver before receiving and sending acknowledgement by the receiver only. In such case there will be less overhead on the network as there is no need to do repeat transmission due to attack (Yu M, et al., 2009). Based on the requirement of routing protocols either source based routing or distance vector routing takes place or link state routing is used. The mechanism of secure source based routing adds the identification of nodes to the dynamically created routing paths (Shakshuki, 2013; Miglani et al., 2017). This helps to prevent the intermediate nodes from changing their routing list. In secured link state routing, a particular source node identifies its neighbour nodes and broadcast its routing table list to every other node in that network. Purpose is to authenticate the process of discovering neighbouring nodes and broadcast information to neighbours. Some protocols also use digital signature for authentication (Jain et al., 2014; Sharma et al., 2017)).

VULNERABILITIES IN MANET

The various vulnerabilities faced by MANET are listed as follows:

- **Lack of Centralized Management:** It does not have centralized monitor server so for this reason, it is not easy to keep track of the traffic in a highly vibrant and large-scale ad-hoc network.
- **Scalability:** As nodes, move freely and openly so scaling of ad-hoc network changes frequently. Therefore, security should be capable of handling a bulky as well as tiny network (Al-Nahari et al., 2013).
- **Resource Constraints:** Due to limited access to resources, sometimes the MANET workstations are drained out of the network due to sudden exhaust of the limited battery power or some abnormal atmospheric condition, In such case, the resources held by them are unlocked and they do not have any controller which leads to easy access to intruders (Bhatsanghave et al., 2012).
- **Topology Change:** Due to the high frequency of change in network topology, the network information shared among the group of nodes under a particular category such as a specific real-time group (Pease et al., 2016) are exposed to neighbour nodes that leads to leakage of information to the rest of the network due to flooding. Nodes in MANET behave in a selfish manner if there is the limited power supply (Patil et al., 2012).

GOALS OF COMPUTER SECURITY IN MANET

To develop a secure MANET, we have to follow the goals that have already been standardized and we will discuss them here. They are as follows:

- **Availability:** A node always provides services it is designed. It concentrates crucially on Denial-of-Service attacks. Some selfish nodes make some network services unavailable (Qiankun, et al., 2011).
- **Integrity:** It refers to the process of guaranteeing the identity of the messenger. There are challenges such as malicious attacks and accidental altering (Sharma et al., 2012). The difference between the two is intent i.e., in the malicious attack, the attacker intentionally changes information whereas, in accidental altering, the alteration is accidentally done by a benign node.
- **Confidentiality:** Sometimes, some information ought to be accessible only to few, who have been authorized to access it. Others, who are unauthorized, should not get hold of this confidential information.
- **Authenticity:** Authenticity checks if a node is an impersonator or not. It is imperative that the identities of the participants are secured by encrypting their respective codes (Baozhu Li et al., 2010). The opponent could mimic a gentle node and can gain a way to private resources or even distribute some harmful messages.
- **Non-Repudiation:** Non-repudiation guarantees that the sender and the receiver of a message cannot refuse that he/she has not sent/received such a message. The instance of being compromised is established without ambiguity. For e.g. if a node identifies that the message it has received is invalid or not genuine (Nicola et al., 2011). The node can then use the incorrect message as a proof to alert other nodes that the nodes have been compromised (Zhu et al., 2011).
- **Authentication:** Bonafide credentials to be issued by the appropriate authority, which will be mandatory to assign access rights to users at different levels. It usually uses an authorization process.

SECURITY ISSUES IN MANET PROTOCOLS

Many security-based protocols have been designed by eminent researchers (Sridhar et al., 2013) while their study on security aspects of MANET. Protocols such as Adhoc on Demand Distance Vector (Rango et al., 2011), Secured -AODV protocol and the proposed method identifies about the various attacks on network layers (Madan Mohan et al., 2013). The SMC (Secure Multiparty Computation) protocol and the proposed method focuses on AODV and Secured AODV protocols and it analyzes the S-AODV protocol to identify unresolved threats to the algorithm such as MAC layer misbehavior, jellyfish etc. In another approach authors have used DSR protocol, where the proposed method involves identification mechanism needed between nodes and is done using identification and credentials and this leads to privacy problems (RSA Algorithm, 2017) i.e. the author uses service-oriented MANET, the Distributed methods must be taken care so that the availability of the service is maintained (Nishanthini et al., 2013) . In some other novel approach, the author has focussed on how to transmit audio securely and this done by providing double security in encrypting and decrypting the audio at each node in the route using stream ciphering method (Naqi. et al., 2013). A summary of few security mechanisms in MANET

(Rath et al., 2016) based on the functionality of the MANET protocols that are studied in this chapter and are presented in Table 1.

TYPES OF ATTACK IN MANET

Attacks can be classified into two broad categories in MANET (Schweitzer et al., 2016). According to the type of mechanism used during the attack to a computer or computing device during transmission

Table 1. Summary of MANET based protocols with their basic security mechanism

Sl. No	Literature	Year	Protocol/ Proposal	Full Name	Mechanism Used for Security
1	Choudhury et al.	2015	MAODV	Modified AODV	Black hole attack prevention mechanism
2	Huang et al.	2014	MEP-AODV	Multipath Energy Efficient Probability AODV	Carefully selection of next hop node after checking its authentication
3	Jain et al.	2014	EESM-AODV	Energy Efficient secure Multipath AODV	Multipath routing is determined using security based energy efficient technique
4	Mohan et al.	2013	PC-AODV	Power Control AODV	On-demand and as per requirement the power level of the selected node is checked
5	Nishanthini et al.	2013	E-AODV	Enhanced AODV	Link failure and the affected security issues are addressed during selection of next hop
6	Sridhar et al.	2013	EN-AODV	Energy AODV	Novel secured technique is used based on energy level for new path selection
7	Ali et al.	2012	NCLBR	Node Centric Load Balance Routing	A threshold criterion of load balancing approach is checked to avoid overhead.
8	Nahari et al	2013	RB-AODV	Receiver-Based AODV	Receiver sends notification of all possible and available path in order to avoid transmission in invalid path
9	Patil et al.	2012	E AODV	Enhanced AODV	To support Quality of Service, link failures are handled carefully.
10	Chirchi et al.	2012	O-AODV	Optimized AODV	A threshold value for energy level is determined and accordingly, route request packets arrival time is delayed.
11	Sharma et al.	2012	AODV-PP	Priority and Power AODV	As per priority the next level nodes are selected with strengthened power so that link failure due to sudden loss of energy can be avoided and further attacks can be prevented
12	Nakhaee et al.	2011	A novel communication Model	Petri Net based Model	Reliable communication is achieved using a PetriNet Model
13	Zhu et al.	2011	Improved AODV	Web-based Time Delay AODV	Security is controlled by providing the channel capacity to small functions, which handles the critical tasks on the mobile nodes.
14	Li et al.	2010	AODV_BD	Broadcast AODV	Considering link failure as the central cause of vulnerability, a broadcast approach is used to inform all the neighbor nodes regarding repair or failure of a link.
15	Kumar et al.	2010	MRAODV	Modified Reverse AODV	Depending on the stability of the nodes for longer period, a suitable path is selected during routing

over a network, the attack may be active or passive (Huang et al., 2007). In passive attack type, an attacker eavesdrops without altering the original information. But in active attack, the attacker carries the information and manipulates it or can also delete the information (Liu et al., 2014)

External Attacks

Here the attacker causes network jamming and this is done by the propagation of fake routing information. The attack disrupts the nodes to gain services.

Internal Attacks

In internal attack, the intruders are also involved in the network functions by using some malicious technique to interfere with the network. Sometimes the attacker captures an isolated node and uses it as the carrier to gain the network information. In Table 2 various types of attacks are specified which are commonly found in Mobile Ad-hoc Networks.

Black Hole Attack

In normal routing process of MANET, any intermediate node with a new route towards the destination can use RREQ message sent by the sender. By considering such case, an attacker node sends route reply information to the sender demanding that it has a route towards the destination. Actually, that attacker node has no route towards the destination (Debarati Roy et al., 2015), so it is a false message. After sensing such a message, the source node sends the important data to the attacker node assuming that it is the correct intermediate node towards the destination. However, this node makes the data drop without sending it to the proper channel resulting in transmission failure. When a group of such attacking nodes performs this attack collectively, it is known as cooperative black hole attack.

Table 2. Details of various attacks in different layers in MANET

Name of the Layer	Attacks	Description
Application Layer	Repudiation	It is a demonstration of refusal in taking an interest in all or some portion of correspondence.
	Malicious Attacks	In this attack, a pernicious hub aggravates the ordinary operation of alternate hubs in the system by assaulting the procedure framework.
Transport Layer	Session Hijacking	In this aggressor gets a path into the session condition of a specific client by taking session ID that is utilized to get into a framework and watches the information.
Data Link Layer	Denial of Service	There is a solitary remote channel shared by every one of the hubs so a malignant hub keeps this channel occupied by sending false parcels to deplete hub's battery control.
	MAC Targeted Attack	The MAC procedure is interrupted.
Physical Layer	Device Tampering	Hubs in specially appointed remote systems are little, smaller and hand-held like not at all like wired gadgets so they can be effortlessly stolen or harmed.
	Jamming	The assailant screens the remote medium with a specific end goal to discover recurrence at which goal hub is getting from sender hub. An aggressor must have the capable transmitter to send the signs to the goal of that recurrence, in this way meddling its operations. The most common types of jamming are random noise and pulse.

Cache Poisoning Attack

The assailant sends a fashioned DNS reaction, the degenerate information is given by the aggressor and it gets reserved by the genuine DNS name server. It is now that the DNS reserve is considered as "harmed". Thus, future clients that endeavour to visit the degenerate space will rather be directed to the new IP address chose by the aggressor. Clients will keep on receiving inauthentic IP addresses from the DNS until the harmed store has been cleared. Table 3 shows important types of attacks that are performed in the network layer of MANET.

CONGESTION CONTROL RELATED SECURITY ISSUES IN MANET

Mobile devices become vulnerable to insecurity and attack due to heavy congestion in the transmission channel. So, while considering congestion control and quality of service, it is indispensable to plan the security mechanism in data traffic. Commonly three types of traffic profiles work in the network, Constant Bit Rate (CBR), Variable Bit Rate (VBR) and Bursty. Congestion in a network may take place if the load on the network that is the number of packets engaged to the network is higher than the capacity of the network, i.e. the number of packets a network can handle. Secured congestion control highlights the method and techniques adapted to control the congestion and keep the load below the capacity of the network so that attacks may be disallowed. Packet Delay and Throughput are exaggerated greatly due to congested traffic as they act as the function of network load. The delay increases when the load increases and the throughput keep varying till the load reaches the network capability but when the load exceeds the network capability, there is the reduction in throughput due to congestion. Table 4 depicts details of contributed security mechanism studied in the current article.

Table 3. Various attacks in network layer of MANET

Attacks	Description
Worm-Hole Attack	A noxious hub gets bundles at one area in the system and massages them to another area in the system where these parcels are resent into the system. This tunnel between two colliding attackers is referred to a wormhole.
Black-Hole Attack	In this assault, a malignant hub publicizes legitimate and most limited course to a casualty hub and from there on furtively drops information and control bundles as they go through it.
Byzantine Attack	It includes different aggressors that work in the conspiracy to debase the system execution, for example, making circles, specifically dropping bundles, picking non-ideal ways for parcel sending.
Routing Table Poisoning	In this assault, the vindictive hub sends manufactured directing refresh and blunder messages or adjusted authentic updates to approved hubs in the system.
Routing Cache Poisoning	A malevolent hub can dispatch DOS attack on any hub by just communicating ridiculed parcels with source courses.
Replay Attack	An aggressor as opposed to changing parcels content simply replay stale bundles with a specific end goal to endeavor battery power, transfer speed and computational limitation of portable hubs.
Rushing Attack	This assault includes whole system moves to go through an assailant. The source hub can't locate any protected way without the assailant.
Jellyfish Attack	It is a specific dark gap assault in which noxious hub assaults the system by reordering the parcels or expanding jitter of the bundles that go through it keeping in mind the end goal to keep it from being identified and it appears to the system that misfortune or deferral is because of ecological reasons.

Table 4. Details of Contributed Security Mechanism studied in the article.

S. No.	Literature	Year	Contribution	Secured Congestion Control	Description
1.	Tang et al.	2002	RALM	Designing a reliable multicast transport protocol	When subjected to network conditions such as traffic load, number of multicast sources and mobility it achieves reliability and exhibits low end to end delay and minimal control overhead
2.	Peng et al.	2003	Congestion Control improved Scheme	It presents a multicast congestion control scheme for MANET	This scheme overcomes the disadvantage of existing multicast congestion control protocols but also achieves good performance in terms of traffic stability, robust against misbehaving receiver etc.
3.	Yerajana et al.	2009	TASR	A new routing protocol for the ad-hoc wireless network is proposed.	A scheme is proposed to distribute load between multiple paths according to time stamp values of the packets associated paths.
4.	Rashidi et al.	2009	AODV	This scheme presents a developed trust protocol based on congestion control.	The congestion control section guarantees the stability of network and does the distribution of the load on the most highly trust nodes. Its performed by the agents on the network nodes.
5.	Kumaran et al.	2010	EDAODV	This scheme presents early detection and congestion control routing protocol for the wireless ad-hoc network.	This protocol detects congestion at the node level and it finds congestion status by utilizing non-congested predecessor and successor nodes of a congested node.
6.	Yuanzhou et al.	2010	Analysis of Conventional AODV	To overcome the disadvantage of AODV i.e. localized network congestion.	AODV protocol doesn't take into account the current load of nodes in the process of route discovery, so it leads to localized network congestion, so this deficiency is overcome and is improved with fuzzy control theory and random early detection ideas are used.
7.	Tabash et al.	2011	FL-TCP	This scheme is based on fuzzy inference system.	It is based on the factors of expected throughput & actual throughput to dynamically adjust the congestion window size that leads to the improvement in the performance of TCP in MANET. This scheme does not rely on explicit from the network; it requires only the sender side modification.
8.	Ikeda et al.	2012	OLSR	This scheme deals with congestion control for multi-flow traffic in wireless MANET.	Here the MANET performance that considers the random waypoint mobility model for different no. of nodes and different area sizes by sending multi-flow traffic in the network.
9.	Ikeda et al.	2012	AODV and OLSR analysis	This scheme deals with TCP congestion control for multiple traffic in MANETs.	Here the MANET performance is considered by using random waypoint mobility model for different no. of nodes by sending multiple traffic in the network.
10.	Sreenivas et al.	2012	Scheme for Link Layer Congestion	This scheme designs link layer congestion control for ad-hoc wireless MANET.	Here the bandwidth and delay are measured at each node along the path. Based on the cumulated values, the receiver calculates the new window size and transmits the information to the sender as feedback.

CONTROLS IN MOBILE AD-HOC NETWORKS AGAINST SECURITY ATTACKS

There are increasing numbers of new types of security attacks in the network with increasing technology. There are several strategies for security concern such as confidentiality and integrity with confidentiality and access control with reference monitors (Shakshuki et al., 2013). Network protection also takes place because of such controls. Firewalls, Intrusion Detection system and encrypted email are three basic control mechanisms used for network protection and these are discussed at various places in this chapter in details. Other control mechanisms are discussed briefly in the following section.

Use of Authorized Software and Integrity Checking

A list of authorized software should be maintained for the concerned organizations at the higher management level. Software that is required for the specific system should be licensed including servers, workstations, and necessary peripheral devices and they should be continuously monitored by the authorized group of people. Continuous checking of the software listed in the above section should be carried out in order to check the integrity of the software to validate that the software has not been modified. If an automated system is used, then the status of the software should be crosschecked with its previous version. In case of emergency if any unapproved software is installed in the computer, then regular scanning must be performed and alert messages must be generated in case of any violation of configuration (Liu et al., 2014). The techniques used for cross-checking of validity of the authentication procedures and correctness of information needs to be refreshed and changed periodically and such changes should be made under the supervision of authentic authority only.

Application Deployment With Authorized Technology and Logbook

Application white listing technology should be employed which allows computing systems to run only those approved software and restricts the use of other software on working systems. Hardware vendors who provide operating system software may be negotiated beforehand for this issue. Software inventory tools may be deployed in the entire organization to keep track of any minor change to the repository and immediately to be noticed to the authority (Paramasivan et al., 2015). Security based programs will be successful only if they are handled by logbook maintenance.

Automated Scanning Tool and Regular Vulnerability Report

The automated scanning tools should not only check the upload/download of applications to the system, additionally, they should also monitor the version no. and patch level. Regular vulnerability report - A vulnerability report (Security, 2017) should be produced periodically and it should highlight the level of vulnerability associated with each hardware and software components associated with the organizational network. This report should be directed to threat intelligence services to fix vulnerable software actively. The discussed software inventory system must be connected to the hardware asset inventory system so that all devices and associated software can be tracked and monitored from a single point of control. The inventory tool and program that keeps track of software should also keep track of individual unauthorized software installed at the individual workstations. This practice is carried out to check the installations of software without the knowledge of authorized monitoring program. Monitoring exchange of suspicious file types over the network, various dangerous file types with extensions such as .exe .zip and .msi should be carefully monitored and if required blocked. If such file types are sometimes required by the organizations, then all such files need to be scanned closely before given for use. Virtual machines are also secured systems, which should be used to run applications, which are based on higher risk factors and should not be installed within a network environment.

INTRUSION DETECTION SYSTEM IN MANET

Intrusion Detection System (IDS) (Pattanayak et al., 2014) have turned out to be most indispensable part of the guard. Now a day's advanced Intrusion Detection Systems are designed to protect the network from outside attacks, as normal methods of encryption techniques and authentication mechanism are very easy to be broken by intruders. As more customized functionalities are added to the system hence, the complex systems become more venerable leading to exposure to more security attacks. Therefore, Intrusion Detection Systems (IDS) can be used as a secondary source of protection to a network system (Kang et al., 2013). If an attack is detected by the system, an immediate preventive mechanism is alarmed to protect the system. IDS can be designed as host based or network based (Yi et al., 2015). Packets capturing and their analysis in a traffic are done in a network-based IDS while in a host-based IDS the log directory of the operating system and application manuals are analyzed to find out the problem. As per their detection technology, IDS can be either anomaly detection system, misuse detection system or specification based detection system. Many researchers have proposed the design of a mobile agent in IDS network because mobile agents help the nodes by contributing their intelligence to the host node for which they have been previously registered or there is some negotiation with them. The basic purpose of the IDS can be scattered among the mobile agents in a distributed approach (Bridges et al., 2013). Advantages of using Mobile Agents in IDS include reduced power consumption by nodes and secured transmission in the network. IDS are a strategy for observing PC framework or systems for unapproved affirmation, development or document adjustment (Yang et al., 2017). It can likewise be utilized to check arranged movement, with the goal that it can detect the framework whether it is been focused by a system assault, for example, dark opening or dissent of administration assault. IDS (Dolk et al., 2017) can accomplish location by ceaselessly observing and dissecting the system for strange movement, some exceptional assaults, and action, which are not same as day-by-day action. IDS can be ordered into two sorts relying upon information accumulation system and identification instrument. Sorts of IDS relying upon the information accumulation system incorporates Network based IDS (NIDS) and Host-based IDS (HIDS).

EMERGENCE FROM MANET TO SECURED IOT TECHNOLOGY

In the current technological scenario, the Internet of Things (IoT) is developing as a promising trend towards interconnecting physical object (Miorandi et al., 2012). Conceptually the IoT provides a platform to enable the objects to interact with each other or with end users by forming the network of interconnected things. Recent advancement in Mobile Adhoc Networks (MANET) that enables dynamically formation of network and networking without pre-defined infrastructure shows great success incorporating many IoT based application domain in smart cities. Internet of things (IoT) and ubiquitous computing, such as

MANET becomes increasingly popular in current technology (Reina et al., 2013). This section focuses on major security aspects due to handshaking of IoT with MANET and issues related to IoT based applications in MANET and they are analyzed with the special focus on the need of smart protocols for the smart environment.

With the rapid increase of internet users, more people have access to global information and communication technology, as a result of which the issues of using the internet as a global platform and enabling the smart objects and machines to coordinate, communicate, compute and calculate gradually emerges (Bellavista et al., 2013). Every day billions of people across the world use the Internet for browsing and accessing the World Wide Web for many purposes like send and receive email, download high volume audio and video files, games, animation using social networking sites etc. At the same time, another problem of the use of the internet as a common platform for communication and message transmission by smart objects and coordination among them also gradually increases. In this context, the term "Internet-of-Things" (IoT) is basically used to refer smart objects with advanced Internet Technology (Airehrour et al., 2015) and all supporting technology used to realize such ideal vision and to put together properly application and service technology to open new business opportunity. It is very much essential to design highly efficient and secure routing protocols for both MANET and IoT. Cryptographic techniques are used in many secured routing for the security of mobile nodes by authentication at every hop during hop-to-hop transmission (Hua et al., 2011). The authentication mechanism is carried out among the nodes and t every intermediate node to cryptographically ensure after checking the digital signatures, which are attached to the encrypted routing information. Sometimes a trust metric is used as the parameter to check the authenticity of the data packets. The final objective of having secured protocol is to store more valid information to the routing messages, efficiently calculating the routing table updates and other security-based operations that are embedded into the routing protocols thereby securing it most. Excessive overhead sometimes makes inefficient decisions. So the final objective is to design energy and delay efficient routing protocols for IoT environment (Qin et al., 2014) keeping all the possible security aspects into consideration.

This section provides a detailed survey and analysis of security in IoT and wireless networks. IoT technology views all the objects in the inter-connected world as virtual objects (Silva et al., 205). Such objects can be either device, services, and processes, which are capable of offering methods to remain, connected to the Internet. Therefore, IoT is a part of the future Internet that can be understood as a paradigm, which integrates different technological solutions. Therefore, there is a need for standard transmission protocols, which can support this particular aspect of IoT. MANET can be understood as a self-organized and self-configured group of mobile nodes in a wireless network capable of doing communication with each other dynamically (Tan et al., 2015). Nowadays this important ubiquitous computing along with IoT technology gradually becomes popular as this pair of network environment works efficiently on Smart Objects. According to Paolo et al. (2013), wireless networks such as WSN and MANETs have become the main technology for many IoT applications and similar domains in smart cities. Due o their self-configuration ability their role in IoT has become more efficient (Caroline et al., 2013). These application areas range from academic interest to research and very soon these combined technology is going to be implemented in Environment Monitoring, traffic management and for public safety-related systems. It is a very challenging task to manage security at the IoT environment as here many heterogeneous devices are networked together. Current research shows that the networks due to IoT are prone to many attacks such as malware, botnet, DoS (Denial of Service) attack; Web-based malware, Android malware, and spam (Shrivastava et al., 2010). Therefore, there is need of developing a standard secured framework for communication in IoT (Hua et al., 2011). The basic requirement of the Internet of Things, which is also any kind of Adhoc Network, is availability, authenticity, and non-repudiation that are features of basic security regulations. Confidentiality refers to the feature that ensures that information should never be revealed to the wrong source. In MANETs, there are security provisions not to allow malicious nodes to get unauthorized access to important information regarding routing neither from any genuine node or while the transmission goes on this information does not reveals outside. Similarly, another feature of security Integrity refers to confirming the data accepted by destination node should not be directed to the wrong destination while in transit.

Designing secure and efficient routing protocols for MANETS is a primary challenge but, extremely useful in maintaining network route information and security. Cryptographic techniques are used to keep the routing information secured during the transmission. Security protocols are embedded in routing mechanism to authenticate and validate the packets during hop-to-hop transmission. All intermediate nodes are required to authenticate and check the digital signature attached to the packets before forwarding to the next hop node.

In Communication, the system used in battlefields, tanks, ground soldiers and real-time aerial vehicles comprises an IoT network where MANET technology used for communication. A password-based group key exchange system was developed by Byun (2006) for such network. A more developed password based communication scheme is proposed in (for IoT environment that can be used in battle field and it supports dynamic group scheme. In this method, the group nodes of the heterogeneous MANET understand the broadcast message and direct communication is possible in real-time systems. Simulation of this scheme proves that it is dynamic and robust. In Software Defined Networking Architecture the main importance is given to the network statistics such as transmission rate, bandwidth consumption rate, delay rate (Qin et al., 2014). Whereas in IoT due to multiple networking state information about many devices are stored in a loosely coupled manner over the distributed network. To measure the performance of IoT network it is difficult to select a parameter just like bandwidth consumption etc due to heterogeneous type and time-sensitive issue of different data types. In recent technology SDN, techniques are mostly used in wireless network. Silva et al. (2015) proposed a symbiotic resource sharing mechanism in IoT platform and its architecture is designed to choose a better performance metric in IoT network. The data collection component and device-related information from the multi-networking environment of IoT and the information are stored in the database. Then the information is used by the layered component. The Analyst also controls the process by incorporating external software tools to the system. Conceptually the controller is centralized to improve the throughput as per increase of large volume of data. Due to the Emergence of MANET equipped IoT technology, prompt communication and interaction among Smart Objects in a highly mobile and dynamic environment has been successfully achieved. Handshaking of MANETs with IoT play significant role in many challenging and advanced application domains like smart cities, traffic Management, controlling, monitoring and Logistics.

CONCLUSION

Security of the network being the primary factor of data communication, the said chapter focuses on the most important security issues and controls in Mobile Adhoc Network (MANET). Introduction part of this chapter highlights on security issues at different levels of routing and how those issues have been handled by incorporating intelligent prevention control strategies. Other than the general and conventional security issues in MANET, this chapter provides more stress on security problems at different layers of the network with more emphasis on network layer where the basic routing mechanism takes place. Different attacks in MANET has been discussed and Control mechanisms have been highlighted in the context of business organizations. IDS as a security framework has also been emphasized in the last part of the chapter. Similarly, security in IoT technology has been discussed with the various mechanisms where there is convergence from MANET to secured IoT transformation.

REFERENCES

Ahmed, A. S., Kumaran, T. S., Syed, S. S. A., & Subburam, S. (2015). Cross-layer design approach for power control in mobile ad hoc networks. *Egyptian Informatics Journal*, *16*(1), 1–7. doi:10.1016/j.eij.2014.11.001

Airehrour, D., & Gutierrez, J. A. (2015). An analysis of secure MANET routing features to maintain confidentiality and integrity in IoT routing. In CONF-IRM (p. 17).

Ali, A., & Huiqiang, W. (2012, March). Node centric load balancing routing protocol for mobile ad hoc networks. In *Proceeding of International MultiConference of Enginners Computer Scientists*.

Al-Nahari, A., Mohamad, M. M., & Al-Sharaeh, S. (2013, December). Receiver-based AODV routing protocol for MANETs. In *Proceedings of the 2013 13th International Conference on Intelligent Systems Design and Applications (ISDA)* (pp. 126-130). IEEE. 10.1109/ISDA.2013.6920721

Basurra, S. S., De Vos, M., Padget, J., Ji, Y., Lewis, T., & Armour, S. (2015). Energy efficient zone based routing protocol for MANETs. *Ad Hoc Networks*, *25*, 16–37. doi:10.1016/j.adhoc.2014.09.010

Bellavista, P., Cardone, G., Corradi, A., & Foschini, L. (2013). Convergence of MANET and WSN in IoT urban scenarios. *IEEE Sensors Journal*, *13*(10), 3558–3567. doi:10.1109/JSEN.2013.2272099

Bhatsangave, S. P., & Chirchi, V. R. (2012). OAODV routing algorithm for improving energy efficiency in MANET. *International Journal of Computers and Applications*, *51*(21).

Bridges, C. P., & Vladimirova, T. (2013). Towards an agent computing platform for distributed computing on satellites. *IEEE Transactions on Aerospace and Electronic Systems*, *49*(3), 1824–1838. doi:10.1109/TAES.2013.6558023

Brindha, C. K., Nivetha, S. K., & Asokan, R. (2014, February). Energy efficient multi-metric QoS routing using genetic algorithm in MANET. In *Proceedings of the 2014 International Conference on Electronics and Communication Systems (ICECS)*. IEEE. 10.1109/ECS.2014.6892695

Chibelushi, C., Eardley, A., & Arabo, A. (2013). Identity management in the internet of things: The role of manets for healthcare applications. *Computer Science and Information Technology*, *1*(2), 73–81.

Choudhury, D. R., Ragha, L., & Marathe, N. (2015). Implementing and improving the performance of AODV by receive reply method and securing it from Black hole attack. *Procedia Computer Science*, *45*, 564–570. doi:10.1016/j.procs.2015.03.109

Corriero, N., Covino, E., & Mottola, A. (2011). An approach to use FB-AODV with Android. *Procedia Computer Science*, *5*, 336–343. doi:10.1016/j.procs.2011.07.044

Da Silva, E., Dos Santos, A. L., Albini, L. C. P., & Lima, M. N. (2008). Identity-based key management in mobile ad hoc networks: Techniques and applications. *IEEE Wireless Communications*, *15*(5), 46–52. doi:10.1109/MWC.2008.4653131

De Rango, F., Veltri, F., & Fazio, P. (2011). Interference aware-based ad-hoc on demand distance vector (IA-AODV) ultra wideband system routing protocol. *Computer Communications*, *34*(12), 1475–1483. doi:10.1016/j.comcom.2010.09.011

Dolk, V. S., Tesi, P., De Persis, C., & Heemels, W. P. M. H. (2017). Event-triggered control systems under denial-of-service attacks. *IEEE Transactions on Control of Network Systems*, *4*(1), 93–105. doi:10.1109/TCNS.2016.2613445

Forouzan, B. A., & Mosharraf, F. (2012). *Computer networks: a top-down approach* (p. 931). McGraw-Hill.

Halder, T. K., Chowdhury, C., & Neogy, S. (2014, August). Power aware AODV routing protocol for MANET. In *Proceedings of the 2014 Fourth International Conference on Advances in Computing and Communications (ICACC)* (pp. 331-334). IEEE. 10.1109/ICACC.2014.84

Harishankar, S., Woungang, I., Dhurandher, S. K., Traore, I., & Kaleel, S. B. (2015, March). E-MAnt Net: An ACO-Based Energy Efficient Routing Protocol for Mobile Ad Hoc Networks. In *Proceedings of the 2015 IEEE 29th International Conference on Advanced Information Networking and Applications (AINA)* (pp. 29-36). IEEE.

Hua, Z., Fei, G., Qiaoyan, W., & Zhengping, J. (2011). A Password-Based Secure Communication Scheme in Battlefields for Internet of Things. *China Communications*, *8*(1), 72–78.

Huang, Y. M., Yeh, C. H., Wang, T. I., & Chao, H. C. (2007). Constructing secure group communication over wireless ad hoc networks based on a virtual subnet model. *IEEE Wireless Communications*, *14*(5), 70–75. doi:10.1109/MWC.2007.4396945

Huang, Z., Yamamoto, R., & Tanaka, Y. (2014, February). A multipath energy-efficient probability routing protocol in ad hoc networks. In *Proceedings of the 2014 16th International Conference on Advanced Communication Technology (ICACT)* (pp. 244-250). IEEE. 10.1109/ICACT.2014.6778932

Ikeda, M., Kulla, E., Hiyama, M., Barolli, L., Miho, R., & Takizawa, M. (2012, July). Congestion control for multi-flow traffic in wireless mobile ad-hoc networks. In *Proceedings of the 2012 Sixth International Conference on Complex, Intelligent and Software Intensive Systems (CISIS)* (pp. 290-297). IEEE. 10.1109/CISIS.2012.83

Jain, H. R., & Sharma, S. K. (2014, August). Improved energy efficient secure multipath AODV routing protocol for MANET. In *Proceedings of the 2014 International Conference on Advances in Engineering and Technology Research (ICAETR)*. IEEE. 10.1109/ICAETR.2014.7012847

Jain, H. R., & Sharma, S. K. (2014, August). Improved energy efficient secure multipath AODV routing protocol for MANET. In *Proceedings of the 2014 International Conference on Advances in Engineering and Technology Research (ICAETR)*. IEEE. 10.1109/ICAETR.2014.7012847

Kishor, A. (2008, December 11). Scan your network for security vulnerabilities using GFI languard. *Helpdeskgeek*. Retrieved on August 25, 2017 from http://helpdeskgeek.com/product-reviews/scan-your-network-for-security-vulnerabilities-using-gfi-languard/

Kumar, P., Kumar, R., Kumar, S., & Kumar, R. D. (2010). Improved modified reverse AODV protocol. *International Journal of Computers and Applications, 12*(4), 22–26. doi:10.5120/1665-2242

Li, B., Liu, Y., & Chu, G. (2010, August). Improved AODV routing protocol for vehicular Ad hoc networks. In *Proceedings of the 2010 3rd International Conference on Advanced Computer Theory and Engineering (ICACTE)* (Vol. 4, pp. V4-337). IEEE.

Li, Y., & Hu, W. (2010, September). Optimization strategy for mobile ad hoc network based on AODV routing protocol. In *Proceedings of the 2010 6th International Conference on Wireless Communications Networking and Mobile Computing (WiCOM)*. IEEE. 10.1109/WICOM.2010.5601193

Liu, L., Zhu, L., Lin, L., & Wu, Q. (2012). Improvement of AODV routing protocol with QoS support in wireless mesh networks. *Physics Procedia, 25*, 1133–1140. doi:10.1016/j.phpro.2012.03.210

Liu, W., & Yu, M. (2014). AASR: Authenticated anonymous secure routing for MANETs in adversarial environments. *IEEE Transactions on Vehicular Technology, 63*(9), 4585–4593. doi:10.1109/TVT.2014.2313180

MadhanMohan, R., & Selvakumar, K. (2012). Power controlled routing in wireless ad hoc networks using cross layer approach. *Egyptian Informatics Journal, 13*(2), 95–101. doi:10.1016/j.eij.2012.05.001

Malek, A. G., Chunlin, L. I., Zhiyong, Y., Hasan, A. N., & Xiaoqing, Z. (2012). Improved the energy of ad hoc on-demand distance vector routing protocol. *IERI Procedia, 2*, 355–361. doi:10.1016/j.ieri.2012.06.101

Mall, R. (2009). *Real-time systems: theory and practice*. Pearson Education India.

Mejri, M. N., & Ben-Othman, J. (2017). GDVAN: A New Greedy Behavior Attack Detection Algorithm for VANETs. *IEEE Transactions on Mobile Computing, 16*(3), 759–771. doi:10.1109/TMC.2016.2577035

Miglani, A., Bhatia, T., Sharma, G., & Shrivastava, G. (2017). An Energy Efficient and Trust Aware Framework for Secure Routing in LEACH for Wireless Sensor Networks. Scalable Computing. *Practice and Experience, 18*(3), 207–218.

Miorandi, D., Sicari, S., De Pellegrini, F., & Chlamtac, I. (2012). Internet of things: Vision, applications and research challenges. *Ad Hoc Networks, 10*(7), 1497–1516. doi:10.1016/j.adhoc.2012.02.016

Nakhaee, A., Harounabadi, A., & Mirabedini, J. (2011, October). A novel communication model to improve Mobile Ad hoc Network routing reliability. In *Proceedings of the 2011 5th International Conference on Application of Information and Communication Technologies (AICT)*. IEEE. 10.1109/ICAICT.2011.6110971

Nishanthini, C., Rajkumar, G., & Jayabhavani, G. N. (2013, January). Enhanced performance of AODV with power boosted alternate path. In *Proceedings of the 2013 International Conference on Computer Communication and Informatics (ICCCI)*. IEEE. 10.1109/ICCCI.2013.6466148

Paramasivan, B., Prakash, M. J. V., & Kaliappan, M. (2015). Development of a secure routing protocol using game theory model in mobile ad hoc networks. *Journal of Communications and Networks (Seoul)*, *17*(1), 75–83. doi:10.1109/JCN.2015.000012

Patil, V. P. (2012). Efficient AODV Routing Protocol for MANET with enhanced packet delivery ratio and minimized end to end delay. *International journal of scientific and Research Publications*, *2*(8).

Pattanayak, B. K., & Rath, M. (2014). A mobile agent based intrusion detection system architecture for mobile ad hoc networks. *Journal of Computational Science*, *10*(6), 970–975. doi:10.3844/jcssp.2014.970.975

Pease, S. G., Phillips, I. W., & Guan, L. (2016). Adaptive intelligent middleware architecture for mobile real-time communications. *IEEE Transactions on Mobile Computing*, *15*(3), 572–585. doi:10.1109/TMC.2015.2412932

Peng, J., & Sikdar, B. (2003, December). A multicast congestion control scheme for mobile ad-hoc networks. In *Proceedings of the Global Telecommunications Conference GLOBECOM'03* (Vol. 5, pp. 2860-2864). IEEE.

Qiankun, Z., Tingxue, X., Hongqing, Z., Chunying, Y., & Tingjun, L. (2011). A Mobile Ad Hoc Networks Algorithm Improved AODV Protocol. *Procedia Engineering*, *23*, 229–234. doi:10.1016/j.proeng.2011.11.2494

Qin, Z., Denker, G., Giannelli, C., Bellavista, P., & Venkatasubramanian, N. (2014, May). A software defined networking architecture for the internet-of-things. In *Proceedings of the 2014 Network Operations and Management Symposium (NOMS)*. IEEE. 10.1109/NOMS.2014.6838365

Rashidi, R., Jamali, M. A. J., Salmasi, A., & Tati, R. (2009, October). Trust routing protocol based on congestion control in MANET. In *Proceedings of the International Conference on Application of Information and Communication Technologies AICT '09*. IEEE. 10.1109/ICAICT.2009.5372623

Rath, M., & Panda, M. R. (2016, December). MAQ system development in mobile ad-hoc networks using mobile agents. In *Proceedings of the 2016 2nd International Conference on Contemporary Computing and Informatics (IC3I)* (pp. 794-798). IEEE. 10.1109/IC3I.2016.7918791

Rath, M., & Pattanayak, B. K. (2017). MAQ: A Mobile Agent Based Quality of Service Platform for MANETs. *International Journal of Business Data Communications and Networking*, *13*(1). doi:10.4018/IJBDCN.2017010101

Rath, M., Pati, B., & Pattanayak, B. K. (2017, January). Cross layer based QoS platform for multimedia transmission in MANET. In *Proceedings of the 2017 11th International Conference on Intelligent Systems and Control (ISCO)* (pp. 402-407). IEEE. 10.1109/ISCO.2017.7856026

Rath, M., Pati, B., Pattanayak, B. K., Panigrahi, C. R., & Sarkar, J. L. (2017). Load balanced routing scheme for MANETs with power and delay optimisation. *International Journal of Communication Networks and Distributed Systems*, *19*(4), 394–405. doi:10.1504/IJCNDS.2017.087386

Rath, M., Pattanayak, B. K., & Pati, B. (2015). Energy Competent Routing Protocol Design in MANET with Real Time Application Provision. *International Journal of Business Data Communications and Networking*, *11*(1), 50–60. doi:10.4018/IJBDCN.2015010105

Rath, M., Pattanayak, B. K., & Pati, B. (2016). Energy Efficient MANET Protocol Using Cross Layer Design for Military Applications. *Defence Science Journal, 66*(2), 146–150. doi:10.14429/dsj.66.9705

Rath, M., Pattanayak, B. K., & Pati, B. (2016). QoS Satisfaction in MANET Based Real Time Applications. *International Journal of Control Theory and Applications, 9*(7), 3069-3083.

Rath, M., Pattanayak, B. K., & Pati, B. (2016). Resource Reservation and Improved QoS for Real Time Applications in MANET. *Indian Journal of Science and Technology, 9*(36). doi:10.17485/ijst/2016/v9i36/100910

Rath, M., Pattanayak, B. K., & Pati, B. (2016, March). Inter-layer communication based QoS platform for real time multimedia applications in MANET. In *Proceedings of the International Conference on Wireless Communications, Signal Processing and Networking (WiSPNET)* (pp. 591-595). IEEE. 10.1109/WiSPNET.2016.7566203

Rath, M., Pattanayak, B. K., & Pati, B. (2017). Energetic Routing Protocol Design for Real-time Transmission in Mobile Ad hoc Network. In *Computing and Network Sustainability* (pp. 187–199). Singapore: Springer. doi:10.1007/978-981-10-3935-5_20

Rath, M., Pattanayak, B., & Pati, B. (2016). A Contemporary Survey and Analysis of Delay and Power Based Routing Protocols in MANET. *Journal of Engineering and Applied Sciences (Asian Research Publishing Network), 11*(1).

Rath, M., Pattanayak, B., & Pati, B. (2016). Comparative analysis of AODV routing protocols based on network performance parameters in Mobile Adhoc Networks. In *Foundations and Frontiers in Computer, Communication and Electrical Engineering* (pp. 461-466).

Rath, M., Rout, U. P., Pujari, N., Nanda, S. K., & Panda, S. P. (2017). Congestion Control Mechanism for Real Time Traffic in Mobile Adhoc Networks. In *Computer Communication, Networking and Internet Security* (pp. 149–156). Singapore: Springer. doi:10.1007/978-981-10-3226-4_14

Reina, D. G., Toral, S. L., Barrero, F., Bessis, N., & Asimakopoulou, E. (2013). The role of ad hoc networks in the internet of things: A case scenario for smart environments. In *Internet of Things and Inter-Cooperative Computational Technologies for Collective Intelligence* (pp. 89–113). Springer Berlin Heidelberg. doi:10.1007/978-3-642-34952-2_4

Geeksforgeeks.org. RSA. (n.d.). Algorithm in Cryptography. Retrieved May 25, 2017 from http://www.geeksforgeeks.org/rsa-algorithm-cryptography

Safa, H., Karam, M., & Moussa, B. (2014). PHAODV: Power aware heterogeneous routing protocol for MANETs. *Journal of Network and Computer Applications, 46*, 60–71. doi:10.1016/j.jnca.2014.07.035

Sankaranarayanan, V. (2010, September). Early detection congestion and control routing in MANET. In *Proceedings of the 2010 Seventh International Conference on Wireless And Optical Communications Networks (WOCN)*. IEEE.

Schweitzer, N., Stulman, A., Shabtai, A., & Margalit, R. D. (2016). Mitigating denial of service attacks in OLSR protocol using fictitious nodes. *IEEE Transactions on Mobile Computing, 15*(1), 163–172. doi:10.1109/TMC.2015.2409877

Shakshuki, E. M., Kang, N., & Sheltami, T. R. (2013). EAACK—a secure intrusion-detection system for MANETs. *IEEE Transactions on Industrial Electronics*, *60*(3), 1089–1098. doi:10.1109/TIE.2012.2196010

Sharma, K., Bala, S., Bansal, H., & Shrivastava, G. (2017). Introduction to the Special Issue on Secure Solutions for Network in Scalable Computing. Scalable Computing. *Practice and Experience*, *18*(3), iii–iv.

Sharma, S., & Patheja, P. S. (2012). Improving AODV routing protocol with priority and power efficiency in mobile ad hoc WiMAX network. *International journal of computer technology and electronics engineering*, *2*(1), 87-93.

Shrivastava, G., Sharma, K., & Rai, S. (2010, December). The Detection & Defense of DoS & DDoS Attack: A Technical Overview. In *Proceeding of ICC* (Vol. 27, p. 28).

Silva, R., Silva, J. S., & Boavida, F. (2015, April). A symbiotic resources sharing IoT platform in the smart cities context. In *Proceedings of the 2015 IEEE Tenth International Conference on Intelligent Sensors, Sensor Networks and Information Processing (ISSNIP)*. IEEE. 10.1109/ISSNIP.2015.7106922

Sreenivas, B. C., Prakash, G. B., & Ramakrishnan, K. V. (2013, February). L2DB-TCP: An adaptive congestion control technique for MANET based on link layer measurements. In *Proceedings of the 2013 IEEE 3rd International Advance Computing Conference (IACC)* (pp. 1086-1093). IEEE.

Sridhar, S., Baskaran, R., & Chandrasekar, P. (2013). Energy supported AODV (EN-AODV) for QoS routing in MANET. *Procedia: Social and Behavioral Sciences*, *73*, 294–301. doi:10.1016/j.sbspro.2013.02.055

Sun, E., Zhang, X., & Li, Z. (2012). The internet of things (IOT) and cloud computing (CC) based tailings dam monitoring and pre-alarm system in mines. *Safety Science*, *50*(4), 811–815. doi:10.1016/j.ssci.2011.08.028

Sun, Y., Bai, J., Zhang, H., Sun, R., & Phillips, C. (2015). A Mobility-Based Routing Protocol for CR Enabled Mobile Ad Hoc Networks. *International Journal of Wireless Networks and Broadband Technologies*, *4*(1), 81–104. doi:10.4018/ijwnbt.2015010106

Tabash, I. K., Ahmad, N., & Beg, S. (2011, October). A congestion window control mechanism based on fuzzy logic to improve tcp performance in manets. In *Proceedings of the 2011 International Conference on Computational Intelligence and Communication Networks (CICN)* (pp. 21-26). IEEE. 10.1109/CICN.2011.5

Tan, S., Li, X., & Dong, Q. (2015). Trust based routing mechanism for securing OSLR-based MANET. *Ad Hoc Networks*, *30*, 84–98. doi:10.1016/j.adhoc.2015.03.004

Tang, K., Obraczka, K., Lee, S. J., & Geria, M. (2002, October). A reliable, congestion-control led multicast transport protocol in multimedia multi-hop networks. In *Proceedings of the 5th International Symposium on Wireless Personal Multimedia Communications* (Vol. 1, pp. 252-256). IEEE. 10.1109/WPMC.2002.1088171

The Cisco Network Simulator. (n.d.). Router Simulator & Switch Simulator. Retrieved June 6, 2017 from http://www.boson.com/netsim-cisco-network-simulator

Tsikoudis, N., Papadogiannakis, A., & Markatos, E. P. (2016). LEoNIDS: A low-latency and energy-efficient network-level intrusion detection system. *IEEE Transactions on Emerging Topics in Computing*, *4*(1), 142–155.

Umamaheswari, S., & Radhamani, G. (2015). Enhanced antsec framework with cluster based cooperative caching in mobile ad hoc networks. *Journal of Communications and Networks (Seoul)*, *17*(1), 40–46. doi:10.1109/JCN.2015.000008

Valikannu, R., George, A., & Srivatsa, S. K. (2015, February). A novel energy consumption model using Residual Energy Based Mobile Agent selection scheme (REMA) in MANETs. In *Proceedings of the 2015 2nd International Conference on Signal Processing and Integrated Networks (SPIN)* (pp. 334-339). IEEE.

Wei, W., Zhang, J., Wang, W., Zhao, J., Li, J., Shen, P., ... Hu, J. (2013). Analysis and Research of the RSA Algorithm. *Information Technology Journal*, *12*(9), 1818–1824. doi:10.3923/itj.2013.1818.1824

Yang, Y., Xu, H. Q., Gao, L., Yuan, Y. B., McLaughlin, K., & Sezer, S. (2017). Multidimensional Intrusion Detection System for IEC 61850-Based SCADA Networks. *IEEE Transactions on Power Delivery*, *32*(2), 1068–1078. doi:10.1109/TPWRD.2016.2603339

Yerajana, R., & Sarje, A. K. (2009, March). A timestamp based multipath source routing protocol for congestion control in MANET. In *Proceedings of the IEEE International Advance Computing Conference IACC '09* (pp. 32-34). IEEE. 10.1109/IADCC.2009.4808975

Yi, Z., & Dohi, T. (2015). Toward Highly Dependable Power-Aware Mobile Ad Hoc Network–Survivability Evaluation Framework. *IEEE Access: Practical Innovations, Open Solutions*, *3*, 2665–2676. doi:10.1109/ACCESS.2015.2507201

Yu, M., Zhou, M., & Su, W. (2009). A secure routing protocol against byzantine attacks for MANETs in adversarial environments. *IEEE Transactions on Vehicular Technology*, *58*(1), 449–460. doi:10.1109/TVT.2008.923683

Chapter 3
Cross–Layer Based Intrusion Detection and Prevention for Network

Reema Kumari
Galgotias University, India

Kavita Sharma
National Institute of Technology Kurukshetra, India

ABSTRACT

Day by day technologies for mobile computing growing rapidly and its network security changed according to their need. The attacker always trying to learn some new techniques to break those security walls of the wireless network. To prevent our network from attacker various defense techniques are used. Firewalls and encryption are used to prevent our network from malware but it is not sufficient for protecting the networks. Many researchers implement new architecture and techniques or mechanism that protect and detect malicious node and their activity over the network that is intrusion detection system (IDS). IDS provides security wall and it provides network security as well as it has continuously monitored and taken appropriate action against the threat. In this Chapter, we are trying to explain some network attack that is resolved or detect through intrusion detection system by exploiting the technology or information that available across different layers of the protocol stack in order to improve the accuracy of detection.

BACKGROUND

The meaning of intrusion is "…any set of actions that attempt to compromise the integrity, confidentiality, or availability of a resource…" (Heady et al. 1990). In the wired network, there are no vulnerabilities but when we talk about wireless network then in each step and each ways attacker is ready for attack. Firewall and encryption software is used to protect our system but it is no longer sufficient for network security. Therefore, we need to develop a new architecture and mechanism that protect our wireless network. Internet worm called Code Red that infects many Windows-based server machines in 2001. To prevent our wireless network from this type of worm attacks, many companies trust on firewalls. It protects an

DOI: 10.4018/978-1-5225-4100-4.ch003

internal network of intranet (Zhang, Lee, & Huang, 2003). Wireless network does not have the underlying infrastructure. Its infrastructure continuously changes according to their node movement. Many hosts connect at a time and make their own topology or infrastructure. These networks create a number of vulnerable network attacks. The wireless network does not communicate directly, it communicates through the intermediate node. To detect and provide the security we need to complement traditional security mechanism with efficient intrusion detection system. Intrusion detection system (IDS) is used to prevent our network. An ID is continuously monitoring our network and warns or detect if any suspicious behavior of the network is occurring (Mishra, Nadkarni, & Patcha, 2004). Wireless sensor network is mainly composed of sensor sink and sensor nodes. The main advantage of the sensor network is self-organizing and self-healing. It mainly used in such areas where wired networks are impossible. There are various applications of wireless sensor networks, which is detecting changed the climate, monitoring habitats, monitoring environment and it is used in military applications and surveillance. Nevertheless, there is one problem in WSN's, WSN nodes are always exposed their physical security attacks. To prevent such type of attacks, WSN proposed various security mechanisms such as key exchange, authentication, and secure routing. However, these security mechanisms are not capable to ensure security at all level, if not eliminate all security attacks. One possible solution having to address a wide range of security attacks in WSNs that is Intrusion Detection System (IDS) (Ananthakumar, Ganediwal, & Kunte, 2015).

INTRODUCTION

Cross layer-based intrusion, detection system utilizes information across the layers; it effectively identifies intrusion over the network. Before detecting malicious node on the network, first, it performs multi-level detection on multiple layers. The main objective of adopting cross-layer design is, 1) Detecting attack at multi-level of the protocol layer; 2) Exploiting information so that energy and congestion; and 3) It detects intrusion more accurately on multiple layers.

1. **Detecting Intrusion:** It detects intrusion on two levels that is level-1 detection and level-2 detection. The two levels are using two methods i.e.
    a. **CIDS-1:** Information is obtained through detecting DoS attacks at one layer and it is shared on another layer.
    b. **CIDS-2:** In this attack, multiple detections of a DoS is detected on the same layer.
2. **CIDS (Cross-Layer Based Intrusion Detection)-1:** It is level-1 detection method. It detects malicious node from different layers. In addition, level 2 detects truly malicious nodes in the network.
3. **CIDS (Cross-Layer Based Intrusion Detection)-2:** It is the second method for detection; 2-level detection occurs at the same layer. It is similar to the first method. In level-1 detection, only passive monitoring is done but in level-2 detection, detection is applied on the same layer (Thamilarasu, Balasumbramanian, Mishra, & Sridhar, 2005).

Cross-layer-based prevention technique is used for securing multi-path routing (CLDASR). This approach is used for dropping the malicious packet and enhances the performance of authentication and prevention. In authentication method, when any source wants to send data packets, then it generates a hash value to encrypt data or packet with destination private key. If intermediate node receive packet then encrypts with the hash value, append their ID, and lastly encrypt the whole message with share symmetry key. When a message is received at destination then destination nodes decrypt the message in reverse order by using the private key and verify hash sent by source (Babu & Sekharaiah, 2014).

In Mishra, Nadkarni, and Patcha (2004), the author explained about, how to prevent intrusion. In traditionally, intrusion detection system is only identifying the attack when they occur but it has some limitation that makes fail IDS to prevent the detection. There is various detection techniques are used to detect the intrusion, some of them are like a firewall. Firewall only block port number when an attack is detected but it fails to analyze traffic that uses that port number. Nevertheless, in case of IDS, it can monitor and analyzed the traffic that passes through the open ports but fails to prevent attacks. To resolve this problem some researcher discovers a new system i.e. Intrusion Prevention System (IPS) that provides prevention during the attack and takes appropriate action against attacks. IPS is very much similar to IDS, both system aim is to provide and distinguish unauthorized activity from the normal activity. An IPS has several predefined conditions like a set of signature or trigger response. All IPS condition is processed according to IDS system. We need some new approach that protects our system and network resources. IPS protects our system before any damage is done.

Intrusion Prevention System: It defined as an ability to detect any types of attacks were unknown, known, and able to prevent that attack is called Intrusion Detection System (IPS). It is proactive and Inline devices that detect and drop packets as well as disconnect the connections before reaching the destination and block all traffic with the same IP sources (malicious source) (Khari, Shrivastava, Gupta, & Gupta, 2017). It also generates some false alarm when an intrusion is detected. There are some IPS requirements that are listed below:

- **Accuracy:** It is the most top-level requirement of the IPS system. That generate false positive whenever any unknown activity is detected. However, it is unacceptable in IPS, the reason is false positive is only generated through a system that relies on a single detection method. Whenever any legitimate traffic is blocked then it creates the problem for authorized users and it causes DoS attacks. DoS attack is originating from the prevention system itself (Shrivastava, Sharma, & Rai, 2010).
- **Reliable and Available:** IPS should be reliable and high availability. It must be available in any situation whenever an attack occurs. Reliability means an ability to perform any kind of function incorrect way without interfering with other systems.
- **Performance:** It is also an important requirement for IPS system. Performance of any system will degrade when an attacker creates a bottleneck on the network.
- **The Anticipation of Unidentified Attacks and Simple Signature Revise for Latest Attacks:** IPS must have to provide flexible methods to update new signatures as well as the capability to response new class of attacks and this system must have a method that responds to new attacks without requiring their signature.
- In Smaha (1988), Author explained, How To Detect Intrusion: There are various processes are available that detect intrusion.
    - The method is to look for the behavior of system whether it is good or not. For example, if clients print an output and rapidly it increases by 3000% and its absolute value is larger than security officer might become doubtful and investigate the security leakage.

○ The second technique of intrusion detection is monitoring the behavior that is "bad" by its definition. For instance, if any person tries to print the secret word file then security officer should investigate the behavior of a user, whether or not authorized to read or access that files.

In Viadya, Mirza and Mali (2016), the author stated systematically about intrusion, intrusion detection, and intrusion detection system.

- **Intrusion:** Some unofficial person not permitted to access, read and edit any data via information sources.
- **Intrusion detection:** By using the automated software system, try to steal and break security breaches.
- **Intrusion detection system:** A security system that detects and tries to discontinue intrusion detection activities.

Sometimes intrusion is too called hacker or cracker that tries to attempt to obliterate and exploitation the system. Intrusion detection system is a software application that can observe networks and system behavior for detect unofficial users. IDS system is like an alarm system, it alerts when malicious activities occur. Its aim to detect computer attacks. There are two types of IDS

- **NIDS (Network Intrusion Detection Systems):** A NIDS network capture or observe all traffic. This system looking at the network when any packets on the network. It matches the packet with their signature if its match and any suspicious is occurring packet are dropped.
- **HIDS (Host Intrusion Detection Systems):** It not only looking at the network traffic and out of the single computer but it checks the all of the computer files and watching malicious processes. However, one demerit has loaded the software on every computer. It is more effective than NIDS because it detects insider attacks.

In Hashmi, Saxena, and Saini (2012), Author states the different types of intrusion attack on the network.

- **Manual Attack:** In this attack, attacker scanned remote machines for vulnerabilities, and broke and installed the malicious code.
- **Semi-Automatic Attack:** In DoS network, it consists of a master and various slave machines. And attacker deploys automatic scripts for compromising of those machines & installed malicious code. Then the uses master machine to specify the attack type.
- **Automatic Attack:** In this attack, it generates automatic attack thus it avoiding the need for communication between slave machine and attacker machine. In this attack, attacker preplanned all things related to attack types and victim address and duration of an attack.

The author also explained types of attack through communication. There are two types attack through communication.

- **Attacks with Direct Communication:** Indirect communication when an attack occurs, master and slave machines both know how to communicate each other and in which ways. This communication is in various ways. Like
  - ◦ The responsibility of master is hard coding the IP address that later installed on slave machine to create zombies.
  - ◦ Slave machine store that IP address in our files.
  - ◦ The major disadvantage of this approach is the detection of one malicious machine can depiction the entire DDoS network.
  - ◦ When any machine is exposed then master and slave is also exposed through network scanner.
- **Attacks With Indirect Communication:** It is the attack that indirectly communicates and deploys a level of indirection to increase the continuity of a DDoS network.

A dynamic honeypot is a Design for intrusion detection in Kuwatly, Sraj, Al Masri and Artail (2004). Definition of the honeypot is "A honeypot is an information system resource whose value lies in the unauthorized or illicit use of that resource" all the honeypot is work in a similar manner. In honeypot system, they store resources that are unauthorized and there have no production values. If we are talking about honeypot then they should not observe any traffic because it has no authorized activity. Any connections attempts to a honeypot are probes, compromises, and attacks. There are two types of honeypot i.e.

- **Low-Interaction Honeypot:** It is an emulation of services and operating systems, an example of emulation services is FTP services. Port number of FTP is 26; the development of Low-interaction system is simple and does not have much risk. However, there is some maintains is required to connect the network. The system Log only has partial information and is intended to detain the recognized activity. However, an attacker can identify Low-interaction honeypot by accomplishing the commands. Example of the low-interaction honeypot is Specter, KFSensor, and Honeyd. To overcome the problem of Low-interaction honeypot can be redirected to the high-interaction honeypot.
- **High-Interaction Honeypot:** It has a complex solution, and it involves direct real operating system and applications. It captures a huge amount of information and allowing the attackers to interrelate with authentic systems where their attacker scenario will be recorded and studied. Example of High-interaction honeypot is Honeynets and Sebek.

In Ramanujam (2009), Author states the architecture of Intrusion Detection System using advance Honeypot.

The activity at each step is defined as follows:

- **Load Balancer:** It receives a request from the virtual IP address. If the data packet is fragmented then it reassembled it. The main functionality of load-balancer is maintaining a TCP connection between IDS process and send packets over the connections.
- **IDS:** IDS system checks the upcoming data packets alongside its database of recognized attacks and proceeds a Boolean result to its load balancer via TCP connections. When the result is received by load-balancer then it terminates the connection.

Figure 1. Architecture of IDS using advance honeypot

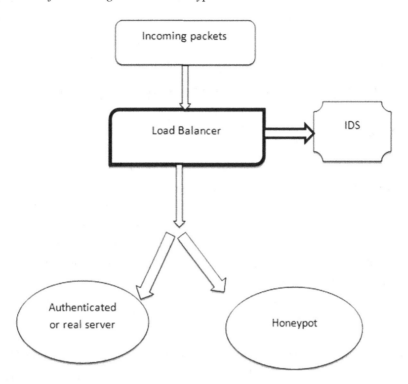

- If the result of load-balancer is indicating true means any attacks is present then that packet is forwarded to honeypot otherwise forwarded to the real server or original server or authenticated server.

Load-balancer provide secure communication between user and server, it has three functionality namely: high availability by handling hardware failure, high speed to the cluster and the third one is ensuring the balancer itself does not become a security hole. High availability means, simply ping the servers at regular intervals and remove from server pool when no response is generated. The challenges of load-balancer are protecting it from irrelevant traffic. Load balancer only processes that traffic that having some known port number and it discards unknown port traffic. The load balancer uses 'proxy-ARP'.

The second main part is IDS system that protects our system from malicious attacks. It runs on TCP server and senses a client requests on a known port. When a connection is established then IDS fork a child process when it receives a bunch of packets then it checks against a database of known attacks. If any intrusion is detected then it takes the decision, whether it forward to the production server or the honeypot.

In Beqiri (2009), Authors defined TCP SYN Flooding and Port Scanning Attacks; author focuses on detection network protocol attacks that are TCP SYN flooding attack and port scanning attacks. Both attacks are common over the network. TCP SYN flooding is a DoS attacks, in this attack, attacker firstly sends a bunch of SYN packet using unique IP address then server send acknowledge and then wait for the response, which never arrives. At last, the memory of server that partially occupies by the attacker will be exhausted.

Second attacks are Port scanning attack, it is a kind of probing and surveillance attacks. In this attack, an attacker has no intention to damage the network data. However, the attacker tries to gather information from victim network. In our network, there are various port scanning attacks.

INTRUSION DETECTION AND PREVENTION RESEARCH AREA

Mobile Ad-Hoc Network

It is a compilation of wireless mobile hosts which forming a momentary bridge or network lacking any centralized administration node. It is based on dynamic topology, which means nodes automatically enter and leave the network continuously. There is no centralized control in MANET. Example of the MANET is emergency meetings, disaster relief situations, military communication, sensor network and wearable computers. In MANET routes address must be addressed to keep network fully connected. In the wireless network, there are having limited communication range. There is one advantage of MANET is, each device is free to shift anywhere separately in any direction. The main challenge of MANET is to furnish every device to preserve the proper information of route traffic (Jayakumar & Gopinath, 2007; Mobile ad hoc network, 2017) There are various types of MANET.

- **Vehicular Ad-Hoc Network (VANETs):** It is used to provide communication between vehicles and roadside apparatus. It helps the vehicle to perform in intelligent manners during a vehicle-to-vehicle accident.
- **Smart Phone Ad-Hoc Network (SPANs):** The existing hardware like Bluetooth and Wi-Fi, it makes the available smartphone to create peer-to-peer networks.
- **Internet-Based Mobile Ad Hoc Networks (iMANETs):** It is the Ad-hoc network that links mobile node and fixed its internet gateway nodes. (Mobile ad hoc network, 2017).

Attacks in MANET

Attack have occurred at the network layer and there are two types of attack is occurring at network layer that is classify below.

- **Passive Attack:** In this attack, the attacker gets all valuable information related to network and their nodes without disturbing routing protocol. The attacker gets crucial information's about nodes i.e. information about network topology, the location of nodes and identity of nodes. There are various types of passive attack that are listed below.
  - **Eavesdropping:** MANET provides the wireless link for all network nodes. If any node sends information to another node within the radio range attacker get all crucial information about the node, if encryption is not used.
  - **Location Disclosure:** Attacker does not harm network node directly in the passive attack. In this attack, the attacker only eavesdrops to traffic to get victim location even if the network is encrypted.
  - **Traffic Analysis:** traffic analysis still performed when the network is encrypted. In military communication, important information disclosure is done through traffic analysis.

- **Active Attack:** In this attack, attacker manually lunches intrusive activity like a modification of data set, injecting new code, forging data, fabrication, dropping or deleting some packets. This attack degrades the pre-formation of network services. Some of this attack is caused by single activity and some of them cause by the colluding attack.
  - **Routing:** All nodes find the best route to send their packets and meanwhile malicious node try to exploit the vulnerabilities and lunch routing attack (Nadeem & Howarth, 2013).
    - **Sleep Deprivation:** it is distributed of denial attack, in this attack attacker try to interact with a node in a manner that emerges to be a legitimate node. The main purpose of the attacker is keeping the victim node in sleep mode. The attacker creates a flood in following ways.
- Attacker broadcast route requests to a destination that is within the network address range.
- All nodes forward the route request to destination IP address.
- After forwarding route request to nodes, an intruder is not idle it continuous send route request to the same destination.
  - **Black Hole:** Whenever any node needs to send a packet to a destination in the network then its first require routes between sender and the receiver node. When the node requires route towards the destination node then node send route request (RREQ) to all node that presents in a network. When intruder receives route request then intruder act as fresh route and maybe succeed in becoming part of many routes in the network. When intruder chooses as an intermediate node then it receives a packet and maybe drops all packets instead of forwarding it, which is called Black Hole (BH) attack.
  - **Grey Hole:** Gray hole is a little bit different from black hole attack. In gray whole attack, first, it captures routes and become part of the routes in the network, same as black hole attack. In this attack, attacker when receiving node packet and drop selected node packet instead of forwarding it.
  - **Rushing:** Firstly, any node that sends a route request to all nodes in the wireless network. In addition, the meanwhile Attacker is present in the in the network and receive route packet. Then attacker sends route packet to his neighbor node with high speed. Because of high transmission speed, attacker request reaches first at the destination node. When the destination node receives route packet request then accept it first and reject another route request, which is reached later. Receiver thinks this route is valid for further communication. And in this way intruder is successful to make attack between sender and receiver (Babu & Sakharaiah, 2014)
  - **Sybil:** Each node having a unique address in the wireless network, through which nodes are identified. By using this benefit attacker exploit this property and make many more fake identities and this known as SYBIL ATTACK. In this attack, an attacker may use random identities or use the identity of any node to create misunderstanding in the routing process.
    - **Malicious Packet Dropping:** A path amid the source and destination node is recognized by route discovery process. When the connection is established then sender starts sending data packets to the corresponding node in the path, the intermediate node identifies next hop node toward the destination node. This procedure is continuing until the packet is delivered to the destination. The responsibility of intermediate is a forward

packet to all source nodes, however, any malicious node might decide to delete or drop this packet instead of forwarding. Because of malicious misbehavior, some cases nodes are unable to carry packet due to overloaded or even unable to forward the data packet to the destination.

Illustration of Network Layer Attack (Nadeem & Howarth, 2013)

- **Sleep Deprivation Attack Illustration:** In this attack, whenever any source node broadcast RREQ over the wireless network if there is an intermediate node (intruder), that receives the RREQ. It may be unicast the RREP or rebroadcast the RREQ over the network. The main purpose of this attack is sending useless control traffic and forcing the node to forgo their sleep mode. So that they completely exhausted or stop working (Ierace, Urrutia, & Bassett, 2005).
- **Black Hole Attack Illustration:** In this attack, intruder receives node packet and simply drop instead forwarding it. In Figure 2 and 3, it shows how source node sends a packet and how the intruder rebroadcast RREQ. N5 is the malicious node in Figure 2 & 3 (Sen, 2011).
- **Grey Hole Illustration:** In gray hole Illustration, intruder drops the packet of only selected node and pass other node packets.
- **Rushing Attack Illustration:** This attack is happening due to early transmission of RREQ to the destination and tries to stop legitimate node RREQ. Whenever any source node tries to send a packet to the destination then intruder hear the RREQ and try to add some delay and send "RUSH" to RREQ to suppress any later legitimate RREQs.

Wireless Sensor Networks

Wireless sensor network is a combination of nodes and sinks. The capability of sensor nodes is self-organizing and self-healing. In the network there is no any centralized node, all communication is taking place via intermediate nodes. The main aim of the sensor node is to collect information from its surrounding environment and send to the sink. There is the various application of WSNs such as:

Figure 2. Network without any attack node N5 is an intruder

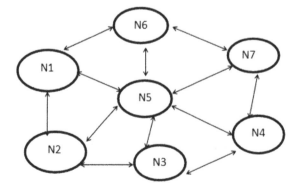

Figure 3. Intruder generates malicious RREQ

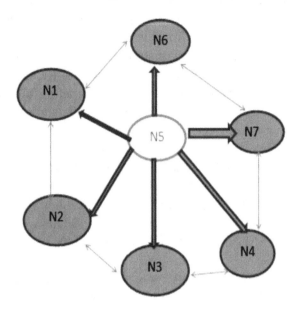

- Detection of Climate Change.
- Monitor environment and their habitats.
- In military application and Surveillance.
- Self-Organizing Nature.
- Low battery power supply.
- Limited Bandwidth Support.

Mostly sensor network is used in such areas where impossible to deployed wired network. Its nodes are always exposed numerous security attacks at every layer of the OSI model. To detect an attack in WSN, the much security-related solution is proposed for authentication, secure routing, and key exchange. This security mechanism is capable to detect the attack at some level but fail to eliminate high-level security attack. The possible solution to detect all high-level attack in WSN is IDS. However, one demerit of IDS is not to prevent attacks as it only detects intrusion. Whenever intrusion is detected by IDS, it raises an alarm to notify controller to take appropriate action against the intruder (Ananthakumar, Ganediwal, & Kunte, 2015; Butun, Morgera, & Sankar, 2014; Messai, 2014).

Attacks in WSN

There is a various attack is occurred in WSN because of its decentralized multi-hoping nature. It is categorized into

1. **Active Attack:** This attack is used to delete, drop and alter the network packets. An attacker can also inject some crafted message to disturb network operation. It causes the denial of services attacks.

2. **Passive Attack:** Passive attack have silent in nature and it extracts significant information from the network. It does not harm the network resources and network. It is easier to realized and difficult to detect. When it retrieved information from the network then it not modifies any information on the network. The intention of an attacker is gain more knowledge about network information and analyzed routing information to prepare the active attack.

3. **Wireless Mesh Network:** It has potential to deliver internet broadband access, WLAN coverage and provides network connectivity for mobile host and stationary at low costs for together network operators and customers (Sichitiu, 2005). It is made by radio node that organized in a MESH TOPOLOGY. Wireless Mesh Network is consisting of mesh router, mesh client and mesh gateways. Here mesh client is user laptop, cell phone, and other wireless devices, while mesh router is forwarding traffic to and from gateways. A mesh network is always consistent and offers idleness. In mesh topology when one is not in working condition still other nodes, communicate with each other. It is implementing with various wireless technologies including 802.16, 802.15, and 802.11 (Sharma & Shrivastava, 2011). It is forming an Ad-hoc network by sending data one node to another one.

4. **Homogenous Wireless Sensor Networks:** Wireless sensor network is used to monitor sensitive information like enemy movement at battlefield or location of any building in any area. Mainly it is used in an application like military, health, ecological area. It is sensing node sense around them and detect an anomaly in the industrial environment. Main issues in the industrial application are to detect intrusion on the wireless medium. To detect these attacks, we need intrusion detection system. It consists of autonomous sensors that used to monitor our physical environment. Thousands of small sensor networks make wireless sensor network, it automatically senses and finds the route and transmit sense data to the base station. The main drawback of sensing node is energy consumption, it has limited energy. To save energy clustering based routing protocol is required. WSN is used to gather information from the real-time environment. There are two types of the wireless sensor network.

   a. **Unstructured or Heterogeneous Wireless Sensor Network:** In this sensor network, sensor nodes are deployed in an ad-hoc manner. It means there is no any fixed structure. All sensor nodes having different functionality and different battery consumptions. In the heterogeneous network, different topology is used and this makes the network more complex as compared to HWSN.; (Al-Hamadi & Chen, 2015; Uplap & Sharma, 2014).

      i. **Structure or Homogenous Wireless Sensor Network:** In this network, all nodes are same in term of battery energy and hardware complexity. It is not complex network, it used in the single network topology. All sensor nodes are expired at the same time because of this it wastes less energy. However, one drawback is all sensor nodes act as cluster heads and they possess the required capabilities related to hardware requirements. in this network there is need of extra battery energy and more complex hardware is embedded in any cluster head (Uplap & Sharma, 2014).

5. **Wireless Ad Hoc Network:** Wireless network becomes an important face in our everyday life. It deployed in various applications. There growing popularity is challenged in insure environment (Thamilarasu, Balasubramanian, Mishra, & Sridhar, 2005) Wireless ad-hoc network having a heterogeneous infrastructure. It consists of various mobile nodes that are capable of communication

with each other. In addition, the interconnection nodes are interchanging their position without any restrictions. To provide network security in Wireless ad-hoc network, such as intrusion detection system is used to reduce intrusion but cannot remove the intrusion. It has an inherent vulnerability, which is not easy to prevent (Zhang & Lee, 2000).

DOS Attack

1. **Collision:** In wireless networks, when already any node is transmitting data and meanwhile another node tries to transmit data on the same channel then a collision occurs. The main intention of this attack is to thwart access to a convinced node or to completely exhaust the transmitting node's resources through continuous retransmission (Thamilarasu, Balasubramanian, Mishra, & Sridhar, 2005) .
2. **Packet Drop:** It affects the availability of the node by denying services to the destination nodes. The main purpose of this attack is randomly dropped data packets at the network layer.
3. **Misdirection:** This attack is occurred due to the adversary node forwards the data packets to the wrong destination node. The adversary node sends false route error message to the destination to deny the availability of nodes services (Thamilarasu, Balasubramanian, Mishra, & Sridhar, 2005).

Types of Intrusion Detection

1. **Anomaly-Based Intrusion Detection System:** This intrusion detection system continues to monitor the network activity and classifies them as either normal or abnormal. It detects intrusion based on threshold values. If any activity is below the threshold is normal otherwise it is detected as unusual or intrusion. But anomaly-based IDSs is capable to identify new and unidentified intrusion but sometimes fail to detect even well-known security attacks (Ananthakumar et al., 2015; Nadeem & Howarth, 2013)
2. **Knowledge-Based Intrusion Detection System:** This system contains knowledge-based data that contains signature and patterns of well-known attacks. This system has knowledge about attacks and looks for attempts to use them. Whenever any attempt occurs, then an alarm has triggered. When series of event is occurring then it degrades the performance of the network and it detected by unknown attacks, the reason is not matching existing rule (Nadeem & Howarth, 2013)
3. **Signature or Misuse Based Intrusion Detection System:** It is also known as rule-based IDS; it has predefined regulations for different security attacks. It detects when any predefined rules are breaks and classify as an attack. It is well suited for the known intrusion, but it fails to detect a new attack that having no predefined rules. In the wireless network, all nodes having its own IDS. The architecture of IDS has various components like packet monitoring, cooperative engine, detecting and response engine (Mishra, Nadkarni, & Patcha, 2004, Nadeem & Howarth, 2013).
4. **Specification-Based Intrusion Detection System:** It defines set of constraint that tells about correct protocol and correct operation of the program. This detection technique monitors the execution of the program with respect to the defined constraint. This detector is detecting the intrusion alongside the background of the normal traffic. These detectors correctly detect the malicious event. Few

steps detect normal and abnormal traffic (Mishra, Nadkarni, & Patcha, 2004; Nadeem & Howarth, 2013).

    a.   Extract the specification.

    b.   IDS system monitors the correct execution of the protocol with respect to the given constraint and specification.

    c.   If any deviation occurs, then it is treated as an intrusion.

5.   **Hybrid Intrusion Detection System:** It is an amalgamation both anomaly and signature-based intrusion detection system. It generally contains two detection modules that are; one module is liable for detecting the known attack by using their signature. In addition, another module is used to detect and learn the malicious pattern and learning the normal and abnormal behavior of nodes profiles. It generates less number of false positive. It is more accurate in terms of attack (Ananthakumar et al., 2015)

Component of IDS

To increase the efficiency of the MANET nodes we have to use data mining techniques in this component but data mining technique is not used to detect all attack in MANET. So we use clustering based intrusion detection techniques instead of data mining techniques, it detects new attacks. Traditional IDS only detect predefined data set; it fails to detect real data set values. Traditional IDS is more expensive and time-consuming to manually collect all pure normal data set and then perform analysis on the wireless network. To detect new types of attack we use association algorithm that is apriori. Apriori algorithm used to increase efficiency and performance of IDS system. There are various components in IDS that are defined below.

1.   **Local Data Collection:** In this component, it collects all information related to a client like traffic pattern and traces attack from MAC and network layers via association modules (Shrestha, Han, Choi, & Han, 2010).

2.   **Monitoring Component:** It monitors all local events and its neighboring nodes activity. This component monitor, event activity, traffic pattern (Ananthakumar et al., 2015).

3.   **Analysis and Local Detection:** It analyzed and detects the network activity, network operation, and their behavior (Ananthakumar et al., 2015).

4.   **Cooperative Detection:** It detects intrusion and anomaly on the basis of voting. In this detection, if sustain and confidence are low or intrusion evidence is weak over the detecting node then at that time it makes the collaborative decision by gathering the knowledge from its neighboring nodes via channel (Shrestha, Han, Choi, & Han, 2010).

5.   **Alarm Management:** Whenever any intrusion is detected then an alarm is initiated and sends the message to a controller to take appropriate action against the intrusion.

6.   **Intrusion Response:** Intrusion response is depending upon type's intrusion. It identifies the malicious node and re-organized the network connection. It also sends re-authentication to legitimate users and provides the new communication channel (Zhang & Lee, 2000).

Architecture for Intrusion Detection System

As per Figure 4, an architecture for intrusion detection system is worked as:

1. **Data Collection:** Data collection is the first module of IDS architecture. It collects real-time from various sources. It gathers client activity within the mobile node as well as their communication activity within the radio range that is observable by IDS agent (Zhang & Lee, 2000).
2. **Local Detection:** Local detection is second modules of IDS architecture. It consists of anomaly detections. It analyzed the local data, which is gathered by the upper module that is data collection module. It detects the normal and abnormal profile of users. The normal profiles consist of normal behavior pattern and abnormal profiles contain abnormal behavior pattern. On the wireless network, there is a number of new types of attacks are mounted. These attacks are increasing according to there more use of wireless applications. We cannot use the simply expert rule to detect these attack we need to update rile-base with new detections rules that are secure and reliable. Soto detects new types of attack on the wireless network we use anomaly detection. During the testing process, the local detection module detects normal and abnormal activity and abnormal activities are recorded (Shrestha, Han, Choi, & Han, 2010;Zhang & Lee, 2000).
3. **Cooperative Detection:-**In this detection stage, it detects two types of data.
    a. If any node detects locally knows as intrusion or anomaly and it has very high accuracy and strong evidence. It determines independently and tells to all networks about their attack and initiated their response.
    b. If any node detects weak evidence that is also known as anomaly or intrusion. In this case, warrant investigator investigates broader and instigate a cooperative global intrusion detection process. In this process, it propagates IDS information among all their neighboring nodes (Zhang & Lee, 2000).
4. **Intrusion Response:** Intrusion response is depending upon types of intrusion, the certainty of the evidence and types of network applications and network protocols. Little response is listed below.
    a. Reconnect communications between network nodes.
    b. Identifying the compromised nodes.

Figure 4. The architecture of intrusion detection system

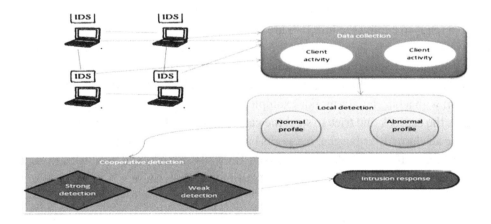

c.   IDS agent identify all end-user node to on their investigations and take appropriate action against the attack.

d.   IDS agent also sends the re-authenticate request to all end user using visual contacts.

e.   Only authenticate channel will recognize as the legitimate user. Moreover, suspicious nodes can exclude from network (Zhang & Lee, 2000).

Cross-Layer Techniques in IDS

If we compared with wired networks then MANET faces various challenges because of its wireless nature and ad-hoc structure. To detect all intrusion in the network we need intrusion detection techniques. However, some time IDS also fails to detect some new types of attack so we have used CROSS LAYER TECHNIQUES in IDS. The tradition way to provide layering between routers, scheduling, rate and power control but it is not efficient for the ad-hoc wireless network.

- Routing is measured in a routing layer.
- Medium access to MAC layer.
- Power control and rate control in the physical layer and sometime in MAC layer.

If there is no cross-layer is provided then routing is select between several routes, because of this there is no routing information is maintained so IDS is unable to detect any malicious nodes and congestion. So it selects congested route or the second option is it the select route that having the malicious node. With the help of cross-layer interaction, it provides network security at MAC layer and decides the possible routes. We select correct combination of layers in CROSS LAYER IDS. It is very vital to detect any attacks from any layer. DoS attack is enhanced to detected at MAC layer. Routing and MAC layer is used to detect routing attack inefficient ways. This cross-layer techniques detection is higher and it increased their true positive in the MANET to reduce the attack in the MANET (Shrestha, Han, Choi, & Han, 2010).

The Need for Intrusion Detection

Intrusion is prevented through encryption and authentication and it is used in ad-hoc networks, but it cannot eliminate them because encryption and authentication cannot detect intrusion at mobile nodes. If we provide any intrusion detection techniques for network there are always present some weak link in the network that ready to exploit the link.IDS are the second wall to defense the attack and it is necessary for any survivability network. To provide secure communication in the network we need to provide IDS and response techniques (Zhang, Lee, & Huang, 2003). Why we need intrusion detection system, it is a big question for us. To answer this question we take one scenario, in this scenario we compare intrusion detection system with a burglar alarm. For example, the lock system in a car to protect from theft but if someone breaks the car lock and tries to steal the car, in this case, burglar alarm detection and alerts the owner by raising an alarm. Like burglar, networks have intrusion detection system that detects malicious attacks when it occurs. If the intruder tries to break firewalls security and even tries to access any data from the authorized side then IDS alerts the administrator of the system.

Challenges of Intrusion Detection

There are various challenges of intrusion detection system in MANET. The main challenges in intrusion detection are, it is fixed networks and it not directly implement on the wireless network. In the fixed network, traffic is monitored on fixed gateways and routers but in the unstructured network, it observes an only node that lies within the radio range. The main drawback of the unstructured network is, outside attacker of radio range is easily escaped (Nadeem & Howarth, 2013).

Intrusion detection system is a defense mechanism tool that provides security. However, there are some challenges in Intrusion detection systems that are discussed below.

- IDS technology itself is undergoing an assortment of enhancements. It is most significant for organizations to clearly describe their need and prospect from the IDS implementation. IDS technology has various automation that notifies the administrator when an intrusion is detected. But it is still important to monitor all the malicious activity continuously and stay on top of the incidence of events. However, the problem with IDS is, it unable to give a past analysis of the intrusion that detected over a period. It is still a manual activity to analysis chronological activity.
- The IDS implementation depends to a large extent on how it has been deployed. A lot of planning is requisite in the implementation phase as well designing phase. There are two types of IDS system one is network based and another one is the host-based system. Many organizations choose network-based IDS instead of host-based because of its monitoring power. It has the ability to monitor numerous systems and it does not require any software that installs on the production system, unlike host-based system.
- The main challenge of IDS technology is, it proactive rather than reactive. IDS technology is work on attack signatures. And the signature database is needed to update whenever any unknown attack occurs. And the frequency of signature varies from person to person (Sarmah, 2001).

Problem of Current Intrusion Detection Techniques

It is extremely complicated to detect intrusion detection- techniques in any environment. The main reason is the fixed infrastructure of an ad-hoc network. If researcher evaluate with wired networks where traffic monitoring is done at switches, routers, and gateways, and mobile ad-hoc don't have traffic attentiveness points and IDS can collect audit data for the all over the network. IDS fail to detect real or false alarm. There is little point that describes the problem on IDS techniques (Zhang, Lee, & Huang, 2003; Zhang & Lee, 2000).

- Do not apply IDS techniques on fixed infrastructure or wired network.
- Due to communication pattern in the wireless ad-hoc network.
- IDS unable to detect intrusion on slower links, limited bandwidth and battery power consumption and higher cost (Zhang & Lee, 2000).

CONCLUSION

A better intrusion detection system based on cross-layer is presented in this chapter. In this chapter, explained the different types of intrusion attack as well as their prevention techniques. In cross-layer IDS, tried to detect new unknown intrusions at the different layer. We also observe that single layer detection is unable to detection attack at some layer. By using the cross-layer detection, it enhances the performance of authentication and detection. In this chapter, honeypot and their various types' attacks and their architecture and challenges are discussed. Also explained different types of attack in MANET as well as the structure and unstructured types of ad-hoc networks.

REFERENCES

Al-Hamadi, H., & Chen, I. R. (2015). Integrated intrusion detection and tolerance in homogeneous clustered sensor networks. *ACM Transactions on Sensor Networks*, *11*(3), 47. doi:10.1145/2700830

Ananthakumar, A., Ganediwal, T., & Kunte, A. (2015). Intrusion detection system in wireless sensor networks: A review. *International Journal of Advanced Computer Science and Applications*, *6*(12), 131–139. doi:10.14569/IJACSA.2015.061218

Babu, K. S., & Sekharaiah, K. C. (2014). CLDASR: Cross Layer Based Detection and Authentication in Secure Routing in MANET. *International Journal of Computer Networks and Wireless Communications*.

Beqiri, E. (2009). Neural networks for intrusion detection systems. In *Global Security, Safety, and Sustainability* (pp. 156-165).

Butun, I., Morgera, S. D., & Sankar, R. (2014). A survey of intrusion detection systems in wireless sensor networks. *IEEE Communications Surveys and Tutorials*, *16*(1), 266–282. doi:10.1109/SURV.2013.050113.00191

Hashmi, M. J., Saxena, M., & Saini, R. (2012). Classification of DDoS attacks and their defense techniques using intrusion prevention system. *International Journal of Computer Science and Communication Networks*, *2*(5), 607–614.

Heady, R., Luger, G., Maccabe, A., & Sevilla, M. (1990, August). The architecture of a network level intrusion detection system (technical report). University of New Mexico.

Ierace, N., Urrutia, C., & Bassett, R. (2005). Intrusion prevention systems. *Ubiquity*, *2005*(June), 2–2. doi:10.1145/1071916.1071927

Jayakumar, G., & Gopinath, G. (2007). Ad hoc mobile wireless networks routing protocols–a review. *Journal of Computational Science*, *3*(8), 574–582. doi:10.3844/jcssp.2007.574.582

Khari, M., Shrivastava, G., Gupta, S., Gupta, R. (2017). Role of Cyber Security in Today's Scenario. *Detecting and Mitigating Robotic Cyber Security Risks*, *177*.

Kuwatly, I., Sraj, M., Al Masri, Z., & Artail, H. (2004, July). A dynamic honeypot design for intrusion detection. In *Proceedings of the IEEE/ACS International Conference on Pervasive Services ICPS '04* (pp. 95-104). IEEE.

Messai, M. L. (2014). Classification of Attacks in Wireless Sensor Networks. arXiv:1406.4516

Mishra, A., Nadkarni, K., & Patcha, A. (2004). Intrusion detection in wireless ad hoc networks. *IEEE Wireless Communications, 11*(1), 48–60. doi:10.1109/MWC.2004.1269717

Nadeem, A., & Howarth, M. P. (2013). A survey of MANET intrusion detection & prevention approaches for network layer attacks. *IEEE Communications Surveys and Tutorials, 15*(4), 2027–2045. doi:10.1109/SURV.2013.030713.00201

Ramanujam, T. (2009). Intrusion Detection System Using Advanced Honeypots. *International Journal of Computer Science & Information Security, 2*(1).

Sarmah, A. (2001). Intrusion detection systems; definition, need and challenges. Retrieved March 2017 from https://www.sans.org/reading-room/whitepapers/detection/intrusion-detection-systems-definition-challenges-343

Sen, J. (2011). Secure Routing in Wireless Mesh Networks. In Wireless Mesh Networks. InTech. doi:10.5772/13468

Sharma, K., & Shrivastava, G. (2011). Public Key Infrastructure and Trust of Web Based Knowledge Discovery. *International Journal of Engineering, Sciences and Management, 4*(1), 56–60.

Shrestha, R., Han, K. H., Choi, D. Y., & Han, S. J. (2010, April). A novel cross layer intrusion detection system in MANET. In *Proceedings of the 2010 24th IEEE International Conference on Advanced Information Networking and Applications (AINA)* (pp. 647-654). IEEE. 10.1109/AINA.2010.52

Shrivastava, G., Sharma, K., & Rai, S. (2010, December). The Detection & Defense of DoS & DDoS Attack: A Technical Overview. In *Proceeding of ICC* (Vol. 27, p. 28).

Shrivastava, S. (2013). Rushing Attack and its Prevention Techniques. *International Journal of Application or Innovation in Engineering & Management, 2*(4), 453–456.

Sichitiu, M. L. (2005, May). Wireless mesh networks: opportunities and challenges. In *Proceedings of World Wireless Congress* (Vol. 2).

Smaha, S. E. (1988, December). Haystack: An intrusion detection system. In *Proceedings of the Fourth Aerospace Computer Security Applications Conference* (pp. 37-44). IEEE.

Thamilarasu, G., Balasubramanian, A., Mishra, S., & Sridhar, R. (2005, November). A cross-layer based intrusion detection approach for wireless ad hoc networks. In *Proceedings of the IEEE International Conference on Mobile Adhoc and Sensor Systems Conference*. IEEE. 10.1109/MAHSS.2005.1542882

Uplap, P., & Sharma, P. (2014, May). Review of heterogeneous/homogeneous wireless sensor networks and intrusion detection system techniques. In *Proceedings of Fifth International Conference on Recent Trends in Information, Telecommunication and Computing* (pp. 22-29).

Vaidya, H., Mirza, S., & Mali, N. (2016). Intrusion Detection System. *International Journal of Advanced Research in Engineering, Science & Technology, 3*.

Wang, X., Wong, J. S., Stanley, F., & Basu, S. (2009, July). Cross-layer based anomaly detection in wireless mesh networks. In *Proceedings of the Ninth Annual International Symposium on Applications and the Internet SAINT'09* (pp. 9-15). IEEE. 10.1109/SAINT.2009.11

Wikipedia. (n.d.). Mobile ad hoc network. Retrieved May 2017 from https://en.wikipedia.org/wiki/Mobile_ad_hoc_network

Zhang, Y., & Lee, W. (2000, August). Intrusion detection in wireless ad-hoc networks. In *Proceedings of the 6th annual international conference on Mobile computing and networking* (pp. 275-283). ACM.

Zhang, Y., Lee, W., & Huang, Y. A. (2003). Intrusion detection techniques for mobile wireless networks. *Wireless Networks*, *9*(5), 545–556. doi:10.1023/A:1024600519144

Chapter 4
Security Issues in Web Services

Priyanka Dixit
Rajiv Gahndi Prouodyogiki Vishwavidyalaya University, India

ABSTRACT

This chapter describes how security is an important aspect in today's digital world. Every day technology grows with new advancements in various areas, especially in the development of web-based applications. All most all of the web applications are on the internet, hence there is a large probability of attacks on those applications and threads. This makes security necessary while developing any web application. Lots of techniques have been developed for mitigating and defending against threats to the web based applications over the internet. This chapter overviews the important region of web application security, by sequencing the current strategies into a major picture to further the future research and advancement. Firstly, this chapter explains the major problem and obstacles that makes efforts unsuccessful for developing secure web applications. Next, this chapter distinguishes three basic security properties that a web application should possess: validation, integrity, accuracy and portray the comparing vulnerabilities that damage these properties alongside the assault vectors that contain these vulnerabilities.

INTRODUCTION

In the distributed environment the World Wide Web is the source that delivers static pages called as web application (Li & Xue, 2011). It is most prominent technology in the world for providing web services, information, and data access over the internet (Li & Xue, 2011). The technological improvements in data frameworks are necessary for the automation of various applications in different business and commercial areas. Information becomes turned into a basic asset in various associations, organizations along these, efficient access to information, distribution of information, and extract data from the information, and making exploitation of the data has turned to a dire necessity. Therefore, there has been needed security from the numerous attackers, which not just modification of data but misusing and destroying data from various sources scattered over the internet (Thuraisingham, 2003; Shrivastava, Sharma, & Bawankan, 2012).

Web applications and services are self-described or modular that can be published, access from anywhere on the internet. These applications can be written in any programming language and run on

DOI: 10.4018/978-1-5225-4100-4.ch004

any platform over the internet. A web service serves three of the basic responsibility in the web service framework these are Service requester, service broker, service provider. The service provider can be any business model, organization, the enterprise that is capable of providing services. The service requester can be any organizations that have the need for the service and service broker that acts as the intermediate between the service provider and requester (Kuyoro Shade et al., 2012).

The Web services are most attractive and important area for the research to the scientist and researchers. It is an important technology for the development and advancement of the distributed environment. Besides all of these merits of web services, there are some major challenges too that makes the deployment of web services over the internet is the critical one. The most challenging area for the web services is security and privacy. The secure service deployment is difficult today and the major issue for the distributed and heterogeneous applications. There are the following e-commerce models due to which the services provided to the customer business or vice versa like B2C and B2B but security is the important issue for providing secure web service.

All the web applications and services are run on the WWW so there is need of strong security architecture for protecting and make them securely running over the internet. This chapter presents the basic terminologies of security and privacy measures for Web Services also defines the security threads that makes difficult to provide secure web services over the internet.

FUNDAMENTAL PRINCIPLES OF SECURITY

Some of the fundamentals of security for the end to end services and application security in the distributed applications over the internet. Here describe the basic security principles that are necessary for the security architecture of web services and applications.

1. **Authentication:** This security term is basically verified the end users, registered system entities, and other components that are claiming. The authentication is the process by which authenticity of the user is checked on the internet it may any credentials, which may explain the following attributes like the identity of the person, role, group etc that can be integrated with the authentication principle.
2. **Authorization:** Is the term of security that granting any permission for accessing of resources, providing the access control, through which only authenticated users may access the resources, services via internet it acts like prevention against threats and unauthorized access. Access controls ensure that only the authorized users can access, control and modify the resource and no unauthorized access can be happened by this principle.
3. **Cryptography:** It provides security mechanisms and techniques that useful for protection of data from alteration and misuse. There are Encryption algorithms are used at the sender side which provides data confidentiality by encrypting the original data or message into some unreadable form that cannot be read by the third party and reverse algorithm at the receiver end, which contained decryption key that helps to decrypt the encrypted data. There are other algorithms like RSA, Diffie Hellman algorithms etc are used for secure key generation that responsible for the confidential information sharing and other terminology digital signature that ensures integrity and non-repudiation so that the data should be valid that send by the authentic person it is not been altered or modified during transmission over the medium.

4. **Availability:** It is one of the important principles of security that ensures that whatever the resources, service on the internet is available to the users. This may be important issue in internet to makes the resources available to the internet for the genuine users there are various attacks and threads that restricts user to access the resources in which Dos is one the major attack on availability of resources these type of attacks create huge traffic over the internet and makes services unavailable to the users.

5. **Accountability:** It ensures that necessary to have accountability for every action of an event happens. It provides the security auditing of record of secure events and also granting the monitoring events into the system. The term Non-repudiation in security ensures indisputable verification of data sending and receiving.

6. **Security Administration:** It provides the good security architecture that includes various security policy, maintenance, risk management, assessments, authentication, authorization mechanisms that ensures the security framework for any service and application (Sharma, Shrivastava, & Singh, 2012) .

7. **Integrity:** Its basically describes the correctness and precision of data and ensures the data originally from source to destination. This is one of the important parameters of security that provides the precision of data from sender to the receiving end that each of the bit that sends by the sender is received by another end is correct and unmodified form. The Data integrity is maintained by various security methods like digital signatures. Messages integrity is necessary for various areas especially in confidential information sharing medium where identity and confidential information of the sender is important hence that high degree of is required.

8. **Confidentiality:** It ensures that message secret and confidential to the third party during the transmission. This is the process requires some encoding of the message by which message is unreadable to the other users and data is confidential. The encryption is the technique that creates ciphertext (encrypted message) and this can be decrypted and read by the authenticated user for whom the message is generated. For this process to be accomplished secret key is shared among the communication between sender and receiver that key is responsible for the confidentiality of the users. In this technique, the encryption algorithm is designed by the complex mathematical calculation and functions to make it hard to decrypt.

9. **Non-Repudiation:** It basically used to ensure the identity of the sender that original generator of the message. By this principle neither the party can deny that the particular message is not sent by them it is a kind of identity proof of the originator of the message. It is useful when any transaction is legally challenged by any person or authority. The digital signature provides non-repudiation among the communicating parties. During this process, both of the parties digitally signed to confirming their identities that can be stored as electronic document due to which none of the party can deny of sharing any information between them.

WEB SECURITY ATTACKS

There are many vulnerabilities are present in security system by which the attacks and threads may enter by gaining the advantage of these security loops. Hence it is necessary to develop and designed the security architecture that fulfills all the basic principle of security and having the complex architecture that hard to break. Due to the certain vulnerabilities, numerous threats can compromise the security principles like availability, integrity, authentication of a Web service and can have backside entry to harm the web service. Here discussing some of these threats that can easy enters with conventional Web application systems or hacks the web services like websites etc. The following are the basic threats and attacks that can happen in various different Web applications for disturbing and harmful to the web services over the internet.

SQL Injections

The SQL injection is one of the serious vulnerability in web applications. The database can be accessed, created or stored by the use of SQL statements many of these vulnerabilities are created by input validations and dynamically execution of SQL statements. When the attacker is successful to break the security parameters then they pass input SQL statements then this inserted input will be run as SQL statements. SQL injections are initiated by inserting some random values alphabets and characters as the requests in URL parameter values or via Web login form submission. To prevent from SQL injection there are various methods and techniques are available but most important to resolve from these types of attacks is to overcome the vulnerabilities from the applications. The following are the very common vulnerability due to which the SQL injection can be possible like by web application authentication and validation procedures, having knowledge of database, injection with various SQL queries like by union, destruction of the database by the different injected query, by remote procedures calls (Saijadi & Pour, 2013; Sharma & Shrivastava, 2011).

Buffer Overflows

This is one of the serious attacks on application layer to the web application. This attack can happen due to the large size of input data. The input validation is the basic vulnerability of a buffer overflow attack. Buffer overflow attacks occur when an attacker over data writes to the outside of allocated memory boundaries and then it overrun the butter limitation. Buffer overflows may result crashing, memory access error, incorrect result and break the security of the system (Gupta, 2012). The following are the basic vulnerabilities for buffer overflow attack are Null terminated strings, format string it consists various formats like print f _ print for formatted output to the standard output, W print f _ wide-character version of printf stream, Fprintf _ print formatted data to a stream etc (Ggupta, 2012).

Denial-of-Service Attacks

It is the attack on the availability of the services from the web applications and resources. There are most prominent attacks on the application layer over the internet. Denial of Service attacks are initiated by applying the common procedure of attack, there is the necessity of strong approach like in architecture or security protocol for protecting various networks and resources against such type of destructive security attacks. There is a necessity to facilitate security among various application servers, network hosts machines, or other web resources over the internet from the harmful actions by the cyberattacks that is one of the important challenges to the network security. Today due to the advancement in technology a lot of application runs on the internet to provide services hence necessary that the resources of web applications like servers, network resources, and network functionality may be protected from the most serious attacks on web applications like Denial of service attack (DoS), SQL Injection, Cross scripting and other application layer attacks. The main objective of Denial of Service attacks to denying any authentic client machine from accessing web application services. The DoS attacks are very different from the other categories of system threats or other application layer attacks. The main ambition of such threat is to the stole or mistreats the personal information but the main target of creating a huge traffic on the network or overloads the various application or web servers by creating the huge amount of network traffic that pointing to the target machine. Typically, such attacks block valid users from using internet or web applications by draining or damaging the important assets of the target machine. Denial of Service attacks are pointing or targeting any device, system, host over the network but mostly at web application resources or web servers like SMTP servers, domain name servers or other web application servers to make the most frequently or important services cannot be provided to the requesting client machines hence numerous methods used, but most commonly by overwhelming the network bandwidth (Shrivastava, Sharma, & Rai, 2010).

Handling Errors Improperly

These types of attacks occur when the attacker intentionally adding or inserting malicious code in the web application request due to which a large number of error messages generated.

Eavesdropping

Eavesdropping is one of the important and serious threats to web services security. These types of attackers have carefully examined the data and online transactions that are mostly transfer using Web applications. The attackers can snoop messages and access all of the information and use that information. Therefore, necessary to maintain a secure transmission so that eavesdropper cannot access important information and only the authorized user can access the information.

Capturing and Replay Attacks

The messages or the information are transmitted over the Internet hence that transmitted messages are captured by the attackers. Such type of attack mostly happens when a third party or the attackers can gain access to some information between the information sharing. Hence hacker can capture and replay a SOAP request for money transferring, or modify the request.

Session Hijacking Attack

For the information sharing over the internet, the connection is established between client and servers. Hence for the secure communication like in bank transactions can be done via creating sessions. Session hijacking can control sessions of user's and gain access to the credentials. It can happen when the hackers steal a valid session ID and can take advantage of this id to the particular user's privileges and important information. By session hijacking, the attack can access the service as a valid or authenticate the user by sniffing user details. There are generally three types of session hijacking are an active session, passive session, and hybrid session hijacking. The active session hijacking is generally between the client and server machine and some time they drop the connection between them by dos attack that creates huge network traffic by sending the continuous request to the server machine (Bharti & Chaudhary, 2013). The passive session hijacking is similar to the active session hijacking besides that attacker silently examines and captures the data during the transmission for the future use. The hybrid session hijacking is the combination of active and passive session hijacking attacks. They can hijack the session and listen to the traffic and captures the information, then gain access to that information illegally (Bharti & Chaudhary, 2013).

WEB SERVICES VULNERABILITIES AND COUNTERMEASURES

There are the following vulnerabilities in web services with its countermeasures.

1. **Invalidated Input:** It is one of the important vulnerability due to which maximum attacks can be done. Hence it is necessary to validate the input request before to process it. Because of this vulnerability when the attacker wants to pass any malicious information, they can easily through the websites (Garfinkel & Spafford, 2002).
   a. Users request should be properly validated with all the input values data types, size of fields.
   b. Input request should follow particular format with all input parameters.
   c. Check the valid input values and their patterns
   d. Ruing all input values against the library.
2. **Handling Error Improperly:** Sometimes the error handling procedures are not proper which vulnerability of programming also is. Attackers can insert error intentionally to the input due to which the error messages generated. It is very difficult to handle lots of error messages (Garfinkel & Spafford, 2002).
   a. Checking each error response by testing the websites.
   b. In the error messages do not provide the important detail it should be hidden.
   c. Not using error messages facility with the important credentials.
   d. Developer level information is restricting to the other users.
3. **Parameter Modifications:** In this type of vulnerability the attackers can modify the input parameters values or data without accessing the site by using URL, query string, get method etc. (Garfinkel & Spafford, 2002).
   a. Don't allow input parameters to the users.
   b. Detect and examine the HTTP request origin carefully before the process.
   c. Dynamic parameter detection used.
4. **Directory Traversal:** The attackers can access the file, directories from the web servers. For this access, an attacker can use HTTP request to penetrate the web servers and web applications (Garfinkel & Spafford, 2002).
   a. Do not allow to access root directory.
   b. Always updates the web application serves.
   c. Web application filters used and input validation.
   d. Web solutions for vulnerabilities used.

CONCLUSION

Now a day's web services security and its challenges become very popular among many of researchers and scientists. This area is very important because every day new technological development is going on hence a lot of new web applications are created for the global connectivity. In this chapter discussing web service, its related issues, various security principle, web services threats and vulnerability and its countermeasures. Here discussing almost all the important issues of web applications and services security. This survey may cover all important points and help the researchers for the future direction for their research work and further growth.

REFERENCES

Bharti, A. K., & Chaudhary, M. (2013). Prevention of Session Hijacking and Ip spoofing with Sensor Nodes and Cryptographic Approach. *International Journal of Computers and Applications*, *76*(9).

Curphey, M., & Arawo, R. (2006). Web application security assessment tools. *IEEE Security and Privacy*, *4*(4), 32–41. doi:10.1109/MSP.2006.108

Durai, M. K. N., & Priyadharsini, K. (2014). A Survey on Security Properties and Web Application Scanner. *International journal of computer science and mobile computing*, *3*(10). 10.4018/978-1-59904-280-0.ch001

Garfinkel, S., & Spafford, G. (2002). *Web security, privacy & commerce*. O'Reilly Media, Inc.

Gupta, S. (2012). Buffer Overflow Attack. *IOSR Journal of Computer Engineering*, *1*(1), 10–23. doi:10.9790/0661-0111023

Kimbahune, V. V., Deshpande, A. V., & Mahalle, P. N. (2017, January). Lightweight Key Management for Adaptive Addressing in next Generation Internet. *International Journal of Ambient Computing and Intelligence*, *8*(1), 50–69. doi:10.4018/IJACI.2017010103

Kuyoro Shade, O., Frank, I., Awodele, O., & Okolie Samuel, O. (2012). Security issues in web services. *International Journal of Computer Science and Network Security*, *12*(1).

Li, X., & Xue, Y. (2011). A survey on web application security. Vanderbuilt University, Nashville, TN.

Matallah, H., Belalem, G., & Bouamrane, K. (2017, October). Towards a new model of storage and access to data in Big Data and Cloud Computing. *International Journal of Ambient Computing and Intelligence*, *8*(4), 31–44. doi:10.4018/IJACI.2017100103

Rafique, S., Humayun, M., Gul, Z., Abbas, A., & Javed, H. (2015). Systematic Review of Web Application Security Vulnerabilities Detection Methods. *Journal of Computer and Communications*, *3*(09), 28–40. doi:10.4236/jcc.2015.39004

Sajjadi, S. M. S., & Pour, B. T. (2013). Study of SQL Injection Attacks and Countermeasures. *International Journal of Computer and Communication Engineering*, *2*(5), 539–542. doi:10.7763/IJCCE.2013.V2.244

Sharma, K., & Shrivastava, G. (2011). Public Key Infrastructure and Trust of Web Based Knowledge Discovery. International Journal of Engineering. *Sciences and Management*, *4*(1), 56–60.

Sharma, K., Shrivastava, G., & Singh, D. (2012). Risk Impact of Electronics-Commerce Mining: A Technical Overview. In *Proceedings of the International Conference on Computing Communication and Information Technology 2012* (pp. 93-96).

Shrivastava, G., Sharma, K., & Bawankan, A. (2012, May). A new framework semantic web technology based e-learning. In *Proceedings of the 2012 11th International Conference on Environment and Electrical Engineering (EEEIC)* (pp. 1017-1021). IEEE. 10.1109/EEEIC.2012.6221527

Shrivastava, G., Sharma, K., & Rai, S. (2010, December). The Detection & Defense of DoS & DDoS Attack: A Technical Overview. In *Proceeding of ICC* (Vol. 27, p. 28).

Thuraisingham, B. (2003, November). Security issues for the semantic web. In Proceedings of the 27th Annual International Computer Software and Applications Conference COMPSAC '03 (pp. 633-638). IEEE.

Zhang, L. J. (2007). Challenges and opportunities for web services research. In *Modern Technologies in Web Services Research*. Hershey, PA: IGI Global.

Chapter 5
Flawed Security of Social Network of Things

Rohit Anand
G.B.Pant Engineering College, India

Akash Sinha
National Institute of Technology Patna, India

Abhishek Bhardwaj
G.B.Pant Engineering College, India

Aswin Sreeraj
G.B.Pant Engineering College, India

ABSTRACT

This chapter deals with the security flaws of social network of things. The network of things (NoT) is a dynamic structure that is basically an interface of real world and virtual world having capabilities of collection and sharing data over a shared network. The social network of things (SNoT) is a versatile way of connecting virtual and real world. Like any other device connected to internet, objects in SNoT are also vulnerable to the various security and privacy attacks. Generally, to secure Social Network of Things in which human intervention is absent, data capturing devices must be avoided. Types of security attacks that are huge threats to NoT as well as SNoT will be discussed in the chapter. The huge collection of information without necessary security measures allows an intruder to misuse the personal data of owner. Different types of attacks with reference to the different layers are also discussed in detail. The best possible potential solutions for the security of devices in SNoT will be considered.

INTRODUCTION

The Network of Things is basically internetworking of physical devices embedded with different sensors, actuators and network connectivity which enable these objects to collect and share data over and again. These devices are provided with some special sensors to perform some specific task. The Network of

DOI: 10.4018/978-1-5225-4100-4.ch005

Things (NoT) allows an object to be sensed or controlled remotely across a network established by connecting different objects (Atzori, Iera, & Morabito, 2010). This also creates an opening to establish a relation between the physical world and artificial world. When the Network of Things grows, it becomes a more general intense case of network security that can also be used as a growing technology for smart grids, virtual power plants, smart homes and smart cities. Typically, NoT is expected to offer advanced connectivity of devices, systems, and communication that go beyond machine-to-machine (M2M) communication. These devices collect some important data using sensors and other devices and have an ability to share data. That data flows among the network of these devices and can be accessed by any of the devices. This term was coined by Kevin Ashton of Procter & Gamble.

The above concept of Network of things was discussed in as early as 1982, with a modified coke machine at Carnegie Mellon University becoming the first connected device. The concept of Network of Things became popular in 1999, at Auto-ID centre of Massachusetts Institute of Technology, Cambridge. Despite many applications and potential in the industry, there is a barrier to adopt Network of Things among industry leaders and consumers. Many of NoT devices have failed to prove their relevance in society. This is a major reason that is boarding this gap. To bridge this gap, companies must identify the value that lies in order to make these devices sounder.

In some application environments, some of the NoT devices may be integrated. The resulting paradigm is Social Network of Things. The Social Network of Things has a potential to support many novel applications and networking applications in more efficient way. The Social Network of Things can be moulded to any desired shape to achieve any desired application in more effective manner. It also increases a level of trustworthiness and security. The SNoT server encompasses network layer and application layer. SNoT devices are not the proposed solution for networking but they make a world of trillions of interconnected devices more manageable. Another term of interest is Web of Things (WoT) that is used to describe approaches, software architectural styles, and programming patterns so as to allow real-world objects to be a part of World Wide Web.

As discussed above, SNoT is a very versatile way of connecting virtual and real world but since all the data and processes are connected to the internet, there is always a possibility of getting it attacked or hacked by someone. In such a case, the data must be protected and other useful information by using some special techniques. The existing SNoT security system has many flaws resulting in the need for some modern techniques to improve this flawed network security. This can be achieved by protecting the network with firewalls and protocols but the devices that are present at the endpoint will impose major problems. Each device has its own specific task but there are some devices that are linked to each other and are discardable. It is hard to detect and fix the problem for such devices. Mainly, there are two kinds of attacks or threats presented to a network. The first one is interface attack that is collecting data from the channel. It can be done by studying the data transmission through a link. The other one is Distributed Denial-of-Service (DDoS) attack. DDoS can be carried out by hindering M2M communication (Shrivastava et al., 2010). There are basically three layers in SNoT architecture: application layer, transport layer, and perception layer. The last one is responsible for interaction with the external world. Radio Frequency Identification (RFID) and Wireless Sensor Networks (WSNs), flooding, wormhole and sewage pool, witch attack, broadcast authentication, external attack, link layer security, selective forwarding attack and HELLO flooding attack are some techniques used to attack the perception layer.

NETWORK OF THINGS

The Network of Things (NoT) is a scenario where objects are enhanced by network connectivity, computing capabilities, sensors and everyday items that allow these devices to generate, exchange, store and consume data without or with minimal human interventions (Rose, Eldridge, & Chapin, 2015). These devices must not be confused with computers because these devices are producing, exchanging and storing data, yet are not considered as computers. Although any single or reliable definition of a device based on NoT is not there as it varies from device to device but we can safely say that an integration of real and virtual world gives birth to a NoT device. These devices are connected to the internet with the help of short-range wireless technology such as RFID (Radio Frequency Identification), NFC (Near Frequency Communication) or WSNs (Wireless Sensor Networks) (Winter, 2015). To increase instrumentation, tracking and both natural and social process, some special devices by merging the physical world and the virtual world may be made. This hybrid device is the NoT device (Sinha & Kumar, 2016).

These devices find application in many fields. Such an Industrial NoT is nothing but a distributed network of some versatile sensors that can precisely control and monitor many complex processes over an arbitrary distance (Huberman, 2016). In a vast, dynamic and expanding world, every object in the internet infrastructure is a NoT Device (Farash, Turkanović, Kumari, & Hölbl, 2016). The main idea of using a NoT device is to bridge the gap between the physical world of humans and virtual machine world by the use of smart objects in day-to-day life. These smart objects help in human-machine interaction by processing and providing any sort of useful information or command. Hence, sensors or actuators can be integrated into buildings or vehicles and the interfacing environment can indicate about their state and surrounding (Makhoul, Guyeux, Hakem, & Bahi, 2016). At the very high level of abstraction, the NoT can be understood as a hyper-scale, hyper-complex human-machine interface environment (Delic, 2016). The NoT not only facilitates human to machine interactions but promotes machine to machine interactions also. While the definition of Network of Things has no rigid definition and is elusive in general, use of the term NoT refers to the use of sensors, actuators or motors in the physical day to day life objects that can sense their surroundings and physical parameters (Fjäder, 2016). These devices are connected irrespective of their functions or use and can communicate over transmission protocols. The NoT envisions the world with smart objects that can communicate over the internet, exchange or share the data that they collect or store and cooperate with each other to provide a value-added product (Yachir, Amirat, Chibani, & Badache, 2016). In a broad sense, NoT is adding some additional values to a product by use of the internet (Lee, 2016). Many other definitions are provided by various standardization groups such as ITU, IEEE, 3GPP, and IETF.

A different type of NoT could be a Local Area Network (LAN), with none of the 'things' connected to the Internet. Social media networks, the Industrial Internet, and sensor networks are all variations of NoT. This distinction in terminology provides ease in splitting out cases from varying vertical and quality domains (e.g., medical, transportation, financial, safety-critical, agricultural, security-critical, high assurance, performance-critical, to name a few). Some recent researches are conducted to integrate social networks and NoT. It is called Social NoT (Kleinberg, 2008). The network of things is a medium to connect things to the internet and using the connection to share data, useful information, and controlling these things. Network of Things is existing as the machine to machine market in today's world. Network of Things works on the principle of an invisible intelligent network fabric that can be sensed, controlled, and programmed. NoT enabled products can communicate with each other either directly or indirectly because they are embedded with sensors and latest technology. In initial 1990s, the internet connectivity was not that good in industry hence the NoT devices were not mostly used but in 2000s internet connectivity became the norm of many applications and as expected, Network of Things became a major part of today's technology. Today over 50 Billion devices are in a network of things (Sinha et al., 2017).

Manufacturers have been connecting things to the internet before we call it internet. By the mid of the 1990s, embedded products were added to web servers. Current M2M manufacturers have connected highly integrated high-value asset tracking system, alarm system, and fleet management system. While on the other hand consumers have connected things like thermosets, energy systems, lighting control systems and remote video streaming boxes etc. and much more to come. Most of these systems are connected to web browsers and can be accessed through a mobile app or using a smartphone. These systems may also use the same protocols as other websites are using in the present scenario. It is scientifically proven that a certain problem, when answered by a large number of individuals, is always more accurate than answered by the small and more knowledgeable group of people. It is the same philosophy behind NoT, making it accurate and reliable.

The primary architecture of NoT is shown in Figure 1.

Since RFID is a fundamental technology in the Network of Things, the history (Minerva, Biru, & Rotondi, 2015) starts from the inception of RFID and how it led to the emergence of NoT. The origin of RFID technology can be traced back to the World War II. A Scottish physicist Sir Robert Alexander Watson-Watt discovered that the RADAR technology can be utilized for creating a passive RFID system ("Identify friend or foe" {IFF} system), that can detect if an aircraft is a friend or foe. Afterwards, further advances in the field of RFID had been developed through the 1950s and 1960s. Electronic article surveillance tags (1bit) were invented by the application of radio waves. Thus, the RFID was commercialized. Later in the 1970s, the RFID system was used to track nuclear materials. Further, the RFID technology found application in a variety of fields, with the expansion of the range of operating frequencies (VHF, UHF, etc.).

Between 1999 and 2003, an agency named Auto-ID Center got aid from various companies, RFID vendors and U.S. Department of Defence, for research and development of RFID technology. This agency formulated two air interface protocols for RFID devices, the Electronic Product Code (EPC) numbering

Figure 1. Primary architecture of NoT

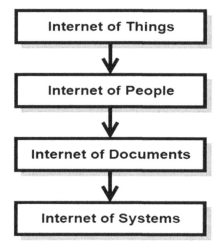

system, and network architecture to search for data related to the RFID tag on the Internet. The term "Network of Things" was used by the Auto-ID Center in 2000 and advocated the ideas and concepts of a world connected with the EPC system as a base for connecting things to the Internet.

NoT is not the result of a single novel technology. Instead, several complimentary technical developments provided capabilities that taken together help to bridge the gap between the virtual and real world. These capabilities include:

- Communication and cooperation
- Addressability
- Identification sensing actuation
- Embedded Information processing
- Localization
- User interface

The NoT can be viewed as a gigantic network consisting of networks of devices and computers connected through a series of intermediate technologies where numerous technologies like RFIDs, wireless connections may act as enablers of this connectivity.

- **Tagging Things:** Real-time item traceability and addressability by RFIDs.
- **Feeling Things:** Sensors act as primary devices to collect data from the environment.
- **Shrinking Things:** Miniaturization and Nanotechnology have provoked the ability of smaller things to interact and connect with the "things" or "smart devices."
- **Thinking Things:** Embedded intelligence in devices through sensors has formed the network connection to the internet. It can make the "things" realizing the intelligence control.

According to a study, by 2020 the world will be having 50 billion NoT devices whereas total world population would be 7.6 billion. That means on an average there would be 6.58 devices per person. It means that NoT will dominate the future technologies.

SOCIAL NETWORK OF THINGS

Social Network of Things (SNoT) utilizes pretty much everything that emerged as a part of the already existing Network of Things, but additionally gives a new model for the structure of this so-called "network". SNoT, even though a novel paradigm, is basically a revamped form of Network of Things. It adopts the newly evolved technologies like the cloud computing, machine learning, and other platforms and explores the implications of those technologies. The Network of Things (NoT) was proposed to have several structures, like the human nervous system and the social network of humans (Ning & Wang, 2011), for its future applications. Out of those proposed structures, the social network of humans is the most felicitous structure for the ubiquitous nature of NoT. The social network is a software platform where many individuals, who share same backgrounds, interests and do similar activities or have real-life connections, come together (Shi, Wan, Cheng, Cai, Li, & Li, 2015). By utilizing the expanding pervasiveness of smartphones, people are continually producing content and sharing it with others with ease through their social networks (Kim, Maron, & Mosse, 2015). These can be perceived as analogous to devices that constantly generate data and share this data with other devices for completing some task. Thus SNoT is derived from the application of architecture of the social network of humans into the concept of Network of Things. This "social network of intelligent objects", analogous to the Social Network Services for humans, introduces a social relationship between the objects in the network (Atzori, Iera, & Morabito, 2011). The devices in the SNoT, based on their "social roles", actively engage in their respective task either collaboratively or independently (Kim, Maron, & Mosse, 2015).

The main target of Social Network of Things is to let the objects to have their own social network analogous to that of humans, thus by defining two distinct levels for people and things, but at the same time giving people the authority to establish rules for the protection of their privacy. The users are allowed to access only the result of the autonomous intercommunication between the objects in the SNoT (Geetha, 2016). Thus, things in the Network of Things, already being smart, get the added feature of sociality when they become a part of the SNoT (Atzori, Iera, & Morabito, 2014). These social things acquire the ability to not only inform other things in the network but to negotiate with them to produce an efficient way of interoperability (Petroni, n.d.). For instance, when the driverless cars are connected to the SNoT, they will not only be able to communicate (like today's driverless cars) but negotiate with each other and other objects available nearby (traffic cameras, sidewalk sensors) as well to derive an outcome, for example, prevent an impending accident or at least reduce its impact (Geetha, 2016).

Several benefits (Atzori, Iera, & Morabito, 2011) have resulted from the adoption of the social network architecture for the Network of Things:

- The models for the social network of humans can be exploited for addressing various issues (inherently related to the broad network of interconnected objects) in this network architecture.
- The level of communication between the "friendly" objects can be maximized by the creation of a degree of trustworthiness.
- This network architecture can be modified to assure network navigability, for the effective detection and identification of objects and services; the scalability is also warranted like that in a social network of humans.

Various social relationships (Atzori, Iera, Morabito, & Nitti, 2012) have been proposed and implemented for SNoT, which includes:

- **Parental Object Relationship:** It is implemented among objects manufactured in the same production batch. This relationship gets updated in case of device failure and obsolescence of devices.
- **Co-Location Object Relationship:** Established between objects belonging to the same place (actuators, RFID, sensors).
- **Co-Work Object Relationship:** Established among devices which repeatedly collaborate with each other to provide shared applications such as telemedicine and emergency response.
- **Ownership Object Relationship:** Implemented between devices possessed by the same individual (smart TV, smartphone, PC, etc.).
- **Social Object Relationship:** Established between devices which occasionally or regularly come into contact with each other due to the relation between the users (friends, classmates, and family).

SNoT has an architecture which is established upon 3 main objectives, the discovery of objects and related services, composition and management of trustworthiness. Basic components of the structure of this network include ID management, Object Profiling, and Owner Control. Additionally, this structure has components like Relationship Management, Service Discovery, Service Composition, Trustworthiness Management and Service Application Program Interfaces (APIs). The architecture of SNoT consists of three layers (Atzori, Iera, & Morabito, 2011):

1. **Perception Layer:** This layer may be viewed as the physical layer in the architecture of SNoT. This layer is also known as sensing layer due to the fact that it contains sensors for collecting data from and about the surrounding (Sethi & Sarangi, 2017). The sensor can be seen as a type of transducer which detects some physical parameters in the environment and sends the corresponding data to another electronic device, like a microcontroller. Devices in the perception layer include Sensor network, Smart card, Reader, and RFID tag.
2. **Transport Layer:** This layer is responsible for the connection to other smart things, servers, and network devices. Sometimes, this layer is also referred to as network layer. It comprises of a mixture of various networks, including the 3G/4G communication network, Internet, databases, big data modules and the cloud computing platform. It takes care of the transmission and processing of the data collected from the perception layer. Long distance wired and wireless communication protocol, magnanimous intelligent information processing technology, and network integration technology are the fundamental technologies of the transport layer (Jain, 2015).
3. **Application Layer:** This layer deals with the delivery of specific services, which are application oriented, to the user. It acts as an interface between the consumers and Social Network of Things. It governs the entire SNoT. It establishes various applications of SNoT, like smart health, smart homes and smart city (Sethi & Sarangi, 2017). This layer employs methods like cloud computing, fuzzy recognition, data mining and various other smart techniques and machine learning methods for processing the humongous amount of data and providing the calculated and effective information (Jain, 2015).

Different trust models have been proposed for the SNoT. Various researchers have been made to establish a successful interface between the humans and SNoT. SNoT is anticipated to have the potential of connecting a vast number of smart devices in the physical world, like Smartphone, actuators, radio frequency identification (RFID) tags, sensors together with the virtual objects like virtual desktops and data on the cloud (Chen, Bao, & Guo, 2016). A variety of applications, such as smart community, smart city, e-health and smart home will be built on the top of this novel paradigm.

FLAWED SECURITY OF SOCIAL NETWORK OF THINGS

Since the inception of the computer network, which was simply the connection between two computers, safeguard of information and unauthorized access have been subjects of concern (Shipley, 2013). Emerging of the Internet has widened these concerns to a large extent. With the dawn of Network of Things, the cyber security risks are more and more jointly affecting the privacy as well as the physical safety of the users (Gupta et al., 2017). As Network of Things (NoT) is the cardinal concept of Social Network of Things (SNoT), it inherits everything from the NoT, including the security and privacy concerns and complications, in addition to its own individual vulnerabilities. The inherited security and privacy complications include vulnerability to unauthorized access, privacy breaches, data theft and various critical threats to the safety of the network. In SNoT, security is essentially indivisible from safety. Whether intentionally or accidentally, manipulation of devices in SNoT, for example, nuclear reactors, vehicles or pacemakers, can be potentially hazardous to humans, who are operating them or are near to them (Shipley, 2013).

The risks become more complicated in the SNoT than in the NoT. The processes and communication between objects in SNoT should be automated, which means the human intervention is restricted. Thus, it is very difficult to address the security in SNoT because the introduction of objects to active control process without human intervention will supplement to the complexity of the system (Romdhani, 2017). Albeit device authentication is not a serious concern in NoT but while implementing SNoT it is going to be a crucial part of strengthening the security. There is another factor for the huge potential risk in the SNoT. This factor is embedding of sensors and other data acquisition devices into commonplace devices which will record the activities of users (Hajdarbegovic, n.d.). When such a device with ubiquitous data collection and faulty security is hacked, it could leak all that information to a person with malicious intent. This will conceivably welcome the hacker to browse around the confidential information and collect critical details about the user of the devices in the SNoT. For instance, smart TVs and tablets collect the browsing history and track the user's online activity and this information, when used without permission, can potentially breach the user's privacy and cause inconvenience and distress to the user (Ramirez, 2015).

The re-engineering of conventional network security measures is required before implementing them in the architecture of SNoT. The flow of high-level of data traffic through the internet can be managed by network firewalls and protocols, but the devices at the endpoint which are thoroughly embedded, having a distinct and defined mission with finite resources available to accomplish are still going to pose a problem while implementing Social Network of Things. These embedded devices are designed and manufactured with small silicon form factor for low power consumption. Their task-oriented memory capacity and processing capability, making them "headless" (Shipley, 2013) and the lack of human intervention could result in its inability to decide the authenticity of applications and lack of judgment capabilities for differentiating undesired commands from required commands. This would also result in suppression of encryption and degraded error-free performance. Moreover, some linked devices are cheap and essentially discardable. If vulnerability of such type of devices is detected, it would be hard to apply a patch or a software update or even to inform the consumers about the fix.

The discussion regarding the network security generally initiates by introducing the topic of security attacks in the network, whether it is simply the Internet or the SNoT. According to Internet Engineering Task Force, an attack is defined as an assault carried out on the security of a system, deriving from an intelligent threat, hence, a smart act that is a calculated attempt (a technique or method) for eluding security services and contravening security protocols of a system (Shirey, 2000). Generally, based on the effect on the system, the attack can be active or passive. An active attack is intended to modify the resources of a system and alter its operations. Whereas a passive attack is carried out only to leak or acquire information from or about the system, without modifying anything in the system. The attack may have been carried out by an insider or from the outside of the system or organization. An inside attack is an attack perpetrated by someone inside the security perimeter or simply an "insider", who is authorized to access and utilize the system resources. The insider instead of using it in an intended way, utilize them in a fashion which is against the protocols of the organization or the system. An outside attack is executed from beyond the security perimeter, by an illegitimate or unauthorized user. Outside attacks are commonplace attacks in the realm of the Internet, carried out by pranksters, black hat hackers, and international terrorist and belligerent governing bodies (Shirey, 2000).

There are two types of security attacks in communication between two devices in SNoT. These include:

- **Inference Attack:** This attack is a privacy attack, which is carried out by analytically and logically studying the data transmission between devices and forming specific patterns. This is a case of violated information security (Jain, 2015). Information security or InfoSec is described as the safeguard of information and the related systems from illegitimate access, exposure, use, destruction, alteration or disruption (Vacca, 2012). This attack is generally carried out at the primary levels of security and gaining information and compiling these to derive information guarded at the top and complex levels of security. In SNoT, for instance, a hacker can simply use the data, like the user's activity and information that may seem trivial, from general devices in the network to intrude into private information and other confidential and sensitive systems.

- **Denial-of-Service (DoS) Attack:** DoS attacks are those which are carried to inhibit legitimate users from connecting to a specific website or accessing a particular network resource or to downgrade regular services for valid users by sending an enormous undesirable traffic to a server or a machine (victim) for exhausting services and bandwidth or connection capacity (Prasad, Reddy, & Rao, 2014). Even in the era of the Internet, the internet servers and network devices were at huge risks due to DoS. In SNoT, a social thing can be made incompetent by flooding its interface with unwanted requests and traffic. This will definitely have some adverse effects on other devices in the network, due to the interconnection between devices and the overall structure of the SNoT. This will degrade the activity of an individual (user) or an organization (in which SNoT is implemented) which may cause distress, financial loss or even loss of life. There is an extended type of this attack called distributed denial-of-service attack. A DDoS attack is a DoS attack on a large scale. It is essentially a coordinated attack on the services of a victim server or device, launched by the utilization of "botnets" on the internet. Botnets are those computers or devices which are acquired by the attacker by stealthy installing malicious hacking software. The degree of attack depends on the size of the botnet, for example, a large botnet can be used to bring down a conglomerate (Criscuolo, 2000).

The general architecture of a Distributed Denial-of-Service attack is shown in Figure 2.

There are individual vulnerabilities in every layer of the SNoT architecture. Each layer is to be considered for discussing the overall flaws in the network security of Social Network of Things.

PERCEPTION LAYER

The primary vulnerabilities of this layer are the sensor network and the RFID tags. The nodes in the sensor network have the responsibilities like data acquisition, integration, collaboration, and transmission. The low cost of sensor network hinders them to have an effective and tailored security system. Cost is also a shortcoming for the security of the RFID tags (Bhabad & Bagade, 2015). The lack of an effective security of RFID allows illegal access to it and the corresponding social object, by counterfeiting. The tag can be altered or decoded, which may leak sensitive information, like money (in digital form), to the malicious hacker. Major security complications (Hu, 2016) in the sensor network include the following:

Figure 2. General architecture of a distributed denial-of-service attack

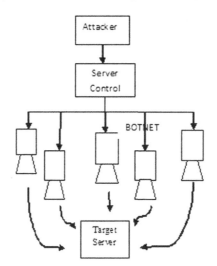

- **Flooding Attack:** It is a type of DoS attack. The device is flooded with the huge amount of data that cause the overload of the memory buffer of the device and as a result, the service provider is hindered. In the perception layer, the potential victims of this attack may be sensors. Devices whose entire operation depends on sensors may become futile when sensors are compromised. Flooding can be caused by:
  - **Attackers:** Flooding of malicious or undesirable data or packets towards the devices in the SNoT.
  - **Legitimates (Flash Crowd):** When many authentic users request for device services and resources simultaneously, the interface of the device gets flooded with request resulting in memory buffer overload.
  - **Aggressive Legitimates:** These are those legit users who repeatedly request for service within a short period of time. These frequent requests overload the device, degrading its performance.
- **Wormhole Attack:** Wormhole attacks predominantly occur in Mobile Adhoc Networks (MANETs). Variety of devices (static or dynamic) exist in the SNoT, which is connected heterogeneously (wired or wireless) with each other. The need to get access to the host in a network is absent in a wormhole attack. The attacker creates a shorter path for the data transmission, misusing the routing algorithms, picks up the data and retransmits it to another node in the network. Wormhole attacks are different from conventional network security attacks and thus, are very hard to be detected.
- **Sinkhole Attack:** In the sensor network, the sensors which are the nodes, when left unattended for a long period of time, are highly vulnerable to sinkhole attack. The node, which is compromised, starts attracting information from other nodes in the network. Thereafter, this attack precedes other attacks like selective forwarding attack, network hijacking, modification of network, etc.
- **Sewage Pool Attack:** Sewage pool attack is similar to sinkhole attack. In sewage pool attack, the malicious node attracts all the information from a particular region of the network towards it and replaces the base station node.

- **Trust Related Attacks by Malicious Nodes:** A malicious node is deceitful and uncooperative socially and it can break the fundamental functionality of the SNoT. The ill-intentioned node displays behavior similar to humans in a social network. The node thus executes the following trust related attacks (Chen, Bao, & Guo, 2016):
  - ○ **Self-Promoting Attack:** An infected or malicious node starts promoting its relevance (by providing useful suggestions) in the SNoT so that it can be preferred as a service provider, then eventually starts providing faulty services.
  - ○ **Whitewashing Attack:** In this attack, the malicious node suddenly vanishes and re-joins the network to erode its bad reputation.
  - ○ **Discriminatory Attacks:** An infected or malicious node distinctively commences attacking nodes without any social link or unfamiliar nodes. This is based on a social behavior, which is the inclination towards friends in a social network.
  - ○ **Collusion Attack:** This attack involves a malicious node, which displays human nature in a social network, boosting friendly nodes and targeting specific nodes for victimizing. There are two types of collusion attack (Chen, Bao, & Guo, 2016):
    - ▪ **Bad-Mouthing Attack:** One or more malicious nodes in a network begin to spoil the reputation of a legitimate node by giving negative recommendations for reducing the likelihood of that node becoming a service provider in the SNoT.
    - ▪ **Ballot-Stuffing Attack:** This is another type of collusion attack. In this attack, the malicious node improves the reputation of another ill-intentioned node by providing positive recommendations. This increases the probability of that bad node becoming a service provider. In this attack also, the malicious node can collaborate with other malicious nodes to boost the reputation of each other.
- **Witch Attack:** The infected node in the witch attack utilizes the failure of an authentic node. When a node in the network fails, the real link takes a detour through the malicious node for further communication, which may open doors to other attacks, like selective forwarding attacks, causing data loss, data theft, and data manipulation.
- **External Attack:** This attack arises from the concern of trustworthiness of the service providers in SNoT. While implementing SNoT, the organizations and individual may share information (both sensitive and trivial) with the service providers (like cloud service providers) for acquiring their service. The safeguard of those provided information lies with the administrator. The information may be misused by the provider or personnel of the service providing company or the information may be leaked to an outsider from the provider.
- **Selective Forwarding Attack:** In selective forwarding attack, one of the nodes is infected or it may succeed wormhole attack. The malicious node selectively filters out some data coming from the node of the infected network and retransmits it to the next node. The dropped data may contain sensitive information that may be essential for the operation of a device in the network.
- **HELLO Flooding Attack:** It is a type of flooding attack. In SNoT, every object has a neighboring device. In HELLO flooding attack, every object will announce itself with HELLO messages to all the neighbors that are accessible according to its bandwidth. A malicious node will have a huge bandwidth and thus becomes the neighbour to the maximum number of nodes in the network. Eventually, this malicious node will flood the neighboring nodes with HELLO messages and degrade its availability to the legitimate users.

- **Broadcast Authentication:** Base stations are required to broadcast data and commands to the sensor nodes in a network. Sensors may carry out unwanted operations and fail to meet the requirements laid out for the network when there is no security for the communication. Existing security solutions for the wired and wireless network do not apply to the wireless sensor network due to the limited resources and memory of the later. Broadcast authentication based on the existing techniques cannot handle these resource-constrained devices. New methods have to be introduced or existing methods have to be revamped for these wireless sensor networks (Eldefrawy, Khan, Alghathbar, & Cho, 2010).
- **Buffer Overflow Attack:** This attack is intended to inundate a predefined space in a buffer, which can possibly lead to data overwriting and corruption in the memory. This is a major risk for those SNoT objects that have a control system for their operation. There are two basic types of buffer overflow attack (Ayala, 2016):
  - **Function Pointer Attack:** This type of buffer overflow attack is carried out by overwriting an exception handler or function pointer that is eventually executed.
  - **Stack Smashing Attack:** This is a cyber-attack that uses the buffer overflow to dupe a system into executing a random code.

TRANSPORT LAYER

- **DDoS/DoS Attack:** DDoS attacks are those which are launched and carried on by several zombie devices (botnets). It is commenced by populating unnecessary traffic data or packets with massive size for capturing and entirely exhausting the memory resources and diminishing the bandwidth of the device. As a result, valid users will not be able to access the device or request service. DoS/ DDoS also attacks the cloud, by overwhelming the resources and restricting normal access by licit devices.
- **Masquerade Attack:** It is a type of attack that utilizes fake identity to gain unauthorized access to devices or servers through authentic access identification. A flawed authorization process can open doors for masquerade attackers. These attacks can be initiated using stolen passwords and login credentials, by detecting loopholes in programs and finding a way around the process of authentication. The extent of access a masquerade attacker gets depends upon the degree of authorization he has managed to achieve (Prasad, Reddy, & Rao, 2014).
- **IP Spoofing Attack:** This attack is similar to the masquerade attack, in the way that it pretends to be a valid user to get access to the various resources that are otherwise restricted or to steal information that may be confidential and sensitive. The attacker impersonates itself as a legitimate user by counterfeiting source IP address of that user and sends IP packets to the vulnerable system, which could be an object in the SNoT, for gaining authorized access and carrying out a malicious activity afterward (Hu, 2016).
- **Man-in-the-Middle Attack:** The man-in-the-middle attack is a prominent security attack in the network layer of the Internet, NoT and SNoT. Basically, this attack uses various techniques that are intended to intercept a communication between two nodes. When the attacker successfully discontinues the connection of his victims, he can supplant the proxy server (Cekerevac, Dvorak, Prigoda, & Cekerevac, 2017). It is illustrated in Figure 3. This attack can be carried out by the following methods:

Figure 3. Illustration of man-in-the-middle attack

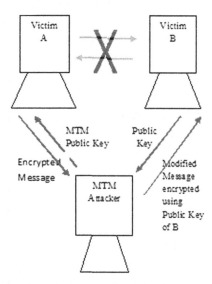

- ○ **Address Resolution Protocol (ARP) Cache Poisoning:** ARP cache poisoning is one the earliest methods of the man-in-the-middle attack. This method is considered to be the simplest to execute, but the most effective after successful implementation by the attacker. In this attack, the attacker joins the same subnet as his victims and eavesdrops on the network traffic between those victims, by utilizing the insecure nature of the ARP (Sanders, March 2010).
- ○ **DNS Spoofing:** DNS spoofing is another method used for the man-in-the-middle attack. It is utilized to provide fake DNS information to a host so that when they try to access a server or website, the host is redirected to a fraudulent replica of the original server or website that is created by the attacker for stealing classified and sensitive data from the innocent victim (Sanders, April 2010).
- ○ **Session Hijacking:** A session may be defined as an established dialogue which contains well-defined set-up, maintenance, and termination of connections among a variety of devices. A session hijacking is the malicious exploitation of this session between devices (Sanders, May 2010).
- ○ **SSL Hijacking:** Secure Socket Layers (SSL) or Transport Layer Security (TLS) is a set of protocols which are designed for the safeguard of network communication by utilizing encryption. The SSL hijacking exploits the transition of connection from a non-encrypted to an encrypted one, for example, the conversion of HTTP to HTTPS in browsers (Sanders, June 2010).
- • **Smurf:** This cyber-attack is a type of address spoofing. It is carried out by transmitting a steady stream of Internet Control Message Protocol (ICMP) packets that are modified by the attacker, to the victim network, keeping the sender address identical to one of the addresses of the target computer. In the context of the SNoT, the device, which responds to the packets, may crash unexpectedly or carry out undesired operations (Zhu, Joseph, & Sastry, 2011).

- **Loop/Chain Attack:** In this attack, the attacker shifts through multiple nodes to remain anonymous, thus creating a chain of connections across these nodes. The loop attack is very similar to the chain attack, but the chain of connections forms a loop. Thus, loop attack is worse than chain attack because it is harder to track down the origin and identity of the attacker in the former in SNoT (Ayala, 2016).
- **Sybil Attack:** Sybil attack is a major threat to vehicular ad-hoc networks (VANETs). In this attack, the attacker attempts to contravene the unique vehicular ID by counterfeiting or fabrication and further displaying multiple identities. This type of attack can cause the massive-scale denial of service or various other types of security attacks (Hu, 2016).

APPLICATION LAYER

- **Doorknob-Rattling Attack:** In this type of cyber-attack, the attacker tries a few commonplace combinations of password and username on various systems. Clearly, this will result in a few failed login attempts. If these failed login attempts from a particular host or several hosts are not traced for detecting the doorknob-rattling attack, this attack will go unnoticed and may cause potential system breach in the future (Ayala, 2016).
- **The Revelation of Sensitive Information:** A potential breach in the cloud service or a system in the SNoT can leak much private and sensitive information to an ill-intentioned person. This can possibly result in physical as well as psychological trauma or loss of finance or property.
- **Data Destruction:** An attacker can hack the cloud service or another data storage system involved in the SNoT by means of various attacks mentioned previously. This illegitimate takeover can eventually result in data destruction by the attacker, which may lead to heavy financial and crucial information losses. This may even lead to loss of intellectual property.

Even after the implementation of security measures, there are various other cyber-attacks which are aimed to either bypass the security or debilitate it. Several of those cyber-attacks include:

- **Cinderella Attack:** It is a type of cyber-attack which incapacitates the security software by maliciously exploiting the internal clock of a system or a network. This manipulation results in the premature termination of the security software license, resulting in the exposure of the system or the network to potential cyber-attacks (Ayala, 2016).
- **Side-Channel Attack:** This attack analyses information (power consumption, timing information, electromagnetic leaks or even sound) acquired from the physical implementation of a cryptographic system (Singer, 2004). This can be considered as a type of inference attack. The deduced information can be used to decrypt encrypted information without the need of possession of the original key.
- **Hardware Tampering:** Even though the software level of SNoT can be secured as much as possible, it is very difficult to prevent the hacking of an attack on the physical system. That is, the devices in the SNoT are not tamperproof; its hardware can easily be accessed by opening it and manipulating the probes and pin headers.
- **Theft:** Since the objects in SNoT do not require human intervention, leaving those devices for a long duration of time can unavoidably lead to thievery (Hu, 2016).

The devices also have limited processing power and the design and the programming are not sophisticated in most cases, thus an attacker can simply produce a clone of the device or manipulate the data and the software in order to make the operation of that device useless or erroneous.

POSSIBLE SOLUTIONS

Albeit many of the complications, which are also present in the conventional networks, in the Social Network of Things were already addressed in the era of the Internet, they may have to be revamped in order to implement in the SNoT. The automation in SNoT has led to the development of various novel threats, which are yet to be detected or addressed adequately. The required security measures should be established at the first time boot of a "Social Thing". Security should not be considered as an add-on to a machine, but rather an integral part of the activity of the social thing. For the security of devices in SNoT, the following requirements (Hu, 2016) should be met:

- **Data Confidentiality and Integrity:** Data confidentiality is maintained through cryptographic processes (encryption and decryption) whereas data integrity is retained via authentication codes or cryptographic hashes annexed to data payload. Data confidentiality along with data integrity ensures trustworthiness in the data sent or received among the devices. Both these can act as a support for dealing with various attack vectors of interception, interruption, and modification
- **Peer Authentication and System Availability:** Peer authentication is closely associated with system availability. Peer authentication consists of a peer validating another peer's identity before establishing a communication link. Thus the ability of the peer to discard or accept another peer's request for the link based on the authentication can avert possible external attacks like denial-of-service attack. Additional device descriptors, which can be made mutually available and validated, can augment the peer authentication.
- **Proof of Authorization:** This can prohibit unauthorized entities to communicate with the device and execute a certain action. Thus, proof of authorization can avoid fabrication by a malicious outsider.
- **Non-Repudiation:** Since the action of a peer (sender or receiver) is linked to its token, it cannot renounce its action after communicating.

Various techniques can be used to safeguard the devices in the SNoT. Some of them are mentioned below (Shipley, 2013):

- **Digital Signatures:** Currently digital signatures of users are attached to a document or a software for the authentication and authorized execution in a system. This way, a degree of trustworthiness is maintained among the users and the system. If this concept is incorporated in SNoT, that is, if we assign a cryptographically developed digital signature to objects in the SNoT, a foundation for trust can be established among the socially linked devices. During the booting up of a "Social Thing" for the first time, its integrity and genuineness can be validated using this digital signature. But this method cannot protect the device from different run-time complications and malicious intents.

- **Restriction of Access:** The access privileges of devices in a network can be regulated using various methods. In SNoT, the access privileges of a social thing may have to be restricted according to their role in the network. This regulation ensures that the device can only access resources and information that are essential for their operation. The benefit of this restriction is that if a device is compromised, the access control ensures that the attacker has a minimal access to the remaining part of the network. Thus, the effectiveness of any security breach can be diminished by access control.

- **Device Verification:** When a device is connected to SNoT, prior to sending and receiving data, it should validate itself. In the conventional social networks, a user authenticates him/her based on a pair of username and password. Similarly, in SNoT, prior to authorization, the authentication of the machine should be carried out based on a set of credentials (also called trust tokens), which should be stored in a secure storage space. This may assist the automated operation of devices in the Social Network of Things. The secure storage facilities (also called keystores) are of two types based on the execution of cryptographic operations, namely passive keystores and active keystores. Passive keystore stores and retrieves the credentials in encrypted form and the cryptographic operations are carried out by the CPU of the device whereas inactive keystores the cryptographic operations are executed using an application program interface (API), this ensures that the credentials are never disclosed. Keystores can be of hardware type or software type, where the former is employed for devices that require high security and extensive cryptographic requirements and the latter is used for low cost embedded systems with mediocre security requirements.

- **Firewall:** In SNoT, in order to prevent vulnerability exploits and various cyber-attacks, the devices should be installed with a deep packet inspection capability and a firewall in order to regulate the flow of traffic which is destined to reach the machine. The necessity of a firewall or an intrusion prevention system (IPS) arises from the fact that protocols in embedded systems differ from general network protocols. The deep packet inspection capability ensures the identification of malicious payloads hiding in device-specific protocols. The regular Internet traffic is handled by network appliances, so the device does not need to filter higher-level traffic but should handle the device-specific traffic with optimum resources utilized for the same.

- **Patches and Software Updates:** The devices in the SNoT should be receiving necessary patches and software updates after their operation has initiated. The necessary security patches and software updates should be authenticated before they are implemented into the device. The authentication and implementation should not deplete the bandwidth and affect the recurrent connectivity of a social thing. Also, the delivery of patches should never impair the functional safety of the machine in the SNoT.

Several types of trust models have been proposed and some of them have been implemented, for assisting the security measures to be taken. Those include (Hu, 2016):

- **Direct Trust Model:** The credentials of the nodes are pre-distributed among all the participating nodes before the network is established.

- **Web of Trust Model:** The credentials of a peer are accepted by another peer only if the credentials have already been validated by another trusted peer.

- **Hierarchical Trust Model:** This is a complex trust model. In this model, the trust is handled by various trust anchors forming a hierarchical infrastructure. This infrastructure can be Trust Centre Infrastructure (TCI) or Public Key Infrastructure (PKI).
- **Subjective Trust Model:** The node evaluates the trustworthiness of another node on the basis of its own experience and on the judgment of common friendly nodes with potential service providers (Nitti, Girau, Atzori, Iera, & Morabito, 2012).
- **Guarantor and Reputation-Based Trust Model:** This trust model is formed on the basis of Guarantor and Reputation for Social Network of Things. The former requests a device to discover a guarantor at a complied commission rate for receiving service from another device; the latter utilizes reputation of a device for evaluating its trustworthiness (Xiao, Sidhu, & Christianson, 2015).

Usually, when the device is deployed, its security and trust credentials are assigned at the time of manufacturing or at a later stage of the life cycle of that device that is utilized for establishing the trustworthiness of that device. Even though this trustworthiness is usually diminished over the passage of time, it is based on the following expectations (Hu, 2016):

1. The device's hardware and its stages of fabrication and assembling are robust and trustworthy so that the tampering of hardware components should not leak any sensitive information about the operation of the device.
2. The design of the firmware and its further development should be sound, complete and authentic. Most of the loopholes in the software should be documented and fixed before the firmware is installed.
3. The creation, management, and distribution of digital signatures using cryptography should be trustworthy and safeguarded sufficiently.

Even though the firmware designing is carried out securely, an attacker can modify the firmware and insert malicious code into it. This can result in manipulation of credentials used by various system processes in order to carry out an internal cyber-attack. So firmware image validation plays a crucial role in the security of the device in the SNoT. Devices with factory-flashed or static firmware image can manage a higher level of trustworthiness than a device with dynamic firmware image (downloadable firmware image). If there are many variations of the firmware image for the upgradation of individual components of a firmware, the authentication of those firmware images will be the tiresome task (Hu, 2016). This issue can be reduced by having an efficient firmware patching mechanism. A firmware update (patching) mechanism over the network should include an effective and effortless patching process, which incorporates authenticity check and robust integrity, reduces the service disruptions and supports a version rollback if required.

The trust related attacks can be countered by enforcing honesty, community-interest, and cooperativeness among the nodes to prevent invasion of malicious nodes to SNoT. Generally, intrusion detection techniques can be used to identify bad nodes and the attacking node can be expelled from the network upon detection (Chen, Bao, & Guo, 2016). The advancement of data tracing competence, the network forensics capability and the network crime forensics mechanism can also aid in preventing the security and privacy threats of SNoT in the future.

As far as research roadmap is concerned, this chapter has introduced a mechanism based on the current Domain Name System (DNS) architecture, developed especially for the application of Network of Things. The feasibility of DNS architecture has been assessed and a three-level caching strategy for that architecture is also analyzed. The suggested mechanism is particularly developed for the domain of transport logistics.

CONCLUSION

In this chapter, various security threats found in the newly emerged technology of Social Network of things have been discussed. Most of the security threats have been passed on to SNoT from the Internet. SNoT is a revamped form of Network of Things. According to OASIS, the network of things is an infrastructure where the physical world is connected to the Internet by utilizing ubiquitous sensors. In NoT, both physical as well as virtual objects have identities, attributes, and personalities. They use smart interfaces and are entirely integrated into the network of information. The things in NoT participate actively in information, business and social processes and are able to interact with external surroundings (real world) as well as with other devices. SNoT is relatively a novel paradigm. The SNoT may be simply defined as the implementation of the concept of the social network of humans into the architecture of NoT. In SNoT, the intelligent devices become socially active, interacting with neighboring 'Social Things' and negotiate with them to achieve a particular task for the user.

The infrastructure of SNoT, like every other system on the Internet, is susceptible to various security threats. This will make implementation of SNoT challenging if those vulnerabilities are not addressed properly. Most of the vulnerabilities are already present on the Internet as well as the NoT, hence these vulnerabilities are already addressed to some extent. But novel vulnerabilities, which emerge due to the nature of SNoT, have to be detected and addressed as soon as possible. One of the principal factors for these vulnerabilities is the automation of devices in SNoT. Even the security of sensor networks and RFID tags are yet to be addressed adequately. The Even cryptographically secured system can be sometimes susceptible to cyber-attacks.

This chapter has also discussed some of the possible solutions to strengthen the cyber-security of the Social Network of Things. Data confidentiality and integrity, peer authentication, proof of authorization and non-repudiation are fundamental requirements for implementing security measures in SNoT. Most of the devices can be secured using cryptographic systems to some extent. Trustworthiness is a critical determinant for establishing peer authentication and for proof of authorization. For promoting the trustworthiness among objects in SNoT, various trust models have been proposed and implemented. Out of those trust models, few of them have been discussed briefly in this chapter. Since the technologies of Network of Things as well as Social Network of Things are novel phenomena and the progress of the today's innovation is happening at a rapid rate, there is a common anticipation that a novel and radical security solution will be developed which is customized uniquely for these technologies, with the assumption that 25 years of security will be compressed into the compact time frame in which the posterior generation devices will commercially be made available.

REFERENCES

Atzori, L., Iera, A., & Morabito, G. (2010). The internet of things: A survey. *Computer Networks, 54*(15), 2787–2805. doi:10.1016/j.comnet.2010.05.010

Atzori, L., Iera, A., & Morabito, G. (2011). Siot: Giving a social structure to the internet of things. *IEEE Communications Letters, 15*(11), 1193–1195. doi:10.1109/LCOMM.2011.090911.111340

Atzori, L., Iera, A., & Morabito, G. (2014). From" smart objects" to" social objects": The next evolutionary step of the internet of things. *IEEE Communications Magazine, 52*(1), 97–105. doi:10.1109/MCOM.2014.6710070

Atzori, L., Iera, A., Morabito, G., & Nitti, M. (2012). The social internet of things (siot)–when social networks meet the internet of things: Concept, architecture and network characterization. *Computer Networks, 56*(16), 3594–3608. doi:10.1016/j.comnet.2012.07.010

Ayala, L. (2016). Cyber Standards. In *Cybersecurity Lexicon* (pp. 199–200). Apress. doi:10.1007/978-1-4842-2068-9_28

Bhabad, M. A., & Bagade, S. T. (2015). Internet of things: Architecture, security issues and countermeasures. *International Journal of Computers and Applications, 125*(14).

Cekerevac, Z., Dvorak, Z., Prigoda, L., & Cekerevac, P. (2017). Internet of things and the man-in-the-middle attacks–security and economic risks. *Journal MESTE, 5*(2), 15–25.

Chen, R., Bao, F., & Guo, J. (2016). Trust-based service management for social internet of things systems. *IEEE Transactions on Dependable and Secure Computing, 13*(6), 684–696. doi:10.1109/TDSC.2015.2420552

Criscuolo, P. J. (2000). *Distributed denial of service: Trin00, tribe flood network, tribe flood network 2000, and stacheldraht (No. CIAC-2319)*. California Univ. Livermore radiation lab. doi:10.2172/792253

Delic, K. A. (2016). On Resilience of IoT Systems: The Internet of Things (Ubiquity symposium). *Ubiquity, 2016*(February), 1.

Eldefrawy, M. H., Khan, M. K., Alghathbar, K., & Cho, E. (2010). Broadcast Authentication for Wireless Sensor Networks Using Nested Hashing and the Chinese Remainder Theorem. *Sensors (Basel), 10*(9), 8683–8695. doi:10.3390100908683 PMID:22163679

Farash, M. S., Turkanović, M., Kumari, S., & Hölbl, M. (2016). An efficient user authentication and key agreement scheme for heterogeneous wireless sensor network tailored for the Internet of Things environment. *Ad Hoc Networks, 36*, 152–176. doi:10.1016/j.adhoc.2015.05.014

Fjäder, C. O. (2016). National Security in a Hyper-connected World. In Exploring the Security Landscape: Non-Traditional Security Challenges (pp. 31-58). Springer International Publishing. doi:10.1007/978-3-319-27914-5_3

Geetha, S. (2016). Social internet of things. *World Scientific News, 41*, 76.

Gupta, M., Shrivastava, G., Gupta, S., Gupta, R. (2017). Role of Cyber Security in Today's Scenario. *Detecting and Mitigating Robotic Cyber Security Risks*, 177.

Hajdarbegovic, N. (2017). Are we creating an insecure internet of things (iot)? security challenges and concerns. *Toptotal. Accessed Feb, 1.*

Hu, F. (2016). *Security and Privacy in Internet of Things (IoTs): Models, Algorithms, and Implementations*. CRC Press. doi:10.1201/b19516

Huberman, B. A. (2016). Ensuring Trust and Security in the Industrial IoT: The Internet of Things (Ubiquity symposium). *Ubiquity, 2016*(January), 2. doi:10.1145/2822883

IEEE Internet Initiative. (2015). Towards a definition of the Internet of Things (IoT) (Revision-1). Retrieved from http://iot.ieee.org/images/files/pdf/IEEE_IoT_Towards_Definition_Internet_of_Things_Revision1_27MAY15.pdf

Kim, J. E., Maron, A., & Mosse, D. (2015, June). Socialite: A flexible framework for social internet of things. In *Proceedings of the 2015 16th IEEE International Conference on Mobile Data Management (MDM)* (Vol. 1, pp. 94-103). IEEE. 10.1109/MDM.2015.50

Kleinberg, J. (2008). The convergence of social and technological networks. *Communications of the ACM, 51*(11), 66–72. doi:10.1145/1400214.1400232

Lee, D. W. (2016). A Study on Actual Cases & Meanings for Internet of Things. *International Journal of Software Engineering and Its Applications, 10*(1), 287–294. doi:10.14257/ijseia.2016.10.1.28

Makhoul, A., Guyeux, C., Hakem, M., & Bahi, J. M. (2016). Using an epidemiological approach to maximize data survival in the Internet of Things. *ACM Transactions on Internet Technology, 16*(1), 5. doi:10.1145/2812810

Neha, J.A. (2015). Social Networking and Securing the IoT. *International Journal of Science and Research.*

Ning, H., & Wang, Z. (2011). Future internet of things architecture: Like mankind neural system or social organization framework? *IEEE Communications Letters, 15*(4), 461–463. doi:10.1109/LCOMM.2011.022411.110120

Nitti, M., Girau, R., Atzori, L., Iera, A., & Morabito, G. (2012, September). A subjective model for trustworthiness evaluation in the social internet of things. In *Proceedings of the 2012 IEEE 23rd International Symposium on Personal Indoor and Mobile Radio Communications (PIMRC)* (pp. 18-23). IEEE. 10.1109/PIMRC.2012.6362662

Petroni, M. J. (n.d.). The Social Network of Things. *CauseIT.* Retrieved June 05, 2017, from http://www.causeit.org/the-social-network-of-things/

Prasad, K. M., Reddy, A. R. M., & Rao, K. V. (2014). *DoS and DDoS attacks: defense, detection and traceback mechanisms-a survey*. Global Journal of Computer Science and Technology.

Ramirez, E. (2015). *Privacy and the IoT: Navigating policy issues*. US FTC.

Romdhani, I. (2017). Security Concerns in Social IoT. In Securing the Internet of Things (pp. 131–132). Cambridge, MA: Syngress. Retrieved May 08, 2017. doi:10.1016/B978-0-12-804458-2.00008-1

Rose, K., Eldridge, S., & Chapin, L. (2015). The internet of things: An overview. *The Internet Society (ISOC)*.

Sanders, C. (2010). Understanding Man-in-The-Middle Attacks-Part 2 DNS spoofing. *Windows Security. com*.

Sanders, C. (2010, June). Understanding Man-In-The-Middle Attacks-Part 4: SSL Hijacking.

Sanders, C. (2010, March). Understanding Man-in-the-Middle Attacks - ARP Cache Poisoning (Part 1).

Sanders, C. (2010, May). Understanding Man-In-The-Middle Attacks - Part 3: Session Hijacking.

Sethi, P., & Sarangi, S. R. (2017). Internet of Things: Architectures, Protocols, and Applications. *Journal of Electrical and Computer Engineering*.

Shi, T., Wan, J., Cheng, S., Cai, Z., Li, Y., & Li, J. (2015, October). Time-bounded positive influence in social networks. In *Proceedings of the 2015 International Conference on Identification, Information, and Knowledge in the Internet of Things (IIKI)* (pp. 134-139). IEEE. 10.1109/IIKI.2015.37

Shipley, A. J. (2013). Security in the internet of things, lessons from the past for the connected future. *Security Solutions, Wind River, White Paper*.

Shirey, R. (2003). RFC 2828–Internet security glossary. Retrieved from http://www.faqs.org/rfcs/rfc2828.html

Shrivastava, G., Sharma, K., & Rai, S. (2010, December). The Detection & Defense of DoS & DDoS Attack: A Technical Overview. In *Proceeding of ICC* (Vol. 27, p. 28).

Singer, A. P. (2004). U.S. Patent No. 6,724,894. Washington, DC: U.S. Patent and Trademark Office.

Sinha, A., & Kumar, P. (2016). A Novel Framework for Social Internet of Things. *Indian Journal of Science and Technology*, *9*(36). doi:10.17485/ijst/2016/v9i36/102162

Sinha, A., Kumar, P., Rana, N. P., Islam, R., & Dwivedi, Y. K. (2017). Impact of internet of things (IoT) in disaster management: A task-technology fit perspective. *Annals of Operations Research*.

Vacca, J. R. (2012). *Computer and information security handbook*. Newnes.

Winter, J. (2015). Algorithmic discrimination: Big data analytics and the future of the internet. In *The future internet* (pp. 125–140). Springer International Publishing. doi:10.1007/978-3-319-22994-2_8

Xiao, H., Sidhu, N., & Christianson, B. (2015, August). Guarantor and reputation based trust model for social internet of things. In *Proceedings of the Wireless Communications and Mobile Computing Conference (IWCMC), 2015 International* (pp. 600-605). IEEE. 10.1109/IWCMC.2015.7289151

Yachir, A., Amirat, Y., Chibani, A., & Badache, N. (2016). Event-aware framework for dynamic services discovery and selection in the context of ambient intelligence and Internet of Things. *IEEE Transactions on Automation Science and Engineering, 13*(1), 85–102. doi:10.1109/TASE.2015.2499792

Zhu, B., Joseph, A., & Sastry, S. (2011, October). A taxonomy of cyber attacks on SCADA systems. In *Proceedings of the 2011 international conference on Internet of things (iThings/CPSCom) and 4th international conference on cyber, physical and social computing* (pp. 380-388). IEEE. 10.1109/iThings/CPSCom.2011.34

Chapter 6
Artificial Intelligence Based Intrusion Detection System to Detect Flooding Attack in VANETs

Mannat Jot Singh Aneja
Thapar University, India

Tarunpreet Bhatia
Thapar University, India

Gaurav Sharma
Université libre de Bruxelles, Belgium

Gulshan Shrivastava
National Institute of Technology Patna, India

ABSTRACT

This chapter describes how Vehicular Ad hoc Networks (VANETs) are classes of ad hoc networks that provides communication among various vehicles and roadside units. VANETs being decentralized are susceptible to many security attacks. A flooding attack is one of the major security threats to the VANET environment. This chapter proposes a hybrid Intrusion Detection System which improves accuracy and other performance metrics using Artificial Neural Networks as a classification engine and a genetic algorithm as an optimization engine for feature subset selection. These performance metrics have been calculated in two scenarios, namely misuse and anomaly. Various performance metrics are calculated and compared with other researchers' work. The results obtained indicate a high accuracy and precision and negligible false alarm rate. These performance metrics are used to evaluate the intrusion system and compare with other existing algorithms. The classifier works well for multiple malicious nodes. Apart from machine learning techniques, the effect of the network parameters like throughput and packet delivery ratio is observed.

DOI: 10.4018/978-1-5225-4100-4.ch006

INTRODUCTION

Vehicular ad hoc networks (VANETs) are the special category of Mobile Adhoc Networks (MANETs). In MANETs the node can move randomly whereas in VANETs the node does not follow the random movement. The nodes simulate like vehicle and move along the direction of roads. Due to increase in population, there has been the exponential increase in the number of vehicles. This increase in vehicles tends to increase the chance of road accidents. According to the survey, there have been 12 lakhs life are lost daily worldwide (Raw et al., 2013). We need to have a mechanism by virtue of which the vehicles can be made smart enough so that they are able to handle the road safety on their own. This concept was the laid under VANETs to provide secure and reliable driving environment. VANETs allow mainly two types of interactions-V2V (vehicle to vehicle) and V2I (vehicle to infrastructure) (Al-Sultan et al., 2014). Apart from these basic interactions, there is yet another interaction that takes care of crucial information like fatigue detection of the driver. This type of interaction is known as intra-vehicular interaction. VANETs have complied with IEEE 802.11p dedicated short range communication (DSRC). The vehicles have the On-Board Units (OBU) which consists of sensors. The communication has to be sent in form of cooperative awareness message (CAM) and has to pass through Road Side Units (RSU) (Alheeti et al., 2015). In VANETs, the OBU is responsible for interacting with outside network which includes other vehicles and roadside unit infrastructure.

VANETs have the huge number of applications. These are safety applications which let other vehicle know about the status of road and can protect some mishap. There is also the user based application which lets the user be entertained on the go where the driver can download some media file or access the weather conditions etc. (Kabir, 2013). VANETs are highly mobile and lack a fixed infrastructure. There is no guarantee of the end to end connection. The auto-configuration adds to its demerits. With the huge number of applications some involving life-saving applications; there are few challenges associated with VANETs such as high mobility, scalability and fault tolerance. Among these challenges, the most crucial is the security. There are two types of solutions to tackle these attacks- cryptography-based solutions and Intrusion Detection Systems (IDS). In this chapter, we have used IDS based solutions as cryptographic solutions do not prove to be robust while determining the new type of attacks and are also resource intensive. There are various types of attacks that can arise due to vulnerabilities in VANETs. We have focused on RREQ Flooding attack as it forms basis of various other attacks like distributed denial of service (DDoS) (Shrivastava et al., 2010) in which an intruder node tries to send multiple numbers of route request messages to a node which does not exist thereby consuming the channel that was supposed to be dedicated to a legitimate node for service. Security is the indispensable component in any industry or in any field. We need security as it gives the sense of surety of wellness. The vehicular networks also need to be secured. The ill effects could also lead to loss of life. There has been a lot of research in the field of security but still, there are lots of demerits, so there is a need to have the research go on in the field of network security especially vehicular networks as driverless cars are trending to become the hot topic in near future.

The remainder of the paper is organized as follows. Section 2 discusses the work done in the related field by various researchers. Section 3 gives an outline of Intrusion Detection System. Section 4 gives an overview of Artificial Intelligence techniques. Section 5 explains the proposed work. The results and conclusion part is covered in Section 6 and 7 respectively.

RELATED WORK

The solutions to various security attacks are classified into cryptographic and IDS. Zhou et al. (2007) proposed Public Key Infrastructure (Sharma & Shrivastava, G., 2011) wherein each node has public-private keys. While sending the information the sender signs the message with its private key and add Certificate Authority (CA) certificate. The receiver verifies the signature. Another alternative proposed by Hao et al. (2011) was group signature but this is complex in nature as every time a vehicle enters the group its public key and vehicle session key has to be changed and transmitted to the group. Another solution is to provide authentication is where the vehicles will sign the message with its private key and add the certificate along with it. This solution was proposed by Daeinabi et al. (2016). Grover et al. (2010) proposed a solution to combat Sybil attack by the use of session keys and the digital signature with sequence numbers.

Tajbakhsh et al. (2009) proposed Fuzzy Association Rules IDS (FARIDS) and Association Based Classification (ABC). The detection model comprises of learning and the detection phase. In the learning phase features were transformed into items based on fuzzification, the rules were induced and formed after selecting appropriate items and later filtered. The detection phase used the classifier to match and label the rule for identifying an attack. The model is used for both known and unknown attacks.

Hoque et al. (2012) proposed an intrusion detection system using the genetic algorithm to detect different network intrusions. The famous KDD Cup99 dataset was used. The paper presented two phases-the first phase gave rise to new chromosomes by proving the network data. The second phase outputs the type of data whether attack or normal by taking the previous phase as input. The detection rate gave remarkable results but can be improved with more hybrid techniques used in detection phase.

Jongsuebsuk et al. (2013) proposed Fuzzy Genetic IDS to detect known and unknown attacks by conducting an experiment for each. Later in case of unknown attack, the Fuzzy Genetic is compared to Decision Tree as well. The arguments of fuzzy rules are passed to GA in this model.

Panja et al. (2014) proposed a hybrid intrusion detection system that used Adaptive Neuro-Fuzzy Inference System (ANFIS) in the first place and later uses Genetic Algorithm (GA) and application-level filtering. The ANFIS is the combination of fuzzy logic and neural networks. This module consists of 4 stages namely data collection, processing, classify and response. The ANFIS has 5 input layers for classifying the attacks as normal, probe, DOS, R2l, and U2R. After this, it is passed to fuzzy inference module where fuzzification and defuzzification take place. The GA is applied to improve the efficiency of detection. The application level filtering is used for making the detection more accurate by filtering the result from GA

Benaicha et al. (2014) proposed IDS using GA. The features extracted from five different attack types and rules are formed for each of them. The paper builds 80 rules for each attack type which are then fed to GA model. After these 400 rules, the evolution process takes place and the fitness function is calculated and rule set are formed.

Alheeti et al. (2015) proposed a multi-stage intrusion detection system. The model is composed of 3 stages. At the first level, the data is aggregated and processed. The second stage consists of the training dataset. The data after processing from the previous stage is passed to Artificial Neural Network for the training of data. The last stage is detection engine where the data is classified as normal or abnormal. The paper is designed for detection of DOS attack.

Sen et al. (2014) proposed back propagation Neural Network (BPNN). The BPNN is composed of multiple hidden layers. This chapter performs 2 experiments one with 70-30 split and another with 80-20 split of the dataset and uses a different number of nodes in each hidden layer. The training is done on 1000 epochs and the number of hidden layers is fixed to 4. The number of features selected is 40 and then all of them are assigned a numeric value for normalization to take place and the confusion matrix is formed.

Saied et al. (2016) proposed an intrusion detection system based on ANN to combat known and unknown DDOS attack (Gupta et al., 2010). It used SNORT IDS to monitor the network. The IP identifier identifies the IP address and is then passed to ANN engine which compares it with an existing pattern to detect the attack. After the detection phase, it is passed to defense phase whose role is to stop the attack and allow only legal packets to pass through. It also took the output from other snort ids as well to determine if it has an outdated algorithm in which case retraining is required. The last phase is knowledge share where each detector sends the message to other IDS. These messages were encrypted. The dataset uses 80% training and 20% testing set.

Barati et al. (2014) proposed a network-based anomaly IDS to detect DDOS attack using GA and MLP of ANN. The ANN is composed of 3 layers. The data received from GA is passed to internal layer. The middle layer processes the data and the external layer gives the output.

Sandhya G et al. (2014) presented a model by combining k means clustering and genetic algorithm to detect unknown attacks without the presence of any actual signatures. The population in current iteration depends on the fitness function for survival in next iteration. The crossover phase was determined by k means operations which include calculation of center and reassignment of each data to closest cluster

Shanmugavadivu et al. (2011) proposed fuzzy logic based intrusion detection system. It used KDD Cup 99 dataset and selected 34 continuous attributes. These attributes were mined to form the most critical attribute that affects the whole attack. After this, fuzzy rules were created and passed to the inference engine to test on testing data. It provided good accuracy for all types of attack-DOS, U2R (user to root), probe and R2l (remote to local).

Selim et al. (2011) proposed IDS using ANN and Decision trees. The decision tree is if-else statements used as an effective classifier. The system consists of 3 layers. The first layer classifies the data. The second layer is responsible for determining the type of attack. The last layer consists of modules for each type of attack.

OVERVIEW OF INTRUSION DETECTION SYSTEM

As we saw, VANETs are vulnerable to many security attacks, so there need to be some measures to combat these attacks. We saw some of the solutions like group keys, encryption policies etc. These solutions do not prove to be successful when a new attack is to be examined. These solutions can only be used as the entry level of protection. After these solutions, there needs to be another layer. This layer is of Intrusion Detection System (IDS). IDS is hardware or software that tries to detect any abnormal behavior in the network. IDS functions in 3 phases. First one is event monitoring which includes aggregation of data for any abnormal behavior and the second one is analysis process which includes various techniques like statistics, pattern matching, machine learning etc. The last phase is response generation which alarms about the abnormal behavior and reports to admin. We classify IDS into following categories:

1. **Anomaly-Based IDS:** This system monitors the network and on the basis of behavior, it either passes the nodes (or network) if found normal else raises an alarm if it finds something abnormal. The normal behavior of the network is studied by these IDS known as training data sets. The study of the normal behavior of the network is known as profiling. There are various ways to train the data set. Some of them are semi-supervised learning and unsupervised learning. The merit of this IDS is the detection of new attacks for which signature is not present.
2. **Signature-Based IDS:** This IDS monitors the network and look for abnormal patterns. These abnormal patterns are also known as the signature. So, these IDS compare the signature of the acquired event against known signatures to detect any attack. These types of IDS are effective to detect known attacks and are suitable for outsider attacks. The problem with these IDS is complexity to update signatures and its inefficiency to detect new attacks.

In this chapter, we have used Artificial Intelligence approach to implement IDS. We have used Artificial Neural Networks (ANN) to detect the RREQ Flooding attack and later on uses the Genetic algorithm (GA) to reduce the number of features from the dataset.

ARTIFICIAL INTELLIGENCE TECHNIQUE

Artificial Neural Networks

Artificial Neural Network (ANN) is a branch of machine learning techniques which are influenced by the central nervous system of humans specifically the brain. ANN is the system of connected neurons wherein each neuron is connected to all other neurons. The neurons are the generally the most important processing unit. The brain processes the information by interchanging the pulses among neurons. The neurons are connected to each and every input with the weight associated with particular input and results in the outcome. The same idea is applied by ANN in computer science for classification or prediction based issues. ANN is the flexible system by virtue of which the organization of network changes due to change in the inputs, weights associated with inputs or any other parameter. In this neural network, there is another layer known as the hidden layer. The Multi-Layer Perceptron consists of the input layer, one or more hidden layer and finally the output layer. The number of the hidden layers depends on the application. Also, the number of neuron in each hidden layer is application specific. The hidden layer is also referred to as the processing layer. The input layer consists of as many neurons as the number of features in the dataset. The processing takes place at hidden layer and finally the output is formed at the output layer. Each input is associated with a weight. The ANN works in two phases- the training phase and the testing phase. During the training phase, the weights are calculated and performance metrics are noted. However, there needs to be changed in weights and biases values; if the performance metric thresholds are not obtained. Due to change in weights and biases values, we need to move back at the first layer and again calculate the values using the training function (Balkanli et al., 2014). Since we move from the last layer to the first layer back, it is known as backpropagation. This back propagation works by calculating gradient at each layer known as the local gradient.

Genetic Algorithm

The genetic algorithm is an artificial intelligence heuristic approach which imitates the methodology of natural evolution. Evolution is the process by virtue of which the organisms improve successively over generations through the GA operators described later in this section. The Genetic Algorithm is used for optimization problems. It follows the principle of survival of the best which means the best feature individual will be selected over successive generations and hence improving and making the system more efficient. The Genetic algorithm starts with an initial population. This initial population is randomly chosen from the list of the population. After initializing the initial population, the fitness function is evaluated. Based on the result of evaluating the genetic algorithm operators like selection, crossover and mutation are applied. The whole procedure is repeated until stopping criteria is matched. In this chapter, GA has been for feature subset selection

-

PROPOSED APPROACH

The proposed system is used to detect RREQ Flooding attack using ANN. It is optimized in terms of feature subset selection using GA. The network simulator ns-2.35 is used for launching the RREQ Flooding attack. This algorithm works well for multiple numbers of malicious nodes and gives remarkable results on evaluating the performance metrics like accuracy and false positive rate. The simulation of VANET environment is done through SUMO. The .tcl file which is generated by MOVE simulator is used as input to NS-2.35. The implementation generally involves three stages. The first stage is the creation of dataset by launching the attack. The second step is Data Preprocessing and the last step is the classification and optimization engine. Figure 1 shows the proposed system architecture.

Creation of Dataset

For the creation of data set, a VANET environment was set up by integration of SUMO, MOVE and NS-2.35. The output of MOVE file is a tcl script used by NS-2.35. The output of trace files was collected as output for two different scenarios- normal AODV and AODV under RREQ Flooding attack. The purpose of this attack is to consume the network bandwidth and to exhaust the network resources all the time.

Data Preprocessing

The real data consists of erroneous data and might also be not very useful as it is raw data. There is a need to convert this raw data into meaningful information. To achieve this objective, data preprocessing is required. The data preprocessing phase as described above in our proposed architecture involves three main steps- extraction of features from the dataset, data cleaning, and data normalization.

- **Extracting Features From Dataset:** The normal.tr and malicious.tr files obtained while launching the attack collectively forms a data set. These trace files contain many fields and are separated by space delimiter. The trace file is divided into three traces namely Basic Trace, IP trace and AODV trace.

- **Data Cleaning:** It refers to correcting or removing of inconsistent records from the data set. In this phase, we try to make the data set robust and unbiased. The redundant data or the data that assumes value zero all the time are removed. Handling of missing values is also done in this phase

- **Data Normalization:** This phase is further subdivided into two stages- Converting the values into numeric and the second stage is normalizing the data set so that the whole data set lies in one particular range.

- **Converting Non-Numeric Into Numeric Fields:** In this phase, the non-integer values like TCP, AODV, MAC, RTR, AGT, etc., are converted into the integer. The columns which consist of hexadecimal values are also converted into integers. This phase is important to be performed for the dataset to be normalized.

- **Converting Data Into Standardized Form**: The dataset in the previous phase contains only integer values. But those integer values have a wide range. It would be the selfish act to let that wide range of inputs. As when we apply the detection techniques the comparison between the fields would make no sense if they have huge deviation. The data with huge values will affect the data with lesser values; hence converting the data into standard form becomes indispensable.

Algorithm 1: Creation of Data Set

```
Input: MOVE.jar
Output: Two trace files normal.tr and attack.tr
1.       no_of_vehicles ←20
2.       simulation_time ← 200
3.       for each node n
4.               set node's cordinates
5.       end for
6.       for each edge e
7.               lanes ← 20
8.               speed ←30
9.               priority ←70
10.              initialize edge id
11.      end for
12.      for each flow f
13.              initialize flow id
14.              no_of _vehicle_per_flow ←no_of_vehicles/no_of_ flow
15.      end for
16.       CreateVehicle()
17.      ConfigVehicle()
18.      call Visualize()
19.      add_Connection()
20.      normal.tr ←NS2()
21.      RREQ_Flooding()
22.      Attack.tr ‹NS2()
```

Figure 1. Proposed System Architecture

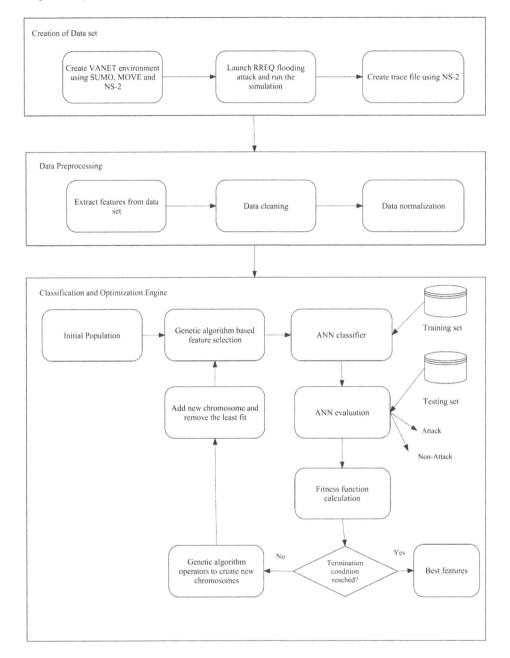

Classification Engine

The ANN is used as classification engine which classifies the features into two main categories- the normal class and the attack class based on knowledge learned in training phase. The inputs are passed to the hidden layer where the processing takes place with the help of transfer function and later the output of these are passed to next hidden layer (in case of the multiple number of hidden layers) or to the output layer (in case of single hidden layer) which finally gives the output. Since the procedure is from the first layer to the last layer it is feedforward network. The backpropagation technique is used to update the weights which are associated with each input in order to improve the training functions. This update of weights is done from the outer layer to the inner layer, hence the name backpropagation. The Levenberg-Maquardt algorithm is used as backpropagation and is given as:

$$x_{k+1} = x_k - [J^TJ + \mu I]^{-1}J^Te$$

where x_k is current value, x_{k+1} is the updated value, I is the identity, e is the network error, J is Jacobian matrix and μ is scalar. The whole process of training and testing which includes calculating the output and update of weights is known as the feed forward back propagation network. Figure 2 shows the workflow of classification engine.

Optimization Engine

The GA is used as optimization engine to reduce the number of features. The initial population is randomly chosen, and feature subset selection is applied to it. It is passed to the ANN classifier. The classification accuracy is considered as the fitness function. The fitness value of each feature set chromosome is calculated. The features which do not contribute to enhancing the accuracy of the system are dropped.

Figure 2. Workflow of the classification engine

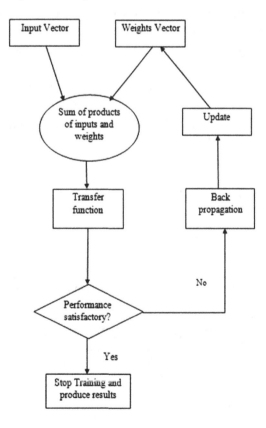

In this chapter, we have used wrapper method for subset selection. The best set of features are retained and the least one is removed from the list hence modifies the feature set.

Algorithm 2: Feature Subselection

```
Input: Initial population
Output: Feature subselection
1.          do{ For each chromosome c
2.                  Calculate fitness function
3.                  Create vector using mutation
4.                  Create new individual using crossover
5.          end for
6.          if fitness value is greater than the previous individual
7.                  add the individual to the list
8.          else
9.                  remove the least fit individual
10.         }while(stopping criteria is not met)
```

RESULTS AND DISCUSSION

The performance metrics have been evaluated in two scenarios- misuse detection and anomaly detection. In both the scenarios 10-fold cross-validation is used. The whole dataset is split into ten equal subsets with 10% records set for testing in each dataset. The average of all these results has been taken into consideration to avoid any biased results. The genetic algorithm has been implemented for feature sub-selection. The final number of features left in the system is 18. The performance metrics are calculated using the four parameters- True Positive (TP), True Negative (TN), False Positive (FP) and False Negative (FN). The accuracy of the system is evaluated. Table 1, Table 2 and Table 3 shows the parameter settings for simulation environment, ANN, and GA respectively.

Table 1. Simulation environment parameters

Parameter	Value
No of nodes	20
No of malicious nodes	2
Channel Type	Wireless
Routing Protocol	AODV
MAC_TYPE	802.11
Packet Size	1000
Interface Queue Type	Queue/Drop Tail/Priority
Simulation Time	200

Table 2. ANN parameters

Parameter	Value
Network Type	Feedforward backdrop
Training Function	Levenberg-Maquardt
Performance Function	Mean Square Error
No of layers	2
No of neurons per layer	10
Transfer Function	Transig
Maximum Epochs	1000
Validation check	6
Data Division	Random

Table 3. GA parameters

Parameter	Value
Genetic Operations	Scattered crossover, single point mutation
Selection Method	Stochastic
Crossover Rate	0.8
Mutation Rate	0.02
Population Size	200
Max Generations	100
Stall Generations	50

The various performance metrics have been evaluated and the outcome is shown in Table 4 and Table 5. Table 4 shows the results for misuse detection and Table 5 shows the result for anomaly detection. A comparative analysis of our approach with existing algorithms has been shown in Table 6. Our approach shows remarkable results especially in terms of accuracy and false positive. A graphical comparison of the accuracy of our approach with other existing approaches has been shown in Figure 3.

CONCLUSION

As security is the indispensable part of wireless networks especially vehicular networks, there was a need to tackle the threats which could arise in vehicular networks. One of the most serious security threats

Table 4. Results (misuse)

Precision	1
Specificity	1
Sensitivity	0.99
Accuracy	0.99
F_measure	1
False Positive Rate	0

Table 5. Results (anomaly detection)

Precision	0.97
Specificity	0.97
Sensitivity	0.99
Accuracy	0.95
F_measure	0.98
False Positive Rate	0.03

Table 6. Comparison of different performance metrics of proposed approach with other existing approaches

Algorithms	Precision	Specificity	Sensitivity	Accuracy	F_measure	False Positive
Proposed approach	1	1	0.99	0.99	1	0.01
ANN and Decision Tree-based IDS (Selim et al., 2011)	NA	NA	NA	0.95	NA	0.10
SNORT	0.96	0.97	0.9	0.93	NA	NA
GA and MLP based IDS (Barati et al, 2014)	1	NA	0.99	NA	0.99	0.03
ANN-based driverless car (Alheeti et al, 2015)	NA	.87	.98	NA	NA	0.12
ANN-based IDS (Saied et al., 2016)	1	1	0.96	0.98	NA	NA

Figure 3. Accuracy graph of different protocols

is RREQ flooding in which the legitimate user is denied access to the service due to unavailability of resources. In our chapter, we have launched the flooding attack in ns-2 and evaluated the packet delivery and throughput of the network. There was sharp fall in packet delivery and throughput. We proposed our algorithm based on ANN to detect the attack and further applied GA for feature sub-selection to obtain better results under two different scenarios misuse and anomaly. Our proposed algorithm can detect multiple malicious nodes with higher accuracy as compared with existing approaches. The accuracy of our system came to 99%.

Moreover, the number of features was reduced to 18. There is no need for any hardware, hence simple and cost-effective. This chapter showed remarkable results but the future scope lies in detecting the attacks with encrypted malicious entries. Also, the data set used is specifically for flooding attack. We would like to extend our proposed algorithm to make it more generic by adding more records of other attacks as well. There could be the use of other techniques as well to reduce the number of features to even lesser than 18.

Research is never ending process. This chapter showed remarkable results but the future scope lies in detecting the attacks with encrypted malicious entries. Also, the data set used is specifically for flooding attack. We would like to extend our proposed algorithm to make it more generic by adding more records of other attacks as well. There could be use of other techniques as well to reduce the number of features to even lesser than 18

REFERENCES

Al-Sultan, S., Al-Doori, M. M., Al-Bayatti, A. H., & Zedan, H. (2014). A comprehensive survey on vehicular Ad Hoc network. *Journal of Network and Computer Applications*, *37*, 380–392. doi:10.1016/j. jnca.2013.02.036

Alheeti, K. M. A., Gruebler, A., & McDonald-Maier, K. D. (2015). An intrusion detection system against malicious attacks on the communication network of driverless cars. In *Proceedings of the 2015 12th Annual IEEE Consumer Communications and Networking Conference (CCNC)*, Las Vegas, NV (pp. 916-921). IEEE. 10.1109/CCNC.2015.7158098

Balkanli, E., Alves, J., & Zincir-Heywood, A. N. (2014). Supervised learning to detect DDoS attacks. In *Proceedings of the 2014 IEEE Symposium on Computational Intelligence in Cyber Security (CICS)*, Orlando, FL. IEEE. 10.1109/CICYBS.2014.7013367

Barati, M., Abdullah, A., Udzir, N. I., Mahmod, R., & Mustapha, N. (2014). Distributed Denial of Service detection using hybrid machine learning technique. In *Proceedings of the 2014 International Symposium on Biometrics and Security Technologies (ISBAST)* (pp. 268-273). IEEE. 10.1109/ISBAST.2014.7013133

Benaicha, S. E., Saoudi, L., Guermeche, S. E. B., & Lounis, O. (2014). Intrusion detection system using genetic algorithm. In *Proceedings of the Science and Information Conference (SAI)*, London, UK (pp. 564-568). IEEE.

Daeinabi, A., & Rahbar, A. G. (2013). Detection of malicious vehicles (DMV) through monitoring in Vehicular Ad-Hoc Networks. *Multimedia Tools and Applications, 66*(2), 325–338. doi:10.100711042-011-0789-y

Grover, J., Gaur, M. S., & Laxmi, V. (2010). A novel defense mechanism against sybil attacks in VANET. In *Proceedings of the 3rd international conference on Security of information and networks* (pp. 249-255). ACM. 10.1145/1854099.1854150

Gupta, B. B., Joshi, R. C., Misra, M., Meena, D. L., Shrivastava, G., & Sharma, K. (2010). Detecting a Wide Range of Flooding DDoS Attacks using Linear Prediction Model. In Proceedings of the 2nd IEEE International Conference on Information and Multimedia Technology (ICIMT 2010) (Vol. 2, pp. 535-539).

Hao, Y., Cheng, Y., Zhou, C., & Song, W. (2011). A distributed key management framework with cooperative message authentication in VANETs. *IEEE Journal on Selected Areas in Communications, 29*(3), 616–629. doi:10.1109/JSAC.2011.110311

Hoque, M. S., Mukit, M., Bikas, M., & Naser, A. (2012). An implementation of intrusion detection system using genetic algorithm. *International Journal of Network Security & Its Applications, 4*(2), 109–120. doi:10.5121/ijnsa.2012.4208

Jongsuebsuk, P., Wattanapongsakorn, N., & Charnsripinyo, C. (2013, January). Network intrusion detection with Fuzzy Genetic Algorithm for unknown attacks. In *Proceedings of the 2013 International Conference on Information Networking (ICOIN)*. IEEE. 10.1109/ICOIN.2013.6496342

Kabir, M. H. (2013). Research issues on vehicular ad hoc network. *International Journal of Engineering Trends and Technology, 6*(4), 174–179.

Panja, B., Ogunyanwo, O., & Meharia, P. (2014, June). Training of intelligent intrusion detection system using neuro fuzzy. In *Proceedings of the 2014 15th IEEE/ACIS International Conference on Software Engineering, Artificial Intelligence, Networking and Parallel/Distributed Computing (SNPD)*. IEEE. 10.1109/SNPD.2014.6888688

Raw, R. S., Kumar, M., & Singh, N. (2013). Security challenges, issues and their solutions for VANET. *International Journal of Network Security & Its Applications, 5*(5), 95–105. doi:10.5121/ijnsa.2013.5508

Saied, A., Overill, R. E., & Radzik, T. (2016). Detection of known and unknown DDoS attacks using Artificial Neural Networks. *Neurocomputing, 172*, 385–393. doi:10.1016/j.neucom.2015.04.101

Sandhya, G., & Julian, A. (2014, May). Intrusion detection in wireless sensor network using genetic K-means algorithm. In *Proceedings of the 2014 International Conference on Advanced Communication Control and Computing Technologies (ICACCCT)* (pp. 1791-1794). IEEE.

Selim, S., Hashem, M., & Nazmy, T. M. (2011). Hybrid multi-level intrusion detection system. *International Journal of Computer Science and Information Security*, 9(5), 23–29.

Sen, N., Sen, R., & Chattopadhyay, M. (2014). An effective back propagation neural network architecture for the development of an efficient anomaly based intrusion detection system. In *Proceedings of the 2014 International Conference on Computational Intelligence and Communication Networks (CICN)*, Bhopal, India (pp. 1052-1056). IEEE. 10.1109/CICN.2014.221

Shanmugavadivu, R., & Nagarajan, N. (2011). Network intrusion detection system using fuzzy logic. *Indian Journal of Computer Science and Engineering*, 2(1), 101–111.

Sharma, K., & Shrivastava, G. (2011). Public Key Infrastructure and Trust of Web Based Knowledge Discovery. International Journal of Engineering. *Sciences and Management*, 4(1), 56–60.

Shrivastava, G., Sharma, K., & Rai, S. (2010, December). The Detection & Defense of DoS & DDoS Attack: A Technical Overview. In *Proceeding of ICC* (Vol. 27, p. 28).

Tajbakhsh, A., Rahmati, M., & Mirzaei, A. (2009). Intrusion detection using fuzzy association rules. *Applied Soft Computing*, 9(2), 462–469. doi:10.1016/j.asoc.2008.06.001

Zhou, T., Choudhury, R. R., Ning, P., & Chakrabarty, K. (2007). Privacy-preserving detection of sybil attacks in vehicular ad hoc networks. In *Proceedings of the Fourth Annual International Conference on Mobile and Ubiquitous Systems: Networking & Services MobiQuitous '07*, Philadelphia, PA. IEEE. 10.1109/MOBIQ.2007.4451013

Chapter 7
Detection of Botnet Based Attacks on Network:
Using Machine Learning Techniques

Prachi
The NorthCap University, India

ABSTRACT

This chapter describes how with Botnets becoming more and more the leading cyber threat on the web nowadays, they also serve as the key platform for carrying out large-scale distributed attacks. Although a substantial amount of research in the fields of botnet detection and analysis, bot-masters inculcate new techniques to make them more sophisticated, destructive and hard to detect with the help of code encryption and obfuscation. This chapter proposes a new model to detect botnet behavior on the basis of traffic analysis and machine learning techniques. Traffic analysis behavior does not depend upon payload analysis so the proposed technique is immune to code encryption and other evasion techniques generally used by bot-masters. This chapter analyzes the benchmark datasets as well as real-time generated traffic to determine the feasibility of botnet detection using traffic flow analysis. Experimental results clearly indicate that a proposed model is able to classify the network traffic as a botnet or as normal traffic with a high accuracy and low false-positive rates.

INTRODUCTION

Scalability in computer networks, its architecture and a variety of software applications allows people to carry out their most mundane of tasks to most complex activities from remote locations in time efficient manner with great ease. There is the tremendous change in people's daily lives and business model of organizations across the world. More and more people are getting connected to the Internet in order to complete their daily chores and get benefits of the new business model. Although Internet brings lots of new ways to reach the end users it also brings the risk associated with it. Unfortunately, criminals have gained these revolutionary technological advances to commit offenses against an individual or groups of individuals in order to physically or mentally harasses victim for personal gains using modern tele-

DOI: 10.4018/978-1-5225-4100-4.ch007

communication systems in form of Cyber Crimes (Shrivastava, 2016). Acceleration in growing usage of Internet and technological advances leads to integration of information from multiple sources that reflects scaling of volume and type of information (Matallah et al., 2017). Constant advancement in Next Generation Internet enhances the requirement of secure and efficient communication against the new sort of challenges posed by the emerging applications (Kimbahune et al., 2017). In recent times, botnets are used to launch a number of distributed cyber-attacks such as ransomware, Distributed Denial of Service (DDoS) (Shrivastava et al., 2010), distributed computational tasks, spam emails, etc. The high infection rate, a large number of unlawful activities and strong comebacks make botnets one of the most destructive attacks (Cox, 2013; David, 2012). Destruction impact of the botnet is becoming more and more critical nowadays (Guntuku, 2014).

In general, botnets can be characterized based on the characteristics of Command & Control server that is used for the communication between the bot-master and bot-client. Command & Control server facilitates a bot-master to issue some queries and waits for their responses in a time efficient manner while evading the security measures deployed by the victim to detect a botnet. Although, the different types of command and control are presented in literature two of them are most significant: centralized and distributed. In case of the distributed botnet, individual bots are hard to detect and hence increase the resiliency of botnet. However, both of them have their own benefits and drawbacks. To address their drawbacks, peer-to-peer botnets came into existence. Till date, these are most robust and hard to detect by most of the existing security mechanisms.

Although a significant number of security solutions have been developed in recent past in terms of firewall and cryptographic solutions they have their limitations in terms of security solutions. Defense solutions that identify network intrusions are another way of identifying the recent type of attacks (Shrivastava et al., 2016). The research community is actively working towards detection of botnets and a number of detection techniques have been proposed in the literature. Botnet mitigation techniques can be classified into 2 categories: active botnet detection and passive botnet detection.

Active botnet detection involves all sorts of analysis techniques that inform Command &Control server or bot-master either directly or indirectly about botnet analysis. Although, active botnet detection techniques appear promising they suffer from the drawback of early detection. Once identified, they can easily circumvent any actions taken against the botnets.

During passive analysis of network traffic, the analysis is performed without interrupting the activity of botnet. In such type of scenario, network activities are traced (Shrivastava, 2017). Most common technique in a passive analysis is the inspection of network packets. Parameters of network packets are analyzed against a large database of malicious behavior for identification of botnets. Packet inspection techniques can be easily incorporated into existing Intrusion Detection Systems (IDS). Intrusion Detection System is considered as most effective technology against the network attacks by identifying and analyzing the traffic (Denning, 1987). Most of the Intrusion Detection System designed for botnet detection is rule-based. Performance of such Intrusion Detection System depends on the rule set defined by the experts (Zhang et al., 2005; Roesch, 1999). In this type of Intrusion Detection System, signatures of incoming network traffic are compared against signatures of previously identified botnets. Such detection mechanism may work well for existing botnet but fail against rapidly changing network traffic. Such dependencies make rule-based Intrusion Detection System inefficient, time-consuming and tedious process against botnets.

Behavior or anomaly based Intrusion Detection System (Huang et al., 2016) cannot perform the complete inspection of packets when network flow is high. Techniques such as packet filtering and packet sampling increase the possibility of missing malicious packets. Moreover, behavior-based IDS increase a large number of false alarms.

In order to counter these issues, analysis of flow records can be considered as one useful technique. In case of flow-based analysis, the headers of several packets are aggregated in a flow and then flows are analyzed (Strayer et al., 2008; Zhao et al., 2012). Consequently, flow-based analysis uses only packet headers, behavior-based packet analysis use payload and some of them use a combination of both (Zeidanloo et al., 2010; Wurzinger et al., 2009). To evade behavior-based packet analysis techniques, attackers started employing data encryption techniques on the data embedded in the messages.

Haddadi et al., 2016 used traffic analysis techniques for detection of the botnet. Traffic traces of normal and malicious traffic for evaluation of botnets were generated by setting HyperText Transfer Protocol and Domain Name System communication with publically available domains of authentic web server and botnet Command & Control server. Features were extracted from the packet header and machine learning algorithms (Naïve Bayes and C4.5) were employed for detection of botnets. The proposed approach is able to achieve the Detection rate of 97% and False Positive Rate of 3%.

Authors investigated four different botnet detection systems: packet based detection system, flow-based detection system, BotHunter (The unique network defense solution that quickly isolates the infected machines and helps you to determine who actually owns your system) (Gu et al., 2007) and Snort (IDS) (Roesch, 1999). After analyzing the botnet traffic on CTU-13 (13 botnet datasets) (Gracia et al., 2014), authors concluded that flow based botnet detection system outperformed all other detection systems.

Therefore, this chapter aims to design a detection model that doesn't use payload but only packet headers in order to detect the botnet. Machine learning techniques will be used to automate the process of botnet detection because flexibility and automated learning capability of machine learning algorithms provide them an edge over other mitigation methods.

We will use a flow exported tool to extract the important features from the network traffic. Exporter tools are generally used to aggregate the network packets into flows. Netflow (Cisco IOS Netflow, 2017), is a standard by CISCO for the collection of IP-flow. This chapter uses its open-source version, softflowd (softflowd, 2017) to collect data in form of flows. Later on, machine learning is applied to differentiate botnet and normal traffic.

BACKGROUND

In current times, detection of botnets has been one of the prominent research areas of researchers. Although a number of techniques are present in literature, a majority of them are not able to detect the recent type of botnets. Previously proposed botnet detection methodologies majorly focused on the analysis of payloads for mischievous content. Payload examination approaches consume more data because they require a massive amount of data. Also, bots nowadays use techniques such as data encryption and code obfuscation to hide their malicious content.

A framework is presented in 2007 for detection of botnets, named as BotHunter, based on the Snort to implement a rule-based Intrusion Detection System (Gu et al., 2007). This framework relates bot activities with alarms from the Snort Intrusion Detection System. This framework exploits the concept that bots perform similar sort of actions during their lifecycle, for example, scanning of the host, infection with some sort of virus, download of binary, connection with Command & Control server, etc. BotHunter closely monitors the traffic of a network to identify the different phases of botnet lifecycle.

Thereafter, BotHunter performs the analysis of payload on the basis of different rules of the Snort and correlation engine of BotHunter is used to calculate the score. The score determines the amount of probability that network is infected by a bot. BotHunter possesses high accuracy when a bot covers all the phases of its lifecycle. Although such type of system provides quite accurate results they don't scale well with voluminous and varied network traffic. Moreover, it can't cope up with encrypted data as it is based on payload analysis.

A botnet detection system was proposed (Strayer et al., 2008) on the basis of network behavior. Authors particularly focused on Internet Relay Chat-based Command & Control activities by examining different flow characteristics of Internet Relay Chat flows such as packet timing, bandwidth, and burst duration. This approach is divided into four different phases: During the first phase, filtering is applied on the generated traffic to differentiate Internet Relay Chat from normal traffic by eradicating traffic that is possibly normal Internet Relay Chat. Filters are designed by taking into consideration the commands of Internet Relay Chats bots, white and blacklists of Internet domains and some of the network flow characteristics. During the second phase, clustering is applied to filtered flows using machine learning algorithms on the basis of pre-defined network applications clusters. Authors didn't specifically mention which machine learning techniques have been used in this paper during this stage. Thereafter, clustered flows are passed on to correlator stage. During the third stage, clustered flows are again clustered according to similarity among characteristics. Consequently, the topological analysis is applied on the correlated flows in order to identify the common controller. Flows that belong to the common controller are analyzed by a human analyst to evaluate whether they belong to a botnet or not. As preciseness of this approach is dependent on the expertise of a human analyst, this is a noticeable drawback of the proposed approach.

Authors have used classification for filtering the traffic and clustering is used to identify different activities. Authors were successfully able.

BotMiner was developed in 2008 for detection of the botnet on the basis of group behavior analysis of individual bots that belongs to a single botnet (Gu et al., 2008). It analyzes and clusters the similar behavior that is being performed continuously on a group of machines in the network for detection of the botnet. They first applied clustering in order to group the behavior for a similar type of communication and later on applied activity clustering. Network flows of popular safe protocols were filtered from the network traffic to increase the accuracy of detection. Consequently, the second phase of clustering is applied to group flows according to the malicious activities identified by the Snort. After applying both types of clustering, BotMiner associates bots that possess similar behavior and perform malicious activities. During this process, BotMiner was able to detect most of existing popular botnets with a detection rate of 99% and false positive rate of approximately 1%.

BotSniffer was proposed on the concept of network-based anomaly detection when there is no previous knowledge of Command and Control server signatures (Gu et al., 2008). This approach can be used to identify both, the Command & Control server as well as the bots. It worked on the assumption that all the bots that belong to the same botnet depict strong synchronization and spatial as well as the temporal correlation between their response behavior as well as activities. The proposed system captures this strong correlation among activities and responses of several bots that belong to a single botnet and utilized various statistical techniques to identify botnets with a restricted number of false positives and false negatives. Authors have evaluated the proposed approach on a large number of real-world network traces.

A system was proposed for detection of general botnets such as Internet Relay Chat and Peer-to-Peer based botnets (Zeidanloo et al., 2010). This approach focused on the similarity in behavior as well as communication pattern among multiple bots that belongs to a single botnet. Moreover, this work doesn't rely on any previous knowledge about the botnets or their signatures.

Authors used classification and clustering to distinguish between normal and botnet traffic.

In 2012, authors presented a methodology for botnet detection by observing network traffic characteristics (Zeidanloo et al., 2012). This approach works very similar to that of BotMiner. The proposed methodology was divided into 3 different stages: filtering, detection of malicious activity and monitoring of network traffic. These different stages are used to group the different types of bots by their group behavior. Proposed approach segregates the flows in six hours' time period. However, effects of different size of flow intervals were not presented. Therefore, the correctness of this approach is not identified.

All the group behavior-based approaches are not suitable for early detection of botnets because they require botnets to perform malicious activities before their detection. Additionally, group behavior-based approaches assume that multiple machines are infected by botnet on the monitored network. Subsequently, this methodology became infeasible if a single system is affected by the botnet on the monitored network.

An approach that detects botnet on the host end without requiring the group behavior analysis was presented (Giroire et al., 2009). Authors worked upon the assumption that bot needs to frequently communicate with its bot-master to perform its desired function. Frequent communication is required between bot-master and bot-client in form of commands and responses. Therefore, there is a form of regularity in communication among bot and its bot-master that may be spread over a large span of time. This sort of communication can be easily captured by monitoring the incoming and outgoing network traffic to/from mischievous destinations with some sort of regularity in time. In order to distinguish normal destination from the malicious ones, the author designed a white-list of authentic destinations. The persistent feature is used to capture the temporal regularity of visited destinations. Botnet detection is implemented by identifying persistent communication from/to non-white listed source/destinations beyond a certain level of threshold. Performance evaluation of proposed approach on real-world network traffic generated the low number of false positives.

On the basis of correlation among commands and responses of monitored traffic, network nodes of a monitored network are evaluated to determine their relation to botnets (Wurzinger et al., 2009). It finds responses within network traffic and then observes the earlier traffic for recognizing the corresponding commands. On the basis of command and responses patterns, detection models are build to identify similar sort of activity and presence of botnet. However, the models generated in this form are specific to the particular type of botnets. In order to evaluate the performance of proposed methodology, 18 models were automatically generated for the different type of botnets say, Internet Relay Chat (IRC) System, Hyper Text Transfer Protocol (HTTP) and Peer-to-Peer (P2P) and their performance was evaluated on publicly available datasets. Performance results depict low false positive rate during evaluation.

Authors have used packet payload information for detection so such type of systems can easily fail when encryption is employed in botnet traffic.

An anomaly-based system was presented (Arshad et al., 2011) that doesn't require any prior information about signatures of bots, addresses of Command & Control and botnet protocols. In the proposed approach, inherent characteristics of botnets were used. In general, all the bots connect to their bot-master, receive and then execute those commands. It became obvious that all the bots that belong to a single botnet receive same instructions. This results in the similarity between NetFlow characteristics and thereby they perform the same type of attacks. This method clusters bots that possess alike net flows and attacks in various time windows and perform the correlation to identify all the hosts that are infected by a botnet. Authors this paper evaluated proposed method against various normal and malicious network traces available over the Internet.

A system was designed for detection of botnets using flow intervals and traffic behavior analysis (Zhao et al., 2012). Features extracted with the help of packet headers were used with classifiers for detection of botnets. Network flow features along-with Bayesian network and decision trees were used for detection of botnets. Authors focused on Peer 2 Peer (P2P) botnets that utilized Domain Name System (DNS) technique and Hyper Text Transfer Protocol (HTTP). The proposed technique was evaluated on the combination of malicious and normal traffic that is collected from various sources LBNL datasets were used for normal traffic and malicious from traces from Honeynet Project. Evaluation results clearly depict that detection rate is above 60% while the false positive rate is below 5%.

A system for detection of Hyper Text Transfer Protocol (HTTP) based botnets on the basis of traffic flow using multilayer feed-forward neural network was proposed (Kirubavathi & Anitha, 2016). They focused on features such as packet ratio, the initial length of packets for detection of botnets. In general, HTTP based botnets don't maintain a persistent connection with Command &Control server but bots send the periodical request to the Command & Control server in order to download all the instructions given by Command & Control server. Authors extracted Transmission Control Protocol features from packet headers. Different botnets are simulated in a laboratory for performance evaluation of the proposed system.

Some researchers used active DNS probing on a large scale to evaluate the query of DNS characteristics based on the values of DNS cache (Ma et al., 2015). However, this method raises high-security alarms and increases the probability of detection by the attackers.

Studies by various researchers on detection of periodic communication in HTTP and their limitations were reviewed (Eslahi et al., 2015). Authors proposed three measures for determining the different communication patterns on the basis of periodicity. The levels of periodicity were explored in order to characterize the traffic for botnets by matching the likeness among messages. Authors were able to detect communication of Hyper Text Transfer Protocol botnet with 80% accuracy. However, this work suffers from the problem of a large number of false positives. Therefore, it became necessary to combine it with other features for better results.

A number of security threats launched by attackers at the network level (Suriya & Khari, 2012). Author classified the attacks in 2 major categories: active attack and passive attack. Further, authors presented a number of security issues that should be taken into consideration while designing a secure routing protocol for networks (Miglani et al., 2017).

The vulnerable features of mobile ad-hoc network and various security measures such as cryptography, intrusion detection system, secure protocols, etc., are reviewed so that they can be used to secure the network nodes against these vulnerabilities (Saini & Khari, 2011).

The numbers of techniques used by attackers to attack web applications that are running on victim system to retrieve confidential and sensitive details are discussed (Khari
& Kumar, 2016). Attackers can exploit the vulnerabilities of web applications via a number of attacking techniques such as SQL Injection, cross-site scripting, etc.

A paper was presented where different types of web applications vulnerabilities are presented (Khari & Sangwan, 2016). Authors also discussed various dynamic and static analysis approaches proposed by researchers to tackle against these types of vulnerabilities. Particularly, authors focused on the research done by researchers on cross-site scripting attack.

A novel user authentication technique is presented in order to prevent unauthorized access to the database during SQL Injection attack (Khari & Kumar, 2016). In case of SQL Injection attack, the attacker exploits the vulnerabilities of web applications to gain access to admin credentials hence control of the entire website. In this paper, authors present a SQL Injection Protector for Authentication where salt and the hash value of username and password are used while authentication in addition to username and password. Since these values are created during the dynamic time so an attacker will not be able to get access to these values.

Various methodologies presented by researchers such as IDS, black hole testing, etc to prevent against SQL Injection attacks were discussed (Khari & Karar, 2013).

It is clear from the above discussion that a number of researchers have presented different botnet detection techniques by a variety of methods. However, most of them were able to detect a specific type of botnet either Internet Relay Chat Based or Hyper Text Transfer Protocol based or Peer-2-Peer-based. In this chapter, the objective of the author is to propose a botnet detection system that can identify all types of botnets with high accuracy and low false positives.

MAIN FOCUS OF THE CHAPTER

This section discusses the advantage of using flow analysis during detection of botnets, generation, and collection of the botnet and normal traffic and different type of machine learning algorithms used for network flow analysis.

Most of earlier presented work focuses on payload analysis that analyzes contents of TCP or UDP protocol based payloads to identify the malicious behavior. This type of analysis offers high accuracy when compared with many other algorithms but also suffers from a number of limitations. Payload-based analysis techniques are resource consuming operations that consume lots of time while performing the analysis. Such techniques fail when the amount of network traffic is quite high. Additionally, new bots started used data encryption, code obfuscation techniques in order to hide the content from the user and hence defeat the purpose of packet inspection techniques. Furthermore, packet inspection techniques also raise the concern regarding violation of privacy.

Flow analysis techniques counter most of the concerns raised by payload inspection techniques. Flow analysis techniques are based on the concept that all bots within a botnet exhibit similar behavior. These techniques use flow generation tools to consolidate data according to the information in packet headers. Network behavior is characterized by a set of features. Therefore, these features can be used to differentiate the normal traffic from the botnet traffic. The flow-based analysis doesn't use payload, so this technique is invulnerable to code encryption and code obfuscation techniques.

Therefore, this chapter explores the possibility of detecting botnets with the help of packet headers. Network traffic is aggregated in form of flows to extract useful features from network traffic. Later on, an effective machine learning model will be designed to detect botnets in real time with high accuracy. Our proposed work is divided into different phases: Dataset collection, Flow extraction, Flow Analysis and Feature extraction

Data Collection

To design a machine learning based botnet detection system, a dataset is required in order to train the models. The dataset should also comprise of real-world network traffic with all the essential features. During analysis, selected models will be evaluated on the ISOT dataset (Saad et al., 2011) from University of Victoria. The ISOT dataset is a collection of various normal and malicious botnet dataset available online on many public sites. To represent the non-malicious data, normal data in ISOT comprises of 2 different datasets i.e. Traffic Lab at Ericsson Research in Hungary and from Lawrence Berkeley National Lab. The malicious dataset actually comprises of 2 different botnets: storm and waledac. In addition to this, the CTU (Gracia et al., 2014) dataset by CTU University is used for botnet traffic dataset. Further, Zeus botnet is used to capture data in real time. Zeus botnet is very popular botnet to steal sensitive details. In addition to above-collected data, Alexa Internet, Inc (Alexa, 2017) is used to gather normal traffic. This site displays 500 benign sites. Softflowd (open source version of NetFlow (a CISCO software)) is also used to capture the traffic in real time. In order to homogenize the network traffic, TCPRelay is used to replay the trace files of these datasets. In the end, the replayed traffic is captured with the help of Wireshark.

Flow Extraction

In order to build the flows out of the captured data, nfcapd and nfdump (NfDump, 2017) are used. Nfdump is an open source and user-friendly flow exporter that can work with a number of NetFlow versions. It can easily export flows out of already captured traffic and real-time traffic captured with the help of softflowd. As input, it can use live network traffic as well as pre-captured data in form of pcap files to extract the important features. By default, nfdump extract 48 features from the flows.

Flow Analysis

In order to classify the flows as botnet or normal, it is important to analyze values of a set of attributes. Functioning of the proposed approach is divided into 2 phases: training and detection phase. Classifiers were trained with the help of malicious and non-malicious attributes values during the training phase for segregation of data in two different classes: normal and malicious. Once the training phase is complete, detection phase starts observing the traffic network and classifies the flows on the basis of the value of different attributes. Whenever attributes show malicious values then flows are flagged as suspicious.

For the analysis purpose, three most prominent machine learning algorithms (Alpaydin, 2004): SVM, Random Tree and REPTree are used to distinguish the botnet and normal traffic accurately:

1. **Support Vector Machine:** In Support Vector Machine, each data instance can be classified according to a hyperplane. The objective of this algorithm is to determine an optimal hyperplane to ensure the biggest minimum distance between training examples.
2. **Random Tree:** This algorithm repeatedly classifies the dataset by randomly selecting a subset of features at each node for constructing the trees. This algorithm creates a number of trees and in the end, each tree makes a vote. This algorithm decreases the risk of over-fitting. It works efficiently even on large datasets and possesses high accuracy even if a large amount of data is missing.

3. **REP Tree:** Reduced Error Pruning Tree uses the concept of regression tree and creates multiple trees in different iterations. Afterwards, the best one is chosen among all the available trees. REP Tree is the fast version of the decision tree that uses information gain as the splitting criteria and prunes the tree according to mean square error.

Feature Extraction

In order to develop an accurate, scalable and real-time machine learning model, it is very important to use feature selection techniques on high-dimensional data. Selection of the right set of features reduces the complexity, increases the accuracy and reduces the time.

Feature selection techniques can be broadly classified into two categories: wrapper and filter.

In case of wrapper method, subsets of features are selected on the basis of the classifier that is being used for performance evaluation i.e. effectiveness of features is determined from the performance of the classifier. Therefore, the performance of a particular classifier is evaluated using the different subset of features and set of features with which classifier performs best is selected as the final output.

Filter method chooses a subset of features regardless of any particular classifier. It evaluates the utility of features and assigns rank according to their relevance in performance evaluation. Their performance is independent of any classifier.

This chapter uses correlation feature selection (CFS) as filter method and WrapperSubsetEval as wrapper method. Best First Search will be used to identify the best set of features with the help of above-mentioned feature selection approaches.

RESULTS

In order to determine the performance of classifiers, WEKA machine learning framework is used in this chapter. To extract and export important features from a given pcap file, nfcapd and nfdump are used. Cross-validation method is used to evaluate the performance and effectiveness of evaluated models. During the assessment, the dataset was distributed into 10 sub-datasets, out of which 9 are used for training purpose and 1 is used for testing purpose. The same phenomenon is repeated again and again until all the subsets are used for testing purpose precisely once.

Different performance measures such as detection rate (DR), false positive rate (FPR), Accuracy are used to assess the performance of various classifiers. DR defines the ratio of intrusions detected out of a total number of intrusions in network traffic. FPR specifies the percentage of normal traffic identified as intrusions. Accuracy determines the percentage of traffic classifier is able to distinguish properly as the botnet and normal traffic. The objective of this chapter is to achieve high DR and Accuracy and low FPR.

The above-mentioned are determined with the help of following formulas:

$$DR = \frac{TP}{TP + FN}$$

$$FPR = \frac{FP}{TN + FP}$$

$$Accuracy = \frac{TP + TN}{TP + TN + FP + FN} * 100$$

where, True Positive (TP) is the ratio of intrusions that are correctly identified as intrusions, True Negative (TN) is the number of normal traffic instances that are correctly classified as normal traffic instances. False Positives (FP) defines the number of normal traffic instances that are incorrectly classified as botnet type. False Negative (FN) defines the number of instances of botnet traffic incorrectly classified as normal traffic.

The DR, FPR, and Accuracy for SVM, Random Tree, and REP Tree are listed in Table 1. These values are an average of results of 10 simulations.

It became clear from Table 1 that all the algorithms performed really well in terms of accuracy, more than 99%. Further, they possess a detection rate of more than 96%. It is clear from the table that Random Tree and REP Tree outperform SVM in terms of accuracy and performance of REP Tree is marginally better than Random Tree. Further, the detection rate is above 99% in case of Random Tree and REP Tree so they only less than 1% of the botnet instances will remain undetected.

Table 1 results make it more evident that botnets possess certain unique features in comparison to normal network traffic.

Figure 1 demonstrates the performance of different algorithms: SVM, Random Tree, and REPTree in terms of accuracy. Out of all the 3 algorithms, REP Tree and Random Tree are more accurate than SVM, classifying more than 99.98% instances accurately while inaccurately classifying less than .02% instances.

Table 1. Performance of algorithms on different performance metrics with full feature set

	DR	FPR	Accuracy
SVM	0.9651	0.00016	99.9411
RandomTree	0.9902	0.00007	99.981
REPTree	0.9932	0.00012	99.982

Figure 1. Accuracy of SVM, Random Tree, and REP Tree

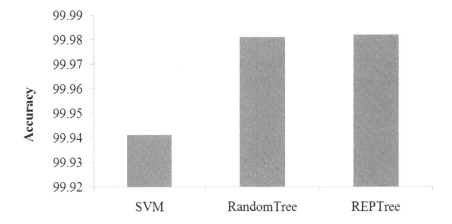

Figure 2 demonstrates model performances in terms of DR. Detection rate is highest in REP Tree followed by Random Tree. Performance of SVM is not up to the mark when compared with Random Tree and REP Tree.

Figure 3 demonstrates model performances in terms of FPR. The false positive rate should be minimum for a good classifier. During analysis, it was determined that SVM possess highest FPR in comparison to other two. FPR is minimum in case of Random Tree.

During the overall assessment, the author concludes that Random Tree is best among all the classifiers because while achieving the similar level of detection rate and accuracy with REP Tree it offers the minimum amount of false positive rate. False positive rate is an important parameter while assessing the performance of a classifier in botnet because a large number of false positives will interrupt the normal functioning of a user and hence not desired.

Figure 2. DR of SVM, Random Tree, and REP Tree

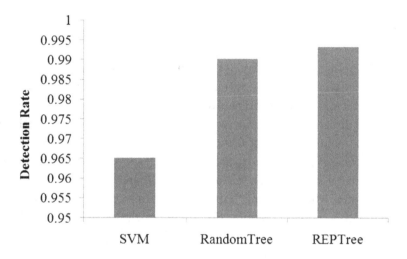

Figure 3. FPR of SVM, Random Tree, and REP Tree

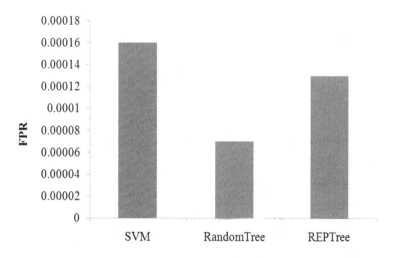

In order to determine some of the crucial discriminating attributes and the effectiveness of above-mentioned algorithms on a subset of features, ML algorithms are then re-evaluated (Table 2 and Table 3) using wrapper and filter feature selection methods: CFSSubsetEval (Filter) and Wrapper method.

Table 2 depicts the performance of different models when a subset of features was selected using CFS algorithm (correlation based attribute evaluation). In case of CFSSubsetEval, each feature is evaluated or ranked w.r.t information gain. If information gain is high, the feature will have the lowest rank and so on. It is clear from the Table 2 that, in general, the performance of SVM, Random Tree, and REP Tree decreases when evaluated with a subset of features determined by CFSSubsetEval in comparison to the evaluation with the entire feature set.

Table 3 shows the performance of models when a subset of features was selected using Wrapper algorithm. In case of wrapper method, the subset of features was different for different classifiers. Although DR of REP Tree increases when evaluated with feature set generated by wrapper method but wrapper method doesn't increase the performance of other algorithms.

CONCLUSION

This chapter proposed a botnet detection model that can detect bots with high accuracy and minimum false positive rate on the basis of network flow characteristics. To train and test the models, the author generated real-world botnet and normal traffic as well as utilized existing datasets. Since machine learning algorithms cannot be directly applied to network traffic so Flow collector (softflowd) and exporter (nfdump) are used for extracting important features vectors. Thereafter, machine learning algorithms (Random tree, REP Tree, and SVM) are used to analyze these feature vectors and to differentiate between the botnet traffic and normal traffic. Further, feature selection is applied to extract important features and discard the irrelevant features. After analyzing the performance of various models on different metrics with the full feature set and with a subset of features, the author concluded that Random Tree and REP Tree performed much better than SVM. In case of the real-world scenario, the author recommended Random

Table 2. Performance of algorithms on different performance metrics with CFS feature set

	DR	FPR	Accuracy
SVM	0.9641	0.00018	99.9339
RandomTree	0.9882	0.00011	99.9712
REPTree	0.9945	0.00017	99.975

Table 3. Performance of algorithms on different performance metrics with Wrapper feature set

	DR	FPR	Accuracy
SVM	0.9646	0.00016	99.94
RandomTree	0.9889	0.00011	99.9756
REPTree	0.9964	0.00017	99.9803

Tree over REP Tree because it possesses minimum FPR while DR, Accuracy is quite comparable with REP Tree. FPR is very important metric while designing real-life botnet prevention solutions because high FPR will generate a large number of false alarms and create a really annoying solution for the user.

REFERENCES

Alexa. (2017) Retrieved March 1, 2017, from https://www.alexa.com/topsites

Alpaydin, E. (2004). *Introduction to Machine Learning*. MIT Press.

Arshad, S., Abbaspour, M., Kharrazi, M., & Sanatkar, H. (2011). An anomaly based botnet detection approach for identifying stealthy botnets. in *Proceedings of the IEEE International Conference on Computer Applications and Industrial Electronics*, Penang, Malaysia (pp. 564–569).

Cisco. (n.d.). IOS NetFlow. Retrieved March 1, 2017 from http://www.cisco.com/en/US/products/ps6601/products_ios_protocol_group_home.html

Cox, O. (2013). Citadel's defences breached. *Symantec*. Rederived March 13, 2017, from http://www.symantec.com/connect/blogs/citadel-s-defenses-breached

David. (2012). Open DNS Security Talk: The Role of DNS in Botnet Command & Control. *Open DNS Inc*. Rederived March 13, 2017, from info.opendns.com/rs/opendns/images/WB-Security-Talk-Role-Of-DNS-Slides.pdf

Denning, D. E. (1987). An intrusion-detection model. *IEEE Transactions on Software Engineering*, *13*(2), 222–232. doi:10.1109/TSE.1987.232894

Eslahi, M., Rohmad, M., Nilsaz, H., Naseri, M., Tahir, N., & Hashim, H. (2015). Periodicity classification of http traffic to detect http botnets. In *Proceedings of the IEEE Symposium on Computer Applications Industrial Electronics*, Langkawi, Malaysia (pp. 119–123). 10.1109/ISCAIE.2015.7298339

García, S., Grill, M., Stiborek, J., & Zunino, A. (2014). An empirical comparison of botnet detection methods. *Computer Security Journal*, *45*, 100–123. doi:10.1016/j.cose.2014.05.011

Giroire, F., Chandrashekar, J., Taft, N., Schooler, E., & Papagiannaki, D. (2009) Exploiting Temporal Persistence to Detect Covert Botnet Channels. In: E. Kirda, S. Jha, & D. Balzarotti (Eds.), *International Workshop on Recent Advances in Intrusion Detection: Recent Advances in Intrusion Detection*, LNCS (Vol. 5758, pp. 326-345). Springer, Berlin, Heidelberg 10.1007/978-3-642-04342-0_17

Gu, G., Perdisci, R., Zhang, J., & Lee, W. (2008). BotMiner: clustering analysisof network traffic for protocol- and structure- independent botnet detection. In *Proceedings of the 17th conference on Security symposium,* San Jose, CA (pp. 139-154).

Gu, G., Porras, P., Yegneswaran, V., & Fong, M. (2007). BotHunter: Detecting malware infection through IDS-driven dialogcorrelation. In *Proceedings of 16th USENIX Security Symposium on USENIX Security Symposium*, Boston, MA (pp. 167–182).

Gu, G., Zhang, J., & Lee, W. (2008). BotSniffer: Detecting botnet commandand control channels in network traffic. In *Proceedings of the Network and Distributed System Security Symposium*, San Diego, CA.

Guntuku, S. C., Hota, C., Singh, K., & Thakur, A. (2014). Big data analytics framework for peer-to-peer botnet detection using random forests. *Information Sciences*, *278*, 488–497. doi:10.1016/j.ins.2014.03.066

Haddadi, F., Phan, D. T., & Zincir-Heywood, A. N. (2016). How to choose from different botnet detection systems? In *Proceedings of the IEEE/IFIP Network Operations and Management Symposium,* Istanbul, Turkey (pp. 1079–1084). 10.1109/NOMS.2016.7502964

Huang, C. T., & Sakib, M. N. (2016). Using anomaly detection based techniques to detect HTTP-based botnet C&C traffic. In *Proceedings of the IEEE International Conference on Communications*, Kuala Lumpur, Malaysia.

Khari, M., & Karar, A. (2013). Preventing SQL-Based Attacks Using Intrusion Detection System. *International Journal of Science and Engineering Applications*, *2*(6), 145–150. doi:10.7753/IJSEA0206.1006

Khari, M., & Kumar, M. (2016). Comprehensive study of web application attacks and classification. In *3rd International Conference on Computing for Sustainable Global Development*, New Delhi, India (pp. 2159-2164).

Khari, M., & Kumar, N. (2013). User Authentication Method against SQL Injection Attack. *International Journal of Scientific & Engineering Research.*, *4*(6), 1649–1653.

Khari, M., & Sangwan, P. (2016). Web-application attacks: A survey. In *Proceedings of the 3rd International Conference on Computing for Sustainable Global Development*, New Delhi, India (pp. 2187-2191).

Kimbahune, V. V., Deshpande, A. V., & Mahalle, P. N. (2017). Lightweight Key Management for Adaptive Addressing in Next Generation Internet. *International Journal of Ambient Computing and Intelligence*, *8*(1), 50–69. doi:10.4018/IJACI.2017010103

Kirubavathi, G., & Anitha, R. (2016). Botnet detection via mining of traffic flow characteristics. *Computers & Electrical Engineering*, *50*, 91–101. doi:10.1016/j.compeleceng.2016.01.012

Ma, X., Zhang, J., Li, Z., Li, J., Tao, J., Guan, X., ... Towsley, D. (2015). Accurate DNS query characteristics estimation via active probing. *Journal of Network and Computer Applications*, *47*, 72–84. doi:10.1016/j.jnca.2014.09.016

Matallah, H., Belalem, G., & Bouamrane, K. (2017). Towards a New Model of Storage and Access to Data in Big Data and Cloud Computing. *International Journal of Ambient Computing and Intelligence*, *8*(4), 31–44. doi:10.4018/IJACI.2017100103

Miglani, A., Bhatia, T., Sharma, G., & Shrivastava, G. (2017). An Energy Efficient and Trust Aware Framework for Secure Routing in LEACH for Wireless Sensor Networks. Scalable Computing. *Practice and Experience*, *18*(3), 207–218.

NfDump. (2017). Retrieved March 1, 2017 from http://nfdump.sourceforge.net/

Roesch, M. (1999). Snort—Lightweight intrusion detection for networks. In *Proceedings of the 13th USENIX conference on System administration*, Seattle, WA (pp. 229-238).

Saad, S., Traore, I., Ghorbani, A., Sayed, B., Zhao, D., & Lu, W. et al. (2011). Detecting P2P botnets through network behavior analysis and machine learning. In Proceedings of ninth annual international conference on privacy, security and trust, Montreal, Canada (pp. 174–80).

Saini, R., & Khari, M. (2011). An Algorithm to detect attacks in mobile ad hoc network. In *International Conference on Software Engineering and Computer Systems* (pp. 336-341). Springer, Berlin, Heidelberg 10.1007/978-3-642-22203-0_30

Shrivastava, G. (2016, March). Network forensics: Methodical literature review. In *Proceedings of the 2016 3rd International Conference on Computing for Sustainable Global Development (INDIACom)* (pp. 2203-2208). IEEE.

Shrivastava, G. (2017). Approaches of network forensic model for investigation. *International Journal of Forensic Engineering, 3*(3), 195–215. doi:10.1504/IJFE.2017.082977

Shrivastava, G., Sharma, K., & Kumari, R. (2016, March). Network forensics: Today and tomorrow. In *Proceedings of the 2016 3rd International Conference on Computing for Sustainable Global Development (INDIACom)* (pp. 2234-2238). IEEE.

Shrivastava, G., Sharma, K., & Rai, S. (2010, December). The Detection & Defense of DoS & DDoS Attack: A Technical Overview. In *Proceeding of ICC* (Vol. 27, p. 28).

Softflowd. (n.d.). Retrieved March 1, 2017 from http://www.mindrot.org/projects/softflowd/

Strayer, W. T., Lapsely, D., Walsh, R., & Livadas, C. (2008). Botnet Detection Based on Network Behavior. In W. Lee, C. Wang, & D. Dagon (Eds.), *Botnet Detection. Advances in Information Security* (Vol. 36, pp. 1–24). Boston, MA: Springer. doi:10.1007/978-0-387-68768-1_1

Supriya, K. M. (2012). Mobile Ad Hoc Netwoks Security Attacks and Secured Routing Protocols: A Survey. In N. Meghanathan, N. Chaki, & D. Nagamalai (Eds.), *Advances in Computer Science and Information Technology, Networks and Communications* (Vol. 84, pp. 119–124). Berlin, Heidelberg: Springer. doi:10.1007/978-3-642-27299-8_14

Wurzinger, P., Bilge, L., Holz, T., Goebel, J., Kruegel, C., & Kirda, E. (2009) Automatically Generating Models for Botnet Detection. In M. Backes & P. Ning (Eds.), *Computer Security – European Symposium on Research in Computer Security, LNCS* (Vol 5789, pp. 232-249). Springer, Berlin, Heidelberg 10.1007/978-3-642-04444-1_15

Zeidanloo, H. R., Manaf, A. B., Vahdani, P., Tabatabaei, F., & Zamani, M. (2010). Botnet detection based on traffic monitoring. In *Proceedings of the International Conference on Networking and Information Technology*, Manila, Philippines (pp. 97-101).

Zeidanloo, H. R., & Rouhani, S. (2012). *Botnet detection by monitoring common network behaviors.* Lambert Academic Publishing.

Zhang, J., & Zulkernine, M. (2005). Network intrusion detection using random forests. In *Proceedings of the Third Annual Conference on Privacy, Security and Trust,* St. Andrews, Canada (pp. 53–61).

Zhao, D., Traore, I., Ghorbani, A., Sayed, B., Saad, S., & Lu, W. (2012). Peer to Peer Botnet Detection Based on Flow Intervals. In D. Gritzalis, S. Furnell, & M. Theoharidou (Eds.), *Information Security and Privacy Research: IFIP Advances in Information and Communication Technology* (Vol. 376, pp. 87–102). Berlin, Heidelberg: Springer. doi:10.1007/978-3-642-30436-1_8

Chapter 8
Denial-of-Service (DoS) Attack and Botnet:
Network Analysis, Research Tactics, and Mitigation

Arushi Arora
Indira Gandhi Delhi Technical University for Women, India

Sumit Kumar Yadav
Indira Gandhi Delhi Technical University for Women, India

Kavita Sharma
National Institute of Technology, Kurukshetra, India

ABSTRACT

This chapter describes how the consequence and hazards showcased by Denial of Service attacks have resulted in the surge of research studies, commercial software and innovative cogitations. Of the DoS attacks, the incursion of its variant DDoS can be quite severe. A botnet, on the other hand, is a group of hijacked devices that are connected by internet. These botnet servers are used to perform DDoS attacks effectively. In this chapter, the authors attempt to provide an insight into DoS attacks and botnets, focusing on their analysis and mitigation. They also propose a defense mechanism to mitigate our system from botnet DDoS attacks. This is achieved by using a through access list based configuration. The artful engineering of malware is a weapon used for online crime and the ideas behind it are profit-motivated. The last section of the chapter provides an understanding of the WannaCry Ransomware Attack which locked computers in more than 150 countries.

DOI: 10.4018/978-1-5225-4100-4.ch008

INTRODUCTION

In recent years, changes in cybercrime techniques have become more pronounced and menacing. One of the evident examples is DDoS (Distributed Denial-of-Service) Attacks, which are now appearing with a new twist, using IoT (Internet of Things) to expand their target area (Bhatt et al., 2017; Yadav et al., 2018). IoT has impacted the digital technology in a way, altering how we think or live (Dey et al., 2017). The technology promises to ease our living by providing convenience and practically improving our communication with our surroundings (Jain & Bhatnagar, 2017; Elhayatmy et al., 2018). The concept of "Anonymity of Internet" is used in the cyber attacks, changing their scale and scope. The Internet is one area where assiduousness is mandatory and security should be a priority. "The Internet is becoming the town square for the global village of tomorrow" was rightly stated by Bill Gates, co-founder of the Microsoft Corporation. The Internet provides us with a huge range of resources and services and has become a platform for numerous commercial activities like online banking, online shopping, publicity, marketing, advertising etc. (Tayal, 2017). The Internet is an open platform when compared to the current circuit-switched networks (ATMs, the analog telephone network, etc.); hence this makes it easier for attackers to enforce a cyber attack on devices connected to the Internet. The reason behind this is that the former is implemented in software using general-purpose computing hardware. Also, standardized and open technologies using servers are reachable through the Internet. Therefore, services like these suffer from internet threats just like HTTP-based services (Mukherjee et al., 2016). This chapter will focus on the Denial-of-Service attacks (Carl et al., 2006) and Botnet analysis (Alejandre et al., 2017), their detection (Park & Lee, 2001) and mitigation (Zhang et al., 2016). It has been appropriately said by Art Wittmann that, "As we've come to realize, the idea that security starts and ends with the purchase of a prepackaged firewall is simply misguided", therefore, in this chapter hybrid mitigation techniques for DoS attacks and botnets are presented (Shrivastava et al., 2010).

Man is a curious being. From the very beginning, communicating and curiosity have encouraged and led to underground research. Over these years, online financial transactions, attackers have shifted their focus from communicating to commercialization and monitory profits. Most computer systems that belong to large organizations contain valuable information about the users or business activities. The attackers are well experienced and know the methods for information retrieval, its location, and extraction for financial gain. Therefore, to protect their resources, organizations are setting up system security, staffing and defensive technologies to protect their information and computer systems (Matallah et al., 2017; Yamin & Sen, 2018). This can reduce the risk of successful attacks but it does not cure the problem completely (Kimbahune et al., 2017). Some attackers, on the other hand, are attracted to individual machines because of lack of security measures taken by the user.

The first section of the chapter explains the DoS attack types; DoS attack techniques along with its symptoms and defense techniques (Desai et al., 2016; Saha et al., 2016). The attacker of a DoS attack prevents the utilization of the resources by the user. In the attack, the bandwidth of the user is reduced and the network is flooded, thereby disrupting a service. Distributed attacks also came into existence soon after Denial of Service attacks. In Distributed attack, separate sites are used for execution to as Distributed Denial-of-Service (DDoS) attacks. The types of DoS attacks that are explained in the chapter are Denial-of-service as a service, Advanced persistent DoS (APDoS) and Distributed DoS (Mirkovic & Reiher, 2004; Feinstein et al., 2003) after which its symptoms are listed. These symptoms comprise of speed issue or slow *network performance,* unreachable websites, drastic number of spam emails or email bomb attack, networking wire issue, connection failure issue and internet access denial for a long period of time. DoS attack techniques including Internet Control Message Protocol (ICMP) flood, attack tools (Kumar et al., 2009) that are Predators Face, Rolling Thunder, *MyDoom, Stacheldraht* and Low Orbit Ion Cannon, Peer-to-peer attacks, application-layer floods (*LAND* attack, *XDoS*), Degradation-of-service attacks (Poturalski et al., 2010), permanent denial-of-service attacks, reflected/spoofed attack, Distributed DoS attack, DDoS extortion, Nuke, Telephony denial-of-service (TDoS), Teardrop attacks, (S)SYN flood, R-U-Dead-Yet? (RUDY), Shrew attack and sophisticated low-bandwidth Distributed Denial-of-Service Attack is explained in detail along with various research work done on these attacks (Long & Thomas, 2001; Gupta et al., 2010)). The defense techniques (Hasbullah & Soomro, 2010) and the solutions proposed on these attacks are then presented. The defense techniques include an amalgam of attack detection, response, and traffic classification. These defense techniques function to block traffic that is identified as illegitimate or illegal and allow traffic that on the other hand is identified as legitimate or illegal (Senie & Ferguson, 1998). Some of the defense techniques that are explained in this chapter are upstream filtering, DDS based defense, blackholing and sinkholing, firewalls, routers, IPS based prevention, switches and application front-end hardware.

The focus of the chapter then shifts to botnets (Cooke et al., 2005). A network of robots can be defined as the botnet. It refers to a number of devices that are connected to the internet and can be used to perform attacks like the DDoS attack, sending of spam and stealing of data. It consists of compromised networks wherein each compromised device is referred to as a "bot." In the second section of this chapter, botnets are explained in detail. Botnets are now rented out as commodities for a number of purposes, by *cybercriminals* (Danchev & Dancho, 2010). These bots over the time have progressed to dodge their detection. Its application and architecture models including peer-to-peer and client-server model are discussed in the chapter (Ullah et al., 2013). In peer-to-peer model, digital signatures might be used by these, for example, a botnet can be controlled by a person who has access to a key of that network (Kang et al., 2009). Newer botnets communicate with a server, which is centralized. In a client-server model, botnets are operated by using Internet Relay Chat (IRC) networks, domains, and websites. Infected clients await incoming commands from the server as they access a predetermined location (Ollmann & Gunter, 2009). The person having the key of the botnet may send commands to the server, which is further forwarded to the clients. The results of the command executed are then sent back to that person called the bot herder. After the architecture, common botnet features of e-mail spam, spyware, Bitcoin Mining, Distributed denial-of-service and click fraud are listed. Botnet detection techniques (Mathews et al., 2016) are discussed along with various researches done on these techniques. The first detection technique that is discussed is the Honeypot-based botnet detection technique that is further divided into low-interaction honeypots and high-interaction honeypots (Provos et al., 2007). The second detection technique that is explained in the chapter is the network-based botnet detection technique wherein different models like BotMiner (Gu et al., 2008), SBotMiner (Yu et al., 2010) and BotSniffer (Gu et al., 2008) are elaborated. The differences in the implementation can sometimes be used to identify the botnets. For example, some botnets use services like DynDns.org, No-IP.com, and Afraid.org that are free Domain Name System (DNS) hosting services which themselves do not host attacks. They point to a *subdomain* towards an Internet Relay Chat server. This server caters to the bots. Rather, they provide the reference points, which can be, removed (Choi et al., 2007). These can incapacitate an entire botnet. Countermeasures like these to curb botnets are discussed along with the exiting software(s) that fulfill this purpose like the Norton AntiBot.

The authors then propose a botnet DDoS mitigation system through access list based configurations. They are designed at the ISP (Internet Service Provider's) edge routers in order to prevent DDoS attacks over ISPs' network traffic. Access Control Lists secure the system by restricting user and device access to a network using packet filtering. The last section of the chapter provides an understanding of the WannaCry Ransomware Attack, which locked the computers in more than 150 countries. In total, the chapter covers the following topics and focuses on:

- **Denial-of-Service Attack:**
  - Types of DoS attacks
  - DoS attack techniques
  - DoS attack symptoms
  - DoS attack defense techniques
- **Botnets:**
  - Botnet architecture
  - Botnet applications
  - Botnet features
  - Botnet detection techniques
  - Countermeasures against botnets
- An approach to secure a network from botnet DDoS attacks using access control lists
- **Case Study:** WannaCry Ransomware Attack

BACKGROUND

In a denial of service attack, the attacker prevents the utilization of resources of an authenticates legal user. In other words, services are disrupted by flooding the network. This also reduces the bandwidth provided to the user. According to 2004 CSI/FBI survey report[1], 17 percent of respondent's detected DoS attacks directed against them, with the respondents indicating that DoS was most common and costly cyber attack on them, even before the theft of proprietary information. These DoS attacks can be classified into two general forms listed below:

- **Crashing Attacks:** Sending the target information leading to a crash.
- **Flooding Attacks:** Flooding the target with traffic, depriving the legitimate users of the services.

Distributed attacks also came into existence soon after Denial of Service attacks. In such attacks, separate sites are used for execution to as Distributed Denial-of-Service (DDoS) attacks. In a distributed denial-of-service (DDoS) attack, which is a cyber attack, a large number of IP addresses that are unique are used. Thousands of IP addresses may be used by the perpetrator. The scale of DDoS has risen tremendously after it was discovered. In 2016, it exceeded a terabit per second. In the past years, the tools, methods, and techniques used for DDoS attacks have improved and have become more sophisticated and effective. This has made difficult to trace and find to the real attackers. The attacking techniques have become so advanced that the present technologies have to surrender to such large-scale attacks. A DoS attack resembles a group of people standing at the entry door or gate to a movie theatre, having valid tickets. The normal service is said to be disrupted when they are not being let in. Usually high-profile web servers of high-profit organizations, multi-nationals, finance companies etc. are targeted by the cybercriminals. Blackmailing and activism in the form of ransom may be done. Incoming traffic is flooded into the system in a distributed denial-of-service (DDoS) attack. Numerous unique IP addresses are used for DDoS attack. This effectively creates problems like:

- Blocking one IP address doesn't curb the attack
- Differentiating or distinguishing between legitimate and illegitimate traffic from user and attacker respectively is very tedious
- Involvement of IP address spoofing which defeats ingress filtering

The number of savages abusing the internet for their mean purposes has increased with the popularity of the internet. Bots are the most common choice to attack networks. In other words, a bot is nothing but a type of malware. A bot is written and programmed in a way to access the Internet and hijack the hosts. Botnets are used as a kick-start for denial of service (DoS) attacks, sending spam and junk mails. It is also used as a platform to host scam pages. Usually, the victim is tricked to install the bot himself. This is generally achieved by taking advantage of software or browser vulnerability. A channel called the command and control channel is then established by the bot with compromised machine. As the name suggests its function is to send commands to the compromised machine thereby taking the full control., This feature of bots separates it from other types of malware. A malicious entity, called the bot-master is used to control all other bot-infected machines. The whole system is referred to a botnet.

There are many traditional means of defense against bots that are available in the market, for example, installation of anti-virus software on the end users' machines. Unfortunately, these methods do not provide enough protection against attacks like DDoS, which is becoming more efficient with its evolution. It is mainly because of the reason that this antivirus software's have been programmed and made based on the already known samples, making the defense difficult. In order to keep up with the fast-rising malware, a large number of defense systems that are host-based have come into play. The behavior of unknown programs is captured by using static or dynamic analysis techniques. However, these systems have a disadvantage of runtime overhead and are problematic in practice. Installation of a platform for analysis is also required by every user. It is desirable to have a network-based detection system for host-based analysis technique, in order to supervise and identify the symptoms of traffic on computers that are bot-infected. The next section gives an insight of the chapter.

INSIGHT OF THE CHAPTER

In this chapter, an overview of DoS attack types is given after which, DoS attack techniques are elaborated in a tabular form by the authors. Its well-known symptoms and defense techniques are then listed. The types of DoS attacks that are explained in the chapter include Denial-of-service as a service, Advanced persistent DoS (APDoS) and Distributed DoS. Some of the DoS attack techniques that are explained in the chapter include Internet Control Message Protocol (ICMP) flood, attack tools that are Predators Face, Rolling Thunder, *MyDoom, Stacheldraht* and Low Orbit Ion Cannon, Peer-to-peer attacks, application-layer floods (LAND attack, *XDoS*), Degradation-of-service attacks, Distributed DoS attack, DDoS extortion, Nuke, Telephony denial-of-service (TDoS), Teardrop attacks, (S)SYN flood, Shrew attack, sophisticated low-bandwidth Distributed Denial-of-Service Attack etc. The defense techniques and the solutions proposed on these attacks that are presented include a composition of attack detection, response, and traffic classification such as upstream filtering, DDS based defense, blackholing and sinkholing, firewalls, routers, IPS based prevention, switches, and application front-end hardware. A detailed explanation of botnets is then presented in the chapter. Its application and architecture models including peer-to-peer and client-server model are discussed. Some of the common botnet features such as e-mail spam, spyware, Bitcoin Mining, Distributed denial-of-service, etc. and its detection techniques like honeypots, BotMiner, etc. are discussed in the section following architecture models. The authors then propose a botnet DDoS mitigation system through access list based configurations. In the section below an analysis on DoS attacks is done.

DENIAL-OF-SERVICE (DOS) ATTACKS

Denial-of-service attacks have used several techniques to crash or hang up machines with large volumes of traffic. The attackers may scan millions of computer devices connected to the internet and search unsecured ports and other loopholes. Daemons on intermediate machines are then installed through batch processes, which then wait for orders from master machine. The section below focuses on types of DoS attacks, their symptoms and defense techniques along with various research works done in the field. The types of DoS attacks are listed below.

Types of Denial-of-Service Attacks

A few prominent examples show the different types of DDoS techniques that hackers use: This section elaborates on the various types of DoS attacks such as DDoS, Advanced persistent DoS (APDos), Denial-of-service as a service, which is as follows:

- **Distributed DoS:** In this cyber attack, more than one unique *IP address,* crossing over a thousand, are used. These multi-person attacks are harder to deflect, due to more number of devices involved. DDoS attacks target the network infrastructure. They fill it with a large volume of traffic. A Trojan usually infects these systems using a Denial of Service (DoS) attack. Figure 1 shows a botnet DDoS attack.
- **Denial-of-Service as a Service:** These are the "booter" or "stresser" services that are now provided by some of the vendors and accept payment over the web. Unauthorized denial-of-service attacks can be performed by these services by allowing technical access of the attacker to the tool without understanding its use. The next section lists the symptoms of DoS attacks identified by US-CERT.
- **Advanced Persistent DoS (APDoS):** These attacks require a specialized monitoring and present an obvious and growing threat involving massive network layer DDoS attacks. Characteristics of APDoS attacks include tactical execution, large computing capacity, advanced reconnaissance and extended period persistence. An APDoSis more likely to be led by exceptionally artful and skilled actors having high-level resources and capacity. APDoS attacks have proved to be a clear threat. They require a lot of monitoring and defensive services. In the section below, the symptoms of DoS attacks have been listed.

Figure 1. Botnet diagram showing DDoS attack

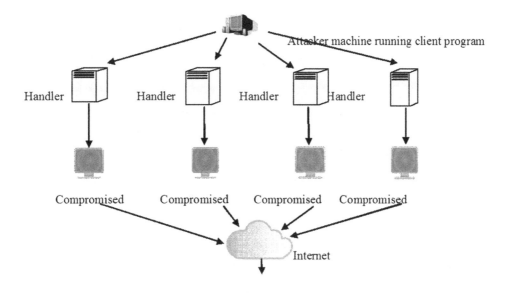

Symptoms of Denial-of-Service Attacks

Symptoms of a denial-of-service attack have been identified by the United States Computer Emergency Readiness Team (US-CERT)[2]. These are as follows:

- Speed Issue or slow *network performance.*
- Website not reachable or reachability issue.
- A drastic number of spam emails or email bomb attack.
- Networking wire issue, connection failure issue.
- Internet access is denied for a long period of time.

In the following section, DoS attack techniques have been elaborated in a tabular form along with their description.

DoS Attack Techniques

A broad spectrum of programs is used to commence DoS-attacks. In this section, various DoS attack techniques are listed in table 1. Figure 2 shows the structure of a land attack (Damon et al., 2012) and Figure 3 shows the architecture of a normal BitTorrent swarm (Hoßfeld et al., 2011).

The section below gives an overview of the techniques providing defense against DoS attacks.

Figure 2. Structure of land attack

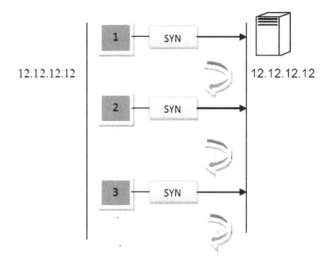

Figure 3. Architecture of a normal BitTorrent swarm

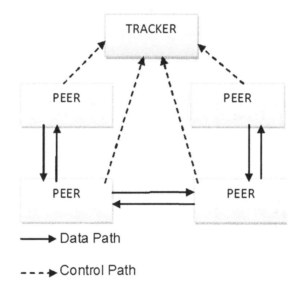

DoS Attack Defense Techniques

The defense techniques include a combination of attack detection (Jin et al., 2004), traffic classification (Douligeris et al., 2004) and response tools. Their purpose is to block traffic that they identify as illegitimate and allow traffic that they identify as legitimate. A list of techniques is given below in Table 2.

The next section gives an overview of botnets.

Table 1. DoS attack techniques

DoS ATTACK TECHNIQUES	DESCRIPTION
Attack tools	Government Communications Headquarters has PREDATORS FACE and ROLLING THUNDER tools built for DDoS. In MyDoom[3] the attacks are launched without the system owner knowing it whereas Low Orbit Ion Cannon (LOIC)[4] is used with user's consent. Stacheldraht[5] uses a layered structure. A client program is used by the attacker to connect to handlers.
Application-layer floods	Various exploits affect the memory of the system by eating up all the available memory or taking up all the disk space. Application level attacks focus their attack on one or a few applications, e.g. LAND attack, XDoS, etc. Some examples of application specific targets Web-based email apps, WordPress, Joomla, and forum software. Figure 4 shows the percentage of application layer attacks[6].
Degradation-of-service attacks	These attacks disrupt websites for time and can be more difficult to detect than a regular zombie invasion. It causes more concentrated floods, slowing server response times.
Distributed DoS attack	It is a cyber attack similar to DoS attack using numerous unique IP addresses.
DDoS extortion	A ransom is asked from the user of the attacked system against the warning of carrying out a larger attack or leaking the user information stored on it. The ransom is usually paid in Bitcoin[7].
Internet Control Message Protocol (ICMP) flood	In this type of flooding, a huge amount of IP packets are sent, affecting the bandwidth of the network. The packets never reach the required destination, as the address sending the packets is dummied with that of the victim. The "ping" command from Unix-like hosts is used to flood the network with ping flooding.
Nuke	The computer is slowed down and finally halted by sending invalid ICMP flood packets to the target in this attack via a modified ping utility. This is done by repeatedly sending corrupt data.
Peer-to-peer attacks	In this attack, the attacker plays the role of a "ringmaster". It instructs clients to connect to the website of the victim and disconnect to their peers.
Permanent denial-of-service attacks	It is an attack that damages hardware of a system such as memory crash, ports failure etc.
Reflected/spoofed attack	It requires sending counterfeit requests of a particular type to thousand of systems that will then reply to them.
Telephony denial-of-service (TDoS)	Calls have become inexpensive and automated with the introduction of Voice over IP. Through caller ID, spoofing fake calls can be placed.
Teardrop attacks	This attack can crash various operating systems as it involves sending mangled IP fragments because of which overlapping of packets occurs. The target machine cannot reassemble these packets because of a bug in TCP/IP fragmentation reassembly (Marin & Gerald, 2005).
(S)SYN flood	In this attack, a number of TCP/SYN packets, with counterfeit source address are sent by the host. Therefore, the response to legitimate requests never comes, causing saturation of half-open connections. (Lemon & Jonathan, 2002). The SYN-ACK communication process involves three steps. It is like handshake protocol which involves SYN & ACK message packet sending and receiving.
R-U-Dead-Yet? (RUDY)	The sessions on the web server are denied by making them unavailable to the victim web applications.
Sophisticated low-bandwidth DDoS Attack	This attack aims at a fatal flaw of the target machine by sending complicated requests to the system.
Shrew attack	This attack disrupts TCP connections by using short synchronized bursts of traffic.
UDP Flood	User Datagram Protocol is a networking protocol wherein flooding of packets is done on random ports of the target machine. They then report back with an ICMP packet.
Ping of Death	Ping of death overwrites the IP packet by sending packets larger than the maximum capacity. Large packets are fragmented across multiple IP packets. They are then reassembled and the resulting packet causes servers to reboot or crash.
Slowloris	Slowloris establishes a low bandwidth consuming connection with the target machine and keeps it open for a long time, affecting its web server. This is achieved using partial HTTP requests that are sent to the target machine and remain uncompleted.

Figure 4. Percentage targets of application-layer attacks

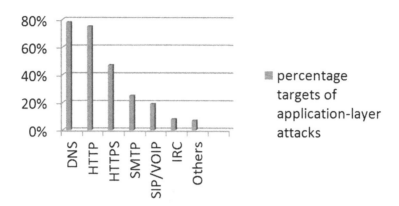

Table 2. List of DoS attack defense techniques

DEFENSE TECHNIQUES	DESCRIPTION
Application front end hardware	It is used along with routers and switches analyzing data packets as they enter the system. These data packets are then categorized as a priority, regular, or dangerous.
DDS based defense	It can address both protocol and rate-based attacks by blocking a DoS attack with legitimate content but bad intent.
Blackholing and sinkholing	In blackholing routing, traffic to the attacked IP address is forwarded to non-existent server i.e. a 'black hole'. In sinkholing, traffic is forwarded to a valid IP address for the analysis purpose which then rejected the Bad Packets.
Firewalls	They can prove to be very useful in a simple attack as they can cater to a simple rule which denies all incoming traffic from the attacker.
Routers	Routers reduce the effects of flooding and are set manually. They have some rate-limiting and Access Control List capability.
IPS based prevention	Intrusion Prevention System (IPS) works on the principle of content recognition. They find their use if the attacks have footprints associated with them. It cannot block DoS attack which is based on the behavior.
Switches	Most switches support access control list capabilities to detect and reform DoS attacks.
Upstream filtering	Different methods like proxies, digital cross-connects, tunnels etc. separating the unwanted traffic and sending only the 'good' traffic to the server. It uses the concept of "cleaning center" or a "scrubbing center".

BOTNETS

In the section below, botnet application, its architecture, features, detection techniques and ways to mitigate have been mentioned (Liu et al., 2009).

Botnet Application and Architecture

Botnets are now rented out as commodities for a number of purposes, by *cybercriminals*. It consists of compromised networks wherein each compromised device is referred to as a "bot". These bots over the time have progressed to dodge their detection. Figure 5 depicts typical botnet architecture. The two botnet architectures are as follows:

1. Client-Server Model

Initially, botnets on the internet used this architecture to fulfill their task. Clients that are infected by the attack await incoming commands from the server as they access a location which is already specified. These commands generated by the person operating the botnet called as the bot herder are then further forwarded to the clients. Power engines of the botnets include Internet Relay Chat (IRC) networks, domains, or websites. These commands are then performed by the client the result obtained is reported back to the bot herder.

2. Peer-to-Peer

Now, the bot herders have started to input traffic and malware on P2P networks as a result of detection of Internet Relay Chat (IRC) botnets. Digital signatures might be used by these bots allowing only a person with access to the key of the botnet network to control the botnet. Newer botnets communicate with a centralized server, where command distribution server and a client who receives commands, both are performed by a P2P bot.

Common Botnet Features

The common botnet features are listed in Table 3.
Botnet detection techniques have been listed in the section below.

Figure 5. Architecture of a Botnet

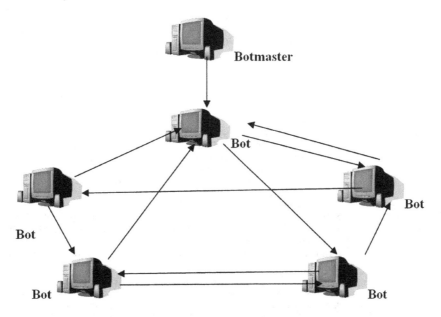

Table 3. Common botnet features

COMMON BOTNET FEATURES	DESCRIPTION
Distributed denial-of-service	In order to connect to the network, the victim receives a lot of requests by the bots.
Spyware	Private and confidential information like bank account and credit card numbers is sent to the creator of the Spyware who could further misuse or sell the data.
Bitcoin Mining	This feature generates profits for the operator of the botnet.
E-mail spam	E-mail messages are disguised as messages from people. In reality, they are malicious.
Click fraud	User's computer visits websites without his/her knowing it. Fake web traffic is hence created for monitory benefits and commercial gain.

Botnet Detection Techniques

The common detection techniques for botnet are mentioned in Table 4.

Measures Against Botnet

Some botnets use services like DynDns.org, No-IP.com, and Afraid.org that are free Domain Name System (DNS) hosting services which themselves do not host attacks. They point to a subdomain towards an Internet Relay Chat server. This server caters to the bots. Rather, they provide the reference points, which can be removed. The attacks are not hosted by these free DNS services. Rather, they provide the reference points which can be removed. These can incapacitate an entire botnet. Some botnets inherit the properties of customized versions of famous protocols and hence are based on them. The differences in implementation can be analyzed in order to detect the botnets. Software to counter botnets has now been released by computer and network security companies, e.g. Norton AntiBot. In the next section, solutions and recommendations to botnet DDoS attack have been proposed.

Table 4. Botnet detection and Identification techniques

BOTNET DETECTION TECHNIQUES	DESCRIPTION
Honeypot-based botnet detection	A honeypot is a resource, used to detect and deflect unauthorized use of information system (Weiler, 2002). The two types of honeypots are: • Low-interaction honeypots: They affect only the frequently requested services by attackers. Hosting multiple virtual machines is easy in this case. E.g. Honeyd • High-interaction honeypots: They provide more security by being difficult to detect. A number of honeypots can be used by using virtual machines. Therefore, restoration of honeypots is quick after being compromised.
Network-based Botnet Detection	Some of the models proposed for Network-based Botnet detection are as follows: • BotMiner: To identify malicious activity manner accomplished by a bot, BotMiner performs a cross-cluster correlation. • SBotMiner: The main goal of the approach is to find a group of bots that generate low rate traffic. • BotSniffer: This detection approach can identify both C&C (Command and Control) servers and infected hosts in the network. The process is carried out using network-based anomaly detection and without any known information about signatures or C&C server addresses.

BOTNET DDOS ATTACK: SOLUTIONS AND RECOMMENDATIONS

In the above section, we studied that botnet is a group of hijacked devices that are connected to the internet. Each device injected with malware that is hidden from the owner of the device and is controlled by a remote region. Figure 6 shows the distribution of botnet Command and Control (C&C) servers in quarter 4 of 2016. A botnet DDoS attack may have multiple origins, i.e. it may be controlled by multiple individuals working in a coordinated manner. Many solutions have been proposed to prevent and to defend against botnet DDoS attack. One of the effective solutions proposed was using dynamic reconfiguration in 5G Mobile Networks (Pérez et al., 2017). Solutions in cloud computing environment have also been proposed (Somani et al., 2017; Osanaiye et al., 2016) that presented a conceptual cloud DDoS mitigation framework. Blackholing at ixps was another effective technique proposed (Dietzel et al., 2016).

From various sources, botnets-for-hire are available. Their services are usually auctioned and traded among attackers. Figure 7 shows the distribution of unique DDoS attack targets. We propose a botnet DDoS mitigation system through access list based configurations. They are deployed at the ISP (Internet Service Provider's) edge routers in order to prevent DDoS attacks over ISPs' network traffic. Access Control Lists secure the system by restricting user and device access to a network using packet filtering. The efficiency of the system is strongly dependent on the responsiveness of ISPs in implementing the system. This coordinated effort by participating ISPs filters out attacks, reducing the load on other routers. Most attacks can easily be stopped close to their point of origin, once each ISP has been implemented in the system. The suspicious traffic is first filtered out based on their source IP address. The first technique spawned as much traffic with different spoofed IP addresses as possible and the second technique generated without spoofed IP addresses. After the testing, it was observed that the bulk of malicious DDoS traffic can be effectively filtered out using proper configuration and filtering rules on the routers. Hence, this mechanism efficiently eliminates bogus traffic from their source, ensuring

Figure 6. Distribution of botnet C&C servers in Q4 2016[8]

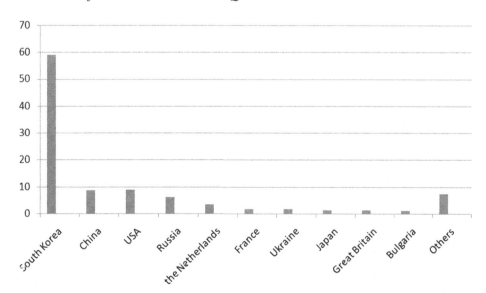

Figure 7. Distribution of unique DDoS attack targets by country, Q3 2016 vs. Q4 2016[9]

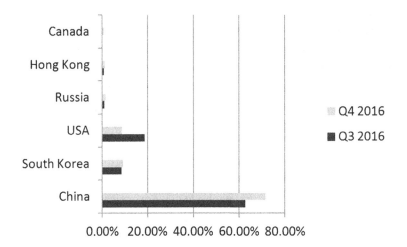

that high priority packets pass through the network and reach the destination and such services are not denied to the clients. Figure 8 classifies the defense mechanisms against network/transport-level DDoS flooding attacks based on their deployment location in a simple network of Autonomous Systems (AS). Figure 9 shows different areas for performing DDoS response and detection.

Setting up the Environment

To test the setup, we were required to generate DDoS traffic ourselves. To generate a lot of traffic to the attacked host, we used two different techniques. We used hping2 as the main tool for generating traffic. Hping is a TCP/IP packet crafter that is command-line oriented. It can be used for creating IP packets containing UDP, TCP or ICMP payloads. Using the command line, all header fields can be controlled and modified.

Figure 8. A classification of the defense mechanisms against network/transport-level DDoS flooding attacks based on their deployment location in a simple network of Autonomous Systems (ASs)

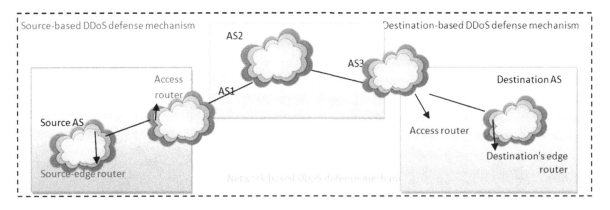

Figure 9. Different areas for performing DDoS response and detection

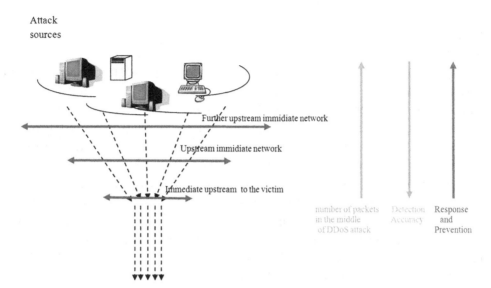

Filtering Rules 1

Only traffic with source addresses belonging to the customer network should be accepted by the ISP edge router. Any source address outside of the customer's network is readily a spoofed IP address. This is required to be implemented on the part of the ISP to prevent customers from participating in such malicious activities. Only traffic with source addresses other than the customer network address-block should be accepted by customer network.

Filtering Rules 2

As opposed to the previous filtering where the source address is filtered, the destination address or port is checked and filtered for filtering. Whatever is not included in the permit list will be rejected. Most of the time ICMP echo and echo-reply packets are allowed to pass through the network as it is an important tool for network troubleshooting and for checking connectivity. However, care must be taken when allowing ICMP traffic coming from the external networks. Although it has been a recommended practice to block known malware ports to prevent misuse of the network through such programs and to reduce the chances of individual computers participating in such activities as zombies, this system of ingress-filtering implicitly blocks any traffic targeted at ports not utilized by the publicly accessible server and thus effectively prevents unused ports from being manipulated. Emsisoft, an anti-malware vendor, has a publicly viewable list of such malware ports. It can be seen from the list that even some well-known ports have been exploited and used to run malicious activities. So, by explicitly allowing access only to specific ports where verified services are being provided is the most effective way to prevent networked systems from being manipulated. The next section covers a case study on the recent WannaCry attack.

CASE STUDY

In a cyber attack, malicious techniques are used to hijack computer machines or a network from an autonomous source, which may be handled, by an individual or an organization. Over the years, these attacks have become more sophisticated and dangerous. Robert Tappan Morris and the Morris Worm which was created in 1988 by a student of Cornell University encountered an error and repeatedly replicated itself and resulted in Denial of Service. 6000 computers were affected by this cyber attack. In 1999, a teen accessed the computers of a US Department of Defense division and installed a 'backdoor' on its servers. Thousands of internal emails from different government organizations were intercepted by him. This included the ones containing usernames and passwords for various military computers.

James used this information and was able to steal a piece of NASA software that cost the space exploration agency $41,000. Their systems were shut down for three weeks. In 2000, another 15-year-old boy named Michael Calce caused problems in the cyberspace by unleashing a number of Distributed Denial of Service attack on leading commercial sites like Amazon, Yahoo!, CNN and eBay. The attack resulted in a $1.2 Billion dollar damage bill. In 2009, a security breach was detected in Google's Chinese headquarters. Intellectual property was stolen, and various Google's servers were accessed by the hackers forcing it to shifts its headquarters to Hong Kong.

One of the biggest data breaches occurred on 3rd October 2013, when Adobe claimed that customer credit card records and login data were stolen and the source code of Adobe's software- Photoshop, Adobe Acrobat Reader, and ColdFusion was exposed. The hackers removed information relating to 2.9 million Adobe customers, including customer names, encrypted credit or debit card numbers, expiration dates, and other information relating to customer orders from the systems. The economic impact of cyber attacks is explained in CRS Report for Congress (Cashell et al., 2004). One of the research works done on cyber attacks by Carnegie Mellon Software Engineering Institute explains their tracking and tracing (Lipson & Howard, 2002). Countermeasures and challenges of cyber attacks were also presented in one of the research works (Li et al., 2012). In a brief issue, cyber attacks on US companies in the year 2014 have been mentioned (Walters & Riley, 2014). In this section, a case study of Wannacy Ransomware Attack is presented.

WannaCry Ransomware Attack

On 14 May'17, computers across the world were hit by a cyber attack, which resulted in locking up of the machines. The files and important documents of the users were held for ransom. The cyber attack mainly focused on government organizations, hospitals, health centers, and multinational companies. Ransomware is a type of Malware (harmful software) that hijacks a system. The user cannot access this system unless the ransom is paid. The ransom is usually paid in Bitcoins.

This type of ransomware was called "WannaCry". The attack halted the systems running banks, transportation, and other multinationals. In total, the cyber attack affected 200,000 victims in more than 150 countries. According to the Japan Computer Emergency, Response Team Coordination Center, a nonprofit group, at 600 locations in Japan was affected which in total included 2,000 systems. The attack also shut down various social media sites disrupting its access. In addition, many people could not take their online driving tests in some regions as the transportation sites of the police department were also affected. Russia's interior ministry and companies including Spain's Telefonica and FedEx corporation in the US where some of the companies that were hit. Multinationals like Hitachi and Nissan Motor Co

Figure 10. Most affected countries of the WannaCry Ransomware

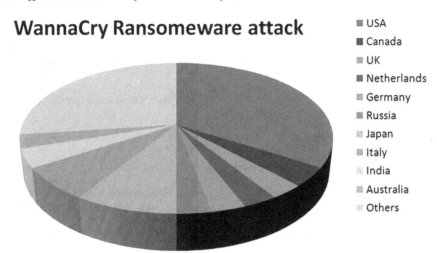

*For a more accurate representation see the electronic version.

were also affected. Chinese media reported 29,372 institutions were infected along with hundreds of thousands of systems. Because schools and universities tend to have old and slow computers with less security and use old versions of operating systems, hence they were the hardest hit. In Indonesia, the locking down of systems affected the hospitals, as the files on the systems could not be accessed. This caused delays. Although, South Korea had a very small amount of cases. Figure 10 shows the percentage of most affected countries.

The idea behind this cyber attack was to trick the user to run a malicious code. In most cases, ransomware affected the systems through the links and attachments that were generally forwarded through e-mail. These e-mails are called phishing e-mails. The malware is hidden in these e-mails in the form of links and attachments. Once this piece of code is run, the malware takes over the system leaving the victim helpless. The important files and documents in the system are then held for ransom. All these files are encrypted by the malware and a message for ransom appears. In order to decrypt these files, the ransom has to be paid. The data may be lost if the ransom is not paid. The key for the encryption is only known to the attacker. People are mining for Bitcoins and various other forms of currency. Cryptocurrency has taken the world by storm. Cryptocurrency in some places has been accepted as a payment for goods and services. Figure 11 shows how do Bitcoins work. When this cyber attack occurs, the malware takes over the computer and the demands of the attacker are mentioned explicitly. Usually, the wallpaper of the affected system is changed. It contains a message specifying the amount to be paid and the method through which it is to be paid in order to recover the files. The attackers mostly demanded between $300and $500 to remove the malicious ransomware. In addition, the price was doubled if the required amount was not paid within the specified time. Although, in many regions, the victims were discouraged to pay the ransom by the law enforcement.

To avoid any cyber attack, one must be cautious. Users should regularly do the following things:

- Users should back up their files and important documents.
- Users should ensure that security and anti-virus updates and patches are installed on their computer as soon as they are released.

Figure 11. Working of Bitcoins

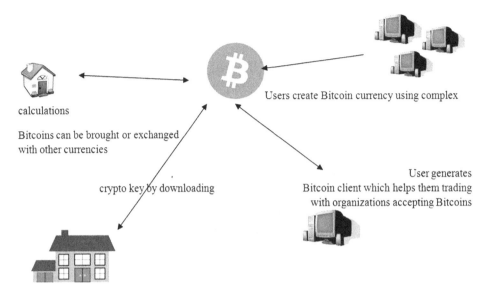

calculations

Bitcoins can be brought or exchanged with other currencies

crypto key by downloading

Users create Bitcoin currency using complex

User generates Bitcoin client which helps them trading with organizations accepting Bitcoins

Business organization accepts payments through Bitcoins and sells to users using unique crypto key

- Backups should be up-to-date. This makes restoration of lost data easy. The user is then not required to pay any ransom.
- It was seen that some loopholes in older versions of Microsoft operating systems were taken advantage of in WannaCry cyber attack. Therefore, it is important to keep the operating system up-to-date.
- Users should also look for malicious or spam email messages that often masquerade as emails from companies or people you often interact with online. Users should not click on these unknown links or download any such unknown files.

The challenge for hospitals was to keep patient data private, secure access to sensitive areas like operation theatres and ensure smooth operations. Some of the steps taken include:

- **Hiring Experts:** All top private hospitals have cybersecurity experts to secure patient information and private hacking.
- **Dedicated Fund:** Hospitals spend anywhere between Rs20 Lakh and Rs 2 Crore for cybersecurity.
- **Strong Password:** Access to Sensitive areas and equipment is controlled with strong passwords.
- **Regular Monitoring:** In a few cases, third-party agencies specializing in cybersecurity are engaged to periodically monitor safeguards.

The Reserve Bank of India (RBI) asked banks to follow instructions issued by Nation' cybersecurity unit CERT-in to prevent the worm from creeping into their systems. Some ATM is running on old the Microsoft Operating System was shut as a precaution.

FUTURE RESEARCH DIRECTIONS

Although users can take, steps to minimize the threat posed by DDoS attacks there are several reasons for concern about the future. Over the time, hackers will become more tempted and may use new fast-growing technologies to plan an attack and overwhelm victims with traffic. This may also overcome the proposed technique or packet filtering techniques. The key to protecting devices is keeping antivirus signatures up-to-date to prevent any future attacks like WannaCry Ransomware. As a part of our future work, detectors in various sub-networks can be introduced. These detectors communicate amongst themselves and warn other sub-networks if they are under attack. For this, we may use multi-agent system approach which has often been used in artificial intelligence. Another challenge is to develop a hypothesis to trace back the source of the attacks since the attacks follow a common pattern. Also, the performance of the technique proposed in this paper needs to be compared with other techniques that are currently being used in terms of false-alarm possibility and response time.

Another evolution in malware would be brought in IoT in the form of thingbots. Thingbots are a variant of botnets that are made up of contaminated IoT devices. These IoT devices can be controlled and supervised to:

- Theft of important sensitive information
- Launching of the attacks
- Other activities that come under cyber crime

In recent years, such activities of thingbots have been observed possessing a threat to cybersecurity. Therefore, there is an urgent need to address IoT related vulnerabilities, especially:

- IoT security
- Adherence to high standards in IoT devices
- Manufacturer and ISP levels should have best standards practice

A cryptocurrency is a value that can be cryptographically secured, and digitally represented and transmitted via the Internet. It is interoperable i.e. it is convertible and transferable. Interoperability is a more practical and credible outcome that requiring less damage to the incumbent. The future development in cryptocurrency is shown in Table 5.

CONCLUSION

Botnet DDoS attack is currently one of the most cardinal threats on the Internet. Moreover, its early detection is also a big challenge. This is mainly because of the characteristics and volume of traffic change at a rattling pace. Therefore, updating the filtering rules and antivirus software is of utmost importance. This chapter mainly included an overview of DoS attacks and botnets. It further improves the measuring and understanding of botnet DDoS attacks and how to deal with them. We also proposed a defending methodology against botnet DDoS attacks. The case study of WannaCry ransomware attack showcases the current situation of malware existing and how much preparation we are for these attacks. In this chapter, the authors did an analysis on DoS attacks like Denial-of-service as a service, advanced persistent DoS

Table 5. Developments in cryptocurrency

DEVELOPMENT AREA	DESCRIPTION
Online Shopping	Bitcoin wallets are now available in most of the leading online shopping websites. It was observed that 2.3 billion people now shop on Amazon using Bitcoins.
Education	Cryptocurrency transactions will soon be moving beyond the digital boundaries and will be accepted as investment opportunities.
Prioritizing privacy	It is very easy to find the details and spending habits of the sender of Bitcoins participating in a transaction. In the future cryptocurrencies like Monero will gain more popularity because of its privacy settings.
Significant capacity	Researchers are working on new algorithms (Ahuja & Yadav, 2013) (Bhushan, Gupta & Yadav, 2016) (Bhushan & Yadav, 2014) (Kamal 2016) (Tayal 2016) and programs in order to overcome blockchain issues. This will expand the reach of cryptocurrencies beyond its present limitations.

(APDoS) and Distributed DoS is done. An overview on DoS attacking methodologies including attack tools, Low Orbit Ion Cannon, application-layer floods (LAND attack, XDoS), Degradation-of-service attacks, Nuke, Distributed DoS attack, Peer-to-peer attacks, DDoS extortion, R-U-Dead-Yet? (RUDY), Shrew attack, Internet Control Message Protocol (ICMP) flood, Telephony denial-of-service (TDoS), Teardrop attacks, (S) SYN flood and so on. The defense techniques and the solutions proposed in these attacks were then presented. Botnet application and architecture models including peer-to-peer and client-server model were successfully discussed in the chapter. Common botnet features of e-mail spam, spyware, Bitcoin mining, distributed denial-of-service and click fraud and botnet detection techniques were listed.

It was also seen that the bulk of malicious DDoS traffic could be effectively filtered out using proper configuration and filtering rules on the routers. This mechanism efficiently eliminates bogus traffic from their source and based on the type of packet and the volume of traffic at that instance, it is either allowed to pass through the network to the targeted host or queued or completely dropped at the destination. This ensures high priority packets to pass through the network and reach the destination and such services are not denied to the clients. From the above, it can be seen that proper filtering of packets at the point of origin can greatly reduce the amount of malicious traffic going through a network. Once such packets are filtered, they do not reach their intended destination. A coordinated effort across all ISPs would reduce such malicious packets and ultimately reduce the load on targeted hosts and the target network. This also prevents the individual internet users from participating in such activities. A case study on WannaCry Ransom Attack was also done.

REFERENCES

Ahuja, Y., & Yadav, S. K. (2013). Statistical Approach to Support Vector Machine. [IJEAT]. *International Journal of Engineering and Advanced Technology*, 2(3), 556–559.

Alejandre, F. V., Cortés, N. C., & Anaya, E. A. (2017, February). Feature selection to detect botnets using machine learning algorithms. In *Proceedings of the International Conference on Electronics, Communications and Computers (CONIELECOMP)*. 10.1109/CONIELECOMP.2017.7891834

Bhatt, C. M., Dey, N., & Ashour, A. (2017). Internet of Things and Big Data Technologies for Next Generation Healthcare (Vol. 23).

Bhushan, M., Gupta, A., & Yadav, S. K. (2016). Big Data Suite for Market Prediction and Reducing Complexity Using Bloom Filter. *The Human Element of Big Data: Issues, Analytics, and Performance*, 281.

Bhushan, M., & Yadav, S. K. (2014). Cost based Model for Big Data Processing with Hadoop Architecture. *Global Journal of Computer Science and Technology*, *14*(2-C), 13.

Carl, G., Kesidis, G., Brooks, R. R., & Rai, S. (2006). Denial-of-service attack-detection techniques. *IEEE Internet Computing*, *10*(1), 82–89. doi:10.1109/MIC.2006.5

Cashell, B., Jackson, W. D., Jickling, M., & Webel, B. (2004). The economic impact of cyber-attacks. *Congressional Research Service Document,* Retrieved from http://www.au.af.mil/au/awc/awcgate/crs/rl32331.pdf

Choi, H., Lee, H., Lee, H., & Kim, H. (2007, October). Botnet detection by monitoring group activities in DNS traffic. In *Proceedings of the 7th IEEE International Conference on Computer and Information Technology* (pp. 715-720). 10.1109/CIT.2007.90

Cooke, E., Jahanian, F., & McPherson, D. (2005). The Zombie Roundup: Understanding, Detecting, and Disrupting Botnets. *SRUTI*, *5*, 6.

Damon, E., Dale, J., Laron, E., Mache, J., Land, N., & Weiss, R. (2012, October). Hands-on denial of service lab exercises using slowloris and rudy. In Proceedings of the 2012 information security curriculum development conference, 21-29. doi:10.1145/2390317.2390321

Danchev, D. (2010). Study finds the average price for renting a botnet. *Zdnet.com*. Retrieved from http://www.zdnet.com/article/study-finds-the-average-price-for-renting-a-botnet/

Desai, M., Patel, S., Somaiya, P., & Vishwanathan, V. (2016). Prevention of Distributed Denial of Service Attack using Web Referrals: A Review. *International Research Journal of Engineering and Technology*, *3*(4), 1994–1996.

Dey, N., Ashour, A. S., & Bhatt, C. (2017). Internet of Things Driven Connected Healthcare. In Internet of Things and Big Data Technologies for Next Generation Healthcare (pp. 3-12). doi:10.1007/978-3-319-49736-5_1

Dietzel, C., Feldmann, A., & King, T. (2016, March). Blackholing at ixps: On the effectiveness of ddos mitigation in the wild. In *Proceedings of the International Conference on Passive and Active Network Measurement* (pp. 319-332). 10.1007/978-3-319-30505-9_24

Douligeris, C., & Mitrokotsa, A. (2004). DDoS attacks and defense mechanisms: Classification and state-of-the-art. *Computer Networks*, *44*(5), 643–666. doi:10.1016/j.comnet.2003.10.003

Elhayatmy, G., Dey, N., & Ashour, A. S. (2018). Internet of Things Based Wireless Body Area Network in Healthcare. In Internet of Things and Big Data Analytics Toward Next-Generation Intelligence (pp. 3-20). doi:10.1007/978-3-319-60435-0_1

Feinstein, L., Schnackenberg, D., Balupari, R., & Kindred, D. (2003, April). Statistical approaches to DDoS attack detection and response. In DARPA Information Survivability Conference and Exposition (pp. 303-314). doi:10.1109/DISCEX.2003.1194894

Gu, G., Perdisci, R., Zhang, J., & Lee, W. (2008, July). BotMiner: Clustering Analysis of Network Traffic for Protocol-and Structure-Independent Botnet Detection. *USENIX Security Symposium*, 5(2), 139-154.

Gu, G., Zhang, J., & Lee, W. (2008). BotSniffer: Detecting botnet command and control channels in network traffic. In *Proceedings of the Network and Distributed System Security Symposium*, San Diego, CA.

Gupta, B. B., Joshi, R. C., Misra, M., Meena, D. L., Shrivastava, G., & Sharma, K. (2010). Detecting a Wide Range of Flooding DDoS Attacks using Linear Prediction Model. In *Proceedings of the 2nd International Conference on Information and Multimedia Technology (ICIMT 2010)* (Vol. 2, pp. 535-539).

Hasbullah, H., & Soomro, I. A. (2010). Denial of service (DOS) attack and its possible solutions in VANET. *International Journal of Electrical, Computer, Energetic, Electronic and Communication Engineering*, 4(5), 813–817.

Hoßfeld, T., Lehrieder, F., Hock, D., Oechsner, S., Despotovic, Z., Kellerer, W., & Michel, M. (2011). Characterization of BitTorrent swarms and their distribution in the Internet. *Computer Networks*, 55(5), 1197–1215. doi:10.1016/j.comnet.2010.11.011

Jain, A., & Bhatnagar, V. (2017). Concoction of Ambient Intelligence and Big Data for Better Patient Ministration Services. *International Journal of Ambient Computing and Intelligence*, 8(4), 19–30. doi:10.4018/IJACI.2017100102

Jin, S., & Yeung, D. S. (2004, June). A covariance analysis model for DDoS attack detection. In *Proceedings of the IEEE International Conference on Communications* (Vol. 4, pp. 1882-1886).

Kamal, S., Ripon, S. H., Dey, N., Ashour, A. S., & Santhi, V. (2016). A MapReduce approach to diminish imbalance parameters for big deoxyribonucleic acid dataset. *Computer Methods and Programs in Biomedicine*, 131, 191–206. doi:10.1016/j.cmpb.2016.04.005 PMID:27265059

Kang, J., & Zhang, J. Y. (2009, May). Application entropy theory to detect new peer-to-peer botnet with multi-chart CUSUM. In *Proceedings of the Second International Symposium on Electronic Commerce and Security* (Vol. 1, pp. 470-474). 10.1109/ISECS.2009.61

Kimbahune, V. V., Deshpande, A. V., & Mahalle, P. N. (2017). Lightweight Key Management for Adaptive Addressing in Next Generation Internet. *International Journal of Ambient Computing and Intelligence*, 8(1), 50–69. doi:10.4018/IJACI.2017010103

Kumar, R., Arun, P., & Selvakumar, S. (2009, March). Distributed denial-of-service (ddos) threat in collaborative environment-a survey on ddos attack tools and traceback mechanisms. In *Proceedings of the IEEE International Advance Computing Conference* (pp. 1275-1280).

Lemon, J. (2002, February). Resisting SYN Flood DoS Attacks with a SYN Cache. In *BSDCon* (pp. 89-97).

Li, X., Liang, X., Lu, R., Shen, X., Lin, X., & Zhu, H. (2012). Securing smart grid: Cyber attacks, countermeasures, and challenges. *IEEE Communications Magazine*, 50(8), 38–45. doi:10.1109/MCOM.2012.6257525

Lipson, H. F. (2002). Tracking and tracing cyber-attacks: Technical challenges and global policy issues. Retrieved from https://resources.sei.cmu.edu/library/asset-view.cfm?assetid=5831

Liu, H. (2010, October). A new form of DOS attack in a cloud and its avoidance mechanism. In *Proceedings of the 2010 ACM workshop on Cloud computing security workshop* (pp. 65-76). 10.1145/1866835.1866849

Liu, J., Xiao, Y., Ghaboosi, K., Deng, H., & Zhang, J. (2009, December). Botnet: Classification, attacks, detection, tracing, and preventive measures. *EURASIP Journal on Wireless Communications and Networking, 2009*(1), 1184–1187. doi:10.1155/2009/692654

Long, N., & Thomas, R. (2001). Trends in denial of service attack technology. *CERT Coordination Center*. Retrieved from https://resources.sei.cmu.edu/library/asset-view.cfm?assetid=52490

Marin, G. A. (2005). Network security basics. *IEEE Security and Privacy, 3*(6), 68–72. doi:10.1109/MSP.2005.153

Matallah, H., Belalem, G., & Bouamrane, K. (2017). Towards a New Model of Storage and Access to Data in Big Data and Cloud Computing. *International Journal of Ambient Computing and Intelligence, 8*(4), 31–44. doi:10.4018/IJACI.2017100103

Mathews, M. L., Joshi, A., & Finin, T. (2016, February). Detecting botnets using a collaborative situational-aware idps. In *Proceedings of the Second International Conference on Information Systems Security and Privacy* (Vol. 1, pp. 290-298). 10.5220/0005684902900298

Mirkovic, J., & Reiher, P. (2004). A taxonomy of DDoS attack and DDoS defense mechanisms. *Computer Communication Review, 34*(2), 39–53. doi:10.1145/997150.997156

Mukherjee, A., Dey, N., Kausar, N., Ashour, A. S., Taiar, R., & Hassanien, A. E. (2016). A disaster management specific mobility model for flying ad-hoc network. *International Journal of Rough Sets and Data Analysis, 3*(3), 72–103. doi:10.4018/IJRSDA.2016070106

Ollmann, G. (2009). Botnet communication topologies. *Retrieved from* http://www.technicalinfo.net/papers/PDF/WP_Botnet_Communications_Primer_(2009-06-04).pdf

Osanaiye, O., Choo, K. K. R., & Dlodlo, M. (2016). Distributed denial of service (DDoS) resilience in cloud: Review and conceptual cloud DDoS mitigation framework. *Journal of Network and Computer Applications, 67*, 147–165. doi:10.1016/j.jnca.2016.01.001

Park, K., & Lee, H. (2001, August). On the effectiveness of route-based packet filtering for distributed DoS attack prevention in power-law internets. *Computer Communication Review, 31*(4), 15–26. doi:10.1145/964723.383061

Pérez, M. G., Celdrán, A. H., Ippoliti, F., Giardina, P. G., Bernini, G., Alaez, R. M., ... Carrozzo, G. (2017). Dynamic Reconfiguration in 5G Mobile Networks to Proactively Detect and Mitigate Botnets. *IEEE Internet Computing, 21*(5), 28–36. doi:10.1109/MIC.2017.3481345

Poturalski, M., Flury, M., Papadimitratos, P., Hubaux, J. P., & Le Boudec, J. Y. (2010, September). The cicada attack: degradation and denial of service in IR ranging. In *Proceedings of the IEEE International Conference on Ultra-Wideband* (Vol. 2). 10.1109/ICUWB.2010.5616900

Provos, N., & Holz, T. (2007). *Virtual honeypots: from botnet tracking to intrusion detection*. Pearson Education database.

Saha, S., Nandi, S., Verma, R., Sengupta, S., Singh, K., Sinha, V., & Das, S. K. (2016). Design of efficient lightweight strategies to combat DoS attack in delay tolerant network routing. *Wireless Networks*.

Senie, D., & Ferguson, P. (1998). Network ingress filtering: Defeating denial of service attacks which employ IP source address spoofing. *Network. Retrieved from* https://buildbot.tools.ietf.org/html/rfc2267

Shrivastava, G., Sharma, K., & Rai, S. (2010, December). The Detection & Defense of DoS & DDoS Attack: A Technical Overview. In *Proceeding of ICC* (Vol. 27, p. 28).

Somani, G., Gaur, M. S., Sanghi, D., Conti, M., & Buyya, R. (2017). Service resizing for quick DDoS mitigation in cloud computing environment. *Annales des Télécommunications*, *72*(5-6), 237–252. doi:10.100712243-016-0552-5

Tayal, D. K., & Yadav, S. K. (2016). Fast retrieval approach of sentimental analysis with implementation of bloom filter on Hadoop. In *Proceedings of the 2016 International Conference on Computational Techniques in Information and Communication Technologies (ICCTICT)* (pp. 14-18). IEEE. 10.1109/ICCTICT.2016.7514544

Tayal, D. K., & Yadav, S. K. (2017). Sentiment analysis on social campaign "Swachh Bharat Abhiyan" using unigram method. *AI & Society*, *32*(4), 633–645. doi:10.100700146-016-0672-5

Ullah, I., Khan, N., & Aboalsamh, H. A. (2013, April). Survey on botnet: Its architecture, detection, prevention and mitigation. In *Proceedings of the 10th IEEE International Conference on Networking, Sensing and Control (ICNSC)* (pp. 660-665). 10.1109/ICNSC.2013.6548817

Walters, R. (2014). Cyber attacks on US companies in 2014. *Heritage Foundation Issue Brief, 4289*.

Weiler, N. (2002). Honeypots for distributed denial-of-service attacks. In *Proceedings of the Eleventh IEEE International Workshops on Enabling Technologies: Infrastructure for Collaborative Enterprises* (pp. 109-114).

Yadav, P., Sharma, S., Tiwari, P., Dey, N., Ashour, A. S., & Nguyen, G. N. (2018). A Modified Hybrid Structure for Next Generation Super High Speed Communication Using TDLTE and Wi-Max. In Internet of Things and Big Data Analytics Toward Next-Generation Intelligence (pp. 525-549). doi:10.1007/978-3-319-60435-0_21

Yamin, M., & Sen, A. A. A. (2018). Improving Privacy and Security of User Data in Location Based Services. *International Journal of Ambient Computing and Intelligence*, *9*(1), 19–42. doi:10.4018/IJACI.2018010102

Yu, F., Xie, Y., & Ke, Q. (2010, February). Sbotminer: large scale search bot detection. In *Proceedings of the third ACM international conference on Web search and data mining* (pp. 421-430). 10.1145/1718487.1718540

Zhang, H., Cheng, P., Shi, L., & Chen, J. (2016). Optimal DoS attack scheduling in wireless networked control system. *IEEE Transactions on Control Systems Technology*, *24*(3), 843–852. doi:10.1109/TCST.2015.2462741

ENDNOTES

[1]   See http://www.crime-research.org/news/11.06.2004/423/

[2]   See https://www.us-cert.gov/ncas/tips/ST04-015

[3]   MyDoom is a type of a computer worm, which affects MS Windows.

[4]   Low Orbit Ion Cannon is a torture testing and DoS attack application developed by Praetox Technologies

[5]   Stacheldraht is a malware acting as a DoS attack agent.

[6]   See http://www.thewhir.com/web-hosting-news/cloud-and-application-layer-increasingly-popular-attack-targets-report

[7]   Bitcoin is a cryptocurrency that is accepted and used globally. The transactions are decentralized.

[8]   See https://securelist.com/ddos-attacks-in-q4-2016/77412/

[9]   See http://www.csoonline.in/analysis/ddos-attacks-q4-2016

Section 2
Cyber Crime and Cyber Forensics

Chapter 9
Role of Cyber Security and Cyber Forensics in India

Gulshan Shrivastava
National Institute of Technology Patna, India

Kavita Sharma
National Institute of Technology, Kurukshetra, India

Manju Khari
Advanced Institute of Advanced Communication Technologies and Research, India

Syeda Erfana Zohora
Taif University, Saudi Arabia

ABSTRACT

This chapter describes cyber forensics, also known as computer forensics, which is a subdivision of digital forensic science, relating to evidence detection in computers and digital storage media. The purpose of cyber forensics is the forensically-sound investigation of digital media with the intent to: identify, preserve, recover, analyze, present facts, and opinions; concerning the digital information. Even though it is generally allied with the analysis of cyber-based crimes, computer forensics may also be used in civil proceedings. Evidence composed from cyber forensic analysis is typically subjected to similar procedures and performs as supplementary digital evidence. With these advancements, it was desired that cyber forensics be to protect users and remain citizen-centric. This chapter shows that there is additional research needed to understand the implications of cyber forensic research to improve detection of cyber crimes.

INTRODUCTION

Cyber forensics, which is likewise known by the name of computer forensics, is a branch of digital measurable science, which identifies with confirming found in PCs and computerized stockpiling media. The goal of the cyber forensics is to look at computerized media painstakingly in a forensically solid way with the point of distinguishing, protecting, recuperating, investigating and showing realities and suppositions about the advanced data (Shrivastava, 2017).

DOI: 10.4018/978-1-5225-4100-4.ch009

In spite of the fact that it is for the most part connected with the examination of a wide assortment of cyber-based wrongdoings, PC legal sciences may likewise be utilized as a part of common procedures. The train includes comparable procedures and standards for data recuperation, yet with extra rules and practices intended to make a legal audit trail.

Proof gathered from digital crime scene investigation examinations are generally subjected to indistinguishable rules and practices from other computerized prove. It has been utilized as a part of various prominent cases and is picking up acknowledgment as very solid inside the U.S. what is more, European court frameworks (Guo et al., 2010).

Scientific strategies and master information are utilized for clarifying the present condition of a digital antiquity, for example, a PC framework, stockpiling medium (e.g. hard disk or CD-ROM), an electronic document (e.g. an email message or JPEG picture) (Gupta et al., 2011). The extent of a scientific investigation fluctuates from straightforward data recovery to recreating a progression of occasions. By and by, it is utilized to explore an assortment of wrongdoings, including child erotic entertainment, fraud, espionage, cyber-stalking, murder, and assault. This train is likewise utilized as a part of common procedures as a type of data gathering (for example, Electronic revelation) (Shrivastava & Gupta, 2014).

In a court, PC criminological confirmation is subjected to the standard necessities for digital prove. This requires the data must be real, dependably got, and admissible. Different nations have particular and diverse sorts of rules and practices for the recuperation of computerized prove. In the United Kingdom, analysts frequently follow Association of Chief Police Officers guidelines that assist them to guarantee the credibility and honesty of proof. While deliberate, the rules are broadly acknowledged in British courts.

National driven administrations like Railways are those sorts of administrations that have been outlined from the point of view of the administration client as opposed to of the legislature. These administrations are essentially planned to remember the advantages of the residents of the nation (i.e. Railroads), which legitimizes the name "national driven" Such administrations are made accessible by the different government associations of the nation and are government financed too. These administrations, for example, Railways, aeronautics administrations, saving money administrations and so forth are made accessible at a reasonable and less expensive rate to general society of the nation with the goal that all classes of individuals can utilize the administrations as per their requirements and conditions.

Both central and state governments have contributed a ton to the Information and Communication Technology (ICT) to improve their working. In this way, a resident-driven way to deal with benefit conveyance is basic if the administration needs to receive the reward of its past interest in the e-administration field. It will likewise help the administrative divisions to streamline their future speculations to receive most extreme pick up in return. In native driven approach, the subjects are dealt with as clients, as on account of the item or administration based organization, while giving the administrations to the resident. A subject driven approach empowers the administration to keep a beware of the nature of administration and enhance it as and when required, which thusly increases the national fulfillment.

While the arrangement of these administrations is basic and need have great importance, developing risk scene is likewise a reality frequenting the internet exchanges. Late bargain of 21.5 million individuals in a monstrous information break at Office of Personnel Management - US, accepted to be one of the greatest ruptures of resident's PII (Personally Identifiable Data) information; additionally, raised the significance of digital security for planning the national administrations.

Citizens living in digital era expect increased transparency about the government decisions, services, and data. In addition, these expectations are rising. To instill confidence in services, build trust, provide accessibility, reduce the digital divide and broaden it across social strata (Baggili & Breitinger, 2015) security and privacy should be the key considerations for designing and implementing thee-Government strategies.

Building a modern and innovative citizen-centric services requires utilization of new age digital technologies. Technology plays a significant role in enabling:

- Anywhere, anytime access for services.
- Interoperability across multiple systems.

It isn't just a vital driver for enhancing people in general area proficiency yet can likewise bolster adequacy of strategies and can make a more open, straightforward, creative, participatory and reliable government (Peltier, 2016).

CYBER FORENSICS: DEMAND OF THE ERA

With the advancement in technology in the modern era, the threats, and vulnerabilities to the computer-based services have also increased. Along with the benefits being made available to the citizens, the maintenance of these services has become a huge task. Some of these services contain confidential and private information about various aspects and resources of the country, which may be of much interest to the enemy nations and the terrorists, need especially secure techniques to protect such information. Thus, information security and cyber forensics go hand-in-hand in order to solve the cybercrime issues and make sure that such acts of crimes, once happened, does not take place again in future.

Applicability of Cyber Forensics

Cyber Forensics is the demonstration of making computerized information reasonable for incorporation into a criminal examination. In the modern era, information security and cyber forensics go hand-in-hand to make information security and reduce the rate of cybercrime.

Any type of cybercrime taking place around the world involves cyber forensics. It has become much easier and faster to solve cybercrimes with the advancement in technologies, saving much effort and time. Cyber forensics is well known in criminal law; however, it also has many applications in private and corporate investigation. Beyond the criminal domain, cyber forensics might commonly be used to ensure unauthorized network intrusions or to identify a network attack or hacker. Whenever such an attack takes place, various forensic tools (Hui et al., 2007) can be used to find evidence of the attack, which may be helpful in catching the attacker. The most probable attacks in the cyberspace take place due to activities of cyber terrorists and hackers. Thus, highly advanced forensic equipment is required to find the evidence and traces of attacks. This also requires highly advanced and skilled professionals, who have a very good understanding of information security and cyber forensics (Abdullah et al., 2008).

The key concentration of digital criminology is to recuperate confirmation of the criminal action. The lawful term is "Actus reus in legitimate speech". The grouping of information inside computerized gadgets is helpful to diffcrent territories of request also. cyberforensics sciences are picking up signs for the legal authorization group for an assortment of reasons, not the slightest of which is that PCs and the Internet speak to the quickest developing innovation devices utilized by hoodlums, a pattern, which is probably going to proceed for the fore observe capable future. Cybercrimes and professional violations are especially lucrative on the grounds that they are for the most part peaceful wrongdoings, return higher benefits (a current report recommended that cybercrime in the U.S. yielded more pay than the unlawful medication exchange), have generally brought down danger of being caught, and, if gotten and indicted, normally result in moderately shorter jail sentences. Judges and juries appear to have a "sentimental" perspective of cybercriminals as astute and misinformed people as opposed to as the cyberthugs that they seem to be (Britz, 2009).

PCs are fit for yielding confirmation of an extensive variety of criminal and other unlawful exercises; lawbreakers occupied with arrange based wrongdoings are by all account not the only ones who store data on PCs. Numerous different sorts of crooks occupied with kill, seizing, rape, coercion, medicate managing, auto robbery, undercover work and psychological warfare, weapon managing, theft/thievery, betting, financial violations, certainty amusements, and criminal hacking (e.g., Web disfigurement and burglary of PC documents) additionally keep up records with implicating proof on their PC. This kind of data on the PC is vital to distinguishing a suspect. The best barrier organizations of the nation are always occupied with keeping up and refreshing their criminal database at general interims so they can perceive any criminal by their unique mark match or face acknowledgment or some other sorts of comparative coordinating.

Consider, for instance, the instance of a pipe bomb kill that occurred in 1998 in the lethargic town of Fair Haven, Vermont. For this situation, a 17-year old kid named Chris Marquis was offering CB radios on the Internet. The issue was that he didn't really have radios to offer and was cheating the purchasers. One of his casualties was a 35-year-old man Chris Dean from Pierceton, Indiana, who was conned for a few hundred dollars. In the wake of acknowledging what had happened, Dean endeavored to contact Marquis, notwithstanding sending a few debilitating messages; be that as it may, nothing happened, as he was not able to connect with Marquis. On March 19, a pipe bomb touched base at Marquis' home by UPS; when it detonated, it slaughtered Marquis and gravely harmed his mom. Examination of the wrongdoing scene yielded bits of the bundle and the UPS shipping mark that drove the FBI and nearby experts to Dean. Having discovered the undermining messages from Dean on Marquis' PC, specialists looked through Dean's PC and found the messages there, also, notwithstanding an electronic form of the mailing name of the bundle, which had the pipe bomb. That data was entering in indicting Dean, who is presently serving a 20-to-life sentence in the government jail.

Challenges to Cyber Forensics

The cyber forensics eventually helps in the confirmation administration to demonstrate a wrongdoing. A definitive point is to demonstrate that the confirmation gave to the court is the proof gathered from the place of authorizing of the wrongdoing. However, there are always some challenges that pose obstacles in this regard. There may be different factors that pose limitations to the processes of cybercrime investigation. The different challenges to the forensic investigation are:

- **Windows OS "Handicap" Factor:** Although, other operating systems like Linux and MAC OS are widely used, most of the forensic-based tools and training works well on windows platform. As a result, of this feature of the forensic tools, the professionals are habituated working on windows platform, heavily dependent on it, due to which, they are unable to investigate "live non-windows" system with equal efficiency. Network infrastructure devices are often ignored.

- **Forensic Training and Education:** Training is predominately certification-based rather than a proper understanding of the concepts and learning to solve real-world problems with broad tools. The focus is always on completing the course structure in the given time duration, which means teaching a little of everything without properly explaining the logic and the concept as to why that particular tool is being taught and how it is supposed to help in the forensic investigation. Also, one of the major drawback, especially in the education system in India is that less focus is given to practical education and more to theoretical knowledge, as a result of which the fundamental knowledge is inadequate in broader skill areas, including Operating Systems (Unix/ Linux, Mac OS, Mainframe, Windows), Networking, Software Development (Scripting), System Administration, System/Network Security, System Exploitation and Countermeasures, Incident Response, Intrusion Detection, Log Analysis and Reverse Engineering.
- **Emerging Technologies:** There have been many emerging technologies such as cloud computing, virtualization technology, emerging devices etc., which makes life easier but the question arises that whether the existing tools and the professionals are able to keep up with these emerging technologies or not (Saxena et al., 2012). Some of the challenges in forensics due to cloud computing may be as follows:
  - Logging may be minimized due to limited storage capability (Bhopal and MP).
  - There is a possibility of data being spread across an ever-changing set of hosts and data centers.
  - Sometimes, the data stored in the RAM is no longer being accessible to the cloud.
  - A chain of custody issues may arise all of a sudden.
  - And law of other countries may prevent or limit retrieval of stored data due to privacy issues.

Some of the latest emerging devices in the market may be Apple iPad, Amazon Kindle, HP Slate etc. Hackers and attackers are more interested in using such devices as the source of the attack or the target since it is easier for them to find vulnerabilities and loopholes in these devices as soon as it hits the market. Some of the issues found in these devices are as follows:

- Secure deletion of data from these devices could be problematic.
- The existing forensic tools cover only a small fraction of mobile and portable devices in circulation.
- The forensic tools in use may not be compatible with the Android and iOS platforms, which are being used in these devices, and hence may be a source of a drawback.
  - **Emerging Cyber Threats:** Cyber threats are evolving day-by-day and are on the increase. The only objective of these threats creates backdoors and steals data and other confidential information on the target. Although, well-known threats can be easily detected and mitigated the new emerging threats, about which there is no stored information in the databases, cannot be easily handled. It also depends on the security expert largely, how well equipped and skilled they are in handling an emergency.
  - **Live Volatile Data:** Forensic artifacts and data are always in a volatile state, which means they can be lost when the power of the computing device is switched off. Some of the reasons to collect volatile data are as follows:
- It helps to determine the criminal activity that can get lost in the system is powered off.
- It may contain passwords used for encryption.
- Sometimes, it also shows indication of anti-forensic use.

- It can help avoid backlog of cases – performing live data collection helps to avoid waiting for months for a full-blown investigation

While there are many important reasons to collect volatile data, there are quite a few drawbacks to it as well. Some of them are:

- It gets difficult to ensure the integrity (using Hash) of collected information.
- There is always a lack of incident response capabilities or forensics readiness plan.
- Untested or lack of established processes and procedures may hinder the investigation process.
- Malicious software, rootkits, or booby traps may alter the outcome of information collected. This may also damage the authenticity and integrity of the collected evidence, which may ultimately lead to false results.
- Command time stamping – helps to answer the questions such as which commands were run, at what time, and with what output.
- Not taking verbose notes.
  - **Malware Analysis:** Malware must be well tamed. Some malware may exhibit different behavior if they are being investigated. Custom Packing and Encryption make investigations challenging. VM environment may not always be the best environment to study them, as malware are capable of "jumping out" of the VM onto Host OS. Hence, a full-blown simulated network may be needed and Research "lab" systems must be cleaned for the next analysis (Shrivastava et al., 2016).

RISKS TO CITIZEN CENTRIC SERVICES

Citizen-centric services are those types of services that have been designed from the perspective of the service user rather than of the government. These services are mainly designed keeping in mind the benefits of the citizens of the country, which justifies the name "citizen-centric." Such services are made available by the various government organizations of the country and are government funded as well. These services such as Railways, aviation services, banking services etc. are made available at an affordable and cheaper rate to the public of the country so that all classes of people can use the services according to their needs and conditions.

Technology and Types of Citizen Services

Building a modern and innovative citizen-centric services requires utilization of new age digital technologies. Technology plays a significant role in enabling:

- Anywhere, anytime access for services
- Interoperability across multiple systems

It isn't just a key driver for enhancing the proficiency of the general population segment yet can likewise bolster the viability of strategies and make more open, straightforward, inventive, participatory and dependable governments.

In India, National e-Governance Plan comprises of 31 mission mode ventures, which are additionally delegated a state, focal and coordinated activities. Through utilization of innovation different native administrations, for example, affirmation of birth and demise, Issuance of declarations, Collection of water charges, Issuance of duty leeway testaments, Property assess, Trade License and so forth and ventures concentrating on the parts of electronic administration, for example, managing an account, arrive records or business charges and so forth are being digitized by different centre and state government departments. The table below depicts the different mission mode project areas classified as Central, State, and Integrated.

Some of the different types of citizen-centric services offered by the central government are as follows:

- Banking
- Income Tax
- Life Insurance Scheme
- Pension Scheme for retired Government servants
- Unique Identification Number(UID) i.e. Adhaar card facility
- Passport and VISA service

Some of the citizen-based services made available by the various state governments are:

- Municipality services for different localities of every city
- Education and Health facilities
- Road Transport facilities for interstate transportation.
- e-Panchayats
- Agriculture facilities to farmers
- Public Distribution Schemes
- Employment Exchange

Major Issues

The Internet is under seized and the volume, speed, assortment and multifaceted nature of the dangers to the web and comprehensively associated foundations are relentlessly expanding. Critical infrastructure and classified data are much more susceptible to the malicious attacks. For administration, Cyber defense vs. Cyber opportunity is always a debate, which needs to be balanced out to reap the benefits of technology and assure citizens and nation's interest. Few elements of cybersecurity that have to be considered for citizen-centric services as mentioned in an international journal are:

- Dependency on information systems
- Increased use of remote access
- Challenges of controlling information from spreading or leaking to unauthorized parties or individuals.
- Laws relating to information security
- National security, which should be of high priority.
- Consequences of a security breach can be detrimental and can have adverse effects.

Typical concerns related to technology alone e-Government system is:

- Virus Attacks
- Outside and Inside Attacks
- User Frauds
- False Identity/Impersonation
- Unauthorized disclosure
- Misinformation and Propaganda
- Failure to recover business information
- Loss or theft of monetary value

Latest Trends

Digital government maturity model in the figure on the right depicts the transformation of electronic governance to smart governance with the role of technology at each stage. The concept of 'civic moment', an event that triggers a series of cascading actions and data exchange across a network of people, businesses and government will become possible with the synergistic value from mobile, information (data analytics, cloud and social technologies supplemented by the internet of things.

There may be number of value-added services which may be built around civic moments which do not exist today and will become possible with usage of data such as tax advice coming from tax agencies that have real-time view of tax payer's situation, from preventive healthcare using data from environmental monitoring to smoother and rapid management of emergency situations based on data coming from various government and non-government sources.

NEED OF CYBER FORENSICS IN CYBER SECURITY

Cyber forensics is the securing, examination, and detailing of data found on PCs and systems that are engaged with a criminal or common examination, in spite of the fact that similar procedures and techniques can likewise be connected to corporate and other "private" examinations. About everything that somebody does on a PC or a system leaves follows, from erased records and registry sections to the Internet history reserve and programmed Word reinforcement documents. These hints of wrongdoing or unlawful exercises can turn out to be negative for the aggressor unless expelled shrewdly, without upsetting the ordinary working of the framework. Email headers and texting logs uncover data about the middle of the road servers through which data has crossed. Server logs give data about each one of those PC frameworks, which have been getting to any Web webpage.

PCs are fit for yielding proof of an extensive variety of criminal and other unlawful exercises; culprits occupied with organizing based wrongdoings are by all account not the only ones who store data on PCs. Numerous different sorts of lawbreakers occupied with kill, abducting, rape, coercion, tranquilize managing, auto burglary, reconnaissance and psychological oppression, firearm managing, theft/robbery, betting, financial wrongdoings, certainty amusements, and criminal hacking (e.g., Web disfigurement and robbery of PC documents) likewise keep up records with implicating proof on their PC. This kind of data on the PC is critical to recognizing a suspect. The best resistance organizations of the nation are continually occupied with keeping up and refreshing their criminal database at general interims so they can perceive any criminal by their unique mark match or face acknowledgment or some other sorts of comparable coordinating.

A fundamental level comprehension of PC crime scene investigation is basic for all law requirement officers, who are associated with the scientific examination process. Agents need to know when data on a PC may have a nexus to a wrongdoing, how to compose a suitable warrant for seizing and looking through a PC, which may have been a piece of a wrongdoing, and how to accumulate and seek digital confirmation from such frameworks. Prosecutors and judges need to comprehend the part of advanced proof and ought to have the capacity to characterize their part all through the case, as and when required suitably. High innovation wrongdoing teams have just been framed in the bigger metropolitan zones where this is an especially difficult issue, however, the issue is in reality much more boundless than simply the huge urban communities. In the present day, where every last little thing is done electronically with the utilization of devices and PCs, such digital based issues will undoubtedly emerge and all classes of examiners, regardless of whether a piece of the cybercrime unit of the nation, ought to have a fundamental comprehension and learning about PCs and their operations, so that in any event they can give legitimate occurrence reaction moves, making fitting measures. Indeed, even a watch officer who isn't engaged with PC violations has to realize what moves to make when a PC is found at a wrongdoing or capture scene.

Cybercrime scene investigation and computerized examinations have turned into a key piece of cybersecurity and police work in the cutting edge time. PCs are currently as much a piece of the cutting edge law authorization officer's day by day normal as the cudgel, sidearm, two-way radio, or binds. Hence, we can say that both cyber forensics and cyber security go hand-in-hand and are complementary to each other. There is always a need of one for the smooth working of the other (Khari et al., 2017).

PREDICAMENTS TO CYBER SECURITY

The internet involves IT systems, PC assets, and all the settled and cell phones associated with the worldwide Internet. A country's the internet is a piece of the worldwide the internet; it can't be disengaged to characterize its limits since the internet is borderless. This is the thing that makes the internet exceptional. Dissimilar to the physical world that is restricted by geological limits in space—arrive, ocean, waterway waters and air—the internet can and is proceeding to grow. Expanded Internet entrance is prompting the development of the internet since its size is relative to the exercises that are brought through it.

Countries are putting intensely in their ICT frameworks with a view to giving higher transfer speeds, coordinate national economies with the worldwide commercial center, and to empower subjects or "netizens" to get to increasingly e-administrations.

Given the security issues, there is expanded accentuation on, and interest in, the security of the cyber infrastructure. Center Internet conventions are unreliable, and a blast of cell phones keeps on being founded on the same shaky frameworks. This is signifying expanded utilization of the Internet to more defenseless the internet.

Insurance of basic framework operations has risen as a noteworthy test. This is on the grounds that trillions of dollars travel through the systems consistently including an expansive scope of exercises, including web-based business, e-administration, travel, friendliness, medicinal services, and general interchanges. Power conveyance, water circulation, and a few other utility administrations depend on ICT frameworks. The barrier part depends intensely on electronic frameworks.

A few security studies point to this need. They uncover an absence of sufficient information among officials about security strategy and episodes, the most recent innovative arrangements, information spillage, money related misfortune, and the preparation that is required for their representatives.

Since the internet is generally new, legitimate ideas for "principles of care" don't exist. Is there a case for governments to offer motivating forces to create aggregate activity? For instance, they could give lessened obligation or duty motivating forces as an exchange off for enhanced security, new administrative prerequisites, and consistency mechanisms.12 Governments need to give impetuses to industry to put resources into security at a level that isn't supported by corporate marketable strategies.

The Cyber Security Dilemma

A "cybersecurity situation" exists when endeavors by one state to improve the security of its advanced framework, either through the improvement of hostile or protective cyber warfare abilities, diminish the cybersecurity of others. Because of cyber fighting's novel properties, the cybersecurity problem might be harder to break than the ordinary security situation.

Cybersecurity is from numerous points of view a weapons contest amongst aggressors and safeguards. ICT frameworks are extremely mind-boggling, and assailants are always examining for shortcomings, which can happen at many focuses. Protectors can secure against feeble focuses, however particularly, three are testing purposeful activities by insiders by getting to the framework; store network dangers, which can permit the inclusion of malevolent equipment and programming amid the presumption procedure; and already obscure or dangers with no characterized settle. Notwithstanding for dangers where arrangements are known, they may not be executed in numerous situations due to operational requirements or budgetary.

It is possible to remove and mitigate the known threats; however, it becomes very difficult to detect the unknown threats. As the newer threats emerge daily, the professionals require updating their skills and knowledge level to deal with such threats.

John Herz, an American researcher of worldwide law and relations are credited for characterizing the expression "security quandary". The difficulty indicates how both the solid and frail states can influence the adjust of energy that could really turn into an explanation behind the war. The security difficulty could increment from the state's gathering of energy in view of vulnerability and dread about the other states' goals. Before-9/11, progressive US organizations have generally endeavored to deal with worldwide confusion by gathering more "power". Not abnormally, since 2007, the US has been breaking down and gathering the pertinent measure of information open on the internet.

Cybersecurity issue of the US was as of late gotten by the US shriek blower Edward Snowden, giving the insights about the US National Security Agency's questionable Prism program. The US unmistakably has been investigating the worldwide e-activity furtively and during the time spent minding cyber precedes onward Facebook, Skype, Google, YouTube, and so on. This has brought about a lot of metadata (the information about information). The metadata clarifies how and when and by whom a specific arrangement of information was accumulated, and how that information is altered. A case of it, a statement following the exercises of the people, for instance, which legal advisors or writers were in contact with whom (phone/visit), for to what extent and where and so on. Such information could be utilized for deductions.

To gather it just, the US organization has been feigning on whatever is left of the world. Not shockingly, the US specialists are flabbergasted at Snowden, who is stowing away in Hong Kong, and even claims against him for treachery. Snowden's introduction has raised the significant verbal confrontation amongst security and protection.

In the 21st century, with the quantity of PC and web clients is expanding significantly, the cyber situation has practically turned out to be essential to a country's 'presence'. Throughout the years Information and Communication Technologies (ICT) have turned out to be particular to various divisions from financial, political, and social to the barrier. The opposite side to it is that different unlawful, unapproved, against national, psychological militant and criminal exercises have additionally turned out to be wild. Shocking as it might sound, however, the third most popular nation after China and India isn't any land range yet a 'virtual state' called Facebook.

The present idea of digital innovation is the end goal that any action occurred in the digital world would each time leave a 'track' behind. Clearly, any actually unrivaled state or even an individual having a precondition financing would endeavor to stroke this innovation to their advantage.

Any digital design can be seen as a multiplied edged sword – either disregard it and be uncovered or utilize it further bolstering one's good fortune. Digital surveillance is staying put. Today, the US is forthright a direct result of its innovative prevalence and capacity over 'deal with' the ICT business and keep few demonstrations of fear-based oppression from really happening. All the more imperatively, the information assembled would have utility in different fields as well.

It is critical to realize that digital claim to fame offers a lot of hilter kilter advantage to the client. In future, it isn't just the US yet numerous different states that are likewise liable to utilize this mystery technique. A significant number of the states may have effectively organized operationally. It is horrible that any insight organization could give-up such an apparatus with loaded with benefits.

The Offense-Defense Balance

There are numerous courses in which cyber warfare is not the same as active and customary fighting. These attributes tend to help the offense. For one, digital assaults can be executed immediately. Under customary military, portability is expected to support the offense. This is on the grounds that the more noteworthy versatility assent focuses with less opportunity to make a nice safeguard. Versatility is identified with the two unique factors that have assumed a vital part in "dynamic fighting". As Jervis examinations, "anything that expands the measure of the ground an aggressor needs to cross… builds the favorable position collecting to the protection." Whereas in motor fighting element may fill in as a boundary to the assault.

The absence of landscape likewise helps in amaze assaults on prior unrecognized system dangers. As Jervis notes, "weapons and methodologies that rely upon for their viability on astounding are quite often hostile." Therefore, the speed with which cyber assaults should be possible makes safeguarding against them troublesome, thus incredibly benefits the offense.

Cyber warfare has low expenses of the section with significant yields on the venture. As a report by the U.S. Flying corps Research Laboratory notes, "anybody with a PC and an Internet association can dispatch assaults… ." An investigation by the U.S. Armed forces also asked that cyber warfare is "a generally economical approach to pick up equality with the U.S. when contrasted with purchasing tanks and airship or preparing a large number of warriors." Related to this, the truth of the matter is that cyber assaults are an imperative apparatus for seeking after the deviated war. Frail on-screen characters can be associated with cyber warfare with low expenses.

The potential abuse coming about because of the viable cyber assault on the main mechanical country like the US could be expansive. Amid a similar time, if the frail performing artist does not have a likewise advanced economy or foundation, a return assault may not be so viable. In this way, where a weaker or less "wired" state goes head to head against a more grounded, more industrialized country, cyber protection methodology may not be critical.

Like distinctive types of fighting, cyber assaults are methods through which states can smother their foes. In any case, not at all like other military alternatives, cyber assaults require not be lead to more human expenses. Cyber assaults have a tendency to stifle by influencing correspondence and economies by not taking lives. Many states are reluctant to rehearse their political closures through savage means. Similarly, states endeavor to restrict their own particular impacts amid the war. Cyber fighting gives methods for pressuring and upgrading the security of others with no death toll to the two sides. Thusly, it isn't just a contrasting option to different methods of fighting, yet it might likewise give expresses a reason to include in a contention that they generally would not have confronted. Along these lines, the accessibility of cyberwarfare could influence the general clash recurrence.

The Offense-Defense Differentiation

Amid offense may have the advantage in cyber warfare, participation is conceivable if states can segregate amongst guarded and hostile digital approaches, projects and weapons. This issue is really attached to the confirm issue that influences many arms control endeavors. Improbable, the viewpoint is similarly bleak. One protest with this is the contraption required to actualize cyber fighting exists in the virtual world. The main identifiable, physical apparatus utilized as a part of this is a PC. Both cyber resistance and cyber assaults are drilled through this non-threatening stage.

A significant number of the world's biggest militaries have gathered cyberwarfare projects and units; a cyber assault could without much of a stretch be completed from a private concern or home. The best test for sorting amongst guarded and hostile cyber weapons is to distinguish a weapon prior. Clearly, this issue isn't one of a kind to the cyberwarfare. States can also think that it's hard to distinguish whether a foe's atomic practices are expected to make bombs or to control urban communities.

Consolidated insight endeavors can uncover whether a plant is making atomic power or the atomic bomb. PCs are more typical and have utilizes that are more unique. Regardless of the possibility that a cyber weapon can be identified, it stays hard to separate amongst guarded and hostile abilities. Numerous military associations pointed at organizing cyberwarfare have both protective and hostile capacities, both of which are performed by similar machines and systems.

The line amongst protective and hostile modes isn't clear, and as the one reporter puts it, "the contrast between having the capacity to test and infiltrate a foe's PC system or assault comes down to two or three keystrokes… ." In that same setting, a weapon's ruinous trademark can be nearly unrealistic to characterize until the point that it has been utilized. As a cybersecurity master, Paul Kurtz thinks of: "You can have a little bit of code that can do an entire of a considerable measure of harm or only a smidgen of harm contingent upon how you utilize it."

The most valuable weapons of cyberwar are the "cyber warriors" that execute it. Be that as it may, it can be extremely hard to identify a cyber warrior. Numerous militaries have "formally assigned" cyber fighting units, yet obligation for both cyber guard and the cyber offense can without much of a stretch be spread all through various security and insight organizations, and even in the private segment. Notwithstanding when cyber warriors are noticeable, it is almost impractical to separate between their cautious and hostile capacities and aims. This is on the grounds that similar instruments and learning that cyber warriors use to secure against the assaults, similar to interruption recognition projects and firewalls, can be utilized to sidestep similar insurances. In this way, it needs abilities and a sharp cerebrum with skill in that specific field to help against cyber warriors.

THE CYBER SECURITY FRAMEWORK

The cybersecurity framework has been proposed to in order to safeguard the security of cyberspace at the national level, particularly in the citizen-centric services. This proposed framework collaborates baseline security approach along with the principles supporting today's requirements such as simplifying the information security and attack driven defense approach in citizen-based services.

The key aspects of this framework are the users, resources, transactions, discernibility, analysis, and alliance. The user indicates the different types of actors or users of cybersecurity around the world. They can be hackers, government organizations, NGOs, cyber terrorists etc. Some of the users such as ethical hackers and government organizations employ cybersecurity for protecting confidential information, i.e. in a positive manner while others such as cyber terrorists, hackers etc use cyberspace in a negative way, in order to hack confidential data, using which they can plan attacks against a country or blackmail someone etc. Government organizations collect and maintain different kinds of data and resources concerning the citizens. Sharing of personally identifiable information among different government organizations is not a good practice due to privacy-related issues. Un-integrated security architecture and poor discernibility across tools and processes provide many opportunities for cybercriminals to exploit vulnerabilities and security loopholes. Once exploited, it becomes very easy for these cybercriminals to take full control of the system and steal the private and confidential information. In the case of a cybercrime, proper collection of evidence, documentation of the evidence and the analysis needs to be done in order to solve the incident. It is important that sometimes, the government agencies should form an alliance among themselves for fighting against cyber terrorism, by sharing important facts and data among themselves. This will definitely help to take corrective steps and in prevention at a much faster pace as and when compared to the situation if the agencies work individually.

Figure 1. Framework of cyber security

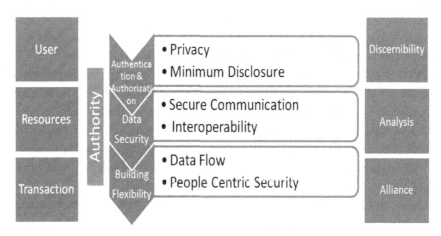

Authentication and authorization are the key aspects of cybersecurity to protect confidential data from unauthorized usage. The top-level government agencies within a country always use secure communication channels to communicate information among each other, to prevent other agencies from sniffing the information. The architecture is flexible and can be applied in most of the citizen-centric services.

Roles and Applications of the Security Framework

User/Actors

For safeguarding the security of cyberspace at the national level (especially the citizen-centric services) cognizance of all the actors in cyberspace including the "enemies" operating should be understood and factored20.

- **Users, Operators, Administrators:** These groups do not have a negative influence on cybersecurity. They are actors who use the cyberspace in an ethical manner.
- **Non-Hostile Hackers:** As a rule, they unintentionally have a negative impact on cybersecurity, whether they are doing so for fun only (settling a bet or dispute, for example) or to show off. They do not provide any harm knowingly. It mainly includes young people, who learn to hack as a part of hobby or passion.
- **Hostile Hackers:** Their motives include revenge, envy, and self-interest. Thus, these types of hackers have a negative impact on the cybersecurity. They can cause damage to a good extent if not to a very large extent. Examples include hacking the bank account of influential or famous personalities or someone from whom they want to take revenge, setting up fraud and forged websites in order to hack the login id and passwords of different users, consuming the network bandwidth to create unnecessary network traffic causing a denial-of-service attack to the target system etc. (Shrivastava, 2016).
- **Cyber Criminals:** Criminals using cyber as their weapons of choice. Their main purpose is to breach the defensive strategies of the government of the country and get hold of confidential information, which can be used to blackmail the government, to act on their wish.
- **Cyber Terrorists:** Terrorists using cyber as their weapons of choice. They use the cyberspace to hack the confidential military information of the country, so that they can get to know about the highly confidential and private information concerning the defensive strategies and weapons of the country such as the number of fighter jets belonging to the country, positions of the ballistic missiles in the country, number of army tanks etc. This type of information is highly useful for the terrorists, as it can help them to plan an attack against the country.
- **Governments:** State bodies that may use cyberspace for military-political purposes. They mainly use cyberspace for ethical purpose and not in any unethical sense. The government organizations employ ethical hackers so as to keep the confidential defense and military information of the country protected so that it does not go into the hands of the enemy country and terrorists. Different governmental organizations such as railways, aviation industry, telecom industry etc deploy cybersecurity techniques in order to keep information and data confidential away from the hands of unauthorized users.
- **Non-Governmental Organizations:** Groups that may use cyberspace to promote their political agendas but do not have any type of negative impact on the cyberspace.

Resources

Government organizations collect and maintain different kinds of data concerning the citizens. Sharing of personally identifiable information cannot be exchanged among different government organizations due to privacy-related issues. In paper-based official processes, the security requirements are generally accomplished by identifying the citizen by means of an identity card, deeds or witnesses. Confidentiality is generally provided by envelopes or by classified records. Handwritten signatures, forms, stamps and a notary public provide the integrity, data origin authentication, and non-repudiation. The equivalences in electronic processes are well known by technologies such as encryption, digital signatures, and PKI.

Transactions

It is essential to understand the role of the actor in cybersecurity. For this, one must understand the flow of information in different stages for e-Governance initiatives. The figure on the left depicts the four stages for the e-Governance; wherein first three e-governments can be seen as a process of modernization of the public sector from paper-based tasks and processes to digital ones. The information in these stages is typically flowed in one direction from government to the public, with limited feedback from citizens. While the fourth stage of e-Gov initiatives is the predominately-Open government with more participation from citizens leading to transformative and participatory model. This will include the use of web 2.0 technologies such as blogs, wikis, social networking hubs, communication modes, photo-sharing, videocasts, audio sharing, virtual worlds etc. These emerging e-government services will be increasingly advanced transaction types that will share personal data for personalization and collaboration among government departments. Actor identity intelligence and behavior of users forms a critical element for ensuring cyber security whether it is trusted insiders, end users or rogue actors.

Discernibility

Un-integrated security architecture and poor discernibility across tools and processes provide many opportunities for cybercriminals to exploit vulnerabilities and security loopholes. Once exploited, it becomes very easy for these cybercriminals to take full control of the system and steal the private and confidential information. In addition, they are able to manipulate the whole system according to their discretion. Most of the times, all these activities happen without the knowledge of the system user because he feels that the system is functioning normally, as the normal operations are not disrupted, although, the cybercriminal is able to compromise the whole system. Sophisticated cyber criminals are increasingly taking advantage of the rapid business digitization and the evolving IT infrastructure to exploit Internet-enabled enterprise networks; putting cyber threats at the top of enterprise and government decision-makers' minds. Thus, it is indeed important to integrate the complete architecture and improve the visibility so that the loopholes and the vulnerabilities are well protected from the sight of the hackers and it becomes very difficult or impossible to compromise the complete system.

Just as it is said that in order to catch a criminal, it is necessary to think like a criminal, in the same manner, to design such an integrated and risk-free system. It is necessary to think like a cybercriminal and not like a security designer or security tester because only then the actual loopholes and the weaknesses of the system can be found out. This will help to cover all the vulnerabilities properly so that at least the known vulnerabilities cannot be exploited. Also, it is very important for the security designers to keep updating and educating themselves about the latest threats and vulnerabilities in the cyber world so that it can be of help while doing the vulnerability assessment of the system and lead to a risk-free system.

Analytics

Incident reporting systems are an integral part of operations of citizen-centric services, because if an incident is not reported and the case is not documented, then no further action can be taken on it ;Once an incident of cybercrime is reported and course of action is followed, then it can be expected that the action taken can be helpful in preventing future incidents of crime, however, reporting of the raw number such as number of privacy breaches may not necessarily prevent the future incidents from happening. Once an incident is reported, then after documenting the case, the proper study should be done to analyze why the incident took place and what course of action can be taken to prevent it from happening in the future, which is one of the prime procedure of cyber forensics. Operational managers should understand the relationships that connect danger signals to potential changes in operations to improve programs. Most government agencies use equipment that has started to become obsolete as compared to the present day technologies and systems, which makes them vulnerable to the new threats and vulnerabilities emerging in the day-to-day world. Detection of threats and vulnerabilities should not be limited to the signature based utilities rather there should be comprehensive pattern analysis for transactions and behavior to unearth the zero-day threats (Choras et al., 2015).

Alliance

Semantic interoperability is the ability to interact network entities different agency systems, citizens and technology to have a consistent understanding of shared information and ability to resolve differences in the conceptualization of entities. Privacy-preserving data integration is a problem; however, integration is required for having a common platform for the security, identity and threat intelligence. Data sharing between controls is paramount to identify the root cause and take preventive/correctives measures based on the intelligence. It is also important that sometimes, the government agencies should form an alliance among themselves for fighting against cyber terrorism, by sharing important facts and data among themselves. This will definitely help to take corrective steps and in prevention at a much faster pace as and when compared to the situation if the agencies work individually.

Authentication and Authorization

In order to maintain privacy and prevent the disclosure or leakage of confidential information, the first thing that needs to be done is to authenticate the user, who is trying to access the particular piece of information. For authenticating the user, the login id, and the password is needed from the user, which is matched by the system against an already stored database of login ids and passwords. On matching, the user is authenticated. Only authorized users within the organization have the right to access the information and upon authentication only. Different people within the organization have different access privileges depending on their rank within the organization. The employee, who is at a very senior position within the company, can access all the types' confidential information as compared to an employee, who is at a junior level.

Data Security

Since its discovery, the sole aim of cybersecurity has been to secure the data of any organization so that it does not fall into any type of unauthorized party, who can use it for their benefit against the particular organization. In addition to this, it becomes extremely important and necessary for the government organizations to implement data security because it contains highly classified and confidential data that may be used by cybercriminals or terrorists to plan attacks against the nation, causing huge damage to human lives and national property. One of the vital aspects of data security is to set up a secure communication between the two parties, who would like o share some kind of confidential and secret data so that no unauthorized third party is able to sniff the communication channel. The best way is to send the data in an encrypted manner that will be understandable only to the two parties involved.

Advantages of the Security Framework

The proposed security framework has been designed carefully keeping in mind the security risks that may pose a challenge to most of the citizen-centric services and help the government institutions to protect their confidential information and data. It covers all the aspects of a citizen-centric service such as users, resources, transactions etc. One of the most important advantages is that it has shown how the security will be implemented for the individual entities of a public based service rather than covering the whole thing as a single entity.

It covers different features of security such as privacy, the minimum disclosure of information, secure communication, interoperability, data flow and people-centric services. Once all these aspects are taken care of, then the framework developed will be secured enough to protect the data from intruders. The computer systems used in the government organizations are mostly not up-to-date, which makes them obsolete at some point in time and their defenses against malware, viruses, and worms weaken. This type of framework will help such systems to overcome the attacks by viruses and worms. In addition, preventing such attacks will help to conserve the bandwidth of the connection, which, otherwise, is mostly consumed by the worms and by the hackers and intruders.

This type of framework cannot only be used by the government institutions but also by private organizations as well in order to secure their private networks and secure communication.

Shortcomings of the Security Framework

Some of the shortcomings of the framework can be as follows:

- **Costly Equipment:** In order to implement the above-proposed security framework, advanced communication, and hacking equipment are needed along with a high-speed internet connection, which will not be interrupted at any point in time. Installation and maintenance of such equipment need a huge amount of funds, which might be beyond the scope of medium and small-scale private organizations. In the case of government institutions, the sanction of such amount takes a lot of time and a long procedure. All these obstacles and issues pave way for the hackers and intruders to steal information in the given amount of time when there is no defensive barrier in these top-level organizations.

- **Difficult to Configure:** Once the equipment is installed and setup, the next step will be to configure the complete system, so that it works perfectly according to the way it should. This needs expertise and skills, for which professionals are needed. In order to implement the framework, these configurations are extremely necessary.
- **Update at Regular Intervals:** In order to maintain the systems and ensure that the security framework is keeping the needed confidential information secured, it is necessary to update the software and the applications being used, at regular intervals. In addition, for the purpose of forensic investigations, the tools should be updated as and when needed, so that they are able to prevent most of the vulnerabilities and threats from infiltrating the system. Most of the government officials do not possess so much expertise and knowledge for these types of works, which becomes a major issue. Thus, special experts and a separate wing of professionals should be recruited and nurtured for this job.

CONCLUSION

The above work tries to establish a connection between cybersecurity and the different types of citizen-centric services. Citizen-centric services are important and vital for the functioning of a nation, as they are meant to benefit the citizens and in order to maintain such services, several important data needs to be stored and maintained over time. This type of data is confidential and hence, needs to be safeguarded. Therefore, the intervention of cyber security and cyber forensics is necessary for the whole picture.

The chapter gives a brief overview of the applicability of cyber forensics in different fields of life and the challenges to it. Overcoming these challenges is a necessary and important task to prevent dangerous and intelligent criminals from committing cyber crimes. The flow then goes on to describe the different types of citizen-centric services and the major issues faced by them, including their latest trends.

The next section has given an overview as to why cyber forensics in needed in cybersecurity. As highlighted earlier, cyber forensics is an integral part of cybersecurity and both go hand-in-hand. They are in some ways, complementary to each other. On one hand, there are many benefits and advantages of cyber-based security techniques, whereas, on the other hand, the same do possess some drawbacks, which are necessary to overcome, as has been explained earlier in the text.

The proposed cybersecurity framework has been designed, keeping in mind all those areas of the citizen-centric services, which may be vulnerable to exploitation by intruders and hackers. It addresses all such aspects and promises to put forward a good defensive barrier for the confidential and private information, thus protecting the national properties and assets.

REFERENCES

Abdullah, M. T., Mahmod, R., Ghani, A., Azim, A., Abdullah, M. Z., Sultan, M., & Bakar, A. (2008). Advances in computer forensics. *International Journal of Computer Science and Network Security*, *8*(2), 215–219.

Baggili, I., & Breitinger, F. (2015). Data Sources for Advancing Cyber Forensics: What the Social World Has to Offer. In *Proceedings of the 2015 AAAI Spring Symposium*.

Bhopal, M. P., & MP, I. B. (2012). A Review of Computer forensic & Logging System. *International Journal (Toronto, Ont.)*, *2*(1).

Britz, M. T. (2009). *Computer Forensics and Cyber Crime: An Introduction, 2/E*. Pearson Education India.

Choras, M., Kozik, R., Torres Bruna, M. P., Yautsiukhin, A., Churchill, A., Maciejewska, I., & Jomni, A. (2015). Comprehensive approach to increase cyber security and resilience. In *Proceedings of ARES (International Conference on Availability, Reliability and Security)*, Touluse (pp. 686-692). 10.1109/ARES.2015.30

Guo, H., Jin, B., & Huang, D. (2010). Research and review on computer forensics. In *Proceedings of the International Conference on Forensics in Telecommunications, Information, and Multimedia* (pp. 224-233). Springer Berlin Heidelberg.

Gupta, P., Singh, J., Arora, A. K., & Mahajan, S. (2011). Digital forensics: A technological revolution in forensic sciences.

Hui, L. C., Chow, K. P., & Yiu, S. M. (2007). Tools and technology for computer forensics: research and development in Hong Kong. In *Proceedings of the International Conference on Information Security Practice and Experience* (pp. 11-19). Springer Berlin Heidelberg

Khari, M., Shrivastava, G., Gupta, S., Gupta, R. (2017). Role of Cyber Security in Today's Scenario. In *Detecting and Mitigating Robotic Cyber Security Risks* (pp. 177).

Peltier, T. R. (2016). *Information Security Policies, Procedures, and Standards: guidelines for effective information security management*. CRC Press.

Saxena, A., Shrivastava, G., & Sharma, K. (2012). Forensic investigation in cloud computing environment. *The International Journal of forensic computer science*, *2*, 64-74.

Shrivastava, G. (2016, March). Network forensics: Methodical literature review. In *Proceedings of the 2016 3rd International Conference on Computing for Sustainable Global Development (INDIACom)* (pp. 2203-2208). IEEE.

Shrivastava, G. (2017). Approaches of network forensic model for investigation. *International Journal of Forensic Engineering*, *3*(3), 195–215. doi:10.1504/IJFE.2017.082977

Shrivastava, G., & Gupta, B. B. (2014, October). An encapsulated approach of forensic model for digital investigation. In *Proceedings of the 2014 IEEE 3rd Global Conference on Consumer Electronics (GCCE)* (pp. 280-284). IEEE. 10.1109/GCCE.2014.7031241

Shrivastava, G., Sharma, K., & Kumari, R. (2016, March). Network forensics: Today and tomorrow. In *Proceedings of the 2016 3rd International Conference on Computing for Sustainable Global Development (INDIACom)* (pp. 2234-2238). IEEE.

Chapter 10
Cyberattacks, Cybercrime and Cyberterrorism

Saurabh Ranjan Srivastava
Malviya National Institute of Technology, India

Sachin Dube
Malviya National Institute of Technology, India

ABSTRACT

This chapter describes how with growing reliance of modern society over internet and web-based services in every nook and corner of our daily lives, the threats of disruption and damage to these services has also evolved at a parallel rate. One of these threats having a potential of severe and life-threatening devastations is 'Cyberterrorism.' Contrasting to non-lethal terms such as 'internet vandalism' and 'hacktivism,' cyberterrorism encompasses a daunting reach to destruction to the fabric of our modern society. Because of its nature, despite its rapid growth, contrary to conventional terror attacks, cyberterrorism still seems distant from creating a direct threat to civilian life and society. Due to this distance, there is a lack of attention and focus on counter mechanisms against cyberterrorism. By applying effective techniques and keeping our eyes open, establishments can go a long way to avert cyberterror attacks and also recover quickly in the occurrence of an attack. The conclusion of this chapter is that additional research is needed to identify the areas in which personal and professional functions on the internet are still vulnerable.

INTRODUCTION

A cyberattack or simply an attack on computer systems and services can be considered as an intentional and planned activity targeted to disrupt and/or damage the normal functioning of equipment, corruption or theft of stored data and alteration in process control of running systems (Collin, 2013). Cybercrime or more commonly 'internet crime' is the crime committed in the cyberspace, by making use of computer and internet services.

As mentioned by Gaub (2017), since several past years, terrorist organizations have aimed and struggled to build well-trained terror squads globally. On encountering the financial, organizational

DOI: 10.4018/978-1-5225-4100-4.ch010

and workforce difficulties, they started moving towards the sleeper cell and leaderless, low resistance models of operations.

In continuation of the search for such low resistance models of operation, the possibility of occurrence of a cyber-attack has increased greatly with modernization and computerization of civilian as well as army infrastructures. With the evolution of distributed systems and growing network capabilities, devices and equipment are now attaining the ability to communicate and respond to each other. Threats of a cyberterror attack may arise from militants, terrorist groups, professional criminals, disruptive anti-state bodies and even from governments of rogue nations. Such threat can eventually result in break-in and theft of government documents, corruption of databases or damage of financial data, which presents the possible impact of such threats.

But the technical know-how and even acceptance towards the existence of terror threats in cyberspace has yet to claim its space. Due to this gap, policies and mechanisms to counter cyberterrorism have yet to be created at national and international levels. Unlike physical terror attacks, expensive logistic trail and the organized workforce is not a compulsion for cyberterror activities. Even a single hacker with justified computer resources and practical sense of attack implementation skills is capable enough of committing a cyberterror attack across the borders from a distant country. An example of such attack can be capturing the control of traffic system of a city and manipulation of signaling services causing multiple accidents at numerous spots throughout the city.

In case of conventional terrorism, pre-planned groundwork and physically dynamic mediums such as explosives and suicide bombers are crucial to execute an attack. By invoking injuries, property destruction and civilian deaths, this class of attacks are generally successful in generating an environment of fear and anxiety among the targeted population. This environment of fear is in turn, used to demoralize and pressurize a government to adopt or abort a policy specific decision. An example of such attack is the Madrid terror bombings killing 191 people in the year 2004 that led to the departure of Spanish armed forces from Iraq (Sciolino, 2004).

Furnelb and Warren (1999) stated that, contrary to conventional terrorism, cyberterrorism utilizes the malicious internet and computer technologies to achieve similar ideological, religious or political goals. The activities for the achievement of these goals may involve stealing money, data or identities, rupturing services and infrastructures, shutting down functions of organizations and much more. In the current scenario, the targets and motivation of all cyberterrorists may not be clearly obvious. Instead of executing any financial scam or ransom, they target to disrupt social fabric and damage public confidence in its administrative mechanism.

For the major part of the world, the internet is not constrained by national borders. This leads to the possibility of a cyberterrorist conducting a computer hack from another country across the globe. Such a hack will consume only a few compromised systems in its track to hide the trail of the attack.

Apart from such transnational attacks, possibilities of insider threats are also existent. An insider such as an annoyed ex-employee can cause compromise of the considerable amount of information. Additional to data and identity theft, such insider compromise can inject malware into the system or can even leak details of the victim system or service to the attacker.

During a cyberterrorist attack, such compromised systems as discussed above may be private computer servers, public internet or even secure government networks. As compared to costs of arms and explosives, the purchase and scaling costs of computer and internet facilities are far less expensive. Additional to costs, the anonymity of attacker and the range of damage are the other benefits that make cyberterrorism an attractive option for the terrorist organizations.

In earlier times, the culprits or perpetrators accused of internet crimes used to be young hackers, who were inquisitive of technological experiments and curious about issues related to information security. However, with the change of times and advance in technology, highly organized and professional groups have replaced these experimenting youngsters. Now, these groups utilize computer attacks for creating sources of income, executing military and industrial espionage and accomplishing even international electronic warfare. Such possibilities of mass disruption and destruction cannot be expected to go unnoticed by terrorist organizations for a long time.

Methods of Computer Attacks

Different mechanisms of computer attacks involving various techniques can target different vulnerabilities of the prey systems. As discussed by Bayles (2001), according to types of weapons used and effects on the victim systems, the attacks on computer systems can be categorized into 3 major categories.

1.   Physical attack
2.   Electronic attack (EA)
3.   Computer network attack (CNA).

A Physical attack (also known as the Cyber-physical attack) comprises of use of conventional weapons (explosion, disconnection, etc.) against a computer system or its transmission infrastructure.

Common damage mechanisms such as blast, heat, fragmentation, and tripping are employed in the physical attack to upset the service availability and reliability of computing architecture. For this purpose, generally unauthorized physical access is achieved to execute direct manipulation of wiring or equipment. Cyber-physical attacks on critical infrastructure such as refineries, power generation plants, manufacturing units and oil pipelines can damage the physical assets to result from widespread losses. Here, an unauthorized access of a system gained by a hacker can result in a major cyber-physical attack on critical infrastructure causing risk not only for owners but also for customers, suppliers, business partners, investors and all dependent entities. Additional to this, the population located in the vicinity of the location of the attack is always at a risk of life and property.

Therefore, damages caused by a physical attack can be widespread, highly interconnected, massively destructive and affect multiple economic sectors simultaneously.

The 9/11 attacks conducted by Al-Qaeda against Pentagon and World Trade Center are an example of physical attacks that destroyed multiple critical computer databases as well as damaged globally connected financial and military communication systems

Electronic attacks (EA) encompass the use of electromagnetic energy (EM), anti-radiation weapon mechanisms or directed energy pulses to attack systems, equipment, and populations to disrupt or destroy infrastructure as well as civilian assets.

Here, the main objective remains to destroy an enemy's communication and connected physical infrastructures by attacking the electronic equipment as well as the electronic spectrum by using the electromagnetic energy.

The EM energy pulse can be used to inject a malicious digital code into the microwave radio transmission. Otherwise instantaneous high-energy EM shock pulse can be used to overload and crash the computational circuitry, transistors, and other devices to disrupt the enemy communication.

During such electronic attacks, electrical systems connected to any wired transmission line remain prominent targets. Besides this, the EM pulse may be sufficiently capable of penetrating the boundaries of the architecture to corrupt data, disrupt software functions or even damage electronic circuitry permanently. An EM pulse attack can be also considered as a DDoS attack on all electronic equipment in the target area. The considerable amount of time required for revival from such EMP attack makes it worse in terms of damage and casualty scales. EMP generator weapons or devices for an electronic attack can be acquired by terrorist outfits through the organized criminal channels.

The third type of attack is the computer network attack (CNA) that involves the injection of a malicious entity to infect adversary systems and services by exploiting a pre-existing weakness of the computational infrastructure. This may include any vulnerability in hardware configuration, software error, the absence of antivirus protection or even security practices being followed in the organization.

BY making use of a malicious code, a computer network attack (CNA) is capable of damaging the authenticity and integrity of the data in the system. An example of this scenario may be the modification in the logic of the running program, resulting in erroneous output signal for associated systems. On infecting a vulnerable computer system with a malicious code, the attackers can remotely control it for data theft, espionage or disrupt the functioning of even other connected computers also. Such CAN attack can be further extended to degrade, deny or even disrupt the information stored on infected computer networks.

Here, the distinction of EA attacks from CAN attacks must be mentioned. For example, damaging the CPU of a computer system by an EM shock pulse can be considered as EA attack. Execution of same by injecting a malicious program or instruction into the system will be counted under CAN attack.

Till now, the probability of CAN and EA class of attacks is estimated lower compared to that of physical attacks. In contrast, physical attacks are expected to prove more destructive as they may involve unpredictable consequences and provide unexpected advantages to the adversary.

Cyberattack, Cybercrime, and Cyberterrorism

All the terms relevant to Internet-based technologies are encircled under the umbrella term 'cyberspace'. As mentioned by Furnelb and Warren (1999), cyberspace can be considered as the collective set of all computer, communication and network service infrastructure. It is a technology-enabled domain that enables processing, control, and management of all critical services today.

Internet as the major component of cyberspace is built upon the telecommunication infrastructure composed of landlines, wireless public phone services as well as satellite communication networks. All these technologies work in coherence with computing services for synchronization and data transfer for critical infrastructure services. These critical infrastructure services involve banking and finance, power generation and distribution, medical, transportation and emergency response.

Any attack on these services, launched in cyberspace (over the internet) can be classified as a cyberattack. A cyberattack is launched against a targeted website, individual computer system or even a complete network of computer systems from another computer system to disrupt or damage the confidentiality, authenticity, and integrity of the data and services of the victim systems.

Types of Cyberattacks

From disruption of services to damage or espionage of data, cyberattacks can be classified into multiple categories. The various types and techniques of cyberattacks can be broadly classified into following major categories (Khanse, 2014):

- Denial of service attacks from single or distributed systems (DoS, DDoS) (Gupta et al., 2010)
- Hacking or defacing a website (XSS)
- Gaining unauthorized access to a computer system and/or data (Brute force)
- Injecting malicious code into a computer system or a network (Virus, worm)
- Holding or hijacking the functioning of a computer system using a hack mechanism (Ransomware)

Cybercrime is a generic term for a wide spectrum of criminal activities. Very often, cybercrimes reveal to be a conventional crime performed only by making use of the internet (Dennis, 1998). One such example is child pornography and kidnapping via chatrooms. Here the use of internet only facilitates remote and more hidden execution of the crime compared to the conventional approach. Forging of documents on a non-networked computer system is also a conventional crime committed with help of computer technology.

In the same sequence, DDoS attacks are also a common method of online extortion. As stated by Shrivastava et al. (2010), a DDoS attack comprises of series of disruption attacks on a website. Later the owner of the website is threatened of continuation of such attacks if a 'protect' or 'ransom' money is not paid.

Types of Cybercrimes

Other faces of cybercrime that involve theft of identity, data and service disruption are as follows:

- Email phishing
- Credit card frauds
- Bank account robbery
- Illegal downloading
- Industrial espionage
- Malware injection
- Domain name hijacking
- Online extortion
- Social engineering

In the light of above discussion, now cyberterrorism can be considered as the use of computer and internet technologies to execute terrorist activities. Since 'terrorism' and 'crime' are both concentrated on disruption of the law and order of the society, thus, cybercrime and cyberterrorism are often used as synonymous terms.

According to Collin (2013), cyberterrorism can be defined as a politically motivated crime committed in cyberspace (against computer systems, program, data and internet technologies) that results in creating havoc, loss of human lives and property, violence with a purpose of compelling the state government to change its policies. In all forms, cyberterrorism is the use of information technology to target critical infrastructure of a society by a terrorist group or organization.

The prime categories of objectives of cyberterrorism are elaborated ahead.

1. **Organizational:** Recruitment of new terrorists, training, attack planning, fundraising and communication activities are counted under the organization objectives of cyberterrorism. With the

growing knowledge and skill levels of terrorist groups about computer technologies, these activities are now being executed by terror groups on a regular basis.

2. **Destabilization:** Deterring the normal functioning of websites, computer systems, and services by defacing, denying and disrupting them is another main goal of cyberterrorist attacks. The more is the administration and society is dependent on internet-based services, the better are the prospects of destabilization objectives of cyberterrorists.

3. **Destructive:** From damaging property and equipment to injury and even death of civilians can result to be the major tool of suppression for terror groups. Hence, any cyberterror attack on critical infrastructure services, e.g. Power supply in hospitals, can prove to be a major shock to the society and administration.

Motivation of Cyberterrorism

A cyberterrorist attack is commonly an outcome of religious, ideological or political purpose, with an intention of constructing an environment of extreme panic, havoc, and horror in the common civilian population or the state body to modify its policies.

The motivation of terrorism in modern times is no more limited to creating physical harm to society for a political objective. Today religious beliefs provide a necessary motivational ground to enable and accept terrorism. Lewis (2003) mentions that, in parallel to religion, it is also essential to recognize the specific aspect of culture in order to comprehend the motives behind terrorism. For example, the glory of the ancient powerful Islamic empires is a major motivation behind the functioning of Al-Qaeda in various parts of the world. In view of religious and cultural aspects, a drift towards violence and destruction due to twisted religious validation is a major cause of terrorism.

In this sequence, the impact of the cyberterrorism is measured by the degree of violence, severity, and loss of human life as well as damage to critical infrastructure services.

As stated by Weimann (2005), while analyzing the motivation of cyberterrorist activities, the different judgment parameters to be kept under consideration are explained ahead.

Casualty Rate

Terror groups with fundamental religious beliefs often attempt to implement maximum casualties during a cyberterrorism attack. On the contrary side, non-religious and groups with secular ideologies remain highly selective and discriminative for the achievement of their political or social objectives.

Target Type

Groups motivated by secular, political or social motivations, restrict to administrative targets such as banks, government offices, multinational corporations and stock market to represent their rage against the established order. While religious terror groups tend towards greater physical damage of religiously affiliated persons, activities, worship services and spots etc.

Date and Timing

Secular or nationalist terror groups execute their cyberterror attacks on dates representing victory or defeat of a national war or struggle. On the other side, religious terror groups often strike with cyberattacks on days of religious celebrations, observances, and festivals.

Although, the fundamental motive of cyberterrorism always remains to create an environment of panic and terror among the victim population. However, from the study of Veerasamy (2010), on classifying the cyberterror attacks according to above-mentioned parameters, this motivation can be further fragmented into following categories.

1. **Political:** The major actors of cyber terrorism are the same groups or individuals responsible for the execution of physical terrorist attacks. In this class, terror organizing groups, as well as sponsoring nations, are both present. A major goal of cyberterrorism remains the opposition of the government or administrative policies of state to create political dominance and pressurize the existing government to obey or abort certain policies. Political cyberterrorism targets to disrupt, damage, capture control, broadcast political announcements, protests, and retaliatory actions. For these activities, fear, and panic among civilian population act as prominent tools. The main methods to achieve this include attacks on accounts of eminent leaders on social networks, blogs, and their media websites.

2. **Religious:** To motivate certain religious beliefs, cyberterrorist attacks are executed. Such attacks include disruption of services towards a targeted population, broadcast of hate messages against a community, etc.

3. **Economic:** Besides creating panic among the masses by attacking the financial establishments of the state, managing the financial transactions of the terrorist organization is also a major concern of the cyberterrorists. For implementing financial management objectives, cyberterrorists target banking systems and payment gateway services for extortion, payment of attacks conducted via outsourcing, money laundering and funding to terror agents etc. For disruption of civil routine life, attack on stock exchange services, forging false cases against public officials and corruption or modification of bank databases are preferred choices for cyberterrorists. With advances in technology, the virtual currency like bitcoin is now being used for storing and transferring money anonymously across borders. By making use of virtual currency, accurate tracking and taxation of money can be made almost impossible for any government.

4. **Communication:** Establishing untraceable and secure communication channels among the operative agents of a terror group is another prime objective. Secure communication is vital for recruitments, execution of attacks, planning of future attacks and message passing for any purpose. For this, electromagnetic transmission, landline, mobile, satellite, and VoIP communication mediums are frequent options. On the internet, communication applications such as chat programs, emails, and even social media are noticeable. It should be noticed that the communication in a business group and a terrorist outfit is not too distinct except their objectives. Here the business group aims at the sales of its product or services, while the terror group is focused on producing havoc among the masses. However, the basic aim of both groups remains to motivate the individuals at the other end to respond. Hence, the same technology used for legitimate transactions by a business group can be used by a terrorist group in dual mode.

5. **Propaganda:** For broadcast of terror messages across public, terrorist makes use of websites of media outlets, organizations and popular accounts on social media platforms. Additional to these, chat applications and text messages from cell phones are also a tool for creating panic in society. As stated by Furnelb and Warren (1999), with the advent of the Internet of Things (IoT), cyberterrorists can use any underlying infrastructure connected to World Wide Web to deliver messages. For example, smart televisions, hoardings on the highway and even electronic billboards may be hacked to spread messages. For implementing propaganda, cyberterrorists have a wide choice of selecting targets from an electronic billboard on a highway to the twitter account of a political leader to the website of a media channel. In such case, where security of each of these mediums remains an issue of concern, in parallel, compromise of any of these may cause havoc and horror in public.

6. **Deprivation:** Various forms of deprivations such as lack of education, poverty or even political freedom can be a motivational goal for a cyberterrorist group. Such goals can lead to theft of intellectual properties, financial data assets like bank and credit card details, fraud, espionage etc.

7. **Fundraising:** Like any other social or business organization, terror outfits also require economic funding to implement their ideology. According to Furnelb and Warren (1999), similar to any startup business, terror groups receive funding from supporting enemy nations and donations from supporters of terrorist ideology. For such fundraiser operations, simple messages through email services and social media platforms are circulated to reach out to the supportive audience and raise funds. Here also, virtual currency systems like bitcoin are used to maintain the anonymity of fundraising operations of cyberterrorist organizations.

8. **Arms Procurement:** Acquisition and development of malicious tools against cyberspace are as critical as procurement of physical weapons for conventional attacks. Internet relay chat (IRC) channels, dark web sources, closed forums and secret groups on social media are some of the many ways to acquire malicious codes in exchange for money. Underground industries involved in illegal development and commercialization of malicious software provide tools, support, and even updates to conduct a cyberterrorist attack on a professional basis.

9. **Recruitment:** Like fundraising operations, recruitments are also operations vital for the functioning of terror groups. To recruit terror operatives, online forums, mailing lists, chat applications, social media platforms like twitter are used by terror groups.

10. **Intelligence Collection:** Terror groups utilize the World Wide Web as a resource for intelligence gathering for targets from third parties; plan the course of actions for execution of operations and coordination of operations. Similar to a business organization, terror groups also execute their operations by making use of intelligence for implementation of their objectives.

11. **Training and Knowledge Acquisition:** From knowledge of assembling explosives and bombs to the execution of a cyberterrorist attack, learning and training are crucial for terror operatives. Specifically, for implementing a cyberattack, working knowledge of programming languages, writing malicious codes and finding practical methods to inject them into target systems are essential for conducting a cyberattack. Cyberterrorists exploit the infrastructure of cyberspace to learn and acquire such knowledge. Besides computer systems, the internet is the vital resource of knowledge about various other fields of chemistry, physics, engineering etc. This knowledge proves useful during the ground implementation of attacks in the live environment from assembling of bombs to blasting them at the exact scene with high accuracy of timing.

Some examples of these motivations for cyberterrorist attacks are enumerated here. A cyberterrorist group can execute attacks to:

1. Attain recognition for their cause at global, national or local levels by drawing attention of media.
2. Create suspicion and fear among civilians against administrative establishments.
3. Pressurize and harass the existing government forces to invite their reaction.
4. Damage communication channels and critical service infrastructures to create doubt that the government can protect its civilians.
5. Deter and discourage economic growth factors like tourism, foreign investments, assistance programs to affect the country.
6. Gain freedom of imprisoned fellow terrorist members of the group.
7. Ego gratification and satisfying vengeance against a community or government.
8. Extortion of money, weapons, and equipment for executing further operations.

How Different Is Cyberterrorism

According to Lewis (2003), in terms of objectives and motivation, no visible difference is presented between conventional and cyber terrorism. The only noticeable variance here is that cyberterrorism consumes cyberspace to craft panic and horror in civilian population to achieve its political and religious goal. In addition, contrary to conventional physical terrorism, direct massive physical causalities of life and property have yet to be observed due to cyberterrorism (Stohl, 2007).

To understand the detailed differences of cyber terrorism, first, we need to distinguish terrorism from other threats dominant in cyberspace such as espionage, cyberwarfare, organized cybercrime and hacktivism.

As discussed earlier, terrorism can be envisioned as the intentional and illegal act of aggression by an individual or group, to attain political objectives against a state or government by influencing its policy-based decisions.

Dual Use of Legitimate Tools

Unlike the bodies mentioned above, a cyberterrorist organization functions in a manner closely similar to a business group or organization. Similar to a business group, cyberterrorists are all involved towards making gains. The only difference here remains that instead of financial profit like a business, cyberterrorism is concentrated over making political gains. Hence, most of the times, cyberterrorists also use the tools and technologies to make political gains, which are used by business organizations to make the economic profit in the market. Such dual use of technologies makes it hard to distinguish and counter cyber terrorism activities.

High Intensity

Due to its nature of goals, terrorism is essentially composed of acts of very high intensity. Here, the intensity corresponds to the possible impact on the target, amount of risk involved and the degree of demoralizing the sense of security in civilians. Such acts are generally executed by secret and undercover groups that may benefit from the support of local population as well as the absence of physical boundaries.

Panic and Horror

The other prominent feature of terrorism is its intention of creating panic and fear among civilian population through violent means. It should be noted that hacktivism is also an approach of influencing political verdicts, but without pressurizing the public to do so. The mediums of violence employed in cyberterrorism are capable of damaging the civilian population through manipulation or corruption of information services running on physical system infrastructures. Even in its minimal form, cyberterrorism is capable of disrupting the normal routine life a modern civil society functioning on information-based services such as banks, ATMs, railway reservations, etc.

Instead of any major physical disruption, till now cyberterrorist groups make use of cyberspace and computer technologies for rational practices like intelligence gathering, arms procurement, fundraising, terror recruitments, purchases and even money transfers. In addition, similar to an authentic business group, cyberterrorists make every use of cyberspace, to run their necessary operations.

Less Expensive

Cyberterrorism is less expensive in terms of execution, risk as well as causalities as compared to conventional physical terrorism. Apart from lower prices of weapons and equipment, a major cause is also lack of awareness among state bodies. As far as physical terror attacks are concerned, today every nation has evolved its own defense and intelligence organizations to counter and foil such attacks.

Cyberterrorism as Terrorism in Cyberspace

The conjuncture of cyberspace and terrorism is known as Cyberterrorism. According to Furnelb and Warren (1999), it usually refers to illegitimate attacks on computer systems, networks, and the information stored on various devices in a computer system. The attack can be carried out to threaten or bully organizations or government for financial, social or political gain. An attack can be classified as cyberterrorism if it violates property or privacy of individual, group or an organization. An attack done to terrorize and spread fear is also considered as cyberterrorism. Apart from that such attacks can cause explosions, plane hijacking, water/air contamination or economic loss, critical infrastructures.

Targets for such attacks can be day-to-day electronic devices such as Smartphone, Smart televisions, home appliances such as Microwave, Automated Parking gate etc. For causing greater damage large-scale infrastructures such as traffic control systems, public transport, hospitals, the backbone of the smart city, modern weapons etc. can be targeted (Campbell et al., 2003). Some commonly available but neglected points susceptible of a cyberattack are mentioned as follows.

- Remotely accessible appliances such as microwave ovens, televisions and coffee makers.
- Domestic utilities like electricity and LPG.
- Pacemaker devices.
- Air traffic controllers.
- Communication equipment.
- Body control module of old cars containing the programmable chip.
- Automated garage doors.

- Road or railroad crossing systems.
- Almost all modern weapon systems.

Potential Attack Trajectories for Cyberterrorism

By making use of sensors, devices are now becoming interactive under the umbrella technology term of "Internet of Things." The latest and most obvious target of cyberterror attack is expected to be these IoT devices, which on comprise can leave the society in panic and havoc.

Possible Attack Vectors for Cyber Terrorists

A few possible instances of cyberterror attacks may be as follows:

- Block of email services throughout the country.
- Broadcast of tweets or messages to craft panic with a fake rumor of a highly transmissible and deadly disease is spreading through the population.
- Permanently disabling the civilian connectivity at the individual level and blocking access to utilities, health, and emergency services.
- Accessing and disabling the signals which to command and control drones and other military technologies.
- Simply hack or break into the private corporate servers of a corporation in order to learn trade secrets, steal banking information, or even the private data of their employees.
- Causing physical damage to homes and property by capturing control of the embedded Internet of things (IoT) devices in use to control heating, refrigeration, lighting, security and other domestic systems, and increasingly vehicles (Campbell et al., 2003).
- Executing a distributed denial of service attacks (DDOS) by bot or zombie computer systems operating as part of a bot network is already a common and widely used hacking technique for corrupting, modifying and spying the corporate databases as well as in industry, commerce, and defense (Shrivastava et al., 2010).
- Using hackers to spy on intelligence and military communications to acquire the location and strategies of troops for gaining a tactical advantage at war.
- Blocking the traffic of a website, that publishes content with which the terror group disagrees.
- Deface or dysfunction a government website or social media platform site to create a public nuisance or inconvenience.

Factors Critical to Success of Cyberterror Attack

According to Collin (2013), The major factors which act as drivers of success for a cyberterrorist attack are enumerated here.

1. **Access:** To the universal interface of cyberspace for attack execution.
2. **Control:** For attaining capabilities of command and control with remote administration.
3. **Mining:** To acquire field intelligence and ground level execution knowledge of attacks.

Channels to Achieve These Goals can be Divided into Following Four Categories:

1. **Transmission:** Longer lines across land and through space;
2. **Connections:** More links to more points;
3. **Aggregation:** More information centralized, and disconnected information linked; and
4. **Retrieval:** More ways of retrieving information, and more importantly, knowledge.

Realization of Cyberterrorism Goals

Modus operandi of a cyberterrorist is similar to any other terrorist. A Cyberterrorist rigorously exploits the goals of the intended population in areas where they are careless.

There are three potential acts in Cyberterrorism at the point of convergence:

1. Destruction;
2. Alteration; and
3. Acquisition and retransmission (these are a unit).

As we will see, these three types of acts are most heinous at the point where the physical and virtual worlds converge.

Dominant Players in the Domain of Cyber Terrorism

U.S.A.

According to review of Breene (2016), The United States of America started improvisation of its cyber warfare capabilities from the year 2010 by integrating the cyber capabilities of its army, navy and air force under a common division named US cyber command. In the year 2012, Pentagon released an official statement announcing the major extension of its cyber warfare capabilities.

As stated by Juzenaite (2015), the National Security Agency (NSA) of US operates a special unit named Tailored Access Operations (TAO), with an estimated number of 1000 military and civilian hackers for its operations in the domain if international cyber warfare. Intelligence gathering, infiltration, and surveillance of enemy operations are the major activate performed by TAO. TAO is believed to be penetrating Chinese computer networks for intelligence gathering from the People's Republic of China for more than last 15 years. Juzenaite (2015) further mentions that similar to China, TAO also adopts an aggressive employment strategy to select highly potential hackers as specialists from major hacker conferences organized around the US.

Russia

Russia is considered as a nation with advanced cyber capabilities and is using it to fulfill its political and military motives. According to Batashvili (2017), a significant example of Russian cyberattack is believed to have influenced the results of American elections of 2016. Nevertheless, the first noticeable evidence of a massive Russian cyberattack appeared in Estonia in the year 2007 in form of a massive

DDoS attack. Estonia is a former Russia colony, a dispute for a historical legacy between Russia and Estonia provoked this attack resulting into damage of multiple government and business websites.

Breene (2016) and Batashvili (2017) further state that in August 2008, with the start of the war against Georgia, Russia cyberattack also initiated and continued till the ceasefire. During this period, massive Russian cyberattacks damaged websites of government, media, business and financial groups of Georgia including the website of Georgian president for 24 hours.

As Russia is now believed to utilize all its available means and tools to achieve its political objectives, the domain of cyberspace is expected to be a major platform for the political and military aggression of Russia.

China

China is considered among one of the most active nations in the domain of cyberspace. Similar to the US, China is also investing sizable manpower, equipment, attack methodologies and money for development and expansion of its cyber capabilities (Breene, 2016).

As per the review by Green (2015), the People's Liberation Army has staged a special cyberwarfare unit named 'Unit 61398' in Shanghai to attack American targets. Trained in multiple network espionage and monitoring capabilities, Unit 61398 is believed to be involved in covert cyber operations throughout the world. These operations involve interception of telecommunication signals, investigation of satellite signals and hacking of computer as well as mobile service networks.

Iran

The swift advancement of the cyber program by Iran has paved its entry in the group of strongest nations in cyber capabilities. Due to a developed military industry and a strong academic infrastructure, Iran has quickly emerged as a prominent cyber power. According to the article by Rafizadeh (2016), currently, Iran is making heavy investments in internet, social media and cyberwarfare capabilities considering cybersecurity as a matter of national security. In the year 2013, the involvement of Iranian attackers was pointed by US intelligence agencies in cyberattacks on multiple US banks and financial groups. Now, Iran is reportedly exporting its cyber capabilities to Syria to suppress any revolt or uprising.

Hezbollah

According to Coleman (2008), Hezbollah showcased its advancing sophistication in technological and attack capabilities during Lebanon war with Israel in the year 2006. Believed to be an extension of Iranian cyberwarfare unit, Hezbollah receives full support from Iran in terms of modern tools, knowledge transfers, and training.

Technologies in Use for Cyber Terrorism

Synonymous with conventional physical terrorism, terrorist organization also outsource cyberterrorist assignments to professionals and criminal groups in exchange for monetary favors. This fact establishes a proven connection between organized crime and terror groups driven by money. Similarly, rogue states and hacker groups are also indispensable associates of cyberterrorism groups. Any technological trend in practice is directly influenced by the connections of these groups in cyberspace. Leakage of Stuxnet code into internet space, and later its use for cyberattacks was a noticeable example of such influences.

As mentioned by Lindsay (2013), like Stuxnet, any program code developed as a weapon by the army of a nation to attack enemy assets, if gained by cyberterrorist groups and supporting rogue nations, can be misused to target critical infrastructures and create havoc. Here we discuss some technologies of similar potential as mentioned above.

Malicious Programs

Malware such as viruses, worms, ransomware etc. comprise a major part of the arsenal of a cyberterror groups. Besides malware, malicious scripts are also a common tool for hacking accounts on social media, databases, financial services, and website defacement. Parallel to the development of such tools, cyberterrorists also opt to purchase them from professional cybercriminals or even hire hackers to perform cyberattacks on their behalf. With evolving technology, it can be expected that similar attacks will only grow in numbers and severity as cyberterror groups improvise their knowledge and skill levels in cyberspace.

Algo Trading and Big Data

Use of computer programs for automatic and fast response stock trading is termed as Algo trading. It is an emerging field of computational sciences catching up the pace in the financial world. Big data has been a popular term for storage and computation of massive datasets. Bigdata is a preferred technique for analysis of data collected in real time. Now, technologies such as algo trading and big data are being employed for analysis of real-time military data for decision making on the battlefield. Nevertheless, parallel to the military, cyberterrorists have also started the use of these technologies for decision making of attack scenarios in cyberspace or even conventional physical terror attacks. For example, live

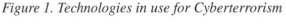

Figure 1. Technologies in use for Cyberterrorism

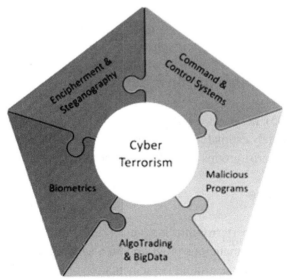

data from real-time devices such as traffic cameras and air traffic control applications can be misused to cause damage to the road or air traffic. Hence, access to such real-time decision-making technologies like also trade and big data can enhance the casualty impact of a cyberterror attack for a terror outfit.

Biometrics

Like other pattern matching technologies, biometric scans are also becoming a preferred and secure technique for verification of individuals in cyberspace. It consists of creating and storing biometric imprints of professional in organizations such as banks, financial services, military operations and political bodies. On part of cyberterrorism, any method of manipulating, forging, recreating and corrupting these biometric imprints can enable illegitimate framing and conspiracy against these officials to diminish their credibility and image. Possession of such capabilities can give the edge to cyberterrorists in committing cyberterror attacks and craft panic in society.

Command and Control Systems

Command and control technologies are essentially used to make coordination in physical or cyberspace environments. Their major use is observed in functioning and management of financial services, stocks, and equipment. Cyberterrorists have embraced these systems to establish coordination for operations such as intelligence acquisition, plan designing and organizing an attack. Utilization of carpooling services running over the web for organizing a meeting of sleeper cell unit members is a visible example of such misuse of technology.

Encipherment and Steganography

Use of data hiding techniques is also becoming a common practice among cyberterrorists. With the growth in their knowledge and technical skill levels, terror outfits are now well aware of the rigorous monitoring systems running over the internet and electromagnetic transmission channels. In order to safeguard their activities in form of image, data, text, video or voice messages from security services, terrorists have adopted encryption and Steganography as de-facto standard practice. Today terrorist groups are capable of encrypting communications over Cellphones, emails, chats, file sharing and even radio communication. They even make use of social media platforms, websites and even porn sites to hide and transfer messages by using Steganography technique.

Fascination of Cyberterrorism for Terrorist Groups

According to Weimann (2005), the exact level of practical ability and technical know-how to execute a cyberattack, cannot be accurately estimated for a terrorist organization. But still, there are many factors that elevate the interest of terrorist groups towards a cyberterror attack.

Higher Chances of Success

To execute a well-coordinated cyberterror attack against critical infrastructure services maintained by computers, injecting an automated malicious program into a network of computers with visible vulnerabilities is preferred the option. For the ground implementation of this attack, merely copy pasting such procedures from a hacker website may be sufficient to take down and compromise a system without any special training and investment.

Lower Risk

With the constantly evolving measures in the domain of conventional physical and ground level security, executing a conventional terror attack is not easier compared to earlier times. In this scenario, an attack through the cyberspace can be minimum risk option for the terror groups. Since, for detection as well as prevention of a cyberterror attacks, there is still a considerable gap of technical ability in the security forces, hence its execution is a more secure alternative.Besides this, due to the interconnectivity of systems and infrastructure services, compromise of a single vulnerable system can result in corruption and downfall of the complete system.

Less Dramatic

According to observers, compared to a conventional terrorist attack, a cyberterror attack is considered of less intensity and lower impact. Unless a cyberattack results into actual physical damage or violence, it cannot be considered as lethal as a chemical, biological or nuclear attack of terrorism.

Abundance of Vulnerable Computer Systems

Vulnerable or misconfigured computer systems can be easily targeted to enslave and make the part a bot network. Such network of compromised systems can be remotely controlled to shut down, spy, corrupt or even manipulate infrastructure services. Through this technology of bot networks, a single hacker can control the compromised systems via an encrypted channel of communication. It can be further used as a collective swarm of bots to search and attack new systems and spread the network.

Fast Expansion of Automated Cyberattacks

The prevalent use of automated tools of attacks by cyberterrorists has worsened the number of network attacks to an alarming state. Such scenario of cyberattacks has rendered the current security measures of the minimum of very little relevance. In this situation, the parameters for assessment for effects and scope of cyberattacks against Internet-connected systems requires through improvisation.

Poor and Inadequate Security Practices

General purpose users of computers and internet services, mostly have minimal or zero training of standard security practices for securing home computer networks and equipment. In this case, vulnerabilities continue to thrive due to the poor quality of software products, outdated security procedures and practices and inadequate training in computer security. Insufficient resources devoted to staffing the security purposes also escalate the chances of compromise of systems and services. Eventually, these chances result into entry points for a cyberattack or invite chances of cyberterrorist outbreak.

Errors in New Software Products

To keep pace with business and profit objectives, the technology vendors lay more focus on marketing and simply keep ignoring the evolving security demands of the systems by. This results into launch and release of new software products with old persisting errors, that keep the vulnerabilities alive in the whole infrastructure service. This scenario can be expected to change only with higher awareness and larger demand for security features by customers.

Delay in Installation of Security Updates

In spite of the periodic and regular release of upgrades, patches and security fixes of latest discovered security challenges, such fixes are updated on the vulnerable systems for a considerable gap of time. Due to various reasons, any delay of these type can let the systems remain unguarded, leaving networks susceptible for any cyberattack for long durations. Hence, such delays in the update of security fixes can cost into comprising and collapse of whole service infrastructure due to a cyberterrorist attack.

Prevention of Cyber-Terrorism

Cyberterrorism affects the national as well as business sectors on the same impact scale. Business groups being a part of the national economy and state machinery also, are the obvious major contributors of the society. Nevertheless, combating cyberterrorism for business and national sectors is and should not be alike. Hence, alike conventional physical terrorism attacks, threats of cyberterror have to be also dealt in a much different manner. Synonymous with conventional terrorism, 100% prevention or eradication of cyber terror is impossible for any group or individual. In light of this fact, government and business organization must include cyberterrorism as a compulsory part of their structuring policies. This will always assist them in countering and responding to cyberattacks in a better manner.

In spite of such degree of severity of cyberattacks, there are no standard or hard-and-fast rulebooks, or even a universal policy agreement on the definition, types, and causes, eradication or even prevention of cyberterror attacks in all cases.

According to their approach and impact, as stated by Goodman (2007), security testing practices can be categorized into 2 major categories:

- **Verification Procedures:** Techniques used to evaluate and assess the predefined security methods and protocols being strictly followed by the organization or not.
- **Validation Procedures:** Methods that are used to check the accuracy and performance of the implemented security procedures in the organizations.

Similar to any other quality control mechanism, both of these procedures are required to generate a comprehensive evaluation of security levels in an organization.

But the best security practices for proactive prevention or cyberattacks and cyberterrorism can be found with the documentation of Computer Emergency Response Team's (ICERT, 2017). This resource presents the basic guidelines for any individual or organization to safeguard its information and digital assets from a cyberterror attack.

1. Harden and secure your systems by establishing secure configurations. Secure your systems with updated intrusion detection systems and latest hardware and software protection. Constantly update the security patches and fixes provided by software vendors.
2. On detection of an intrusion, respond quickly to the possible threat to minimize damage. At minimum measure, immediately change the network configuration as well as the passwords when defects become known.
3. Connect with antivirus firms or defensive organizations, preferably in a partnership to track and respond to threats.
4. Secure your computers and network with strong passwords, active firewalls, and latest antivirus systems. Keep each of them updated and run regular checks to detect and remove any possible problems. Also, apply filters to screen out suspicious material or messages from known sources of threats such as specific countries.
5. Use your national database of cyberthreats as a resource manual to stay updated with latest threats and defense machinery. Follow news and computer information reports about new threats, such as a new worm or other malware being circulated, even if it is not in your immediate area.
6. Create a firm security policy. In case of any doubt about the safety and integrity of your systems due to unusual network activities or suspicious logs, report and respond according to security policies.
7. On receiving any doubtful emails or even chat messages on social media platforms from unknown accounts or addresses, never access it. They may invite trouble.
8. Train the employees of your organization to guard against such things as opening email attachments or responding to messages from unknown sources. Institute regular checks to make sure security precautions are followed.
9. Get your defense mechanisms tested on a regular basis preferably by employing a testing or security service to regularly run demo-attacks over system and network to investigate and report any insufficiencies or flaws. Regularly audit systems and check logs to help in detecting and tracking an intruder.

Case Study

Stuxnet is a potential example of a sophisticated computer worm designed to attack computers running Windows operating system (Lindsay, 2013). Stuxnet was originally designed to target only specific SCADA systems for industrial control. The first version of Stuxnet worm was identified in the year 2010 as a spyware capable of reprogramming industrial systems running control and monitoring processes. It may affect critical infrastructure services such as nuclear power plants and assembly line systems by reprogramming specific PLC (programmable logic controller) devices.

According to Kushner (2013), by using 0-day vulnerability attacks, Stuxnet exploits the vulnerability of a system, much before it is known to its developers. It also uses rootkits and digital certificates to hide from users and anti-malware software.

Stuxnet is believed to be developed by experts of US and Israel for targeting and derailing Iran's uranium enrichment program. By attacking the infrastructures using only a specific 'cascade' physical layout, Stuxnet can reprogram or damage the supportive systems. The centrifuge layout at Natanz enrichment plant of Iran is of cascaded design where multiple centrifuge pipes are connected in parallel in a cascaded manner.

Figure 2. Working of Stuxnet Worm

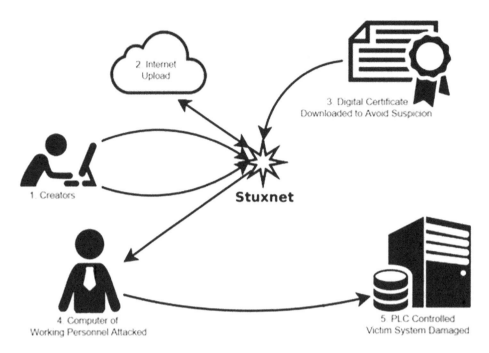

By damaging around 1000 centrifuges at Natanz, Stuxnet reduced the production of enriched uranium and spread disorder within the Iranian nuclear facility.

CONCLUSION

As given by Stohl (2007), Cyberterrorism is in many ways similar to physical terrorism. Its conceptual similarity allows drawing conclusions from one dimension to the other. However, there are few main differences.

The first difference arises from the fact that cyber terrorism targets the business sector directly. While in the physical dimension, the government has the proper infrastructure to shield the business sector from terrorism through its security services. However, in the cyberspace, the state-based security services are almost non-existent and the business owners are left with the responsibility for handling cyber terrorism all on their own. This fierce reality forces the organizations to be responsive to the threats arising from cyberterrorism, and to adopt the necessary measures to preserve and recover from it with minimal support from the government.

A second difference is that it is harder to deter a cyberterrorist organization completely. A prominent reason for this is the problem of detecting and assigning responsibility for attack due to lack of physical, as well as evidences. In case, if we cannot assign responsibility for a cyber-attack to a specific group or individual, there arises no question of punishing anyone, which leads to zero deterrence.

The cyberterrorism threat is actual and people are not sufficiently prepared to prevent or detect such an attack. Besides them, this affects even other organizations that may be well prepared. Cybersecurity is a public concern of security. Like everything else, testing can only authenticate what has already been prepared. However, quality professionals can be imperative promoters for the consciousness of IT safekeeping. The potential impact that can be caused due to a cyber-attack on public infrastructures of a nation-state.

For example, if credit cards are stolen from a retailer and the incident is publicized on the internet, that message drives out to all consumers around the world. This results in weakening and diminishing of the sense of security of consumers around to world to shop online. This communicational change leads to a drop in encouragement of public from online transactions thousands of kilometers away from the origin of the incident. Cyberspace makes the transmits any such change in consumer behavior into global trends at a very fast pace. The responsibility for dealing with cyber terrorism rests on the shoulders of the business organization. The fact that the government is out of the equation forces the business organization's executive team to prepare and react to such event. This additional operational and managerial overhead cost that is added to the daily operation of the business.

Cyber terrorism is an undoubted challenge for modern business organizations. The economic connectivity based on the World Wide Web forces business globally to deal with the infectious changes in one place in the world to quickly affect businesses on the other side of the globe. Modern cyberterrorist organizations can utilize this reality to its full potential. Ignoring the threat from cyberterrorism threat will not make it go away and would certainly not prevent it. Cyber terrorism is here to stay and will almost certainly toll its price from the business sector.

REFERENCES

Batashvili, D. (2017). EUobserver - Russia's cyber war: past, present, and future. *EUobserver*. Retrieved from https://euobserver.com/opinion/136909

Bayles, W. J. (2001). The Ethics of Computer Network Attack. *Information Warfare Site*. Retrieved from http://www.iwar.org.uk/iwar/resources/ethics-of-cna/bayles.htm

Breene, K. (2016). World Economic Forum - Who are the cyberwar superpowers? *WEForum*. Retrieved from https://www.weforum.org/agenda/2016/05/who-are-the-cyberwar-superpowers/

Campbell, R., Al-Muhtadi, J., Naldurg, P., Sampemane, G., Mickunas, M.D. (2003). Towards Security and Privacy for Pervasive Computing, Springer-Verlag Berlin Heidelberg. 1–15

Coleman, K. (2008). Hezbollah's Cyber Warfare Program. DefenseTech. Retrieved from https://www.defensetech.org/2008/06/02/hezbollahs-cyber-warfare-program/

Collin, B. C. (2013). The Future of CyberTerrorism. In *Proceedings of the 11th Annual International Symposium on Criminal Justice Issues*. Retrieved from http://www.crime-research.org/library/Cyberter.htm

Dennis, M. A. (1998). Cybercrime. *Encyclopedia Britannica*. Retrieved from https://www.britannica.com/topic/cybercrime

Furnelb, S. M., & Warren, M. J. (1999). Computer Hacking and Cyber Terrorism: The Real Threats in the New Millennium. *Computers & Security*, *18*(1), 28–34. doi:10.1016/S0167-4048(99)80006-6

Gaub, F. (2017). Trends in terrorism, European Union Institute for Security Studies (EUISS). doi:Retrieved from https://www.iss.europa.eu/sites/default/files/EUISSFiles/Alert_4_Terrorism_in_Europe_0.pdf. 10.2815/66788

Goodman, S. E. (2007). Cyberterrorism and Security Measures, Science and Technology to Counter Terrorism. In *Proceedings of an Indo-U.S. Workshop*. Retrieved from https://www.nap.edu/read/11848/chapter/6

Green, M. A. (2015). China's Growing Cyberwar Capabilities. *The Diplomat*. Retrieved from https://thediplomat.com/2015/04/chinas-growing-cyberwar-capabilities/

Gupta, B. B., Joshi, R. C., Misra, M., Meena, D. L., Shrivastava, G., & Sharma, K. (2010). Detecting a Wide Range of Flooding DDoS Attacks using Linear Prediction Model. In Proceedings of the IEEE 2nd International Conference on Information and Multimedia Technology (ICIMT 2010) (pp. 535-539).

ICERT - Indian Computer Emergency Response Team. (2017). Ministry of Electronics & Information Technology, Government of India. Retrieved from http://meity.gov.in/content/icert

Juzenaite, R. (2015). Infosec Institute - The Most Hacker-Active Countries. Retrieved from http://resources.infosecinstitute.com/the-most-hacker-active-countries-part-i/#gref

Khanse, A. (2014). Cyber Attacks – Definition, Types, Prevention, The Windows Club. Retrieved from http://www.thewindowsclub.com/cyber-attacks-definition-types-prevention

Kushner, D. (2013). The Real Story of Stuxnet. Retrieved from http://www.nytimes.com/2012/06/04/technology/cyberweapon-warning-from-kaspersky-a-computer-security-expert.html?pagewanted=all

Lewis, J. (2003). Cyber Terror: Missing in Action. *Knowledge, Technology & Policy*, *16*(2), 34–41. doi:10.100712130-003-1024-6

Lindsay, J. R. (2013). Stuxnet and the Limits of Cyber Warfare. *Security Studies*, *22*(3), 365–404. doi:10.1080/09636412.2013.816122

Rafizadeh, M. (2016). Al Arabiya - Iran's asymmetrical warfare: The cyberattack capabilities. Retrieved from http://english.alarabiya.net/en/views/news/middle-east/2016/04/02/Iran-s-asymmetrical-warfare-The-cyberattack-capabilities.html

Sciolino, E. (2004). Bombing in Madrid: The Attack. *New York Times*. Retrieved from http://www.nytimes.com/2004/03/12/world/bombings-in-madrid-the-attack-10-bombs-shatter-trains-in-madrid-killing-192.html

Shrivastava, G., Sharma, K., & Rai, S. (2010). The Detection & Defense of DoS & DDoS Attack: A Technical Overview. In *Proceeding of ICC*, December 27-28 (pp. 278–282).

Stohl, M. (2007). Cyber terrorism: a clear and present danger, the sum of all fears, breaking point or patriot games? In *Crime Law and Social Change*. Springer Science + Business Media B.V. doi:10.1007/s10611-007-9061-9

Veerasamy, N. (2010). Motivation for cyberterrorism. In *Proceedings of ISSA*. Retrieved from http://icsa.cs.up.ac.za/issa/2010/Proceedings/Research/02_paper.pdf

Weimann, G. (2005). The Sum of All Fears. *Studies in Conflict & Terrorism, Taylor & Francis., 28*(2), 129–149. doi:10.1080/10576100590905110

Chapter 11
Cyber Crime Toolkit Development

Aarthee R.
VIT University, India

Ezhilmaran D.
VIT University, India

ABSTRACT

This chapter describes how cybercrime, likewise called computer crime, is any illicit activity that includes a PC or system associated gadget. While numerous magnificent items have been produced to secure our information correspondence frameworks, these items must be upgraded significantly more. What is additionally required more are the individuals who know how to explore PC network security episodes and the individuals who have both investigative gifts and specialized knowledge of how the internet truly functions. This allows for an investigative structure which can withstand attack, alongside information of how the internet functions and the instruments to examine cybercrime apparatus to tell the who, where, what, when, why, and how. Cybercrime apparatus make our work substantially more productive.

INTRODUCTION

The earth will not keep running with weaponry, vitality, and cash. An electron which contains zeros-little bits of information will control the world. As a result of the world wars which not have the most shots. World war is about the information that will have what will people think, see and hear and how people will work (Sneakers, 1765).

Computer crime is famously known as cybercrime. Cybercrime is characterized as illicit movement using web, networks and computer frameworks. Cybercrime includes the control, get to and misuse of data and in a roundabout way, individuals. As PC offense transforms into the most in all cases criminal development in the world, there are dependable crooks hunting down new and unprotected PC innovations to abuse. These hoodlums who work in the electronic world change in age, sexual orientation, identity,

DOI: 10.4018/978-1-5225-4100-4.ch011

social, monetary status and that's just the beginning, suggesting that people who execute cybercrimes could be anyone. Regardless, most cybercriminals share comparable points of view and inspirations to execute these infringements regardless.

Individuals do cybercrime, after all, it is unquestionably not difficult to be dark utilizing improvement. A major motive for the crime of information technology is typical and typical for the guilty parties is a compromise of the "Deficient Legal Jurisdiction". The issue has been included in the computer encryption system if there is an impracticable effort to create or maintain processing devices if remote processing can be performed.

Frequently individuals spread pernicious computer codes, for example, worms and viruses since they try to make hurt an individual or organization. Such assaults expect to crush or challenged person their objectives for the individual fulfillment of seeing them endure. For some computer culprits, the energy, popularity, and test of misusing a computer framework basically are the thing that incites their way into cybercrime.

The digital security group and real media have to a great extent agreed on the forecast that cybercrime harm will cost the world $6 trillion every year by 2021, up from $3 trillion only a year back. Worldwide spending on digital security items and administrations are anticipated to surpass $1 trillion throughout the following five years from 2017 to 2021. Microsoft gauges that by 2020 four billion individuals will be online double the number those are online at this point. Worldwide ransomware harm costs are anticipated to surpass $5 billion out of 2017. Amid the following five years, cybercrime may turn into the best danger to each individual, place, and thing in the world.

To conquer the previously mentioned issues, Forensic authorities examining computer crimes require a game plan of devoted apparatuses and furthermore the use of particular systems. Contingent upon the kind of PC contraption and the kind of automated prove experts may pick instrument or another. This chapter organized as follows, section 1 described about crimes which are related to computer, section 2 deals with different types of cybercrime cases, section 3 detailed about different types of cybercrime tools, which presents a variety of tools along with case examples that demonstrate their usefulness, section 4 discuss about summary of the paper. The scope of subjects highlights the lavishness and imperativeness of the discipline and offers promising avenues for future advancement in cyber crime kit tools.

BACKGROUND

Dangers postured to associations by cybercrimes have expanded quicker than potential casualties or digital security experts can manage them, setting focused on associations at extensive hazard (Khari et al., 2017). The development of the risk of cybercrime has outpaced that of other digital security dangers. Right now digital offenders are progressively skillful at increasing unnoticed access and keeping up a determinedly low profile. A few analysts have distinctive sorts of discernment. Dark and dim markets for hacking devices, hacking administrations and the products of hacking are increasing boundless consideration as more assaults and assault systems are connected in somehow to such markets (Albon et al., 2014). In 2013, a few analysts examined about coherent apparatuses and that instrument separates into Reconnaissance Tools, Scanning Tools, Access and heightening Tools, Exfiltration devices, Sustainment Tools, Assault devices, Obfuscation Tools (Andress et al., 2013). The work of Harbawi (2016) points by point the hole between the developing shrewd innovations and measurable instruments.

It offers an extremely rich zone of research in creating apparatuses that are perfect with ebb and flow brilliant gadgets and it can be accommodated open utilize (Harbawi et al., 2016). Interruption Detection has been vigorously considered in the two businesses and the scholarly world; however digital security experts still want significantly more ready exactness and general risk investigation keeping in mind the end goal to secure their frameworks inside the internet (Zuech et al., 2015). The quantity of effective digital assaults keeps on expanding, undermining budgetary and individual security around the world. Digital criminology is experiencing a change in outlook in which prove is every now and again monstrous in the estimate, requests live securing, and might be deficient to convict a criminal living in another legitimate locale (Harichandran et al., 2016). The best dangers to the security, protection, and unwavering quality of PC systems and other related data frameworks when all is said in done are cybercrimes carried out by cybercriminals, yet in particular programmers. According to the harm caused by past cybercriminal and programmer assaults to PC organizes in organizations, governments, and people, bringing about burden and loss of efficiency and validity, one can't neglect to see that there is a developing group request to programming and equipment organizations to make more secure items that can be utilized to recognize dangers and vulnerabilities, to settle issues, and to convey security arrangements (Kizza, 2017). The approach of advanced media, Internet, web and online web-based social networking has drawn the consideration of important research group fundamentally and made numerous new research challenges on digital security. Individuals, associations, and governments around the globe are losing a colossal measure of cash as a result of having digital assaults. Consequently, digital security has turned out to be a standout amongst the most troublesome and critical issues over the world. (Chowdhury, 2016). To defeat the previously mentioned issues and issues in this part the creator talked about different sorts of cybercrime instruments to confront the digital fighting. Area Based Services (LBS) open client information to vindictive assaults. Methodologies, advanced, up until this point, for saving protection and security, experience the ill effects of at least one oddity, and consequently the issue of securing LBS information is a long way from being settled. Specifically, precision of results versus security degree, protection versus execution, and trust between clients are open issues. (Yamin, 2018). The specially appointed steering convention's outline has gotten a tremendous consideration due to the flighty and quick portability of a hub. It is made progressively with no framework. (Chowdhuri, 2014). The expanded Mobile Ad-hoc Network engineering is a principal examine space because of a wide improvement of PDA and open source Unmanned Aerial Vehicle (UAV) innovation (Mukherjee, 2016). The ubiquity of Wireless Sensor Networks (WSNs) is quickly becoming because of its wide-extended applications, for example, modern diagnostics, condition checking or reconnaissance. (Binh, 2016). Constant channel models are utilized to account the acknowledgment of the way misfortune as far as recurrence and transmission go in Rayleigh blurring condition. Distinctive obstruction levels are experienced over a bundle transmission, making the impedance decent variety that mitigates the different access obstruction impacts. (Chowdhuri, 2015). The ceaseless advancement of Next Generation Internet NGI intensifies the interest for proficient and secure correspondence equipped for reacting viably to the difficulties postured by the rising applications (Kimbahune, 2017). The expanded development of low-control coordinated circuits, physiological sensors and remote correspondence has presented another age of remote sensor systems (Goswami, 2016). The improvement of Intelligent Transportation System (ITS) will change into a next level advancement of differently new necessities combined with the new age remote correspondence innovation (Yang, 2018)

COMPUTER VS. CRIMES

Computers can be the objective of a criminal action, a capacity put for information about a criminal movement (Casey et al., 2001). Crimes that includes a computer and a network, where a computer could possibly have had an instrumental impact on the commission of the crime (www.studymode.com). The term cybercrime really alludes to computer-related crime; in any case, some view computer crime as a subdivision of cybercrime that warrants its own definition and comprehension. The subject of computer crime would bring about a confounding number of articles as more scientists and experts are using the term cybercrime as an umbrella term for all crime including computers and innovation.

Computer Crime Technology

PC offense is portrayed as some encroachment of crook act that incorporates learning of PC development for their execution, examination, and prosecution (C. Laudon, 2004; P.Laudon, 2004). The basic piece of information and correspondence development was to improve the capability and ampleness of affiliations. In any case, the mission of profitability and sufficiency serves more dim goals as charlatans mishandle the automated measurement for singular advantages (Pichard, 2009).

PC offense or PC related offense or development offense, are depictions frequently used equally to suggest any illegal exhibition conferred by the use of PC progressions or utilization of such advances as techniques in the commission of the offense (www.infosec.gov.hk).

Computer-Facilitated Crime

The web, portable applications a data innovation are currently implanted in societal structures of the fund, well-being, training, and business in numerous nations all through the world. More than 3 billion individuals, more than 40% of the total populace, have utilized the web in 2016. The openness and proficiency of the web and data advances in supporting the framework of societal foundations likewise cultivate the improvement of cybercrime and degenerate subcultures (InternetLiveStats, n.d.).

The webs encourage abnormality and wrongdoing through giving permeability and availability to elective legitimizations and regulating view focuses on types of cybercrime. The divided and layered nature of the web additionally invigorates freak and criminal action as there is no brought together government body to build up the standards for suitable direct and to authorize criminal laws in particular nations. Unlawful conduct in a few nations is endured and legitimate conduct in different nations enabling guilty parties to pick wards for their sites that have the slightest hash lawful outcomes.

Computer Crime on the Internet

The web is one of the best vibes of late circumstances. It has turned into an image of our innovative resourcefulness and offers mankind a wonderful exhibit of advantages (Wall et al., 2003). Cybercrime and PC offense are jointly identified with web offense. The web stated a "twofold edged sword" that gives numerous chances to carry out crime (Gottschalk, 2010). The web offense has transformed into an overall problem which demands complete co-operation also contribution of both makings and made nations at the all-inclusive grade. Snap coercion has transformed into a troublesome issue at Google and distinctive destinations that part pay-per-click web advancing. A couple of Association's contracts outcasts to misleadingly tap on a contender's advancements to weaken them by driving up their publicizing cost (S. Pickett, 2002; M. Pickett, 2002).

The other noteworthy part of cybercrime comprises of particularly characterized digital offenses hacking breaking and infection scattering that are online adaptations of real world crimes. Peoples can exist principles to arraign the customary sorts of cybercrime and embrace new, digital particular guidelines for rising assortments of cybercrime. The issue lies in the requirement technique (Jewkes et al., 2013).

Financial Crime on the Internet

Monetary crime can be characterized as an offense against assets, including the unlawful transformation of property having a place with another to one's very own utilization and advantage (Larsson, 2006). Some scientists characterize financial crime as the utilization of misleading for illicit gain, ordinarily including a break of trust and camouflage of the genuine idea of the exercises. A few analysts contend that financial crime, for the most part, portrays an assortment of crimes against assets, including the lawless transformation of assets having a place with another to one's very own usage and advantage as a general rule including extortion additionally bribery, defilement, illegal tax avoidance, misappropriation insider exchanging, assess infringement and the digital assaults (Henning, 2009). The financial and innovative crimes cash falsifying, tax evasion, intellectual assets crime, installment card extortion, computer virus assaults and cyber sabotage can influence all levels of civilization.

Sorted out criminal networks are frequently behind the financial crime, drawn by the possibility of the colossal benefits to be made. Law implementation officers need to respond quickly with a specific end goal to secure confirmation or to solidify and seize illicitly acquired resources. Notwithstanding, various elements make it troublesome, now and then even difficult to follow the criminal or the unlawful resources (Interpol, 2017).

White Collar Computer Crime

PC offense can happen inside white-collar offense, this is a unique area of monetary offense. Cubicle wrongdoing can be described similar to the offenses, the guilty party or both. On the off chance that white-collar crime is characterized as far as crime, it implies offense against assets for individual or administrative gain. If the banner of one of the forms of property confers the means of communication and conceal or misdirection(Simpson,2009). In the event that white-collar crime is characterized regarding the guilty party, it implies crime submitted by high society individuals from society for individual or organizational gain. And the case of this white-collar crime if it portrayed and culpable, implies the crime presented by individuals of the high society or organizational gain. That is the individuals whoever fortunate, outstandingly educated, and socially related, and they are typically used by and in legitimate affiliations (Hansen, 2009).

The most monetarily impeded people from society are not by any methods the main ones carrying out a wrongdoing. People from the unique money related class are moreover involved by culprit lead. This type of the offense might differentiate of lower classes, for instance, legitimate advocates helping criminal clients wash their money, and managers remunerate open experts to fulfill open or accounting contracts that control the accounting relationship to avoid costs. Further fundamental differentiation among both responsible meetings is that the most criminal type is significantly more opposed to being received or reproached in the light of their monetary prosperity (Brightman, 2011).

Offense Offender or Victim

Many examinations appear to solicit the casualty point of view of PC offense. The point of view suggests such as a person, a gathering an association and a general public be a culprit of offense. The guilty party point of view infers that an individual a gathering, an association and a general public is the crook in charge of computer crime. In the victim viewpoint, alongside malware disease and robbery of IT hardware, hacking was the most ordinarily revealed PC offense occurrence. The discoveries of researchers report that PC offense trigger additional work for the casualty and loss of income too. A few of the stated offense episodes in their investigation could be countered by enhanced get to control and information assurance measures notwithstanding mindfulness raising exercises (Hagen, Sivertsen, & Rong, 2008).

CYBERCRIME CASES

All the more as of late, digital hoodlums have broadened their points of view and driven by monetary and political thought processes, have carried out a wide assortment of crimes and caused impressive hardship all around both monetarily and personally. Following the authoritative change, an ever-increasing number of cases have entered the legal procedure. These cases have represented some recognizable difficulties for prosecutors and judges, additionally made might be the new ones (Smith, Grabosky, & Urbas, 2004).

The progress of development has made man subject to the Internet for each one of his needs. The Web has given man easy to everything while in the meantime sitting in one place. Person to person communication, internet shopping, storing data, gaming, web-based examining, online occupations, and each possible thing that man can consider ought to be conceivable through the medium of the web. The Web is utilized as a part of practically every circle. With the improvement of the web and its related advantages additionally built up the idea of cybercrimes. Cybercrimes are perpetrated in various structures. A few years back, there was nonattendance of care about the wrongdoings that could be submitted through the web. In the issues of cybercrimes, India is in like manner not far behind substitute countries where the rate of recurrence of cybercrimes is moreover growing well ordered.

Cybercrimes can be characterized as the lawless demonstrations where the PC is utilized whichever as a tool or a goal both. The term is a general term that spreads infringement like phishing, charge card cheats, bank burglary, illegal downloading, modern surveillance, tyke obscenity, seizing kids by methods for talk rooms, traps, digital fear based oppression, creation as well as a scattering of infections, spam et cetera.

Cybercrime is a sweeping term that is used to portray criminal activity in which PCs or PC systems are an instrument, a goal, or a place of criminal development and join everything from electronic part to dissent of administration assaults. It in like manner covers the customary wrongdoings in which PCs or systems are used to enable the unlawful development (www.helplinelaw.com). Give us a chance to talk about the distinctive sorts of cybercrime cases.

Fake Websites

Culprits make take sites that look live authentic sites keeping in mind the end goal to trap the client into entering their own data, for example, their username, password, credit card, or social security numbers.

These destinations frequently seem to be indistinguishable to genuine one and may even have comparative web addresses to trap the client.

For instance, an imaginary fake site (www.bankofallahabad1.com) could be made to resemble a legitimate bank site (www.bankofallahabad.com) see the distinctive URLs for the sites. At the point when the client enters their data on the fake site, the trickster now has their keeping money accreditations.

Fake sites have turned out to be progressively inescapable producing billions of dollars in deceitful income to the detriment of clueless web clients. The outline and appearance of these sites make it troublesome for clients to physically distinguish them as fake (Abbasi, Zhang, Zimbra, Chen, & Nunamaker, 2010).

Money Laundering

Tax evasion is the path toward concealing the profits of wrongdoing and joining it into the true blue cash related system. Before proceeds of the offense are washed it is unsafe for hoodlums to use the unlawful money since they can't clear up where it began from and it is less requesting to tail it back to the offense. In the wake of being laundered, it ends up noticeably hard recognizing cash from honest to goodness monetary assets, and the assets can be utilized by crooks without recognition.

There are incalculable approaches to dispatch cash. By and large tax evasion can be separated into three phases.

- **Placement:** The underlying section of unlawful cash into the monetary framework.
- **Layering:** The way toward isolating the assets from their source, frequently utilizing unknown shell organizations.
- **Integration:** The cash comes back to the criminal from true blue looking source (www.gfintegrity.org).

Tax evasion is a stream of assets. There is basically a place where the cash is produced and a place where it is laundered. On the off chance that a cheat offers a stolen bike to a second-hand retail shop, it doesn't consider another robbery when the bike is bought from the shop, and each time it along these lines changes hands, yet this kind of obfuscated believing is clear even in the most powerful of reports on illegal tax avoidance (Walker, 1999).

Illegal tax avoidance is one of the greatest obstructions to keeping up a compelling working worldwide budgetary framework. A worldwide wonder and universal test illegal tax avoidance is a money laundering that regularly includes an unpredictable arrangement of exchanges and various budgetary establishments crosswise over numerous outside wards, Money Laundering is additionally greatly troublesome to research and arraign (Buchanan, 2004).

Bank Fraud

Bank extortion is a criminal demonstration that happens when a person utilizes unlawful intends to get cash or resources from a bank or other monetary foundation (legaldictionary.net). Developing effect of banks and monetary establishments on the present society financial perspective, have given current approaches to offenders to ambush individuals' rights notwithstanding to every single huge accomplishment that they had on financial associations advancing; in such way that we witness that convoluted and new sorts of crimes are being dedicated in bank and money related foundations areas, which are not the same as their customary shape (Hidarimanesh & Esfahani, 2016). Money related misrepresentation has been a major worry for some associations crosswise over enterprises; billions of dollars are lost yearly in light of this extortion (Duhart & Gress, 2016).

- As per Deloitte, the explanations behind increment in misrepresentation episodes are the absence of oversight by the senior administration on deviations from existing procedures. Business pressures to meet nonsensical targets. The test confronted in the avoidance of extortion is a lack of customers and staff awareness.
- Difficult to integrate data from various sources.
- Inadequate fraud detection tools and technologies.

A portion of the current misrepresentation episodes in India detailed through the media identify with fixed deposits, loans disbursement or broadening credit facilities for bribes, phishing, and other web/ATM based fakes. Such prominent cases in late time demonstrate that frauds not just undermine benefits, working efficiencies and unwavering quality of administrations yet can likewise severe affect an association's notoriety. Notwithstanding potential fines demanded by administrative bodies, it can negatively affect worker spirit and financial specialist certainty (www2.deloitte.com).

Advance Fee Fraud

Propel charge extortion is when fraudsters target casualties to make progress or forthright installment for products, administrations as well as monetary profits that don't emerge (www.actionfraud.police.uk). The accompanying is some basic cases of propelling expense misrepresentation tricks:

- **Beneficiary Fund Scam:** The tricksters frequently display some kind of tale about requiring your assistance to get cash from a bank in another nation.
- **Lottery Scam:** Scam asserts that you won cash in an abroad lottery. The letter or email will, for the most part, request individual data to affirm your personality.
- **Speculation Scam:** A venture organization contacts and needs help with contributing cash abroad. The letter or email will look just as it is originating from a respectable speculation firm or government official. The letter will make a request to contact the organization, where it will be solicited to pay some sort of charge in advance as an end-result of a weighty benefit that does not exist.
- **Sentiment Scam:** Scammers pull at the heart strings of those on web dating sites and visit rooms by requesting cash for debilitated relatives, or cash for a plane ticket to meet face to face (www.stonebridge.com).

The most infamous sort endeavoured day by day on office laborers everywhere throughout the world, is called propel charge misrepresentation. The sender will try to include the beneficiary in a plan to gain a great many dollars if the beneficiary pays a propel expense (Ampratwum, 2009). Propel charge misrepresentation is a present plague that rakes in a huge number of dollars every year (Cheng & Ma,

2009). Propel charge fraudsters tend to utilize particular techniques that adventure the limited reasonably and programmed conduct of casualties. Strategies incorporate a declaration of specialist and master control, referencing regarded people and associations, giving incomplete verification of authenticity, making criticalness, and suggesting security and benefit.

Malicious Agents

Malignant Agent is a PC program that operation advantage of a potential intruder to help in ambushing a network or system. By and large, a weapons store of such administrators included infections, worms, and trojonized programs. By uniting key components of these masters, at trackers are as of now prepared to make programming that speaks to a veritable peril even to affiliations that support their framework outskirt with a firewall.

A malignant specialist is a PC program that works for the benefit of an intruder potential to help the assault on a chassis or system (Zeltser, 2000). Programming is named noxious programming in light of the apparent plan of the maker instead of a specific component. Malware for advantage consolidates spy product, botnets, and keystroke lumberjacks. In a botnet, the malware sign into a visit structure, while a key lumberjack obstructs the customer's keystrokes when entering a watchword, Visa number and further knowledge that might be abused. Malevolent programming can automate a variety of strikes for evildoers also be fairly accountable as the overall augmentation in cybercrime (Bossler & Holt, 2009).

Identity Theft

The information can be utilized to acquire make stock and administrations for the sake of the victim or to give the cheat false certifications (Bilge, Strufe, Balzarotti, & Kirda, 2009). Sorts of identity theft incorporate criminal, therapeutic, money related and child identity theft. (investopedia.com). Social networking sites have been progressively gaining ubiquity. Understood locales, for example, Facebook have been detailing development rates as high as 3% every week. For potential aggressor, it is anything but difficult to dispatch computerized creeping and fraud assaults against various prominent long range interpersonal communication locales with a specific end goal to access a substantial volume of individual client data (Milne, 2003). Identity theft is a genuine and progressively pervasive crime and buyers need to take precautionary measures to limit the possibility of turning into a victim (Bilge et al., 2009).

Digital Piracy

Digital piracy has turned into a standard wellspring of downloads [weebly.com]. Digital piracy is another type of programming theft has taken the spotlight. Lost incomes because of advanced theft could reach $5 billion before the finish of 2005 (Al-Rafee, &Cronan, 2006).

Since advanced theft has represented a critical danger to the improvement of the product business and the development of the computerized media industry, it has, for the most recent decade, held significant enthusiasm for specialists and experts (Yoon, 2011). The problem of computerized theft has transformed into a subject of colossal worry, with the ultimate objective that it has pulled in the thought of administrators, scholastics and also business authorities (Moore, & McMullan, 2009).

Cyber Stalking

The wonder of cyber stalking and online provocation looks set to be the concentration of the
following Internet-related good frenzy (Ellison & Akdeniz, 1998). Cyber stalking accordingly involves indistinguishable general qualities from customary stalking, yet in being transposed into the virtual condition it is on a very basic level changed. The idea of this change is needy upon what specific parts of the Internet are misused (Ogilvie, 2000). When all is said in done terms, stalking can be named as the rehashed demonstrations of badgering focusing on the victim, for example, following the casualty, making irritating phone calls, executing the casualties pet, vandalizing casualties property, leaving created messages or inquiries. Stalking may be trailed by bona fide savage acts, for instance, physical wickedness to the casualty. Advanced Stalking infers reiterated exhibits of goading or undermining behavior of the computerized criminal towards the setback by using web organizations. Both kind of Stalkers i.e., Online and Offline – need to control the setbacks life (Snyder & Crescenzi, 2009).

Child Pornography

Pornography implies indicating sexual acts keeping in mind the end goal to cause sexual energy. The meaning of explicit entertainment additionally incorporates obscene sites, obscene magazines created utilizing PC and the web pornography conveyed by mobiles. The web is in effect exceedingly utilized as a medium to sexually manhandle youngsters. The youngsters are a suitable casualty to the cybercrime. PCs and the web have turned into a need for each family unit, the kids have a simple access to the web. There is a simple access to the pornographic contents on the web. Pedophiles bait the kids by circulating explicit material and afterward, they endeavor to meet them for sex or to take their bare photos incorporating their engagement in sexual positions. Some of the times paedophiles contact kids in the talk rooms acting like young people or an offspring of comparable age and after that, they begin getting to be plainly friendlier with them and win their certainty. By then step by step pedophiles start a sexual visit to empower children to shed their impediments about sex and a while later gets them out for the singular association. At that point begin genuine abuse of the youngsters by offering them some cash or dishonestly encouraging them great open doors in life. The pedophiles at that point sexually misuse the youngsters either by utilizing them as sexual articles or by taking their obscene pictures keeping in mind the end goal to offer those over the web (Fidelie, 2009).

Intellectual Property Crime

Intellectual assets offense is a genuine monetary worry for auto producers, extravagance great creators, media firms, and medication organizations. Intellectual property crime is that falsifying imperils general well-being, particularly in creating nations, according to WHO exceeding sixty per cent of medicament are fake products (Pontell, Geis, & Brown, 2007).

Protected innovation's rising a motivation in the era of wealth has been reflected by its extending frailty to wrongdoing. Cybercrime generally connected the intellectual assets offense; along with the investigated the dangers of crime innate in intellectual capital and a dispersed digital condition to exhibit that customary legitimate cure is to a great extent insufficient to protect property rights. Not at all like cash or aesthetic manifestations, for example, had which required the culprit to enter a vault or display lobby and thusly take away the filched items, scholarly resources offense demands just such as the culprit makes a technical imitation. A colossal cure for occurrences of robbery is to re-establish the asset to its exceptional proprietor (techtalk.gfi.com).

Internet Gambling

Web betting is general problems which have an outcome on all the autonomous countries of their adjacent block laws or which authorizes betting. By utilizing the police powers state governments generally controlled the Betting. In any case, web betting's national and worldwide augmentation require its organization by overall law.

Antigua is a little Caribbean island that gained its freedom from Britain in 1981. In 1997, web betting is arranged on the small island. Web betting is under the control of the Worlds Sports Enterprise (WSE). For entering the wager, customers are required to transmit $300. Moreover, each wager will get 10% off by the WSE. The organization took $3.5 million for the initial fifteen months of operation. It is contended that sorted out offense has penetrated the Antiguan betting attempt and those underage members are permitted to play (Guan, 2003).

In light of the considerable trouble in prohibiting Internet gambling, a few scientists suggest that administrations everywhere throughout the world should direct and impose online business wanders. On account of the hazy lawful status of Internet gambling, there must be enactment expressly characterizing what is and is not an admissible movement, and in addition an accentuation on control by world governments and self-direction by the web betting organizations.

CYBERCRIME TOOLS

Criminal experts studying pc crimes require an arrangement of devoted tools and further the use of certain approaches. Contingent upon the type of pc gadget and the kind of automated show, dealers may additionally choose little equipment. A typically misguided judgment in the utilization of PC criminological instruments is the conviction these tools are just used to settle cybercrime. While cybercrime is rapidly achieving levels unbelievable only 10 years prior, PC legal sciences are not restricted to this sort of crime. Indeed, just a little extent of cases settled by PC legal experts is identified with cybercrime.

Up to 93% of all data never leaves the digital domain for retrieving Digital Evidence, Methods, Techniques and Issues. This means the lion's proportion of statistics is both made and expanded in the virtual frame. Automated snap shots, electronic correspondence, on line talks and texting are incredible without a PC. For masters performing scientific examinations, this implies increasingly confirm winds up noticeably accessible in the digital form. Truth is advised, many types of affirmation are just handy in automated. Convalescing automatic prove in direction of measurable examinations calls for the utilization of unusual equipment.

The present PC measurable investigators are fit for recuperating information that has been erased, scrambled or is covered up in the folds of cell phones innovation; they can be called to affirm in court and relate the proof found amid examinations. They can be included in testing cases, to incorporate the check of guilty parties' justifications, examination of Internet manhandle, abuse of figuring assets and system use in making PC related dangers. Forensic specialists can be called upon to help real cases including information breaks, interruptions, or whatever another sort of occurrences. By applying strategies and exclusive programming criminological applications to analyze framework gadgets or stages, they may have the capacity to give key revelations to stick who was/were in charge of an examined crime.

Hardware Tools

There are numerous instruments out there assembled particularly for cybercrime. A portion of the devices incorporate cloning gadgets, compose blockers, convenient capacity gadgets, connectors, links, and that's only the tip of the iceberg. Computers are the foundation of any cybercrime lab. In order an inspector you will require the great pc workstation you may manipulate. Cybercrime tests require a large amount of figuring power. a terrific examination gadget has numerous, multicore processors, as a whole lot RAM as you may get 40(the more and more the higher), and expensive, brief difficult drives. Legal programming producers give nitty gritty arrangements of least and proposed equipment necessities. Cybercrime is not any more a "PC Centric" attempt. Little-scale devices, for example, mobiles and Global Positioning Systems gadgets are filling labs the country over. These devices require specific device from that applied on portable PC and desktops. Cellebrite's UFED bolsters greater than 3 thousand phones. Paraben organization, a contender of Cellbrite, brags bolster for greater than 4 thousand telephones, PDAs, and GPS devices.

When managing telephones, having the right link is fundamental. Not at all like PCs, Cell Phones need a significant part of the institutionalization as to connectors and links. Labs need a wide choice of links close by to adapt to the huge swath of handsets that stroll through the entryways. Luckily, the producers of cell phone scientific equipment give a significant number of the required links. A few organizations make equipment cloning gadgets. A forensic clone is a "bit stream" duplicates of a specific bit of media, for example, hard drive. These devices can truly accelerate the procedure, cloning different drives without a moment's delay. They can likewise give compose assurance, hash verification, drive wiping, a review trail, and that's just the beginning.

Software Tools

There is a wide cluster of cybercrime programming items available nowadays. A few are standard instruments that serve an assortment of capacities. Rest is extra focused, filling a genuinely constrained need. Such applications tend to concentrate on a particular kind of proof, email or web, for instance, when choosing to the program, a decision should be made between running with open source instruments or a commercially created item. There are preferences and drawbacks to both. Factors, for example, cost, usefulness, capacities, and support are a portion of the criteria that can be utilized to settle on this choice.

Forensic Toolkit (FTK) from Access Data and Encase from Guidance programming are considered as the most well-known general programming for business instruments. These two programs are phenomenal and can make exams easier and more productive. These applications have "Swiss Army Knife"-like abilities. They play out a large number of errands, including: "Searching,", "E-mail investigation", "Sorting", "Reporting", "Password cracking".

The inquiry tools in these things are particularly exceptional and give investigators the ability to exhaust down to effectively the information they are hunting down. Here is a fast rundown of a portion of the data that can be hunt down: "E-mail addresses", "Names", "Phone Numbers", "Keywords", "Web addresses", "File types", "Data ranges".

As strong as these gadgets can be, they do have a couple of hindrances. Actually, no single instrument does it all. Therefore, spending plan allowing, labs need an assortment of devices accessible. Cybercrime specialists utilize both programming and equipment devices in their duty. No one single instrument does everything or does it well. Most labs will have an assortment of apparatuses available to them to give them the expansive capacity they require given the wide cluster of innovation they see coming in the entryway for investigation [Sammons, 2012]

Tools for System Admin (Taboona, 2017)

Sans Sift

For logical and scene response examination the users can use the SANS Investigative Forensic Toolkit (SIFT) is an Ubuntu-based Live CD. RAW (dd) affirm positions, Advanced Forensic Format (AFF) and Expert Witness Format (E01) are supported by Sans Sift tool. Channel fuses gadgets, for instance, log2timeline for delivering a course of occasions from structure logs, Scalpel for data archive cutting, Rifiuti for examining the reuse compartment, and parts more. When you at first boot into the SIFT condition, the master propose to research the documentation on the desktop to empower you to wind up discernibly common to what instruments are open and how to use them. There is in like manner a tolerable illumination of where to find demonstrate on a system. Use the best menu bar to open a gadget, or dispatch it physically from a terminal window.

ProDiscover Basic

The above-mentioned tool that has an essential advanced legal examination gadget that engages us to picture, particular also cover certify found over the drive. When the users incorporate the criminological

Figure 1. Sans Sift

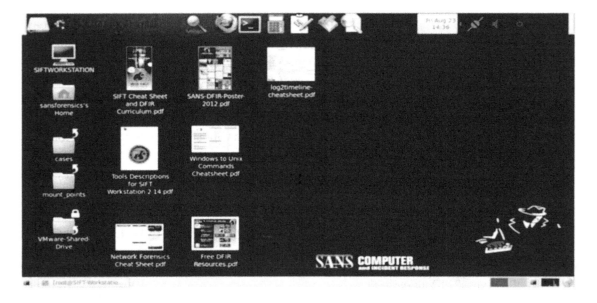

picture the users able to see a database through the content also through observing gatherings that hold such data. A client in like way inspects as information utilizing the Search focus point in the context based on the criteria chosen.

To dispatch Pro Discover Basic, to start with, want to form also heap the meander also fuse show from the "Include" focus. Utilize 'Substance View' and 'Group View' center points for analyzing an information also the Tools menu to act exercises towards the information. Tap a "Report" center point to see fundamental facts almost to wander.

Volatility

For incident response and malware examination, the users can use Volatility is a memory forensics that empowers you to expel propelled old rarities from unusual memory (RAM) dumps. To evacuate information about running methods, open framework connections and framework affiliations, DLLs stacked for every technique, put away registry hives, handle IDs for all above-mentioned methods the users can use Volatility.

By essentially put instability 2.1.standalone.exe through an organizer also open the charge incite window the users can use the independent Windows executable rendition of Volatility. Out of charge incite, examine an area based on viable report and sort "instability 2.1.standalone.exe –f <FILENAME> –pr ofile=<PROFILENAME><PLUGINNAME>" devoid of quotes – Memory dump having the name of FILENAME.PROFILENAME would be the machine the memory dump was gone up against and To remove information the users can use PLUGINNAME would be the name of the module.

The Sleuth Kit (+Autopsy)

To perform inside and out an investigation of various record structures the technicians can use the open source digital forensics toolbox which is known as The Sleuth Kit. For GUI sites over the sleuth

Figure 2. ProDiscover Basic

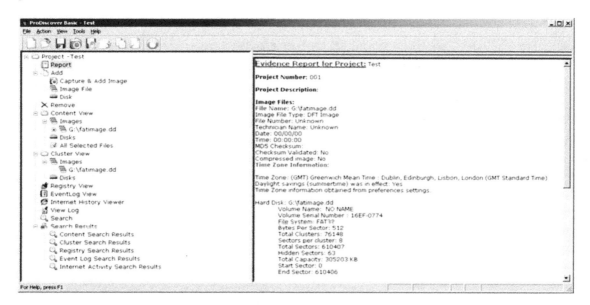

Figure 3. Volatility

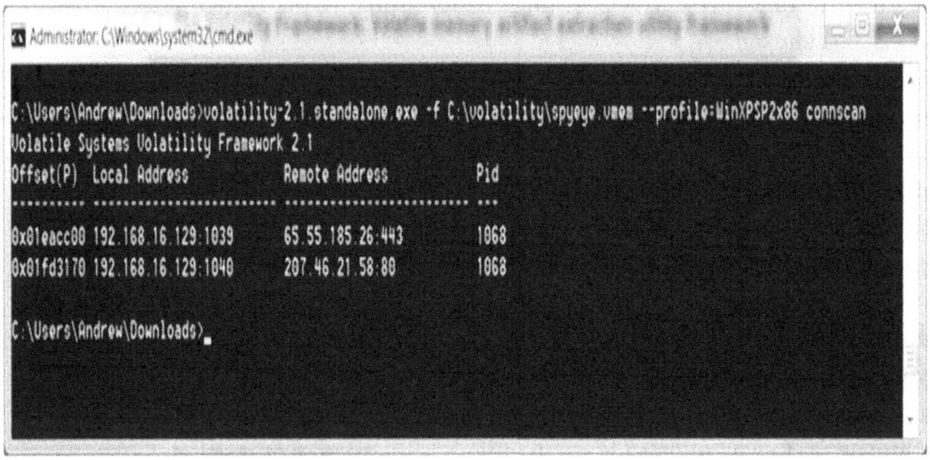

kit, autopsy examination is very essential. The sleuth kit has the ability to incorporate diverse modules for widened helpfulness also it goes with features like Timeline Analysis, Hash Filtering, File System Analysis and Keyword Searching out of the case.

To launch Autopsy, you can put forth another defense or load a present one. On the off chance that you make another case you should stack a measurable picture or a neighborhood circle to begin the examination. After the examination strategy process, the technicians can see the results by using the center points on the left-hand sheet of the tool.

Figure 4. The Sleuth Kit (+Autopsy)

FTK Imager

For an overview the substance of logical pictures or memory dumps also for neighborhood hard drives, arrange drives, CDs/DVDs the analysts can use the FTK Imager. FTK Imager is an information and imaging gadget. The analysts can make SHA1 or MD5 hashes of archives, convey records and envelopes from criminological pictures to circle, review and recover records that were deleted from the Recycle Bin ((giving that their data pieces haven't been overwritten), and mount a quantifiable picture to see its substance in Windows Explorer by using FTK Imager.

To start this tool, Start with 'Record >Include Evidence Item" to stack a bit of proof for the survey. To make a forensic image, go to 'Document > Create Disk Image "for the forensic image the analysts can pick the source.

Linux 'dd'

Currently, some portions of Linux divisions are stopped by dd. (e.g. Ubuntu, Fedora). Linux 'dd' tool could be utilized as unique advanced legal undertakings, for instance, forensically wiping a drive (zeroing out a drive) and making a crude picture of a drive.

dd is an intense apparatus that can have annihilating impacts if not utilized with the mind. It is prescribed that you analyze in a protected domain before utilizing this device in the real world.

To utilize dd, basically, open a terminal window also sort dd took after through an arrangement of order parameters. The essential dd language structure for forensically wiping a drive is:

dd if=/dev/zero of=/dev/sdb1 bs=1024

if = input document, of = yield record, bs = byte estimate

Figure 5. FTK Imager

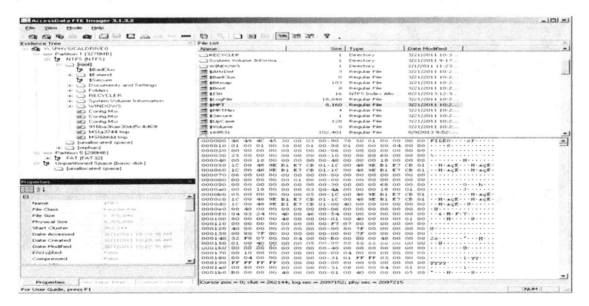

Figure 6. Linux 'dd'

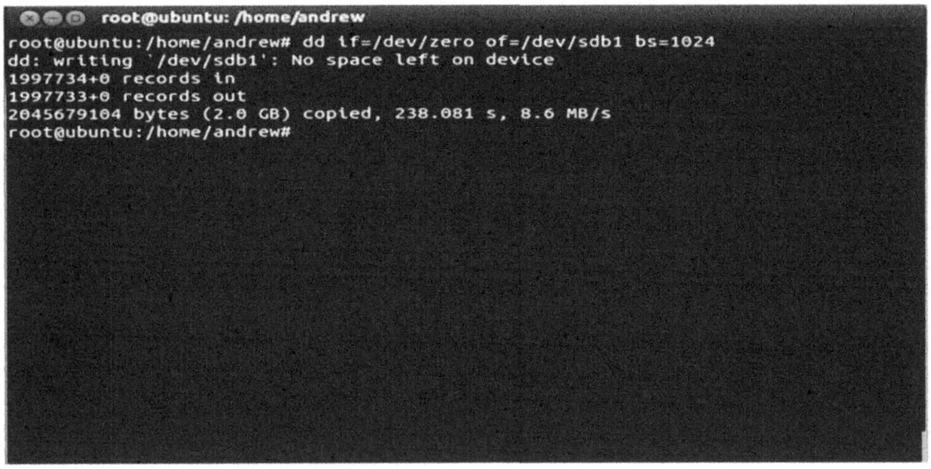
root@ubuntu: /home/andrew
root@ubuntu:/home/andrew# dd if=/dev/zero of=/dev/sdb1 bs=1024
dd: writing `/dev/sdb1': No space left on device
1997734+0 records in
1997733+0 records out
2045679104 bytes (2.0 GB) copied, 238.081 s, 8.6 MB/s
root@ubuntu:/home/andrew#

Computer Aided Investigative Environment

A tool which contains a wealth of advanced legal tools and it is named as CAINE (Computer Aided Investigative Environment). Components join the simple to utilize GUI, partial-robotized record beginning also gadgets for Mobile Forensics, Network Forensics, Data Recovery to say the very least.

When booting into the CAINE Linux condition, launch the advanced scientific instruments from the Computer Aided Investigative Environment interact or against every gadget's simple course on the 'Measurable Tools' envelope upon the applications menu bar.

Figure 7. Caine

caine
interface
Create report
Info
Computer
Trash
C.A.IN.E.
Computer Aided for INvestigative Environment

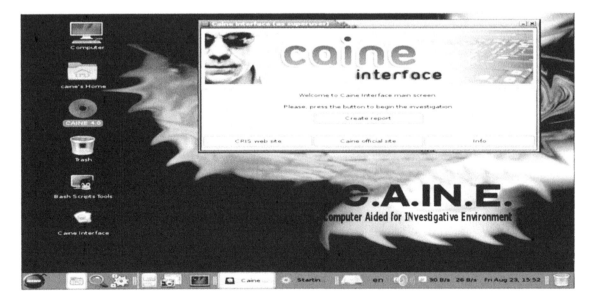

Oxygen Forensic Suite 2013 Standard

Oxygen Forensic Suite is a tool that empowers to finish the case that anticipates that will collect affirm against a wireless. It parts have the ability to gather Device Information, Contacts, Messages, and recovery of eradicated messages, Call Logs and Calendar and Task information. The tool moreover goes among a recorded program that empowers us to get to also separate customer pictures, recordings, files also contraption data's. At the point, while dispatch Oxygen Forensic Suite, smack the 'Interface recent gadget' get the best menu bar to dispatch the Oxygen Forensic Extractor wizard that assists us by picking a gadget also sort of facts you desire to independent.

Free Hex Editor Neo

For dealing the expensive records a fundamental hex supervisor tool was invented and its named as Free Hex Editor Neo. While a considerable measure of the further items is established in the business adaptations of Hex Editor Neo, The main reason for discover this instrument important for stacking enormous reports (e.g. database reports or legitimate pictures) and performing exercises, for instance, manual data cutting, low-level record adjusting, information gathering, or chasing down disguised data. Use 'Record > Open' to stack an archive into Hex Editor Neo. The data will appear in the middle window where you can begin to investigate through the hex physically or press CTRL + F to run a chase.

Bulk Extractor

Bulk_extractor is a PC wrongdoing scene examination instrument that ranges a plate picture, archive, or file of records and focuses information, for instance, Mastercard numbers, spaces, email areas, URLs, and

Figure 8. Oxygen Forensic Suite 2013 Standard

Figure 9. Free Hex Editor Neo

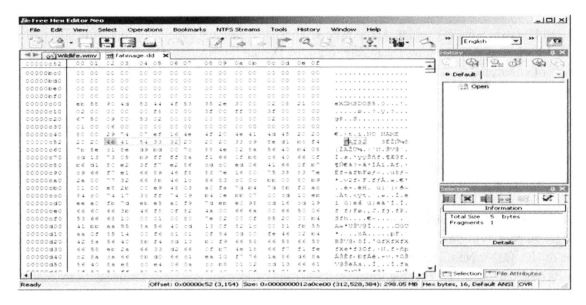

ZIP records. The isolated fact has respected a movement of substance records (which can be reviewed physically or analyzed using distinctive wrongdoing scene examination instruments or substance). Inside the yield content documents, you will discover passages for information that look like a Visa number, email address, area name, and so forth. You will likewise observe a decimal incentive in the principal segment of the content record that, when changed over to hex, can be utilized as the pointer on circle where the passage was found

Figure 10. Bulk Extractor

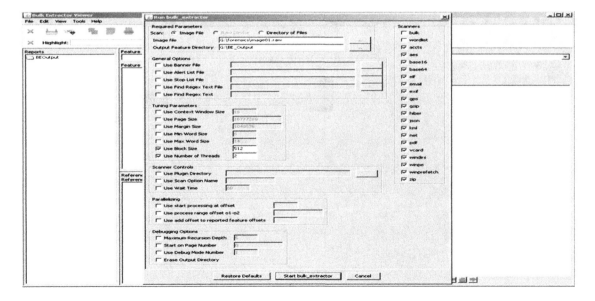

This tool is a summon line instrument or a GUI device. In the case above I set the mass extractor device to separate data from a legal sciences picture I took before and yield the outcomes to an envelope called "BE_Output". The outcomes would then be able to be seen in the Bulk Extractor Viewer and the yield content documents said above.

Deft

The most predominant free and open source PC forensic tools available in the forensic field are DEFT. This is another Linux Live CD. For investigate Incident Response, Cyber Intelligence and Computer Forensics situations DEFT plays a major role. Mobile Forensics, Network Forensics, Data Recovery and Hashing are the part of DEFT tool.

Technicians are requested to use DEFT to stack the live condition or to introduce the DEFT to circle. On the off chance that for stacking the live condition by utilizing the alternate ways upon the application menu bar to dispatch a needed instrument.

Xplico

For isolate applications data from web development, a tool was invented an open source Network Forensic Analysis Tool and it is named as Xplico. Components join help as an extensive number of traditions. TCP reassembly and the capacity to yield information to a MySQL or SQLite database, amongst others.

Formerly, you have introduced Xplico, get to the web interface by exploring to HTTP://<IPADDRESS>:9876 and signing in with a typical client account. The principal thing you have to do is make a case and include another session. When you make another session you can either stack a PCAP record (obtained from Wireshark for instance) or begin a live catch. Once the session has completed the process of disentangling, utilize the route menu on the left-hand side to see the outcomes.

Figure 11. Deft

Figure 12.Xplico

LastActivityView

LastActivityView empowers to perceive what moves had made through customer also whatever events occurred in the device. Any exercises, for example, running an executable document, opening a record/ envelope from Explorer, an application or framework crash or a client playing out a product establishment will be logged. The data can be sent out to a CSV/XML/HTML record.

Figure 13. LastActivityView

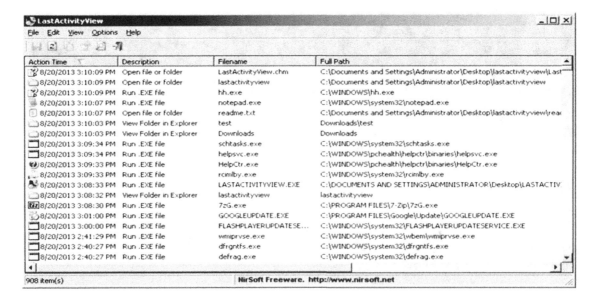

After launching LastActivityView, it will instantly begin showing a rundown of moves made upon the device it is being kept running on. Sort by activity period also utilizes an inquiry catch to begin exploring what moves were made on the machine.

DSi USB Write Blocker

A write blocker that forestalls composes access to USB gadgets and it is named as DSi USB Write Blocker. It is an essential in an examination to forestall adjusting the metadata or timestamps and nullifying the confirmation.

When you run DSi USB Write Blocker, it raises a window that enables you to empower or impair the USB Write Blocker. When you roll out improvements and leave the application, you can watch out for the status from the latch symbol in the taskbar. When playing out an examination of a USB drive, empower the USB Write Blocker first and after that connect the USB drive too.

MandiantRedLine

RedLine offers the capacity to perform memory and document investigation of a particular host. It gathers data about running procedures and drivers from memory and accumulates record framework metadata, registry information, occasion logs, organizes data, administrations, assignments, also, Internet history to help manufacture a general danger evaluation profile.

After launching RedLine, you will be given a decision to Collect Data or Analyze Data. Unless you as of now have a memory dump document accessible, you'll have to make an authority to accumulate information from the machine and let that procedure gone through to culmination. When you have a memory dump record to hand you can begin your examination.

PlainSight

PlainSight is a live Knoppix (a Linux transport) CD that allows you to perform advanced measurable measurements, such as displaying web stories, cutting data, collecting information about using USB devices, examining physical memory dumps, and this is just an indication of a bigger challenge.

Figure 14. DSi USB Write Blocker

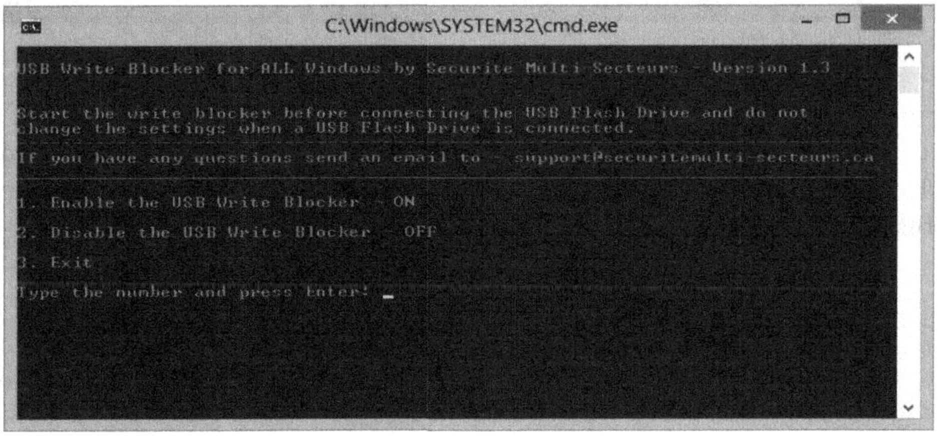

Figure 15. Mandiant RedLine

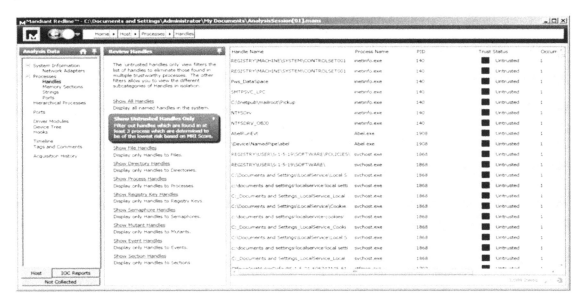

Figure 16. PlainSight

When you start your naked eye, you will see a window asking you to choose whether you need to sweep, stack a document, or run the wizard. Enter an option to start the process of extracting and analyzing information.

HxD

HxD is one of the best choices unquestionable. It is an easy-to-understand hex helper that allows you to make low-level changes and change a rough circle or core memory (RAM). HxD has been designed in the light of the ease of use and execution and can handle extensive recordings without any problems. Pieces gather to chase and replace, carry, checksums/forms and more.

Helix3

HELIX3 is a Linux Live CD that has been worked on for use as part of Incident Response, Computer Forensics, and E-Discovery situations. It is pressed with a bundle of open source devices that are executed by hex editors to program cutting information to keyword divide utilities and this is just the beginning.

The HELIX3 module you need is 2009R1. This variant was the last available free form before HELIX was taken by a businessman. HELIX3 2009R1 is still substantial today and is a valuable expander for its digital forensic toolkit.

To use HELIX3, users must stack the GUI condition or enter HELIX3 on the board. With the ability to stack the configuration of the graphical interface (prescripted) directly, a Linux-based screen seems to give you the alternative to graphically display the bundled devices.

Paladin Forensic Suite

Paladin Forensic Suite is a Live CD in Ubuntu view that is compressed with an abundance of open source scientific devices. The 80 devices found on this live CD are composed of more than 25 classes that feature imaging tools, malware analysis, social network analysis, hash tools, and so on.

After starting the Paladin Forensic Suite, search for the application menu or tap any of the images in the taskbar to get started. A speedy manual for the Paladin Forensic Suite is available to see or download from the Paladin webpage and from the Paladin taskbar.

Figure 17. HxD

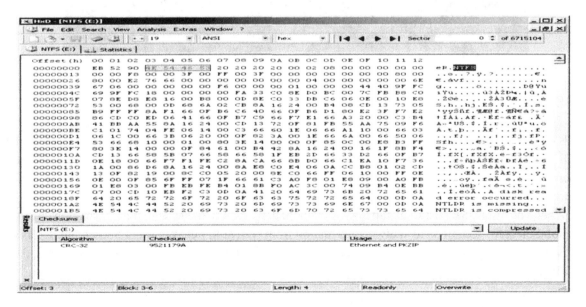

Figure 18. Helix3

Figure 19. Paladin Forensic Suite

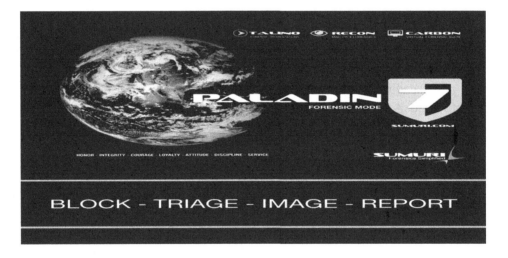

USB Historian

USB Historian investigates USB data, basically from the Windows registry, to give an outline of all the USB drives related with the machine. Indicates information such as USB drive name, serial number, when mounted, and customer account. This data can be extremely useful when conducting an exam for which you need to understand if the information was stolen, moved, or obtained.

When you send USB Historian, tap the "+" symbol in the best menu to send the information analysis wizard. Select the technique to analyze information from (Drive Letter, Windows Folder, and Users or Individual Hives / Files), and then select the separate information to be scanned. Once completed, data will be displayed as in the previous image.

Figure 20. USB Historian

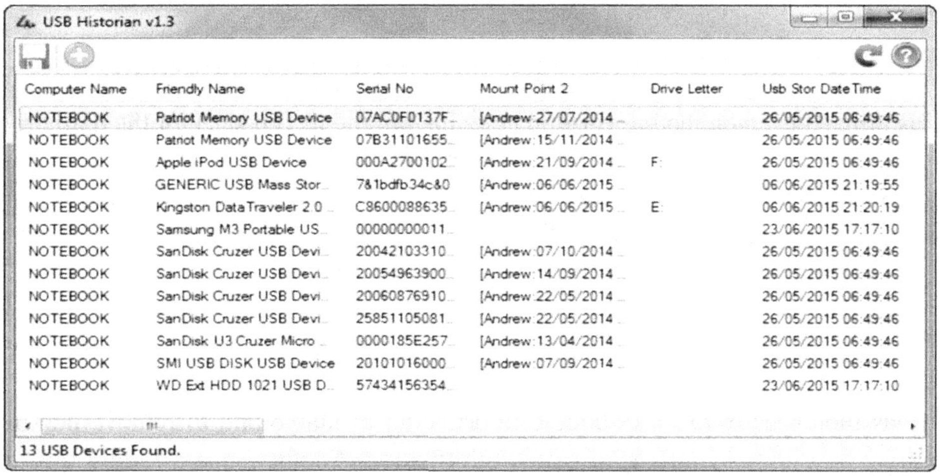

Computer Name	Friendly Name	Serial No	Mount Point 2	Drive Letter	Usb Stor Date Time
NOTEBOOK	Patriot Memory USB Device	07AC0F0137F	[Andrew:27/07/2014		26/05/2015 06:49:46
NOTEBOOK	Patriot Memory USB Device	07B31101655	[Andrew:15/11/2014		26/05/2015 06:49:46
NOTEBOOK	Apple iPod USB Device	000A2700102	[Andrew:21/09/2014	F:	26/05/2015 06:49:46
NOTEBOOK	GENERIC USB Mass Stor	781bdfb34c&0	[Andrew:06/06/2015		06/06/2015 21:19:55
NOTEBOOK	Kingston DataTraveler 2.0	C8600088635	[Andrew:06/06/2015	E:	06/06/2015 21:20:19
NOTEBOOK	Samsung M3 Portable US	00000000011			23/06/2015 17:17:10
NOTEBOOK	SanDisk Cruzer USB Devi	20042103310	[Andrew:07/10/2014		26/05/2015 06:49:46
NOTEBOOK	SanDisk Cruzer USB Devi	20054963900	[Andrew:14/09/2014		26/05/2015 06:49:46
NOTEBOOK	SanDisk Cruzer USB Devi	20060876910	[Andrew:22/05/2014		26/05/2015 06:49:46
NOTEBOOK	SanDisk Cruzer USB Devi	25851105081	[Andrew:22/05/2014		26/05/2015 06:49:46
NOTEBOOK	SanDisk U3 Cruzer Micro	0000185E257	[Andrew:13/04/2014		26/05/2015 06:49:46
NOTEBOOK	SMI USB DISK USB Device	20101016000	[Andrew:07/09/2014		26/05/2015 06:49:46
NOTEBOOK	WD Ext HDD 1021 USB D	57434156354			23/06/2015 17:17:10

13 USB Devices Found.

Evidence Collection Tools (Guan, 2003)

SafeBack

Function: Upon your underlying landing at a customer site, get a bit stream reinforcement of the traded off frameworks. When playing out a bit stream reinforcement of a hard drive, you are getting a little bit at a time duplicate of the hard drive, not simply documents. Each piece on the hard drive is exchanged to your reinforcement medium. On the off chance that it comes as a shock to you that there is concealed information on your hard drive then you are going to enter another world – Cyber Forensic Investigator. Just duplicating documents starting with one medium (e.g., hard drive) then onto the next (e.g. tape, album, compressed media drive, and so forth)

GetTime

Function: By scrutinizing the structure date/time from CMOS GetTimeused to report the time and date settings of a casualty PC system . Take a gander at the date/time from CMOS to the present time on your watch or whatever timepiece being used. Do this before handling the PC for confirming.

GetFree

Function: It is used to secure the substance of all unassigned space (eradicated records) on drive C of your PC and place this data in a singular report. It assesses the measure of filespace anticipated that would hold the unallocated space.

GetSwap

Function: It is used to get a copy of the exchange reports in your structure if bitstream fortification on PC C drive is MS Windows or some different operating systems that contain static exchange records.

Procure data found in PC "swap" or "page" files. Obtain data from both NTFS and FAT-sort packages

GetSlack

Function: It is utilized to catch the information contained in the record slack of the hard drive on your PC. Documents top off at least one bunches on a hard drive. Whatever bit of a group that the record does not totally top off is called slack space. Slack space is utilized by the OS for different things, however, it can't be seen by the conventional PC client. Unique devices are required to see it. As a rule, profitable data relating to an examination can be found here.

Filter_I

Function: It has the capacity to make double information printable and to remove possibly helpful information from an extensive volume of paired information. Another superb use for this device is to help in the production of a catchphrase list for use with another digital legal device, Text Search Plus.

CRCMD5

Function: It is utilized to ascertain a CRC-32 checksum for a DOS record or gathering of documents and a 128-piece MD5 process.

DiskSig

Function: It is used to calculate a CRC checksum and an MD5 process for an entire hard disk. The checksum and process merge all data into the drive, including deleted and unused sectors. By default, the hard disk boot partition is avoided in this calculation.

Doc

Function: It is utilized to report the substance of the index from which it is run.The yield gives a posting of the record/catalog names, document sizes, record dates, and document times (creation time in an hour, minute, second).Read-just and concealed records are additionally shown.

Mcrypt

Function: It is utilized to scramble and unscramble records and gives three level of encryption.
Levels of encryption:

1. Restrictive encryption (low-level default)
2. DES CBF (abnormal state default)
3. Improved DES (double encryption initially utilizing DES, at that point restrictive encryption)

Micro-Zap

Function: When erasing or deleting a file utilizing standard DOS (erase, eradicate) or MS Windows (95/98/NT/2000) systems, the document is not really erased. The record is still there and can be recuperated by the individuals who know how. Miniaturized scale destroys really wipes out the document names and the record substance-related to them. Micro-Zap destroy erases records by overwriting them with a hex F6 design. One overwrite is the default, however, a perpetually lifted measure of security is overseen by the seven overwrites decision.

Map

Function: It is utilized to discover and distinguish TSR (Terminate and Stay Resident) programs. TSR is a program that is running in PC memory, yet you may not understand it.

M-Sweep

Function: It is utilized to evacuate leftovers of these old records (documents you erased by means of DOS or Windows summons, however, whose substance are in reality still on the hard drive or diskette) by overwriting the plate space that is not being utilized by current documents you wish to hold.It is especially critical to guarantee expulsion of these old documents when a PC moves to an alternate office or is sold. M-Sweep safely expels remaining information from hard drives that are 8GB or little.

AnaDisk

Function: It is a utility for investigating diskettes. It can perform:

- Duplicates areas of a diskette to a record
- Repairs diskettes with information mistakes
- Duplicates a diskette without respect to its configuration
- Looks diskettes for content
- Breaks down a diskette to decide thickness, configuration, changes, and blunders
- Modified arranging of diskettes
- Can alter information on a diskette
- ASCII and HEX show of physical divisions and records

Seized

Function: It is utilized to boot the PC and show a message expressing that the PC has been seized as confirmation and that it ought not to be worked.

Scrub

Function: It is utilized to forever expel hard drive information. It overwrites each plate area utilizing every one of the zero bits and after that each of the one bits. The last pass is then done written work a hex F6 to the drive. A number of times the hard drive can be overwritten can be shifted in the vicinity of 1 and 32000. It doesn't take a shot at non-BIOS drives (e.g., Iomega Zip drive).

Spaces

Function: It is utilized to make a document that contains spaces (and nothing else).Each record made by Spaces contains precisely 10,000 spaces. Spaces are perfect for assessing encryption designs.

Network Security Tools (SecTools, 2011)

Wireshark

Wireshark is an amazing open source multi-arrange sort out tradition analyzer. It empowers you to take a gander at data against a current framework also against a capture report over the plate. The analysts may naturally examine the capture data, jumping down into just the level of package detail you require. Wireshark has a couple of successful segments, including a rich show channel vernacular and the ability to see the reproduced stream of a TCP session. It is like manner supports a few traditions and media sorts. A TCP-type distribution of comfort type called shark is included. One single alarming expression is that Wireshark has found many remote securities exploits remotely, so stay tuned and be careful to handle them on systems or untrustworthy opponents.

Metasploit

In 2004, Metasploit overpowered the security world. It is an open source to organize to verify, use and use the code of abuse. The extensible model through which the technicians can compile payloads, encoders, non-operation generators and attempts have allowed the Metasploit Framework to be used as the exit point for the appearance of the bleeding edge malfunction. It comes with many adventures, as it should be evident in the summary of the modules. This makes the composition of your particular adventures simpler and that positively is better than rubbing the darkest corners of the Internet for illegal code questionable. A free extra is Metasploit an unstable Linux virtual machine and intentionally usable to test Metasploit and other malfunctioning gadgets without hitting live servers.

Metasploit was completely free; however, the company was acquired by Rapid7 in 2009 and soon increased its business variations. The framework itself is not yet open and open, but now also offer a free but limited community release, a more guided Express version ($ 5,000 each year per customer), and a full version included in Pro release. Other paid abuse contraptions to consider are Core Impact (all the more expensive) and Canvas (less). The framework Metasploit now joins an official GUI based on Java and the remarkable Armitage of Raphael Mudge. Community, Express, and Pro downloads have electronic GUIs.

Nessus

Nessus is a champion among the most predominant and skillful shortcoming scanners, particularly for UNIX structures. It was at first free and open source, be that as it may, they close the source code in 2005 and cleared the free "Enrolled Feed" frame in 2008. It now costs $2,190 consistently, which still beats an extensive parcel of its adversaries. A free "Nessus Home" frame is in like manner open, be that as it may, it is limited and approved for home system use. Nessus is consistently revived, with more than 70,000 modules. Key segments fuse remote and close-by (affirmed) security checks, a client/server designing with an online interface, and an embedded scripting lingo for forming your own particular modules or understanding the present ones.

Aircrack

Aircrack is a suite of tools to break WEP and WPA 802.11a / b / g. Performs best-known piece counts to retrieve remote keys once accumulated enough encoded packets. The suite includes more than twelve discrete tools, including airodump (802.11), aireplay (802.11 packages), aircrack (WEP and WPA-PSK breaks) and airdecap (WEP / WPA logging decrypting).

Snort

This detection of intrusion and abhorrence of the system exceeds the wishes in the development exam and the marking of packets in IP frameworks. Through exploration of tradition, the pursuit of content and various preprocessors, Snort recognizes a large number of worms, fragile attempts to abuse, port yields, and suspect distinctive lead. Snort uses the versatile vernacular check to represent the action to be mounted or passed and a deliberate motor. While Snort is open source, Sourcefire's parent company offers its VRT certified rules for $ 499 per sensor per year and a complementary range of software and applications with multiple enterprise-level features. Sourcefire also offers a delayed 30-day feed.

Cain & Abel

UNIX clients frequently pompously state that the best free security instruments bolster their stage, to begin with, and Windows ports are regularly an untimely idea. They are typically right; however, Cain and Abel are a glaring exemption. This Windows-just secret key recuperation device handles a tremendous assortment of assignments. It can recover passwords by sniffing the framework, breaking encoded passwords using vocabulary, brute urge and cryptanalysis strikes, recording VoIP discourses, interpreting blended passwords, revealing mystery key boxes, uncovering put away passwords and dismembering coordinating traditions. It is additionally all around recorded.

BackTrack

This phenomenal bootable live CD Linux appropriation originates from the merger of Whax and Auditor. It brags a tremendous assortment of Security and Forensics tools and gives a rich improvement condition. Client measured quality is stressed so the conveyance can be effortlessly modified by the client to incorporate individual contents, extra apparatuses, altered portions, and so forth. BackTrack is prevailing by Kali Linux.

Netcat

This essential utility examines and forms data transversely finished TCP or UDP orchestrate affiliations. It is expected to be a tried and true backend instrument to use clearly or easily drive by various activities and substance. Meanwhile, it is a component rich framework examining an examination instrument, since it can make any kind of affiliation you would require, including port definitive to recognize moving toward affiliations.

The first Netcat was discharged by Hobbit in 1995; however, it hasn't been kept up regardless of its ubiquity. It can here and there even be elusive a duplicate of the v1.10 source code. The adaptability and helpfulness of this device provoked the Nmap Project to create Ncat, a current reimplementation which bolsters SSL, IPv6, SOCKS and HTTP intermediaries, association handling, and that's only the tip of the iceberg. Different goes up against this great instrument incorporate the incredibly flexible Socat, OpenBSD'sNC, Cryptcat, Netcat6, penetrate, SBD, thus called GNU Netcat.

Tcpdump

Tcpdump is the sniffer of the frame that all in all previous cases (Wireshark) preceded to the scene, and a substantial part of us continues to use a significant part of the time. It won't have the favor incidentals, that Wireshark, in any case, is well occupied and with less security risk. It in like manner requires fewer structure resources. While Tcpdump does not often get new components, it keeps itself properly to solve errors and transportability issues. It's amazing to find out about the chassis issues or look at development. There is an alternative Windows port called WinDump. TCP dump is the source of the Libpcap / WinPcap mapping library, used by Nmap and various gadgets.

John the Ripper

John the Ripper is a quick secret word saltine for UNIX/Linux and Mac OS X.Its basic role is to distinguish feeble Unix passwords, however, it underpins hashes for some different stages too. There is an official free form, a group upgraded adaptation (with many contributed fixes yet not as much quality affirmation), and an economic star variant.

Kismet

Kismet is a comfort (ncurses) based 802.11 layer-2 remote system locator, sniffer, and interruption discovery framework. It recognizes arranges by inactively sniffing (instead of more dynamic apparatuses, for example, NetStumbler), and can even decloak covered up (non-beaconing) systems on the off chance that they are being used. It can consequently recognize organize IP obstructs by sniffing TCP, UDP, ARP, and DHCP parcels, log activity in Wireshark/TCP dump perfect organization, and even plot distinguished systems and evaluated extends on downloaded maps. As you may expect, this device is normally utilized for wardriving. Gracious, and furthermore warwalking, warflying, and warskating, and so forth.

OpenSSH/PuTTY/SSH

SSH (Secure Shell) is the now comprehensive program for checking into or executing summons on a remote machine. It gives secure mixed correspondences between two untrusted has over an insecure framework, supplanting the appallingly temperamental telnet/rlogin/rsh choices. Most UNIX clients run the open source OpenSSH server and customer. Windows clients regularly lean toward the free PuTTY customer, which is additionally accessible for some cell phones, and WinSCP. Different Windows clients lean toward the pleasant terminal-based port of OpenSSH that accompanies Cygwin. There are many other free and restrictive customers to consider also.

Burp Suite

Burp Suite is a coordinated stage for assaulting web applications. It contains an assortment of apparatuses with various interfaces between them intended to encourage and accelerate the way toward assaulting an application. The greater part of the apparatuses shares a similar system for taking care of and showing HTTP messages, steadiness, verification, intermediaries, logging, alarming and extensibility.

Nikto

Nikto is an Open Source (GPL) web server scanner which performs finish tests against web servers for different things, including more than 6400 conceivably dangerous records/CGIs, checks for out of date variations of more than 1200 servers, and interpretation specific issues on more than 270 servers. It furthermore checks for server course of action things, for instance, the closeness of various record reports, HTTP server decisions, and will attempt to perceive presented web servers and programming. Compass things and modules are once in a while invigorated and can be normally revived.

Hping

It was powered by the ping call, however, it offers much more control over the tests sent. In addition, it has a useful traceroute mode and backups of IP discontinuity. Hping is particularly valuable when traceroute/ping /test attempts behind a firewall that squares using standard utilities. This allows you to regularly define the firewall control sets. It is also amazing to adapt more than TCP / IP and try different things with IP conventions. Tragically, it has not been upgraded since 2005. The Nmap project has done and takes care of Hping, a comparable program with more current components, such as strengthening IPv6 and one of the reverberation modes.

Ettercap

Ettercap is a suite for the man at the center of the local area's assault. It emphasizes the smell of live associations, screening of the contents of the march and numerous other fascinating traps.It supports the dynamic and latent dismounting of many conventions (even encrypted) and incorporates many components for system and host search.

Sysinternals

Sysinternals offers numerous small window utilities that are very useful for low-level hacking windows. Some are free or potentially incorporate source code, while others are exclusive. The most satisfied were the following:

- ProcessExplorer to monitor open documents and catalogs from any procedure (such as UNIX).
- PsTools to monitor (execute, suspend, kill, enumerate) near and remote procedures.
- Autorun to find out which executables are configured to continue running on the start or access medium structure.
- RootkitRevealer to distinguish between the log and document API differences that can demonstrate the proximity of a client mode or root functionality.
- TCPView, to examine the ending TCP and UDP activity used by each procedure (egNetstat on UNIX).

Huge numbers of the Sysinternals apparatuses initially accompanied source code and there were even Linux forms. Microsoft procured Sysinternals in July 2006, promising that "Clients will have the capacity to keep expanding on Sysinternals' propelled utilities, specialized data, and source code". Under four months after the fact, Microsoft evacuated the vast majority of that source code.

W3af

W3af is an amazingly prevalent, effective, and adaptable system for finding and missing web application vulnerabilities. It is anything but difficult to utilize and expand and highlights many web appraisal and misuse modules. In some ways, it resembles a web-centeredMetasploit.

OpenVAS

OpenVAS is a lack of protection scanner that was forked from the last free type of Nessus after that instrument went prohibitive in 2005. OpenVAS modules are as yet written in the Nessus NASL dialect. The venture appeared to be dead for some time, yet advancement has restarted.

Scapy

Scapy is a capable intuitive bundle control apparatus, parcel generator, arrange scanner, organize disclosure instrument, and bundle sniffer. Note that Scapy is a low-level instrument—you communicate with it utilizing the Python programming dialect. It gives classes to intelligently make bundles or sets of parcels, control them, send them over the wire, sniff different bundles from the wire, coordinate answers and answers, and then some. While there are many propelled front line gadgets out there to help security checking on, bear in mind about the nuts and bolts. Everyone should be to a great degree familiar with these surprisingly with most working systems (besides that Windows rejects who is and uses the name tracert). They can be exceptionally convenient when there's no other option, albeit more propelled usefulness is accessible from Hping and Netcat.

THC Hydra

When you have to break the brutal strength of a remote confirmation benefit, Hydra is regularly the decision maker. You can run quick word reference attacks on over 50 conventions, including telnet, FTP, HTTP, https, smb, some databases, and more. Like THC Amap, this download comes from end-users THC. Other online saltings are Medusa and Ncrack. The Nmap Security Scanner also contains many intelligent online intelligence puzzle modules.

Perl/Python/Ruby

While many canned security devices are accessible on this site for dealing with basic errands, scripting dialects enable you to compose your own (or alter existing ones) when you require something more custom. Brisk, convenient contents can test, abuse, or even fix frameworks. Documents like CPAN are loaded with modules, for example, Net:: RawIP and convention usage to make your assignments significantly less demanding. Numerous security devices utilize scripting dialects vigorously for extensibility. For instance, Scapy communication is through a Python translator, Metasploit modules are composed in Ruby, and Nmap's scripting motor uses Lua

Paros Proxy

A Java-based web mediator for looking over web application shortcoming. It supports adjusting/seeing HTTP/HTTPS messages on-the-go to change things, for instance, treats and casing fields. It incorporates a web movement recorder, web arachnid, hash adding a machine, and a scanner for testing regular web application assaults, for example, SQL infusion and cross-website scripting.

NetStumbler

Netstumbler is the best known Windows device for discovering open remote get too focused ("wardriving"). They moreover scatter a WinCE variation for PDAs and such named MiniStumbler. The mechanical assembly is starting at now free yet Windows-just and no source code is given. It uses a more powerful approach to manage to find WAPs than inert sniffers, for instance, Kismet or KisMAC

ISSUES AND CHALLENGES

The workplaces of PC development have not turned out without hindrances. Regardless of the way that it makes the life so snappy and speedy, yet hurled under the eclipsing of risk from the deadliest sort of culpability named as 'Computerized wrongdoing' without PCs, entire associations and government operations would essentially stop to work. This duplication of poor, powerful, straightforward PCs has engaged a consistently expanding number of people to use them and, more fundamentally, rely upon them as a segment of their run of the mill way of life. As associations, government workplaces, and individuals continue depending on them to a consistently expanding degree, so do the guilty parties Restriction of computerized infringement is liable to a fitting examination of their lead and appreciation of their belongings over various levels of society. In this manner, in the present original copy a precise comprehension of digital violations and their effects over different regions like Socio-eco-political, buyer trust, youngster etc. With the future patterns of digital wrongdoings are clarified. As of late, there has been huge exchange over the amalgamation of sorted out lawbreakers and cybercrime. Such a blending surely forecasts an evil sign for the close term future. With the vast majority of the criminal gatherings working out of Eastern Europe, Russia and Asia, where laws and requirement are channels and focusses on crime and empowers them to be abused for extensive pick up with a low level of hazard. For sorted out wrongdoing it is hard to request more. The outcome that would then be able not out of the ordinary will be an expansion in modern phishing assaults and different means for data fraud that might be two dimensional. For instance, utilizing call focuses to tell "clients" early of some issue, and afterward catching up with messages that demand individual data. The total of individual data in numerous outsider server farms will turn out to be significant focuses to penetrate. It is not hard to envision offenders utilizing information mining strategies to locate the most naïve shoppers, or fitting phishing messages for particular individuals in view of their therapeutic, money related or individual history. Identity theft will likewise move in more robotized bearings. For instance, botnets will move toward becoming vehicles not only for foreswearing of administration assaults and spam, yet additionally as monster look stages for discovering individual data, similar to Visas and government managed savings numbers. Controllers of the botnets will then get installments to run questions on their "database."

With proficient offenders dealing with the illegal tax avoidance and association of such plans, it asks to ask where all the specialized know-in what manner will originate from so as to perform cybercrime. Sadly, there are developing quantities of canny dark caps with college degrees spread far and wide, a considerable lot of them working in nations where the lawful business does not pay too and the odds of being gotten are thin. In any case, more troublesome is that it has turned out to be less demanding than at any other time to be a programmer equipped for causing awesome damage to systems and carrying out cybercrime. The Internet has made a storehouse of information where anybody can take in the essentials of subverting PC frameworks, with various instructional exercises accessible that spell out in almost layman's terms how to play out a support flood or a man in the center assault. Curiously, the best issue is not the individuals who will set aside the opportunity to learn and find new endeavours. Indeed, this gathering will most likely remain a little, profoundly canny system of scientists and security bunches concentrated exclusively on discovering gaps in programming. In this, it is predetermined, that regardless of the possibility that somebody is persuaded to figure out how abuses function, finding another adventure takes a level of examination, ability, and determination that most are not willing to contribute. The genuine danger originates from the significant straightforwardness at which anybody can run a program like "Metasploit," a system for running endeavours against focuses on that enables new modules to be foreign made and run consequently. The aggressor actually has to know nothing about how PCs function, other than how to work one. Actually, for all assaults, the diligent work is finished by a little gathering of individuals, and after that discharged into people in general space, permitting practically anybody to simply run the assault. Botnets are never again hand-made programming made by one gathering who really comprehended the basics, yet rather are open-source shared endeavours that expect to make it as simple as conceivable to control remote PCs, for example, botnet, eggheads and CSharpBot, all accessible from Source Forge.

Hence, the obstruction to the section to the field is low to the point that it permits practically anybody to examination and join the swelling positions of cybercriminals. With the expectation to learn and adapt so low, it should incite discourse on the requirement for another worldview of thought in how to acquire and manage culprits, in a way that is not any more attached to conventional strategies. For instance, for somebody to break into a house, not exclusively do they have to design the helpful minute, yet they may likewise know about bolt picking, security framework avoidance and have a level of get up and go to conquer moral limits. In resistance, the simplicity of cybercrime appears to be conversely relative to the lucrativeness that it offers and also, these patterns hint at quickening.

CONCLUSION

The possible destiny of the Internet is still up for gets among wrongdoers and conventional customers. Fears of an advanced Apocalypse still prosper, while the potential level of mischief that can be caused by wide-scale blackmail is about unbounded. A different report by digital security Ventures anticipated that ransomware harm expenses would surpass $5 billion out of 2017. This mulls over the harm of a few factors past simply the cost of the payoff, including the loss of information, downtime and lost efficiency. The Wannacry ransomware assault that hit the U.K's. National Health Service prior to May, and additionally a great many different associations and organizations around the globe, was a standout amongst the most across the board ransomware assaults that have ever occurred. The assessed harm it caused could surpass $1 billion, as per the report, in spite of just around $100,000 in bitcoins having so far been paid in payoffs to the culprits. To eradicate the above-mentioned issue, in this chapter we detailed about computer crimes, cybercrime cases and different types of tools both in hardware and software. No single device does everything or does everything very well. In spite of everything, it is a dignified practice to have several accessible tools. Utilizing different apparatuses is likewise an incredible approach to approve your discoveries. Similar outcomes, with two distinct devices, altogether increment the unwavering quality of the proof.

REFERENCES

Abbasi, A., Zhang, Z., Zimbra, D., Chen, H., & Nunamaker, J. F. Jr. (2010). Detecting fake websites: The contribution of statistical learning theory. *Management Information Systems Quarterly*, *34*(3), 435–461. doi:10.2307/25750686

Ablon, L., Libicki, M. C., & Golay, A. A. (2014). *Markets for cybercrime tools and stolen data: Hackers' bazaar*. Rand Corporation.

Al-Rafee, S., & Cronan, T. P. (2006). Digital piracy: Factors that influence attitude toward behavior. *Journal of Business Ethics*, *63*(3), 237–259. doi:10.100710551-005-1902-9

Andress, J., & Winterfeld, S. (2013). *Cyber warfare: techniques, tactics, and tools for security practitioners*. Elsevier.

Bilge, L., Strufe, T., Balzarotti, D., & Kirda, E. (2009, April). All your contacts belong to us: automated identity theft attacks on social networks. In *Proceedings of the 18th international conference on World wide web* (pp. 551-560). ACM. Retrieved from http://www.eurecom.fr/en/publication/2782/detail/all-your-contacts-are belong-to-us-automated-identity-theft-attacks-on-social-networks

Binh, H. T. T., Hanh, N. T., & Dey, N. (2016). Improved Cuckoo Search and Chaotic Flower Pollination optimization algorithm for maximizing area coverage in Wireless Sensor Networks. *Neural Computing & Applications*.

Bossler, A. M., & Holt, T. J. (2009). On-line activities, guardianship, and malware infection: An examination of routine activities theory. *International Journal of Cyber Criminology*, *3*(1), 400.

Brightman, H. J. (2011). *Today's White Collar Crime: Legal, Investigative, and Theoretical Perspectives*. Routledge.

Buchanan, B. (2004). Money laundering—a global obstacle. *Research in International Business and Finance*, *18*(1), 115–127. doi:10.1016/j.ribaf.2004.02.001

Casey, E. (Ed.). (2001). *Handbook of computer crime investigation: forensic tools and technology*. Academic Press.

Cheng, H., & Ma, L. (2009). White collar crime and the criminal justice system: Government response to bank fraud and corruption in China. *Journal of Financial Crime*, *16*(2), 166–179. doi:10.1108/13590790910951849

Chowdhuri, S., Dey, N., Chakraborty, S., & Baneerjee, P. K. (2015). Analysis of Performance of MIMO Ad Hoc Network in Terms of Information Efficiency. In *Proceedings of the Emerging ICT for Bridging the Future-Proceedings of the 49th Annual Convention of the Computer Society of India CSI* (Vol. 2, pp. 43–50). Cham: Springer; doi:10.1007/978-3-319-13731-5_6.

Chowdhuri, S., Roy, P., Goswami, S., Azar, A. T., & Dey, N. (2014). Rough set based ad hoc network: A review. *International Journal of Service Science, Management, Engineering, and Technology*, *5*(4), 66–76. doi:10.4018/ijssmet.2014100105

Chowdhury, A. (2016, October). Recent Cyber Security Attacks and Their Mitigation Approaches–An Overview. In Proceedings of the International Conference on Applications and Techniques in Information Security (pp. 54-65). Springer Singapore. doi:10.1007/978-981-10-2741-3_5

Cosmo (1765).From the movie Sneakers, from http://quotegeek.com/quotes-from-movies/sneakers/1765/

Das, S., & Nayak, T. (2013). Impact of cyber crime: Issues and challenges. *International Journal of Engineering Sciences & Emerging Technologies*, *6*(2), 142–153.

Deloitte. (2017). About Deloitte. Retrieved from https://www2.deloitte.com/us/en/pages/about-deloitte/articles/about-deloitte.html

Duhart, B. A. M., & Hernández-Gress, N. (2016, December). Review of the Principal Indicators and Data Science Techniques Used for the Detection of Financial Fraud and Money Laundering. In *Proceedings of the 2016 International Conference on Computational Science and Computational Intelligence (CSCI)* (pp. 1397-1398). IEEE. 10.1109/CSCI.2016.0267

Ellison, L., & Akdeniz, Y. (1998). Cyber-stalking: The Regulation of Harassment on the Internet. *Criminal Law Review (London, England)*, *29*, 29–48.

Fidelie, L. W. (2009). Internet Gambling: Innocent Activity or Cybercrime? *International Journal of Cyber Criminology, 3*(1), 476.

Fokuoh Ampratwum, E. (2009). Advance fee fraud "419" and investor confidence in the economies of sub-Saharan African (SSA). *Journal of Financial Crime, 16*(1), 67–79. doi:10.1108/13590790910924975

Global Financial Integrity (GFI). (n.d.). Money laundering. Retrieved from http://www.gfintegrity.org/issue/money-laundering/

Goswami, S., Roy, P., Dey, N., & Chakraborty, S. (2016). Wireless body area networks combined with mobile cloud computing in healthcare: a survey. *Classification and Clustering in Biomedical Signal Processing, 388.*

Gottschalk, P. (2010). *Policing Cyber Crime.* Bookboon.

Guan, Y. (2003). Evidence and Collection Analyses Tools. Retrieved October 30, 2003, from home.eng.iastate.edu/~guan/course/backup/CprE-592-YG-Fall.../Lecture15.pdf

Hagen, J. M., Sivertsen, T. K., & Rong, C. (2008). Protection against unauthorized access and computer crime in Norwegian enterprises. *Journal of Computer Security, 16*(3), 341–366. doi:10.3233/JCS-2008-16305

Hansen, L. L. (2009). Corporate financial crime: Social diagnosis and treatment. *Journal of Financial Crime, 16*(1), 28–40. doi:10.1108/13590790910924948

Harbawi, M., & Varol, A. (2016, April). The role of digital forensics in combating cybercrimes. In *Proceedings of the 2016 4th International Symposium on Digital Forensic and Security (ISDFS)* (pp. 138-142). IEEE. 10.1109/ISDFS.2016.7473532

Harichandran, V. S., Breitinger, F., Baggili, I., & Marrington, A. (2016). A cyber forensics needs analysis survey: Revisiting the domain's needs a decade later. *Computers & Security, 57,* 1–13. doi:10.1016/j.cose.2015.10.007

Helplinelaw.com. (2000), *Helplinelaw.com is one of the pioneers of the online legal Services.* Retrieved from http://www.helplinelaw.com/docs/indian%20law/aboutus.shtml

Henning, J. (2009). Perspectives on financial crimes in Roman-Dutch law: Bribery, fraud and the general crime of falsity (falsiteyt). *Journal of Financial Crime, 16*(4), 295–304. doi:10.1108/13590790910993771

Hidarimanesh, S. N., & Esfahani, M. S. (2016). Bank fraud. *Recht & Psychiatrie, 724*(2247), 518–525.

Internet Live Stats. (n.d.). Retrieved from www.internetlivestats.com

Interpol. (n.d.). *INTERPOL is the world's largest international police organization, with 190 member countries.* Retrieved from www.interpol.int/public/FinancialCrime/Default.asp

Investopedia. (2017). Identity theft. Retrieved from www.investopedia.com/terms/i/identitytheft.asp

Jewkes, Y. (Ed.). (2013). *Crime online.* Routledge.

Khari, M., Shrivastava, G., Gupta, S., Gupta, R. (2017). Role of Cyber Security in Today's Scenario. *Detecting and Mitigating Robotic Cyber Security Risks*, *177*.

Kimbahune, V. V., Deshpande, A. V., & Mahalle, P. N. (2017). Lightweight Key Management for Adaptive Addressing in Next Generation Internet. *International Journal of Ambient Computing and Intelligence*, *8*(1), 50–69. doi:10.4018/IJACI.2017010103

Kizza, J. M. (2017). Cyber Crimes and hackers. In *Guide to Computer Network Security* (pp. 105–131). Springer International Publishing. doi:10.1007/978-3-319-55606-2_5

Larsson, P. (2006). Developments in the regulation of economic crime in Norway. *Journal of Financial Crime*, *13*(1), 65–76. doi:10.1108/13590790610641242

Laudon, K. C., & Laudon, J. P. (2004). Management information systems: Managing the digital firm.

Legal Dictionary. (n.d.). Bank Fraud. Retrieved from https://legaldictionary.net/bank-fraud/

Milne, G. R. (2003). How well do consumers protect themselves from identity theft? *The Journal of Consumer Affairs*, *37*(2), 388–402. doi:10.1111/j.1745-6606.2003.tb00459.x

Mukherjee, A., Dey, N., Kausar, N., Ashour, A. S., Taiar, R., & Hassanien, A. E. (2016). A disaster management specific mobility model for flying ad-hoc network. *International Journal of Rough Sets and Data Analysis*, *3*(3), 72–103. doi:10.4018/IJRSDA.2016070106

Northeastern University. (1898) Northeastern. Retrieved from www.northeastern.edu/neuhome/academics/departments-programs.html

Ogilvie, E. (2000, December). The Internet and cyberstalking. In *Proceedings of Criminal Justice Responses Conference*, Sydney.

Picard, M. (2009). Financial services in trouble: The electronic dimension. *Journal of Financial Crime*, *16*(2), 180–192. doi:10.1108/13590790910951858

Pickett, K. S., & Pickett, J. M. (2002). *Financial crime investigation and control*. John Wiley & Sons.

Pontell, H. N., Geis, G., & Brown, G. C. (2007). Offshore internet gambling and the World Trade Organization: Is it criminal behavior or a commodity? *International Journal of Cyber Criminology*, *1*(1), 119–136.

Sammons, J. (2012). *The basics of digital forensics: the primer for getting started in digital forensics*. Elsevier.

Sectools.org. (2011), SecTools.Org: Top 125 Network Security Tools. Retrieved from http://sectools.org/

Simpson, S. (2009). *White Collar Crime: An Opportunity Perspective. Criminology and Justice Studies*. Taylor & Francis. doi:10.1007/978-0-387-09502-8

Smith, R., Grabosky, P., & Urbas, G. (2004). Cyber criminals on trial. *Criminal Justice Matters*, *58*(1), 22–23. doi:10.1080/09627250408553240

Snyder, H., & Crescenzi, A. (2009). Intellectual capital and economic espionage: New crimes and new protections. *Journal of Financial Crime, 16*(3), 245–254. doi:10.1108/13590790910973089

Studymode Research. (2010), *Computer Crime and its Effects*. Retrieved May 30, 2010, form www.studymode.com/essays/Computer-Crime-And-Its-Effects-63666883.html

Taboona, A. (2017) Top 20 Free Digital Forensic Investigation Tools for SysAdmins. Retrieved from https://techtalk.gfi.com/top-20-free-digital-forensic-investigation-tools-for-sysadmins/

The Government of the Hong Kong Special Administrative Region (n.d.). InfoSec website is produced and managed by the Office of the Government Chief Information Officer of the Government, from https://www.infosec.gov.hk/english/crime/what_crc_1.html

The National Fraud Intelligence Bureau (NFIB). (n.d.). Advance Fee Fraud. Retrieved from www.actionfraud.police.uk/fraud-az-advance-fee-fraud

Walker, J. (1999). How big is global money laundering? *Journal of Money Laundering Control, 3*(1), 25–37. doi:10.1108/eb027208

Wall, D. (Ed.). (2003). *Crime and the Internet*. Routledge.

Weebly. (n.d.). Cyber Crime. Retrieved from http://cybercrimeproject.weebly.com/sources.html

Yamin, M., & Sen, A. A. A. (2018). Improving Privacy and Security of User Data in Location Based Services. *International Journal of Ambient Computing and Intelligence, 9*(1), 19–42. doi:10.4018/IJACI.2018010102

Yang, W., Wang, X., Song, X., Yang, Y., & Patnaik, S. (2018). Design of Intelligent Transportation System Supported by New Generation Wireless Communication Technology. *International Journal of Ambient Computing and Intelligence, 9*(1), 78–94. doi:10.4018/IJACI.2018010105

Yoon, C. (2011). Theory of planned behavior and ethics theory in digital piracy: An integrated model. *Journal of Business Ethics, 100*(3), 405–417. doi:10.100710551-010-0687-7

Zeltser, L. (2000). The evolution of malicious agents. Retrieved Oct 12, 2006 from http://www.zeltser.com/malicious-agents

Zuech, R., Khoshgoftaar, T. M., & Wald, R. (2015). Intrusion detection and big heterogeneous data: A survey. *Journal of Big Data, 2*(1), 3. doi:10.118640537-015-0013-4

KEY TERMS AND DEFINITIONS

Computer: A computer is a device that can be instructed to carry out an arbitrary set of arithmetic or logical operations automatically. The ability of computers to follow generalized sequences of operations, called programs, enable them to perform a wide range of tasks.

Crime: A crime is an unlawful act punishable by a state or other authority.

Cyber Crime: computer related crime, is a crime that involves a computer and a network.

Hardware: Computer hardware is the collection of physical components that constitute a computer system.

Internet: The Internet is the global system of interconnected computer networks that use the Internet protocol suite (TCP/IP) to link devices worldwide.

Malicious Agents: A malicious agent is a computer program that operates on behalf of a potential intruder to aid in attacking a system or network.

Chapter 12
On Creating Digital Evidence in IP Networks With NetTrack

Diana Berbecaru
Politecnico di Torino, Italy

ABSTRACT

Computer forensic is the practice of collecting, analyzing, and reporting digital evidence in a way that is legally admissible in open court. Network forensics, an offset of computer forensic, is mainly concerned with the monitoring and analysis of network traffic, both local and WAN/internet, in order to identify security incidents and to investigate fraud or network misuse. In this chapter, the authors discuss challenges in creating high-speed network forensic tools and propose NetTrack, a tamper-proof device aimed to produce evidences with probative value via digital signatures for the network traffic. Since digitally signing each IP packet is not efficient, the authors used a specific technique exploiting the Merkle trees to create digital signatures for flows and multicasts and implemented it by using an optimized algorithm for Merkle tree traversal to save space and time. Through experiments, the authors show NetTrack signing is fast as it can produce digital evidence within a short time.

INTRODUCTION

The Scientific Working Group on Digital Evidence (SWGDE, 2017) defines a "digital evidence" as "information of probative value that is stored or transmitted in binary form". Examples of "digital evidence" are: application files (like tests, images), system files (logs) or data ignored by the operating systems but stored on disks. This chapter addresses the problem of creating digital evidence for the network traffic, which is information with probative value about the network activity monitored at the interface of a network node (e.g. router, computer) or on a network link.

Such kind of digital evidence could be very useful in applications requiring both accurate tracing of data as well as the ability to proof its correctness in court. We give in this sense a simple example: two clients C1 and C2 connect almost simultaneously to a company server S providing time-sensitive services (e.g. stock option transactions). Even though the client C1 sends connection requests to S before C2, the IP packets are not guaranteed to arrive at S in this order: the network could actually delay

DOI: 10.4018/978-1-5225-4100-4.ch012

packets of C1 (with respect to the ones of C2) either involuntarily due to the processing of the packets in the intermediate routers, or deliberately due to attacks performed by malware users. In case a dispute is raised, the server S can exploit his internal logs to prove the quality of the service provided to his users. Such logs typically contain timestamped packets, which contain basically an association between the data arrived at the server S' network interface and the time indicated by the internal clock of the system S. In some situations, like for example in some banking applications, the information stored in logs could be accepted as proof in court even though the internal log has not been actually created in such a way to provide non-repudiation of the data stored and even though it could be possible for the internal log to be incomplete, in the sense that parts of the packets might have been lost and not recorded in the internal log.

In other critical scenarios (cyberattacks, financial services), it is highly required to know the *arrival timing* information of a packet. Thus, in this case, it is necessary to trace also the time when the packet is present on the network link or at a device interface. However, such applications do not have actually very strict constraints on the time precision, but rather on the authenticity and/or non-repudiation of time (who states for the time) and the packets' ordering. Thus, companies or entities are highly interested in a solution that can be used to create digital evidence with probative value for their own internal network activity (e.g. to compute forensic analysis) as well as of the client's and that could be subsequently used in case of disputes.

Nowadays, the network monitoring tools do not address the creation of digital evidences asserting packet's arrival time for the network activity. Most of the network monitoring techniques and tools developed so far provide typically essential inputs towards performance tuning, they are normally used to identify and reduce network bottlenecks, troubleshooting, as well as to identify, diagnose and rectify faults, or to perform planning. Such tools are also used to predict the scale and nature of necessary additional resources, to characterize network activity in order to supply data for network modeling and simulation, and to identify and correct the pathological network behavior. We will present some of these techniques and tools further below.

This chapter presents the first steps towards developing the NetTrack device, which is a tamper-proof device that could be employed in several use case scenarios requiring digital evidences of network activity, such as to provide the proof of quality of service, to achieve advanced IP traceback, in the Value Added Networks, or to perform network forensics. The NetTrack operates basically on two elementary pieces of data inputs, the IP packet and the time, and is composed of several modules, like a Network Sampler used to interface with the network node/link to capture and filter packets, an ACTS (Authenticated and Certified Time Source) used to obtain an authenticated and certified time from a time source, a NetTrack Evidence Creator module used to digitally sign the network traffic, and one used to store the evidences for short-term. In this chapter we focus mainly on the NetTrack Evidence Creator and we discuss its design, implementation and the results obtained in testing its performance.

The NetTrack Evidence Creator is the core application of the NetTrack, and is in charge with digitally signing the packet flows. In the current approach, we adopted the (hash) tree chaining technique presented in Wong and Lam (1999) for signing and verifying multiple IP packets. This technique uses a single signing/verifying operation to sign and verify a group of IP packets, called a *block*. In practice, an authentication tree or a so-called "Merkle tree" data structure (Merkle, 1982) is exploited to calculate a "block digest", which is digitally signed by using an asymmetric algorithm, e.g. RSA (Jonsson & Kaliski, 2003), and the appropriate signer's asymmetric key. Since this technique exploits the asymmetric cryptography, it may be used in scenarios requiring data integrity and authentication, and (possibly) the non-repudiation of the data. The Merkle trees have been used so far in many cryptographic applications, like in multicast authentication protocols (Perrig et al., 2002), in multicast authentication scheme with forward security (Berbecaru et al., 2010), for certification refrashal (Kocher, 1998), certificate revocation (Berbecaru, 2004) and to perform micropayments (Rivest & Shamir, 1997).

In the tree chaining technique, each packet is individually verifiable because it contains the signed block digest, named "block signature", together with the "chaining information", which proves that the packet is in the block. Since the cost of signing/verifying operation is spread over many packets, this procedure improves the rate of signing and verification operations by several orders of magnitude with respect to performing the same operations individually on the packets. Moreover, in the implementation, we have improved this technique by using an optimized algorithm for the construction and traversal of Merkle tree in order to obtain a better *chaining time* at the signer. In particular, we used Szydlo's algorithm (Szydlo, 2004), which requires $log_2 N$ time and $3 log_2 N$ space per packet digest output. We describe our implementation of the above algorithm in order to create digital evidences in NetTrack, and we show its performance on several platforms.

BACKGROUND

One of the main issues to be treated in any network forensics tool is the packet capture. In the past, a wide variety of networking monitoring tools and distributed systems have been designed and implemented, (for example, Miessler, 2015; Apisdorf, 1996; Fraleigh, 2001; Ranum, 1997), but none of them actually produced digital evidence for the network traffic. Generally speaking, network monitoring is still used nowadays to observe and quantify exactly what is happening in the network, both on the microcosmic and macrocosmic time scales. Two types of monitoring can be performed: passive and active. Passive network measurement (PNM) denotes "the method of observing packets on a data link or shared network media without generating any additional traffic on that media which may disturb the existing network behavior" (Donelly, 2002). Different types of devices, such as workstations, servers, routers, or dedicated equipment can accomplish passive packet capture. Active network monitoring usually observes the effects of injecting traffic into the network in order to investigate some aspects of the network's performance or functioning. For example, Internet Control Message Protocol (ICMP) ping packets are typically injected to establish reachability, while HTTP requests are exploited to monitor server response times (Shrivastava & Gupta, 2014).

In general, passive network measurement is the best way to observe packets on a network without disturbing their regular behavior. To analyze how packets, protocols, and network equipment interact or to log events of choice, the most important feature to record is the precise time of key events on the network, usually called *time–stamping*. However, copying all the packets into the capturing device memory can be expensive at high packet rates. Since the host cannot keep up with the arrival rate of all packets, or because only some packets are of real interest, the *"packet filters"* might be used in order to reject some packets and accept others, which are passed further on for further elaboration. Many different packet filters have been developed over the years, such as Yuhara (1994), and Engler (1996), but one of the most popular tools exploited for passive network monitoring nowadays is Tcpdump tool (Miessler, 2015). Some network forensic tools exploit packet filters or primitive libraries such as *libpcap* (Garcia, 2008) to perform packet capture, while others use dedicated hardware, due to the reasons explained below.

In some cases, like in safety-critical infrastructures that must run continuously without interruption (Perry et al., 2016), the standard network monitoring tools are unsuitable to perform forensic analysis and security-related anomalies because they cannot guarantee that all data packets are being captured and/or the original packet ordering is preserved. Moreover, they might introduce their own traffic into the network. In time, the network monitoring tools have been also integrated with systems able to provide precise time. For example, hardware-based measurement system named Dag (Donnelly, 2002) has been designed with the precision in mind: its main purpose is to capture and timestamp the network packets as precisely as possible so that to reflect packet's arrival order at the system's network interface. One of the main reasons for which the Dag cards were designed is that the internal clock of a computer based on crystal oscillators is not suited for creating time indications because of the drift effect, which can cause the frequency to change by hundreds of Hertz in case the temperature changes by few degrees. Moreover, the frequency skew of the clock can lead to an error of the time indication of over 8 seconds in just 24 hours, much poorer than the average digital watch. The second motivation of creation of Dag cards was the inaccuracy of the timestamps due to the errors have driven from the interrupt latency, buffering, and processing time of the hosts running software network measurement tools.

Endace measurement systems manufacture nowadays special-purpose Dag cards, which have a dedicated hardware enabling them to perform full line-rate packet acquisition at network speeds up to 40 Gbps (Endace, 2017). Contrary to commodity network adapters, Dag cards can "retrieve and map network packets through a zero-copy interface to user space, which avoids the interrupt processing. The arriving packets are stored in a large static circular buffer memory mapped to user-space, which avoids wasting time for costly packet copies. Moreover, user applications can directly access this buffer without the invocation of the operating system kernel." Thus, Dag cards are a good solution for applications that need very precise information on the network traffic.

The Dag card, namely the Endace Data Acquisition and Generation Card (EndaceDAG, 2015), has been exploited in (Perry et al., 2016) to build a network forensic tool, which allows all network traffic to be captured accurately in a Supervisory Control and Data Acquisition (SCADA) network and it does not affect the original order. Moreover, the tool allows also replaying data traffic to precisely reproduce the original timing of packets. This work is highly related to the proposed NetTrack in part, however, it does not create cryptographic proofs on what it has been recorded. The tool proposed in (Perry et al., 2016) is aimed to be used in "live" safety-critical systems (such as in electricity substations) to reproduce security incidents and to capture anomalous events. So, it is assumed that the end-user is trusted or anyway the data does not have to be provided further on to another external application and would not be used as proof in court. Some schemes apply cryptographic processing on the traffic traced. For example, Kim and Kim (2011) proposed a scheme named "Network Forensic Evidence Acquisition (NFEA)" that produces secured tracking data at edge routers. The tracked data is protected for authenticity and integrity by using a so-called Authenticated Evidence Marking Scheme, in which a router encrypts part of the IP packet and router's time by using the AES-256 algorithm in ECB mode and a router' secret key for authenticity and integrity.

Actually, to digitally sign generic network flows, several solutions have been proposed so far and we have studied some of them as resumed in Berbecaru et al. (2010). Some multicast authentication protocols exploit MAC (Message Authentication Code) and symmetric cryptography, while other solutions exploit asymmetric cryptography. TESLA (Perrig et al., 2005), for example, is based on symmetric cryptography and exploits time as the source of asymmetry, while more recent proposals like Bamasag and Toumi (2016) exploit a secretly shared scheme to achieve continuous authentication in the Internet of Things. The multicast authentication protocols that exploit asymmetric mechanisms provide the integrity, source authentication, and non-repudiation of the packets, but on the other hand they need to use some technique to spread the cost of creating or verifying the signatures over multiple packets in order to avoid time delays at the signer or verifier. Moreover, they have to support also various types of redundancy at signature generation in order to resist to packet loss (Tartary et al., 2011; Perrig et al., 2000; Golle & Modadugu, 2001; Miner & Staddon, 2001).

It is clear that any system performing network forensic has to capture and process huge amount of data and it generates also lots of data in every event of action. Thus, it might be difficult for forensic investigators to find out the clue and analyze the whole data. Even though the Network Sampler and storage modules in NetTrack are subject to future work, it's worth mentioning some solutions that can provide useful insights for their development. The ever-growing speed of network links (reaching 100 Gbit/s) will make it very difficult to perform online analyses or to store traffic for subsequent forensic investigations. Some authors propose to filter the network traffic, e.g. (Ruiz et al., 2016) propose a "method able to identify plain text (human readable) in the IP packet payload", which is extremely useful for forensic and real-time analyses. The authors of this method provide also details on its implementation in a Field Programmable Gate Array (FPGA). On the other hand, the Network Forensic Tool proposed in Mate and Kapse (2015) directly capture the network packets in order to recognize data like the hosts, open ports, sessions, etc. without injecting traffic on the network.

Visualization of data becomes also an issue because a good visualization tool would allow an analyst to discover new anomaly and application traffic patterns easily or even to see other details of the anomaly traffic. Fatima et al. (2017) propose a method of data fusion together with visualization techniques to handle data in forensic investigation and analysis. Promrit and Mingkhwan (2015) also proposed an iterative visualization technique to illustrate network communication for forensic analysis.

NETTRACK USE CASE SCENARIOS

Proof of Quality of Service

Suppose two clients C1 and C2 are both trying to connect to an online stock options server S to perform financial online transactions, in a very short time one from another. Even though C1 sends connection request packets to S before C2, the Internet infrastructure does not guarantee that C1 would actually get served by S in the first place: the IP packets can be delayed on their way to the destination S unintentionally (e.g. by the routing infrastructure) or by malware attacks (i.e. intentionally). In case of a dispute, the company managing the server S could provide their internal log files, proving that client C1's packets actually arrived at S after C2. But server's internal log files are not enough, especially if a proof (of the quality of service provided by S) is required and the proof should be valid in court.

A solution could be to use NetTrack, which is attached to the interface(s) of the server S: in this way the company could provide evidence (proof) about the order and the arrival time of the IP packets at their server's network interfaces, by means of the data provided by NetTrack, as illustrated in Figure 1.

Advanced IP Traceback

This usage scenario can be seen an extension of the usage scenario explained in the previous paragraph. Since the IP protocol is anonymous, it is difficult to accurately identify the true source of an IP datagram. IP addresses can be spoofed using simple widely-available tools or even more spoofed source addresses

Figure 1. NetTrack exploitation for the proof of Quality of Service

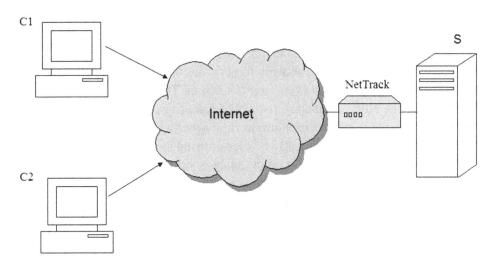

are legitimately used by Network Address Translators (NATs) or Mobile IP. On the other hand, the network routing infrastructure is stateless (that is routers do not keep track by default of the IP packets they forwarded) and it is based largely on destination addresses, which means that no entity in an IP network is officially responsible for ensuring the IP source address is correct.

The solution to this problem is a technique called *IP traceback*: by using these techniques a victim is able to identify the true source of an IP packet and maintains a track of the path traversed by a single IP packet. In other words, it is possible to identify the path followed by an IP packet from the source to the destination. Among IP traceback techniques mark each packet with partial information probabilistically (Dean, 2001;Doeppner, 2000;Goodrich, 2002;Savage, 2000;Song, 2001), while the technique proposed in Snoeren (2001) stores the packet digests in the form of Bloom filters at each router.

If it is necessary to identify not only *where* (i.e. the path) an IP packet passed through from his way from the source to the destination, but also *when* it passed through a particular network point, some IP traceback systems allow to associate a timestamp (whose time indication is taken from a global clock source, e.g., a GPS receiver) to the packet, which is named "packet trace" (PatentBBNT, 2005). NetTrack could be employed for IP traceback either if it is extended to allow for IP traceback too, or if NetTrack is attached to a separate system that performs the IP traceback task (e.g. IP traceback-enabled router) in case the NetTrack maintains his primary role of associating IP packets to the precise time. In the latter case, in case of a cyber attack, the data must be read and processed by both devices.

Value Added Networks

By definition, a value-added network (VAN) is *"a private network provider hired by a company to facilitate electronic data interchange (EDI) or provide other network services "*. In the past, some companies hired dedicated networks to transfer data between different operational locations belonging to their company or to exchange data between their company and other trusted companies. Nowadays, many companies move their data over the Internet by exploiting VAN technologies, while contemporary value-added network providers now focus on offering more advanced services for their customers. For example, if the clients C1 and C2 are both connected to the same VAN, the VAN could provide a service aimed to be able to track the packet delivery between them. In case of a dispute, in order to o prove this to third parties, the VAN could use NetTrack devices at the entrance points, as illustrated in Figure 2.

Forensic Analysis and Investigation

Forensic analysis is "the process of understanding, re-creating and analyzing events that have occurred previously" (Peisert, 2005). At the basis of successful forensic analysis stay the ability to re-create any event regardless of the intent of the user whether the cause of the events was an illegitimate intruder or an authorized insider, independently of the nature of the previous events. The tools that address forensic analysis should follow 5 principles - enumerated in Peisert (2005) - otherwise, the tool will fail to record actions or result in enough detail to understand their meaning. One of the 5 principles states that: "Assumptions about expected failures, attacks and attackers should not control what is logged. Trust no user and trust no policy, as we may not know what we want in advance. For example, ignoring insiders to focus on outsiders places too much attention on access control mechanisms rather than recording system events". By placing several NetTrack devices in various points of the network, outside but also inside the trusted network domain, an analyst should be able to recover the IP traffic that passed through that network points at specific time instants and use it for forensic analysis. Due to a large amount of storage required, NetTrack devices could be activated only under circumstances or for some time intervals, for example only during the night.

NetTrack Design Issues

Generally speaking, the probative value of data depends on the following (general) properties:

P1 - Authenticity: It can be proved that the data has been recorded by a specific device.
P2 - Integrity: It can be proved that the data has been recorded unaltered and have not been changed afterward.

Figure 2. NetTrack exploitation in a VAN

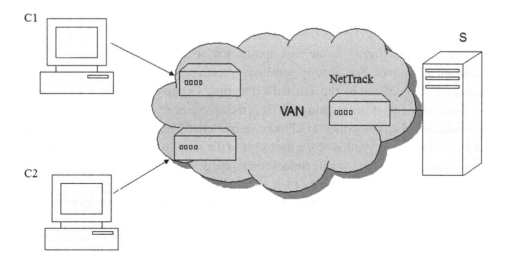

P3 - Accuracy: The data are a faithful copy of the original, including the time information.

P4 - Completeness: All relevant information (as agreed in a *specific contract*) has been collected and nothing has been omitted.

P5 - Law Compliance: The data are collected and handled in accordance with all applicable legal regulations, including those on personal privacy.

P6 - Access Control: The data are available only to the duly authorized individuals.

These properties must hold for all the data (input & output) handled by NetTrack. Since NetTrack operates basically on two elementary pieces of data (inputs), the IP packet and time, it must check properties P1-P4 on these inputs. As output, the NetTrack produces a digital evidence in the form *(IP packet, T, SV)*, which serves as a probative value that the IP packet captured from the network was traced at the authenticated and certified time *T* on the NetTrack's interface, and *SV* is the cryptographic data used for integrity and authenticity purposes (properties P1 and P2).

In our view, the NetTrack device should meet the following requirements:

C1: Is fine-grained, that is the device operates on the smallest unit of data handled in the IP network that is in the IP packet.

C2: It produces timing attestations, that is the device has the role to attest when an IP packet was ``seen'' in a specific point of the network at a specific, precise time.

C3: It should support accurate, authenticated and certified time-stamping of the packets that are individual IP packets are associated with a timestamp that reflects the sequencing of the packets. The time included in the timestamp must be obtained from an authenticated and certified time source.

C4: The device must be tamper-proof and it should produce information with legal-value. Tamperproofing and `law compliance' of the NetTrack are very important features, which distinguishes it from other previous network monitoring tools.

C5: The device should be seen as a closed box, which means access to the data stored into the device should be allowed specialized parties, for example to police personnel investigating a cyber attack. Thus, the device should ideally have no open communication ports towards network infrastructure, except for the dedicated network card used for sampling the network flow.

In this chapter, NetTrack is a device based on the PC architecture, whose main components are illustrated in Figure 3. The full description of the components is out of the scope of this chapter; in the following, we will detail mainly the NetTrack Evidence Creator.

The NetTrack Evidence Creator is the core application of the NetTrack device in charge with the creation of the digital evidence. For security-sensitive operations such as the creation of *SV*, the Trusted Platform Module (TPM) defined by the Trusted Computing Group can be used. We assume the TPM as the root of trust for the platform running the NetTrack Evidence Creator. TPM can also be used for measuring the integrity of all components of NetTrack Evidence Creator: therefore it is possible to use a TPM capability to bind the decryption of the user keys to the status of the platform. Only if the platform is in a good status the signing keys can be unlocked and used. This way the NetTrack Evidence Creator can be considered tamper-proof. Furthermore, it should be possible at any time to remotely verify the integrity status of NetTrack Evidence Creator through the so-called remote attestation. By exploiting the

Figure 3. NetTrack components

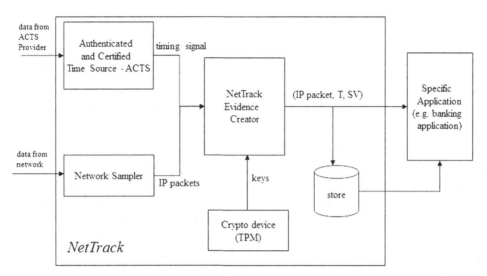

TPM, usage responds to P2 and P6 properties for what it concerns the security sensitive material used by the NetTrack Evidence Creator.

NETTRACK EVIDENCE CREATOR IMPLEMENTATION

IP Packet Timestamp Resolution

By considering the smallest event on a network a single bit, the highest useful IP packet timestamp resolution would be a clock running at the bit-rate of the physical layer, which would produce a unique timestamp for each bit time. However, most networks nowadays are byte oriented, which means packets are typically expressed as an integer number of bytes in length. By considering the smallest network event a byte, a clock running at the byte rate of the media would be sufficient. But when a computer architecture is used for network monitoring and timestamping of packets, the frequency of the system's clock determines the resolution of the timestamps attached to the IP packets. For example, a minimum size packet is transmitted in only 57.6 microseconds even on a 10Mb/s network.

Thus with a packet timestamps of 10 milliseconds resolution, many sequential packets may have identical timestamps. In this case, we cannot derive from the timestamp the packet arrival order, and consequently, the ordering information may be lost in processing. In case multiple packets have identical timestamps, the packet inter-arrival time distributions cannot be accurately generated. The minimum requirement is that the timestamps associated to a pair of immediately consecutive minimum sized packets should be different. In this way, the packet arrival ordering information can always be determined solely from the timestamps of the packets. The IP packet timestamp resolution then must be less than the transmission time of a minimum sized packet on the media.

Some Linux kernels, and also FreeBSD kernels could timestamp packet arrivals with 1 μs resolution, easily meeting the minimum requirement for 10Mb/s Ethernet. Also in case of a 100Mb/s Ethernet, the minimum packet time is 5.7microseconds, so the kernel clocks could meet the requirement here also. Nevertheless, the system clock alone is not a good solution in NetTrack for timestamping the packets because the source of time information is not authenticated or certified. The time contained in the timestamp would be just the internal time of the PC sampling the network and this could be manipulated easily by a user. In case of a 1Gbit/s Ethernet, the minimum packet time drops to only 576 nanoseconds, and so kernel timestamping resolution of 1microseconds is not sufficient.

One possible solution to solve the timestamp resolution problem would be to use dedicated hardware, like the Dag cards. Dags have a clock that provides timestamping resolution less than the transmission time of a minimum sized packet even on high-rates networks, enabling thus full line-rate data acquisition at speeds up to 10 Gbit/s.

Let's assume that NetTrack is sampling a network at 100 Mb/s and that the size of an IP datagram is 128 bytes, then this means that approximately 97.656 packets/s are conveyed through the network. Consequently, one IP packet is conveyed in approximately 10 μs and approximately 100.000 packets are captured by the Dag in one second and are transferred into the NetTrack's memory area. User applications (e.g. NetTrack Evidence Creator) can directly access this buffer, without invoking the operating system kernel. Let's assume that not all NetTrack's recorded packets have to be provided to an external application (e.g. a banking application) according to the contract stipulated between the NetTrack owner and the bank but only a portion of them, let's say 10% of the packets. This means that 10.000 packets need to be digitally signed in the time interval considered as the example for sampling the network, which is 1 second. Obviously, the T=1 second time period given as the example for sampling the network can be shortened or extended, based on the requirements of the application that receives the data from NetTrack. Clearly, in NetTrack we need an efficient and scalable solution for digitally signing a significant amount of data within a short amount of time and saving space also. This solution is explored and tested next.

Digital Signatures for IP Packet Flow With Tree Chaining Technique

Let's consider N packets that constitute a block. In the tree chaining technique, an "*authentication tree*" is built and the "*block digest*" is the root node of this *tree*. For example, in Figure 4 is shown an authentication tree of degree two (binary) for a block of eight packets "p_1", "p_2", ..., "p_8", where the packet digests "H_1", "H_2", ..., "H_8", are assigned to the leaf nodes, while the internal nodes of the tree are computed as message digests of their children, e.g. "$H_{1-2}= h\ (H_1|H_2)$" where "h" denotes the hash function and "$|$" is the concatenation.

The root of the authentication tree represents the "*block digest*", which is digitally signed to obtain the "*block signature*" (BS). Each packet carries its own "*authentication data*", called also "*packet signature*" (PS), which is composed of three elements: the block signature, the packet position in the block, and the siblings of each node (at every level in the tree) in the path from the packet to the root. For example, the packet signature of p_1 is composed of the block signature (i.e. digital signature applied on H_{1-8}), the position in the block (i.e. 1) and the PS containing "H_2", "H_{3-4}" and "H_{5-8}". To verify the packets in a block, the verifier has to build also an authentication tree from packet signatures as the packets arrive. For example, to verify the third packet digest, the verifier computes the digest "H_3'" of the received packet and each of its ancestors in the tree, i.e. "$H_{3-4}'=h\ (H_3',H_4)$", "$H_{1-4}'=h(H_{1-2},H_{3-4}')$" and "$H_{1-8}'=h(H_{1-4}',H_{5-8})$", where "$H_4$", "$H_{1-2}$", and "$H_{5-8}$" are part of the packet signature. The verifier then checks whether "H_{1-8}'" is equal to the block digest "H_{1-8}" obtained from the block signature "BS

Figure 4. Tree chaining technique

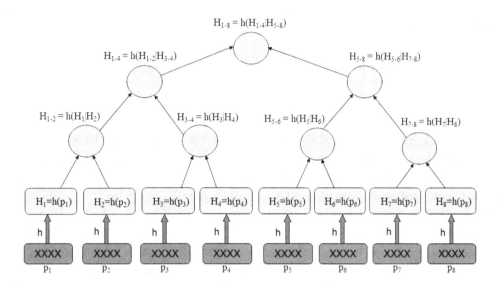

= Sign (H$_{1-8}$)", where Sign denotes the "classical" digital signing operation, e.g. signature is created by using an RSA key pair.

The *"chaining overhead"* denotes all that data in a packet signature with the exception of the block signature. It can be noted that the number of elements in PS is the same as the height of the authentication tree, and is also equal to the number of hash operations to be performed to check the correctness of a packet digest stored in a leaf of the tree. In our approach, the time required to build an authentication tree for a block of *N* packets is called *"tree build time"* and includes also the time required to compute packet digests. Note that in the original technique described in Wong and Lam (1999), the tree build time excludes the time to compute packet digests. The time required to compute a packet signature is called *"packet signature build time"*, while the *"chaining time"* for a block at a signer is "the sum of the tree build time and packet signature build time for all packets in the block (excluding the time required to digitally sign the block digest)". The *"chaining time"* for a block at a verifier is "the sum of tree build time and time to verify the chaining information in the packet signature of every packet in the block".

NetTrack requires a solution, which has to be efficient both in terms of the time required for constructing and traversing the authentication tree for a block of N packet digest, as well as in terms of storing the nodes of the authentication tree at the signer. In the following section, we present such a solution, based on the use of the Merkle trees.

TREE CHAINING IMPLEMENTATION: PURSUIT AND IMPLEMENTATION OF OPTIMALITY IN NETTRACK

Merkle (1982) proposed a method to sign multiple messages by using a binary tree, named also Merkle tree. The Merkle trees are actually used in the tree chaining technique, and one of the most important issue to be solved to save space and time is the tree traversal when the tree gets bigger. The Merkle tree traversal problem consists in finding an efficient algorithm to output the authentication data (at the signer) for successive leaves in the tree. For its solving, several algorithms have been defined in the literature, as presented further below.

The Classical Algorithms

Setup Phase

One of the real problems of all classical algorithms, such as the ones proposed by R. Merkle for Merkle tree traversal (Merkle, 1982, 1998), is that the root node's generation (or setup) has a cost. In fact, a tree of height H has $N=2^H$ leaves, and a generic node at height h ($0 \leq h < H$) will depend on 2^h leaf values, which means that it is required to calculate all *N* leaf values plus 2^H-1 hash function evaluations in order to obtain the root value. Another problem is the tacit assumption of having all node values saved, but it is intuitive that a useful Merkle tree has many leaves, like in our case. In case all $N=2^H$ leaves and *N-1* interior nodes are stored, it will be required a significant amount of space. Additionally, the decision of recalculating the authentication tree from the scratch requires much time; in fact, an interior node near the top of the authentication tree requires 2^H-1 hash operations.

Traversal Phase

The traversal of a Merkle tree deals with generating a "sequence of outputs" by the signer, one for each leaf. In our particular case, the NetTrack will have to generate such an output, one for each packet digest. Each output has two components: the "*leaf pre-image*" (i.e. the packet digest) and the "*authentication path*" of the leaf (i.e. the packet signature), which is used by the verifier in order to verify the value of a leaf pre-image. The verifier has to (re)compute the root value, by applying hashing on the leaf pre-image and the components of the authentication path. The leaf pre-image (i. e. the packet digest) is accepted as correct by the verifier if the computed root value is equal to the received/published digitally signed root value. It is known that neither storing all node values nor recalculating the node values on the fly to compute the *authentication path* would be an efficient use of resources at the so-called "*Prover*" who creates the authenticated data. By storing all the nodes, the space occupied increases exponentially with the height of the tree, while the time cost increases also exponentially if the nodes are recalculated on the fly to compute the authentication path.

To face these aspects, some Merkle tree traversal algorithms use amortization techniques that are more efficient in terms of the space consumed to hold the nodes and the time required to traverse the tree. In these techniques, the costly nodes are computed over many "rounds", where one "round" is the output required for the verification of one leaf in the tree. In the classical Merkle traversal algorithm, at each round the algorithm outputs the value of a leaf together with its sibling values, it discards the ``expired'' sibling values and, for each height, it works on preparing the ``upcoming'' siblings. With this technique, the upcoming sibling values should be ready on time. For medium-size trees, the classical algorithm embodies a reasonable degree of storage and computation efficiency but it is not an "optimal" one; in fact, there have been proposed other approaches with smaller costs, which are briefly described below. The challenge of Merkle tree traversal is to ensure that all node values are ready when needed, but are computed in a manner which conserves space and time.

Logarithmic Algorithms: Fractal, Recursive and Log-Log Algorithms

The works of Jakobsson (2003), Berman (2004, 2007), and Szydlo (2004) improved Merkle hash-tree traversal in order to process more efficiently the hash trees containing large amounts of data (that is big trees). These algorithms provide a tradeoff of the storage occupied by the data and the time required for computation in the traversal of a Merkle tree, which is aimed to output the *"leaf pre-images"* and the *"authentication paths"* sequentially.

The Fractal algorithm (Jakobsson et al., 2003) requires a worst-case computational effort of $T_{max} = 2logN/loglogN$ hash function evaluations per output, and a total storage capacity less than $Space_{max} \leq 1.5log^2N/loglogN$ hash values for an authentication tree with N leaves. This algorithm has been exploited in (Naor et. al, 2006) to create a new one-time signature scheme, which creates a signature very fast (about 35 times faster) with respect to a traditional 2048-bit RSA signature.

The Recursive algorithm proposed in Berman (2004) instead works in $O(logN/h)$ time and $O((logN/h)2^h)$ space per round for an arbitrary parameter h used to split the Merkle tree in L sub-trees of height h used to compute and store them initially, where L=H/h. Thus, this algorithm was considered to have the worst complexity in space and time.

M. Szydlo proposed the so-called Log-Log algorithm (Szydlo, 2004) that computes sequentially the Merkle tree leaves and the authentication path for the leaves, requiring thus the storage of $3Log_2(N)-2$ node values and the computation of only $Log_2(N)$ elementary operations per round.

EXPERIMENTAL EVALUATION OF LOG-LOG ALGORITHM IN NETTRACK

We have implemented the *Log-Log* algorithm by following a layered approach, based on a preliminary implementation that we have documented in Berbecaru and Albertalli (2008). The main characteristics of this implementation are resumed in brief further below.

We defined a dedicated *node* structure, which contained the packet digest to be associated to a leaf and the node index in the Merkle tree. Next, we implemented function for creating new nodes (*node_create*), for calculating the hash of a node (*node_hash*) and for deleting the nodes that are not needed anymore (*node_destroy*). To construct the Merkle tree, we implemented the tree-building algorithm introduced by Merkle itself, namely the TREEHASH algorithm. This algorithm uses basically a stack, and a *node stack* is built upon the *node* structure. For the creation, generation of output data and the verification of the Merkle trees, we have implemented dedicated tree management functions, which can easily be used from external applications. We have also developed some utility modules, such as *calchash*, which is to calculate hash values by using different hash algorithms supported by OpenSSL library (OpenSSL), the *errorchecker* module, which is used to check and diagnose error conditions, and the *timespacelogger* module, which is used for estimating the time/space costs of the Log-Log algorithm.

Time and space cost evaluation. Szydlo exploited the hash size and the computation time to estimate space and time complexity, and showed through a formal proof that time cost is bounded by log_2N and the space cost is bounded by $3log_2N$. In Berbecaru and Albertalli (2008), we have provided a preliminary estimation of the time and costs of our implementation of Szydlo's algorithm independently of the machine or operating system on which the implementation runs. In brief, we have estimated that time cost increases every time the function *node_hash* is called. The used space increases by calling the *node_create* function and decreases by calling the *node_destroy*. These estimations do not depend on the type of machine running the algorithm, or on operating system, or on any other running applications, but they measure to which extent our implementation keeps the properties of the algorithm. We have observed that both space and global time calculated for all the *N* leaves are below their theoretical bounds, respectively $3\log_2 N$ and $N\log_2 N$ outlined by Szydlo himself. The results we have obtained for our estimations of time and space costs are provided in Figures 5 and 6.

Experimental Evaluation

Next, we have evaluated through experiments the time required to sign medium-size Merkle trees containing about 131072 packet digests and big Merkle trees containing about 1 million packet digests to be signed, corresponding to a Merkle tree with $N=2^{20}=1'048'576$ leaves. The time required for the traversal of the big Merkle tree on different platforms is shown in Table 1.

On the worst case, on the Sun4U Enterprise 250 platform, it took 2.55 seconds to setup a Merkle tree with 131072 leaves and 20.62 seconds to setup a Merkle tree with 1'048'576 leaves containing the packet digests to be signed. For the traversal of the whole tree by using the Log-Log algorithm, on the same architecture, it took 24.36 seconds for a tree with 131072 leaves and 243.45 seconds for a tree

Figure 5. Space cost (theoretic bound: $3\log_2 N$). Space cost is below its theoretic bound. Traversal requires more space than setup because of the intermediate data saved, it is the price of achieving a better time cost. The space unit is ``one node''.

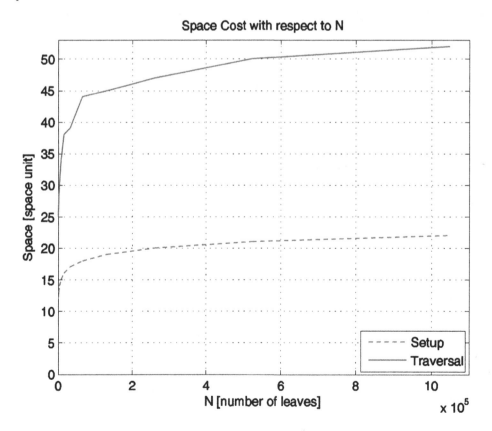

Figure 6. Time cost (theoretic bound: log_2N).Time cost is logarithmic for traversal and linear for setup. The traversal time is intended per-leaf and the time unit is ``one hash computation''.

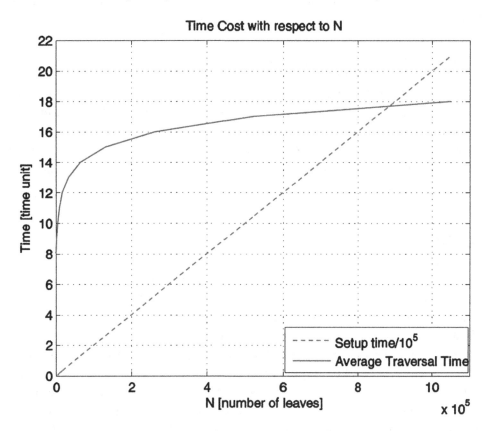

Table 1. Computation time for traversing a Merkle tree with 2^{20} leaves on different platforms.

Processor	RAM	Time [s]
AMD Turion 1.8 GHz	1 GB	31.07
Intel Core2 2.4 GHz	2 GB	41.39
Sun4U ULTRA Enterprise 250 (2 X UltraSPARC-II 400 Mhz)	512 MB	243.45
Dual Intel Pentium 4 3GHz	1 GB	22.26

with 2^{20} leaves. In the worst case, on Sun 4U platform, the time required to sign the block digest was 0.0655 seconds using 1024-bit RSA and 0.0345 seconds using 1024-bit DSA. We used a 1024-bit RSA key because we considered the key to be employed for short-time, and according to IETF, a 1024-bit RSA key should be used for 1 year (Weis, 2006). Note also that unlike the approach in Wong and Lam (1999), the time required to build the tree includes also the time for calculating the packet digest values stored in the leaves of the tree.

The block digest signing time was calculated by using the "openssl speed" utility tool of OpenSSL v 1.0 running on the platforms considered. Thus, on the Sun4U architecture, we obtained a *chaining time* at the signer equal to $2.5 + 0.06 + 24.36 = 26.92$ seconds for a block of 131072 packets. Consequently, the average signing time for one packet was $26.92/131072 = 0.20$ milliseconds, which was much faster than signing each packet, digest individually by using 1024-bit RSA. In terms of delay, the NetTrack may provide digital evidence for the 131072 packets it captured within 30 seconds in the worst case (Sun4U), while for the other platforms the delay is significantly lower. For example, on a machine equipped with an Intel Pentium Mobile 1.7 GHz and 1 GB RAM, the chaining time we have obtained for signing 131072 packet digests was 9.44 seconds, that is on average a packet digest has been signed in 0.07 milliseconds.

The authors of tree chaining technique (Wong & Lam, 1999) noted that for real-time applications, the period T during which at most N packets are generated must be larger than T_{sign} plus $chain_s(N)$ at the signer, where T_{sign} is the block digest signing time and $chain_s(N)$ is the chaining time for a block containing N packets. We have shown that this requirement can be reached by our implementation on medium to powerful platforms.

CONCLUSION

The ability to capture network traffic and to create digital evidence that is legally admissible in court is a big challenge in network forensic tools. Our research was motivated by the need to create a system, named NetTrack, which is aimed to create such evidence for IP traffic by using cryptographic algorithms, more specifically by digitally signing the network traffic together with an indication of the time when the packet was seen on a network link or at a device network interface. Such system may be used in several scenarios, such as for proof of the quality of service by a company, in a VAN, or to provide data required performing forensic analysis. Due to the ever-increasing network speeds, capturing and storing the traffic to be cryptographically processed in real-time is itself a challenging issue: specific hardware might be needed to capture packets in critical networks in order to avoid packet reordering and packet loss. Moreover, specific hardware might be needed for precise timestamping of the packets.

In this chapter, we focused on the creation of the evidence by digitally signing packets together with the timestamp attached. To the best of our knowledge, this characteristic has not been covered yet in other network forensics tools. Signing the large amount of traffic data captured by the NetTrack is a challenge because the classical digital signing techniques are not adequate for this purpose. Thus, we have adopted and tested a solution for digitally signing the IP packet flow based on the use of Merkle trees. Such trees themselves present the traversal problem, which means they require optimized algorithms for creating 'proofs' at the signer for the data in the tree leaves. Through experiments, we obtained encouraging results with NetTrack: the digital evidence created by the NetTrack can be delivered to external applications within a reasonable amount of time, e.g. within 10 seconds.

FUTURE RESEARCH DIRECTIONS

Since NetTrack is an application of trusted computing, further work may be done on the exploitation of TPM for tamper-proofing. Moreover, the interface of the NetTrack Evidence Creator with the Authenticated and Certified Time and with the Network Sampling and Filtering modules may be extended to allow dynamic configuration based on application requirements. For example, some applications may require high time precision, while other applications may require the creation of evidence for specific types of flows. We will also investigate other Merkle tree traversal algorithms, such as Berman et al. (2007), and Buchmann et al., (2008) that could be employed by the NetTrack Evidence Creator to further improve the signing operation in terms of space occupied and time required to produce the digitally signed evidence.

REFERENCES

Apisdorf, J., Claffy, K., Thompson, K., & Wilder, R. (1996). OC3MON: Flexible, affordable, high-performance statistics collection. In *Proceedings of the 10th USENIX conference on System administration* (pp. 97-112). Chicago, IL: USENIX Association.

Bamasag, O., & Toumi, K. Y. (2016). Efficient multicast authentication in internet of things. In *Proceedings of International Conference on Information and Communication Technology Convergence (ICTC)* (pp. 429-435). Jeju, South Korea: Academic Press. 10.1109/ICTC.2016.7763512

BBNT Patent. (2005). *Systems and methods for network performance measurement using packet signature collection.* Patent 6978223, Issued 20 December 2005 to BBNT Solutions LLC (Cambridge, MA). Retrieved July 11, 2017, from http://www.patentgenius.com/patent/6978223.html

Berbecaru, D. (2004). MBS-OCSP: an OCSP based certificate revocation system for wireless environments. In *Proceedings of the Fourth IEEE International Symposium on Signal Processing and Information Technology (ISSPIT 2004)* (pp. 267-272). Rome, Italy: IEEE. 10.1109/ISSPIT.2004.1433737

Berbecaru, D., & Albertalli, L. (2008). On the Performance and Use of a Space-Efficient Merkle Tree Traversal Algorithm in Real-Time Applications for Wireless and Sensor Networks. In *Proceedings of IEEE International Conference on Wireless and Mobile Computing, Networking and Communications (WIMOB 2008)* (pp. 234-240). Avignon, France: IEEE. 10.1109/WiMob.2008.14

Berbecaru, D., Albertalli, L., & Lioy, A. (2010). The ForwardDiffSig Scheme for Multicast Authentication. *IEEE/ACM Transactions on Networking, 18*(6), 1855–1868. doi:10.1109/TNET.2010.2052927

Berman, P., Karpinski, M., & Nekrich, Y. (2004). *Optimal Trade-Off for Merkle Tree Traversal.* Report No. 49, Electronic Colloquium on Computational Complexity. Retrieved July 13, 2017, from http://preprints.ihes.fr/2004/M/M-04-29.pdf

Berman, P., Karpinski, M., & Nekrich, Y. (2007). Optimal Trade-Off for Merkle Tree Traversal. *Theoretical Computer Science. Elsevier Science Publishers., 372*(1), 26–36. doi:10.1016/j.tcs.2006.11.029

Buchmann, J., Dahmen, E., & Schneider, M. (2008). Merkle Tree Traversal Revisited. In *Post-Quantum Cryptography: Proceedings of PQCrypto 2008 (LNCS)* (vol. 5299, pp. 63-78). Berlin, Germany: Springer. doi: 10.1007/978-3-540-88403-3_5

Dean, D., Franklin, M., & Stubblefield, A. (2001). An algebraic approach to IP traceback. In *Proceedings of Network and Distributed System Security Symposium (NDSS 2001)* (pp. 3-12). Retrieved July 13, 2017, from http://www.csl.sri.com/users/ddean/papers/ndss2001a.pdf

Doeppner, T., Klein, P., & Koyfman, A. (2000). Using router stamping to identify the source of IP packets. In *Proceedings of the 7th ACM conference on Computer and communications security* (CCS) (pp. 184-189). Athens, Greece: ACM. 10.1145/352600.352627

Donnelly, S. F. (2002). *High Precision Timing in Passive Measurements of Data Networks* (Ph.D. Thesis). University of Waikato, Hamilton, New Zealand. Retrieved July 14, 2017 from https://wand.net.nz/pubs/1/pdf/stephen-thesis.pdf

Endace. (2017). *Endace Delivers High Performance, Reliability and Affordability with new 1/10/40 Gbps Packet Capture Card*. Endace.

Endace, D. A. G. (2015). *Endace Ltd. Datasheet: Endace DAG 7.5G4 network monitoring card*. Retrieved September 26, 2017 from https://www.endace.com/dag-7.5g4-datasheet.pdf

Engler, D. R., & Kaashoek, M. F. (1996). DPF: Fast, flexible message demultiplexing using dynamic code generation. In *Proceedings of ACM SIGCOMM '96 conference on Applications, technologies, architectures, and protocols for computer communication* (pp. 53-59). Palo Alto, CA: ACM. 10.1145/248156.248162

Fatima, H., Satpathy, S., Mahapatra, S., Dash, G. N., & Pradhan, S. K. (2017). Data fusion & visualization application for network forensic investigation - a case study. In *Proceedings of the 2nd International Conference on Anti-Cyber Crimes (ICACC)* (pp. 252-256), Abha, Saudi Arabia: ICACC. 10.1109/Anti-Cybercrime.2017.7905301

Fraleigh, C., Diot, C., Lyles, B., Moon, S. B., Owezarski, P., Papagiannaki, D., & Tobagi, F. A. (2001). Design and deployment of a passive monitoring infrastructure. In *Evolutionary Trends of the Internet (LNCS)* (Vol. 2170, pp. 556–575). Berlin, Germany: Springer; doi:10.1007/3-540-45400-4_36

Garcia, L. M. (2008). Programming with libpcap: Sniffing the network from our own application. *Hakin9*, *3*(2), 38-46. Retrieved September 28, 2017 from http://recursos.aldabaknocking.com/libpcapHakin9LuisMartinGarcia.pdf

Golle, P., & Modadugu, N. (2001). Authenticating Streamed Data in the Presence of Random Packet Loss. In *Proceedings of Network and Distributed System Security Symposium (NDSS 2001)* (pp. 13–22). San Diego, CA: Internet Society.

Goodrich, M. T. (2002). Efficient packet marking for large-scale IP traceback. In *Proceedings of the 9th ACM conference on Computer and communications security* (pp. 117–126). Washington, DC, USA: CCS. doi:10.1145/586110.586128

Jakobsson, M., Leighton, T., Micali, S., & Szydlo, M. (2003). Fractal Merkle Tree Representation and Traversal. In *Proceedings of Topics in Cryptology - CT-RSA 2003: The Cryptographers' Track at the RSA Conference 2003 (LNCS)* (vol. 2612, pp. 314-326). Berlin, Germany: Springer. 10.1007/3-540-36563-X_21

Jonson, J., & Kaliski, B. (2003). *Public-Key Cryptography Standards (PKCS) #1: RSA Cryptography Specifications Version 2.1*. IETF, RFC-3447. Retrieved July 12, 2017, from https://tools.ietf.org/html/rfc3447

Kim, H. S., & Kim, H. K. (2011). Network Forensic Evidence Acquisition (NFEA) with Packet Marking. In *Proceedings of the 9th IEEE International Symposium on Parallel and Distributed Processing with Applications Workshops* (pp. 388-393). Busan, Korea: IEEE. 10.1109/ISPAW.2011.27

Kocher, P. C. (1998). On certificate revocation and validation. In R. Hirchfeld (Ed.), *Financial Cryptography: Proceedings of Financial Cryptography 1998 (LNCS)* (Vol. 1465, pp. 172–177). Berlin, Germany: Springer; doi:10.1007/BFb0055481

Malan, G. R., & Jahanian, F. (1998). An extensible probe architecture for network protocol performance measurement, In *Proceedings of ACM SIGCOMM '98 conference on Applications, technologies, architectures, and protocols for computer communication* (pp. 215-227). Vancouver, Canada: ACM. 10.1145/285237.285284

Mate, M. H., & Kapse, S. R. (2015). Network Forensic Tool -- Concept and Architecture. In *Proceedings of the Fifth International Conference on Communication Systems and Network Technologies (CSNT)* (pp. 711-713), Gwalior, India: Academic Press. doi: 10.1109/CSNT.2015.204

Merkle, R. C. (1982). *Secrecy, Authentication and Public Key Systems*. UMI Research Press.

Merkle, R. C. (1988). A digital signature based on a conventional encryption function. In Proceedings of Advances in Cryptology - CRYPTO '87 (LNCS) (vol. 293, pp. 369-378). Springer Berlin Heidelberg. doi:10.1007/3-540-48184-2_32

Miessler, D. (2015). *A tcpdump Tutorial and Primer with Examples*. Retrieved September 28, 2017, from https://danielmiessler.com/study/tcpdump/

Miner, S., & Staddon, J. (2001). Graph-based authentication of digital streams. In *Proceedings of IEEE Symposium on Security and Privacy (S&P)* (pp. 232–246). Oakland, CA: IEEE. doi: 10.1109/SECPRI.2001.924301

Naor, D., Shenhav, A., & Wool, A. (2006). One-Time Signatures Revisited: Practical Fast Signatures Using Fractal Merkle Tree Traversal. In *Proceedings of the 24th Convention of Electrical & Electronics Engineers in Israel* (pp. 255-259). Eilat, Israel: Academic Press. doi: 10.1109/EEEI.2006.321066

OpenSSL library. (2016). *Welcome to OpenSSL!* Retrieved from http://www.openssl.org/

Parry, J., Hunter, D., Radke, K., & Fidge, C. (2016). A network forensics tool for precise data packet capture and replay in cyber-physical systems. In *Proceedings of the Australasian Computer Science Week Multiconference (ACSW)* (pp. 1-10). Canberra, Australia: Academic Press. 10.1145/2843043.2843047

Peisert, S., Bishop, M., Karin, S., & Marzullo, K. (2005). Principles-Driven Forensic Analysis. In *Proceedings of the 2005 New Security Paradigms Workshop (NSPW)* (pp. 85-93). Lake Arrowhead, CA: Academic Press. 10.1145/1146269.1146291

Perrig, A., Song, D., Canetti, R., Tygar, J. D., & Briscoe, B. (2005). *Timed Efficient Stream Loss-Tolerant Authentication (TESLA): Multicast source authentication transform introduction*. IETF, RFC-4082. Retrieved July 14, 2017 from https://tools.ietf.org/html/rfc3447

Perrig, A., Tygar, J., Song, D., & Canetti, R. Efficient. (2000). Authentication and Signing of Multicast Streams over Lossy Channels. In *Proceeding 2000 IEEE Symposium on Security and Privacy* (pp. 56–63). Berkeley, CA: IEEE. 10.1109/SECPRI.2000.848446

Promrit, N., & Mingkhwan, A. (2015). Traffic Flow Classification and Visualization for Network Forensic Analysis. In *Proceedings of 29th International Conference on Advanced Information Networking and Applications* (pp. 358-364). Gwangiu, South Korea: Academic Press. 10.1109/AINA.2015.207

Ranum, M. J., Landfield, K., Stolarchuk, M., Sienkiewicz, M., Lambeth, A., & Wall, E. (1997). Implementing a generalized tool for network monitoring. In *Proceedings of the 11th Conference on Systems Administration* (pp. 1-8). Berkeley, CA: USENIX Association.

Rivest, R. L., & Shamir, A. (1997). PayWord and MicroMint: Two simple micropayment schemes. In M. Lomas (Ed.), *Security Protocols: Proceedings of Security Protocols 1996. (LNCS)* (Vol. 1189, pp. 69–87). Berlin, Germany: Springer; doi:10.1007/3-540-62494-5_6

Ruiz, M., Sutter, G., López-Buedo, S., & de Vergara, J. E. L. (2016). FPGA-based encrypted network traffic identification at 100 Gbit/s. In *Proceedings of International Conference on ReConFigurable Computing and FPGAs (ReConFig)* (pp. 1-6). Cancun, Mexico: Academic Press. 10.1109/ReConFig.2016.7857172

Savage, S., Wetherall, D., Karlin, A., & Anderson, T. (2000). Practical network support for IP traceback. In *Proceedings of the 2000 SIGCOMM conference on Applications, Technologies, Architectures, and Protocols for Computer Communication* (pp. 295-306). Stockholm, Sweden: ACM. doi: 10.1145/347059.347560

Scientific Working Group on Digital Evidence (SWGDE). (2015). Retrieved from http://www.swgde.org

Shrivastava, G., & Gupta, B. B. (2014, October). An encapsulated approach of forensic model for digital investigation. In *Consumer Electronics (GCCE), 2014 IEEE 3rd Global Conference on* (pp. 280-284). IEEE.

Shrivastava, G., Sharma, K., & Kumari, R. (2016, March). Network forensics: Today and tomorrow. In *Computing for Sustainable Global Development (INDIACom), 2016 3rd International Conference on* (pp. 2234-2238). IEEE.

Snoeren, A. C., Partridge, C., Sanchez, L. A., Jones, C. E., Tchakountio, F., Kent, S., & Strayer, W. T. (2001). Hash-based IP traceback. In *Proceedings of the 2001 SIGCOMM conference on Applications, Technologies, Architectures, and Protocols for Computer Communications* (pp. 3-14). San Diego, CA: ACM.

Song, D., & Perrig, A. (2001). Advanced and authenticated marking schemes for IP traceback. In *Proceedings of IEEE INFOCOM 2001 Conference* (pp. 878–886). Anchorage, AK: IEEE.

Szydlo, M. (2004). Merkle Tree Traversal in Log Space and Time. In C. Cachin & J. L. Camenisch (Eds.), *Advances in Cryptology - EUROCRYPT 2004: Proceedings of Eurocrypt 2004 (LNCS)* (Vol. 3027, pp. 541–554). Berlin, Germany: Springer; doi:10.1007/978-3-540-24676-3_32

Tartary, C., Wang, H., & Ling, H. (2011). Authentication of Digital Streams. *IEEE Transactions on Information Theory*, *57*(9), 6285–6303. doi:10.1109/TIT.2011.2161960

Weis, B. (2006). *The Use of RSA/SHA-1 Signatures within Encapsulating Security Payload (ESP) and Authentication Header (AH).* IETF, RFC-4359. Retrieved July 14, 2017, from https://www.ietf.org/rfc/rfc4359.txt

Wong, C. K., & Lam, S. S. (1999). Digital Signatures for Flows and Multicasts. *IEEE/ACM Transactions on Networking, 7*(4), 502–513. doi:10.1109/90.793005

Yuhara, M., Bershad, B. N., Maeda, C., & Moss, J. E. B. (1994). Efficient packet demultiplexing for multiple endpoints and large messages. In *Proceedings of the Winter 1994 USENIX Technical Conference* (pp. 13-13). San Francisco, CA: USENIX Association.

KEY TERMS AND DEFINITIONS

Authentication Path of a Leaf in a Merkle Tree: The siblings of all nodes on the path from the leaf to the root of the Merkle tree.

Digital Evidence: Information of probative value that is stored or transmitted in binary form.

Forensic Analysis: The process of understanding, re-creating, and analyzing events that have occurred previously.

IP Traceback: Technique used to identify the true source of an IP packet and maintain a track of the path traversed by a single IP packet.

Merkle Tree: A tree in which every non-leaf node is labelled with the hash of the labels or values (in case of leaves) of its child nodes.

Merkle Tree Traversal: The problem of consecutively outputting the authentication path for every leaf in the tree.

Passive Network Measurement: Method of observing packets on a data link or shared network media without generating any additional traffic on that media.

Chapter 13
Digital Forensics in Distributed Environment

Asha Joseph
VIT University, India

K. John Singh
VIT University, India

ABSTRACT

This chapter is about an ongoing implementation of a digital forensic framework that could be used with standalone systems as well as in distributed environments, including cloud systems. It is oriented towards combining concepts of cyber forensics and security frameworks in operating systems. The framework consists of kernel mechanisms for data and event monitoring. The system monitoring is done in kernel mode by various kernel modules and forensic model mapping is done in user mode using the data collected by those kernel modules. Further, the authors propose a crime model mapping mechanism that makes use of rule sets that are derived from common cyber/digital crime patterns. The decision-making algorithm can be easily extended from a node in a computing cluster, to a cloud. The authors discuss the challenges to digital forensics in distributed environment and cloud extensions and provide some case studies where the proposed framework is applied.

INTRODUCTION

This chapter is about an ongoing implementation of the framework in the field of digital forensic which could be used with the standalone system as well as for forensics in the distributed environment. It is oriented towards combining the concepts of cyber forensics, security frameworks in Operating Systems, digital forensic support integrated with Operating Systems, challenges of digital forensics and proposed solution for such challenges in a typical distributed computing environment.

Digital forensics is around for a while and is rapidly becoming a specialized and accepted investigative technique with its own tools and legal precedents that validate the discipline. The aim of digital forensics is not to prevent the crime as and when it happens, but to identify the victim and criminal either proactively or after the attack or incident occurs in the system or in the network; analyze it in depth

DOI: 10.4018/978-1-5225-4100-4.ch013

and record it for further reference. Computer forensics can be defined as "the application of computer investigation and analysis techniques in the interests of determining potential legal evidence"; while digital forensics can be defined as "the application of scientifically established methods in preserving, collecting, validating, identifying, analysing, interpreting and presenting digital evidence to the court of law after obtaining the evidence from reconstruction of events if possible". Digital forensics can be categorized into different groups such as Cyber Forensics, Disk Forensics, Memory Forensics, Cloud Forensics, Network forensics etc. And the attackers are usually referred as cyber criminals not as digital criminals and the crime is referred as cybercrime.

BACKGROUND

Digital Forensics

The application of scientifically established methods in collecting, preserving, validating, identifying, analyzing, interpreting and presenting digital evidence to the court of law after obtaining the evidence from the reconstruction of events if possible.

Memory Forensics

It is the forensic analysis of a computer's memory dump. Advanced computer attacks will use stealth techniques to avoid leaving traceable evidence data on the computer's non-volatile memory (hard drive, SSD etc). In those situations, the computing system's memory (RAM) dump is taken using OS tools or third-party tools for further forensic analysis. Using OS tools and symbolic debugging information of the OS components, it is possible to substantially recreate the state of the computing system to a reasonable analysis at the process and resource level.

Disk Forensics

It is the analysis of storage devices which comes in numerous categories in terms of physical interfaces and storage technologies. The forensic analysis of disks mainly consists of the application and operating system logs, picture analysis, signature/keyword analysis of known digital entities of criminal nature, timeline analysis, mailbox, databases, cookies, registry – virtually any persistent data that is commonly used by various application software and operating system.

Network Forensics

It is all about the monitoring and analysis of computer network traffic for evidence collection, information gathering or even intrusion detection. Compared to the other areas of digital forensics, network forensics deal with more volatile data and thus it is considered as a proactive approach to forensic investigation (Sammons, 2015)

Network security should be a huge concern to all of us since the networks are under near-constant attack from lone hackers, organized criminals, and foreign countries. Cybercrime, Cyberwar, and cyberterrorism are major problems threatening not only our countries and companies but our personal computers as well. Networks represent a far greater challenge, from a forensic standpoint. They vary wildly in size and complexity. There are several tools to help us protect our critical network infrastructure, including firewalls and intrusion detection systems. Smart organizations plan for security breaches enabling them to respond efficiently and effectively minimizing the damage and increasing the odds that they can identify the perpetrator(s) (Shrivastava et al., 2016; Shrivastava, 2016).

Cloud Forensics

Cloud computing can be viewed as digital computing using the shared collection of networked resources. So, it is evident that cloud forensics is closely related to network forensics. In a cloud, resources are shared and often duplicated (to avoid data losses) and a cloud service provider typically has hundreds to thousands of tenants from various jurisdictions whose computing needs are satisfied by the shared networked resources that the service provider owns. Information security in terms of privacy and access control to these shared resources are of paramount importance in such a multi-tenant environment. Further to complicate the matters, huge sets of resources can be provisioned and de-provisioned dynamically in a cloud. Thus, it is apparent that legacy methods of digital forensics tend to be lesser effective in a cloud environment. Instead of trying to analyze the huge amount of data for evidence – which itself may require a cloud service in terms of required computing power, a proactive approach will be more practical. In a proactive approach (as we saw in network forensics), we monitor and analyze the cloud system in real time using a distributed monitoring framework. We will see more of this proposed framework as we progress through the chapter.

Digital forensic tools are application programs and utilities that automate various or specific digital forensic functions. These tools are credited for amongst other things reducing the time required to analyze large volumes of data, case management, and standardized reporting and making it possible to carry out tasks that would otherwise have been impossible to complete manually. It is acknowledged that automation results in the reduction in costs and significantly shortens the time needed for training forensic professionals (Saxena et al., 2012).

David Bennett (2011) states that legal evidence might be sought to constitute a wide range of computer crimes or misuses such as child pornography, use of abusive languages, audio or video, including theft of trade secrets, theft of or destruction of intellectual property and fraud. Usually, digital evidence is the event logs generated by application software as well as operating system software. In modern Operating Systems, any application process will be running in a much-closed environment and Operating System will make sure that an application has minimal knowledge of any other application process that is running in the system. So, naturally, evidence data as event logs generated by such application processes lack the overall system perspective. The data discovered is important in forensic analysis and in solving various computer crimes through the proper log or record preservation, which leads to profiling.

The Statistics

These are some of the statistics of the study conducted on cyber-crimes in India. In the last 2+ years, about 200 zero-day exploits unleashed. 11.6 million mobile devices are infected at any given time. In 2014, more than 348 million identities stolen. Overall, about 594 million people were affected by cybercrime. The statistics followed by the predictions by cyber security analysts are as follows:

It was predicted that 2017 would be the year of online extortion. More than 30% of crimes by criminal networks will involve the theft or use of stolen data moved across international boundaries. Cyber/digital crime will cost the global economy over the US $650 billion, climbing over to over US$1 trillion by 2020. It would be more than 1.5 billion people will be affected by data breaches by 2020.A graphical representation of rising crime rate in India and specifically in the southern part of India are given in Figure 1.

The following are some of the statistics by the study conducted by National Cyber/digital Safety and Security Standards Summit, India:

The cybercrime rate has reached its peak in the year 2015. Cyber security analysts predict that 2016 will be the year of online extortion. By 2019, more than 30% of crimes committed by transactional criminal networks will involve the theft or use of stolen data moved across international boundaries (Joseph & Singh, 2016). By 2020, more than 1.5 billion people will be affected by data breaches. The following Figure 2 represents the recent statistics.

More Recent Findings

Small and midsized organizations (SMBs), defined as those with 100 to 1,000 employees, are hardly immune to cyber/digital crime.

According to the recent Keeper Security's "The State of SMB Cybersecurity" report, a staggering 50 percent of small and midsized organizations reported suffering at least one cyber-attack in the last 12 months. The average cost of a data breach involving theft of assets totaled $879,582 for these SMBs. They spent another $955,429 to restore normal business in the wake of successful attacks. For these

Figure 1. Rise of crime rate in Southern India

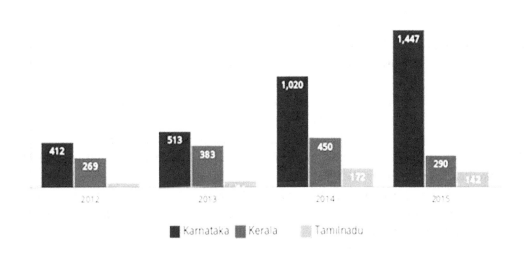

Figure 2. Number of cybercrime cases reported

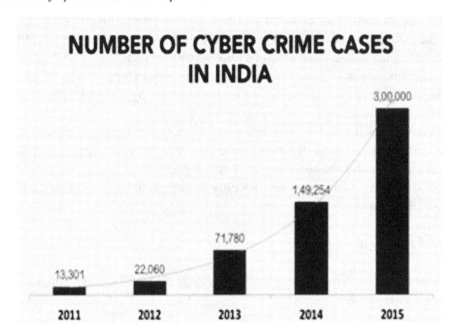

SMBs, 60 percent of employees use the exact same password for everything they access. Meanwhile, 63 percent of confirmed data breaches leverage a weak, default or stolen password. (Techpayments, 2016)

Research Challenges in the Field of Digital Forensics

Constant developments in Information Technology and communication have posed many challenges in the field of digital forensics. Based on the advancements existing digital forensic models (Shrivastava, 2017), these are some of the major challenges in this field:

1. The lack of real data sources for study and analysis purposes (Baggili & Breitinger, 2015)
2. The lack of efficient and readily available tools for data acquisition and analysis
3. The limitation of the operating environment during the acquisition of data
4. The accessibility to the data – especially if the data is on distributed systems
5. The volume of data and the time is taken to undertake an investigation
6. The ultimate lack and differences of laws across the countries
7. Multitude of OS platforms and file systems
8. Cloud system that has multi-tenancy and involves multiple jurisdictions

Legal support and forensic standardization are also challenges encountered in network forensics. As stated by Chen et al. (2015) real-time and comprehensive audits in distributed environments like cloud are very difficult and post audits can be rather challenging. The capacity of comprehensive investigations and the collection of web exception information are also limited.

Evidence disappearance is also a major challenge in the distributed digital environment, especially in cloud networks. Environmental or regional factors such as, the collection of evidence should be in accordance with local laws and regulations that may increase the difficulty in time and costs of forensic investigations. Privacy issues of legitimate users are again a problem that is encountered in digital forensics. In a multi-tenant environment, how to qualify forensics range to protect the privacy of legitimate users is still a challenge that needs to be faced. Evidence fixation/collection/preservation can be very complex in the cloud and distributed environments, because investigation involves non-standard data sets, such as processes, workflow information etc. Long-term preservation of evidence is a huge challenge.

PROPOSED WORK

Crime follows humanity from the Garden of Eden and human being is confronted with interesting mental conflicts such as whether to declare the world he is dared to commit a crime and get away with it or protect himself. This conflict, deepest in our minds manifests itself in actions: the criminal commits mistake and leaves traces, always; evidence is the digital footprint left out during the commission of cyber/digital/digital crimes such as terrorism, fraud identity theft or child pornography. Considering these aspects to get more from the interpretation of digital evidence, suggests for a new method - "crime and criminal profiling". Nykodym (2008) Point out that "the idea that an individual committing the crime in cyber space can fit a certain outline (a profile) may seem far-fetched, but evidence suggests that certain distinguishing characteristics do regularly exist in cyber/digital criminals". Therefore, the possibility of using the tools and techniques discussed by Tennakoon (2016) might be worth testing in a practical scenario.

The steps/stages in criminal profiling are shown in Figure 3 (Adapted from Tennakoon,2016)

Figure 3. Stages in criminal profiling

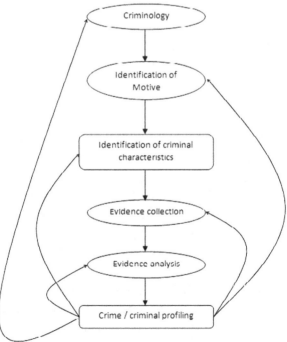

The criminal profiling has six stages:

1. Understanding what aspect of the victim attracted the criminals ("criminology")
2. Identification of a motive
3. Identification of characteristics of the criminal (expert, script-kiddie)
4. Collecting Evidence
5. Analysis of evidence
6. Repeat the above to refine the deductions.

From the research point of view, this analysis should give insights into what all data is to be collected from the system in the first place.

The rest of this chapter is dedicated to the proposed framework, explaining the fundamental concepts and technologies behind its operation. It is to be noted that the system is designed to be scalable and can be easily tailored from a single host solution to a distributed digital forensic system that can be an integrated part of a cluster, grid or even a cloud.

Typical Scenario

To illustrate the fundamental concepts on which the proposed architecture is conceived, the following scenario is considered:

An attacker gets all the credentials of a victim's internet banking account - including his mobile phone or an illegally duplicate SIM. With the security measures currently in practice, such an attacker can have open access to the victim's bank account - because even the 2-factor authentication using mobile One Time Password (OTP) will be circumvented by the attacker. However, the proposed architecture can detect, log and even alert the authorities in runtime when this happens. This is how it is proposed to achieve:

The proposed system is installed on the server where the banking application server runs. The banking server application does not have any dependency or relation with the proposed software framework. For simplicity, we are assuming that the server is not part of a distributed system. To maintain anonymity, such an attacker will usually try to login to the bank account from many public proxies available on the Internet. We can get an exhaustive database of such proxy servers from many government authorities' private sources. Have such a database ready for the forensic model-matching component (fraud detection) in the architecture (Shrivastava & Gupta, 2014). The kernel network subsystem hook detects that a TCP connection is initiated to a socket belonging to the banking server process and notifies the model-matching component that a connection attempt is made to the banking server process. The model-matching component notes that the connection is made from one of the proxies in its database. The username and password information is encrypted end to end from the attacker's host to the server process and hence our framework cannot access such details, but we do have a kernel process subsystem hook, which can monitor file access and network access of each process in the server. The security model-matching component tells this process subsystem hook to watch out for imminent local or network database access from the banking server process.

In the cases, such as, the scope of the digital crime is not limited or only if the OS kernel has access to all events; a trigger is made by the model-matching component as soon as these happen in a configurable time window (some hundreds of milliseconds). The logs generated by the banking server process and all other relevant logs for that time is tagged and archived for further analysis. This way, the evidence of a possible crime is collected in real time, without the burden of a huge data set and low rate of false positives. More than that, none of the existing server applications are to be modified (Shrivastava et al., 2012).

The Role of Operating System

The operating system is the most powerful software, the brain of the computer system, so how can it assist in cyber/digital forensics? From a conventional criminal forensics perspective, it is very well equivalent to the most intelligent and knowledgeable person assisting an autopsy. Being the master software running on a digital computing platform, it is evident that Operating System software has the ultimate knowledge and control over an event that is happening in the system. In other words, any software running as a part of Operating Systems has the capability to monitor all events from a system-wide perspective. At the same time, popular general-purpose Operating Systems has minimal security mechanisms enforced by default because it will affect the overall system experience by the end user (e.g. the infamous User Authentication Module – UAM – in Windows) and event logging from a cyber/digital-forensic perspective is not even a secondary priority of popular Operating Systems.

Many server applications are not configured or maintained properly for security and security oriented auditing. The scope of a digital crime may not be limited to the event logs generated by a single server/ user application. It may be spread across much different software (and even hardware) and at present, there is no centralized entity to co-relate and then analyze them to make a coherent security decision. Only the operating system kernel has access to all the events in the system and hence a kernel-oriented approach is required for the effective generation and logging of security events in a host/server system.

The authentication and authorization enforced by popular operating systems do not enforce the security policies on many user actions that can potentially be a security threat. This is usually justified in terms of user-friendliness and system performance. The amount of data to be analyzed for finding a valid evidence of the crime is huge. This is primarily because all usual logging schemes are very primitive in nature and do not differentiate between normal logs and logs that can be potential candidates for cyber/ digital forensic evidence. Many digital services are cloud-based and are inherently distributed across host machine boundaries. From a cyber forensic point of view, coordinated monitoring of potential security threats and related events in such a distributed system is virtually non-existing.

It is evident from the above-listed reasons that, digital evidence collection can only be performed satisfactorily by a security-enhanced operating system kernel, which has the following capabilities: It should have a subsystem to enforce security policies based upon one or more digital forensic models. It also should have a subsystem for monitoring the logs from such policy enforcement and logically coordinate them using one or more digital forensic models.

In this work, a new security architecture for is proposed, which tries to incorporate the above capabilities into a typical operating system kernel. For this purpose, Linux Operating System is selected and existing methods for enhancing securities and enforcing security policies in Linux kernel are studied. Various digital forensic models are analyzed and suitable mechanisms to incorporate them as policies into the said subsystem are identified. A mechanism to collect events generated from enforcing these policies is also identified and possibilities to make the system distributed are discussed.

The Targets of Proposed Framework

The target of the proposed work is to find out and classify if there is any cyber security / digital forensic models in place for general purpose Operating Systems at present. If there are, in what all ways it can be further improved and made more effective? If not, propose a practical approach and model for it. It is noted that for profiling crimes and criminals, access to evidence digital data is most important. Since real life evidence data for analysis of cybercrimes are difficult to come by, - a problem that is practically very difficult to take care of - mechanisms that can enable sophisticated logging and tracing in existing systems is identified as a very important area where much research is yet to happen.

Primarily, it is difficult to get access to the run-time state of the systems, and as a result, there can be important information that is not part of the analysis, such as network connections, encryption keys, decrypted data, process lists, and modified code running in memory. It is also noted that in recent times more and more data are stored and managed in distributed hosts (mostly hosted in clouds using virtualized hosts). Hence, the monitoring and logging of events that are related to cyber security in a distributed environment are getting more and more importance. The work mentioned by Chou (2009) opens a new methodology for securing the logs using virtualization tools and comparing it with kernel module approach. It is noted that evidence data acquisition from a computer system can be accomplished in two distinct methods:

One is using logs generated by the applications like web server, FTP server etc. and the another method is using kernel mode analysis and logging system that functions as a part of operating system and thus having exclusive access to all events and data in the system.

The second approach is significantly different from the first because, in operating system kernel, the data and events can be analyzed from the perspective of the whole system – whereas in the first case the information in the logs is severely limited by the scope of the concerned application. However, the second approach involves the additional complexity of kernel mode implementation (that is significantly more advanced and less documented than application level implementations).

The problem further extends to how the event logs generated by the Operating System can be used for forensic analysis. In other words, how the above-described security mechanisms and models can be further extended so that the evidence is made more useful in criminal profiling, another related domain in cyber forensics. Obviously, this work needs access to design and development details of a typical general-purpose Operating System. Considering the Open Source development model that gives us complete access to all such information, Linux is selected as the platform for all practical purposes for this work. The research area of evidence data acquisition system in kernel mode is briefly mentioned in Chou (2009).

Proposed Framework

In this work, security architecture is proposed, which tries to incorporate Information Flow Control and provenance approaches (Pohly et al. 2012) into a typical operating system kernel – and the target of this work is evidence collection and application of digital forensic modeling on the collected evidence. For this purpose, Linux Operating System is selected and existing methods for enhancing securities and enforcing security policies in Linux kernel are studied (Wright, Cowan & Smalley, 2002; Wright, Cowan & Morris, 2002). Various digital forensic models are analyzed and suitable mechanisms to incorporate them as policies into the said subsystem are identified. A mechanism to collect events generated from enforcing these policies is also identified and possibilities to make the system distributed are discussed.

The framework consists of kernel mechanisms for data and event monitoring that encompasses virtually all subsystems of the OS kernel. In addition, a user mode entity is defined that can monitor, classify and store these data and events. This user mode entity can make decisions based on predefined forensic models. We have designed such a system where whole system monitoring is done in the kernel by various kernel modules and forensic model mapping of the provenance data collected by those kernel modules is done by the user mode application modules, shown in Figure 4.

The Linux Security Modules (LSM) allows the Linux kernel to support a variety of computer security models while avoiding favoritism toward any single security implementation. The framework is licensed under the terms of the GNU General Public License and is the standard part of the Linux kernel since Linux version 2.6. AppArmor, SELinux, Smack, TOMOYO Linux, and Yama are the currently accepted modules in the official kernel.LSM was designed to provide the specific needs of everything needed to successfully implement a mandatory access control module while imposing the fewest possible changes to the Linux kernel (Bates, Tian & Butler, 2016). LSM avoids the approach of system call interception. Instead, LSM inserts "hooks" (upcalls to the module) at every point in the kernel where a user-level system call is about to result in access to an important internal kernel object.

Figure 4. The framework

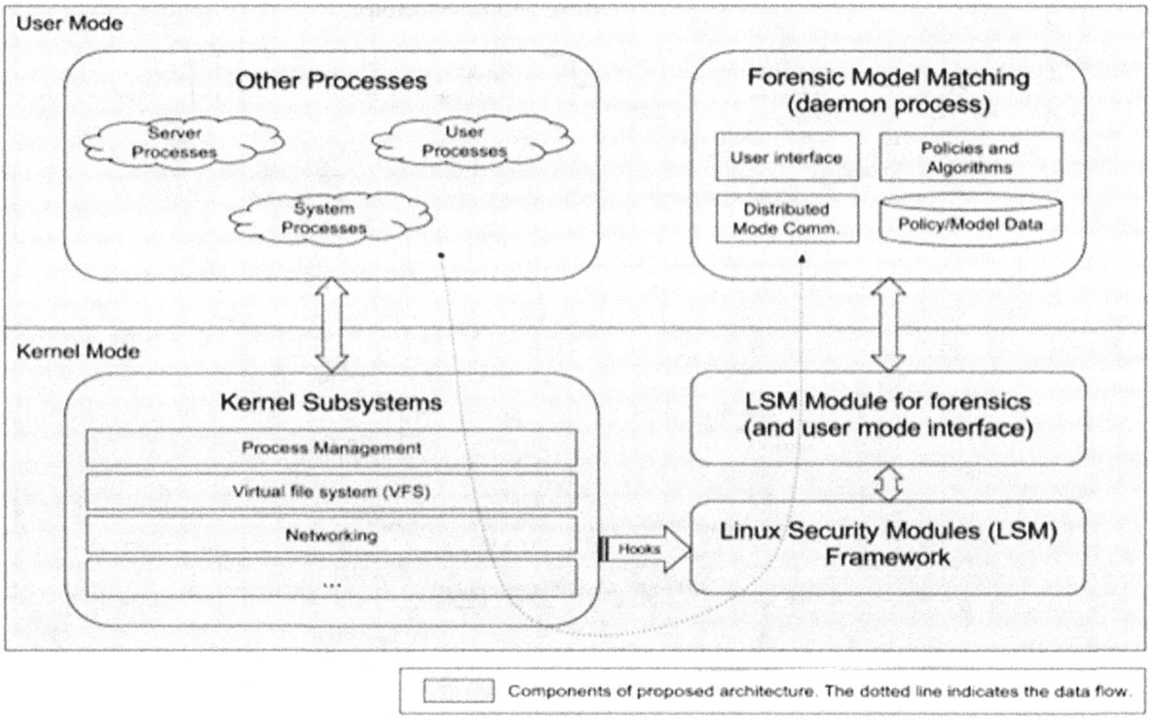

LSM Module for Forensics

This is one of the two core components of the proposed architecture. This module acts as a kernel mode counterpart of the Forensic Model Matching (FFM) component that is a user mode component. It essentially uses the LSM framework to monitor all relevant creation and access of kernel objects (files, network interfaces, network data packets, IPCs) by other processes in the system. The processes and other objects to be monitored are set by the user mode counterpart (FFM) which does it based upon policies currently set.

Forensic Model Matching (Daemon Process) (FMMD)

This is the most important component in the designated architecture. This module runs as a privileged (as root) daemon process. It provides the configuration interface using which policies pertaining to a particular forensic model, which can be further defined and set. It also implements necessary algorithms for implementing that model. As described in the previous section, it uses the kernel mode counterpart to facilitate the required fine-grained access to all objects maintained by the kernel in the system.

The access control rules enforced on the user by the OS is assumed to be in place. The model does not include those rules in the crime model mapping. This is because digital crimes are made regardless of the access controls in place. Criminals either find loopholes in the access restrictions in place

Figure 5. Crime model mapping module

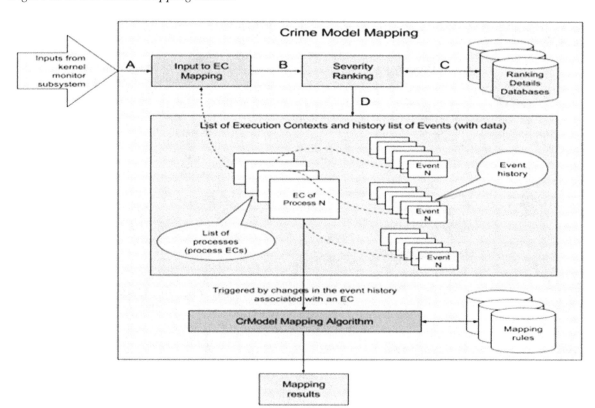

(administrative errors) or exploits the vulnerabilities in a process or system (bugs in software) to gain access to the targeted resource. From a cyber forensics point of view, the model to identifies a crime as and when it is committed rather than trying to prevent it (even though this model can be extended for that purpose). Another reason to exclude the access control enforced by the system from this model is to avoid too many unknowns and variables in the model that system administrators have the multitude of ways to set access controls for processes and users.

The Crime Model Mapping Algorithm

The crime model-mapping algorithm makes use of rule-sets, which are derived from common cyber/digital crime patterns. Each of these patterns has parameters that are readily available in the EC and event history associated with it. This includes (but not limited to) the list of known server processes in the system, the database of safe IP addresses which can act as valid source and destinations of network connections, the list of blacklisted IP addresses which are generally proxy IP addresses and attack sites, the network ports to which connections are made from outside, the network ports to which connections are made from the host, the checksum of known malicious binaries and so on.

Cloud and Other Distributed Computing Environments

Distributed computing, especially cloud computing presents some hard challenges for digital forensics. One of the major challenges is that the evidentiary material could be distributed over many servers that can be located in countries (or even continents). This implies a multi-jurisdiction and multi-tenancy environment, which can hinder or delay the investigation severely. Another problem is that the servers can be provisioned and unallocated in a matter of minutes. Because of this dynamic nature of the cloud resources, data (and logs) for multiple customers can be spread across a volatile set of hosts and data centers in the cloud.

Another major problem for traditional forensics applied on the cloud is that users will most likely choose not to store local copies of their data on the local storage of their PCs and other digital devices, given the security, synchronization and share features offered by the cloud. Interaction with data stored in the cloud is normally carried out through a web browser. So, hardly any useful evidence data can be obtained from the storage of a client device.

The discussion so far logically points to the following three options for carrying out effective forensic investigations in a cloud system:

1. Collect evidence data from client devices known to have connected to the cloud
2. Eavesdrop network traffic between client and the cloud
3. Get evidence from the cloud server by legal means

These observations are pointing at the requirement of having a proactive forensic framework - such as the proposed framework discussed here - built into the popular end-user Operating Systems so that a forensic system is in place before and during the attacks. Such a framework can provide effective evidence data with scarcely any performance impact on the devices. We will now see that that the proposed framework can fulfill these requirements and it can be implemented in two distinctly different ways as follows:

1. The framework implemented in each Virtual Machine in the cloud
2. The framework implemented in the client devices of the cloud

The first implementation is more intrusive as it requires the cloud infrastructure changes whereas the second implementation is less intrusive as it involves only the client side of the cloud. We will see each of these approaches in detail as follows:

The Proposed Framework Implemented in Cloud

The system we discussed so far has the boundaries set solely by the host on which it is implemented. The decision-making algorithm can be easily extended to be a node in a computing cluster, grid or even a cloud. Here in this chapter, we are considering cloud environment for such an analysis. We will analyze a proposed technology and framework to monitor and manage resources in a cloud environment which can be readily extended to include the previously explained forensic features.

In cloud computing, the underlying large-scale computing infrastructure is often heterogeneous, not only because it's not economical and reliable to procure all the servers, network devices, and power supply devices in one size and one time, but because different application requires different computer hardware, e.g. workflow extensive computing might need standard and cheap hardware; scientific computing might need specific hardware other than CPU like GPU or ASIC.

There are kinds of resources in the large-scale computing infrastructure need to be managed, CPU load, network bandwidth, disk quota, and even type of operating systems. To provide the better quality of service, resources are provisioned to the users or applications, via load balancing mechanism, high availability mechanism and security and authority mechanism. To maximize cloud utilization, the capacity of application requirements shall be calculated so that minimal cloud computing infrastructure devices shall be procured and maintained. Given access to the cloud-computing infrastructure, applications shall allocate proper resources to perform the computation with time cost and infrastructure cost minimized.

To implement flexible and fine-grained resource monitoring and management in a cloud deployment scenario, such an Advanced Resource Management and Monitoring System (ARMS) must have the following characteristics:

Firstly, it should provide a well-defined method for the cloud operator and his clients to properly communicate with each other and arrive at a set of Service Level Agreements in terms of resource usage.

Secondly, the heterogeneous nature of physical resources (in physical hosts) shall be manageable by a resource management paradigm, which can be used to define the conceptual entity, which can be used uniformly by the resource allocation algorithm. This paradigm must be made simple enough so that the cloud operator and clients can use the underlying concept in their resource negotiations.

Thirdly, the system shall be distributed across the cloud so that it must run in each of the host systems where virtual machines are run by one or more hypervisors. This component integrates itself with host OS as well as the hypervisor (and hence the VMs and virtual networks present in the host), providing complete control over the host system and hosted VMs. The distributed system shall be able to communicate together in the cloud whenever a resource management decision is taken which has the global impact on the cloud operation. This also can be used to take system snapshots as described in Alamulla, Iraqi, and Jones, (2013).

Finally, the resource management system must be able to run in a heterogeneous environment of different operating systems and different hypervisors. Thus, the implementation shall be portable across popular server class operating systems and it shall be able to support all popular hypervisors.This earlier work, in the field of cloud, was to realize these requirements by the design and development of such an advanced resource management system (ARMS) for clouds.

The fine-grained control and monitoring capabilities over resource usage such as bandwidth and memory based upon user-defined rules and conditions demand some components that are a part of the host operating system. Without direct interaction of the host OS as well as with the hypervisor, this kind of control is not possible in a virtual hosting environment. This kind of a component as shown in Figure 6 is the key part of the proposed solution.

To provide the complete access control over the cloud system, it is required to have control over the physical network of hosts within the cloud (the real LAN of hosts) as well as over the virtual networks managed by the hypervisors residing in the hosts. In order to achieve this, ARMS is designed as a distributed system, running on all physical hosts in the cloud setup. This distributed nature of ARMS is also illustrated in Figure 6.

Figure 6. ARMS architecture

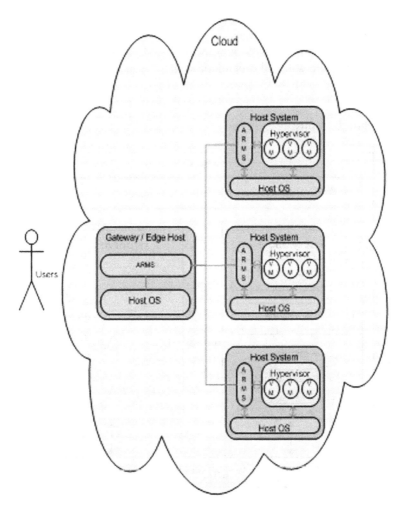

Thus, ARMS have access control and resource management over the whole cloud in a physical and virtual level by distributing itself over the host network of the cloud. Also, being present on the edge host device (gateway), ARMS can also act as a highly efficient firewall, which has reached to the whole host network with its distributed architecture, as shown in Figure 7.

This is particularly effective in a cloud environment as a proactive forensic approach if it can be integrated with the cloud resource provisioning system as shown in ARMS where resource usage allocation and monitoring are implemented using agent software running on each physical host in the cloud. If the proposed system is integrated with the agent module of a system such as ARMS, it has the potential to become a viable solution as a proactive digital forensic framework for any distributed system.

The Proposed Framework Implemented in Cloud Client

Here we will have a case study, where the proposed framework will be able to show that by searching local artifacts, it is possible to find interesting evidentiary material about the user-cloud interaction.

Case Study: Dropbox Client

Dropbox is a very popular cloud-based storage system where the user can install a software application that acts as a client to Dropbox cloud storage service. The user can typically define a directory (folder) on his device (PC or mobile). We will call this folder as his "Dropbox local folder". The client software

Figure 7. ARMS system architecture

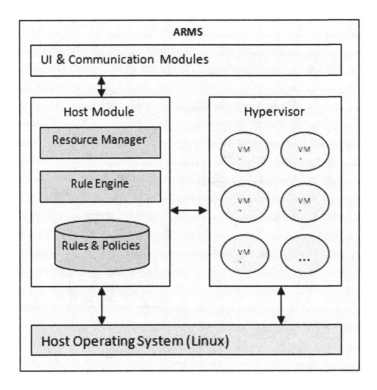

application will monitor the "Dropbox local folder" for changes and keep the contents of it synchronized with the storage allocated for the user in Dropbox storage servers.

In this case study, the following scenario is considered:

1. The user is installing Dropbox client software on his Linux workstation and "MyDropbox" as his "Dropbox local folder" in his home directory.
2. The user is creating a new a file in the Dropbox local folder and saving it.
3. The user then deletes that file in the Dropbox local folder.

The FFMD has this simple policy definition:

```
[policy]
name=cloud_local_client;
id=1001;
type=file_monitor;
process=dropbox;
monitor=open,read,write,execute,delete;
directory=$home/*;
rank=1;
dependency=nil;
action=log;
```

Note that the policy definition is relatively straightforward. It has a name and id and specifies which process is of interest and what action it can take on files in the folder "MyDropbox" that is present in any of the user's home folder. This rule need not be matched with further and it is indicated by the "nil" dependency attribute of the policy, its rank (importance) is highest and action to be taken is simple logging.

When the user carries out the above described operations, the following is the output log of the framework:

```
Event: Policy match: name=cloud_local_client, id=1001, type=file_monitor
timestamp= 1488643352 (03/04/2017 4:02pm UTC)
process=dropbox, proc id: 12876, user: ashajoseph2015
file_path=/home/ashajoseph2015/MyDropbox/test.txt
file_action=open [flags: read | write] [success]
```

As we can see, the kernel file monitor and process monitor together has hooked the file created by "Dropbox" process and passed it as an event to FFMD module. It analyzed the event using the simple policy and logged the event with all relevant details such as process id, user id, time, file path etc.

```
Event: Policy match: name=cloud_local_client, id=1001, type=file_monitor
timestamp= 1488643693 (03/04/2017 4:08pm UTC)
process=dropbox, id: 12876, user: ashajoseph2015
file_path=/home/ashajoseph2015/MyDropbox/test.txt
file_action=unlink (delete) [success]
```

Again, the kernel file monitor and process monitor together has hooked the file deletion by "Dropbox" process and passed it as an event to FFMD module. It analyzed the event using the simple policy and logged the event with all relevant details.

Case Study: Google Documents Accessed Via Web Browser

1. User logs on docs.google.com
2. User creates a word document
3. User deletes a word document

In this case, the FFMD has this simple policy definition:

```
[policy]
name=cloud_local_client;
id=1002;
type=network_monitor;
process=*firefox*,*chrome*;
monitor=connect,disconnect,timeout;
server=docs.google.com/*;
url=*;
protocol=http,https;
rank=1;
dependency=nil;
action=log;
```

The policy describes the browser processes to look for (namely processes that have 'firefox' or 'chrome' in their process names) and asks the framework to monitor the network for HTTP and https communications with the server under docs.google.com. This simple policy has no dependencies; its rank (importance) is highest and the action to be taken is simple logging.

The following is the output log of the framework implementation:

```
Event: Policy Match: name=cloud_local_client, id=1002, type=network_monitor
timestamp= 1488648660 (03/04/2017 5:31pm UTC)
process=firefox, id: 12876, user: ashajoseph2015
url: https://docs.google.com/document/u/0/create?usp=docs_home&ths=true
type: request
rank=1;
dependency=nil;

Event: Policy Match: name=cloud_local_client, id=1002, type=network_monitor
timestamp= 1488648662 (03/04/2017 5:31pm UTC)
process=firefox, id: 12876, user: ashajoseph2015
url: https://docs.google.com/document/u/0/create?usp=docs_home&ths=true
type: response 302
```

```
rank=1;
dependency=nil;

Event: Policy Match: name=cloud_local_client, id=1002, type=network_monitor
timestamp= 1488648665 (03/04/2017 5:31pm UTC)
process=firefox, id: 12876, user: ashajoseph2015
url: https://docs.google.com/document/u/0/d/1CdAfCImh-0oIIWOEM8w1PXZtwsBC56Wd-
pjUNaq5WmSU/edit
type: request
rank=1;
dependency=nil;

Event: Policy Match: name=cloud_local_client, id=1002, type=network_monitor
timestamp= 1488648669 (03/04/2017 5:31pm UTC)
process=firefox, id: 12876, user: ashajoseph2015
url: https://docs.google.com/document/u/0/d/1CdAfCImh-0oIIWOEM8w1PXZtwsBC56Wd-
pjUNaq5WmSU/edit
type: response 200
rank=1;
dependency=nil;
```

These logs clearly show the creation of a new file with an id *1CdAfCImh-0oIIWOEM8w1PXZtwsB-C56WdpjUNaq5WmSU* by the user ashajoseph2015 at 03/04/2017 5:31 pm UTC.

This case study showcases some important limitations of the client-side network monitoring. Because the connection is HTTPS (secure HTTP), after the initial HTTPS handshaking, all communication will be encrypted. So the forensically useful information is only the URL. However, the positive side is that the URL itself will give some important clues such as the document ID as seen in the logs above. With this information and the IP address of this device, it is legally possible to obtain rest of the details such as file name, its owner, and contents from Google.

CONCLUSION

Forensic computing and cyber/digital crime investigation emerged because of increase in digital crime due to the development of the Internet and proliferation of computer technology. In this chapter, we reviewed the literature in computer forensics and identified many categories of active research in computer forensics. A few research categories are framework, trustworthiness, computer forensics in networked /virtualized environments and acquisition and analysis of evidence data. The advances such as components, approaches, and the process of each category have been reviewed and discussed.

After conducting the extensive literature review, it is understood that lack of effective mechanisms in place to collect the data, lack of effective frameworks to classify the data, the volume of evidence data and the time taken to undertake an investigation based upon the data are key limiting factors for future advancements in this domain. Further exploring techniques and technologies for potentially reducing these issues resulted in focusing on approaches such as criminal profiling and better methods of tracing and logging events in the system under observation.

In this chapter, we put forth a proposal, which accomplishes the crime and criminal profiling, using the data collected from a sophisticated operating system level evidence acquisition scheme thus achieving integrity and correctness of the forensic analysis results from distributed and non-distributed systems. If the proposed system is integrated with the agent module of a system such as ARMS, it has the potential to become a viable solution as a proactive digital forensic framework for any distributed system.

REFERENCES

Alamulla, S., Iraqi, Y., & Jones, A. (2013). A Distributed Snapshot Framework for Digital Forensics Evidence Extraction and Event Reconstruction from Cloud Environment. *Proceedings of IEEE International Conference on Cloud Computing Technology and Science*, 699-704. 10.1109/CloudCom.2013.114

Baggili, I., & Breitinger, F. (2015). Data Sources for advancing cyber forensics: What the social world has to offer. *Proceedings of AAAI Spring Symposium*, 6-9.www.aaai.org/docs

Bates, A., Tian, D., & Butler, K. R. B. (2016). Trustworthy Whole-System Provenance for the Linux Kernel. *Proceedings of 24th USENIX Security Symposium*, 319-334.

Bennett, D. W. (2011). *The Challenges Facing Computer Forensics Investigators in Obtaining Information from Mobile Devices for Use in Criminal Investigations*. Retrieved from http://articles.forensicfocus.com

Chen, L., Xu, L., Yuan, X., & Shashidhar, N. (2015, February). Digital forensics in social networks and the cloud: Process, approaches, methods, tools, and challenges. In *Computing, Networking and Communications (ICNC), 2015 International Conference on* (pp. 1132-1136). IEEE.

Chou, B. H., & Tatara, K. (2009). A Secure Virtualized logging scheme for digital Forensic in comparison with Kernel Module approach. *Proceedings of the international conference of ISA*.

Hu, L., Zhang, X., Wang, F., Wang, W., & Zhao, K. (2012). Research on the Architecture Model of Volatile Data Forensics. *Procedia Engineering*, *29*, 4254–4258. doi:10.1016/j.proeng.2012.01.653

Joseph, A. (2012). Cloud Computing with Advanced Resource Management. *International Journal of Advanced Technology and Engineering Research*, *4*, 21–25.

Joseph, A. (2013a). *Enhanced Resource Management on cloud systems using Distributed Policy and Rule Engines* (Master's Thesis). VTU Bangalore, India.

Joseph, A. (2013b). Enhanced Resource Management using Distributed Policy and Rule Engines. *Proceedings of International Conference on Advanced Computing and Information Technology*.

Joseph, A. (2017). Provenance of Digital Assets-Blockchains and Bitmarks. *IEEE ComSocNwesletter*, *1*, 5.

Joseph, A., & Singh, K. J. (2016). The latest Trends and challenges in cyber forensics. *Proceedings of International Conference ICMCECE*, 107.

Morris, J., Smalley, S., & Kroah-Hartman, G. (2002, August). Linux security modules: General security support for the Linux kernel. *USENIX Security Symposium*.

Nykodym, N., Ariss, S., & Kurtz, K. (2008). Computer addiction and cyber-crime. *Journal of Leadership, Accountability and Ethics, 35*, 55–59.

Pohly, D., McLaughlin, S., McDaniel, P., & Butler, K. (2012). Hi-Fi: Collecting High-Fidelity Whole-System Provenance. *Proceedings of Annual Computer Security Applications Conference*.

Sammons, J. (2015). *The Basics of Digital Forensics - The Primer for Getting Started in Digital Forensics. 2nded*. Syngress Publications.

Saxena, A., Shrivastava, G., & Sharma, K. (2012). Forensic investigation in cloud computing environment. *The International Journal of Forensic Computer Science, 2*, 64-74.

Shinder, D. (2010). *Profiling and Categorizing Cyber Criminals*. Retrieved October 2016, from www.TechRepublic.com/blog/it-security

Shrivastava, G. (2016, March). Network forensics: Methodical literature review. In *Computing for Sustainable Global Development (INDIACom), 2016 3rd International Conference on* (pp. 2203-2208). IEEE.

Shrivastava, G. (2017). Approaches of network forensic model for investigation. *International Journal of Forensic Engineering, 3*(3), 195–215. doi:10.1504/IJFE.2017.082977

Shrivastava, G., & Gupta, B. B. (2014, October). An encapsulated approach of forensic model for digital investigation. In *Consumer Electronics (GCCE), 2014 IEEE 3rd Global Conference on* (pp. 280-284). IEEE. 10.1109/GCCE.2014.7031241

Shrivastava, G., Sharma, K., & Dwivedi, A. (2012). Forensic computing models: Technical overview. *CCSEA, SEA, CLOUD, DKMP, CS & IT, 5*, 207–216.

Shrivastava, G., Sharma, K., & Kumari, R. (2016, March). Network forensics: Today and tomorrow. In *Computing for Sustainable Global Development (INDIACom), 2016 3rd International Conference on* (pp. 2234-2238). IEEE.

TechPayments. (2016). *20 Eye-Opening Cybercrime Statistics*. Retrieved from http://www.fitech.com/news/20-eye-opening-cybercrime-statistics/

Tennakoon, H. (2016). *The need for a comprehensive methodology for profiling cyber-criminals*. Retrieved on November 2016, from http://www.newsecuritylearning.com

Watson. (2013). *ExtremeXOS Operating System*. Technical Specification Report. The University of Cambridge.

Wright, C., Cowan, C., Morris, J., Smalley, S., & Kroah-Hartman, G. (2002, June). Linux security module framework. In *Ottawa Linux Symposium* (Vol. 8032, pp. 6-16). Academic Press.

Zhang, S., Meng, X., & Wang, L. (2016). An Adaptive Approach for Linux Memory Anaysis based on Kernel Code Reconstruction. *Eurasip Journal of Information Security, 14*, 13.

Chapter 14
Successful Computer Forensics Analysis on the Cyber Attack Botnet

Kavisankar Leelasankar
Hindustan Institute of Technology and Science, India

Chellappan C.
GKM College of Engineering and Technology, India

Sivasankar P.
National Institute of Technical Teachers Training and Research, India

ABSTRACT

The success of computer forensics lies in the complete analysis of the evidence that is available. This is done by not only analyzing the evidence which is available but also searching for new concrete evidence. The evidence is obtained through the logs of the data during the cyberattack. When performing analysis of the cyberattack especially the botnet attacks, there are many challenges. First and the foremost is that it hides the identity of the mastermind, the botmaster. It issues the command to be executed using its subordinate, the command and control (C&C). The traceback of C&C itself is a complex task. Secondly, it victimizes the innocent compromised device zombies. This chapter discusses the analysis done in both proactive and reactive ways to resolve these challenges. The chapter ends by discussing the analysis to find the real mastermind to protect the innocent compromised system and to protect the victim system/ organization affected by the botnet cyberattack.

INTRODUCTION

Successful prosecution of computer-based crime is dependent upon the investigation. The investigator should be asking all these questions like who, what, how and when a criminal event occurred. It depends upon how the evidence is examined. The general public will not understand or even know that they are under some kind of cyber attack. Victim of these attacks is not only the large corporations but also the

DOI: 10.4018/978-1-5225-4100-4.ch014

unaware public. The hackers come with the number of ways to bypass or intrude the network using the number of methods. First and foremost thing they do is that they hide their identity or they use the trusted source identity to intrude the network. They try to compromise the number of cyber devices, where these cyber devices become the compromised zombies. These compromised zombies cyber devices belong to the unaware public. The hackers use the internet which provides them the borderless environment. The internet, compromised zombies are used and they are brought into a network. This network is very powerful and it can be used to launch the intended attack on the intended victim.

Botnets are networks of robots or robot net. A software program bot obeys the instructions of command-and-control (C&C). They act as remotely located, a single coordinated central collection point of the bots. They would be taking over a remote machine (victim 1) and using that, attack another machine (victim 2). Botnets are compromised hosts under a common C&C (command and control) server. Their purpose is to produce Denial of Service attacks (DOSs), id theft, flood the user with spams, and many more.

A large number of the system is compromised using Active worms. These compromised systems are the bots or zombies. The botnet is formed by these large number bot or zombies when networked together with help of the C&C. The number of destruction done using botnet: (i) large-scale distributed voluntary advertisement through emails spam or malware. (ii) large scale sniffing of traffic which gives access to critical information that can be misused. (iii)The network components are destroyed by launching the massive DDoS attack.

Botnet when comparing with customary malware is more dangerous because of the C&C channel. It is one of the high-risk security threats. Where the malware used for fun is now turning to be malware used for financial benefit.

The detailed analysis and discussion are made on onetime request flooding using a Botnet are generally detected and defended against, using a number of schemes. The detection schemes provide the detection of three major components of Botnet architecture, namely, Bot, C&C, and Botmaster. These detection schemes are in two modes, active and passive. First, the passive detection of Bot is done by two major ways i.e. Correlation and Behavioral analysis.

There are various Botnet Detection Schemes; a few botnet detection schemes developed are Mining-based Detection, Signature-based Detection, and Anomaly-based detection techniques. Most importantly the detection scheme like Host-based detection is a detected scheme built on the host system. Some of the Host-based detection is a detected schemes are HoneyPots / Virtual HoneyPots, DNS- based detection techniques, Infiltration, Filtering, Packet Filtering, Remedial measure and Index Poisoning Attack.

For performing the forensic analysis the trace back to botmaster is required. Packet marking Techniques is used to Traceback of Botmaster, similarly Probabilistic Packet Marking Schemes is also used in Traceback of Botmaster, Other Schemes like Deterministic Packet Marking Schemes, and Probabilistic Packet Marking Schemes.

Even using all these techniques one of the most challenging tasks of the botnet network is that the identity of the botnet master is hidden, Traceback to command and control is also very difficult, since the attack is from the compromised zombies, these compromised zombies are the unaware public who get victimized by the crime they haven't done. A proper computer forensics investigation is required here. In the first instance, you will criminalize the compromised zombies. But when you criminalize you have to criminalize a huge number of compromised system that is legally impossible adding to that point they are totally unaware what is happening. It is the part of the security experts to build all the cyber devices with additional security features.

There is the number of methods that perform the forensic analysis of the cyber attack which has taken place. The scenario discussed here is the Distributed Denial of Service (DDoS) attack performed using the botnet network. Now when the forensics investigation happens the first step is to analyze the intensity of the attack. It needs to validate that the cyber crime has happened using the botnet. In case of botnet attack, it would have come from the number of compromised systems. The attack is traced back using the traceback mechanism. The honeypot installed in the compromised zombies operates like a computer forensics analyst provides a concrete evidence to find the real source of cyber attack (Shrivastava et al., 2010).

DDoS Attacks by Botnet

Botnets are networks of robots or robot net. A software program bot obeys the commands of command-and-control (C&C). The C&C is remotely located and they act as a single coordinated central collection point of the bots. They would be taking over a remote machine (victim 1) and using that, attack another machine (victim 2). Botnets are compromised hosts under a common C&C (command and control) server. Their purpose is to produce Denial of Service attacks (DOSs), id theft, flood the user with spams, and many more.

A large number of the system is compromised using Active worms. These compromised systems are the bots or zombies. The botnet is formed by these large number bot or zombies when networked together with help of the C&C. The number of destruction done using botnet: (i) Large-scale distributed voluntary advertisement through emails spam or malware. (ii) Large-scale sniffing of traffic which gives access to critical information that can be misused. (iii)The network components are destroyed by launching the massive DDoS attack.

Figure 1 represents the Botnet Architecture. Botnet when comparing with customary malware is more dangerous because of the C&C channel. It is one of the high-risk security threats. Where the malware used for fun is now turning to be malware used for financial benefit.

Botnet Life-Cycle

- **Initial Infection Phase:** In the initial phase vulnerabilities are exploited by scanning. This scanning is done on the entire targeted subnet. The scan is followed by infection of the target victim

Figure 1. Botnet architecture

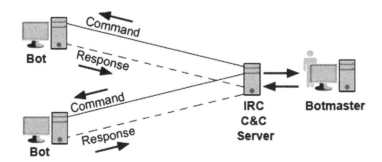

using the discovered vulnerabilities. For infection of the target, the number of exploitation methods is used.

- **Secondary Injection Phase:** Once the infection is done. The shell code is executed. This Shell code/ script using FTP, HTTP, or P2P from the particular location get the image of the actual binary. Target machine is installed with the bot program and it is made has "Zombie". Whenever the compromised zombie system is booted the bot application is started automatically.

- **Connection Phase:** Channel between Command-and-Control (C&C) is established using bot binary. By establishing the connection with C&C channel, the zombies are attached to attacking botnet group.

- **Malicious Command-and-Control (C&C):** The C&C channel are used by the Botmaster to broadcast the commands to the bot army. Botmaster commands are followed by the compromised zombies.

- **Update and Maintenance:** The update is done mainly by C&C to avoid detection techniques and maintain the botnet network. It is also used to append new functionality, the feature to the bot.

Figures 2 and 3 represent the life cycle of the botnet.

There are various botnet taxonomies given by Hachem et al. (2011). Botnets are classified, based upon their structure, as centralized and decentralized bots; they are the based on their language as compilers (C, C++) and as interpreted (Perl, PHP, JavaScript), and lastly they are also classified based on their features as attacks (DDOS, Exploit), server (HTTP, FTP, RLOGIN) and as proxy (socks4, socks5, HTTP). Botnets have so many taxonomies because bots are multifaceted and complex beasts. Bots in malware taxonomy have worm characteristics and spyware components. Bots spread along the network through emails as Trojans, or attach mentors installed by explicit tools, as link spams, websites, or by even by explicit attacks on hosts. We have different types of bots because of their pride, purpose, different languages and their actions on different platforms. The Bot family is very vast; they are pBot, Kaiten which are mostly used in a Linux environment, agobots, sdbots, spybots, and gtbots in the windows environment. Bots receive commands from the C&C server and accordingly attack the target hosts. If the command and control server is corrupted, so that the commands do not reach the bots, they remain dormant (Gupta et al., 2010).

Figure 4 shows the example scenario of DDoS attack generation using Botnet.

Figure 2. Botnet life-cycle

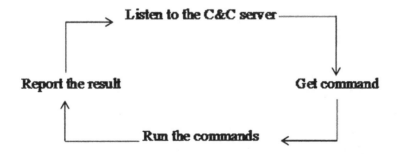

Figure 3. Detailed Botnet life cycle

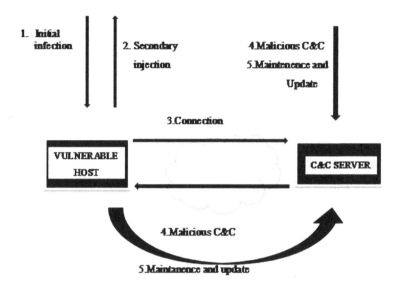

Figure 4. DDoS attack generation using Botnet

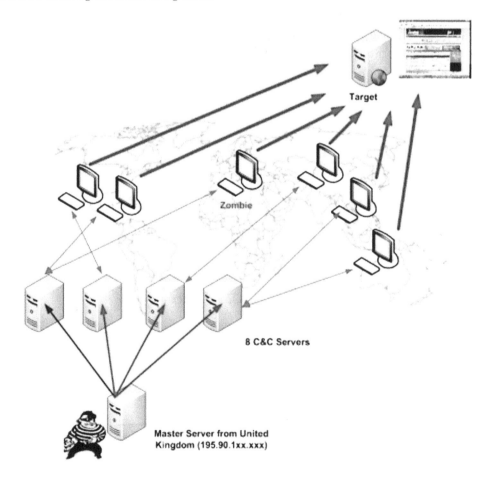

ONE TIME REQUEST FLOODING (BOTNET) DDOS ATTACK DETECTION

Distributed Denial-of-Service (DDoS) attacks are generated by large number of the request at one instance. It consumes large volume of server resources using malicious traffic or utilizing the large-scale botnet to mimic the average request rate of the normal users and produce the low rate attack flows. These aspects contribute to the factors in difficult in identifying the botnet. Now, in order to concentrate more on the basic methodologies used in the proposed approach, we shall discuss the existing models to detect the botnets and their respective C&Cs.

Onetime request flooding using a Botnet is generally detected and defended against, using a number of schemes as given in Figure 5. The detection schemes provide the detection of three major components

Figure 5. One time request flooding Botnet taxonomy

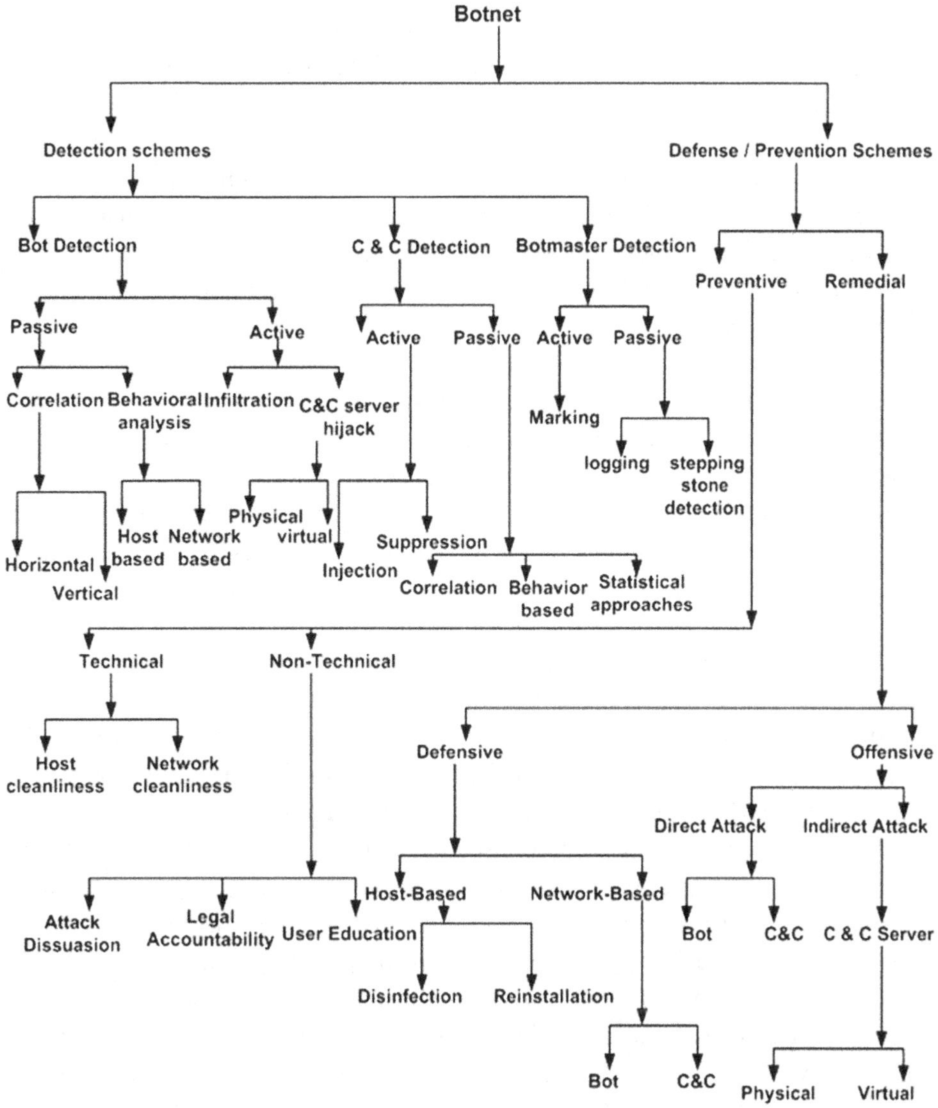

of Botnet architecture, namely, Bot, C&C, and Botmaster. These detection schemes are in two modes, active and passive. First, the passive detection of Bot is done by two major ways i.e. correlation and Behavioral analysis.

Botnet Detection Schemes

A Few botnet detection schemes developed are discussed below.

- **Anomaly-Based Detection Techniques:** Anomaly detection on network traffic based on several network traffic anomalies that could point out the existence of malicious bots in the network is huge volumes of traffic, towering network latency, unusual system behavior and unusual ports used with sudden increase in traffic. Gu et al. (2007) BotHunter uses dialog trace of Intrusion Detection System in that network and a novel system, botfinder, by Tegeler et al. (2012) analyses bot's network traffic using the properties of high-level to detect compromised zombie machines. It works based on machine learning so it has two phases, first phase is training and second phase is detection. The first training phase requires a trace file to be maintained; hence, this needs a higher space complexity. The main drawback is that it needs a history to be maintained.

Pratik Narang et al. (2013) discussed algorithms of feature selection like Correlation-based feature selection; Consistency based subset evaluation, and Principal component analysis using Machine learning techniques. The merit is that problem of detecting unknown botnets is solved by anomaly detection techniques. The drawback is that if no anomaly is found it cannot detect bot. It cannot detect encrypted bot and has no real-time detection.

- **Signature-Based Detection:** Intrusion detection systems (IDS) find signs of intrusion. This is done by the real-time log of network traffic Snort (2009) an open source intrusion detection system (IDS) is the best example. The spatial-temporal behavioral similarity is used in BotSniffer Gu et al. (2008a) to identify botnets. The merit is that detection of known botnets is done by using signature-based detection techniques. There are low false positives as long as attacks are clearly defined in advance. The drawback is that unknown bots cannot be detected using this method. Another drawback is that the Antisignature techniques make the malware evade these techniques.
- *Mining-Based detection is* based on characteristics of the flow, like pushed packets, bytes per packet, TCP flags, bits per second, and duration. It is done to classify network flows using Bayesian net algorithms, Naive Bayes, and decision trees. The BotMiner Gu et al. (2008b) is independent of both structure and protocol. The flows in the BotMiner are classified into groups based on alike malicious activity patterns and communication patterns. The merit is that it produces very low false positive rate while detecting compromised machines even in normal traffic.
- *Host-based detection is a detected scheme built on the host system. It is done based on the symptom modification of windows hosts file,* Random unexplained pop-ups, machine slowness, and antivirus not working. A new technology, called mashups proposed by Santos et al. (2011), integrates several tools to detect such even new evolving botnets. It is the combination of online sandboxes, anti-viruses, and traffic analysis tools. Meaningful results are obtained using the free web-based tools, like map APIs and geocoding services. This method may fall low since it uses only online toolboxes and there are no relevant theoretical or notable proofs for its execution. Hence, this can

only be used to develop a vast view of the problem and helps in approaching a better solution. The drawback is that Real-time detection is not possible.

- **HoneyPots / Virtual HoneyPots:** The very important information about botnet, like botmasters instructions that is issued to the bots and detection of number of bots connected to the network. Choi et al. (2012) monitor the botnet using honeypot and honeynet techniques. The attackers, on the other hand, tried to find honeypots by developing new methods. Meanwhile, the defenders provide the even more enhanced mask for honeypots. The Spy bot is sent to detect malicious activities in the botnet. Honeynet Project and Research Alliance (2008), is developed using a defender employed. The merit is that honeynets understands characteristics and technology of botnet. Infection may or may not be essentially detected in sand it is considered one of its drawbacks. The Honeypot resorts to inactivity or breaks down.

DNS-Based Detection Techniques

DNS-based detection techniques are given by Springer reference (2014) are worked based on botnet generating particular DNS information. The domain names high abnormality or temporally concentrated DDNS query rates are detected, and classify analogous query rates. The DNS holds mappings between IP addresses and name servers, mail servers, and canonical names. These Botnet detection techniques identified based on DNS information produced by a botnet. The most recent approach is Botminer. This approach detects Botnet C&C traffic by using data mining techniques.

The Botminer is advanced than Botsniffer. It clusters similar malicious traffic and communication traffic. Then, it recognizes the hosts by cross-cluster correlation shared by both malicious activity and similar communication patterns. The merit of this method is that it uses IP headers information. So, that it can even find the botnets with encrypted channels. The drawback is that only HTTP and IRC traffics are analyzed. Techniques have the same weakness that when the bogus DNS queries are used it could be easily avoided. Misclassification of legitimate or well-known domains occurs while DNS with short time-to-live (TTL) is encountered and it, in turn, increases the false positives.

Infiltration

Infiltration is done by penetration testing the bot system. The probes are made to C&C and other bots by changing its identity to an actual bot. The replay attack is used by Nappa et al. (2010) on a Skype-based botnet. Crafted bogus messages are issued by the defenders to gain information about the bots.

Timing Analysis

Using Probabilistic Context-Free Grammars by Chen and Richard (2012) automated network processes generally carry timing signatures. The fastflux creates moving targets and resilient to detection. The merit is that it improves the True Positive rate. The demerit is that decreases the False Positive rate, which can be further reduced. If the timing signatures are not considered, the system performance degrades.

Filtering

Saliva (2008) describes in RFC 2827 the filtering techniques is the most basic network level defense. An ISP is used in ingress filter blocks based on IP sources not belong to that end site. It works very effectively on spoofed IP packet along with SYN flooding.

Packet Filtering

Kolias et al. (2011) discusses about Packet Score filtering uses some attributes in the TCP and IP headers, and the Bayes Theorem to score packets. This method is not suitable for handling large amounts of attack traffic. Based on a set of rules, the firewall makes a decision whether to accept or drop the packet. The drawback is that ingress filtering provides low security due to two reasons; it is not universally deployed and wholly ineffective against the policies employed by ISPs.

HTTP Flooding Attack

In case of HTTP flooding attack, The HTTP request to the server is of many types the two main types are GET and POST. GET normally used for the static pages and data. The POST is used with forms. In most of the cases GET is used by the attackers since it is easier for the attackers to execute. Whereas in the case of POST it consumes relatively lot of resources it performs relatively complex process. When the attacker wants to be more successful they try to immerse the entire target with the method that allocates a lot of resources. It basically spams the server with requests, like refreshing a page. With enough people participating in the DDoS attack, the server might not be able to handle all the requests simultaneously, and hence, crashes. Choi et al. (2012) detected the DDoS attack based on Time Slot (TS) and Monitoring Period (MP). It is observed more HTTP requests in MP and TS during attack than normal traffic. The drawback is that parameters should be analyzed for accurate detection.

One of the Remedial Measure is given below:

- Index Poisoning Attack

Wang et al. (2010) proposed copyright content protection with help of Index poisoning attack. In a P2P network, peers try to get a file search for the target file while the target file is poisoned with the bogus record is redirected and return the bogus result in a way that the bogus result is downloaded. It is used to defend the P2P botnet where the communication between zombies and botmaster in the P2P protocol employs pull-based C&C communication mechanism the file index is used.

The detection schemes discussed in the above is helpful in the forensic analysis of the botnet attack. The above schemes try to analyze the behavior of the botnet network especially the compromised zombie devices.

Flow-Based Techniques

There are a number of techniques used for DoS detection, using only the flow information. A sketches data structure is used to collect the aggregate of the flow measures. This approach was proposed by Gao et al. (2006). However, they lack the ability to differentiate between different types of attacks. Another approach proposed by Munz et al. (2007), is TOPAS (Traffic flow and Packet Analysis System). However, it runs based on the requirements given by the network administrator. Banks et al. (2007) provided a review of particle swarm optimization, a natural computing technique. The proposed system uses an ACO technique to traceback the victim of the DoS/DDoS attack to the zombie system. This is done by using the incoming flow information of the routers. Based on the flow and pheromone intensity, the probability is calculated and the path with high probability is taken by the ants.

The detection schemes discussed in the above is helpful in the forensic analysis of the botnet attack. The above schemes try to analyze the traffic behavior of the botnet network especially to traceback to the origin of the attack. The scheme helps in finding out the attack source with the path traveled frequently. It may lead to traceback of two sources first is compromised zombies and the command and control.

Traceback of Botmaster

An Ant algorithm by Kolias et al. (2011) is used for resource scheduling and vehicle routing associated with discrete optimization problem. The Ant colony algorithm was biologically inspired by ants and works based on how the natural ants work. In case of the botnet, the Ant colony algorithm has always been successful in finding the path of attack launch of DOS, though it lagged in finding the C&Cs and tracing back their IP address. The execution of the ant colony algorithm does not even require the complete information about the routers and their route. Swarm intelligence has many different algorithms in it, but among them, the ACO overcomes others with a high performance in source detection.

Figure 6, gives us an overview of the different existing flow based, packet marking, and hybrid IP traceback techniques available.

Figure 6. IP traceback taxonomy

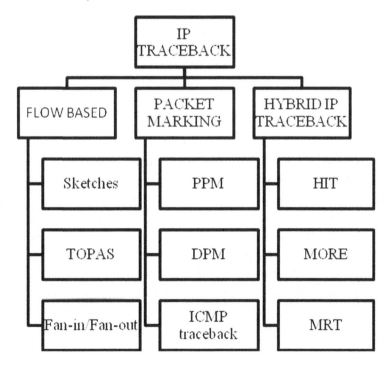

- Packet Marking Techniques

Probabilistic Packet Marking (PPM) is a scheme proposed by Savage et al. (2000) packets are marked by the router. The spoofing of IP address is detected, even though spoofed IP address is used the full path is reconstructed. Similarly, Deterministic Packet Marking was proposed by Belenky and Ansari (2003a, 2003b) where each packet entering a router is marked. The incoming packets are marked with the address information of the interface in the packets identification field and the reserved flag bit is used for marking which part of the address the ID field contains. The received information from this is the address of the ingress routers. Deterministic Packet Marking engages the marking of each and every packet entering the network, which leads to computation delay. The Probabilistic packet marking scheme is similar to this scheme; only the marking is not done based on probability. Both the schemes require a large number of incoming packets for path reconstruction.

- Probabilistic Packet Marking Schemes

It was developed by the Computer Security Institute and Federal Bureau of Investigation (1999). Goodrich (2008) proposed Probabilistic packet marking for large-scale IP traceback. The drawback is that high computational work is required for the path reconstruction process, in particular when there is the number of sources and also creates high false positives the possible rebuilt path branches are actually becoming useless according to Dean et al. (2001).

- Other Probabilistic Packet Marking Schemes

The PPM method proposed by Song and Perrig (2001), and Govindan and Tangmunarunkit (2000) reduce the overhead of reconstruction. Adler et al. (1996) examined on the middle ground between the mark bits required in the IP header and the number of packets required to reconstruct the paths. On the other hand, Savage et al. (2000) used edge sampling PPM scheme, which is known as FMS. Gong and Sarac (2009), Yaar et al. (2005), Al-Duwari and Govindarasu (2006), Lee et al. (2004), and Li et al. (2004) are the other probabilistic packet marking schemes.

- Deterministic Packet Marking Schemes

Belenky and Ansari (2003a) proposed Deterministic Packet Marking (DPM). DPM as by Howard (1998), and Kam and Simpson (1999). Recently, in "A Formal Framework and Evaluation Method for Network Denial of Service," by Meadows, (1999) false positive rates are reduced by marking fields with adding redundant information. The drawback is that repeated spoofing with the different value of the source address may bypass the successful mitigation of DPM. Another efficient scheme named TOPO was proposed by Zhang et al. (2006). Source Path Isolation Engine (SPIE) by Ehrenkranz and Li (2009) is an IP traceback scheme which stores the packet digests alone and not the packets themselves. It makes use of Bloom filters which has the false positive problem. TOPO also has the same storage problem and uses bloom filters with has the same the false positive problem. Full path of the attack is determined by ICMP traceback scheme by Bellovin et al. (2003). It requires the involvement of the ISP for this scheme to be implemented (Gong & Sarac, 2008).

Hybrid IP Traceback Techniques

Many hybrid traceback techniques are available, which make use of packet marking as well as packet logging. These techniques are mainly used to prevail over the problem of IP spoofing. Few of the hybrid IP traceback techniques are discussed below. The Hybrid IP traceback (HIT) is a hybrid scheme proposed by Gong and Sarac (2008) which uses both packets marking as well as packet logging. Packet marking reduces logging burden by reducing the required number of router for logging. A few more hybrid schemes proposed are, Huffman Coding by Choi and Dai (2004), MOdulo/REverse modulo (MORE) and Modulo/Reverse modulo Technique (MRT) by Malliga and Tamilarasi (2010). These schemes make use of interface numbers of the routers and the number of interfaces of a router for marking. In the Huffman coding scheme, the upstream interface number is encoded using Huffman coding, and this is inserted into the marking fields of the packet by Yang and Yang (2012). MORE uses a 16-bit field and MRT uses a 32-marking field. These schemes make use of log tables to store the mark value in the routers, which demands a high storage space. It also requires doing an exhaustive search on the log tables during path reconstruction. During path reconstruction it encounters inefficient search and false positive problem due to big size of the log table and digest in a log table might have a collision.

Since the Distributed Denial of service (DDoS) attacks are on the increase, we propose an efficient approach to detect and defend the botnet from performing DDoS attacks. The solutions to the problem statement can detect, mitigate and filter the DDoS attacks.

The detection scheme discussed in the above scheme is helpful in the forensic analysis of the botnet attack (Shrivastava, 2017). The above schemes try to analyze the traffic behavior of the botnet network especially to traceback to the source of the attack. The scheme helps in finding out the attack origin with help of the marking scheme. It is helpful in finding the ultimate mastermind the botmaster.

Table 1 provides the performance comparison of the existing one Time Request Flooding (BOTNET) detection schemes with various parameters.

From the detailed analysis of the various detection and defense schemes which are discussed above gives us the clear picture that they do not collect all the evidence required for the complete analysis of the various components of the botnet network. Either the compromised zombies or command and control are detected. The detection of the botmaster is even more difficult. It requires special marking scheme to traceback to the botmaster. This kind of special marking scheme is hard to be implemented in ever network. But there is a need for some pro-active measure to be taken to find the real origin of the attack.

Table 1. Performance comparison of the existing detection one Time Request Flooding (BOTNET) detection schemes

Schemes		Bot Miner (2008)	Bot Hunter (2008)	Bot Sniffer (2008)	Heuristic (2012)	Feature (2013)	Timing Based (2013)
Deployment		Not universally Deployed	Easily Deployed	Easily Deployed	Easily Deployed	Router level deployment	Not universally Deployed
Detection rate		74.7%	69.81%	70.23%	80% to 95%	98%	96.7%
False alarm rate		23%	29%	29%	1%	2%	1.6%
Type of attack	Multiple Flooding		√	√	√	√	
	Spoofed Flooding	√	√	√			
	One Time Request Flooding		√	√			

The state-of-art works like Alieyan et al. (2017) discusses the botnet hidden identities using the DNS services and the botnet detection techniques depend on DNS traffic analysis. Al et al. (2016) discuss the about detection of the botnet using machine-learning models. Garg et al. (2017) filters and classifies on data received by Botflex and detects botnet based on this method.

The two important challenges in the trackback of cyber attack botnet are

- The attack is the number of compromised zombies systems they tend to be legitimate.
- The difference between the request from the compromised zombies and the legitimate device is very difficult to identify.
- Since there is the number of compromised zombies system it is difficult to defend by adding the entire compromised zombie's list to the firewall.

The steps taken to identify the Origin of the botnet botmaster (Shrivastava, 2016).

- The cyber forensic analysis is to be done on the behavior of compromised zombies and the comparison is made with the existing behavior of the compromised zombies.
- With the comparison, concrete evidence is taken and the compromised zombies are identified.
- The cyber forensic analysis is to be done on the network traffic and based on the frequent path traversed the command and control are identified.
- The comparisons are made with the existing identified command and control the network traffic behavior and the host behavior of command and control.
- With the comparison, concrete evidence is taken and the real command and control are identified.
- The cyber forensic analysis is to be done based on the special marking scheme applied it is used to uncover the actual origin of the attack.
- The special marking scheme provides us the concrete evidence to identify the real originator of the attack.
- To identify botmaster (origin of the attack) it is necessary to follow these stepwise evidence gathering.
- First the compromised zombies, then the command and control, and then the big fish botmaster.

The ultimate target of the forensics expects is to find the real origin of the attack the mastermind the botmaster. The traceback of the compromised zombies and the command and control is essential. The successful computer forensics analysis on the cyber attack botnet can be fulfilled only when the traceback of the real origin of the attack botmaster is found successful. Since if the identity of the real botmaster is revealed then the attack from that origin can be mitigated easily. It can be used for the future to defend against these kinds of attacks by the cybersecurity professionals. It is helpful in making the entire botnet network becomes inactive.

CONCLUSION

One of the most challenging tasks of the botnet network forensics analysis is that the identity of the botnet hidden master, Traceback to command and control is also very difficult, since the attack is from the compromised zombies, these compromised zombies are the unaware public who get victimized for the crime they haven't done. A proper computer forensics investigation is required here to provide the concrete evidence. This chapter discussed the existing works related to botnet attack and the forensics method to discover the real source of the attack. It not only finds evidence that the botnet attack has taken place. It also finds the evidence that the botnet attack has taken place especially using compromised zombies. It also collects the evidence to justify that the compromised zombies are not the real source of attack. It identifies and collects the evidence that, the Command and Control (C&C) work under the control of botmaster. Forensic analysis does not stop with this it also find evidence to identify the real source of the attack the botmaster, with help of special marking scheme the mastermind botmaster is identified. The real origin of the attack is identified with concrete evidence then the effect of the botnet could be mitigated very easily.

REFERENCES

Al-Jarrah, O. Y., Alhussein, O., Yoo, P. D., Muhaidat, S., Taha, K., & Kim, K. (2016). Data randomization and cluster-based partitioning for botnet intrusion detection. *IEEE Transactions on Cybernetics*, *46*(8), 1796–1806. doi:10.1109/TCYB.2015.2490802 PMID:26540724

Alieyan, K., ALmomani, A., Manasrah, A., & Kadhum, M. M. (2017). A survey of botnet detection based on DNS. *Neural Computing & Applications*, *28*(7), 1541–1558. doi:10.100700521-015-2128-0

Banks, A., Vincent, J., & Anyakoha, C. (2007). A review of particle swarm optimization. Part I: Background and development. *Natural Computing*, *6*(4), 467–484. doi:10.100711047-007-9049-5

Belenky, A., & Ansari, N. (2003a). IP traceback with deterministic packet marking. *IEEE Communications Letters*, *7*(4), 162–164. doi:10.1109/LCOMM.2003.811200

Belenky, A., & Ansari, N. (2003b). On IP traceback. *IEEE Communications Magazine*, *41*(7), 142–153. doi:10.1109/MCOM.2003.1215651

Bellovin, S. M., Leech, M., & Taylor, T. (2003). *ICMP traceback messages*. Marina del Ray, CA: Internet Engineering Task Force; doi:10.7916/D8FF406R

Choi, K. H., & Dai, H. K. (2004, May). A marking scheme using Huffman codes for IP traceback. In *Parallel Architectures, Algorithms and Networks, 2004. Proceedings. 7th International Symposium on* (pp. 421-428). IEEE. 10.1109/ISPAN.2004.1300516

Choi, Y. S., Kim, I. K., Oh, J. T., & Jang, J. S. (2012). Aigg threshold based http get flooding attack detection. *Information Security Applications*, 270-284.

Dos Santos, C. R. P., Bezerra, R. S., Ceron, J. M., Granville, L. Z., & Tarouco, L. M. (2011, October). Identifying botnet communications using a mashup-based approach. In *Network Operations and Management Symposium (LANOMS), 2011 7th Latin American* (pp. 1-6). IEEE. 10.1109/LANOMS.2011.6102273

Ehrenkranz, T., & Li, J. (2009). On the state of IP spoofing defense. *ACM Transactions on Internet Technology*, *9*(2), 6. doi:10.1145/1516539.1516541

Garg, S., & Sharma, R. M. (2017). Classification Based Network Layer Botnet Detection. In *Advanced Informatics for Computing Research* (pp. 332–342). Singapore: Springer. doi:10.1007/978-981-10-5780-9_30

Gong, C., & Sarac, K. (2008). A more practical approach for single-packet IP traceback using packet logging and marking. *IEEE Transactions on Parallel and Distributed Systems*, *19*(10), 1310–1324. doi:10.1109/TPDS.2007.70817

Goodrich, M. T. (2008). Probabilistic packet marking for large-scale IP traceback. *IEEE/ACM Transactions on Networking*, *16*(1), 15–24. doi:10.1109/TNET.2007.910594

Gu, G., Perdisci, R., Zhang, J., & Lee, W. (2008, July). BotMiner: Clustering Analysis of Network Traffic for Protocol-and Structure-Independent Botnet Detection. In USENIX security symposium (Vol. 5, No. 2, pp. 139-154). Academic Press.

Gu, G., Zhang, J., & Lee, W. (2008, February). BotSniffer: Detecting Botnet Command and Control Channels in Network Traffic. In NDSS (Vol. 8, pp. 1-18). Academic Press.

Gupta, B. B., Joshi, R. C., Misra, M., Meena, D. L., Shrivastava, G., & Sharma, K. (2010). Detecting a Wide Range of Flooding DDoS Attacks using Linear Prediction Model. In *2nd International Conference on Information and Multimedia Technology* (pp. 535-539). IEEE.

Hachem, N., Mustapha, Y. B., Granadillo, G. G., & Debar, H. (2011, May). Botnets: lifecycle and taxonomy. In *Network and Information Systems Security (SAR-SSI), 2011 Conference on* (pp. 1-8). IEEE. 10.1109/SAR-SSI.2011.5931395

Honeynet Project and Research Alliance. (2008). *Know your enemy: Tracking Botnets*. Retrieved October 8, 2008, from http:// www. honeynet. org/papers/bots

Kolias, C., Kambourakis, G., & Maragoudakis, M. (2011). Swarm intelligence in intrusion detection: A survey. *Computers & Security*, *30*(8), 625–642. doi:10.1016/j.cose.2011.08.009

Malliga, S., & Tamilarasi, A. (2010). A hybrid scheme using packet marking and logging for IP traceback. *International Journal of Internet Protocol Technology*, *5*(1-2), 81–91. doi:10.1504/IJIPT.2010.032617

Savage, S., Wetherall, D., Karlin, A., & Anderson, T. (2000, August). Practical network support for IP traceback. *Computer Communication Review*, *30*(4), 295–306. doi:10.1145/347057.347560

Shrivastava, G. (2016, March). Network forensics: Methodical literature review. In *Computing for Sustainable Global Development (INDIACom), 2016 3rd International Conference on* (pp. 2203-2208). IEEE.

Shrivastava, G. (2017). Approaches of network forensic model for investigation. *International Journal of Forensic Engineering*, *3*(3), 195–215. doi:10.1504/IJFE.2017.082977

Shrivastava, G., Sharma, K., & Rai, S. (2010, December). The Detection & Defense of DoS & DDoS Attack: A Technical Overview. In *Proceeding of ICC* (*Vol. 27*, p. 28). Academic Press.

Snort I. D. S. (2009). *Snort IDS*. Retrieved January 5, 2009, from http://www.snort.org

Springer reference. (2014). *DNS based botnet detection*. Retrieved July 15, 2014, from http://www.springerreference.com/docs/html/chapterdbid/317753.html

Tegeler, F., Fu, X., Vigna, G., & Kruegel, C. (2012, December). Botfinder: Finding bots in network traffic without deep packet inspection. In *Proceedings of the 8th international conference on Emerging networking experiments and technologies* (pp. 349-360). ACM. 10.1145/2413176.2413217

Wang, P., Sparks, S., & Zou, C. C. (2010). An advanced hybrid peer-to-peer botnet. *IEEE Transactions on Dependable and Secure Computing*, *7*(2), 113–127. doi:10.1109/TDSC.2008.35

Yaar, A., Perrig, A., & Song, D. (2006). StackPi: New packet marking and filtering mechanisms for DDoS and IP spoofing defense. *IEEE Journal on Selected Areas in Communications*, *24*(10), 1853–1863. doi:10.1109/JSAC.2006.877138

Yang, M. H., & Yang, M. C. (2012). RIHT: A novel hybrid IP traceback scheme. *IEEE Transactions on Information Forensics and Security*, *7*(2), 789–797. doi:10.1109/TIFS.2011.2169960

Zhang, L., & Guan, Y. (2006, August). TOPO: A topology-aware single packet attack traceback scheme. In Securecomm and Workshops, 2006 (pp. 1-10). IEEE. doi:10.1109/SECCOMW.2006.359556

Section 3

Security and Privacy in Big Data Analytics and Machine Learning, Biometrics, Audio Watermarking, and Cryptocurrency

Chapter 15
Impact of Big Data on Security

Ramgopal Kashyap
Sagar Institute of Science and Technology, India

Albert D. Piersson
University of Cape Coast, Ghana

ABSTRACT

The motivation behind this chapter is to highlight the qualities, security issue, advantages, and disadvantages of big data. In the recent researches, the issue and challenges are due to the exponential growth of social media data and other images and videos. Big data security threats are rising, which is affecting the data heterogeneity adaptability and privacy preservation analytics. Big data analytics helps cyber security, but no new application can be envisioned without delivering new types of information, working on data-driven calculations and expending determined measure of information. This chapter demonstrates how innate attributes of big data are protected.

INTRODUCTION

Data has transformed into a key bit of every economy, industry, affiliation, business limit and individual. The Big data display unique computational and genuine troubles, including flexibility and limit bottleneck, disturbance accumulating, spurious association and estimation botches. These difficulties are perceived and require new computational and quantifiable perspective. This shows the big data Mining and the issues and challenges with emphasis on the perceived segments of Big Data. It moreover discusses a couple of strategies to deal with tremendous data. Huge data is a total term insinuating data to outperform the getting ready limit of standard data organization structures and programming frameworks (Herland, Khoshgoftaar & Wald, 2014). However with big data come enormous esteems. Information turns out to be enormous information at the point when singular information quits making a difference and just a vast gathering of it or examinations gotten from it are of esteem with numerous enormous information breaking down innovations, experiences can be inferred to empower better basic leadership for basic improvement ranges, for example, social insurance, monetary profitability, vitality, and catastrophic event forecast. The period of Big data has purchased with it a plenty of chances for the headway of science, change of medicinal services, advancement of financial development, upgrade of training framework

DOI: 10.4018/978-1-5225-4100-4.ch015

and more methods for social collaboration and stimulation. safety and insurance are unimaginable matter in tremendous data on account of its epic volume, rapid, broad grouping like immense scale cloud establishment, arrangement of data (Gartner warns of big data security problems, 2014). The utilization of vast scale framework that is fluctuated number of programming stages crosswise over vast systems of PCs expands the area of assault to an all new level of the whole framework. The distinctive defy is to colossal big data and appropriated registering additionally, its safety and assurance concern for motive to show the purposes of intrigue.

QUALITIES OF BIG DATA

The gigantic in enormous information is a result of the absolute amount of huge information that it truly suppose. It insinuates the gigantic measures of data that is made each second moment. It starts as of broad datasets or various little data bit assembled after some time. Reliably more than 200 messages and 2 million photos are exchanged and 1.8 million inclinations are created on social media and more than 2 million recordings are seen (Hoskins, 2014). "Big data" rises up out of this amazing acceleration in the quantity of IP-prepared endpoints. It is truly quite recently the term for all the accessible information in a given range that a business gathers with the objective of finding concealed examples or patterns inside it. These, once uncovered by investigation devices, can be utilized to yield an enhanced result not far off higher consumer loyalty, speedier administration conveyance, more income, et cetera. The other side of that coin is that the design used to store big data additionally speaks to a gleaming new focus of enormous information security issues for criminal action and malware. Should something happen to such a key business asset, the outcomes could be annihilating for the association that accumulated it (Miciuła & Miciuła, 2015). Lamentably, a number of the apparatuses related with enormous information and savvy examination are open source. In many cases they are not outlined considering security as an essential capacity, prompting yet more enormous information security issues. Individuals, process, information and things are the solid pillars of huge information as appeared in Figure 1.

BIG DATA SECURITY ISSUES

Along these lines, because of that, here's a waitlist of a portion of the undeniable enormous information security issues that ought to be considered.

1. **Non-Social Information Stores:** Think NoSQL databases, which without anyone else's input for the most part, need security (which is rather given, kind of, through middleware) (Bhagwath & Mallikarjun Math, 2016).
2. **Storage:** In enormous information design, the information is normally put away on numerous levels, contingent upon business requirements for execution versus cost. For example, high-need "hot" information will as a rule is put away on streak media. So securing capacity will mean making a level cognizant procedure.
3. **Access Controls:** Similarly as with big business IT all in all, it's basically imperative to give a framework in which encoded confirmation/approval checks that clients are who they say they are, and figure out who can perceive what.

Figure 1. Strong pillars of Big Data

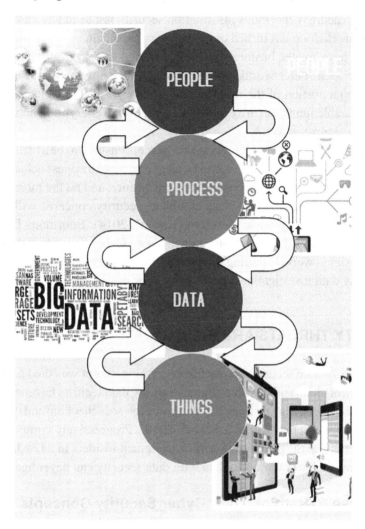

4. **Granular Examining:** It can help decide when missed assaults have happened, what the outcomes were, and what ought to be done to enhance matters later on. This in itself is a great deal of information, and must be empowered and ensured to be helpful in tending to big data security issues (Appelbaum, 2016).

TENDING TO BIG DATA SECURITY ISSUES

Ideally, every one of the nine ranges of big data security issues would be exhaustively secured. In this present reality, approximations might be required on the grounds that the information gathering and examination devices have security that was "blasted onto" the center usefulness as opposed to being "prepared in." Security and data occasion administration (SIEM) arrangements ought to dependably be conveyed to total security logs and consequently recognize potential breaks (Ma & Wu, 2014). One specific purpose of concern, which is the reason I recorded it first above, is Hadoop, which was just not initially intended to address enormous information security issues in any case by any stretch of the imagination. Luckily, as Hadoop has turned out to be more prevalent, an assortment of driving security arrangement suppliers have created business review innovation to help secure it and these are joined by commitments from the open source world, similar to Apache Accumulo. So nowadays it is in any event conceivable to shore up a portion of the more terrible shortages of big data security issues presented by Hadoop (and comparable items) security that stay in zones like encryption and verification. So what lays ahead for big data security issues?

The fate of enormous information itself is everything except ensured to be a brilliant one it's all around perceived nowadays that shrewd investigation can be a regal street to business achievement. So this infers big data engineering will both turn out to be more basic to secure, and all the more every now and again assaulted. Moreover, as more information is accumulated, security concerns will reinforce in parallel, and government directions will be made therefore (Kshetri, 2014). Enormous Data Security Analytics (Win, Tianfield & Mair, 2017): A Weapon against Rising Cyber Security Attacks? The continuous digitalization of the business world is putting organizations at danger of digital assaults like never before some time recently. Big data investigation can possibly offer insurance against these assaults.

DIGITAL SECURITY THREATS ARE RISING

Since the thought of a corporate security border has everything except vanished as of late on account of the developing selection of cloud and portable administrations, data security has encountered a significant outlook change from customary edge insurance apparatuses towards checking and distinguishing noxious exercises inside corporate systems (Kalra & Sekhri, 2016). Progressively complex assault techniques utilized by digital culprits and the developing part of malignant insiders in a few late vast scale security breaks plainly show that customary ways to deal with data security can never again keep up.

Organizations Have to Rethink Their Cyber Security Concepts

Investigation is the key component in utilizing digital flexibility with progressively progressed and persevering assaults and the straightforward certainty that each association must ensure itself against all assortments of assaults while an aggressor just needs one effective endeavor, associations must reexamine their digital security ideas (Horowitz & Lucero, 2016). They need to move past immaculate aversion towards the PDR worldview: Prevent – Detect – Respond.

How Big Data Analytics Fits in

At the center of this approach stands enhanced discovery and that is the place enormous information examination becomes possibly the most important factor. Location must have the capacity to recognize changing use designs; to execute complex examination quickly, near constant; to perform complex connections over an assortment of information sources running from server and application logs to organize occasions and client exercises. This requires both progressed examination past straightforward lead based methodologies and the capacity to run investigation on a lot of present and authentic information big data security investigation. Joining the present condition of examination with security enables associations to enhance their digital flexibility (Hussain & Roy, 2016).

Huge Data Security Analytics: A New Generation of Security Tools

As the security business' reaction to these difficulties, another era of security investigation arrangements has risen as of late, which can gather, store and examine enormous measures of security information over the entire undertaking continuously. Improved by extra setting information and outside risk knowledge, this information is then investigated utilizing different relationship calculations to recognize peculiarities and in this way distinguish conceivable malevolent exercises. Not at all like customary SIEM arrangements, such apparatuses work in close constant and produce few security alarms positioned by seriousness as per a hazard display (Lafuente, 2015). Figure 2 is showing big data security issues. these alarms are enhanced with extra legal subtle elements and can significantly improve a security expert's employment and empower speedy identification and moderation of digital assaults.

What Made Big Data Security Analytics Possible

The greatest innovative leap forward that made these arrangements conceivable is enormous information examination. The business has at long last achieved the point where business insight calculations

Figure 2. Big Data security issues

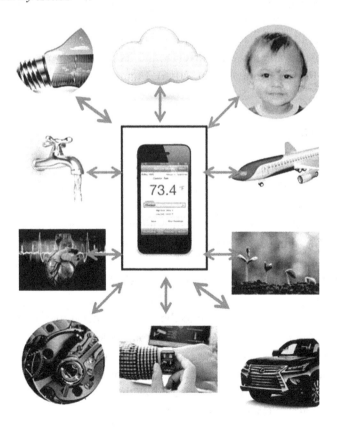

for expansive scale information preparing, already reasonable just too extensive organizations, have progressed toward becoming commoditized. Using promptly accessible systems, for example, Apache Hadoop and cheap equipment, sellers are currently ready to construct enormous information answers for gathering, putting away and breaking down tremendous measures of unstructured information continuously (Tromp, Pechenizkiy & Gaber, 2017).

Joining Data to Predict Suspicious Activity

This makes it conceivable to join ongoing and verifiable investigation and distinguish new episodes that could be identified with others that happened before. Combined with outside security knowledge sources that give current data about the most recent vulnerabilities, this can extraordinarily encourage recognizable proof of progressing progressed digital assaults on the system. Having a lot of recorded information within reach likewise fundamentally streamlines beginning adjustment to the typical examples of movement of a given system, which are then used to distinguish abnormalities. Existing arrangements are as of now fit for mechanized adjustment with almost no info required from managers (Bakare & Argiddi, 2017).

Recognizing Relevant Incidents

In light of demonstrated big data investigation calculations, these arrangements can distinguish exceptions and different peculiarities in security information, which quite often show some sort of malignant or possibly suspicious action. By sifting through the factual clamor, big data security investigation can lessen monstrous streams of crude security occasions to a reasonable number of compact and plainly sorted cautions to permit even an unpracticed individual to settle on a choice on them. All things considered, by keeping all recorded data accessible for later examination, it furnishes a measurable master with a great deal more insight about the occurrence and its relationship to other chronicled inconsistencies (Wang, Tasoulis, Roos & Kangasharju, 2016). Figure 3 is showing the growth of big data and challenges in the future.

Robotizing Workflows

At long last, current enormous information security examination arrangements give various mechanized work processes to reacting to distinguished dangers, for example, disturbing obviously recognized malware assaults or presenting a suspicious occasion to an oversaw security benefit for encourage investigation. Robotized controls for digital security and extortion identification have been distinguished as one of the key business drivers for future selection in this examination (Wang, Crawl, Altintas & Li, 2014).

Key Findings From the Big Data Security Analytics Report

The examination conveys bits of knowledge into the level of mindfulness and current methodologies in data security and extortion location in associations around the globe. It gauges the significance, current state and feasible arrangements of big data security examination activities crosswise over various divisions, and in addition exhibiting a review of the different open doors, advantages and difficulties identifying with those activities. It additionally diagrams the scope of advancements at present accessible to address those difficulties (Wu & Chin, 2014).

Figure 3. Challenges in the future

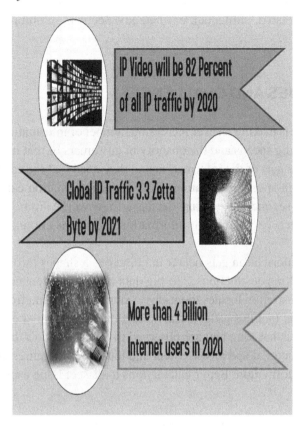

Enormous Data Opportunities Need Big Data Security

The gathering of huge information examination is rapidly creating. If you don't progress past the curve, there's tremendous potential for gigantic issues; however if you do plan, there are immense opportunities to successfully enable the business. You might be considering what the real difficulty is and what makes colossal data extraordinary and moreover troublesome (Wang, 2016). The bother is that enormous information examination stages are filled by huge volumes of oftentimes sensitive customer, thing, associate, tolerant and other data which when in doubt have insufficient data security and address low-hanging characteristic item for cybercriminals.

A CLOSER LOOK AT BIG DATA CHALLENGES

Enormous information examination makes basic open entryways. In any case, affiliations must manage the security challenges they show, for example Big data examination focuses on finding key encounters to push the business. Those encounters are generally gotten from unstable data that is gathered in the tremendous data document. The idea of colossal data high volume, arrangement and speed makes it difficult to ensure data respectability. Mapping less flowed conditions, where data from various sources can be joined and totaled in self-self-assured ways, make it endeavoring to set up get to controls. Enormous data circumstances empower relationship to add up to a consistently expanding number of data, as it were, including cash related, individual, ensured advancement, prohibitive or by and large fragile data (Bradley, 2013).

IMMENSE DATA ISSUES AND CHALLENGES

Data Velocity: Frameworks is making an ever increasing number of information, both operational what's more; diagnostic at expanding speeds and the quantity of customers of that information are developing. Individuals need the greater part of the information and they need it at the earliest opportunity prompting what is inclining as high-speed information. High speed information can mean a huge number of lines of information every second. Customary database frameworks are not sufficiently proficient of performing investigation on such volumes of information and that is continually in movement (Catlett & Ghani, 2015).

Data Assortment: Big information gets nearer in numerous a shapes through text, image, audio and videos in the online networking destinations. The big data are for all intents and purposes new or rather as old as the systems administration locales themselves, similar to the data from informal organizations. Advanced cells and different mobiles gadgets can be sectioned in a similar class. The conventional databases keeps the data that is not long ago are observed to be ill-suited to this information. Quite a bit of this information is unstructured and inconvenient and loud which requires thorough system for basic leadership in light of the information. Better calculations to dissect issue excessively (Dhar, 2014).

BIG DATA TECHNICAL ISSUES AND CHALLENGES

Adaptation to Internal Failure

With the happening to propels like conveyed figuring the indicate must remain such a degree, to the point that at whatever point disillusionment happens the damage done must occur inside commendable utmost instead of the entire work. Accuse tolerant enlisting is dreary and requires to an extraordinary degree complex counts. An imbecile verification, penny percent strong accuse tolerant machine or writing computer programs is essentially an unreasonable idea.

Data Heterogeneity

More than 82% of information in this day and age is unstructured information. It enveloped practically every sort of information we create once a day like web-based social networking connection, archive sharing, fax exchanges, messages, and messages and significantly more. Working with unstructured information is badly designed and costly as well. Changing over these to organized information is unfeasible (Wu & Chin, 2014).

Adaptability

The test in flexibility of gigantic data has provoked appropriated registering. It is prepared for conglomerating different unmistakable workloads with different execution destinations into broad bundles. This needs unusual condition of sharing of advantages that is exorbitant and conveys close by it diverse challenges like executing distinctive businesses with the goal. It in like manner needs to oversee structure frustrations capably as it is extremely general when working with broad bundles (Jabeen, 2016). The kind of limit contraption to be used is henceforth an immense request drawing nearer around huge data accumulating issue.

HUGE DATA STORAGE AND TRANSMISSION

Huge information getting ready and cleared up by the maker of average outline, each time another limit medium is produced the measure of data advances toward getting to be to a consistently expanding degree. The farthest point of current plates is around 4 terabytes for each circle so more than 1 exabyte requires 25000 plates. Despite the likelihood that a lone PC structure is adequately capable of getting ready 1 exabyte, to explicitly work with that other plates is well past its capacity. On the remote possibility that 1 gigabyte for each second framework has an intense sensible swapping scale of 80% its doable information exchange limit is around 100 megabytes. Challenges similarly join finding data centers that are genuinely of importance what's all the more, how to utilize the data to isolate most outrageous preferred standpoint.

HUGE DATA PRIVACY AND SECURITY

Frequently in gigantic data examination, the individual information of people from database and relational correspondence districts ought to be joined with outside huge educational accumulations. Thusly assurances about anyone which may have been characterized ended up being intrigued on the planet. Frequently it prompts taking bits of learning in people's lives. Consistently more educated individual having better learning and thoughts regarding colossal data examination abuses farsighted examination over a man who is less instructed than him. Security and insurance are immense stresses the degree that huge information are concerned and as expansive data creates through volume reliably so are these stresses on the ascent (Ghiglieri & Waidner, 2016). A prime clarification behind security and insurance stress in colossal data is in light of the fact that huge information is by and by and large open.

SECURITY ISSUES AND CHALLENGES WITH BIG DATA

Affiliations assemble data from gear contraptions, programming applications and devices, assembling this data, endorsement of the data and furthermore the source is a test. ID cloning ambushes like Sybil strikes are predominant circumstance in which noxious customer brings contraption, place stock in device and gives vindictive commitment starting. Data wellsprings of material data can be controlled additionally like dishonestly to change the temperature using sensors and contributing vindictive commitment to the temperature gathering process. GPS signs can be controlled comparatively (Batarseh, Yang & Deng, 2017). The threatening customer changes data for transmission to the central data gathering system.

REALTIME SECURITY MONITORING

Consistent security watching has been an advancing test in the tremendous data examination circumstance transcendently as a result of the amount of alerts delivered by security contraptions. The various false positives and due to individual's awkwardness to viably oversee such a gigantic measure speed. Security requires the Big Data system and data structure fuse revolt manager access to applications or centers, application threats, and tuning in remaining in a precarious situation. Establishment which is generally a natural group of particular portions, the security of each fragment and the security blend of the sections must be considered. On the off chance that there ought to be an event of a Hadoop aggregate continue running in an open cloud for the general society cloud, organic arrangement of parts including figuring, storing and framework parts, ought to be viewed as (Lafuente, 2015). The security of the centers and the interconnection among the center points besides, data set away in a center point ought to be considered. The watching application including appropriate association chooses that should take after security guidelines and the data source security starts from exorbitantly ought to be considered.

PRIVACY-PRESERVING DATA MINING AND ANALYTICS

Enormous information security, prominent publicizing, diminishment of normal flexibility and augmentation in state and corporate control. A specialist of an association accountable for the tremendous data store can manhandle his vitality and harm security courses of action.

Data-Centric Security

Guaranteeing data end-to-end by encryption gives an impressively more diminutive especially portrayed attacking surface. It is helpless against in disguise side-channel attack and can remove puzzle keys; in any case it is an ominous endeavor. Diverse risks related with cryptographically approved get the chance to control technique using encryption, the plaintext data looking figure message paying little heed to the likelihood that he needs to pick between a privilege and a wrong plain substance. For a cryptographic tradition for empowering chasing and filtering encoded data the foe should not have the ability to get the hang of anything about the encoded data past the relating predicate, paying little respect to whether satisfied or not.

Granular Reviews

Data security specialists need to have a dynamic impact as fast as time licenses. As a matter of fact weight to settle on smart business decisions can realize security specialists being chosen to keep a safe distance for key decisions or being seen as inhibitors of business advancement (Yang and Yecies, 2016). In any case, the threat of delinquent data security is outstanding and recorded, and it's possible to be an enabling operator rather than a block.

No Opportunities Without Security

Starting at now, a growing number of associations are grasping huge information circumstances. The time is prepared to guarantee security bunches are fused into these decisions and courses of action, particularly since huge data conditions which do avoid comprehensive data confirmation capacities address low-hanging natural item for software engineers since they hold so much possibly productive fragile data. Data security is a separated, relentless obligation that necessities to end up some part of old news for colossal data circumstances. Securing data requires a far reaching approach to manage shield relationship from a psyche boggling hazard scene transversely finished varying systems (Su and Xu, 2017). Data security must supplement other wellbeing endeavors, for instance, endpoint security to make a through approach. By getting ready and being set up for the introduction of gigantic data examination in your affiliation, you will have the ability to help your affiliation meet its objectives securely.

Security Intelligence With Big Data

Increasing Security Intelligence With Big Data

Driving security insight arrangements today depend upon an arrangement of organized and semi-organized information sources, including logs, organize activity and others, to give the Security Operations Center with an on-going constant perspective of their association's security act. The measurements utilized to assess arrangements incorporate the scale and speed of information that can be prepared continuously, pruning the extensive arrangement of crude information to a restricted arrangement of huge security episodes requiring the consideration of the association.

While security insight arrangements do empower security experts to investigate the information and distinguish developing dangers or pinpoint new hazard exposures, the attention is on utilizing a current arrangement of risk and hazard identifiers to empower ongoing examination for identification (Lim, 2015). While this approach is powerful to monitor and keeping up the digital guards of an association and enhancing the reaction time to deal with episodes, another arrangement of difficulties are surfacing which requires security knowledge to be opened up with big data examination.

Proactively Mitigating Risk and Identifying Threats

As the hierarchical edge obscures because of quick market selection of cloud and portable innovations and also shopper engagement in informal communities, an association can't exclusively concentrate on barrier. Or maybe the association must be more proactive in relieving hazard and recognizing dangers. Aggressors are likewise utilizing more modern focused on assault systems, for example, social designing, and lance phishing (Gheyas & Abdallah, 2016). The assault strategies are likewise adjusting to current guarded methodologies endeavoring to either cover up malignant exercises among a lot of harmless movement or mask the goal by giving off an impression of being harmless action. Indeed, even current tumultuous monetary and social conditions are further rousing new sorts of vindictive practices.

The Need for Big Data and Big Data Analytics

Advancing security knowledge to address the issues of the new security challenges requires enormous information and big data investigation. Right off the bat, an association needs to keep its customary security information for longer timeframes to perform examination on the information. Chronicled investigation has the capability of uncovering longer running assault techniques and recognizes backslides in security after some time. Besides, information sources not customarily utilized for security can enable an association to better qualify what resources and elements should be ensured or potentially watched. For instance, recognizing clients who regularly work with delicate information, and frameworks that are basic to center business forms (Diesner, 2015). Information sources, for example, email, online networking content, corporate archives, and web substance may help add extra setting to conventional security information however is overwhelmingly unstructured information.

Affiliation grabs awareness of an enlivened or supported assailant who attempts to conceal or cover the strike as innocuous associations, perhaps completed a drawn out extend of time (months, years). Quick moves in the changing face of medication are inclining at quickened pace toward more different, mind boggling, dynamic, coordinated, and consistent care frameworks. Thus, this is fuelling an expansion sought after and craving for mechanical advancement in therapeutic advances. A wide assortment of advances and instruments are associated with the demonstrative procedure including electronic human records (EHRs) and imaging data frameworks (Balogh et al., 2015). As current drug turns out to be progressively perplexing, the coordination of restorative imaging into a total undertaking wide electronic patient record arrangement additionally turns out to be considerably more intricate, but on the other hand is more proficient, and financially savvy.

Current restorative imaging modalities, for example, processed and computerized radiography, ultrasound, advanced mammography, fluoroscopy, computed tomography (CT) play critical parts in social insurance, as they deliver computerized pictures which contain a riches measure of clinical data. These pictures are critical substances since they are utilized to question anatomical cross-segments of inner organs and tissues, and to give finding and screen the impacts of the treatment (Abd-Eldayem, 2013). As of late, radiology has driven the route in setting up the accessibility of data through restorative pictures whenever and anyplace through the inescapable arrangement of these computerized frameworks (Andriole, 2014). As gadgets turn out to be progressively associated with systems, and information is shared among PCs, security dangers move past the framework to interruptions crosswise over computerized systems (Abd-Eldayem, 2013) in this manner presenting whole systems to cyberattacks and disturbances that put wellbeing, mind quality and notoriety in danger (Quebec, 2017).

DISCUSSION

The reason for the clarified preparing occasions is to set up a relationship among low-level image/video highlights separated from cases, variable substances, factors esteems and time. A human or programmed/algorithmic chief can play out the errand of comment of preparing cases. The boss includes the name of a variable to the rundown of factors contained in the comment of the occasion if the substance speaking to the variable is coordinated decidedly on the case (Kashyap& Gautam, 2015). Such a positive match of an element speaking to a variable on an occasion happens when an example of low-level elements additionally called an element vector that describes the particular element likewise called an element coordinating example are coordinated utilizing an element vector examination work to an arrangement of components separated from the occurrence allude to include extraction above. For instance, if the element related with the variable "Emotion_of_Ram" is Ram, at that point a client can physically explain all preparation cases containing Ram's face with the substance "Dwindle." As another case, a comment calculation can likewise coordinate an element coordinating example containing various low-level components, for example, the state of a human face describing Ram's face and a shading histogram containing extensive canisters of red skin shading since Ram's appearance is red on all preparation cases to naturally clarify the preparation cases that contain Ram's face. In a next explanation step, the estimations of factors recorded in the comment of each preparation example are recognized in the particular case utilizing an approach like that of substance coordinating depicted previously. For instance, the administrator can give all preparation examples commented on with the variable "Emotion_of_Ram" that contain a cheerful outward appearance the clear cut variable esteem "Glad" or "Irate" on account of a furious face. Such esteem can likewise be naturally identified by a calculation in view of an example of low-level components related with the estimation of a variable called an esteem coordinating example (Juneja& Kashyap, 2016). For instance, an esteem coordinating example may depict a specific number of onlookers wearing the shading orange in a image of a football stadium in view of various components, for example,

- A shading histogram with expansive canister of orange shading,
- A polygon that describes the upper portion of the human body, or
- A disparity characterizing the edge.

At last, preparing examples are time stamped for time arrangement examination purposes. We comment on preparing examples related with a specific time an incentive with the string or numerical portrayal of the separate time esteem (Kashyap & Tiwari, 2017). Optalysys is creating optical elite figuring equipment for huge information handling, which works at more elevated amounts than what can be accomplished with customary gadgets at a small amount of the cost and vitality utilization (Kashyap & Gautam, 2016). Optalysys innovation utilizes light, as opposed to power, to perform processor-concentrated numerical capacities, (for example, Fourier Transforms) in parallel at amazingly high speeds and resolutions. Optalysys innovation can be utilized to perform design coordinating, contrasting info information with reference pictures and distinguishing likenesses or irregularities.

Additional scary still, consider the way that the extent of security dangers is frequently corresponding to the measure of information that is powerless against assault. The coming of big data stockpiling and preparing capacities has presented verifiable dangers for huge security breaks Risks that must be secured before a business actualizes major information extend at scale(Abd-Eldayem, 2013). In this fourth post of BMC's enormous information arrangement, you'll get an outline on the fundamental big data security issues you ought to know about (Andriole, 2014).

Practically every big data security issue that is basic to big business wide usage can be followed back to plan exclusions in the first Hadoop circulation. Not that Hadoop's unique outline was flawed or awful, it simply was not intended to be utilized as a part of an undertaking information condition. Enough time has passed; in any case, that compelling adjustments and arrangements have been created to address these security concerns. The trap is to first comprehend what the potential shortcomings are, and after that check that you have avoided potential risk to secure those shortcomings. User Authentication and Access Organizations conveying Hadoop in a common domain must make sure that client confirmation and get to rights are entirely controlled. Apache Sentry is one conceivable arrangement that is accessible to enable you to point of confinement and control client get to rights over a major information framework. With so much information, associations need to try to consent to administrative prerequisites. In big data frameworks, you'd be reasonable to make a couple of strides of additional precautionary measure by guaranteeing that records on client exercises and framework occasions are being produced and put away. You'll require them to complete any client and framework reviews. Several major information security issues revolve around the way that client and administration verification conventions in local Hadoop are to some degree frail. This leaves Hadoop frameworks open to the danger of malevolent information inputs and alters. Ensure you have Kerberos and LDAP conventions set up keeping in mind the end goal to defend against this short coming. Native Hadoop conveyances offer information encryption capacities for information very still; however it's somewhat trickier to ensure information in-movement. System encryption techniques have been produced to secure moving information, however they're excluded with Hadoop's local appropriation, so you'll have to set up that line of insurance for yourself.

CONCLUSION

Big Data is inclining, no new application can be envisioned without it delivering new types of information, working on data driven calculations, and expending determined measure of information. With information putting away and processing situations getting to be more less expensive, cloud conditions winding up plainly more competent of putting away and sharing framework and investigation applications, programming applications ending up noticeably more organized, information security, get to control, pressure encryption and consistence have presented a few difficulties that for all intents and purposes should be taken care of and tended to in an exceptionally orderly way. In this chapter security challenges and have laid a few suggestions for making enormous information preparing and calculation more dependable and thusly making its foundation more secure. The enormous information emerge from the various foundation levels utilized for huge information preparing, the new calculation foundations like NoSQL databases utilized for quick throughput that are vital for enormous volumes of information are not completely secured from real security dangers, the non versatility of genuine time observing methods, the heterogeneous design of gadgets delivering information, perplexity with differing legitimate limitations that some way or another prompt specially appointed methodologies for security and protection. There is a major biological system existing for particular enormous information issues. Points in this paper serve to clear up particular parts of the powerless ranges in the whole huge information preparing foundation that should be broke down for specific dangers. Significant proposals for managing the main five security dangers have likewise been recommended in this chapter. The expectation is that this paper will cooperatively expand the center of the innovative work group towards the main five difficulties, which will eventually prompt more prominent security and protection in separate enormous information stages.

REFERENCES

Abd-Eldayem. (2013). A proposed security technique based on watermarking and encryption for digital imaging and communications in medicine. *Egyptian Informatics Journal, 14*, 1–13. doi:10.1016/j.eij.2012.11.002

Andriole, K. P. (2014). Security of Electronic Medical Information and Patient Privacy: What You Need to Know. *Journal of the American College of Radiology*, *11*(12), 1212–1216. doi:10.1016/j.jacr.2014.09.011 PMID:25467897

Appelbaum, D. (2016). Securing Big Data Provenance for Auditors: The Big Data Provenance Black Box as Reliable Evidence. *Journal of Emerging Technologies in Accounting*, *13*(1), 17–36. doi:10.2308/jeta-51473

Bakare, A., & Argiddi, R. (2017). To Study, Analyze and predict the Diseases using Big Data. *International Journal of Computers and Applications*, *165*(7), 17–19. doi:10.5120/ijca2017913917

Balogh, E. P., Miller, B. T., & Ball, J. R. (Eds.). (2015). *Committee on Diagnostic Error in Health Care; Board on Health Care Services; Institute of Medicine; The National Academies of Sciences, Engineering, and Medicine. Improving Diagnosis in Health Care*. Washington, DC: The National Academies Press.

Batarseh, F., Yang, R., & Deng, L. (2017). A comprehensive model for management and validation of federal big data analytical systems. *Big Data Analytics*, *2*(1), 2. doi:10.118641044-016-0017-x

Bhagwath, S., & Mallikarjun Math, D. (2016). Distributed Systems and Recent Innovations: Challenges Benefits and Security Issues in Distributed Systems. *Bonfring International Journal Of Software Engineering And Soft Computing*, *6*(Special Issue), 37–42. doi:10.9756/BIJSESC.8239

Bradley, P. (2013). Implications of Big Data Analytics on Population Health Management. *Big Data*, *1*(3), 152–159. doi:10.1089/big.2013.0019 PMID:27442197

Dhar, V. (2014). Big Data and Predictive Analytics in Health Care. *Big Data*, *2*(3), 113–116. doi:10.1089/big.2014.1525 PMID:27442491

Diesner, J. (2015). Small decisions with big impact on data analytics. *Big Data & Society*, *2*(2), 205395171561718. doi:10.1177/2053951715617185

Everett, C. (2015). Big data – the future of cyber-security or its latest threat? *Computer Fraud & Security*, *2015*(9), 14–17. doi:10.1016/S1361-3723(15)30085-3

(2014). Gartner warns of big data security problems. (2014). *Network Security*, *20*(6). doi:10.10161353-4858(14)70062-5

Gheyas, I., & Abdallah, A. (2016). Detection and prediction of insider threats to cyber security: A systematic literature review and meta-analysis. *Big Data Analytics*, *1*(1), 6. doi:10.118641044-016-0006-0

Ghiglieri, M., & Waidner, M. (2016). HbbTV Security and Privacy: Issues and Challenges. *IEEE Security and Privacy*, *14*(3), 61–67. doi:10.1109/MSP.2016.54

Herland, M., Khoshgoftaar, T., & Wald, R. (2014). A review of data mining using big data in health informatics. *Journal Of Big Data*, *1*(1), 2. doi:10.1186/2196-1115-1-2

Horowitz, B., & Lucero, D. (2016). System-aware cyber security: A systems engineering approach for enhancing cyber security. *Insight (American Society of Ophthalmic Registered Nurses)*, *19*(2), 39–42. doi:10.1002/inst.12087

Hoskins, M. (2014). Common Big Data Challenges and How to Overcome Them. *Big Data*, *2*(3), 142–143. doi:10.1089/big.2014.0030 PMID:27442494

Hussain, A., & Roy, A. (2016). The emerging era of Big Data Analytics. *Big Data Analytics*, *1*(1), 4. doi:10.118641044-016-0004-2

Jabeen, K. (2016). *Scalability Study of Hadoop MapReduce and Hive in Big Data Analytics*. International Journal Of Engineering And Computer Science; doi:10.18535/ijecs/v5i11.11

Juneja, P., & Kashyap, R. (2016). Optimal Approach For CT Image Segmentation Using Improved Energy Based Method. *International Journal of Control Theory and Applications*, *9*(41), 599–608.

Juneja, P., & Kashyap, R. (2016). Energy based Methods for Medical Image Segmentation. *International Journal of Computers and Applications*, *146*(6).

Kalra, S., & Sekhri, B. (2016). Security threats in big data. *Far East Journal of Electronics and Communications*, 623-633. 10.17654/ecsv3pii16623

Kashyap, R., & Gautam, P. (2013). Microarray Image Segmentation using Improved GOGAC Method. *Science and Engineering*, *2*(4), 67–74.

Kashyap, R., & Gautam, P. (2015, November). Modified region based segmentation of medical images. In *Communication Networks (ICCN), 2015 International Conference on* (pp. 209-216). IEEE. 10.1109/ICCN.2015.41

Kashyap, R., & Gautam, P. (2016, August). Fast Level Set Method for Segmentation of Medical Images. In *Proceedings of the International Conference on Informatics and Analytics* (p. 20). ACM. 10.1145/2980258.2980302

Kashyap, R., & Gautam, P. (2017). Fast Medical Image Segmentation Using Energy-Based Method. *Pattern and Data Analysis in Healthcare Settings*, 35-60.

Kashyap, R., & Tiwari, V. (2017). Energy-based active contour method for image segmentation. *International Journal of Electronic Healthcare*, *9*(2-3), 210–225. doi:10.1504/IJEH.2017.083165

Kshetri, N. (2014). The emerging role of Big Data in key development issues: Opportunities, challenges, and concerns. *Big Data & Society*, *1*(2). doi:10.1177/2053951714564227

Lafuente, G. (2015). The big data security challenge. *Network Security*, *2015*(1), 12–14. doi:10.1016/S1353-4858(15)70009-7

Lim, K. (2015). Big Data and Strategic Intelligence. *Intelligence and National Security*, *31*(4), 619–635. doi:10.1080/02684527.2015.1062321

Ma, X., & Wu, D. (2014). Research on Information Security Issues Facing the Era of Big Data. *Applied Mechanics and Materials*, *651-653*, 1913–1916. . doi:10.4028/www.scientific.net/AMM.651-653.1913

Miciuła, I., & Miciuła, K. (2015). The key trends for business building in the industry of big data. *Zeszyty Naukowe Uniwersytetu Szczecińskiego. Studia Informatica*, *36*, 51–63. doi:10.18276i.2015.36-04

Neela, K., & Kavitha, V. (2017). Enhancement of data confidentiality and secure data transaction in cloud storage environment. *Cluster Computing*. doi:10.100710586-017-0959-4

Ragesh, G., & Baskaran, K. (2016). Cryptographically Enforced Data Access Control in Personal Health Record Systems. *Procedia Technology*, *25*, 473–480. doi:10.1016/j.protcy.2016.08.134

Su, Z., & Xu, Q. (2017). Security-Aware Resource Allocation for Mobile Social Big Data: A Matching-Coalitional Game Solution. *IEEE Transactions on Big Data*, 1-1. 10.1109/tbdata.2017.2700318

Tromp, E., Pechenizkiy, M., & Gaber, M. (2017). Expressive modeling for trusted big data analytics: Techniques and applications in sentiment analysis. *Big Data Analytics*, *2*(1), 5. doi:10.118641044-016-0018-9

Wang, J., Crawl, D., Altintas, I., & Li, W. (2014). Big Data Applications Using Workflows for Data Parallel Computing. *Computing in Science & Engineering*, *16*(4), 11–21. doi:10.1109/MCSE.2014.50

Wang, L., Tasoulis, S., Roos, T., & Kangasharju, J. (2016). Kvasir: Scalable Provision of Semantically Relevant Web Content on Big Data Framework. *IEEE Transactions On Big Data*, *2*(3), 219–233. doi:10.1109/TBDATA.2016.2557348

Wang, Y. (2016). Big Opportunities and Big Concerns of Big Data in Education. *TechTrends*, *60*(4), 381–384. doi:10.100711528-016-0072-1

Win, T., Tianfield, H., & Mair, Q. (2017). Big Data Based Security Analytics for Protecting Virtualized Infrastructures in Cloud Computing. *IEEE Transactions on Big Data*, 1-1. 10.1109/tbdata.2017.2715335

Wu, Z., & Chin, O. (2014). From Big Data to Data Science: A Multi-disciplinary Perspective. *Big Data Research*, *1*, 1. doi:10.1016/j.bdr.2014.08.002

Yang, J., & Yecies, B. (2016). Mining Chinese social media UGC: A big-data framework for analyzing Douban movie reviews. *Journal of Big Data*, *3*(1), 3. doi:10.118640537-015-0037-9

KEY TERMS AND DEFINITIONS

Big Data Security Issues: Security and insurance issues are enhanced by speed, volume, and collection of enormous data, for instance, immense-scale cloud establishments, not too bad assortment of data sources and setups, spilling nature of data getting, and high volume between cloud developments.

Cryptography: It is the training and investigation of concealing data. It is once in a while called code; yet, this is not by any means a right name. It is the science used to endeavor to protect data mystery and present day cryptography is a blend of arithmetic, software engineering, and electrical designing. Cryptography is utilized as a part of ATM (bank) cards, PC passwords, and shopping on the web.

Data Security: Data insurance, in like manner called information security, is the piece of information advancement (IT) that game plans with the limit an affiliation or individual needs to make sense of what data in a PC system can be bestowed to outsiders.

Chapter 16
The Impact of Big Data Analytics and Challenges to Cyber Security

Anandakumar Haldorai
Akshaya College of Engineering and Technology, India

Arulmurugan Ramu
Bannari Amman Institute of Technology, India

ABSTRACT.

In order to scrutinize or evaluate an extremely high quantity of an ever-present and diversified nature of data, new technologies are developed. With the application of these technologies, called big data technologies, to the constantly developing various internal as well as external sources of data, concealed correlations between data can be identified, and promising strategies can be developed, which is necessary for economic growth and new innovations. This chapter deals with the analysis of the real-time uses of big data to both individual persons and the society too, while concentrating on seven important areas of key usage: big data for business optimization and customer analytics, big data and healthcare, big data and science, big data and finance, big data as enablers of openness and efficiency in government, big data and the emerging energy distribution systems, and big data security.

INTRODUCTION

Big data analysis has not been entirely new to the world as it has been around the corner and discussed by a lot of analytics. Though it is been viewed or thought to be a highly sensitive buzzword, big data analytics is just a means to bird's view of extremely large data to identify concealed patterns, new correlations, preference of the customers, marketing trends or priority, and other business-related information. Various business corporate structures are bound to take a leap in their decisions to maintain their stand in the highly competitive business world and they have to definitely control their data to develop strategies that can be put into actions (Xia, Liu, Lee, & Cao, 2016). The last few years have seen a major explosion in the quantity of data and the variety of it generated by individuals and about them. Such a

DOI: 10.4018/978-1-5225-4100-4.ch016

huge data is easily copied at a very low price and is conveniently stored in public databases where they are easily accessed through the Internet.

As per the IBM estimation which is released recently, an awesome amount of 2.5 billion Gigabytes (GB) of data are produced every day all of the world and this volume are ever growing every minute. And what more to add to this along with the Web 2.0 applications, the literally baseline cost of computational storage, the fast-evolving of entirely new range of computing prototypes like cloud computing, the field of artificial intelligence and data mining which is in the process of major breakthrough innovations (Li, Tang, & Xu, 2016), all of which join hands with an extremely wide range of sensor endowed and Internet-friendly mobile instruments helps greatly in enabling the big data phenomenon on itself. The term big data by itself still do not have a strict definition but is widely used to explain the magnanimous development and feasibility and the varied nature of data and the rate of momentum at which these data (different nature, format, and origin) are created and transported.

The NIST (National Institute of Standards and Technology) promoted a feasible definition for big data in cooperate with major areas like Velocity (data speed), Volume (data volume), and the Variety (data source). Big data is entirely different than conventional data warehousing and the other areas of analysis (Jiang & Wang, 2016) of business intelligence which has been in the scenario for quite some time. An unsurpassable amount of big data is quite unstructured and they comprise of literally raw data which is created with an increasing speed unlike anything earlier.

Today's real-time analysts are continuously able to wring out highly difficult patterns, identify correlations and pull out information that is valuable from collections of real-time data which are the cross-domain in nature. This is done with the use of technologies that are high in performance, storage infrastructures that are nominal in pricing, statistical correlation algorithms and strong techniques in data mining (Bhatt, Dey, & Ashour, 2017). The examples of big data sources are quite rich and varied in nature. They range from big corporate companies' Intranets, government directories which are online, the enormous search data, mobile communication finds, the users' data of their live interactions on social communication platforms, as well as the cyber physical systems like the ITS or intelligent transport system, smart energy distribution, smart cars, ultra modern home equipments which merge into the various home entertainment needs as well as domestic appliances to house security devices which have applications that use face, emotion recognition and motion detectors (Shrivastava et al., 2011).

This is a fast-growing trend which is highly used in various services which affect our day to day life and has a great impact on the socio-economic scenario. The big data analysts are derive and relate algorithms and make use of the artificial intelligence which uncovers concealed insights from a large amount of collected data for different areas of life. They range from decision optimization from the given data which can be utilized in the police force by the practical strategic assessment which helps to decrease the public crimes, and in the medical environment, patient's hazard to certain diseases are calculated along with the spreading of contagious diseases. It also helps to understand the nature of human reactions and consequences in typical socio-technical situations. These days the acquiescence of data is a form of currency and is a rich and rare commodity. The holding of such big data reduces to face new privacy challenges of individuals and society in whole as these accumulated data are linked to other databases as well. Based on this big data, its storage, analytics, and decisions which are automated through computational algorithms make a heavy impact on individuals and society and it also poses a great threat to the basic rights on various platforms like unfair discrimination, prejudicial outcomes, and many personal issues.

RELATED REVIEWS

Today's world of business and institution is certainly data driven. By and through, the usage of big data technology and its extensive reach makes a significant impact on productivity, innovation and economic growth. This enables both the society and businesses to benefit extensively.

Big Data for Business Optimization

Using big data is the iconic cornerstone and the key to a new business era, as this means personalized service in delivery of business and the same could do wonders for the marketers and the business pioneers (Shamoto, Shirahata, Drozd, Sato, & Matsuoka, 2016). The hidden patterns can be isolated and viewed by the business analysts and highly in-depth knowledge from the different sources both internal and external data is extracted from the assimilation of both the advanced analysis of big data and the modern warehouse data platforms. The big data knowledge thus acts as leverage to the business leaders as they continuously add more intelligence to their processes, their operational efficacy is greatly improved, and the end results in gaining the advantage in their business competition. The interlinking of the large volume of data which is heterogeneous and extremely complex along with the externally available growing amount of big data leads the business pioneers and their analysts to shortlist and zoom down to optimize the various strategic plans in advertisements as well as marketing (Wu, Zhu, Wu, & Ding, 2014). They also help in knowing the exact needs of the customers, their usage, buying trend and also the new developing patterns can be identified at the very early onset itself.

Most of the online, as well as other company retailers, are relying greatly on these big data technology to sort out their clients and customers' history of purchase, other transactions and inventory to their databases in order to

1. Gather a higher knowledge about their clients,
2. Deliver personalized goods, service and commendable guidance to their existing and potential clients,
3. Identification of changes in client-based needs.

With the help of the growing amount of data of the customers who rely on their mobile devices or smart devices for all their purchase, transactions and usage of electronic cards, and making use of the OSN or social networks where they register their views and share their intimate and personal ideas and whereabouts, allow the marketing personnel of most of the companies to gain leverage with simple analytic technology to reach out to the client with the exact need during the exact time and phase of life. This could be seen very well in the near future as its course has already been set into motion. This means a healthy situation in competitive business intelligence and the continuance of a business is kept stable for a reasonable future keeping in mind the changes in technology and persistent market needs.

Big Data and Big Science

Science could be influenced to change with the help of highly potential big data. The future of the data-intensive science is molded greatly with the developments that are seen in conventional decade. The major areas of computer model along with difficult and practical analytics coupled with the persistent growth in quantity and variety of data derived from different databases like health and medical data, internet browsing and searching pattern data, security and surveillance video data, genomic data, observatories which provide data of the images of the earth, sensor networks, wire free networks, as well as mobile devices help in the growth of the big data as well as its importance in the field of science (Suganya & Anandakumar, 2013).

Virtually a new idea to tackle the challenges of exploration and invention in the field of science looms intensively with the future of data-intensive science in use. The ubiquitous volume of data researched allows a good amount of leverage and needs new simulations, computations, tools, and technology for data management. This approach of data-intensive science allows a new lease of promise in the integration of various features of life in physical and social sciences. This also covers areas of application right from earth computations, genomics, nature and environmental studies, to the ends of computed social research studies. All this is done with the pure aim and hope that mankind will be better enabled and usage of data-intensive study or science will meet out at least a few of the challenges that pose globally like global warming, pandemics, efficacy in delivering and usage of better energy resources, as well as monitoring of global health amongst various other matters.

Big Data in Medicine and Health Care

The healthcare industry, on the whole, has started its reliance in all wakes of the healthcare department like that of monitoring of the public healthcare, delivery, and research of the healthcare industry towards big data. The growing dependence on information technology, the industry's stakeholders and its financial data to be collected, develop and inter distribute numerous data through the systems which adds up to the biological sample data of the person, medical imaging data, patient insurance and claims, medical prescriptions, health notes and other medical related statistics (Anandakumar, & Umamaheswari, 2017a). In the healthcare industry, keeping record of all the above said data has been done through the age, but what is new is the a) the ability to interlink both the internal and external health details when putting on whole allows to develop a pattern in the geographic, behavior and health fitness over a higher quantity of human health data allows to form a pattern and for better understanding of the healthcare industry of a particular geographical location and its people. b) This will help in aiding better understanding of research, exploration new medicinal values and controlled observation of concealed health trends in a particular society and will definitely allow better medical products and service to them.

Big Data in Marketing Economic Services

Big data related technology plays an exorbitant role in financial institutions and its market which has the fastest growth in IT department. The technology is used mainly in the compilation and analyzing high volume of financial data of both personal and economic in nature from live streams of finance like that of both the stock and share markets. This helps to have a clear idea of the risks and challenges faced by the complex system of finance and its possibility of newer investments (Kaseb, Mohan, Koh, & Lu, 2017). These last years, the insurance and credit companies are capitalizing on the IT field and its developments to gain fast access to analyze through social network data. They can go back and find out the complex designs which help to identify fraudulent activities (Yang, Wang, Song, Yang, & Patnaik, 2018).

This financial big data implementation helps in making otherwise hard decisions in newer market areas. Their source data are analyzed, viable and profitable patterns which may not be able to track will be revealed and they would allow valuable knowledge to foresee changes in stock markets and take revolutionary decisions which would have a greater impact in the financial market and institutions.

Big Data in Energy Distribution Environment

Emergence of smart grids in the Energy Distribution Systems is another new field in which the big data analysis remains to gather momentum in its usage. The data-driven techniques and its analytical devices use the smart meters, secure field devices, IT components which latest energy configurations which help in the compilation of newer data. The practical and real-life compilation and scrutinizing big data help the energy sector to come to a conclusion to develop better means in generating power, its supply, distribution, and transmission.

Big Data in Government Sector

The monumental decision of the government sector to display big/open data in the past decade had seen a great impact all over. A great volume of public details like the population census, crime details, real-life traffic status, healthcare data, meteorological statistics has been all over the Internet for public viewing. This is rather done to keep open end accountability and transparency of data which would improve the government respect among the public. The government hopes that by allowing this easy access and use will create a formidable economic growth and create new innovations by the private parties and commercial agencies (Lecuyer, Spahn, Geambasu, Huang, & Sen, 2017). This data provided freely by the government proves to a rich source of monumental data mine. As the British government foresees, this data can be exploited both by the government organizations and individual to unimaginable heights. This ubiquitous amount of poorly used government data will allow the private and other agencies to make use of latest techniques in data processing and analysis and they will be cross-linked to help improve governments' operational efficacy and cost reduction. A $100 billion dollars per annum is saved from the European public sector by disabling the potentiality of big data in its efficacy in operation. The same is expected in other areas as well. In private sectors, for example, the real estate scenario will be changing greatly with its knowledge of the available property, its location and value along with its criminal data. They will be better equipped to advise their customers about where to invest and where not to (Kimbahune, Deshpande, & Mahalle, 2017).

Detecting Cyber Crime With Big Data

Cybercrime is one of the latest criminal scenarios which affect both the public, private and personal area of oneself. Taking up against this crime needs a lot of analysis and a sure knowledge of all the possible evidential tools, making the exact and detailed prediction about the activities of the criminals. The criminals' behavior and their flexible adapting ability to changing and challenging measures should be taken into account. The cyber security personnel or information officers take a great amount of exercise to constantly oversee and secure their corporate companies against these high techno-savvy cybercriminals who evolve constantly in their criminal activities and threats (Park, Chung, Khan, & Park, 2017). Due to this growth rate of cyber crime the private companies tend to move slowly and surely to use big data analytical devices and technology to safeguard themselves. The changing trends of malicious attacks by these cyber criminals and their activities which are deeply hidden are identified. Their pattern of activity, motivation, and intentions are detected and continual supports of insight into security details are thus provided. Also, these type of data is inter-shared among other corporate companies as well as cross-border interstate and inter-country knowledge is shared to identify and reduce the cybercrime rate. This also helps to identify any network activities of similar types across various state and country jurisdictions. This compilation of big data and its analysis of security and information satisfy the craving of the law makers and its enforcement agencies for new information from different sources such as the Internet usage, mobile compatible wireless networks, financial data, travelers' data, and many other means like surveillance videos, satellite images and the like of them. When all these data are cleverly compiled and put together for the analytical purpose, the security personnel are able to detect the criminals' behavioral patterns, their identities, and much more insight (Chowdhuri, Dey, Chakraborty, & Baneerjee, 2015).

REAL-TIME PROBLEMS AND CHALLENGES OF BIG DATA

There is no doubt that the individual personalities, companies, societies, organizations, government and non-government sectors receive a great deal of positive opportunities with the use of big data techniques and its various tools but on the other hand, there is also a query on much more important issues of privacy and ethics. The big data's analytical devices or mechanisms and configurations will have a greater effect which may be negative to the privacy aspect, both legally and morally (Zhang, Shang, Lin, Li, & Tan, 2017). This will be a definite hurdle to the potentiality of the big data theory which has to be foreseen at this juncture.

Challenges in Big Data Security and Privacy

Usage of big data analytical tools on various grounds such as financial, economic, social, and other transactional definitely paves the way to the loss of civil rights as there is the complete deprivation of individual autonomy and privacy. From this aspect, they lose the liberty to maintain control or monitor their private data and prevent any misuse and/or abuse by cybercriminals, data analysts though the utility, growth, and innovation depends on big data preservation and use. The given below areas pose a few relative threat to the concept of big data's privacy and security.

Increased Prospective of Sensitive Data

While the increased amount of data is stored, accessed and shared online through internet by the third parties, the chance of the breach of data is also increased. So there arises an immeasurable list of queries regarding personal data's access, storage, and usage which is of paramount importance.

There are Two Different Opponent Components in Unauthorized Access as Follows

The initial adversary likes to enter into the database of raw data with a plan to compromise the process of interpretation or analysis. This is done by processing wrong data into the database or takes over the immense volume of identity or financial data which are highly sensitive. The other adverse act is to act upon already analyzed databases and steal the actions and intelligence of the legal analysts of the big data (Schmidt, Chen, Matheson, & Ostrouchov, 2017). To perform this breach of privacy in data, both the software and the hardware of these data platforms are scrutinized and their flaws are used.

Therefore the large data infrastructures like the cloud platforms and the data centers which are open to attack are largely protected from security breach and malware attacks. These are the places where all the original information and knowledge are stored highly sensitive data. An individual may suffer from identity exposure, confidential data like credit, debit card details, financial transactions while a company's breach would lead to grave damage to its brand image, loyalty of the partners and its consumers, loss of share market value, intelligence data, and penalties legal in nature due to non compliance of privacy regulations.

Loss of Personal Data in Individual Control

The process of big data technology is ever growing in nature and so the collection of data, its sharing and processing have become very difficult to control the privacy of an individual's personal data. The real reason at the back of this issue is as follows:

1. In the large scenario of big data sets, the information technology infrastructure processes multiple individuals' data by collecting and storing to make an inference. This is not in the hands of the individual.
2. The concept of big data's need to store all data in large measures and the basic privacy regulation needs of individuals and organizations are at war here. The minimization of data and principles of purpose binding are fundamental needs which pose to be highly contradictory and ridiculous to achieve simultaneously with the principles of big data performance.
3. There still remains a controversy over the ownership of data and intelligence derived from the big data analysis like that of the other online platforms of social media and e-commerce.

All the above-cited problems not only raise queries over the individual's right to monitor and control their personal data both implicitly and explicitly but also whether disclosure at proper juncture can be maintained. Also, it is difficult to know if the monitoring and control of private data can be achieved all through the lifetime of the data (Yusuf, Thomas, Spichkova, & Schmidt, 2017). Above all these, there is the major issue of the freedom to access data of individuals as per the norms of European Data Protection Directive which is closely connected to the individual privacy and control of their personal data.

Availability of Sensitive Datasets in Long-Term

The storage prices paired with developing needs to get back all the big data which is perennially legal and business oriented, permits the entire community of government, private organizations and individual researchers to assemble their large data platforms. In this database, only the identity attributes vary rarely, and the rest of the data regarding behavioral styles, lifestyle, personal view, and emotional feeling of an individual is recorded. All these data of an individual is possible (Zong, Ge, & Gu, 2017) to change many times in a person's lifetime. The social digitalization has definitely changed the meaning and discussion in connection with personal digital info. All these information are easy to duplicate and made available in cross-linked data platforms which are easily accessible online and the deletion of this data is not practically expected of. Big database of analytical intelligence that is inferred keeps on record permanently along with all the disclosures and silly blunders have done by the individual person online (Arulmurugan, Sabarmathi, & Anandakumar, 2017). These would rather not be remembered by anyone even after long period of time about the data subject.

Data Integrity and Provenance Issues

All the applications that are enabled by big data are rich in information and sensitive in context. This frequently needs a clear wisdom of the data subjects' genealogy and history, also keeping in view the issues regarding data quality, provenance, and integrity in connection to the proximity of raw and unreliable databases which poses a serious challenge to the analytics of big data. These data analysts do not have the means or method to have a stable integrity as well as quality data and also do not have clear idea to collect or recognize the pedigree nature of the big data and its context (Anandakumar, & Umamaheswari, 2017b). This leads to a difficult condition to derive optimization in businesses, to administer the monumental level of data received and also to run through any important operation or process which is data driven. The quality of the data, its provenance and also the integrity part of it determines the activity part of the analytics on how these data should be interpreted along with their results. Special accordance should be given to sensitive contexts like analysis of data dependency, decision optimization of both tactical and strategic in nature within the constraints of an organization, and as well as detection of criminal and malicious behavior by the law enforcement sector (Matallah, Belalem, & Bouamrane, 2017).

Data Inferences and Correlation

The entire accumulated personal data of individuals which are accessed from multiple sources helps in identifying concealed designs of big data. The big data already has the needed potency to increase the privacy implications of all the database correlations. In almost all the big data platforms or database, compilation and correlation of data from diverse nature is a strenuous operation which also adds up to the challenge of re-identification.

Lack of Transparency and Management

The major two key needs of legal procedures which are needed from the individuals or both the private/public organizations which help in collecting, processing and sharing PII or Personal Identifiable Information are the electric consent and the notion of Notice. All over the world, both these methods have an integral position in the legislation regulations of privacy and protection of data. Although this is common procedure, different countries and different jurisdictions may have multiple definitions to the notion of consent and notice as to the needs and interpretations of its subjects like their advocates, citizens, legislators and legal authorities.

Implementation of all these regulations is a risky task in the big data sets as there is a constant change from the individuals when data is collected where they have an option to check in/out of the privacy notice, to the exact point of time when the decision of consent made is already informed to them. In spite of all this clarity processed to the individual, the recent practice of the individuals seems to have lack of understanding and limited attention is paid to these consent notices during the installation of digital services (Matallah, Belalem, & Bouamrane, 2017). At a later point in time, the consequence of this particular action implies differently and the situation is further aggravated by the entire nature of big data processing. Also, all the details or information gathered at the point of data collection do not have the complete context inference and no prediction can be done based on this data as individuals do not and will not be aptly able to give consent beforehand itself. In addition to this, the different data and information gathered with the use of big data analytics, the numerous reasons, and contexts used by the persons in connection to their private data are far exceeding in nature and have nature to persistently undergo changes. Based on this pattern, it is highly difficult for the users to assess their needs beforehand and make a potential assessment when it is in connection with the analysis of cost-benefit and there is a slight tremor to allow consent to make use of their private details, comprise and reveal all of it for any other different purpose (Mukherjee, Dey, Kausar, Ashour, Taiar, & Hassanien, 2016).

In truth, the individuals are completely unaware of the process of the big data working techniques, their infrastructures, and the functioning of their algorithms. All this is done without the exact knowledge of the data subject. They do not know the context and concept of notice and management of the consent given by them and how it is made use of in the large-scale big data compilation and how it helps in making decisions. So a need for transparency and empowering knowledge to the subject should be done by data controllers of the big data scheme.

These constraints or restrictions in the big data collection of consent calls out for a change in policy with regard to give more clear support in consent specifics and clarification (i.e. signaling of consent decision), transparency in consent management, refining the process of consent or notice management, enforcing or implementation as well as the revoking the data-driven business models of the emerging big data technology (Goswami, Roy, Dey, & Chakraborty, 2017).

Big Accountability

The accountability of the big data algorithms also poses another major challenge along with that of transparency. Although the big data algorithms help to achieve beneficial outputs to the society, on the whole, do have disapproving or harmful effects to the individuals in par with the mounting profiles, surveillance was done and many more discriminatory methods. To react to these problems and finding redressal to all the issues makes it important to change the path from the current approach to algorithmic accountability. There should sufficient leniency and accessibility allowed to the data subjects so that they can personally counter check the information fed into the system for computation is accurate and as per their individual preference for privacy and conceding to the current norms that exist.

ETHICAL ISSUES AND SOCIAL CHALLENGES

Apart from the technological queries and legal challenges which have been discussed extensively in the above-mentioned sections, the moral and ethical implication of big data analytics is yet another huge hurdle that has to be completely addressed to. The following are a few of the issues listed (Yamin, & Sen, 2018).

Issue of Power and Information Asymmetry

Information asymmetry is nothing but the business environments wherein one of the parties have more information and information is nothing but power ready to be used. For example, in a retail business transaction, the buyer has relatively less and few experience compared to the retailer who stands in the business for quite a long time. This knowledge of the retailer about the exact details about the availability, quality and prevailing rates of the goods and the ability to assess market value through long experience is extremely more than that of the buyer. The buyer has to rely on his limited knowledge and peer lent feedback and accepts the retailer's demands. This asymmetry in information permits a selected few to withhold power against the majority of the common with the aid of big data. The larger public or individuals do not have the access to this type of knowledge and this develops into a situation wherein power is accumulated between the state or the respective big business centers and the people or the respective customers. When this amount of unprecedented data is accrued and the ability to manipulate information about citizens and clients is allowed or accessed by the larger organizations, this might lead to having private and selfish agenda, and when authoritarian government bodies or politicians who are intrusive might do away with unwarranted societal control, and unimaginable scale of negative impact is bound to the democracy of many countries there in igniting great harm on the whole.

Big Surveillance

Surveillance is another great field wherein big data technology has its playground. There is a great need for the continuous growing and system based surveillance both offline and online. These are not just used by the law governing bodies and intelligence sectors but also by individuals and business institutions on a commercial basis. The algorithms used by big data and its exceptional infrastructure are used online by many service providers commercially. They, in turn, compile and scrutinize the high volume of information about customer needs and preference much better and in turn help to improve their services for higher client-friendly services and helps in targeted commercial ads. This constant and continuous surveillance over the customers helps them to amass valuable knowledge on the customers' needs, bias, preference, spending habits, interests in social interactions and places visited, daily routines, browsing history, brand preference and continue in all walks of life in a person. Nothing is a secret anymore and all this collection turns out to be the digital treasure trove to the data controller and knowledge definitely turns out to be power. Making use of this digital dossier of individuals, spy sectors of both private and government intelligence derive sensitive knowledge about the selected personalities and help to keep a tab on them through the internet in reality.

Social Sorting and Social Control

Conventionally it is said that the powerless segments of the population and the minority sector needs to be kept in solidarity and they require protection. But with the big data analytics detailing, all these info is accessible to only a select few in power and so the security, privacy, fairness, and morality of all this becomes questionable. Big data permits untoward discriminatory activities aimed at particular individuals and this is made extremely easy with predictable accuracy. Though the positive nature of big data technology allows compilation and analysis of vast amount of data to help in improved efficacy in operations, decision making and provide services to the specific needs of the people, this type of knowledge tends to be used to discriminate the same public if allowed in wrong hands (Anandakumar & Umamaheswari, 2017c). At times when there is discrimination of pricing is there and few other aims like law enforcement, customer scoring, and personal and group behaviors are identified, they could be treated badly and completely stopped in public scenarios. Advanced mathematics models aid in understanding both the differences and similarities of individuals and groups and also help in categorizing them into various cadres. In case used negatively, these poor individuals may face the wrath of discrimination but are kept in dark against why they have been in such state and also do not possess any means to save themselves. In the fields of the healthcare community and insurance companies, they make use of the big data technology to perfection. They identify the entire patients' list of data, their sickness oriented internet browsing history, patients' online group discussions and all these may actually provide better insight and services to the individual. But it also allows them to discriminate certain persons due to their sex and gender biased orientation (Elhayatmy, Dey, & Ashour, 2017).

Moreover, in real estate field, data regarding property and crime statistics revealed by governmental bodies help them to plot the area and thereby discriminate poor people's livelihood and their residential area go down in value. This technique is majorly used by the sophisticated chain of hotels, airline companies for collection and analyzing the extensive volume of data with regard to rooms, seats that are available, their rates and demand in particular. These findings allow them to make variations in price and availability to increase their profits. These particular environments suggest the consumer's interest to spend towards a necessary service or computational skill. They also dispense with scores that are creditworthy which is definitely based on big data models who have all the necessary data about the person's age, sex, religion, income, race, medical conditions, geographical location and their habit of purchase. At this particular point itself, the consumer is discriminated for better or worse and neatly put under the specific category that is treated differently.

In connection with the law enforcement sector or agencies, big data analysis place and divide the community into various segments and without confirmed knowledge, many correlations and inferences are derived. Racial profiles are created thus to encourage the dark nature of preventive policing. They also raise concerns about civil rights and negative stereotypes are thus perpetuated.

CASE STUDY ANALYSIS

NTT DATA Telecommunication Company Case Study for Big Data Analytics

NTT DATA is a leading national service provider of wireless voice, messaging and data services capable of reaching over hundreds million users. NTT DATA engaged with the customer to upgrade their BI systems and revitalized their architecture to increase BI adoption and user acceptance. Currently supporting the application development for all their BI and Data warehouse systems across platforms

NTT DATA faced many business problems including Lack of Reporting in Finance, logistics and point of sales, Low customer service, Inability to track and capture e-commerce and telesales, Supply & Demand Variations, Outdated system versions, Redundant Data, Too many user security Roles, Lack of better data exchange and collaboration.

Big data Analytics can be improved with Upgrade to BW 7.0 & Revitalize, Migrate to Business Objects XI 3.1, Optimize Data models / Universes, Re-design of security, P.I used to connect POS Bwand 3rd party tools.

After upgrade their system to big data analytics and improved 35% reduction in data models, 70% reduction in user roles, Reduce data redundancy, Single version of truth, Optimized BI Security, BI Standardization, Increase in tele & E-commerce sales by 21% annually, Reduce the effort of online order system by 85%, Store/Article analytics, Event Analytics, Cashier analytics.

ZIONS Bancorporation

Big Data analytics used for security purposes n a recently published case study, Zions Bancorporation announced that it is using Hadoop clusters and business intelligence tools to parse data more quickly than with traditional SIEM tools. In their experience, the quantity of data and the frequency analysis of events are too much for traditional SIEMs to handle alone. In their traditional systems, searching among a month's load of data could take between 20 minutes and an hour. In their new Hadoop system running queries with Hive, they get the same results in about one minute (Mythili & Anandakumar, 2013).

The security data warehouse driving this implementation not only enables users to mine meaningful security information from sources such as firewalls and security devices but also from website traffic, business processes and other day-to-day transactions.

This incorporation of unstructured data and multiple disparate data sets into a single analytical framework is one of the main promises of Big Data.

HP Labs

Routinely Enterprises collect and process terabytes of security-relevant data like networking events, software applications, and action events of people for various reasons. This includes regulatory compliance requirements and post forensic analysis. But drastically, this volume of data becomes extremely overwhelming where these enterprises only store the data, rather do anything useful with this data. An estimate states that HP currently (in 2013) generates 1 trillion events per day or roughly 12 million events per second. This amount will grow as enterprises enable event logging via dynamic sources, hire huge employees, deploy more devices, and run parallel software. Prevailing analytical techniques do not work efficiently at this scale and typically produce so many false positives such that their capability is undermined. This problem becomes even worse as enterprises move towards cloud architectures and collect huge data. This results in deriving less actionable information as more data is being collected (Kamal, Ripon, Dey, Ashour, & Santhi, 2016).

An effort in recent research at HP Labs aims to move towards a scenario where more data leads to better analytics and more actionable information. Algorithms and systems are designed and implemented in order to identify actionable security information from large enterprise data sets and drive false positive rates down to a manageable level. The more the data that is to be collected, the more valuable information can be derived from that data. Despite, many challenges must be overcome to realize the actual capability of Big Data analysis. Among these challenges there prevail privacy, legacy and technical aspects regarding scalable data collection, transport, storage, analysis, and visualization. Despite the challenges, the group at HP Labs has successfully addressed various Big Data analytics for security challenges, some of which are highlighted in this section.

At first, a large-scale graph interpretation was undertaken to identify malware-infected hosts in an enterprise network and the malicious domains accessed each enterprise hosts. A host-domain access system was constructed graphically from large enterprise data sets by adding edges between every host in the enterprise and the domains visited by the host. The graph was then seeded with minimal ground truth information from a black list and a white list, and belief propagation was used to estimate the likelihood that a host or domain is malicious. Experiments over 2 billion HTTP request dataset was collected in this huge enterprise and a 1 billion DNS request data set was collected at an ISP and a 35 billion network intrusion detection system alert data set collected from over 900 enterprises worldwide indicates high true positive rates and low false positive rates can be achieved with minimum amount of truth information that is, having limited data labeled as normal events or attack events used to train anomaly detectors.

CONCLUSION

The imminent value of Big Data Analytics has been proved profoundly as global wide business opportunities have opened up ensuring new future and also thereby assuring a great deal of security too. The knowledge that has been revealed through big data has proven to easily convert into valuable business. Decisions that are highly effectual could be made with the available data analysis techniques and tactical data administration by the corporate organizations. As an emerging data analyst, one should be thoroughly equipped to make use of the three V's (volume, variety, and velocity) and should be updated with the latest and new technologies. Better understanding and implementation of this technology by the higher officials in administration aids in better and effective decision-making process. The future will see the rise of democracy in data analysis and big data will be widely used globally by the entire business organizations. To improve the effectiveness, it is necessary to construct strategies of big data, and paving way for futuristic and new databases. Kick starting powerful merging in the BDM organization, trained staff to follow clarity filled governing model, and to help in making business decisions in connection with the budget of the IT field. Though it is not an entirely new concept to compile, store and analyze the large volume of data, banking and finance industries tend to use algorithms that are complex in nature and many devices to deal with this nature of structured data and derive composite meaning from it. This has helped in the long run for many years so far. But the recent emergence of Big Data Analytics is seen to be replacing these old methods and puts on fresh face to the situation with more productive and effective results.

REFERENCES

Anandakumar, H., & Umamaheswari, K. (2017a). Supervised machine learning techniques in cognitive radio networks during cooperative spectrum handovers. *Cluster Computing*, *20*(2), 1505–1515. doi:10.100710586-017-0798-3

Anandakumar, H., & Umamaheswari, K. (2017b). An Efficient Optimized Handover in Cognitive Radio Networks using Cooperative Spectrum Sensing. *Intelligent Automation & Soft Computing*, 1–8. doi:10.1080/10798587.2017.1364931

Anandakumar, H., & Umamaheswari, K. (2017c). A bio-inspired swarm intelligence technique for social aware cognitive radio handovers. *Computers & Electrical Engineering*. doi:10.1016/j.compeleceng.2017.09.016

Arulmurugan, R., Sabarmathi, K. R., & Anandakumar, H. (2017). Classification of sentence level sentiment analysis using cloud machine learning techniques. *Cluster Computing*. doi:10.100710586-017-1200-1

Bhatt, C., Dey, N., & Ashour, A. S. (2017). Internet of Things and Big Data Technologies for Next Generation Healthcare. In *Studies in Big Data*. Springer International Publishing.

Chowdhuri, S., Dey, N., Chakraborty, S., & Baneerjee, P. K. (2015). Analysis of Performance of MIMO Ad Hoc Network in Terms of Information Efficiency. In *Advances in Intelligent Systems and Computing* (pp. 43–50). Springer International Publishing; . doi:10.1007/978-3-319-13731-5_6

Elhayatmy, G., Dey, N., & Ashour, A. S. (2017). Internet of Things Based Wireless Body Area Network in Healthcare. In *Studies in Big Data* (pp. 3–20). Springer International Publishing; .

Goswami, S., Roy, P., Dey, N., & Chakraborty, S. (2017). Wireless Body Area Networks Combined with Mobile Cloud Computing in Healthcare. In *Classification and Clustering in Biomedical Signal Processing* (pp. 388–402). IGI Global.

Jiang, Y.-G., & Wang, J. (2016). Partial Copy Detection in Videos: A Benchmark and an Evaluation of Popular Methods. *IEEE Transactions on Big Data*, 2(1), 32–42. doi:10.1109/TBDATA.2016.2530714

Kamal, S., Ripon, S. H., Dey, N., Ashour, A. S., & Santhi, V. (2016). A MapReduce approach to diminish imbalance parameters for big deoxyribonucleic acid dataset. *Computer Methods and Programs in Biomedicine*, *131*, 191–206. doi:10.1016/j.cmpb.2016.04.005 PMID:27265059

Kaseb, S. A., Mohan, A., Koh, Y., & Lu, Y.-H. (2017). Cloud Resource Management for Analyzing Big Real-Time Visual Data from Network Cameras. *IEEE Transactions on Cloud Computing*, 1–1. doi:10.1109/tcc.2017.2720665

Kimbahune, V. V., Deshpande, A. V., & Mahalle, P. N. (2017). Lightweight Key Management for Adaptive Addressing in Next Generation Internet. *International Journal of Ambient Computing and Intelligence*, *8*(1), 50–69. doi:10.4018/IJACI.2017010103

Lecuyer, M., Spahn, R., Geambasu, R., Huang, T.-K., & Sen, S. (2017). Pyramid: Enhancing Selectivity in Big Data Protection with Count Featurization. *2017 IEEE Symposium on Security and Privacy (SP)*. 10.1109/SP.2017.60

Li, T., Tang, J., & Xu, J. (2016). Performance Modeling and Predictive Scheduling for Distributed Stream Data Processing. *IEEE Transactions on Big Data*, 2(4), 353–364. doi:10.1109/TBDATA.2016.2616148

Matallah, H., Belalem, G., & Bouamrane, K. (2017). Towards a New Model of Storage and Access to Data in Big Data and Cloud Computing. *International Journal of Ambient Computing and Intelligence*, *8*(4), 31–44. doi:10.4018/IJACI.2017100103

Mukherjee, A., Dey, N., Kausar, N., Ashour, A. S., Taiar, R., & Hassanien, A. E. (2016). A Disaster Management Specific Mobility Model for Flying Ad-hoc Network. *International Journal of Rough Sets and Data Analysis*, 3(3), 72–103. doi:10.4018/IJRSDA.2016070106

Mythili, K., & Anandakumar, H. (2013). Trust management approach for secure and privacy data access in cloud computing. In *2013 International Conference on Green Computing, Communication and Conservation of Energy (ICGCE)*. IEEE.

Park, G., Chung, L., Khan, L., & Park, S. (2017). A modeling framework for business process reengineering using big data analytics and a goal-orientation. *2017 11th International Conference on Research Challenges in Information Science (RCIS)*. doi:10.1109/rcis.2017.7956514

Schmidt, D., Chen, W.-C., Matheson, M. A., & Ostrouchov, G. (2017). Programming with BIG Data in R: Scaling Analytics from One to Thousands of Nodes. *Big Data Research*, *8*, 1–11. doi:10.1016/j.bdr.2016.10.002

Shamoto, H., Shirahata, K., Drozd, A., Sato, H., & Matsuoka, S. (2016). GPU-Accelerated Large-Scale Distributed Sorting Coping with Device Memory Capacity. *IEEE Transactions on Big Data*, *2*(1), 57–69. doi:10.1109/TBDATA.2015.2511001

Shrivastava, G., & Bhatnagar, V. (2011). Secure Association Rule Mining for Distributed Level Hierarchy in Web. *International Journal on Computer Science and Engineering*, *3*(6), 2240–2244.

Suganya, M., & Anandakumar, H. (2013). Handover based spectrum allocation in cognitive radio networks. *2013 International Conference on Green Computing, Communication and Conservation of Energy (ICGCE)*. 10.1109/ICGCE.2013.6823431

Wu, X., Zhu, X., Wu, G., & Ding, W. (2014). Data mining with big data. *IEEE Transactions on Knowledge and Data Engineering*, *26*(1), 97–107. doi:10.1109/TKDE.2013.109

Xia, F., Liu, H., Lee, I., & Cao, L. (2016). Scientific Article Recommendation: Exploiting Common Author Relations and Historical Preferences. *IEEE Transactions on Big Data*, *2*(2), 101–112. doi:10.1109/TBDATA.2016.2555318

Yamin, M., & Sen, A. A. A. (2018). Improving Privacy and Security of User Data in Location Based Services. *International Journal of Ambient Computing and Intelligence*, *9*(1), 19–42. doi:10.4018/IJACI.2018010102

Yang, W., Wang, X., Song, X., Yang, Y., & Patnaik, S. (2018). Design of Intelligent Transportation System Supported by New Generation Wireless Communication Technology. *International Journal of Ambient Computing and Intelligence*, *9*(1), 78–94. doi:10.4018/IJACI.2018010105

Yusuf, I. I., Thomas, I. E., Spichkova, M., & Schmidt, H. W. (2017). Chiminey: Connecting Scientists to HPC, Cloud and Big Data. *Big Data Research*, *8*, 39–49. doi:10.1016/j.bdr.2017.01.004

Zhang, C., Shang, W., Lin, W., Li, Y., & Tan, R. (2017). Opportunities and challenges of TV media in the big data era. *2017 IEEE/ACIS 16th International Conference on Computer and Information Science (ICIS)*. doi:10.1109/icis.2017.7960053

Zong, Z., Ge, R., & Gu, Q. (2017). Marcher: A Heterogeneous System Supporting Energy-Aware High Performance Computing and Big Data Analytics. *Big Data Research*, *8*, 27–38. doi:10.1016/j.bdr.2017.01.003

Chapter 17
Security and Privacy Challenges in Big Data Environment

M. Manikandakumar
Thiagarajar College of Engineering, India

E. Ramanujam
Thiagarajar College of Engineering, India

ABSTRACT

In this information era, big data is revolutionizing business. The data are generated by each and every user from servers, terminals, smart phones, appliances, satellites, and a range of other sensors on vehicles: military, agriculture, and the like. Anything the end users does online can be traced, stored, and analyzed. It is also possible to analyze from various diverse sources such as social media postings, credit card or e-cash purchases, internet searches, mobile phone locations, etc. Users are willing to provide their private information, linked to their real-life identities, in exchange for faster or better digital services. But, the companies yet may not have the fundamental rights of the user from a security perspective. More risks are associated with big data security. The main purpose of this chapter is to explore the security concerns and privacy issues in big data environments.

INTRODUCTION

Almost all industries largely implementing the concept of Big Data to store peta bytes data for analyzing, marketing and research based on users perspective to earn superior insights concerning the customers and their business. Since many industries noticed that, storing confidential or private information of the end users in cloud storage (Manikandakumar et al., 2015) or in the dedicated server, those companies have the sole responsiveness for protecting private data from both a legal and a commercial perspective. As with all the new technologies, security and protection seems to be addendum at best. As the definition of Big Data (Gandomi & Haider, 2015), the breaches are also too large, with the possibility of high severe reputational hurt and legal consequence than these recent times.

The new types of data in the organizations that need to analyze the following.

DOI: 10.4018/978-1-5225-4100-4.ch017

- Web streams such as e-commerce, weblogs and social network analysis data.
- Business specific transaction data like Tele Caller records, Geo-spatial data, Temporal and Customer Relational Transaction data.
- Data generated from various types of sensor such as motion, weather, energy, wind, humidity, vibration, airflow, liquid flow, pressure and health-oriented sensors.
- Textual data from the large volume of archived documents, external sources or customer interaction data, e-mails, messages, and tweets.

According to a study by the Economist Intelligence Unit (Unit, 2007)

- Nearly 90% of Industrial experts and business leaders believe that the data is now the raw and fundamental source of production to business such as land, labor, and capital.
- Using Big data in businesses improves the performance by 26% and it is predicted that it may grow up to 41% in next few years.
- 58% of business sectors say that they are planning to increase the investment in big data over the next three years.

According to Gartner (Beyer, 2011)

- About 42% of Information Technology experts stated that, they had invested in big data technology or were planning to do so within a year.
- Organizations those integrate large volume, various information types and sources into a rational information management communications will outperform their industry peers by more than 20%.

Four V's

Big data involves the "four Vs" for the efficient storage of data - volume, velocity, variety and the value. When defining the Big Data it is common to discuss the three major V's: Volume, Velocity, and Variety.

Volume

The main characteristics of "Big" are the absolute volume of data to be stored. There is no effect focusing on minimum storage as the technology and the information utilized to rapidly increasing in a fraction of time even in seconds or lesser. Thomson Reuters (2010) quoted in their 2010 annual report that, the world was "awash with over 800 Exabyte of data growing". Likely another data storage company named EMC reveals it was about to 900 Exabyte and might raise up to 50% per every year.

Velocity

Big Data Applications used in research (Swan, 2013), telecommunications (Hashem et al., 2015), emergency care (Ramanujam et al. 2016; Padmavathi et al. 2015), Agriculture and the like has given much more attention to handling both real-time and simulated data for data access and processing. At the same time frequently received in a series manner also has to be processed. For an example, in telecommunication, the numbers of Short Messages, social media status update and tweets, e-commerce transactions, purchase through credit/debit card swipes are processed by a telecom carrier in every minute of a day.

Variety

Data is normally classified as structured, unstructured or semi-structured data. Big data not only covers "structured" data normalized into a fixed schema and exported from ERP or CRM (Manikandakumar et al., 2015) systems. It also includes semi-structured data, unstructured data such as images, e-mail messages, clippings, and videos. Not all these three Vs must apply for data to be called Big data. For example, data might need to be analyzed in real time, but be relatively small in volume and reside largely in structured formats.

The Fourth V: Value

What makes big data exciting is not the scale and diversity of the data, but the scale and diversity of the things that can do with it. That's why the concept of Big Data adds a fourth V. Big data can generate business value by supporting strategic decisions over the business, accurate predictions, expectations, detecting trends and anomalies and automating processes such as pricing or stock orders.

The Big-Data Lifecycle

Collection

Data from internal and external sources, owned or bought, in a variety of formats, to meet identified business needs. Data can exist in many disparate stores and across several domains and may need special processing during collection.

Aggregation

Organizing and storing data ready to be analyzed according to governance standards. Big data provides a complete centralized view of disparate data.

Processing

Processing includes predictive behavioral modeling, pattern recognition, and summary, producing insights to change business outcomes. Big-data analytics is often performed in cloud-based environments as they allow easy scaling of storage, give access to massive on-demand computing power and are isolated from business as usual workloads.

Sharing, Decision, Access, and Action

Getting the data to the right place so it can be used for a business advantage, through dashboards, data services, and reports to PCs and mobile devices. Cloud computing and web technologies have made it much easier to deliver information and tools to users wherever they are and whatever device they are using. Application programming interfaces (APIs) and services allow outputs from big-data analyses to be integrated into existing systems.

Big Data Specialization Skills Set

A data mart, warehouses, and Relational DataBase systems process the structured data and utilize a huge amount of data. Big Data is in need of high computational facilities such as Hadoop (White, 2012) and MapReduce (Dean et al., 2008) tools to process and generate outputs than the storage utilized. Also, there needs an expert with the specific technical skill set to work with the large volume of data. Lack of proficiency in big data analysis will lead to business failure. Hadoop is implemented to analyze the large set of structured and also the unstructured data. The MapReduce framework of Hadoop works against the difficulty of building web search indexes. MapReduce segregates the process on multiple resources for resolving the issues of huge data collections that not fit into a single resource. Integrating the Big Data techniques with Open source servers gives a cost-effective approach to Big data. Rapid use of Big data tools and the related technologies are increasing the claim for more specific tool skill sets. Statistical Engineers, Analysts, Knowledge Engineers, Predictors, Semantic Analyst, Text Analyst, Social Network Analyst, Data Dredgers are all in demand for this area. The principal aims of these persons are to proceed with the formatted and unformatted data to convey new business approach and intelligence. Professionals of various platforms are also highly in demand to secure, manage, optimize, and cluster and to implement the data in Hadoop. Skill-based training programme to enhance the platform professionalism offered by the providers like IBM, MapR, Cloudera to face the challenges.

Impacts of the Big Data on Information Protection

The impacts of big data in many of the companies are as follows,

- Frequent updates and patches of information.
- Data in transit and at rest.
- Latest analytical and logical workloads.
- Infrastructure necessities required for data engineers to perform analytical process.
- Software tools and other application platforms to collect and analyze big data.
- Multifaceted administrative schemes in large data platforms for providing the data to multiple data stores.
- Data transmission flow from analytical systems to data warehouses.
- Difficult environment for analytical due to multiple analytical stores
- Platform-specific storage space such as Hadoop Distributed File System (HDFS), Analytical RDBMS Columnar Data Store, or a NoSQL Graph database.

Big Data Technologies and Risks

Big Data extends the boundaries of current information security measures and delivers new challenges and issues. The various risks that are related with the Big Data techniques are,

- Any industries that are not well understood will introduce any vulnerability.
- Implementation of Big Data in open and free platforms may increase the probability of unrecognized backdoors and credentials.
- Regulation requirements have to be fulfilled, to access web logs and user audit trails.
- Chance for malevolent input and not enough data validation.
- It's difficult to ensure that all the data is viable when dealing with large amounts of unstructured information.
- Tracking and monitoring the origins of all that unstructured data is also hampered by the sheer volumes in play.
- User verification and access permissions to multiple data locations may not be addressed correctly.

NoSQL like non-relational database systems are analyzing actively, creating the process difficult for security solutions to balance with the ongoing demand. Few distributed systems need to be synchronized with multiple levels of protection. Data transfers in an automated manner need to be facilitated with high-security aspects which is not available nowadays. The unethical way of data mining and processing which includes collecting personal data without permission leads an overhead. Due to the vast amount of information available, thorough and periodical audits are not regularly performed in Big Data environment. Similarly, because of the huge size of big data, the origins of data are not tracked and monitored again and again.

In terms of security, big data may be viewed from two angles:

- Its potential to threaten the security of an enterprise, and measures which need to be taken to prevent this
- Its potential to contribute to the security of an enterprise, and finding ways to make this happen

Usage of open source in big data analysis and applications introduces another level of ambiguity with the potential for code tampering, the installation of backdoors for cyber-criminals to gain unwarranted access, and the assignment of default credentials which end users may neglect to change.

Cybersecurity and Data Privacy

Generating Decisions From Erroneous Data Patterns

Big data analytics deals with large volumes of data which involves more variables with the high probability of spurious patterns or correlations. Establishing relationship among the variables with absolute volume of sample data does not exist. Such results may confuse and misguide the decision making authorities which may lead the analytic managers in making erroneous decisions.

Limitations in using large datasets:

1. The predictive capability of analysts may lead to false confidence.
2. The victims can easily access, manipulate, misinterpret, or misuse the results given by the data analyst.

Data Dependency

The successfulness of decision making in business analytics can't be achieved at all times by only depending on data. Many factors beyond the data are critical as such as trust, respect, strategic goals and instinct when the analyst blindly rely on data. It is highly recommended to understand the data thoroughly. Without a deep knowledge of the associated context, analysts will fail to relate the data to the strategy.

New Security Requirements to Protect Information in Big Data Environments

Big Data Environments should able to define or may apply the following things to protect information with the new security requirements.

- Identify the files being loaded into a Big Data platform (e.g Hadoop HDFS) which may contain sensitive data and to know where it resides.
- Policies to encrypt sensitive data (structured and multi-structured Big data) in transit and at rest.
- Policies that redact the sensitive data at transit or at rest to store in a big data analytical store.
- Possible to encrypt and redact structured and multi-structured data at transit between data and traditional data stored during analytical processing.
- Control access to all sensitive data files stored in a file-based big data analytical store.
- Possible to monitor and maintain log all administrative activity associated with sensitive streams and data files in big data environments.
- Possible to control the user who creates and allow accessing the big data analytical sandboxes on big data analytical platforms. e.g. Hadoop HDFS and/or analytical DBMSs
- Possible to control the data sources loaded into a data stores and sandboxed for analysis and to log what sensitive data files are loaded and when.
- Possible to encrypt and /or redact the sensitive data brought into big data analytical data stores and sandboxes.
- Possible to control the analytical applications and its access to sensitive data streams and to report, the streams which were accessed by the name of the applications with time.
- Possible to control the MapReduce analytical applications which have access to sensitive data files in Hadoop and other NoSQL data stores and to report the files, where accessed by the name of the applications.
- Possible to secure, protect and audit all activity on sensitive big data irrespective of whether it is in test, development or production environments
- With respect to the use of analytics to help protect information the following requirements should be added
- Possible to leverage Big Data platforms and analytics to collect, monitor and analyze security information to help solve advanced security and risk use cases

Industries and institutions have to protect themselves against all kinds of security-relevant Big Data attacks. Identifying the anomalies in device behavior, identifying the anomalies in employee and contractor behavior, detecting the anomalies in the network, Assessment of network vulnerabilities and risks are the major tasks that have to be addressed in a proper manner.

Most of the cut off devices will always try to automatically steal the data. Monitoring systems has to be deployed to ensure the security of data from the inside victims.

Alarming notifications to the right people has sent when a malpractice occurs. Industries also have to secure themselves against all kind of data attacks.

Deploying Big Data for Security

Big Data style analysis detects and prevents advanced persistent threats, which plays a key role in identifying attacks and threats at the early stage by using the refined data pattern analysis. Also, the Big Data environment provides the chance to consolidate and analyze indexes automatically from various data sources which could enhance the Intrusion Detection System (IDS) and Intrusion Prevention System (IPS) via constant modification and effective analyzing of good and worst behavior. The organizational storage structure often reduces the efficiency of secure systems, so the companies should be attentive about the potential effectiveness of the Big Data style analysis can be weaken unless the companies address the issues on storage structure.

Big data technology may be used to provide a centralized storage facility for security event management. Alternatively, there are commercial deployments based on big data technology that can serve as replacements for traditional log management tools.

Cyber Security Approach on Big Data

1. Malware detection and analysis when malware becomes more ambiguous and persistent.
2. Macro trend analysis for analyzes malware movements at better understands and look forward to the direction of the threat landscape.
3. Measuring performance on detection of malware using hypothetical and statistical will provides the clear results.
4. Attribute oriented encryption *techniques and access rights permissions would be required to protect the sensational data.*

Security at Enterprise

With the peta byte levels of information collected from transaction records, website tracking, click streams, and social media analysis, organizations looking to gain insights from big data will typically turn to the remote storage, distributed computing power and hosted infrastructure of the cloud, rather than storing and analyzing everything in-house. So enterprise security for big data will have more of an application rather than the device-specific focus. Organizations should isolate devices and servers on their premises which house sensitive and critical data. Networks and systems should incorporate both Intrusion Prevention Systems and Intrusion Detection Systems. Monitoring regimes should include real-time security information and event management (SIEM).

Ownership Rights

Amongst the masses of unstructured data passing through an enterprise, the big data stream may contain person health information, financial records, social identifiable information, intellectual property, and so on. So an essential aspect of security lies in identifying and classifying these various forms of information and establishing their rights of ownership.

Big data security breaches have the potential to affect millions of people, so steps should be taken within the enterprise to minimize the risk. Unique identifiers must be removed from each data set and the information anonymized before it is stored.

Attribute Level Encryption

Access controls and security protections need to be applied at the data level rather than the infrastructure level in which the data is stored. Attribute level encryption is applied in accordance with the characteristics of the data being encrypted. Options such as Fully Homomorphic Encryption (FHE) may be exercised, to enable operations on encrypted data transferred to the cloud.

Generally there are five features distinguish big data security analytics.

Scalability

Scalability is one of the major key distinctive features of data analytics. These podiums must have the capability to accumulate data in near real time. Network traffic is continues streaming of data packets that should be analyzed as much fast as they are captured. Analysis tools cannot depend on a quiet period in network traffic to catch up on a backlog of packets to be analyzed.

It is important to understand that, the big data security analytics is not only just probing data packets in a stateless manner or carrying out deep packet analysis. These are important and necessary that the capacity to associate events across instant of time that is the key differentiator of big data analytics platforms. This means the flow of events logged by web server like devices.

Reporting and Visualization

The next vital function of big data analytical system is status reporting and support for further analysis. Security engineers and experts might have effective reporting tools to support operations and compliance reporting. Security uses preconfigured security indicators to provide high-level overviews of key performance measures. Both of these existing tools are necessary but not sufficient to meet the recent demands of big data.

Visualization techniques are highly needed to represent the data derived from big sources in such a way that they can be readily and rapidly identifies by security analyst. These visualization techniques are rightly used by sqrrl to assist analyst to understand difficult relationships in networked data across more number of entities such as web transactions and websites.

Persistent Big Data Storage

Big data security analytics gets its name because of the data storage and analytical facilities of these platforms which are differentiating them from other security techniques. These platforms employ big data storage systems, such as the Hadoop Distributed File System (HDFS) and longer latency archival storage. Back-end processing is done with Map Reduce, a well-established computational model for batch processing. While MapReduce is highly resistant to failure, it is at the cost of I/O-intensive processing. Long-term determined storage typically depends on relational or NoSQL databases. The platform assembles between an organization's non-relational data stores and the rest of its application environment. The security framework can consume data from a variety of sources and hence deduplicate attack notifications and associated information from their own custom data collection methods.

Information Context

As security event produces so much data, there is a risk of overwhelming analysts and other information security professionals and limiting their ability to discern key events.

Data without this kind of context is far less useful and can lead to higher than necessary false positives. Contextual information also improves the quality of behavioral analysis and anomaly detection. Contextual information can contain moderately static information, such as the fact that a particular employee works in a specific department. It also includes more dynamic information, such as typical usage patterns that may change over time.

Breadth of Functions

The last distinctive characteristic of big data analytical security is the span of functional security areas. Big data analytics used to gather data from different end devices, which is connected to a TCP or IP network through the Internet. These data source includes any devices ranges from handheld devices to Internet of Things (IoT) based networked devices. Like the physical systems and servers, big data security also must attend to software based security. Vulnerability measurement and assessments are used to establish any possible security weak points in the given environment.

The Differences of Big Data Security Analytics

Security analytics over big data differs from other forms of security analytics. The big data security approach requires scalability, integration tools, visualization of any data, contextual information importance and breadth of security functions.

WAYS TO STRENGTHENING BIG DATA SECURITY

A few recommendations to improve the Big Data Security includes,

- Isolation of devices and servers containing critical data.
- Center of attention on application functional security, rather than the device level security.
- Introducing real time security policy and relevant event management.
- Providing reactive and proactive security protection.

CONCLUSION

Big Data is a significant field of growth in the era of big data has been started. Now it is the time for scholarly identify and apply security involvements into Big Data because the consequences of data security and its infrastructures like policies and laws are not yet regularized. The most practical method to develop the advanced security and privacy in Big Data environment is the continual development of the antivirus and malware protection industries. A massive amount of antivirus providers offers a large number of solutions that addresses enhanced security against the security threats. Antivirus software providers need to generously swap over information about current Big Data security attacks and the industry heads need to work together to cope up with new kind of malicious software attacks. Big data analytics infrastructure can also use intrusion detection services that analyze system and environment behavior in order to spot possible malicious activity.

REFERENCES

Beyer, M. (2011). *Gartner Says Solving'Big Data'Challenge Involves More Than Just Managing Volumes of Data*. Gartner.

Borthakur, D. (2008). HDFS architecture guide. *Hadoop Apache Project*, 53.

Dean, J., & Ghemawat, S. (2008). MapReduce: Simplified data processing on large clusters. *Communications of the ACM*, *51*(1), 107–113. doi:10.1145/1327452.1327492

Gandomi, A., & Haider, M. (2015). Beyond the hype: Big data concepts, methods, and analytics. *International Journal of Information Management*, *35*(2), 137–144. doi:10.1016/j.ijinfomgt.2014.10.007

Hashem, I. A. T., Yaqoob, I., Anuar, N. B., Mokhtar, S., Gani, A., & Khan, S. U. (2015). The rise of "big data" on cloud computing: Review and open research issues. *Information Systems*, *47*, 98–115. doi:10.1016/j.is.2014.07.006

Manikandakumar, M., Mano Sharmi, K., & Shanthini Devi, S. (2015). Analyzing Spam Messages and Detecting the Zombies Using Spam Count and Percentage Based Detection Algorithm. *International Journal of Applied Engineering Research*, *10*(55), 1284–1289.

Manikandakumar, M., & Shanthini Devi, S., & VengaLakshmi, S. (2015). A Survey on Data Warehousing and Data Mining Technology for Business Intelligence. *International Journal of Applied Engineering Research*, *10*(77), 352–356.

Padmavathi, S., & Ramanujam, E. (2015). Naïve Bayes classifier for ecg abnormalities using multivariate maximal time series Motif. *Procedia Computer Science*, *47*, 222–228. doi:10.1016/j.procs.2015.03.201

Ramanujam, E., & Padmavathi, S. (2016). Multi-objective genetic motif discovery technique for time series classification. *International Journal of Business Intelligence and Data Mining*, *11*(4), 318–337. doi:10.1504/IJBIDM.2016.082214

Reuters, T. (2010). *Web of Science*. Retrieved from https://clarivate.com/products/web-of-science/

Swan, M. (2013). The quantified self: Fundamental disruption in big data science and biological discovery. *Big Data*, *1*(2), 85–99. doi:10.1089/big.2012.0002 PMID:27442063

Unit, E. I. (2007). *World investment prospects to 2011: Foreign direct investment and the challenge of political risk*. Academic Press.

White, T. (2012). *Hadoop: The definitive guide*. O'Reilly Media, Inc.

Chapter 18
Impact of Big Data on Security:
Big Data Security Issues and Defense Schemes

Kasarapu Ramani
Sree Vidyanikethan Engineering College, India

ABSTRACT

Big data has great commercial importance to major businesses, but security and privacy challenges are also daunting this storage, processing, and communication. Big data encapsulate organizations' most important and sensitive data with multi-level complex implementation. The challenge for any organization is securing access to the data while allowing end user to extract valuable insights. Unregulated access privileges to the big data leads to loss or theft of valuable and sensitive. Privilege escalation leads to insider threats. Also, the computing architecture of big data is not focusing on session recording; therefore, it is becoming a challenge to identify potential security issues and to take remedial and mitigation mechanisms. Therefore, various big data security issues and their defense mechanisms are discussed in this chapter.

INTRODUCTION

To harness the power of big data, one requires an infrastructure that can manage and process huge volumes of structured and unstructured data in real-time and can preserve data privacy and security.

Security management and data access are primary concerns for both persistent and moving data. Persistent data security is usually managed in layers: Physical, Network, Application, and at the database. Data moving between applications and organizations need additional security to protect the data in transit from unauthorized access.

The focus of this chapter is to high light the impact of security and privacy aspects on capacity and performance implications of big data solutions, which must be taken into account for such solutions to be viable. This chapter gives an overview of root causes for security and privacy challenges in big data and their consequences. It also describes the defense mechanism aspects that must be considered to make secured Big Data environment and suggests good practices to be followed for Big Data solutions, both now and in future.

DOI: 10.4018/978-1-5225-4100-4.ch018

BACKGROUND

What Is Big Data?

The Smartphones, Science facilities, Readers/ Scanners, Programs/ Software, Social media, and cameras are working as data generation points in Healthcare, Security Systems, Traffic Control, Manufacturing Sector, Sales, Sensors, Telecommunication, On-line gaming, Location-based services and Trading are leading to Big Data. The data generated and collected from different sources is doubling in every two years. The Big data become increasingly important in enterprises, government, and sciences. The process of capturing, storing, filtering, sharing, analyzing and visualizing this voluminous data itself is a challenge in Big Data. The purpose of Big Data is to generate value from stored large volumes of information by processing it using analytical techniques. The Big data helps in generating revenue, better services, strategic decisions, executive efficiency, specify needs, determine new trends, and flourish new products.

Characteristics of Big Data

Big data is characterized by 5 Vs: volume, velocity, variety, veracity and value. Volume represents huge data; velocity represents rapidity of data; variety indicates data collected from variety of sources with different data types; veracity defines consistency and trustworthiness of data; and value capture greater insights into data and supports in decision making from huge data sets. Defining characteristics of Big data will be helpful in obtaining hidden patterns available in data.

Big Data Types

Big Data includes structured, semi-structured and unstructured data.

- **Structured Data:** Represents the formal structure of data associated with relational databases or any other form of data tables and which can be generated by humans or software or computers. Structured data are often managed with SQL. Structured data are easy to input, query, store, and analyze. Examples of structured data include numbers, words, and dates.
- **Semi-Structured Data:** Also called self-describing structure, contain marks such as tags to separate semantic elements. Also, the records and fields of data can be arranged in hierarchies. XML, JSON, EDI, and SWIFT are few examples of this kind of data.
- **Unstructured Data:** Has no pre-defined data model. Now a day 80% of data accounts for unstructured data in any organization and which includes data from e-mails, video, social media websites and text streams.

Similar to structured data, this unstructured data can be generated by human or machine. Human-generated data includes text messages, e-mails, and social media data. Machine generated data includes radar and sonar data, satellite images, security, surveillance, traffic videos and atmospheric data. Often data are generated by a combination of these three groups.

Uses of Big Data

According to McKinsey Global Institute (2011), the proper management of Big Data will lead to many advantages, such as:

- Creates transparency by making relevant data readily accessible.
- Enables experimentation to expose variability, discover needs, and improve performance. i.e Data can be analyzed to identify variability in performance and to understand the root causes.
- Segments customers to customize their actions and tailors products and services to meet their specific needs.
- Replaces/supports human decision-making with Machine Learning algorithms in order to minimize risk.
- Innovates new business models, products, and services.

Big Data Classification

Big data can be categorized into ten types based on data type, data source, content format, data usage, data consumer, data analysis, data frequency, data store, data processing propose, and data processing method and is shown in Figure 2.

Issues With Big Data

Need of Privacy and Security Implications and Analysis in Big Data

To a huge degree, Big Data includes reuse of information. But, it requires a sensible framework for its data access ensuring confidentiality due to the following reasons:

Lack of Transparency

Absence of openness and information on how data is compiled and used is resulted in no control over on our own data. For example, an average Internet user has almost no knowledge of how the web-based promoting market works and how their own information might be gathered and used by an extensive variety of business.

Data Compilation May Uncover Sensitive Information

Through the Big Data tools, it is possible to identify a person's inherent qualities related to politics, health etc.

Big Data also involves challenges in terms of data security which may likewise be significant for the protection of privacy. Cases of such security challenges incorporate utilization of several infrastructure layers with a specific end goal to process Big Data, new sorts of the framework to deal with the

Figure 1. Big Data value chain

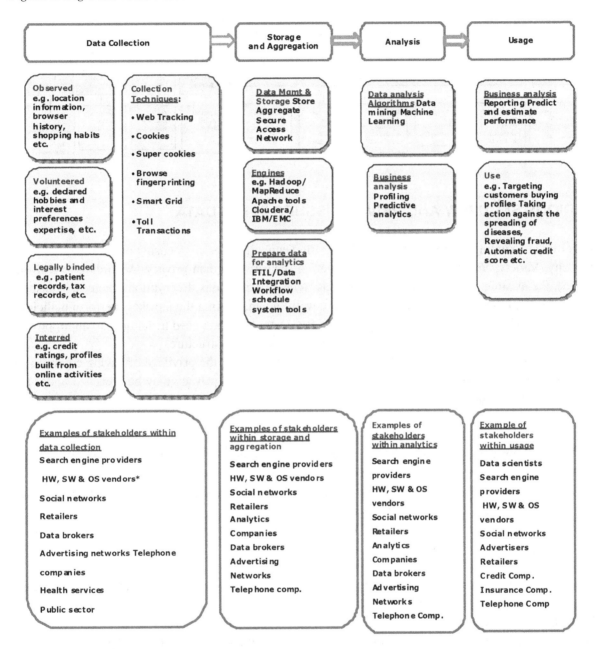

tremendous stream of information and in addition non-versatile encryption of large data sets. Further, a data breach may have more severe consequences when enormous datasets are stored. According to McKinsey Global Institute (2014), enterprises that acquire and maintain large sets of personal data must be responsible stewards of that information.

Figure 2. Big Data classification

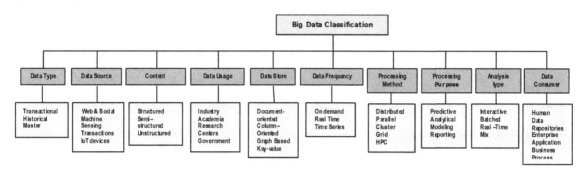

VARIOUS SECURITY AND PRIVACY ISSUES IN BIG DATA

According to Yunling Wang (2016), the existing Big Data initiatives are focusing on Volume, Velocity, Veracity, Variety, Variability, and Value, but not on security and data privacy. According to Kalyani (2015), the existing IT security practices such as Access permissions, Encryption schemes, Transport layer security, Firewalls and their limitations are well-known, making the attackers perform malicious attacks on applications and operating systems in Big Data. Big Data need techniques to audit, protect data processes, and monitor in terms of data, application and infrastructure.

According to Abid Mehmood (2016), Data Privacy represents the privilege of having control over the way in which the personal data is collected and used. User's privacy may be breached under the following circumstances:

- Most of the business organizations are collecting buying preferences of users by gathering personal information such as healthcare records and location-based information etc. to improve their marketing.
- The sensitive data are stored and processed in a location not secured properly and data leakage may occur during storage and processing phases.
- The sensitive data are stored and processed in a location which is not secured properly and data leakages may occur during storage and processing phase.

According to Porambage (2016), one serious privacy issue to the personal data such as medical records, criminal records, political records, financial data, website data or business-related information is identification during transmission over the network. According to Jing (2014), Information Security is protecting data from malicious attacks and misusage of data for profit and ensuring integrity, confidentiality, and availability of data. Therefore, such information security mechanisms are to be extended to achieve Big Data Security.

According to Fei (2016) Cloud Secure Alliance categorized privacy and security issues of Big Data in four different groups as follows:

- Infrastructure Security Issues
  - Insecurity due to Distributed Processing of Data.
  - Insecurity due to Schema-free databases.

- Data Privacy Issues
  - Insecurity due to Data mining and Analytical mechanisms.
  - Insufficient Cryptographic mechanisms for Data Security.
  - Insufficient Access Control mechanisms.
- Data Management and Integrity Issues
  - Insecure Data Storage and Transaction Log Procedures.
  - Ineffective Granular Audits.
  - Data Provenance issues.
- Reactive Security Issues
  - Insufficient End-to-End Filtering & Validation mechanisms.
  - Ineffective Supervising Security monitoring mechanisms in Real-Time.

Infrastructure Security Issues

Impact of Distributed Data on Security

Now a day's data are distributed and new technologies are used for storage and process large volumes of data. For example, the Cloud Computing technologies such as Hadoop are explored for big data storage and processing.

The Big Data uses a distributed programming framework based on parallel programming for computations and storage mechanism to have massive amounts of data processing. One of the popular Big Data techniques is MapReduce framework, which divides an input file into multiple partitions in the initial phase of MapReduce, and then each partition of Mapper reads input data, do some computation activity, and provides a list of key/value pairs as output. In the second phase, the Reducer performs the summary operation based key/value pairs. Insecure Computation is due to distributed environment feature of Big Data, where parallel computation across multiple servers/workstations, lead to an opportunity for the security breach. Identifying a malicious node and securing the sensitive data from the unreliable node is a major challenge. Another issue of concern is sometimes the Mappers leak private records either intentionally or unintentionally. Also, the MapReduce computations may be subjected to replay attacks, the man in the middle attacks and denial of service attacks. According to Fei (2016), malicious data nodes may be added to a network, with an intention to receive replicated data and then to deliver modified MapReduce code. According to Fei (2016) creating the snapshots of corresponding legitimate nodes and re-introducing the concerned modified copies is an avoidable attack in the distributed environment. In healthcare, large volumes of Electronic Medical Records are creating Big Data. These kinds of data collected from networked hospitals are generally stored in a Cloud. A malicious user can make an intrusion attack by using a un-trusted computation program to leak sensitive information, or to perform data corruption and to launch DoS attack. Most of the distributed nodes' computations are having only a single level of protection mechanism, which is not sufficient and hence not recommendable also.

Hadoop and other Big Data technologies for instance: MongoDB, Accumulo does not communicate securely when it comes to inter-node communication where inter-node communication is not protected by using SSL and TLS.

There are several ways a malicious program to create big security risk:

1. Sensitive data such as credit cards, personal profile can be accessed by a malicious program, which can corrupt the data leading to incorrect results.
2. A malicious program can perform even Denial of Service attack into Big Data environment leading to financial loss.

Impact of Non-Relational Databases on Security

The big data storage has migrated from traditional relational database to unstructured NoSQL database. NoSQL database architecture is designed to be a multi-sourced data, hence leaves it vulnerable to attacks. The security in NoSQL databases is embedded in middleware and they are not supported by any dedicated security mechanism. Transactional integrity is not properly maintained in NoSQL databases. It is difficult to inculcate complex integrity constraints into NoSQL databases as it may hamper with functionality and it makes NoSQL databases not to be scalable and inefficient. The authentication techniques are not properly defined in NoSQL databases. There is no mechanism to store the password in NoSQL databases. They use Basic HTTP or Message Digest based authentication schemes and which are subjected to man in the middle attack. The HTTP protocol based on Representational State Transfer (REST) is leading to cross-site scripting, request forgery and injection attacks such as array injection, JSON injection, REST injection, view injection, schema injection, Generalized Query Language (GQL) injection, and others. NoSQL has no support of blocking with the help of the third party as well. Authorization techniques in NoSQL provide authorization at higher layers only. Authorization in NoSQL allows controlling of user access to the database but it is not possible to control user access to specific data collection. Employment of weak security mechanism makes NoSQL databases vulnerable to inside attacks. They may be unnoticed due to poor log analysis mechanisms and other fundamental security mechanisms. The NoSQL Big Data systems either use password or the default system password, therefore making anybody to easily access them.

Data Privacy Issues

Data Privacy and Data security are tightly coupled aspects of Big Data. Even though security and privacy look they are related but they are two different concepts. Infrastructure level restriction which prevents or allows accessing of data or network area on authorization is referred as Security. Whereas privacy is restricting or controlling access for different authorized users to access a specific set of data. According to Kristin Lauter (2011), it is challenging to protect private data on the web. Data Privacy has become a sensitive issue with the evolution of Big Data because it increases the risk of leakage of data. In Distributed Computing environment the data provider with privacy concerns will not expose the data; on the other hand, data demander requires accurate data for analysis. It is very difficult to preserve privacy in distributed data sharing environment using available privacy-preserving mechanisms. Information Technology besides providing convenience in public's daily life it also brings the risk of leakage of data with every transaction they do online. Cyber attackers are creating hidden online markets where personal it is possible to buy and sells stolen information. The recent cyberattacks have demonstrated that there is potential harm to personal data. Because of the reasons stated above, there is a need to continuously enhance the current privacy-preserving mechanisms, which enable the organizations employing data sharing systems to take the benefit of big data analytics.

Impact of Data Mining and Analytics on Security

The data collection, storage, and usage trend are modified by Big Data analytics. Today the consumer data is turned into business intelligence and provide new insights into different industry sectors including manufacturing, financial services, healthcare, consumer goods IT and technology, professional services, pharmaceuticals, and biotechnology. Big data is helpful to predict or forecast organizations' business and to fix optimum price a product, new product development and to enhance the market. Unethical means of information mining methods are allowing gathering personal data without asking users' permission or notification (Shrivastava & Kumar, 2017). In 2013 Cloud Security Alliance published magazine published an article on Top Ten Security Big Data Security and Privacy Challenges and it states that data analytical techniques are leading to untrustworthy, invasion of privacy and decreased civil freedom. It is required to collect and aggregate data from many nodes to perform data analysis. It is challenging to secure data while providing compatibility between nodes which are working in different computing environments. There is an extensive study of Privacy Preserving Data Mining (PPDM) since years, but still, it is a challenge to apply different mining algorithms without reading confidential data. One of the best challenges in PPDM and analytics is making certain that derivation of person acknowledgeable data is not possible (Shrivastava & Bhatnagar, 2011).

Insufficient Cryptographic Mechanisms for Data Security

Data encryption and access control mechanisms ensure the end to end security to the sensitive data and allow only authorized entities to access. The existing techniques, like Attribute-Based Encryption (ABE), are not efficient and scalable. Also, the existing authentication policies need to be improved to ensure secure communication among distributed entities. Traditional Policy of encryption that encrypts everything or nothing is inefficient on large datasets since it makes sharing or searching of records either insecure or time-consuming process. Searching and filtering of encrypted data, securing an outsourced computation are the other challenges to be considered while designing a cryptography mechanism for big data. It is highly challenging to secure data through encryption when distributed file systems are used to store the big data and processed in the cloud. File-system encryption can effectively apply only to data at rest. This requires encryption and decryption of a file every time it is accessed which increases computational time. Sometimes this overhead forces users to choose between security and performance.

Insufficient Access Control Mechanisms

Node and API authentication are concerns due to the limitations and inherent vulnerabilities in the out-of-the-box Big Data Security implementations. Rouge node insertion and stolen ticket issues are at the top of the list for holes that can be exploited. Security Design Flaw: Most of the Big Data technology implementations are built keeping minimal security model in mind. Most of the services do not authenticate users.

In Big Data the data nodes themselves do not implement any access control mechanism. The traditional SQL based database systems have good access control mechanisms for users, even at the table level, row level, and cell level. Big Data NoSQL databases are lack of comprehensive access control mechanisms. It is a complex task to keep track of different roles of users along with preserving access labels during large networked analytical transformations which can be considered as the potential threat. At the same time, granular level access control implementation gives sound security, but the data may move more restrictive category, making data analysis and decision making critical.

Data Management and Integrity Issues

Insecure Data Storage and Transaction Logs

In Big Data environment the data and related transaction logs are stored in a multi-tiered storage media as it is difficult to move data manually between tiers by the manager and to have control on exactly what data is moved and when. The exponential growth of Big Data demands auto-tiering for storage management. But, Auto-tiering based data storage solutions do not keep track of where the data is stored, leading new data storage security challenges. According to Cloud Security Magazine on Top Ten Security Big Data Security and Privacy Challenges (2013), new imperative security mechanisms to thwart unauthorized access and maintain constant availability.

Auto-tiering form of storage enables automatic storing of petabytes of data based on the policies established, which may lead security challenges like unverified storage services and mismatched security policies. Also, transaction logs are to be protected. Two kinds of attacks are possible in auto-tiered environments: collusion attacks, rollback attacks.

- **Collusion Attack:** Interchange of keys and access codes between services providers may allow them to gain excessive privileges to access data for which they are not authorized.
- **Rollback Attack:** The datasets which are outdated will be uploaded back to replace current version of data sets.

Confidentiality, integrity, consistency, and data provenance are the vulnerabilities associated with big data storage. For logging and auditing, several factors create challenges in this area including policy modeling, appropriate access definitions/profiles when someone has breached your cluster and you must find ways to detect it by recording an activity.

The Transactional logs of Big Data are huge and require protection. Data Confidentiality and Integrity is also a matter of concern where encryption and signatures might be important. Authentication, authorization, and encryption may be considered as a challenge at each node since the data is stored at different distributed nodes. Securing communication between nodes, middlewares, and the user is another security concern.

Ineffective Granular Audits

The real-time security monitoring mechanisms will enable to understand when an attack can happen. But, identifying new kinds of attacks is a problem. To identify the missed attacks audit information is needed. Also, understanding the forensics, regulation and compliance reasons are required. Therefore, the auditing should focus on more granularity levels, where one has to deal with more number of distributed data objects.

Data Provenance Issues

When you find some information in big data it is difficult to know from where it has got there since there may be a chance that the data has copied from somewhere. There may be a case where the data has been edited in the copying process. So the trustworthiness of data depends on root from where it has been generated so it is a challenge to find if the data is trustworthy. Metadata of data which is generated by the different applications can be of use to disambiguate the data and also allows reusing of data. According to Craig Gentry (2015) data provenance, one kind of metadata pertains to the derivation history of a data product starting from its original sources. The programming environment of Big Data applications generates a large number of provenance graphs leaving complex metadata. Analyzing and detecting metadata dependencies for security and or confidentiality applications from such large provenance graphs are computationally intensive.

Reactive Security Issues

Ineffective Input Validation and Filtering Mechanisms

End-point Input Validation and Filtering is another challenge as the breadth of data sources and size of the data pool is large. A key challenge of data collection process is input validation: What kind of data is untrusted? And what are the un-trusted data sources? Therefore data filtering is required to filter rogue or malicious data. In Big Data GBs or TBs of continuous data is accumulated and signature-based data filtering has a limitation that what kind of behavior aspect is to be considered for filtering are challenges. Validating the data sources and finding whether data is malicious or incorrect and filter out unreliable data is really difficult. The ID cloning attack and Sybil attack can spoof multiple IDs and also feed fake data to the data collection device, as data collection devices and programs are vulnerable to attacks. Organizations need analysis and monitoring tools in Big Data framework to identify an attack at its very first sign. Security of computational elements such as Hadoop framework has two parts namely mapper and reducer and there is every possibility of leakage of sensitive information, therefore trustworthiness of these computational elements needs to be evaluated through the process of data sanitization and de-identification.

Big data applications require data collection from the variety of sources and this process involves two fundamental security risks:

1. **Input Validation:** If all data sources are known, then only data and its source trustworthiness can be evaluated.
2. Filtering of data is also one of the major concerns since Big Data applications collect huge amount data making it difficult to validate and filter data on the fly. The existing conventional signature-based data filtering techniques may not completely resolve the input validation and data filtering problems.

Ineffective Supervising Security Monitoring Mechanisms in Real-Time

Security monitoring in real time is a challenge, based on the number of alerts generated by security devices. The Big Data technologies allow fast processing of data on the fly, however, humans cannot cope with the correlated effect of these security alerts or false positives due to the shear amount of data and velocity. Therefore, techniques or tools are necessary to detect real-time anomalies, while supporting scalable security analytics.

Renu Kesharwani (2016) has summarized the big data security challenges as follows:

- The Big Data has distributed computing environment, which supports only a single level of protection and is not recommendable.
- The evolution of Non-relational databases (NoSQL) is making it difficult to keep up security solutions in Big Data with demand.
- The auto-tiering mechanism used for automatic data transfer requires additional security mechanisms and are not available.
- When any Big Data system receives huge volumes of information, validation is required to retain trustworthiness and accuracy; however, this is not always practiced.
- During data mining, unethical IT specialists can gather personal data without having users' permission or notification.
- The traditional access control mechanisms, data encryption standards and communication procedures used for security have become dated and insufficient to rely on it.
- In many organizations, the type of access controls is not instituted to divide the level of confidentiality within the company.
- The detailed auditing mechanism is not recommendable Big Data due to the large volume of data involved.
- Consistently monitoring and tracking the origins is a challenge due to the size of Big Data.

DEFENSE SCHEMES FOR BIG DATA SECURITY ISSUES:

Data Management

Data Management Comprises: Data Classification, Data Discovery and Data Tagging

1. **Data Classification:** The organizations which maintain Big Data should be:
   a. Able to identify which data is more sensitive, which fields should be more prioritized for applying for cryptographic protection etc. For this purpose, the organizations should prepare a data classification matrix.
   b. Able to perform security control assessment to determine:
   c. Location of data, such as which data is to be exposed to the Internet and which data should be kept in the secure zone, Number users or systems that can access data and Security controls such as cryptography.
   d. Able to determine data value to the attacker.
   e. Data is available easily for resell by the attacker and belongs to Intellectual Property.
   f. Able to determine the impact on revenue and compliance.
   g. Determining and reporting breaches for distinct fields, loss of a particular data field such as cardholder information may affect the business and estimating cost involved in buying new security products and re-architecting the current system.

h. Able to determine the impact of phishing attacks on personal data such as customer's email IDs or credit card information etc.

2. **Data Discovery:** Programmatically one can protect sensitive fields of structured data such as CSV and JSON files. However, for unstructured data performing classification of sensitive data and finding its location is difficult. Therefore building threat models and profiles and sharing with Data Analysts is useful to prevent data ex-filtration activities. Conditional search routines should be built.

3. **Data Tagging:** Understanding of ingress and egress methods will help in know the end-to-end data flow. One should identify all data ingress methods including manual, automated and methods that go through meta-layer, where the file may be copied and what kind of interface is used, such as Command Line or Java APIs. Similarly, one should know all egress methods, such as reporting jobs through Hive queries, Pig jobs or exporting through Sqoop or copying via REST API etc. This will decide control boundaries and also trust zone. It is also, helpful for data discovery and access management activities.

Identity and Access Management

POSIX Style of Permissions Provides Access Controls in Hadoop Environment

1. **Data Metering and User Entitlement:** Using machine learning algorithms and access models the threshold value should be decided to access a particular data per particular user/application and thereby data metering can be performed. The access policies should be tied to data and not for the accessing methods. Attribute-based access control should be leveraged. Providing permissions is a method to leverage data attributes user and environment or location.

2. **Role Based Access Control (RBAC) Authorization:** The security administration in huge networked systems is very complex challenging to manage. Existing access control mechanism is costly and errors prone since every user are given different privileges by the administrator. The user may be able to access confidential information when he is granted privileges that exceed the need of their job role.

RBAC is becoming popular among the people who are working with big data technologies since it reduces the complexity of administration in security. RBAC is also being adopted in many commercial applications and huge networked applications. RBAC allows you give different roles for different users and give different privileges for different roles; this reduces the risk of a user being given the privileges that exceed the need for his/her job role.

Fine-grained access control can be delivered through RBAC. Data access should be managed by role and not the user. Relations between users and roles should be determined based on group memberships and rules across all data access paths.

Data Privacy and Protection

In Hadoop distributed environment data-at-rest encryption at the file level or block –level, field-level or column level encryption (application level), data tokenization, and data masking/redaction provide security.

1. **Application Level Cryptography:** Security granularities and audit tracking capabilities are enabled by tokenization and field level encryption. Through manual intervention the fields, which need encryption should be decided and where and how to enable authorized decryption.

2. **Transparent Encryption:** To prevent access through the storage medium Full Disk Encryption or HDFS layer encryption should be adopted. Employment of Data – at – rest encryption in Hadoop will result in protecting sensitive data and keeping the disks out of audit scope. Employment of Transparent Encryption scheme at disk level makes residual data, human unreadable format when the disks are removed or deactivated from the cluster.

3. **Data Redaction or Data Masking:** Data redaction or data masking before loading data in ETL process de-identifies the Personally Identifiable Information, therefore no sensitive data in Hadoop. To keep Hadoop environment potentially out of audit scope both static and dynamic masking tools can be deployed for batch or real-time data processing.

Network Security

Network security includes data protection in-transit, authorization mechanisms, and network zoning.

1. **Data Protection in Transit:** HTTPS can prevent information disclose and elevation of privilege threats. Today's Hadoop environment is using TLS protocol to provide authentication and ensuring the privacy of communication name servers, nodes, and applications. To ensure data confidentiality the following controls should be adopted:
   a. From client to Hadoop cluster perform Packet level encryption using TLS.
   b. Between Namenode to Job Tracker and Job Tracker to Datanode apply packet-level encryption within Hadoop cluster.
   c. To prevent Sniffing attack use Lightweight Directory Access Protocol (LDAP) over SSL called LDAPS when communicating with enterprise directories.

2. **Network Securing Zoning:** To allow traffic to the approved levels segment the Hadoop clusters into Choke points such as Rack switches and thereby:
   a. End users are able to connect with only individual Datanodes, but not to the Namenodes.
   b. To control traffic in and out of Hadoop environment Apache Knox Gateway can be used and it provides per-service-level granularity.

Infrastructure Security and Integrity

The infrastructure security and integrity consist of Auditing, Secure Enhanced Linux, File Integrity Checking, Data Tamper Monitoring, Privileged user verification and Activity monitoring.

1. **Auditing or Logging:** Every unique change of Hadoop ecosystem needs to be audited and audit logs should be protected and includes the following:
   a. Addition and deletion of management and data nodes.
   b. State changes in management as well as Jobtracker and Namenodes.
   c. Activities including preventing of the addition of unauthorized node into Hadoop cluster.

d. When data is not limited to only one of the Hadoop components, the data security leads many moving parts and results in the high percentage of fragmentation. To address this fragmentation problem the following technologies are recommendable.

  i. **Apache Falcon:** Focuses on data management and controls data life cycle.
  ii. **Cloudera Navigator:** To address log sprawl of metadata.
  iii. **Zettaset Orchestrator:** Having its own metadata collected from Hadoop components.

2. **Secure Enhanced Linux:** National Security Agency (NSA) of US created the Secure Enhanced Linux called SELinux and has Mandatory Access Control. If any user changes settings of his home directory the SELinux policy prevents other users and processes access it. It prevents command injection attacks. Even any malicious user access the root, still he will not be able to execute anything using any kind of data ex-filtration methods. SELinux makes access decisions depending on all the information available like user, type, role, and level.

REQUIREMENTS FOR SECURITY MANAGEMENT OF A BIG DATA SYSTEM

A successful big data system for organizing the security need to:

*   Reduce tedious manual tasks in a routine assessment and response activities. When an issue is being investigated, the system requires diminishing the number of repetitive and manual tasks which includes executing the same operation on n different tools, toggling between consoles etc. The system should make efforts to consistently decrease the number of steps involved per incident since these tasks cannot be eradicated in an instant.
*   Apply business context in order to point analysts towards the main impact issues. The securities teams should be able to map the systems they consider monitoring and able to manage back the crucial business applications and processes being supported. The dependencies between the system and the third party need to be understood along with understanding their current state of compliance and vulnerability.
*   Present the analysts with only the most appropriate data. "Reducing false positives" is often referred by the security professionals. The system should eliminate the noise and provide the analysts with the pointers to work on the high impact issues. The system should provide the data aiding to highlight the what, why are the likely biggest problems.
*   Supplement human knowledge. The system should extend support to the analyst for analyzing the significant critical items. This involves providing built techniques that identify the current threats as well as the high priority issues. These techniques use to recognize the current tools, methods, and procedures being used by the attacker community.
*   View "over the horizon". Defending the system against the current threats is a "race against time". The system needs to be predictive and able to present early warning. By making aware of the external threat intelligence by the internal situational awareness attending the internal security team to an active defense and prevention state from a passive defense state.

HANDLING BIG DATA PRIVACY CONCERNS

According to the article, Big Data Analytics for Security Intelligence by Cloud Security Alliance Magazine (2013) the possible strategies for the Big data privacy protection can be analyzed by considering the following development strategies of the framework.

1. The privacy policies able to access the stored data in the target platforms.
2. The making of useful enforcement monitors for these policies.
3. The integration of the generated monitors with the target platforms.

Big data privacy can be handled in various phases of Data generation, Data storage, and Data processing etc.

Big Data Privacy in Data Generation Phase

The risk of privacy violation can be minimized at the data generation phase by either access restriction or by falsifying data.

1. **Access Restriction:** The data owner provides the massive amount of data if the data contains sensitive information which cannot be shared by others. For privacy preserving a few measures such as encryption tools, script blockers, anti-tracking extensions need to be taken in to account.
2. **Falsifying Data:** In certain circumstances, in order to prevent the access to the sensitive data, data can be distorted before the data is got. In such cases, true data cannot be obtained easily from the distorted data. Data distortion can be achieved by the following techniques.
   a. A *Socketpuppet* tool is used to hide the online individual identity. By using numerous Socketpuppets to one particular individual data, it is seen as the individual data having the place with different people. Hence, it is difficult to relate the data of different socketpuppets to one individual data.
   b. *Mask Me* is an example of the security tool used to mask the identity of the individual. This is applicable especially in cases of the data having patients' health records, owners' credit card details etc.

Big Data Privacy in Data Storage Phase

According to the article Big Data Analytics for Security Intelligence by Cloud Security Alliance Magazine (2013) with the advancement of data storage technologies, storing large volumes of Big data is not a challenge. According to Kesharwani (2016), the major challenge is ensuring the Big data storage without disclosing the individuals' sensitive data. According to Priyank Jain (2016), the traditional security mechanisms of data protection can be categorized into four groups as the file level data security schemes, database level data security schemes, media level security schemes and application level encryption schemes.

According to Liu (2011) information availability ensures the access of the needed data to the authorized users. Therefore the primary concern of the big data storage is to ensure the privacy of the individual.

For example, public key encryption (PKE) is an existing method to ensure such a requirement where the encrypted can only be decrypted by a valid recipient. User privacy in the data cloud can be achieved by any of the following techniques.

1. **Attribute-Based Encryption:** Access control is granted based on the user's identity to have complete access to all resources.
2. **Homomorphic Encryption:** Can be carried out by IBE/ABE deployment scheme settings by updating the possible ciphertext receiver.
3. **Storage Path Encryption:** Ensures the secured big data storage in the cloud.
4. **Usage of Hybrid Clouds:** Usage of Hybrid cloud environment which is a combination of both public and private cloud environment provides a secure access to the data to a certain extent.

Big Data Privacy in Data Processing Phase

The big data privacy preservation in the data processing phase can be achieved in two phases. It is possible that the collected data contains sensitive data which affect the privacy of data owner. Therefor the first phase is intended for safeguarding this sensitive data from the unsolicited disclosure. The second phase is aimed at extracting significant information from the data without privacy violation.

TECHNIQUES FOR HANDLING BIG DATA PRIVACY

There were traditionally used techniques for providing privacy in big data. The demerits of these traditional techniques led to the introduction of advanced techniques.

De-Identification

According to Cheng (2015) and Mehmood (2016), De-identification is one of such traditional techniques of privacy preserving.

With De-identification there is an increased possibility of re-identification also. There are three types of De-identification privacy-preserving methods,

*   K-anonymity
*   L-diversity
*   T-closeness

1. **K-Anonymity:** The K-anonymity allows maximizing data utility of data while limiting disclosure risk to an acceptable level. Therefore, it is especially suitable for privacy protection But, it is still unaided by attacks such as unsorted matching attack, temporal attack, and complementary release attack. An additional limitation of the problem is where attributes are suppressed in place of individual entries. This limitation was handled by the L-diversity approach of data anonymization.
2. **L-Diversity:** By diminishing the granularity of data representation, the L-diversity group based anonymization safeguards the privacy of the data sets. The k-anonymity model extends to l-diversity model (Distinct, Entropy, Recursive) by utilizing both generalization and suppression methods in

such a way as to map any given record onto at least k diverse records in the data. The setback of this method is that it is dependent on the sensitive attribute value range. Apart from this L-diversity method also tends to skewness and similarity attack.

3. **T-Closeness:** According to Li N (2007), t-closeness is an added enhancement of l-diversity group based anonymization. The l-diversity model is extended to t-closeness model (Equal/Hierarchical distance) by handling the attribute values distinctly by considering into account the data distribution values for that attribute. The major improvement of t-closeness is that it intercepts attribute disclosure. The major setback of t-closeness lies in the increased odds of re-identification with the increased size and variety of data.

Differential Privacy

Differential Privacy is a technique which allows the user to access user data from databases where personal information of people is stored without revealing the identity of the individual. Information is distracted minimally by the database system to achieve Differential Privacy. The distraction should be minimal that it should preserve data privacy as well as provide enough useful information to the analyst.

In DP direct access to the database is not provided to the analyst. Database analyst and database are separated by an intermediate piece of software known as Privacy Guard to protect the privacy.

Identity-Based Anonymization

According to Samarati, P (1998) an open architecture for anonymization was created by Intel allowing the utilization of a wide range of tools utilized for both de-identifying and re-identifying web log records. It is found that the enterprise data has different properties to those of standard anonymization examples. This concept revealed the benefits of big data techniques when working with anonymized data. The anonymized data was found exposed to correlation attacks instead of masking the sensitive personal information.

Anonymization needs to be beyond simple masking or generalizing certain fields. To achieve valuable results Intel used Hadoop to analyze the anonymized data. Anonymized datasets need to be carefully analyzed to determine whether they are open to attack.

VARIOUS ENCRYPTION TECHNIQUES FOR PRESERVING THE PRIVACY OF SENSITIVE DATA

With the rapid growth in demand for improved security and the limitations of the ancient encryption techniques of data, the need for the advanced encryption techniques has increased. In this section, we recommend the employment of new encryption techniques like Searchable, Order-preserving and Homomorphic schemes.

Searchable Encryption

Searchable encryption provides us with the facility to search in the encrypted data. Searchable Encryption is an optimistic method of protecting individuals' sensitive data while retaining the ability to search on the server side. SE allows the search of encrypted data in the server side without information leakage in plaintext data. In addition to the security of the stored documents and keywords on the server side, the security of the query keywords should also be guaranteed in the searchable encryption scheme. Moreover, the search pattern and the access pattern should also be protected. Searchable encryption can be categorized into the main branches as Searchable Symmetric Encryption (SSE), Public-key Encryption with Keyword Search (PEKS), and Deterministic Encryption.

Order Preserving Encryption Scheme (OPES)

An OPES is a deterministic encryption technique where the encryption algorithm generates the ciphertexts that maintain the numerical ordering of the plaintexts. The main objective of the technique is to consider a target distribution provided by the user as an input and alter the plaintext values such that the alteration never changes the order while ensuring that the altered values are following the target distribution. The capability of the Order-preserving encryption technique by directly supporting the range query processing on the encrypted data without decrypting them made the technique important. This technique is exclusively designed to work with the existing indexing structures, hence can be easily integrated with the existing database systems. Without decryption, OPES directly allows comparison operations to be performed on the encrypted data.

Given a series of non-negative integers, Ozsoyoglu (2003) considered attribute-level encryption for relational databases to show that there can be a distinctively determined order-preserving function. The input distribution function is a sequence of strictly growing polynomial functions. Since this distribution method never considers input distribution, the shape of the distribution of the encrypted values varies with the shape of the input distribution.

OPES that makes the encrypted result independent of input distribution was designed by Agrawal (2004). The encrypted result of this technique is statistically indistinguishable which is achieved by introducing the "Flatten" stage.

CryptDB is a system which provides confidentiality for the applications using database management systems by exploring an intermediate design point. This system was presented by Popa (2011).

Homomorphic Encryption

Homomorphic encryption allows us to encrypt the data in such a way that performing a mathematical operation on the encrypted data and decrypting the result produces the same answer as performing an analogous operation on the unencrypted data. The homomorphism is defined as the correspondence between the operations performed on the encrypted data to those of the operations performed on the unencrypted data. This correspondence can be utilized to perform operations which are secure in the cloud. A partially homomorphic cryptosystem is a system that exhibits either additive or multiplicative homomorphism, but not both. Homomorphic cryptosystems are available in many forms which are designed to perform specific operations. A fully homomorphic cryptosystem was recently proposed by Craig Gentry (2015). Few Homomorphic Encryption Techniques are Fully Homomorphic Encryption, Fully Homomorphic Encryption over the Integers, Homomorphic evaluation of AES.

GOOD PRACTICES FOR MANAGING BIG DATA FROM A
SECURITY POINT OF VIEW (ENISA-CSA,2015)

- If big data information is stocking in the cloud, the cloud provider should have good enough security mechanisms in place. Also, the provider should carry out regular security inspections and agree on fines if case sufficient security standards are not met.
- To obtain security in big data Granular auditing must be carried out. The confidentiality and integrity of the audit information are also important. The big data and the audit information are to be stored separately. The audit information is to be regularly monitored and protected with the users' granular access controls. This can be performed by the available open source audit tools.
- Develop a proper access control policy such as allowing access to authorized people users. The access control can be handled in two ways as granting the user access and restricting the user access. Better security is provided by implementing the policy that that chooses the correct trick for a particular scenario. For providing the best access controls, CSA (2013) has suggested the following tips:
  - Normalizing the mutable elements and de-normalizing the immutable elements.
  - Ensuring proper implementation by tracing the secrecy requirements.
  - Maintaining the access labels.
  - Tracing the admin data.
  - Using SSO (Single Sign-ON).
  - Maintaining accurate data federation by using a labeling scheme.
- **Secure the Data:** Both the raw information and the result from analytics should be properly secured. Encryption should be utilized to make sure that no confidential data is leaked.
- Storage management is an important part of the Big Data security. A technique known as secure untrusted data repository (SUNDR) is used to detect the illegal modifications of the file by malicious server agents. This technique recommends the usage of signed message digests for identifying each file by a digital identifier. This is supported by many techniques such as policy based encryption schemes, encryption key rotation and key updating for lazy revocation, digital rights management (DRM) for copyright protection etc. It is better building one's own secure cloud storage over the existing infrastructure.
- **Secure Communications:** Data on transport should be appropriate to make sure its confidentiality and integrity.
- **Real-Time Security Supervising:** Access to the information should be supervised. Tools related to threat intelligence should be deployed to prevent unauthorized access to the confidential data.
- Endpoint security is vital and this can be achieved by using Mobile Device Management (MDM) by connecting only to the trusted devices in the network, performing resource testing, and using trusted certificates. Further, the techniques of outlier detection and statistical similarity detection are used for filtering the malicious inputs while safeguarding against ID spoofing attacks, Sybil attacks etc.
- The application of big data analytics is recommended by implementing tools such as Internet Protocol security (IPsec), secure shell (SSH) and Kerberos in order to handle the real-time data. Data compliance is a major task when dealing with the constant overflow of data. This overhead is can be tackled by considering the security at each level of the stack and also through real-time analytics. The implementation of the security controls at each level of the stack of the cloud, appli-

cation level, and clusters can be achieved by deploying the front end security systems such as the application level firewalls and routers. Care should be taken against the attacks that try to circumvent the infrastructure of the Big Data and also the "data-poisoning" attacks (i.e., the monitoring system is tricked by the falsified data).

- Managing the data privacy in ever increasing data sets is really hard. The key for data privacy is maintaining the Scalability and Composability with the implementation of techniques such as differential privacy and homomorphic encryption. Differential privacy minimizes the record identification while maximizing the query accuracy. Homomorphic encryption provides the feasibility of storing and processing the encrypted data in the cloud. Incorporating awareness among the employees by training them on the latest privacy regulations and making sure of maintaining the software infrastructure with the aid of authorized mechanisms helps in maintaining the data privacy. Encouraging the implementation of the "privacy-preserving data composition" helps in data leakage control from various databases by monitoring and reviewing the infrastructure that is linked to the databases together.

- Mathematical cryptographic techniques were advanced in these days. Constructing a system that allows the operations such as searching and filtering on the encrypted data actually runs Boolean queries on the encrypted data. Searchable Symmetric Encryption (SSL) is one such technique. Relational encryption aids in comparing the encrypted data by matching the identifier values and the attribute values without sharing the encryption keys. The key management is made easy in the public key systems by Identity-based Encryption (IBE). This technique allows the encryption of the plain text for a certain identity. Attribute-based encryption integrates the access controls with the encryption scheme. Identification of the duplicate data in the cloud can be achieved by using the converged encryption scheme which makes use of the encryption keys.

- SSL certificates offer great security and protection. It encrypts all the communications that happen between a website and browser. Therefore SSL certificates are mandatory for web-based data transactions. The security is provided by encrypting the passwords and ensuring the end-to-end encryption by encrypting the data at rest. Apart from Secure Sockets Layer (SSL), algorithms such as Advanced Encryption Standard (AES), Secure Hash Algorithm 2 (SHA-256), RSA, Transport layer security (TLS) can also provide secure encryption.

- Data provenance is referred to as the provenance metadata originated from the big data applications. This is also the category of data that needs considerable protection. Developing a protocol such as an infrastructure access protocol that controls the access is recommended. Making use of the mechanisms such as checksums to set up regular status updates and continuous data integrity verification is also recommended. The finest practice for data provenance includes the implementation of scalable and dynamic granular access controls and also the implementation of the encryption methods.

- Secure big data environments using firewalls. Antivirus applications like Bit defender are used across various organizations who want to secure their big data repository from cyber attackers.

- End-to-end lineage tracking, entity matching, and thorough assessments can help in quickly detecting security breaches.

In summary, various security and privacy practices to be followed are shown in Table 1.

Table 1. Security and privacy methods

Security Mechanism	Purpose	Method
Security in Cloud Environment	Securing the data storage process on cloud	Authentication, Encryption-Decryption, and Compression
		Key Establishment, and ID based Encryption Algorithms
Hadoop Security	Security and privacy of Hadoop	Trust establishment between User and Name node, Random Encryption technique on data
	HDFS Security	Kerberos mechanism, Bull Eye Algorithm, and Name node approach
Monitoring Mechanism	Intrusion detection architecture	Maliciousness attack identification metrics
	Detection of anomalies or predicting network behaviour	Data collection, analysis, integration, and interpretation
	Detection of abnormal user behaviour	Self-assuring network control system
Auditing Mechanism	Auditing Dynamic Storage of Big Data	MuR-DPA: Top Down based on Merkle Hash Tree
Key Management Method	Generating strong keys, and authenticating data centers	Quantum cryptography algorithm and Pair-Hand protocol
	Securing group-key transfer	Online key- generation centre using Diffie-Hellman key Agreement mechanism and linear secret-sharing scheme
	Securing group -data sharing	Outsourcing conditional proxy re-encryption scheme
	Securing unstructured big data	Data analytics such as data- filtering, clustering & classification; security suit for existing security standards and as well as algorithms.
Anonymization Method	Providing privacy for sensitive fields using anonymization	K-anonymity Approaches
	Data mining with privacy preserving	Adaptive utility based k-anonymization model
	Scalable anonymization capability	Techniques such as Hybrid Top Down and Bottom Up SubTree Anonymization
	Scalable privacy- preservation for big data	Two Phase Clustering algorithm

CONCLUSION

Big data is the most important area of the research problem in these days. The commercial impacts of big data have the potential to generate significant productivity growth for a number of vertical sectors. Big data presents the opportunity to create unprecedented business advantages and better service delivery. All the challenges and issues are needed to be handled effectively and in an efficient manner. The major issue is to provide great security to the big data so that the big data could be handled and managed with the Cloud along with the modern systems. A successful big data managed for security has a system that extracts and presents critical data for analysis in the fastest and effective way. This chapter elaborated various security and privacy issues and factors that affect the Big Data storage, processing and communication and the possible defense mechanisms. In this chapter, we presented various privacy-preserving techniques in the big data applications perspective. As far as security of big data is concerned the existing techniques are promising to progress into new vulnerable to big data arose and the necessity for securing the big data increases.

This study reveals that it may be difficult to attain big data with privacy but is not unattainable. Many issues related to the intellectual property rights, Cybersecurity, data privacy along with data integrity, Code of conduct for the big data and the exploitation liability need to be resolved.

The Big Data organizations need to employ three key security controls: Preventive, Detective and Administrative for securing Big data life cycle.

- **Preventive:** Securing the data using encryption techniques while it is at rest/motion and use of access control and identity management.
- **Detective:** Adopting auditing mechanisms to monitor anomalous behavior and to provide compliance reports/alerts about the potential problems throughout the Big Data environment.
- **Administrative:** Implementation of administrative processes and procedures for security through privileged user analysis, sensitive data discovery, encryption key management capabilities, and configuration management.

To achieve the above, the new research direction privacy-preserving data mining should be strong. In this method, data should be published with appropriate suppression, generalization, distortion, and decomposition so that privacy of individuals is not compromised and yet the disclosed data is used for analytical purposes. K-Anonymity algorithm is one of the best ways to achieve security. The data collector is not a trustworthy, hence privacy-preserving pattern publishing is needed so that sensitive information about underlying data is not revealed. Therefore, Pattern hiding method can transform the data in such a way that certain patterns cannot be derived via data mining. The Secure Multiparty Mining a distributed mining method, where the data on which mining is to be performed is partitioned, vertically or horizontally among several nodes. This partitioned data is not shared and hence remains private, but the results of mining process can be combined and shared among participating nodes.

In future, to provide highly secure Big Data environment it is recommendable to implement application security rather than device security, isolating devices and servers having sensitive data, applying reactive and proactive protection mechanisms, regular auditing, analyzing logs, and updating attack information across the organizations can help for better organization of data.

REFERENCES

Agrawal, R., Kiernan, J., Srikant, R., & Xu, Y. (2004). Order-preserving encryption for numeric data. *Proceedings of SIGMOD '04*, 563 – 574. 10.1145/1007568.1007632

Big Data Analytics for Security Intelligence. (2013). Retrieved from www.cloudsecurityalliance.org/research/big-data

Big Data and Privacy principles under pressure in the age of Big Data analytics. (2014). Retrieved from https://dzlp.mk/en/node/2736

Boneh, D., Di Crescenzo, G., Ostrovsky, R., & Persiano, G. (2004). Public key encryption with keyword search. Advances in Cryptology – EUROCRYPT '04, 506–522.

Boneh, D., & Waters, B. (2007). Conjunctive, subset, and range queries on encrypted data. *Theory of Cryptography Conference (TCC '07)*, 535–554. 10.1007/978-3-540-70936-7_29

Brakerski, Z., Gentry, C., & Vaikuntanathan, V. (2011). Fully Homomorphic Encryption without Bootstrapping. *Cryptology ePrint Archive Report*.

Brakerski, Z., & Vaikuntanathan, V. (2011). Efficient Fully Homomorphic Encryption, LWE. *Proceedings of FOCS*.

Chang, Y. C., & Mitzenmacher, M. (2005). Privacy preserving keyword searches on remote encrypted data. *ACNS 05*, *3531*, 442–455.

Cheng, H., Rong, C., Hwang, K., Wang, W., & Li, Y. (2015). Secure big data storage and sharing scheme for cloud tenants. *China Communications*, *12*(6), 106–115. doi:10.1109/CC.2015.7122469

Cheon, Coron, Kim, Lee, Lepoint, Tibouchi, & Yun. (2013). Batch fully homomorphic encryption over the integers. *EUROCRYPT,* 315-335.

Collins, T., Hopkins, D., Langford, S., & Sabin, M. (1997). *Public Key Cryptographic Apparatus and Method.* US Patent #5,848,159.

Coron, Naccache, & Tibouchi. (2012). Public key compression and modulus switching for fully homomorphic encryption over the integers. EUROCRYPT 2012, 446-464.

Coron, J. S., Lepoint, T., & Tibouchi, M. (2014). Scale-invariant Fully Homomorphic Encryption over the Integers. *PKC 2014*, *8383*, 311–328.

Differential Privacy for Everyone. (2012). Retrieved from http://download.microsoft.com/Differential_Privacy_for_Everyone.pdf

Fei, H. (2016). Robust cyber-physical systems: Concept, models, and implementation. *Future Generation Computer Systems*, 449–475.

Gentry, Halevi, & Nigel. (2015). *Homomorphic evaluation of the AES circuit* (Updated Implementation).

Gentry, C. (2009). Fully homomorphic encryption using ideal lattices. *Symposium on the Theory of Computing (STOC)*, 169-176.

Goh, E. J. (2003). Secure indexes. *Cryptology ePrint Archive*. Retrieved from https://eprint.iacr.org/2003/216.pdf

Hussain, N. I., & Saikia, P. (2014). *Big Data ppt*. Retrieved from http://www.slideshare.net/nasrinhussain1/big-data-ppt-31616290

Jain, Gyanchandani, & Khare. (2016). Big data privacy: A Technological Perspective and Review. *Journal of Big Data*, *3*(25).

Jing, Q., Vasilakos, A. V., Wan, J., Lu, J., & Qiu, D. (2014). Security of the internet of things: Perspectives and challenges. *Wireless Networks*, *20*(8), 2481–2501. doi:10.100711276-014-0761-7

Kesharwani, R. (2016, August). Enhancing Information Security in Big Data. *International Journal of Advanced Research in Computer and Communication Engineering*, *5*(8).

Lauter, Naehrig, & Vaikuntanathan. (2011). Can homomorphic encryption be practical? ACM-CCSW, 113–124.

Li, N. (2007). t-Closeness: privacy beyond k-anonymity and L-diversity. *IEEE 23ʳᵈ international conference on Data engineering (ICDE)*.

Liu, S. (2011). Exploring the future of computing. *IT Professional, 15*(1), 2–3. doi:10.1109/MITP.2012.120

Machanavajjhala, A., Gehrke, J., Kifer, D., & Venkitasubramaniam, M. (2006). L-diversity: privacy beyond k-anonymity. *Proceedings of 22nd International Conference Data Engineering (ICDE)*. 10.1109/ICDE.2006.1

McKinsey Global Institute. (2011). *Big data: The next frontier for innovation, competition, and productivity*. Author.

Mehmood, Natgunanathan, Xiang, Hua, & Guo. (2016). Protection of Big Data Privacy. *IEEE Access on Special Section on Theoretical Foundations for Big data Applications: Challenges and Opportunities,* 1821 – 1834.

Mehmood, A., Natgunanathan, I., Xiang, Y., Hua, G., & Guo, S. (2016). *Protection of big data privacy*. IEEE Translations and Content Mining.

Meyerson, A., & Williams, R. (2004). On the complexity of optimal k-anonymity. *Proceedings of the ACM Symposium on Principles of Database Systems*.

Ozsoyoglu, Singer, & Chung. (2003). Anti-tamper databases: Querying encrypted databases. *Proceedings of the 17ᵗʰ Annual IFIP WG 11.3 Working Conference on Database and Applications Security*.

Popa, R. A., Zeldovich, N., & Balakrishnan. (2011). *CryptDB: A practical encrypted relational DBMS*. Technical MITCSAIL-TR-2011-005, MIT Computer Science and Artificial Intelligence Laboratory, Cambridge, MA.

Porambage, P., Ylianttila, M., Schmitt, C., Kumar, P., Gurtov, A., & Vasilakos, A. V. (2016). The quest for privacy in the Internet of Things. *IEEE Cloud Computing, 3*(2), 36–45. doi:10.1109/MCC.2016.28

Rivest, R., Shamir, A., & Adleman, L. (1978). A method for obtaining digital signatures and public-key cryptosystems. *Communications of the ACM, 21*(2), 120–126. doi:10.1145/359340.359342

Samarati, P., & Sweeney, L. (1998). *Protecting privacy when disclosing information: k-anonymity and its enforcement through generalization and suppression*. Technical Report SRI-CSL-98-04, SRI Computer Science Laboratory.

Sedayao, J., & Bhardwaj, R. (2014). Making Big Data, Privacy, and Anonymization work together in the enterprise: Experiences and Issues. *Big Data Congress*. 10.1109/BigData.Congress.2014.92

Shirudkar & Motwani. (2015). Big-Data Security. *International Journal of Advanced Research in Computer Science and Software Engineering, 5*(3).

Shrivastava, G., & Bhatnagar, V. (2011). Secure Association Rule Mining for Distributed Level Hierarchy in Web. *International Journal on Computer Science and Engineering, 3*(6), 2240–2244.

Shrivastava, G., & Kumar, P. (2017). Privacy Analysis of Android Applications: State-of-art and Literary Assessment. Scalable Computing. *Practice and Experience, 18*(3), 243–252.

Sokolova, M., & Matwin, S. (2015). *Personal privacy protection in time of Big Data*. Berlin: Springer.

Song, D. X., Wagner, D., & Perrig, A. (2000). Practical techniques for searches on encrypted data. *Proceedings of IEEE Symposium on Security and Privacy*, 44–55.

Tarekegn, G. B., & Munaye, Y. Y. (2016). Big Data: Security Issues, Challenges and Future Scope. *International Journal of Computer Engineering & Technology, 7*(4), 12–24.

The Economist Intelligence Unit Ltd. (2012). *Big Data: Lessons from the Leaders*. Retrieved from http://www.bdvc.nl/images/Rapporten/SAS-Big-data-lessons-from-the-leaders.pdf

Top Ten Security Big Data Security and Privacy Challenges. (2013). Retrieved from http://www.cloud-securityalliance.org

Wang, Y., Wang, J., & Chen, X. (2016, December). Secure Searchable Encryption: A survey. *Journal of Communications and Information Networks., 1*(4), 52–65. doi:10.1007/BF03391580

Wiener, M. (1990, May). Cryptanalysis of Short RSA Secret Exponents. *IEEE Transactions on Information Theory, 36*(3), 553–558. doi:10.1109/18.54902

Yogesh, Simmhan, Plale, & Gannon. (n.d.). *A Survey of Data Provenance Techniques*. Technical Report IUB-CS-TR618.

Chapter 19

A Comparative Review of Various Machine Learning Approaches for Improving the Performance of Stego Anomaly Detection

Hemalatha Jeyaprakash
Thiagarajar College of Engineering, India

KavithaDevi M. K.
Thiagarajar College of Engineering, India

Geetha S.
VIT University, India

ABSTRACT

In recent years, steganalyzers are intelligently detecting the stego images with high detection rate using high dimensional cover representation. And so the steganographers are working towards this issue to protect the cover element dependency and to protect the detection of hiding secret messages. Any steganalysis algorithm may achieve its success in two ways: 1) extracting the most sensitive features to expose the footprints of message hiding; 2) designing or building an effective classifier engine to favorably detect the stego images through learning all the stego sensitive features. In this chapter, the authors improve the stego anomaly detection using the second approach. This chapter presents a comparative review of application of the machine learning tools for steganalysis problem and recommends the best classifier that produces a superior detection rate.

DOI: 10.4018/978-1-5225-4100-4.ch019

INTRODUCTION

Steganographers aim is to conceal some undisclosed message inside an innocuous cover file known as digital images, and later it could be send via an unconfident channel as a stego file. In contrary, the anomaly detection called steganalysis aims to detect the presence of steganogram. In the last two decades, both the steganography and steganalysis experienced a precipitous development. There are three reasons are there why the research on steganalysis has attained a greater attention. Originally, sensing the occurrence of hidden messages, that can be castoff as a clandestine communication among terrorists or illegal groups. Then the greater achievement of steganalysis aids to increase the security of information hiding/steganography and watermarking. Steganalysis finds to be helpful in computer forensics, cyber warfare, criminal activities and etc. At last, it stimulates the researchers to construct the enhanced numerical model for multimedia which leads to the great successful application on other fields such as digital forensics. In the recent works, the best detectors are known to be the supervised learning for detecting the steganographic methods. In this chapter, we propose to study several recent machine learning algorithms available for steganalysis of images. The objective of this chapter is to present the efficiency of using machine learning algorithms in detecting stego objects.

Since many image formats are hugely available on the communication networks, JPEG images are the utmost frequently castoff images for data hiding purpose. The primarily steganographic procedures opted for the JPEG format was JSteg (Upham, n.d.), Outguess (Provos et al., 2001), F5 (Westfeld et al. 2001), Steghide (Hetzl et al., 2005) followed by Model-based Steganography (Sallee et al., 2005). Thereby Outguess and JSTEG obviously alters the DCT coefficient histogram, whereas the ancient attacks purely depended on first-order statistics of DCT (Discrete Cosine Transform) coefficients (Zhang et al., 2003). After, substantially more promising detectors were designed as possibility ratio trials with an id of well DCT coefficient cover models (Thai et al., 2015; Hastie et al, 2009).

The promising detectors for F5 and nsF5 (Fridrich et al., 2007) along with for Steghide, Model-Based Steganography are presently designed as classifiers skilled on features since DCT- quantized coefficients, the JRM (JPEG Rich Model) (Kodovský et al., 2012). When the features are mined from the residuals in the spatial domain, namely JPEG – phase – aware features, J-UNIWARD and UED (Guo et. 2012; Lerch-Hostalot et al., 2016) are perfectly detected by using such a feature-based model. Example of such features is GFR (Song et al., 2015), PHARM (Holub et al., 2015), DCTR (Holub et al., 2015) and etc. The concept of such a design is the JPEG phase notion, which is, the residual location in the 8*8 grid of JPEG. By rendering the informations gathered from the residuals by their segment, further promising stego detector can be built.

Steganographic Methods

- **Steghide:** The practical LSB implementation for images and audios are dome by Steghide. It may modify the original algorithm by adds a graph to lessen the amount of pixel modification. To enhance the hiding security, the hidden messages are properly encrypted and compressed before the message is embedded. Following that pseudo-random sequence is generated equation the passphrase as seed. This corresponding sequence belongs to the image pixels and the LSB bits are modified the sequence message bits. To enhance the visual imperceptibility, the LBS bit that differ from the message bit is considered for exchange. This may handle by a graph where every vertex represents the change and every 20 edges is a successful exchange. At the end, the balanced message bits are hidden y replacing the corresponding LSB.

- **LSB matching Revisited:** It customs the couple of pixels as an entrenching part. Binary function (decrement or increment) is used to hide a bit pairs.
- **Model-Based:** The research based on Model-Based steganographic algorithm will preserve the distribution of an image as well as the distribution coefficients. The distribution values have been estimated by using the conditional probability.
- **Edge Adaptive LSB Matching Revisited:** This approach is same as pixel pair, where the data embedding is carried out by regions. At first, the given image is divided by random block size. The random rotation is applied to the block for improving the security. Pixel pair in the threshold is considered and binary function is used for hiding the message.
- **F5 Steganography:** F5 steganography is a transform domain hiding algorithm where password starts a pseudo-random number generator used for permuting DCT coefficients. Then bits are embedded in the certain coefficients based on matrix encoding. To perform such an operation image coefficients are used as a code word with modifiable bits for message bits. Then by using a hash function, the message bits are entrenched with the XOR operation, in the sequence manner. When the message is embedded each time, when the sum is not zero then is the corresponding result the index of the coefficient that must be changed and also the consistent value is decrement, on the other hand, the code word remains are the same. At last, JPEG compression continues followed by the reverted permutation.
- **Spread Spectrum:** Spread spectrum is mainly developed for the purpose of military appliances to reduce the signal jam and interruptions. An example of spread spectrum is frequency hopping. In the case of frequency hopping, message bits are divided and sent via various frequencies controlled by a key. Using spread spectrum in an image, the message bits are modulated as independent and distributed as the Gaussian sequence then the embedding takes place.

Approaches of Steganalysis

The steganalysis finder can be constructed by means of two approaches. The initial approach is numerical signal detection. From the arithmetical perfect of the concealment source, the detector is derived and detector performance error will be obtained. Normalized statistical detection is less sensitive in finding differences among cover sources. Instead adopted cover model is used but it confines the indicator optimality and rationality error to the chosen cover model (Ker et al., 2006). Hence by using this simple model, we could not capture the entire associations between the separate image basics acquired using image sensors. Moreover, it has been successful in detecting the simple embedding operations such as LSB embedding and matching (Hostalot et al., 2013;Zhang et al., 2010; Chen et al., 2016). But it quite difficult in detecting complex and content adaptive steganographic algorithms such as wavelet obtained weights (WOW) (Fridrich et al., 2011), Highly undetectable SteGo HUGO (HUGO) (Pevny et al., 2010), HUGO BD, Universal Wavelet Relative Distortion (UNIWARD) (Houlb et al., 2014), edge adaptive because it is infeasible to measure the local model parameters for highly non-stationary natural images.

Another approach is to consider as a classification problem (stego/clean), it does not need any cover distribution. Individually, the image is characterized as a feature vector and hence it is a heuristic dimensionality reduction. Later by using any machine learning tool, the database consists of both stego and clean image is trained and testing. The key advantage of this approach is constructing detector for arbitrary embedding algorithms is easy. The disadvantage is that the classifiers may be imprecise when examining a particular image of unknown origin. Because it is not possible to have several samples from the concealment source and detect the steganographic channel for a time length.

Designing a practical steganalysis benchmark requires many choices. The first choice is to extract the statistical features (Ho et al., 1995) from each image. The goal of such extraction is to decrease the dimensionality of the space to analyze. It is known that extraction information is a destructive process because the projection is taken place from the image space to lower dimensional space this may cause the information destruction. In the steganalysers point of view, the extracted feature contains the most important relevant features. The second choice is to choose the most appropriate model in order to discriminate the stego image based on the useful devised features. In many cases supervised machine learning model is used for stego image classification.

General Classes of Steganalysis

Since the steganalysis aim is to notice the mere existence of message concealed in a suspicious medium, the field has developed towards improvements. The general types of steganalysis can be categorized as follows

Specific / Targeted Steganalysis

The hypothesis of this method is the steganographic embedding algorithm is already known before detection. It tries to analyze the images for detecting the hidden message and focus on the statistics/features which are modified by the steganographic algorithm.

In more detail, this type of techniques is recognized by examining the entrenching process and finding the image statistics. Accordingly such methods quietly in need of the meticulous embedding process. Hence such a method yields an actual precise result once used in contradiction of the target steganographic technique. Specific steganalysis techniques (Xiong et al., 2010) are used for detecting the secret messages from stego images undergone by steganographic embedding such as LSBM matching, JPEG compression, spread spectrum, and also for other transform domain (Chanu et al., 2012; Qian et al., 2015). Chi-Square is a first specific statistical steganalysis tool for detecting the message bits.

Blind/ Universal Steganalysis

Blind steganalysis aims to detect the stego images and it has been undergone with any type of steganographic algorithms. Blind steganalysers are restricted by the training data. Computational complexity is the severe problem as the training set grows. The limitation of such steganalysers depends on machine learning is that it depends on a range of training set characteristics. For example, for a JPEG image, the characteristics are the resolution, compression ratio, sensor noise and etc. Anyhow with the possible set of cover images, accurately the steganalysers should train.

Quantitative Steganalysis

Quantitative steganalysis intentions to predict the length of the clandestine communication that has been concealed in the cover medium. It is quite difficult to find the hidden message length other than the stego detection. This concept was familiarized by Chandramouli and Memon (2001). In detail, this method inventions to excerpt the further information around the hidden communication in the covert communication. So for many quantitative steganalysis in the literature aimed to goal a specific entrenching algorithm and successfully excerpt the payload information by means of some structural paradigm. In addition to that to calculate the stego message payload, modern steganalysers use supervised machine learning by using some useful set of features.

In the literature, many methods have been proposed for envisaging the stego payload. Nearly of the powerful methods are Sample Pair Analysis (SPA), Regular- Singular steganalysis (RS), Triple/ Quadruple and Difference Image Histogram (DIH) (Fridrich et al., 2001; Sorina et al., 2003; Tao et al., 2003). These methods are mainly focused on image structural correlation based on neighbor pixels characteristics and hence it is called as structural steganalysis. The basic knowledge for all these approaches is that the LSB flipping due to stego communication embedding which may affect the penetrating information of sample pair of signals. Likewise weighted stego (Fridrich et al., 2006), which finds the payload by using estimated cover version. To estimate the cover version, attributes such as local variance, saturation and etc. are used. The main problem of these algorithms is, even though it attains high accuracy, it targets only specific steganographic algorithm.

On the other hand, universal quantitative steganalysis, irrespective of the embedding algorithm used to embed and domain used to embed the stego message, it endeavors to find the secret message length. These works by extracting the useful set of image features and learn such a feature using supervised learning. Many research works have been done for extracting the sophisticated features (Shi et al., 2012; Xiaz et al., 2016) to find the advanced steganographic algorithms. These steganographic algorithms lead to disturbing the weaker enslavements among cover elements and later to find these, there is a need for complex statistical descriptors. But the problem is, the dimensionality is relatively high for such feature sets. A strong framework (Hou et al., 2016; Lerch-Hostalot et al., 2016; Sajedi et al., 2016) is required for handling such a dimensionality problem. Only a fewer research works have been proposed for universal quantitative steganalysis (Guan et al., 2011; Pevny et al., 2012).

Forensic Steganalysis

In addition to the quantitative steganalysis, forensic steganalysis target to obtain the actual concealed message. The first step needs for such a forensic steganalysers is their algorithm should support for universal steganalysis. Because once the detection is done on the corresponding image, then it is a need to know about the hiding algorithm of the particular image to extract the hidden message. In this case, forensic steganalysis is merely close to cryptanalysis.

Using a brute force search is the best method for determining the stego key. That is the dictionary attack and mining the allege communication when searching for a recognized leader as a sign that can originate athwart the stego key. Anyhow this will be unsuccessful when the entrenched informations does not have any detectable arrangement, and also it is very difficult to find because of the stego key, also entirely possible encryption key should be tested. Consequently the complexity of both encryption key space and product of stego size is proportional.

For the stego key search method Fridrich et al. (2012) show the embedding paradigm and whose entrenching device involves of the subsequent points.

1. Hiding laterally a pseudo-random path engendered equation the stego key
2. Bits are hidden as equivalences of separate pixels.
3. In the needed case, pixels parity is change by means of an entrenching process.

By using PRNG (Pseudo Random Number Generator), random path selection has done that is broadcasted with a kernels consequent equation a passphrase or user defied stego key. PRNG (Pseudo Random Number Generator) output is used to create a pseudo-random walk over the pixels. Along the pseudo-random walk, the secret message is embedded as a bitstream element parity. This helps to change the element parity and hence it may probabilistic or deterministic (Shrivastava et al., 2013).

Feature Extraction

When designing classifier using machine learning, it is very helpful to represent images in some manner. Because signal dimensions are high and the stego-signal-to-noise ratio is very low. In the case of feature extraction, images are represented using features. For an effective steganalysis, this feature should sensitively react to steganographic embedding and it should be very insensitive to the image content. In this section, we introduce the most famous feature set done by the existing steganalysers especially in the image domain of spatial and JPEG.

Feature Extraction in Spatial Domain

Fundamentally noise residual values highly depend on the content other than the pixel values. For every pixel, noise residuals are calculated as differences among the pixel value and its predicted value obtained from the pixel neighbors. Based on this idea, from the spatial domain noise residuals, images are represented. Also, the noise residual has a limited dynamic range other than the pixels and hence the stego noise uses a larger SNR. Likewise, it has an advantage of easy in finding a well-fitting model. But the problem is the dimension of this signal is very high, proportional to the original image.

Due to steganographic embedding, the dependency of neighboring samples is disturbed. Hence it is not enough to extract a first order static from the residuals, needs to extract the joint statistics of residuals. To do this the residuals are first quantized into the small number of samples following that co-occurrence matrix (joint probability mass function) are formed. The problem with co-occurrence matrix is the number of co-occurrence bins will increase exponentially with the dimension of co-occurrence. In this section, we are going to discuss the two strong spatial domain feature sets.

Spatial Rich model (SRM) (Kodovsky et al., 2012; Fridrich et al., 2007) is a very strong and promising statistical descriptor of images. Four-dimensional co-occurrence matrices are formed with the quantized residuals and detection is done in a diverse content. Likewise, from the spatial domain, several feature sets are extracted. Subtractive pixel adjacency matrix and subtractive DCT coefficient adjacency matrix (SDAM) (Farsi et al., 2014) LLT histogram coefficient textural features and co-occurrence matrix (Xian et al., 2012) textural features of LLT coefficient histogram, co-occurrence matrix and etc.

Feature Extraction in Transform Domain

In this segment, we provide an evaluation of the feature mining methods for image universal steganalysis. Also, we mainly absorbed on the arithmetical characteristics mined as of the wavelet sub-band of an image. Then, Universal steganalysis is designed built on two choices namely 1. Feature extraction 2. Classifier used for stego detection. So for numerous feature mining systems has been described based on discrete wavelet transform. In 2002, Farid et al. proposed the first universal steganalysis method. A examination image is disintegrated at three stages via QMF (Quadrature Mirror Filter). PDF (Probability distribution function) moments of each subband are mined from the sophisticated frequency wavelet subband coefficient, and also from log-linear prediction fault subband. And hence 72-dimensional features are generated and given as input to the FLD (Fisher Linear Discriminant) classifier for stego detection. Later Farid's feature set has been extended by Lfu and Farid et al (2004), to extract 216 features from first and higher order color wavelet statistics. The classifier used to discriminate the stego image is one- class SVM (Support Vector Machine). Similarly, four-level dwt has used to (Shunquan Tan et al., 2014) to capture PDF moment of wavelet coefficient subband and log-linear prediction error subband.

Guoming et al (2012) extracted the wavelet transformation based features by decomposing an image into three levels using Haar discrete wavelet transform. Likewise, Xiangyand et al. (2011) decomposed an image into three levels to gather 255 features collected of absolute characteristic function moment of histograms obtained from 85 coefficient of each subband. To distinguish the stego images from cover, a back propagation neural network was used.

To capture the first three CF (characteristic Function) moment of wavelet subband, Xuan et al. (2005) disintegrated an image into three stages and the resulting 39 features are given as input to Bayes classifier to organize the stego images. The method proposed by Holotyak et al. (2005) calculated the stego wavelet subband by using message estimation method. PDF moment of higher frequency wavelet coefficient subbands of stego version is mined as 33-dimensional features. Finally FLD 9Filsher Linear Discriminant) is used as a classifier for discriminating the stego version from the clean one. Moreover, Yang et al. (2011) estimated the absolute CF (Characteristic Function) and PDF moments by hypothetical examination and to finding the more sensitive feature to embed the stego message. And their experimental founding's shown that CF moments attained from prediction subband, high-frequency wavelet subband, prediction error subband or wavelet coefficient subband of image noise are additional complex to stego message embedding's rather than the PDF moments. Also aimed at the log prediction fault subband, first order CF moments are not healthier than the PDF moments.

Machine Learning

Support Vector Machine

Support vector machines are a good and more promising algorithm for detecting the stego images. Basically, SVM is a linear and binary learner, when to solve the nonlinear problems; the kernel is used to convert it to linear which can map the feature vector into high dimensional spaces. SVM enlarges the margin of the data samples in two different classes. The success of SVM purely depends on the kernel function. Kernels are used to convert the input data into higher dimensional space; hence decision boundaries are made. The problem of SVM is, for the moderate six problems, the SVM training complexity slows down the development cycle and kernels gram matrix is

$Grammatrix = \left(Featuredimension \times sizeoftrainingset\right)^2$. This may restrict the steganalyst to deliberately project the features set that fitting in the involvedness problems. In other words, training an SVM classifier their complexity cultivates by means of the cube of the amount of features and training examples. The easily solvable problem need of fewer support vectors and thus training process is quick, but in the case of highly overlapped features number of support, vectors are needed to train the samples and hence it is very time-consuming. For a classification problem, based on the amount of features and support vectors complexity grows linearly. As alternative ensemble classifiers significantly give freedom to the steganalyst without any concern about the feature dimension, the training set size and build detectors with a faster development cycle.

Deepa et al. (2016) proposed the steganalysis scheme for wow stego images. Using SPAM and CC-CHEN features set the stego images created by WOW steganographic scheme are detected. To classify the stego images SVM classifier has been used. In Muthuramalingam et al. proposed the steganalysis system built on low dimensional informative features. With the idea of curvelet, sub band image representation provides the discrimination ability; features are formed from the empirical moments. Support vector machine has been employed to distinguish the stego images from the clean images. And their results are outperforming than the previous steganalysis methods. Likewise, support vector machine has been used as a classifier with various kernel functions in stego image detection by many authors such as (Liu Shaohui et al., 2003; Cogranne et al., 2015; Pathak et al., 2014; Shankar et al., 2016).

Artificial Neural Networks (ANNs)

Since in the past little decade neural networks are proficiently used in stego image detection. Artificial neural networks are familiar with significant data analysis tools. It accurately captures both linear and nonlinear models and also it is said to be a powerful tool for data clustering, classification, function approximation and etc. We will see how the authors are using the ANNs in stego detection. Since ANN is a mathematical-like model that pretends the whole structure as of biological neural scheme. It adopts some of the features of the natural nervous system which is a collection of computing units called neurons. These neurons were embodied as the biological model into the conceptual component for circuits which can do the operational tasks. The simple model of the neuron is originated upon the functionality of a natural neuron. ANN comprises of an interrelated collection of artificial neurons and practices data by means of a connectionist method of reckoning. Such model illustrates tough similarity to axons and dendrites in a nervous system. Flexibility, Robustness, collective computation is the gorgeous structures of this model, owing to its self-organizing and adaptive nature. An artificial neuron consists of three interesting basic components; 1. Neurons Synapses are showed as weights. The aforementioned interrelates the neural networks and supports the connection. Here weight is assigned by a number and synapse is represented. 2. The positive value of a weight designates excitatory connection and the negative weight designates inhibitory connection. Hence all the inputs are added together and the modified by weights and it is referred as the linear combination. 3. At last, the amplitude of an output is measured by an activation function. For illustration, the yield is accepted when it is range between 0 and 1 or it could be between -1 and 1.

The structure of a network node looks like a differential equation. The connection among the nodes is either interconnected between nearest layers are interconnected with nearest neurons in the same layer. An activation value outputs from a previous layer is given as an input into the nodes of the subsequent layers. The activation value from an activation function is passed over non- linear function. If the vectors are analog in nature then squash function ID considered, on the other hand, if the vectors are binary of polar then hard – limiting non-linearity is considered. Some of the quash function are given as tanh (+1 or -1), sigmoid (0 or 1), logarithmic, exponential and Gaussian. Likewise, the network is considered either analog or discrete. The analog network is allied with continuous output whereas the discrete network is allied with two states. The discrete network can be considered as synchronous when each neuron state is updated in the network. Then again, the discrete network is considered as asynchronous, when only one particular is updated for a given time.

A feed-forward network delivers input to the following layer with no closed chain of dependence among neural states via a weight set. The entire network is set as static when the network output depends upon the current input, whereas the entire network is set a dynamic if the output depends on the past input or output. Likewise based on the time factor the network is called as adaptive or non-adaptive. In the case of adaptive the interconnection among neurons changes with time, on the other hand, the network is called as non-adaptive when it is not undergone any changes with time.

In the practical scenario, most of the patterns are not separate linearly. In order to achieve virtuous separability nonlinear classifiers are mostly used for pattern classification. The multilayer network is a nonlinear classifier (e.g. Polynomial discriminate function - pdf) since it uses hidden layer. In the case of the polynomial discriminate function, the input vector is basically preprocessed. In practical, neural networks are used for classifying the patterns by learning some samples. To learn the patterns several weight updating methods have been developed so far, that is supervised and unsupervised methods. When both input and output are considered then the problem is dealt under supervised learning methodology whereas in the case of unsupervised learning, the input will be available and target output cannot be provided. Once the sum of the excitatory inputs reaches its threshold value then a neuron is said to be fired. Until the neurons receive any input then this state always remains valid. This model can be used to hypothesis a network which can compute any logical function, but this was un-biological. To overcome such a model deficiency, a model was proposed to learn and generalize.

To scrutinize the texture of the pixel within the neighborhood plane, Lafferty et al. (2004) proposed a steganalysis method based on local binary pattern texture operator. It computes the statistics of pixels among neighbors, the correlation between neighbors. Also, first order statistics and delta among histogram bins are used as features. And back propagation neural networks are used for training and testing the clean and stego images. Likewise, neural networks are used by many authors in stego detection on different domains (Shaohui et al., 2003); Davidson et al., 2005; Sabeti et al., 2010).

Ensemble Classifier

As current steganalysis, have faith in on progressively complicated image models, so there is a need of scalable machine learning tool. To discourse the issue of complexity, an ensemble classifier is used. This background constructed as a combination of judgments of weak base learners. In Kodovský et al., (2011) Kodovský et al. (2014), Kodovský et al. (2012), Fridrich et al. (2011), Tao et al. (2003), and Pevny et al. (2010), the authors used an ensemble classifier as a fully automatized framework and the ensemble classifier research area gets bloomed up.

Ensemble classifiers consist of many individual trained base learners. From the feature space F, unpretentious classifiers are constructed based on the subspaces which are randomly selected. The dimension chosen by the random subspaces are quite smaller than the entire dimension d and thus the training complexity has greatly reduced. Ensemble classifier is finely trained by using training set and when a new unseen test image is given, each base learner will give its own decision and the final decision will be given by accumulating all the decisions given by each base learner. Since the base learner has chosen are the weak base learner, the performance was given by each base learner also weak, but the accuracy of aggregation is an improved one. This strategy will work only in the case of individual base learners are adequately miscellaneous in the sense that makes the error for an unseen new data. In the hope of increasing the mutual diversity of base learners, each base learner is trained in a bootstrap manner, whereas some samples are drawn from the training set other than the complete training set. This is termed as aggregating or bagging which may allow attaining the testing error accurately. We will go little bit deep for explain the full concept of Ensemble classifier.

As an alternative to SVM, the Fisher Linear Discriminant (FLD) ensemble classifier was initially anticipated (Cogranne et al., 2015) as a scalable learning tool which works as a promising detector in high dimensional feature spaces besides set of the huge size of training set. Assume that from an image, $f \in \mathbb{R}^d$ be a row vector of features d mined. Both training and testing set contains cover and stego image features whereas, the features of stego and cover of training set be matrices $N^{training} \times d$ size where the components of $c^{training}$ and $s^{training}$ respectively. FLD considers that between these two classes, means of features are μ_{cover} and μ_{stego}, covariance matrices are Σ_{cover} and Σ_{stego} of size $d \times d$. By using all these linear decisions rile is defined by:

$$R : \begin{cases} H_0 & if \; f.w^T - b < 0 \\ H_1 & if \; f.w^T - b > 0 \end{cases} \tag{1}$$

where b is a threshold, f is a row vector, the FLD determines the weight vector $w \in R^d$ which maximizes the below fisher ratio:

$$Fisher \; ratio \; F(w) : \frac{w\left(\mu_{cover} - \mu_{stego}\right)^T \left(\mu_{cover} - \mu_{stego}\right) w^T}{w\left(\Sigma_{cover} + \Sigma_{stego}\right) w^T} \tag{2}$$

Some experimental observations illustrates that the maximization of fisher ratio from the training samples hints to the resulting weight vector w.

$$w = \left(\hat{\mu}_{stego} - \hat{\mu}_{cover}\right)\left(\hat{\Sigma}_{cover} + \hat{\Sigma}_{stego}\right)^{-1} \tag{3}$$

with

$$\hat{\mu}_{cover_i} = \frac{1}{N_{training}} \sum_{n=1}^{N_{training}} cov \, er_{n,i}^{training} \;\;, \;\; \hat{\mu}_{stego_i} = \frac{1}{N_{training}} \sum_{n=1}^{N_{training}} stego_{n,i}^{training} \;\;,$$

$$\hat{\Sigma}_{cover_{n,i}} = \frac{1}{N_{training} - 1} \sum_{n=1}^{N_{training}} \left(cover_{n,i}^{training} - \hat{\mu}_{cover_i} \right) \left(cover_{n,j}^{training} - \hat{\mu}_{cover_j} \right),$$

$$\hat{\Sigma}_{stego_{n,i}} = \frac{1}{N_{training} - 1} \sum_{n=1}^{N_{training}} \left(stego_{n,i}^{training} - \hat{\mu}_{stego_i} \right) \left(stego_{n,j}^{training} - \hat{\mu}_{stego_j} \right)$$

Let I_d be an identity matrix of size $d \times d$, the inversion of the covariance matrix "between class" is performed directly but in most of the cases, to improve numerical stability λI_d is added with covariance matrix and hence $\hat{\Sigma}_{cover} + \hat{\Sigma}_{cover} + \lambda I_d$. In the case of feature space dimensionality d and the amount of training samples $N^{training}$, order of magnitude is similar then the covariance matrix of between-class is often ill-conditioned. Fisher Linear Discriminant ensemble is a set of L base learners which can be trained on equally randomly selected dimensional subsets of the feature space. To diversify the base learners, such an approach was initially used with decision trees. It works on the majority voting process. That is an ensemble gives a final assessment by combining all the decisions given by all the base learners by means of majority voting. The training scale of the ensemble is a good enough one because of $d_{sub} << d$. Either by using cross-validation set or bootstrapping d_{sub} and L is determined.

In some of the works, the rule of majority voting has substituted with a likelihood ratio. Once the majority voting rule is replaced with LRT then automatically the ensemble turns into a linear classifier. And also both the linear and nonlinear FLD ensemble classifier performance are same. Truly, there is no difference between linear and nonlinear when the high dimensional rich image model decision boundary is near to linear. In the current digital image steganography scenario, the linear classifier may accomplish the identical classification precision as near as the original majority voting – FLD ensemble classifier. Then it makes us rise a question as there exist any simpler approaches based on FLD. Hence four linear classifiers are there such as Ridge regression, l2 regularization of Fisher ratio, solving LLS with LSMR and LASSO regularization.

1.   L2 Regularization of Fisher Ratio

The fisher ratio from L2 regularization can be accomplished by interchanging the Fisher ratio intensification with

$$w = \arg \min F\left(w\right)^{-1} + \lambda \parallel w \parallel_2^2$$

This may lead to the identical weight vector as the w which can attained using Tikhonov regularization.

$$w = \left(\hat{\mu}_{stego} - \hat{\mu}_{cover} \right) \left(\hat{\Sigma}_{cover} + \hat{\Sigma}_{stego} + \lambda I_d \right)^{-1} \tag{4}$$

2. Ridge Regression

The other name of Ridge regression is denoted as Tikhonov regularization- least square estimation. For further explaining this classifier, consider the training samples in a matrix as

$$X = \begin{pmatrix} c^{training} \\ s^{training} \end{pmatrix} \tag{5}$$

And it's label vector $y \in R^{2N^{training}}$ which defines the corresponding class of the examples as of x. Where $y = \left(-1-1-1..... +1+1+1...\right)^T$. Its aim is to find a weighting vector $w_{rr.}$ which can minimize the squared error between actual and the estimated label.

$$w_{rr.} = \underset{w \in \mathbb{R}^d}{\arg \min} \parallel y - Xw^T \parallel_2^2 + \lambda \parallel w \parallel_2^2 \tag{6}$$

3. Solving LLS With LSMR (Least Square Minimum Residual)

On the availability of the large set of optimization methods for solving the linear system, the ridge regression can be implemented using a large optimization method called LSMR. The reason for using LSMR is, this having low computational complexity and also there is a requirement of little memory space. This may involve us in finding regularization λ and forbearance used in LSMR parameter. This greatly panels the trade-off among computational effectiveness and optimal solution.

4. LASSO Regularization

Machine learning group always prefers to use l_1 regularization because of generating the sparse solution and identifying a feature set of linear classifiers and hence it is called as LASSO (Least Absolute Shrinkage and Selection Operator).

Deep Learning

In the preceding few decades deep learning (Krizhevsky et al., 2012; Russakovsky et al., 2015; Szegedy et al., 2015) is the emerging area and it is said to be a particularly promising alternate to steganalysers depends on the rich models of the image with ensemble classifiers. Convolution Neural networks (CNN) is an approach to Deep learning which acts as steganalysers with a set of useful features and new classification procedures. Detection takes place based on 2d shape variation and also is used in many pattern recognition problems. Couchot et al.(2016) proposed a CNN based steganalysis system which entrenches fewer convolutions and larger filters in the final layer of convolution. It efficiently deals with larger payload and outperforms other steganalysis systems with same embedding key. In some steganographic schemes, DNA sequences have been used as a cover medium to hide medium to cover the secret messages. Due to DNA's complex internal structure, hidden message detection is difficult. To detect such a method the author proposed deep recurrent neural network to detect DNA steganalysis. Likewise, Wu et al. proposed deep residual learning based network to catch complex statistics and also preserves stego signal. In addition to that even though there is a cover source mismatch, Pibre et al. (2016) convolution neural network and fully connected neural network are very robust to mismatch problem and their results have been shown that very promising in detecting the stego images than the state of the art steganalysis. In (2017) Sedighi et al. proposed an optimized method for rich features. Since the availability of CNN packages, the feature set such as the projection of spatial rich features are optimized and simulated a new histogram layer from the quantized noise residuals.

Recent many published works on using CNN's mainly focus on detecting spatial domain steganography only (Shuang et al., 2007; Qian et al., 2015; Qian et al., 2016; Thai et al., 2014; Xu et al., 2016a, 2016b). Even though JPEG steganography is more conveniently used in practice, there is a gap on applying CNN for detecting such a JPEG steganography domain schemes. To fill this gap Zeng et al. (2017) proposed a hybrid CNN optimized method upon several DCT quantized sub-bands of decompressed input image files. Three convolutional layers are used in this method and also employed an average pooling that usually appears in spatial domain steganalysis. The experiment has been carried out on 14 million images collected from the Image Net Database and their results showed up that, because of using the huge number of training data, CNN outperforms the usual feature- based steganalysis methods in detecting JPEG steganography schemes. Later Xu et al. (2017) articulate that using "shallow architecture and average pooling layers are too conservative" in bringing the full strength of deep learning. Little more deeply discuss that, spatial domain steganography directly changes the pixel values of an image and hence CNN is very powerful in mining such a local pattern, run the peril of learning the hiding patterns that would ultimately damage the generality of the trained models.

To solve this, authors (Xu et al., 2017; Xu et al., 2016) designed a CNN framework to distinguish the most powerful JPEG steganography method – J-UNIWARD (JPEG universal wavelet relative distortion). The experiment has been conducted on BOSS base database images compressed with JPEG QF (Quality Factor) of 75 and 95. Each compressed image has embedded in J-UNIWARD steganography method using Gibbs simulator with all the rates of 0.1-0.4 bpnzAC (bits per non zero AC Coefficients). Their results discovered that the designed 20 layer CNN worked with batch normalization, shortcut connections for worthy gradient back propagation has more promising performance that the state-of-the-art feature based steganalysers and also 20 layers CNN has cut down error rate by 35% than the large-scale JPEG steganalysis (Zeng et al., 2017).

The architecture of the work is as follow. To project each input into 16 various frequency bands, 4×4 un-decimated DCT was used. When the study has been done in this research various DCT sizes are used such as 2×2, 4×4 3×3, 5×5 and 8×8 but the best result was obtained in the DCT size 4×4. Also, no exact improvement has been observed when removing the highest frequency subbands or DC subband. For the feature extraction purpose, magnitudes of subbands and quantization have been used. The subbands are truncated with a global threshold value of 8 and it greatly helps to prevent some information loss. Truncation is an important step to limit the range of input data and also it attains fast convergence. Ensuring these pre-processing steps is the essential portion of the CNN encompassing 20 convolutional layers plus a global- average pooling layer. This may help the classifier to learn the optimized function to transform every preprocessed input into the 384-dimensional feature vector. To decrease the internal covariant shift and Rectified Linear Unit (ReLU), Batch Normalization (BN) has used. GPUs memory has been fit with12GB memory and single GPU and the convolution kernel used was 3×3 along the spatial dimension.

FEATURE NORMALIZATION

At present, the more promising feature set designed to steganalysis is rich models comprises of co-occurrences (joint probability mass function) of neighboring noise residuals extracted using a bulk of nonlinear and linear pixel predictors. Owing to the problem of features cure of dimensionality and more training complexity, we are in need of low complexity machine such as ensemble classifier (Kodovsky et al., 2014), regularized linear discriminates (Cogranne et al., 2015) and linear version (Cogranne et al., 2015). To achieve the better detection rate and to utilize the feature vector information without using any intricate machine learning tools is, performing a pre-processor transformation on the feature vector before given into classification. To separate the stego and cover features with a plain decision boundary non- linear feature transformation is used in Boroumand et al.(2016). This work was extended to assessing tacit feature maps in kernelized SVM with explicit transformation.

FEATURE SELECTION

In feature selection, the aim is to choose the features subgroup to form the original features to perform the best prediction scheme by confiscating the redundant and irrelevant features. This can be accomplished by appreciative the kindliness of the features in the direction of the steganographic algorithm which aids in plummeting the training time, the difficulty of the features and too aids in improving the classification/ prediction performance.

To improve the efficiency of classifiers, several feature selection methods have been discussed under three categories. 1. Filter approach, 2. Wrapper approach, 3. Hybrid approach. Filtering method assess the feature relevance depends on the numerical characteristic of information and ranks the features. Generally, features with high rank and high discriminatory capability are selected. For steganalysis, various filtering approaches have been proposed based on the distance measures such as Euclidean distance, Bhattacharya distance, and Mahalanobis distance. To remove the redundant features, information gain and mutual information are also proposed. Correlation-based Feature Selection Measures are there, it ranks the feature subsets instead of each feature. The concept behind is that, on behalf of a feature subgroup, it to be relevant each features must have the high correlation with its class variable. In some other research based on Analysis of Variance (ANOVA), the Image Quality Metrics (IQM) are ranked and the images were detected as stego or clean via multivariate regression analysis classifier.

Secondly method namely wrapper method which evaluates the feature subset effectiveness. For individually feature subgroup, the precision has been appraised and the combined features subset with maximum accuracy has been selected. In some steganalysis research, forward selection algorithm has been employed which begins with the best features and starts to add a new feature one by one, until the classifier identifies the maximum accuracy. This may help to overcome the exhaustive search need best it is not an effective one for high dimensional features. On the other hand, many research works have been done based on PSO (Particle Swarm Optimization), GA (Genetic Algorithm), ABC (Artificial Bee Colony) and etc.

The advantage of filtering method is that, its computation simplicity. It may give preference for the high dimensional feature selection as like as it provides good computational efficiency in terms of computational time and cost. Their advantage it does not depends on the classifier, that is it is difficult to know about the performance of the selected subset until a learning model is generated. On the other hand, wrapper approach gives good accuracy as it computes the performance of each feature subset and chooses the combination of feature set with maximum accuracy. The problem is that for the high dimensional feature set, it is computationally exclusive.

To overcome the problems of both wrapper and filtering approaches, hybrid approaches have gained consideration in the recent years. The idea is to use the filter approaches for selecting the feature subset and its output is given as an input into wrapper approach. In this case, the evaluation of wrapper approach is reduced the computational complexity and on the other hand, the enhanced precision may be retained. This hybrid approach has been realistic for various applications such as malware detection, steganalysis, biomedical, internet traffic classification and etc. But using hybrid approach for feature selection in steganalysis is still an unexplored area and also only less research work has been done.

On the emergent of deep learning, the usage of such a feature selection method for pattern recognition like research will be reduced because of not worrying about the size of data in the deep learning.

CONCLUSION

In this chapter, we have attempted to deliver a short introduction to machine learning algorithms used as a classifier in detecting the stego images. Many machine learning algorithms are used in the literature. Since many steganalysers try to detect the recent steganographic algorithms via a high dimensional feature set. Recently, ensemble learning and deep learning are the most promising and fastest learning methods and it is greatly free from the complexity problems. And also, even though the feature set contains lakhs of features and the training the system using lakhs of objects in the dataset, deep learning is the best tool to training such a larger of the amount of dataset. On the other hand to overcome the complexity of training time and space, handling the huge set of high dimensional features, the ensemble learning, and deep learning is the suggested one.

REFERENCES

Boroumand, M., & Fridrich, J. (2016). Boosting Steganalysis with Explicit Feature Maps. *Proceedings of 4th ACM Workshop on Information Hiding and Multimedia Security.* doi: 10.1145/2909827.2930803

Chandramouli, R., & Memon, N. (2001). Analysis of LSB based image steganography techniques. *Proceedings of ICIP 2001.* 10.1109/ICIP.2001.958299

Chanu, Singh, & Tuithung. (2012). Image Steganography and Steganalysis: A Survey. *International Journal of Computer Applications, 52*(2), 1-11.

Chen, X., Gao, G., Liu, D., & Xia, Z. (2016). Steganalysis of LSB Matching Using Characteristic Function Moment of Pixel Differences. Image Detection and Analysis Technique. *China Communications*, *13*(7), 66–73. doi:10.1109/CC.2016.7559077

Cogranne, R., Denemark, T., & Fridrich, J. (2014). Theoretical model of the FLD ensemble classifier based on hypothesis testing theory. *IEEE International Workshop on Information Forensics and Security (WIFS)*, 167–172. 10.1109/WIFS.2014.7084322

Cogranne, R., & Fridrich, J. (2015). Modeling and extending the ensemble classifier for steganalysis of digital images using hypothesis testing theory. *IEEE Transactions on Information Forensics and Security, Volume*, *10*(12), 2627–2642. doi:10.1109/TIFS.2015.2470220

Cogranne, R., Sedighi, V., Pevný, T., & Fridrich, J. (2015). Is Ensemble Classifier Needed for Steganalysis in High-Dimensional Feature Spaces? *IEEE International Workshop on Information Forensics and Security*. 10.1109/WIFS.2015.7368597

Couchot, J.-F., Couturier, R., Guyeux, C., & Salomon, M. (2016). *Steganalysis via a Convolutional Neural Networks using Large Convolution Filters for embedding process with same stego key*. Cornell University Library.

Davidson, Bergman, & Bartlett. (2005). An artificial neural network for wavelet steganalysis. *Proceedings of SPIE- The International Society for Optical Engineering, Mathematical method in Pattern and Image Analysis, 5916*, 1-10.

Deepa, S., & Uma Rani, R. (2016). Steganalysis on images based on the classification of image feature sets using SVM classifier. *International Journal on Computer Science and Engineering*, *5*(5), 15–24.

Farid, H. (2002) Detecting hidden messages using higher-order statistical models. *Proceedings of IEEE International Conference Image Processing, 2*, 905–908. 10.1109/ICIP.2002.1040098

Farsi, H., & Shahi, A. (2014). Steganalysis of images based on spatial domain and two-dimensional JPEG array. *Journal of the Chinese Institute of EngineersVolume*, *37*(8), 1055–1063. doi:10.1080/025 33839.2014.929711

Filler, T., & Fridrich, J. (2010). Gibbs Construction in Steganography. *IEEE Transactions on Information Forensics and Security, Volume*, *5*(4), 705–720. doi:10.1109/TIFS.2010.2077629

Fridrich, J., & Goljan, M. (2006). On estimation of secret message length in LSB steganography in spatial domain. In Proceedings of Security, steganography, and watermarking of multimedia Contents VI. *Proceedings of the Society for Photo-Instrumentation Engineers, 5306*, 23–34. doi:10.1117/12.521350

Fridrich, J., Goljan, M., & Du, R. (2001). Detecting LSB steganography in color and gray-scale images. *IEEE MultiMedia*, *8*(4), 22–28. doi:10.1109/93.959097

Fridrich, J., & Kodovský, J. (2012). Rich models for steganalysis of digital images. *IEEE Transactions on Information Forensics and Security*, *7*(3), 868–882. doi:10.1109/TIFS.2012.2190402

Fridrich, J., Kodovský, J., Goljan, M., & Holub, V. (2011). Breaking HUGO – the process discovery. *Information Hiding, 13th International Workshop*, *6958*, 85–101.

Fridrich, J., Kodovský, J., Goljan, M., & Holub, V. (2011). Steganalysis of content-adaptive steganography in spatial domain. *Information Hiding, 13th International Workshop*, 6958, 102–117. 10.1007/978-3-642-24178-9_8

Fridrich, J., Pevný, T., & Kodovský, J. (2007). Statistically Undetectable JPEG Steganography: Dead Ends, Challenges, and Opportunities. *Proceedings of the 9th ACM Multimedia & Security Workshop*, 3–14.

Guo, Ni, & Shi. (2014). Uniform Embedding for Efficient JPEG Steganography. *IEEE Transactions on Information Forensics and Security, 9*(5), 814–825. 10.1109/TIFS.2014.2312817

Guo, L., Ni, J., & Shi, Y.-Q. (2012). An Efficient JPEG Steganographic Scheme Using Uniform Embedding. *Proceedings of Fourth IEEE International Workshop on Information Forensics and Security*. 10.1109/WIFS.2012.6412644

Guoming, C., Qiang, C., Dong, Z., & Weighing, Z. (2012). *Particle swarm optimization feature selection for image steganalysis*. IEEE Computer Society.

Hastie, T., Tibshirani, R., Friedman, J., & Franklin, J. (2009). *The elements of statistical learning: data mining, inference and prediction* (2nd ed.). Springer. doi:10.1007/978-0-387-84858-7

Hetzl, S., & Mutzel, P. (2005). A Graph-Theoretic Approach to Steganography. *Communications and Multimedia Security, 9th IFIP TC-6 TC-11 International Conference, CMS 2005*, 119–128. 10.1007/11552055_12

Ho, T. K. (1995). Random decision forests. *Proceedings of International Conference on Document Analysis and Recognition*, 278–282.

Holotyak, T., Fridrich, J., & Voloshynovskiy, S. (2005). Blind statistical steganalysis of additive steganography using wavelet higher order statistics. *Proceedings of 9th IFIP Conference on Communication and Multimedia Security, LNCS 3677*, 273–274. 10.1007/11552055_31

Holub, V., & Fridrich, J. (2015). Low-Complexity Features for JPEG Steganalysis Using Undecimated DCT. *IEEE Transactions on Information Forensics and Security, 10*(2), 219–228. doi:10.1109/TIFS.2014.2364918

Holub, V., & Fridrich, J. (2015). Phase-Aware Projection Model for Steganalysis of JPEG Images. *Proceedings of SPIE, Electronic Imaging, Media Watermarking, Security, and Forensics 2015, 9409*, 1–11.

Holub, V., Fridrich, J., & Denemark, T. (2014). *Universal distortion function for steganography in an arbitrary domain*. EURASIP Journal on Information Security.

Hou, X., Zhang, T., & Xu, C. (2016). New framework for unsupervised universal steganalysis via SRISP-aided outlier detection. *Image Communication, 47C*, 72–85.

Ker, A. K. (2006). Fourth-order structural steganalysis and analysis of cover assumptions. Proceedings of SPIE 6072, Security, Steganography, and Watermarking of Multimedia Contents VIII, 6072, 1–14. doi:10.1117/12.642920

Kodovský, J., & Fridrich, J. (2011). Steganalysis in high dimensions: Fusing classifiers built on random subspaces. *Proceedings SPIE, Electronic Imaging, Media Watermarking, Security and Forensics of Multimedia XIII*, 7880, 1–13.

Kodovský, J., & Fridrich, J. (2012). Steganalysis of JPEG Images Using Rich Models. *Proceedings SPIE, Electronic Imaging, Media Watermarking, Security, and Forensics 2012, 8303*. 10.1117/12.907495

Kodovský, J., & Fridrich, J. (2012). Steganalysis of JPEG images using rich models. *Proceedings SPIE, Electronic Imaging, Media Watermarking, Security, and Forensics of Multimedia XIV*. 10.1117/12.907495

Kodovský, J., Fridrich, J., & Holub, V. (2012). Ensemble classifiers for steganalysis of digital media. *IEEE Transactions on Information Forensics and Security*, 7(2), 432–444. doi:10.1109/TIFS.2011.2175919

Krizhevsky, A., Sutskever, I., & Hinton, G. (2012). Imagenet classification with deep convolutional neural networks. Proceedings of Communications of the ACM, 60(6), 84-90.

Lafferty & Ahmed. (2004). Texture based steganalysis: results for color images. *Proceedings of SPIE, Mathematics of Data/Image Coding, compression and encryption VII with applications, 5561*, 145-151.

Lerch-Hostalot, D., & Megías, D. (2013). LSB matching steganalysis based on patterns of pixel differences and random embedding. *Computers & Security*, 32, 192–206. doi:10.1016/j.cose.2012.11.005

Lerch-Hostalot, D., & Megías, D. (2016) Unsupervised steganalysis based on artificial training sets. *Proceedings of EngApplArtifIntell, 50*, 45–59. 10.1016/j.engappai.2015.12.013

Liu, Q., Sung, A. H., Qiao, M., Chen, Z., & Ribeiro, B. (2010). An improved approach to steganalysis of JPEG images. *Information Sciences*, 180(9), 1643–1655. doi:10.1016/j.ins.2010.01.001

Liu, S., Yao, H., & Wen, G. (2003). Neural Network based steganalysis in Still Images. *Proceedings of IEEE International Conference on Multimedia and Expo (ICME)*, 509-512. doi:10.1109/ICME.2003.1221665

Lyu, S., & Farid, H. (2004). Steganalysis using color wavelet statistics and one-class vector support Machines. Proceedings of SPIE security, steganography and watermarking of multimedia contents, 5306, 35–45. doi:10.1117/12.526012

Pathak & Selvakumar. (2014). Blind image steganalysis of JPEG images using feature extraction through the process of dilation. *Digital Investigation, 11*, 97–77.

Pevný, T., Filler, T., & Bas, P. (2010). Using high-dimensional image models to perform highly undetectable steganography. In *Information Hiding, 12th International Workshop, Lecture Notes in Computer Science*. Springer-Verlag. 10.1007/978-3-642-16435-4_13

Pevny, T., Fridrich, J., & Ker, A. D. (2012). From blind to quantitative Steganalysis. *IEEE Transactions on Information Forensics and Security*, 7(2), 445–454. doi:10.1109/TIFS.2011.2175918

Pibre, L., Pasquet, J., Ienco, D., & Chaumont, M. (2016). Deep learning is a good steganalysis tool when embedding key is reused for different images, even if there is a cover source-mismatch. *Proceedings of SPIE, IS&T International Symposium on Electronic Imaging, Media Watermarking, Security, and Forensics*. 10.2352/ISSN.2470-1173.2016.8.MWSF-078

Provos, N. (2001). Defending Against Statistical Steganalysis. *Proceedings of 10th USENIX Security Symposium*, 323–335.

Qian, Y., Dong, J., Wang, W., & Tan, T. (2015). Deep learning for steganalysis via convolutional neural networks. In *Proceeding of SPIE 9409*. Media Watermarking, Security, and Forensics. doi:10.1117/12.2083479

Qian, Y., Dong, J., Wang, W., & Tan, T. (2016). Learning and transferring representations for image steganalysis using convolutional neural network. *IEEE International Conference on Image Processing*, 2752–2756. DOI:10.1109/ICIP.2016.7532860

Russakovsky, O., Deng, J., Su, H., Krause, J., Satheesh, S., Ma, S., ... Li, F.-F. (2015). ImageNet large scale visual recognition challenge. *International Journal of Computer Vision*, *115*(3), 211–252. doi:10.100711263-015-0816-y

Sabeti, V., Samavi, S., Mahdavi, M., & Shirani, S. (2010). Steganalysis and payload estimation of embedding in pixel differences using neural networks. *Pattern Recognition*, *43*(1), 405–415. doi:10.1016/j.patcog.2009.06.006

Sajedi, H. (2016). Steganalysis based on steganography pattern discovery. *Journal of Information Security and Applications*, *30*, 3–14. doi:10.1016/j.jisa.2016.04.001

Sallee, P. (2005). Model-Based Methods for Steganography and Steganalysis. *International Journal of Image and Graphics*, *5*(1), 167–190. doi:10.1142/S0219467805001719

Sedighi, V., & Fridrich, J. (2017). Histogram Layer, Moving Convolutional Neural Networks Towards Feature Based Steganalysis. *Proceedings of IS&T, Electronic Imaging, Media Watermarking, Security, and Forensics*.

Shankar & Upadhyay. (2016). Performance analysis of various feature sets in calibrated blind steganalysis. *International Journal of Computer Science and Network Security, 16*(8), 29-34.

Shi, Y. Q., Sutthiwan, P., & Chen, L. (2012). Textural features for steganalysis. In *Information Hiding. 14th International Conference, IH 2012*. Springer.

Shrivastava, G., Pandey, A., & Sharma, K. (2013). Steganography and its technique: Technical overview. In *Proceedings of the Third International Conference on Trends in Information, Telecommunication and Computing* (pp. 615-620). Springer. 10.1007/978-1-4614-3363-7_74

Shuang, H. Z., & Hong, B. Z. (2007). Blind steganalysis using wavelet statistics and ANOVA. *Proceedings - International Conference on Machine Learning and Cybernetics*, *5*, 2515–2519.

Song, X., Liu, F., Yang, C., Luo, X., & Zhang, Y. (2015). Steganalysis of Adaptive JPEG Steganography Using 2D Gabor Filters. *The 3rd ACM Workshop on Information Hiding and Multimedia Security (IH&MMSec '15)*.

Sorina, D., Xiaolin, W., & Zhe, W. (2003). Detection of LSB steganography via sample pair analysis. *IEEE Transactions on Signal Processing, 51*(7), 1995–2007. doi:10.1109/TSP.2003.812753

Szegedy, Liu, Jia, Sermanet, Reed, Anguelov, … Rabinovich. (2015). Going deeper with convolutions. *Proceedings of IEEE International Conference on Computer Vision and Pattern Recognition (CVPR)*, 1–9.

Tan, S., & Li, B. (2014). Stacked convolutional auto-encoders for steganalysis of digital images. *Signal and Information Processing Association Annual Summit and Conference (APSIPA)*. 10.1109/APSIPA.2014.7041565

Tao, Z., & Xijian, P. (2003). Reliable detection of LSB steganography based on the difference image histogram. *Proceedings of. IEEE International Conference on Acoustics, Speech, and Signal Processing*, 545–548.

Thai, T., Cogranne, R., & Retraint, F. (2014). Statistical Model of Quantized DCT Coefficients: Application in the Steganalysis of Jsteg Algorithm. *IEEE Transactions on Image Processing, 23*(5), 1–14. doi:10.1109/TIP.2014.2310126 PMID:24710399

Thai, T. H., Cogranne, R., & Retraint, F. (2014). Optimal Detection of OutGuess using an Accurate Model of DCT Coefficients. *Sixth IEEE International Workshop on Information Forensics and Security*. 10.1109/WIFS.2014.7084324

Upham, D. (n.d.). *Steganographic algorithm JSteg*. Retrieved from http://zooid.org/ paul/crypto/jsteg

Westfeld, A. (2001). High Capacity Despite Better Steganalysis (F5 – A Steganographic Algorithm). In *Information Hiding, 4th International Workshop* (Vol. 2137, pp. 289-302). Springer-Verlag.

Wu, S., Zhong, S., & Liu, Y. (2017). Deep residual learning for image steganalysis. *Multimedia Tools and Applications*, 1–17.

Xia, Z., Wang, X., Sun, X., Liu, Q., & Xiong, N. (2016). Steganalysis of LSB matching using differences between nonadjacent pixels. *Multimedia Tools and Applications, 75*(4), 1947–1962. doi:10.100711042-014-2381-8

Xiang, Y., & Zhang, W. H. (2012). Effective steganalysis of YASS based on statistical moments of wavelet characteristic function and Markov process. *Proceedings of International conference on computer science and electronics engineering*, 606–610. 10.1109/ICCSEE.2012.218

Xiangyang, L., Fenlin, L., Shiguo, L., Chunfang, Y., & Stefanos, G. (2011). On the typical statistic features for image blind steganalysis. *IEEE Journal on Selected Areas in Communications, 29*(7), 1404–1422. doi:10.1109/JSAC.2011.110807

Xiong, G., Ping, X., Zhang, T., & Hou, X. (2012). XiaodanHou. (2012). Image textural features for steganalysis of spatial domain steganography. *Journal of Electronic Imaging, 21*(3), 033015-1. doi:10.1117/1.JEI.21.3.033015

Xu, G. (2017). Deep Convolutional Neural Network to Detect J-UNIWARD. *Proceedings of 5th ACM Workshop Information Hiding Multimedia Security. (IH &MMSec)*. 10.1145/3082031.3083236

Xu, G., Wu, H.-Z., & Shi, Y.-Q. (2016). Ensemble of CNNs for steganalysis: An empirical study. *Proceeding of 4th ACM Workshop on Information Hiding and Multimedia Security (IH&MMSec '16)*, 103–107. DOI: 10.1145/2909827.2930798

Xu, G., Wu, H.-Z., & Shi, Y.-Q. (2016, May). Structural design of convolutional neural networks for steganalysis. *IEEE Signal Processing Letters*, *23*(5), 708–712. doi:10.1109/LSP.2016.2548421

Xuan, G. R., Shi, Y. Q., & Gao, J. J. (2005). Steganalysis based on multiple features formed by statistical moments of wavelet characteristic functions. *Proc. 7th International Information Hiding Workshop, LNCS 3727*, 262–277. 10.1007/11558859_20

Zeng, J., Tan, S., Li, B., & Huang, J. (2017). *Large-scale JPEG image steganalysis using hybrid deep-learning framework*. arXiv: 1611.03233v2

Zhang, T., Li, W., Zhnag, Y., Zheng, E., & Ping, X. (2010). Steganalysis of LSB matching based on statistical modeling of pixel difference distributions. *Information Sciences*, *180*(23), 4685–4694. doi:10.1016/j.ins.2010.07.037

Zhang, T., & Ping, X. (2003). A Fast and Effective Steganalytic Technique AgainstJsteg-like Algorithms. *Proceedings of the ACM Symposium on Applied Computing*, 307–311.

Chapter 20
Audio Watermarking With Reduced Number of Random Samples

Rohit Anand
G. B. Pant Engineering College, India

Gulshan Shrivastava
National Institute of Technology Patna, India

Sachin Gupta
Vivekananda Institute of Professional Studies, India

Sheng-Lung Peng
National Dong Hwa University, Taiwan

Nidhi Sindhwani
Amity School of Engineering and Technology, India

ABSTRACT

Digital signal watermarking is an indiscernible and safe transmission of freehold data through host signal that includes immersing into and extrication from the actual host. Some algorithms have been investigated for the strong and secure embedding and extraction of watermarks within the host audio files but they do not yet yield good results in compression and re-sampling. In this chapter, an excellent method is suggested for the compressed wave files that uses random carrier to immerse the watermark in the sequence of an audio signal. The watermark is embedded lucently in audio stream after adaptive differential pulse code modulation (ADPCM) before quantization. The proposed scheme has been implemented and its parameters are compared with the finest auditory watermarking method known. A tool has been used to measure the parameters to produce the results and tabular values. The larger PSNR and smaller BER prove that the suggested scheme is robust.

DOI: 10.4018/978-1-5225-4100-4.ch020

INTRODUCTION

A drastic number of changes in the world have been because of the evolution of the online networks and the digital content uprising. The different kinds of wideband transmission webworks/ networks and interactive media information present in a binary format (text, pictures, audio, and video) have unlocked so many challenges and possibilities for modernization and novelty. Easy-to-use as well as versatile software and the shrinking prices of the different kinds of digital devices (for example, compact and movable mp3 players and CD players, camcorders, digital scanners, digital cameras, DVD players, CD and DVD recorders, laptops etc.) have created the possibility for the customers from the different regions of the world to design, modify and interchange the different types of data related to multimedia. Different high-speed internet connections and near-accurate transmission of data ease the people to share the heavy kinds of multimedia files and create their homogeneous digital reprints. Digital interactive media files do not undergo any loss of the superiority due to repetitive processes of copying such as analog audio and Video Home System tapes. Further, recording medium and transportation networks for different kinds of analog media are very uneconomical. These benefits of digital means over the analog means may shift to the drawbacks as far as cerebral copyright supervision is concerned because of the likelihood for boundless replication without a loss of precision results in a large economic loss for the holders of possession rights. The effortlessness of the alteration of the matter and exact replication in the digital sphere have encouraged the safekeeping of phrenic possession and the avoidance of illicit dabbling of the different kinds of mixed media data to become a crucial specialized and inspecting issue (Adya, 2007).

A large usage of the audio-visual data along with a speedy transportation of mixed media to the different customers having gadgets with a very good quality of service is growing into a huge challenge. Copy protection systems based on the hardware have now been sidestepped for the analog media. The digital media are very easier to hack because of the possibilities of the different kinds of mixed media processing platforms. Simple protection mechanisms are obsolete now as header information can be easily be eliminated by a simple format of the data that does not affect the correctness of data.

Applying the coding technique to the mixed media avoids ingress to the different mixed media details to a human without a genuine deciphers key. So, detail providers are rewarded for the carriage of recognizable multimedia and each consumer who has paid the royalties should have a proper decipher key so as to unravel the file that has been received. After the decoding of the mixed media file, it can easily be duplicated and dispensed in a repetitive manner with no hurdles. Present-day software and high-speed internet present the aid to accomplish it with very least amount of skills and awareness needed. A very usual example is the hacking of a system based on digital rights management as well as encryption for digital versatile disks. So, existing protocols related to security remain tend to guard the medium of communication between the user and the person who can provide the data for a mixed media. These protocols are totally insignificant if transaction item is digitally designated.

The type of watermarking discussed above can be used to make the digital media safe and secure from the process of tampering. Digital watermarking refers to the embedding of a lucent digital signature (containing a data useful in the applications like broadcast monitoring, anti-tampering etc.) into a host signal. A watermark embedder has one input as watermark message (i.e. a binary sequence along with a secret key) and second input as host signal (like image, audio or video etc.) while the product of a watermark implanter is a very safe watermarked signal that may be broadcasted later to the watermark detector. The function of watermark detector is to find out whether there is any watermark in the multimedia signal and if there is such a watermark, what kind of message is encoded in that. Watermarking is very much related to the field of steganography as well as information hiding. In steganographic systems, the occurrence of the message is kept confidential. In information hiding, information is made imperceptible i.e. it refers to the concealed communication (Cvejic, 2004, 2007; Foo, 2008)

Initially, algorithms related to watermarking were designed only for the digital still images and digital video sequences but research related to the watermarking in the audio files started slightly later. All the watermarking algorithms used for the audio files take the benefit of the visual characteristics of the human auditive systems for adding the watermark onto a host signal. The embedding of information onto the audio bit sequence is more difficult task than onto the images but many of the attacks feasible on the image watermarking algorithms are almost impossible to implement on the audio watermarking algorithms (Walker, 2004).

Watermarking must be distinguished from Steganography. The purpose of latter is to secrete a data in any audio-visual data (say A) to get some new message (say A') totally resembling with A so that an intruder is not capable to identify A'. On the other hand, watermarking refers to hiding a signal (say S) in any audio-visual file (say A'') so as to get some signal A''' practically similar to A'' so that an eavesdropper should not be able to remove, edit or replace M in D''' (Dey et al., 2013).

In case of digital watermarking, a framework of some bits can be fitted into a digital type of picture, sound or visual file that can recognize the ownership details and facts (such as author, rights etc.) of the file. Further, the actual bits that represent the watermark must be dispersed right through the file in such a way that they must not be recognized and edited. Also, this watermark should be so rigid that it can easily stand firm with the modifications to the file, for example, scaling down from the lossy compression techniques (Adya, 2007). In watermark embedding, the watermark may be embedded with the key. The system security is high because of the uncertainty of the key. The watermark should be such that it can always be restored even in the case of signal distortion. The watermark embedding process is shown in Figure 1.

In watermark extraction, the same key may be used to take out the watermark from the disfigured watermark signal. Unlike the normal and secret cipher systems for security and encryption, it helps to

Figure 1. Watermark embedding process

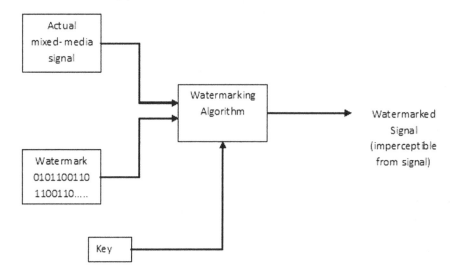

provide the proof of a wrong act after this act has happened. The watermark extraction process is shown in Figure 2.

Digital watermarking may be classified according to

1. Working domain (spatial domain and frequency domain)
2. Type of document (text, image, audio & video)
3. Perception by humans (visible and invisible)
4. Application (source based and destination based)

The watermarking discussed in this paper is only audio watermarking that may be either of blind type or non-blind type. Non-blind methods utilize the actual origin to recover the watermark using easy and elementary correlation or coherent techniques while blind techniques detect the original watermark without the actual source. Non-blind techniques are more secure than the blind ones and hence they have been discussed here (Bassia, Ioannis, & Nikos, 2001).

Some of the parameters that should not be compromised too much are audio quality, reliability, robustness and audio coding.

1. **Quality of Audio:** The system should not impair the quality of audio by the large amount. Any alteration of the original sound/audio from the idealistic position is unacceptable and that needs improvement before describing it to be 'perfect'. Secondly, most of the audience is not in a situation to examine the status of audio to large scale and level because of their restricted vocal and verbal potentials. For those types of audience, a degree of limited but non-perceivable deterioration would be unobjectionable. Thirdly, the people in very poor conditions (like in a car) might withstand some genuinely perceptible deterioration. The very large vicinity of these types of conditions presents a large dilemma for the applications of the watermarking system.
2. **Reliability:** A watermarking system designated to govern access by a client should detect the watermark rapidly and reliably. It is not so crucial that the ingress by an unauthorized human is genuinely barred. It is difficult to develop any safeguard system with satisfactory performance on that issue. Recognition applications may or may not be so faithful in the short term. The required reliability can be attained over longer extracts
3. **Robustness:** A system used for watermarking must be invulnerable to the large indignity of the substance as well as impairments to the substance. The watermark should remain until the contents become 'of no venal value'.

Figure 2. Watermark Extraction Process

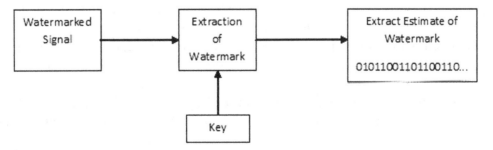

4. **Audio Coding:** The disagreement between the unheard systems having very low bit rate and watermarking systems having the ability to obscure the auxiliary data inaudibly are tangible and discernible.

Further, there are some important properties (Cvejic, 2004) of the watermarking algorithm:

1. **Visual Transparency:** It means that the watermarking embedded algorithm has to embed the watermark without modifying the visual quality of the host signal. The fidelity of the watermarking algorithm refers to the visual similarity between the actual signal and the watermarked sequence.
2. **Bit Rate:** Capacity (bps) requirement of a watermark sequence i.e. set of binary digits of the watermark inserted per unit time of the actual host auditory signal depends upon the application. e.g. many of the applications such as copy control require the embedding of a unique identifying number or the ID of the writer with the mean capacity of 0.6 bit per second. In many other visualized implementations (like speech darkening in host), some techniques must be there to insert watermark sequence with the data rate (capacity) that is a notable fragment of the host data bits per unit i.e. up to few tens of kbps
3. **Strength:** It refers to the ability of extraction of a watermark sequence after management and feature extraction of signal. A large number of feature extraction alterations to which a watermarking technique requires to be strong totally relies on the application. For instance, in case of radio frequency signal broadcasting and supervising, inserted watermark must be resistant against the distortions caused by the transmission process including the filtering of low-frequency signals, compression etc. because the watermark identification is performed straightaway from the telecast signal. In some other techniques, strength may not be advantageous because of being labeled fragile audio watermarking algorithms.
4. **Blind or Non-blind Detection:** Use of the actual host signal to draw the watermark from the watermarked stream refers to non-blind detection that improves the performance of the detector considerably. The original audio signal may be deducted from the watermarked signal that gives the isolated watermarked stream as a result. On the other hand, blind detection does not refer to the ingress to the actual audio that results in the reduction of the aggregate of data concealed in the actual signal. The whole phenomenon of inserting and extraction of the watermark may be modelled as a communication medium in which watermark may be deformed because of the channel effects and intense disturbance. The intense disturbance refers to the existence of actual host and formerly refers to the feature extraction operations.
5. **Security:** It means that an adversary shouldn't have the capability to recover the inserted data. The safety of watermark process may be advantageous just like the safety of the ciphering methods. The security of watermark sequence must be controlled by a secret key to controlling the embedding of the watermark. An eavesdropper must not be able to recover the data although it is known to him that the watermark is contained by the host and the complete inserting algorithm is known to the host. The need for security and safety varies from one application to other application. For example, in some cases, data may be encrypted prior to the insertion of the watermark into host audio.
6. **Cost and Complexity:** The audio watermarking implementation is quite complicated, tedious and uneconomical task that depends upon the application involved, the complexity of the embedding

algorithm and the extraction algorithm. For example, inserting as well as extraction should occur in factual time in case of broadcast monitoring while duration does not affect the realistic execution in case of copyright protection applications.

To evaluate the audio quality, mostly Subjective Testing is used. However, this testing is uneconomical, long-delayed and unrealistic. Some of the instinctive quality testing techniques are Degradation Category Rating (DCR), Pair Comparison (PC) and Absolute Category Rating (ACR). Two different streams (actual and rectified) are displayed to the Volunteers (i.e. humans) and they have to judge the standard of the refined stream on the subject of the original sequence. The complete experiment is partitioned into different phases (keeping the duration of each phase as half an hour at the most). Many of the mock streams are integrated for every phase. These streams may be utilized to upskill the volunteers and may be excluded in the eventual grade. The video stream is graded by the volunteers on the basis of calibration corresponding to their intellectual evaluation of the standard. This is commonly referred to as Mean Observer Score (MOS). MOS score of 1 corresponds to unacceptable score and MOS score of 5 corresponds to the excellent score. For objective testing, the two commonly measured parameters are PSNR and Mean Square Error (MSE). These parameters are used to calculate the absolute difference between input and output. These parameters are very important in Quality Analysis (QA) and Monitoring. PSNR value of 35 dB or more is considered as good.

The choice of the performance evaluation criteria for the characterization of the audio watermarking algorithm represents a key issue for the effective design of a high performance watermarking algorithm. There are four important criteria for the performance evaluation. They may be applied to any watermarking system. The main criteria are (Gordy & Bruton, 2000):

1. Bit Rate
2. Visual Quality
3. Computational Complexity
4. Robustness to Signal Processing

The different application areas (Cvejic, 2004) for the digital watermarking are:

1. **Possession Rights Security:** In the applications regarding possession rights, a watermark having the possession rights details can be inserted in the mixed-media actual signal. The watermark, that is familiar solely to the possession owner, must be very secure and robust. This enables the rights holder to verify the existence of this watermark in case of conflict to prove his possession. The watermark identification should have at least some fictitious likelihood to raise the danger signal. On the contrary, possession rights security needs some inserting capability of the set up because the actual number of bits that are inserted and taken out with a little possibility of error does not necessitate to be substantial.
2. **Proof of Ownership:** It is very much challenging to manage the watermark as an original evidence of possession rights. The real difficulty comes when the contender applies the software to substitute the actual legal right notice with his own and then professes hold the legal right himself. To achieve the security, it is very crucial to limit the accessibility of the recognizer. If any contender does not have the recognizer, the watermark elimination would be utmost troublesome. But, albeit possessor (of rights)'s watermark is not eliminated; a contender might attempt to subvert the possessor. A

contender, using his own watermarking system, might be good enough to frame it look such that that watermark information is available in the possessor's actual host signal. The difficulty may be reduced to some extent by little modification of the problem averment.

3. **Genuineness and Dabbling Identification:** In the content genuineness exercise, a collection of subsidiary data is inserted into the host mixed-media signal and is subsequently employed to find if the original host signal was dabbled or not. The strength of eliminating the watermark or making it unrecognizable does not matter because this incitement from hacker's perspective is not there. But hammering a genuine watermark within an illegal host signal should definitely be avoided. In pragmatic accomplishment, it is also advisable to track and to distinguish the unintended disfigurements. (e.g. distortion caused due to confining of MPEG) from the content dabbling. It is usual to have the watermark insertion capacity high so as to fulfil the need for some extra additional data than in the applications related to ownership protection. The identification must be done with no original host signal required.

4. **Dactylogram:** The supplementary data inserted by the watermark in the dactylogram may be employed so as to follow the founder or receivers of a specific transcript of hypermedia document. For instance, the different watermarks having the different identity numbers are inserted within the distinct transcripts of music disks or video disks prior to assigning them to numerous receivers. The techniques to be used for the dactylogram should have good toughness in resistance to the global attacks and signal processing adjustments like lossy compression or filtering etc. Dactylogram needs excellent counter-complicity features of the various techniques i.e. insertion of two or more identity numbers to the host hypermedia file is almost impossible. If such a thing occurs, the identifier is unable to differentiate about which reprint exists. The extent to which embedding occurs for the dactylogram applications spans in the range of scope required in the applications of possession rights security with quite less bit rate.

5. **Broadcast Tracking:** As far as broadcasting is concerned, a variety of applications are there for the auditory watermarking. Its benefit is that it may be inserted within the hypermedia host. It does not need utilizing a specified segment of the signal to be broadcasted. Therefore, it is generally reconcilable with the previously established support of broadcasting device that includes analog as well as digital transmission medium. The major difficulty is that the watermark insertion is somewhat more complicated than placing an elementary data into the header of the file. One more problem is that the contortion may be introduced by the watermark that may debase the optical or phonic feature of the hypermedia. A few of the broadcast tracking applications that are based on the watermark are available thus far on the lucrative basis e.g. program type identification, advertising approach and broadcast reportage analysis etc. The customers hence acquire a thorough evidence of the potential knowledge that lets the customers to:
    a. Prove the right program and its related promos
    b. Monitor trade marketing within programming
    c. Self-regulatory monitor hypermedia inside programs with the programmed software online

6. **Transcript Regulation and Retrieve Regulation:** In this type, the inserted watermark indicates some regulation of transcript or retrieving. A watermark identifier is mostly united in a sound recorded by reproduction e.g. in video disc transcript regulating technique or in Secure Digital Music Initiative (SDMI). After the detection of a watermark and decoding of all of its matter, the transcript regulation or retrieve control strategy can be imposed by directing a specific hardware or software process like activating or deactivating the record components or elements. Such types

of applications need the watermarking techniques to be immune against the intended reproaches and signal processing refinements so as to be able to accomplish the blind watermark recognition to have the potential of inserting the significant bits in the original signal.

7. **Knowledge Carrier:** The inserted watermarks are envisioned to own a large ability to be identified and decrypted using a blind detection technique. While the strength against the global rebuke is not needed, some level of toughness in resistance to the usual processing (e.g. MPEG compression) may be required. A prominent watermark inserted into the host hypermedia may well be employed as a connection to the extramural directory having specific supplementary details about the hypermedia document like possession rights information and authorizing requirements. One more fascinating use is the communication of data about data (called metadata) along with mixed-media. Metadata inserted within, for example, the auditory clip might have details about the symphonist, artist, generic of melody etc.

First, a brief discussion about the categories of audio watermarking will be done and then very small literature review followed by objective will be studied and then the implementation of the proposed watermarking technique will be studied. At last, the results of the performance parameters will be shown graphically using the various types of audio signals.

CATEGORIES OF AUDIO WATERMARKING

The audio watermarking may be categorized into different categories depending upon the mode of operation (Walker, 2004):

- Time Domain Methods
    - Appending noise
    - Appending reverberation
    - Changing Phase
    - Amplitude Modulation
- Frequency (Transform) Domain Methods
    - Appending modulated carriers
    - Appending noise in any transform domain
    - Deducting frequency bands
    - Combination of adding notches and then adding carriers
    - 'Out of Band' signals
    - Alteration of the spectral spread
- Coded Domain Methods
    - Changing the coded coefficients with the help of biased error distribution
    - Appending noise-like signal to the coding coefficients

All these will be studied in brief.

Time Domain Methods

Adding Noise

The watermark may be superimposed onto the signal simply as a low level signal. If the watermark is not so much different from the random noise, it increases the effective background noise level of the audio signal. The most common way of implementing such type of system is by using the spread spectrum modulation. Other types of modulation systems are also possible. One such scheme is based on least significant bit (LSB) modulation. It may be used in both audio and video systems. It may be used to carry the auxiliary data. Such a system can support high data rate but is not completely robust. Practically, it may be used in digital coherent systems.

Adding Echoes

As it is known that the human auditory system is very insensitive to echoes under certain criteria. On a very short time scale (around 20 ms), a repetition of the signal is not perceptible if the amplitude is somewhat lower than the original host signal. The amplitude of the echo need not be very low for the purpose of watermarking. The data may be embedded by using an echo at 10 ms (say) to represent a binary 0 level and at 30 ms (say) to represent a binary 1 level. The amplitude may be between -20 dB and -40 dB with respect to the original host signal. The binary data sequence may be used to carry the watermark data directly at a slow rate or as a part of the spread spectrum modulation system at a higher rate.

Modifying Phase

Audio is generally phase insensitive as Human Auditory System (HAS) is not aware of absolute or relative phase of a signal or of the parts of the signal relative to the other ports. This is the basis of the current watermarking system. In this method, the signal is changed to the Fourier world in blocks. The relative phases of the Fourier components are then modulated to carry the watermark information. Mostly, the phase of a reference block is set to a reference value and the code information carried by phase is offset from the reference. The signal is converted again to the time domain. In an alternative method, the phase differences between the components in a single block may be set to the specific values. In all cases, the induced changes in phase must be altered to reduce the audibility. Detection is by the same sequence of the transformations and calculation of the differences between the phases of the Fourier components. The modulation again may be raw watermark data or spread spectrum encoding.

Amplitude Modulation

In this, the time domain envelope of the signal may be changed to carry the watermark data. The overall envelope may be modulated on a large timescale. Although no audio system works in this way, a commercial video system intended for the cinema may work by the introduction of a virtual flicker or frame rate variation in the overall brightness.

Frequency Domain Methods

The watermark may be added in some transform domain. Most of the commonly used transforms are Fourier, DCT, Hadamard and Wavelet Transforms. All of these are readily computable. It is best to use a domain in which the properties of the human perceptual system can be expressed in the best way. The following methods are based on the modification of the common frequency domain i.e. Fourier transform domain. In some of the cases, the methods can also be implemented by linear filtering or analog systems.

Adding Modulated Carriers

Such a system requires a system for calculating and making use of psychoacoustic audibility thresholds. Almost all the added tones will be audible sometimes if their amplitude is not controlled by any masking threshold function. The tones are additionally modulated to convey the watermark information. Such a system is quite simple and capable of being made imperceptible but not secure. It would not take long for a hacker to determine the frequencies and distort them sufficiently to result in the failure of the detector.

Adding Noise in Transform Domain

Instead of a noise like signal being added in the original signal domain, the watermark may be embedded in a suitable transform domain. The same domain may easily be used to calculate the perceptibility and masking functions.

Subtracting Frequency Bands

The idea of eliminating the narrow frequency bands is the very simple idea. However, the potential data rate is somewhat low because the audio normally contains periods having some unused bands. Such a system would be easy to detect and overcome.

Combination of Adding Notches and Adding Carriers

It refers to the combination of the previous two methods. If the added carriers had the similar characteristics to the audio that had originally been in each band, the system would definitely be less perceptible. It would also be very robust especially to digital encoding where the watermark signal would be more likely to be seen as a part of the audio signal. The method of Spectral Band Replication (SBR) for the MPEG audio standards might form a basis to calculate such computationally distinct (but visually similar) signals.

'Out of Band' Signals

The addition of signals outside the normal audio spectrum is a very old idea. It has been used many a time as a 'spoiler' to interfere with copying using analog tape recording. But it would cause the audible inter-modulation components with the bias signal in the record amplifier/ head. It is completely obsolete now. Any watermarking system based on 'out of band' carriers would be similarly trivial to overcome even if it would pass through the modern digital processing systems with their sharp band-limiting filters.

Modification of the Spectral Distribution

Some of the systems have been proposed that can modify the spectral weighting. It would be the same as adding noise in the transform domain (provided that it is carried out in a high-resolution Fourier domain) but the addition in that method is replaced with the multiplication in this method. If carried out over a broad spectrum, it would be the frequency domain method with the similar limitations.

Coded Domain Methods (MPEG, DTS, ATRAC etc.)

Changing the Coded Coefficients With the Help of Biased Error Distribution

The signal is coarsely quantized in an audio coder used for the reduction of bit rate. The decision thresholds for that quantization are based on the subjective modelling of the perception thresholds in a number of relatively narrow frequency bands. But in a system based on assigned decision thresholds, the thresholds are not immutable. Thresholds can be altered very slightly without too much effect on the output quality. If these decision thresholds were altered in a small and pre-determined way by the watermark signal, then the effect on the quality would be quite small but those alterations could be detectable in a receiver.

Adding Noise-Like Signal to the Coding Coefficients

The watermark data can simply be added to the coefficients (as an alternative to modifying the coding coefficients by biased error distribution) as in any other additive system working in a transform domain.

.NET FRAMEWORK

.NET Framework (Wigley, Sutton, Wheelwright, Burbidge, & Mcloud, 2002) is a platform made with internetworking but old workstation application platform should not be compromised. .NET is a collection of languages, technologies, and tools that are integrated to give the results required to make robust applications that can interact with respect to each other and yield the data and application logic uncorrelated to the languages and the platforms. This platform consists of three layers: user & program interfaces (ASP.NET and Windows Forms), .NET framework base classes and common language runtime. The components of this Framework are shown in Figure 3.

The main basis of this substructure is the common language runtime whose principle is to fill up, implement & organize cipher collated to the transitional configuration of code format of binary digits. This type of code format refers to Intermediate Language (IL). Some languages like C#.NET and Visual Basic.NET have the different compilers that support this type of code format. This component of the .NET Framework employs just-in-time (JIT) compilers so as to collate the Intermediate Language cipher to local cipher of bits just before implementation. The significant features are edition regulation, memory management, interaction for cross-language and conventional data type system.

The second layer of this type of substructure is base classes (for the .NET configuration) whose main aim is to give the service and object prototypes for retrieval of data and its exploitation, sequences of data (input/output), protection, thread governance etc. The Application Programming Interface (API) is brooded within the different base classes. The repositories are stores of classes oriented towards the

Figure 3. Different components of .NET framework

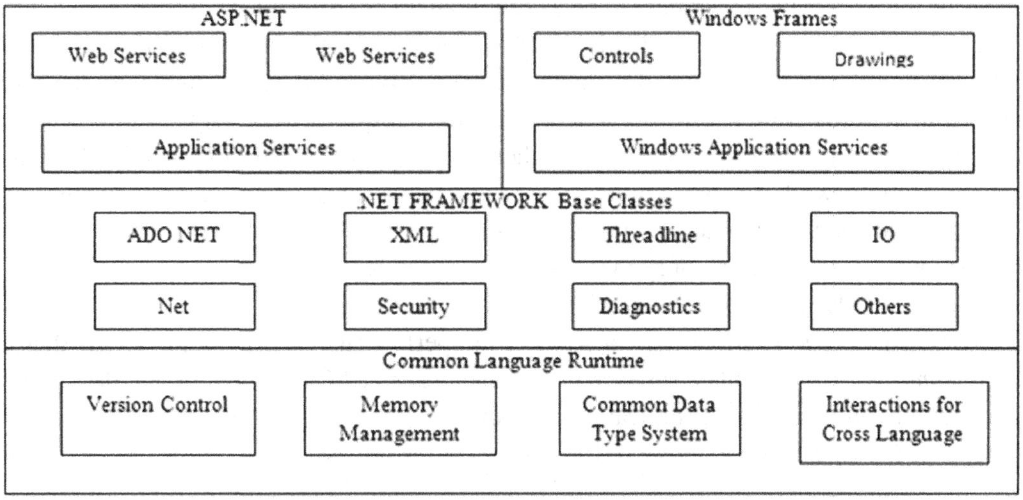

objects. These classes may be rephrased as well as upgraded to permit the brisk evolution of the application. These types of classes encourage the formation of applications ranging from the different types of web services and web pages and web services to the different conventional applications for Windows etc.

This type of framework includes some runtime hosts that are unorganized constituents to store the common language runtime within the mechanisms and start the implementation of organized cipher hence making situation that can benefit from organized as well as unorganized attributes. The kit for the development of the software for .NET framework delivers many runtime hosts and assists the evolution of third-party runtime hosts.

The third layer of this framework includes program and user interfaces. The two sub-components are Windows application services and ASP.NET application services. ASP.NET supports the new kinds of technologies related to web forms and web services.

The main components of the .NET framework may be described as follows:

Common Language Runtime (CLR)

It represents a prosecution framework that organizes the codes destined to the framework. The code organization involves memory management, thread management, safety management, verification of ciphers and code systematization. All the components that are organized must have enough degree of faith. This extent of faith may differ depending upon the desktop/ laptop, type of cyber-link and kind of network connection.

Subsequent to the assignment of the trust level to the component, the component that is managed may or may not perform the functions from within the application. An organized component might behave dissimilarly inside the similar operative application depending on the degree of trust. This degree may be employed to restrict the registry ingress, file ingress or operationality of the network. The common language runtime gives the safety so as to enable the customer to run the different practices without endangering the unsuitable ingress to the delicate level tools or methods e.g. an individual may access an executable by clicking it two times in an e-mail and albeit this can result into playing any kind of aural or visual surge, ingress to the private information present within any desktop/ laptop is having no threat. This allows a cyber-enactment to be as full of attributes as ordinary workstation enactments.

A common type system is also used by the CLR so as to provide the language interoperability. Various third-party compilers can produce the organized classes, types etc. that collate with the CTS. This generation provides protection and conservatism to the framework through the CTS.

One more aim of this type of runtime is the higher throughput of the programmer. With the different languages of the framework, the programmer may select any desired language. Each language may be benefitted from the common language runtime, class library, and components.

The inherent self-activating memory management also tends to increase the application and framework firmness that reduces many usual application inaccuracies.

The common language runtime must also raise the performance of the applications that may be done in two schemes: JIT compilers (used to collate the organized Cipher to inherent device bit cipher at implementation) and server-side applications (to consolidate the application inference and marketing roles and also to permit execution closer to the dependent resources).

Class Library

This is a group of renewable classes that are united with CLR. The applications related to .NET are benefitted from exploiting and expanding the performance from the different types of classes existing in the library of classes.

It starts with very general classes and carries on to the classes with peculiar and accurate serviceability. It is straightforward and easy to learn and use because of its proper management. This model frames it very simple for the other-company sections to be combined effortlessly with the existing library of classes.

.NET framework classes help the developers to perform a variety of usual programming functions that also include tasks such as file retrieval, string organization, and database association. Also, a few of the classes cause the environment related to application development very much pliable and adaptable. The different kinds of applications are assisted in this framework:

- Web services, Console applications, Windows applications (Windows frames), Scripted applications etc.

For instance, the classes of Windows forms may be useful for making applications of Windows graphical user interface (GUI). Further, this may be made easy through a succession of sustainable graphical user interfaces. As an alternative method, classes of web forms along with HTML enable its swift growth to instigate the applications based on the web.

Client Application Development

Client applications indicate the very customary application domain in use. The client applications are those which may be implored with a kind of form and duplicating an action are referred to as client applications. Examples of these applications may vary from manipulation of text to personalized accounting package. Such an application may be started by opening a form from the start menu of Windows. Often, the folders and practicable are saved and run provincially and are connected in association with the local peripherals. The organized control of Windows frames permits the application to be installed over the hyperspace but the customer is able to see the application as a web page.

Earlier, developers made these sorts of applications with either C or C++ along with the Microsoft Foundation Classes (MFC) or with a rapid application development (RAD) environment such as Microsoft Visual Basic. The substructure of .NET subsumes the features of the preliminary commodities into a lone homogeneous blooming scenario. The purpose of the lone scenario is to ease the evolution of applications for clients. This modesty may further be increased by adding the safety and disposition attributes. As all the applications full of features may be located on the web, some of the other applications existing within a user's machine may be built on the web. The application may interpret the cipher-ingress protection bounds that limit what the application can undertake on any device. This provides the developer the attributes related to security although the application is running in the machine language. Every object and web server are having safety virtues dissimilar with respect to other server. Windows forms applications are much better than the applications based on the web. Windows Forms applications have a degree of faith so as to allow binary and native implementing code so as to connect with some of the supports. This may further be employed to do the requisite Graphics User Interface components of the application.

Server Application Development

Web services are application units on the server side. These services can be allocated comfortably just like the websites. The components for Web services are not intended for a particular gateway. These are just renewable elements made so that they may be employed by the other applications. Traditional applications, Applications based on web and the other web amenities may utilize the different services of web. The web services are mobile application development towards the internet. The environment of ASP.NET allows the different developers to use the substructure of .NET to aim towards the applications related to web services. The most important characteristic is the capability to generate the web forms in the framework supporting language. Multiple languages are not needed to be learned to make the distinct kinds of applications as Visual Basic.NET may be used to create the web forms. Web forms can be implemented in the native machine-code and may take advantage of the CLR in the similar mode as various organized applications. This permits the web forms to be collated and prosecuted with a brisk pace.

Besides, .NET substructure gives a group of classes and mechanisms so as to be used in the evolution & exhaustion of the applications concerned with the web services. Web services are made on the various standards like XML (an extensible data format), WSDL (Web Service Description Language) etc. The framework applies these standards to encourage the information exchange and its use with non-Microsoft solutions.

Web forms and web services both take benefit of the adaptable architecture of Internet Information Services. Although these technologies are dependent on Internet Information Services, their concatenation formulates the inceptive layout as well as existing conservation uncomplicated.

Windows Forms

As the languages switch towards the web environment, .NET framework is discouraging conventional Windows application development. The concept of Windows forms eases the evolution of applications and may well be used to make the attribute-rich user interface Windows applications. Windows forms is a new package used to evolve and exploit the various kinds of applications of Windows via the .NET framework. It supports the innovative methods including a common application framework, organized execution environment, coherent protection and the various layout principles related to the objects. Also, Windows forms offer assistance for the web services and may link effortlessly to the stores of information/ data with a particular .NET data model called ADO.NET.

Windows forms in .NET framework assist the evolution of Windows user interface applications. Although the layout is very much identical to that of Web forms, the classes, as well as execution, are quite dissimilar. The development environment is so that it will be very much easy for an application developer to write an application using Windows forms or Web forms.

The main goal of Windows forms is the comfort to use and recyclability. All Windows forms are rested on delegates that are primarily pointers. Every event may be stated a handler such that the handler defining is not required always by any other mode. Windows forms project making with Visual Studio. net results in the creation of only one project file that is collated. There are no header files, no interface definition files, no bootstrap application files, no resource files and no library files. Developers can write the Windows forms applications (or web forms applications) in different languages ranging from C# to COBOL. This results in the reduction of training curve by permitting the developers to be stiff with their desired language. Windows forms are benefitted from Microsoft's next-generation 2-D graphics system.

Web Forms

These are the frames which are driver imparted with ASP.NET. The main aim of them is to have user interfaces based on the application programs. The engineering has further been upgraded to yield a new generation of evolution by including more features like the development of dragging an item and then dropping that item to some other location across the screen.

They contain a template and a module. The template consists of the particulars of the arrangement and the organization for the user interface elements. The module consists of all the cognition and argumentation connected with the user interface. The benefit of Web elements is that they control all the coordination required.

New Programming Language

Visual Studio.NET is .NET substructure deployment environment for Microsoft. This coherent development domain is basically created to assist the different programming languages that collate to Microsoft's Intermediate Language (MSIL).

BRIEF SURVEY

The following section presents a brief survey on the watermarking of the audio signals:

Bassia, Ioannis, and Nikos (2001) developed an audio watermarking method in the time-domain without the use of the actual signal for the detection of the watermark. The watermark signal is generated using a single number key kept only with the owner of the copyright.

Cvejic and Seppanen (2003) developed a very reliable audio watermarking technique in the wavelet domain. In this technique, watermarks are embedded in the visually significant and randomly selected set of audio sub-bands in accordance with a secret key. This embedding is performed in a pre-specified time slot just like frequency-hopping spread spectrum technique.

Larbi and Meriem (2005) developed watermarking as a pre-processing step for the upcoming processing of the audio systems. The watermark signal is used to change the different statistical characteristics of an audio signal.

Lei, Xue, and Lu (2006) proposed a new localized powerful audio watermarking technique. In this technique, firstly strong local regions (that represent music edges or drum sounds etc.) are chosen and then the watermarks are embedded within those strong locations. These locations are of utmost benefit for the better interpretation of music.

Wang, Wei, and Panpan (2007) developed a novel flexible digital audio watermarking technique that is dependent on support vector regression (SVR). In this technique, the watermark is inserted into the audio signal with the help of adaptive quantization in accordance with the local audio correlation.

Chen, Zhao and Wang (2008) presented a new watermarking algorithm for MP3 compressed audio signals. In this algorithm, the watermark may be embedded after discrete cosine transform (DCT) but before quantization.

Zhang and He (2009) developed an invisible and robust audio watermark algorithm on the basis of stochastic resonance (SR) in discrete cosine transform (DCT) as well as discrete wavelet transform (DWT) domain. The domain coefficients of DWT and DCT are used as the inputs of SR System.

Wang (2010) proposed the quantization of mean signal followed by the embedding of the scrambled watermark. The technique is found to be quite robust but is suffered from white noise.

Panda and Kumar (2011) presented an attack resistant and efficient watermark embedded onto the audio host signal. The proposed scheme is found to be very much robust as well as inaudible against attacks like noise adding, requantization & resampling etc.

Ding, Wang, Shen, Lu and Hu (2012) presented a novel non-embedded DWT based audio watermark scheme. The proposed scheme shows that the copyright information may be hidden without degrading the sound quality.

Wang and Bo (2013) demonstrated an excellent method based on the mixture of DWT and DFT followed by the quantization of the amplitude so as to embed the watermark. The advantage of this scheme is that it doesn't require the original audio signal while extraction of the watermark.

Muhaimin, Danudirdjo, Suksmono and Shin (2015) developed a method for the autocorrelation embedded watermarking systems for the stego audio signals. The watermark extraction may also be easily done because of the autocorrelation between stego signal and its own delayed version hiding the watermark.

Elshazly, Nasr, Fuad and Samie (2016) proposed a novel watermarking scheme in which the original audio signal is undergone to wavelet transform followed by the decomposition of low-frequency coefficients by Singular Value Decomposition (SVD) transform. The resultant matrix is a diagonal matrix into which the watermarking bitstream along with the synchronizing code stream is embedded. Inverse SVD and Inverse DWT may then be applied to get the watermarked signal and thereafter watermark may be extracted out. The technique has been found to be robust against the various attacks.

PROPOSED SCHEME

There are some gaps left in the literature survey. In most of the papers, the results are little preliminary and may be improved a lot. The parameters like Peak Signal to Noise Ratio (PSNR) and Bit Error Rate

(BER) will be computed here to show the advantages of this research. This work will be in continuation of the work in research already done (Chen et al., 2008). In this research work, the random carrier will be used (instead of the fixed carrier in the previous research) to embed the watermark onto the audio stream after applying a compression technique called ADPCM i.e. Adaptive Differential Pulse Code Modulation (unlike Discrete Cosine Transform) but before quantization. The proposed scheme may embed a watermark into .wav files so as to impose the copyrights and secure the different types of mixed media from dabbling. A keystream will be used to bypass some samples, grasp the next sample, insert one digit of the message into the lowermost digit of the sample and afterward, register the altered unit to the final stream. After the entire message has been concealed, rest of the samples are copied. The advantage of ADPCM is that it results in the reduction/compression of data but the drawback is that any high frequencies get the little bit distorted.

The main problem is to produce an algorithm to develop the watermarked audio using ADPCM technique followed by Quantization and hence to plot the values of PSNR and BER. The effectiveness of the proposed technique will be shown by its comparison with the results shown in the existing research (Chen et al., 2008).

DESIGN AND IMPLEMENTATION

The steps of the implementation may be divided into the following steps:

1. To develop an algorithm to embed watermark onto an audio file
2. To develop an algorithm to extract the watermarked text from the watermarked file
3. To plot the parameters like PSNR and BER
4. Compare the results with the traditional scheme developed in existing research (Chen et al., 2008)

The proposed watermarking technique is shown in Figure 4. Firstly, the original audio (.wav) file is partitioned into 16-bit frames followed by the ADPCM compression technique (not shown in the figure because this compression is considered as a part of framing). Thereafter some random sample of bits is chosen so that detection of watermark becomes almost impossible. Ultimately, the watermark is embedded in this random sample file. ADPCM is based on the assumption that the differences between the adjacent samples will not be so large. A 4:1 compression ratio is achieved with reduced attenuation with the increase in sampling rate. At the frequency of 44.1 KHz, the compressed signal may be an exact replica of the actual sample.

A wave file is a Resource Interchange File Format (RIFF) along with a "wave" chunk having two sub-chunks: an "fmt" sub-chunk (that specifies the data format of sound) and "data" sub-chunk (that indicates the original raw data sample) (Khan, n.d.).

Embedding Watermark

Adding the watermark is identical to concealing it in the bitmap pixels. The watermark is first added to the compressed wave file and thereafter a key stream is used to skip a number of samples, grab the next sample, insert one bit of message into the lowest bit of the sample and then write the changed unit to

Figure 4. Flow sequence of audio watermarking

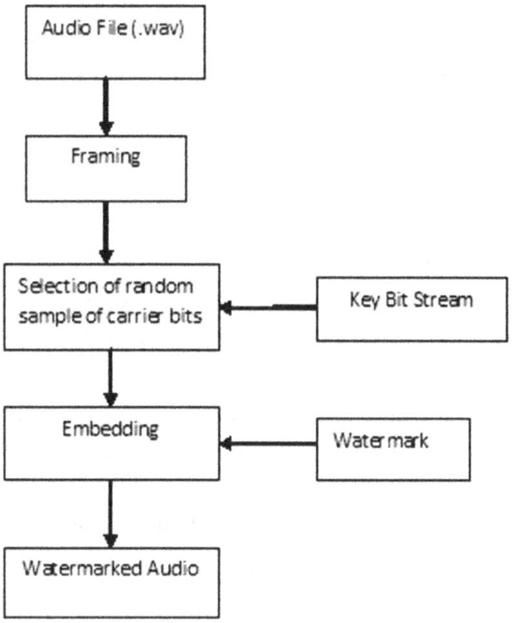

the destination stream. After the entire message has been added like that, rest of the samples are copied. The steps are:

1. Partition the audio file into 16-bit frames.
2. Use commonly used compression technique (ADPCM in this case)
3. Select the random sample using the key and then add the watermark onto the lowest significant bit of the selected sample. This may be done as follows:
   Read the 1st byte of the message. For every message bit, read a byte from the keystream. Leave a couple of samples in accordance with the key byte. Read one sample from the wave stream. Then the upcoming bit from the present message byte is obtained and afterward it is placed in sample's last bit.

Extracting Watermark

In this method, the keystream is used to find the location of the right samples that are required (like in the case of watermark adding). Then the last bit of the sample is read and shifted into the present byte of the message. After the completion of the byte, this is written it into the message stream and then continues with the next one. The steps are:

1. First of all, use the key to know the location of the sample where the watermark is to be added:
   Read a byte from the keystream, leave a couple of samples in accordance with the key byte and read one sample from the wave stream
2. Extract watermark bit from the lowest significant bit of the sample and insert in watermark array.

The complete random sample watermark algorithm may be described using .NET framework. The executable file of the proposed random sample watermarking algorithm consists of all the required fields that are required for the audio encoding as well as decoding (such as adding the encryption key, adding the watermark, uploading the window for the original audio and embed/extract watermark functions.

Embedding Watermarking Algorithm

Steps of embedding watermarking algorithm in the audio signal are:

1. The very first step is to install .NET framework on the system and then the executable form of the proposed random sample audio watermarking scheme is deployed.
2. After installing an icon with the name, the audio watermark is created on the system screen. That icon is double-clicked to get the embed/extract watermark screen. It consists of many buttons like hiding message, browses etc. The watermark may be embedded in the .wav file format of audio files.
3. Browse button is clicked and it is seen that 'Open Dialog Box' has appeared. Thereafter, a compressed audio file from the computer is selected.
4. After selecting the audio file, both key file and name of the watermarked audio file are browsed.
5. The watermark (that is to be encoded) is written in the textbox and 'Hide' button is clicked so as to encode the data in the given audio file.
6. After clicking the 'Hide' message button, the watermark is successfully inserted into the audio file. The watermarked audio file may be saved with the name to be specified in the same result as the textbox. The watermarked audio file is saved in the same file format as the original audio file format.

Extracting Watermarking Algorithm

Steps of extracting the watermarking algorithm from the audio signal are:

1. The very first step is to click on browse button and then the watermarked audio file, as well as the key file on the embed/extract watermark screen, are loaded.
2. The 'Extract' button is clicked so as to retrieve the watermark from the watermarked audio file.
3. If the key is valid, the receiver will get the watermark. The watermark will appear in the Message text box. If the key is not matching, the message box will appear displaying the message "Key is not matching".

RESULTS AND DISCUSSION

The simulation and testing may be done by the following procedure:

1. Select the audio (.wav) file as it has the best quality. Wave audio may be manipulated with very much ease using some software. The usage of the .wav format is not concerned with its simplicity, familiarity, and simple structure.

2. Let the copyright message be "This message will not be visible within the sound file"
3. A private and confidential message is embedded in the audio with the help of "Random sample audio watermarking technique". In this way, a watermarked audio signal is made.
4. The signal formed in step 3 is then transmitted to the receiver through the channel. After this signal being received at the receiver end, the decoding technique recovers the watermark from the watermarked signal only if it knows the valid private key. So the receiver retrieves the watermark text as "This message will not be visible within the sound file"

The different steps to calculate the Peak Signal to Noise Ratio (PSNR) and Bit Error Rate (BER) are:

1. Install .NET framework on the computer. Then there appears an executable form of audio PSNR tool.
2. After the installation, "Audio PSNR" icon is created on the screen. That icon is now double-clicked to have Audio SNR, PSNR and BER screen. BER and either of SNR or PSNR may be chosen as the output parameters. The parameters of interest in this research are PSNR and BER.
3. After clicking "Browse", an "Open Dialog Box" appears and then an audio file is selected from the computer.
4. The last step after selecting the audio file is to click "Browse" for key file and then click on "Find Result" button to get the PSNR and BER of the watermarked audio signals.

Table 1 shows the PSNR and BER values of the proposed and the existing technique. The values are shown for three different types of audio: Pop, Classic, and Vocal. The results indicate that the suggested technique gives higher PSNR than the existing technique and same BER (i.e. zero) as the existing algorithm. Results of PSNR for the proposed and existing algorithms are also displayed in figure 5.

CONCLUSION

The random sample audio watermarking scheme provides much finer results with BER being close to zero under the ordinary conditions of insertion and extraction. Also, the arbitrary sample audio watermarking based method allows complete watermark recovery with not so much distortion of the actual host signal as prescribed by high values of PSNR. The compressed Adaptive Differential Pulse Code Modulation (ADPCM) has been discussed and it gives better results in terms of PSNR with zero BER

Table 1. Techniques with PSNR and BER (for classical, pop and vocal audio)

Algorithm	Audio Signal	PSNR	BER
Adaptive Watermarking Algorithm for MP3 Compressed Audio Signals	Classic (1)	56.4	0
	Pop (2)	53.4	0
	Vocal (3)	55.4	0
Random Sample Watermarking Algorithm	Classic (1)	61.7	0
	Pop (2)	61.3	0
	Vocal (3)	61.2	0

Figure 5. PSNR comparison for proposed and existing algorithms (1-Classic, 2- Pop, 3- Vocal)

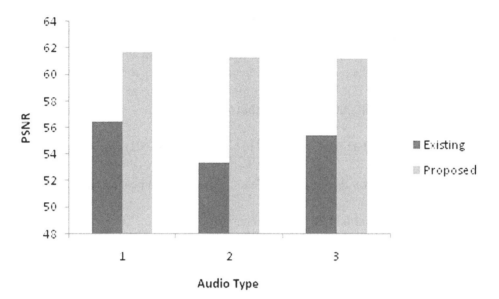

without the actual standard of the signal being degraded. The comparison with the existing technique proves that the suggested technique is quite strong. This technique is commonly used for suitable for keeping the 'first generation' archived files of quite a high standard.

FUTURE SCOPE

There is very large interest in the management and security of intellectual property rights. Embedding some 'secret signal' or watermark in the actual audio can be seen as an excellent method to manage the use of the material. Some techniques have been used to have 'gatekeepers' in audio equipment so that the unlicensed reproduction and unlicensed imitation could be prevented. A lot of research will be on demands in future. The study may be extended in the future with the following directions:

1. In the technique discussed, the only text has been embedded into the audio signal. This technique may further be used to insert a watermark on an image (instead of text) into an audio signal
2. The results discussed are the little bit preliminary and may be improved further in future.

REFERENCES

Adya, M. (2007). *Audio watermark resistant to mp3 compression* (Doctoral dissertation). Department of Computer Science and Engineering Indian Institute of Technology Kharagpur, India.

Bassia, P., Pitas, I., & Nikolaidis, N. (2001). Robust audio watermarking in the time domain. *IEEE Transactions on Multimedia*, 3(2), 232–241. doi:10.1109/6046.923822

Chen, B., Zhao, J., & Wang, D. (2008, May). An Adaptive Watermarking Algorithm for MP3 Compressed Audio Signals. In *Instrumentation and Measurement Technology Conference Proceedings, 2008. IMTC 2008. IEEE* (pp. 1057-1060). IEEE. 10.1109/IMTC.2008.4547194

Cvejic, N. (2004). Algorithms for audio watermarking and steganography. Oulun yliopisto.

Cvejic, N. (Ed.). (2007). *Digital audio watermarking techniques and technologies: applications and benchmarks: applications and benchmarks*. IGI Global.

Cvejic, N., & Seppanen, T. (2003, September). Robust audio watermarking in wavelet domain using frequency hopping and patchwork method. In *Image and Signal Processing and Analysis, 2003. ISPA 2003. Proceedings of the 3rd International Symposium on* (Vol. 1, pp. 251-255). IEEE. 10.1109/ISPA.2003.1296903

Dey, N., Maji, P., Das, P., Biswas, S., Das, A., & Chaudhuri, S. S. (2013, January). An edge based blind watermarking technique of medical images without devalorizing diagnostic parameters. In *Advances in Technology and Engineering (ICATE), 2013 International Conference on* (pp. 1-5). IEEE. 10.1109/ICAdTE.2013.6524732

Ding, F., Wang, X., Shen, Y., Lu, Y., & Hu, J. (2012, June). Non-embedded audio watermark based on wavelet transform. In *Software Engineering and Service Science (ICSESS), 2012 IEEE 3rd International Conference on* (pp. 8-11). IEEE. 10.1109/ICSESS.2012.6269393

Elshazly, A. R., Nasr, M. E., Fuad, M. M., & El-Samie, F. A. (2016, May). Synchronized double watermark audio watermarking scheme based on a transform domain for stereo signals. In *Electronics, Communications and Computers (JEC-ECC), 2016 Fourth International Japan-Egypt Conference on* (pp. 52-57). IEEE. 10.1109/JEC-ECC.2016.7518966

Foo, S. W. (2008). *Audio-watermarking with stereo signals*. Academic Press.

Gordy, J. D., & Bruton, L. T. (2000). Performance evaluation of digital audio watermarking algorithms. In *Circuits and Systems, 2000. Proceedings of the 43rd IEEE Midwest Symposium on* (Vol. 1, pp. 456-459). IEEE.

KhanS. (n.d.). Retrieved from C# from www.programmersheaven.com

Larbi, S. D., & Jaïdane-Saïdane, M. (2005). Audio watermarking: A way to stationnarize audio signals. *IEEE Transactions on Signal Processing*, *53*(2), 816–823. doi:10.1109/TSP.2004.839899

Li, W., Xue, X., & Lu, P. (2006). Localized audio watermarking technique robust against time-scale modification. *IEEE Transactions on Multimedia*, *8*(1), 60–69. doi:10.1109/TMM.2005.861291

Muhaimin, H., Danudirdjo, D., Suksmono, A. B., & Shin, D. H. (2015, August). An efficient audio watermark by autocorrelation methods. In *Electrical Engineering and Informatics (ICEEI), 2015 International Conference on* (pp. 606-611). IEEE. 10.1109/ICEEI.2015.7352571

Panda, J., & Kumar, M. (2011, October). Application of energy efficient watermark on audio signal for authentication. In *Computational Intelligence and Communication Networks (CICN), 2011 International Conference on* (pp. 202-206). IEEE. 10.1109/CICN.2011.40

Walker, R. (2004). *Audio watermarking, R&D White Paper WHP 057.* British Broadcasting Corporation.

Wang, C., & Bo, G. (2014). A novel approach to generate and extract audio watermark. *International Journal of High Performance Systems Architecture, 5*(1), 33-38.

Wang, W. (2010, December). A new average quantized watermark for audio signal. In *Information Science and Engineering (ICISE), 2010 2nd International Conference on* (pp. 1728-1731). IEEE.

Wang, X., Qi, W., & Niu, P. (2007). A new adaptive digital audio watermarking based on support vector regression. *IEEE Transactions on Audio, Speech, and Language Processing, 15*(8), 2270–2277. doi:10.1109/TASL.2007.906192 PMID:20428476

Wigley, A., Sutton, M., Wheelwright, S., Burbidge, R., & Mcloud, R. (2002). *Microsoft. net compact framework: Core reference.* Microsoft Press.

Zhang, L., & He, D. (2009, January). A novel robust audio watermark algorithm based on stochastic resonance. In *Microelectronics & Electronics, 2009. PrimeAsia 2009. Asia Pacific Conference on Postgraduate Research in* (pp. 185-188). IEEE. 10.1109/PRIMEASIA.2009.5397415

Chapter 21
Bitcoin:
Digital Decentralized Cryptocurrency

Feroz Ahmad Ahmad
Galgotias University, India

Prashant Kumar
GCET Noida, India

Gulshan Shrivastava
National Institute of Technology Patna, India

Med Salim Bouhlel
Sfax University, Tunisia

ABSTRACT

In this chapter, a digital decentralized cryptocurrency system where transactions are secured by cryptography and are independent of any centralized third party is discussed. The different characteristics of bitcoins and how transactions occur between two bitcoin users along with some facts and examples are also discussed. The rapid internet development facilitates cyber-attacks to all type of online transactions and also to bitcoin network transactions. Some security issues are also discussed in the chapter along with the cyber-crimes and their punishments.

INTRODUCTION

Online transaction processing using electronic means has revolutionized human society altogether. It has brought the era which leads towards the cashless e-commerce using electronic gadgets. To transfer money into an account one need not wait for hours in bank queues. For buying a laptop or for reserving an air ticket, one needs not to carry a large amount of cash to the shopkeeper. Now there is no need to maintain a lengthy register by a shopkeeper or by a bank employee to keep a record of monthly transactions. Now booking a hotel room or reserving a plane or buying a laptop is just a click away. This is all because of the computing and communication technologies. Though easy and powerful, there are some

DOI: 10.4018/978-1-5225-4100-4.ch021

limitations with these electronic financial transactions and one of these limitations is that these transactions involve some third party as intermediaries for processing electronic payments. In case required financial institutes are not able to reverse the transactions and are unable to handle the intermediate disputes. Involvement of third part becomes costlier as per transaction cost.

To overcome the limitations associated with the conventional approach of electronic financial transactions, Nakamoto (2008) and Moore (2013) proposed a different electronic payment system. An electronic decentralized payment system called Bitcoin cryptocurrency system. This system is based on cryptographic proof and security which provides the customers with this virtual currency to sell or buy services or goods. This currency is called as bitcoin.

Bitcoin was introduced as a peer-to-peer-based digital currency in Nakamoto (2008). The conventional cashless transaction systems which were used before bitcoins are third party dependent which requires that trusted third party for clearing the transaction between the two parties. In bitcoins, unlike other transaction systems, the whole bitcoin network performs the role of the trusted third party to carry out transactions between two accounts. The transactions under process are verified for legitimacy by the nodes in the network. These nodes create a ledger like data recording file that keeps track of the account balances and verifies transactions by using the records in that ledger as per the current state and updates the same accordingly. Unlike other digital transactions systems, bitcoins are the irreversible type of transaction networks. Once the transaction is committed there are no means to reverse the transaction except the receiver returns the amount to the sender through another transaction. As a consequence, bitcoin has no charge-backs and hence has a drawback that the bitcoins lost or being fraudulently stolen are non-refundable.

Bitcoin, a form of electronic digital cryptocurrency is created and controlled by the network itself. These are created by the miners using high computational computers to solve mathematical problems related to bitcoins. Bitcoin is not printed like currencies of the nations and is independent of the boundaries of countries hence accepted and used internationally.

How Are Bitcoins Different From Other Currencies?

Bitcoin can be used for buying thing online like normal currencies which are traded digitally. In that sense, bitcoins are like conventional currencies like dollars, euros, rupees or yen.

However, the characteristic which makes Bitcoin more powerful than the traditional digital currencies is that it is decentralized. In case of currency transactions between two parties, a centralized third party like the bank is responsible for the transaction. But there is no requirement of any third party to control the transactions in bitcoin network. This makes it easy and cheaper to perform a transaction because a large bank is not needed to control the money. A third party like banks charges for the transactions every time, which is not the case in bitcoin network.

Who Created It?

Satoshi Nakamoto named unknown person designed Bitcoin and also created its original implementation. It was an electronic system based on mathematical proof. The basic idea was to produce a digital currency network independent of any third party intervention that is decentralized, should perform instantly electronically transferable, and with very little transaction charges.

Who Prints It?

Bitcoins are not physically printed under any central bank or any other bank or institutions. It is mysterious to the population and controlled by its own protocols. Banks creating printed currency can produce more currency for wrapping the country debt, hence depreciate their currency.

Unlike other currencies, Bitcoins are created electronically or digitally, by a group of people on the network. This group or community is open to all and anyone who is interested can join. This makes it easy to register and use bitcoin facilities. On the other hand, giving flexibility to all might be risky as per security aspects. But it is not like that because the transactions are processed and confirmed when approved by the majority of the users. It is like the democratic voting system, the leader is selected only after acquiring more than half votes. If more than half are fraudulent then there is a chance of 51% attack which is discussed ahead in the paper. Bitcoins are created using some computationally powerful machines in the distributed bitcoin network, called as mining of bitcoins. The network processes the transaction on its own without the intervention of any third party and hence effectively makes a bitcoin network independent network.

Is There Any Limit to the Creation of Bitcoins?

Bitcoins cannot be conceived like traditional currencies rather there are Bitcoin protocols that need to be followed. One of the rules is that not more than 21 million bitcoins can ever be created by miners "What is Bitcoin?". This maintains the value of the Bitcoin, unlike conventional currency which can be printed unconditionally resulting in devaluing the currency. 'Satoshi' is the smallest unit or part of bitcoin named after the creator Satoshi Nakamoto. One Satoshi is equal to one hundred billionths of a Bitcoin.

What Is Bitcoin Based on?

The value of currencies of all nations is decided on the value of Gold or Silver. If one gives some money at the bank, based on the value of the money he could get some gold in exchange. Although this is not practiced in reality it is possible as exchange rates are based on gold or silver. Bitcoins are based on some mathematics rather than gold or silver. Bitcoins are produced using software programs that follow some mathematical formula. The mathematical formula is freely available so, people all around the world can check it. The software program to which the mathematical formula is applied to produce bitcoins is also open source software. So it is freely available to anyone and people can have it without any cost, but make sure it is doing the same job as supposed to.

CHARACTERISTICS OF BITCOINS

Some of the important characteristics of bitcoins that makes them different from normal currencies are:

Decentralized Network

Bitcoin networks are not controlled by any central authority and transactions are not maintained or governed by any third party like banks. But every node involved in the mining of Bitcoin and processes transactions makes a part of the network. The machines or nodes work together to control the transactions in the network. There is no need for the third party to maintain the records of transactions. The transaction acceptance or rejection is decided by the nodes of the network and also maintain the record of the transactions.

Easy to Set Up

To open a simple account in any financial unit like banks a lot of formalities are required. Setting up this account for digital transactions is another hectic task. Bitcoin addresses are easy to create and do not require to go through any security procedure. It is free and need not reveal or verify your identity.

Anonymous

Bitcoin addresses do not need any type of identity or location verifications like banks. A user can have a number of Bitcoin addresses without the user's name, address or any personal information. Bitcoin transactions do not need to reveal the personal information between the two parties performing the transaction.

Completely Transparent

As banks maintain ledgers for every transaction of a client, Bitcoin networks also maintain it for all the transactions. It stores a record of every single transaction that ever occurs in the network in a vast ledger called as Blockchain. The blockchain maintains all the details of the publicly broadcasted Bitcoin address, a number of bitcoins stored at that address are revealed to everyone in the network. But the identity of the user is not open to the other. No one knows whose address it is.

Bitcoins are sent and received through addresses. The different address can be generated for different transactions. The transaction activities can be made more secure and opaque on a Bitcoin network by using different addresses for different transactions. As a security aspect, it is better not to use the same address for a number of transactions and also transfer a reasonable (Not so large) amount of bitcoins to a single address.

Cheaper Transactions

The third party banks and financial institutions charge for transactions. They may charge a pretty good fee for international transfers and also varies as per amount. Bitcoin does not know the boundaries of nations, so every transaction is treated same way in the network. There are some transaction charges also but negligible as compared to the banks.

Fast

Transactions through conventional methods are time-consuming and to send money anywhere has some constraints. In case of Bitcoin, one can send money anytime, anywhere within minutes. It takes a time of few minutes, which bitcoin network takes to process the transaction for its validation.

Non-Repudiable

In commercial banks, sometimes a customer can reverse the transaction called as a chargeback. This is not the case in Bitcoin. Once the Bitcoin is sent, the sender cannot get them back. Once they are gone, they are gone forever. The only way to get them back is if the receiver returns them back.

BACKGROUND OF THE BITCOIN NETWORK

Bitcoin is a decentralized cryptocurrency (Bonneauand, 2015; Barber, 1892) stored and exchanged in the digital form only. It follows open standards and is maintained by peer to peer network with free and open membership. This network is given the name of Bitcoin Network. Bitcoin also is written as BTC are exchanged between two parties using addresses by means of transactions. Blockchain, a public ledger maintains all the transaction details. Each node maintains the record by keeping a copy of this blockchain. The transaction which is validated by the nodes of the network is finally added to the blockchain.

The Bitcoin network is a network in which the nodes share resources without passing through the server. It works on the distributed algorithms and cryptographic tools to allow entities to buy goods or services with digital currencies called bitcoins. Some of the main concepts in the bitcoin are (i) *Transactions* performed by the person who each time wants to send the bitcoins from his account to the other. It can be a buyer who wishes to exchange bitcoins for goods or services. (ii) *Blockchain* which contains the record of the transactions validated by the network. It is maintained collectively by the network units as a ledger of the issued transactions, and (iii) a pool of *Pending transactions* which are in the blockchain for the confirmation. These are maintained locally by all the units of the network. In a bitcoin transaction there are three main entities that participate in the bitcoin ecosystem: *users*, *sender* and the *receiver* of the bitcoins in the network, peers the way of propagation of the transaction in the network and the maintenance of the blockchain and the miners that mine the transaction and decide which transaction to appear in the blockchain and also the sequence of the transactions in which they will appear in the blockchain. These transactional records are of great importance in the bitcoin ecosystem.

THE BASICS OF A BITCOINS BASED SYSTEM

From the above concept of Bitcoin, we come to know that what decentralized digital cryptocurrency is all about. It does not depend upon some central authority to control its functionality, rather depends upon some mathematical calculations and cryptography. Miners create the bitcoins using bitcoin miner devices with very high computational power instead of normal computers. Creation and management of bitcoins depend on mathematical formulas and cryptography. It does not have a single central dedicated server to control the transactions. In Bitcoin network, multiple nodes in the network are responsible for verification of the transactions between two nodes, unlike conventional systems where a central authority controls it. The transactions are recorded in a publically distributed ledger called a blockchain. Bitcoin network consists of some important constituents, some of them are briefly explained below:

Transaction

The transaction (Ladd, 2012; Meiklejohn, 2013) is a process of transferring bitcoins from one Bitcoin account to another Bitcoin account in exchange for goods or services. In other words, it is a signed piece of data that is broadcasted on the network and, if valid, ends up as a record in the blockchain ("Bitcoin Transaction"). The main goal of the process is to transfer the ownership of an amount of Bitcoin to the owner bitcoin address. The transaction occurs when a person wants to transfer bitcoins and is created by the wallet of the sender. This transaction is broadcasted to the network for verification and validation. Nodes in the network will respond to it and rebroadcast the transaction. If the transaction is found valid it is included in the block they are mining. The process of verification is performed by the miners which set up the computers to calculate cryptographic hash functions. It takes some time maybe 10 to 20 minutes and then only the transaction is added to the blockchain. Once it is recorded into the blockchain the transaction will be reflected in the receiver's account and he will be able to see the transaction amount in his wallet.

The process of the transaction is explained with the help of Figure 1.

The color-coded components are the main components of this standard transaction which are as follows:

- *Transaction ID* (the string in the figure highlighted in yellow is the transaction id for this transaction).
- *Descriptors and meta-data* (on the right side blue brace contains the description and other details of the transaction id).
- *Inputs* (is the encrypted detailed amount of bitcoins which are in the address of the sender for transaction shown in transaction example as pink area).

Figure 1. Bitcoin transaction example "bitcoin transaction"

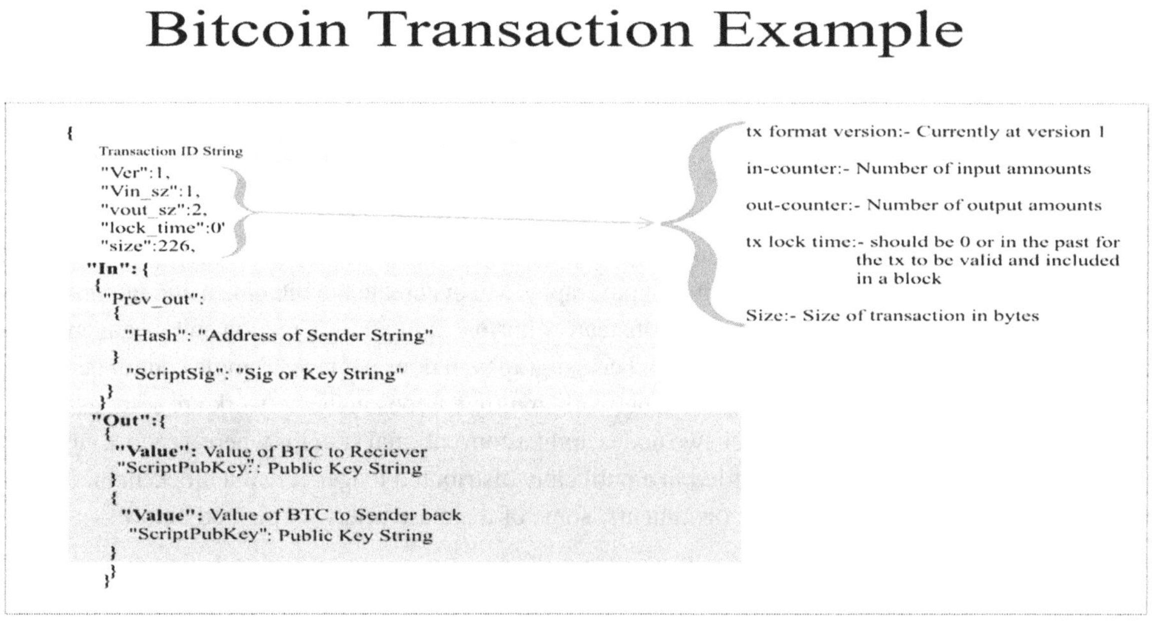

*For a more accurate representation see the electronic version.

- *Outputs* (part of the transaction which contains the details of amount send to the receiver plus the change send back to the sender green area).

Four aphoristic reality regarding transactions:

- Any Bitcoin amounts are sent to the addresses generated by the receiver.
- On the side of the receiver, these Bitcoins are locked to the receiving address, which is usually identified with a wallet.
- While spending the Bitcoins, these bitcoins will come from the amount already present in your wallet. These can be previously received or added to the wallet.
- Addresses receive Bitcoin, whenever a receiver is about to receive the bitcoins, it creates an address to which the bitcoins are sent rather than adding bitcoins directly to the wallet.

When the amount is sent to an account the amount is reflected in the wallet. The amount added to the wallet is not added up to the amount already present in the account as in case of bank accounts. Neither the bitcoins that go in the wallet jumble together like the coins in the physical or normal wallet. The amount received for each transaction remains separate in the wallet. The amount received by the account either from some other sender or the change of the one's self-transactions is kept separate and distinct as the exact amount received by the wallet. These are then used by the sender separately for other transactions. Here's an illustration:

Suppose Bob created a new account and his wallet contains 0.0 BTC. Suppose it received three Bitcoin amounts of 0.5, 5 and 2 BTC as follows: Jerry sends 5 BTC to an address associated with the wallet and two payments, 0.5 and 2 are made to other addresses associated with Bob's wallet by Alice.

The wallet now contains a balance of 7.5 BTC Figure 2. The bitcoin is also represented by Satoshi, the name given because of the developer of the bitcoin. The wallet contains 750,000,000 satoshis. But

Figure 2. Bitcoin transactions

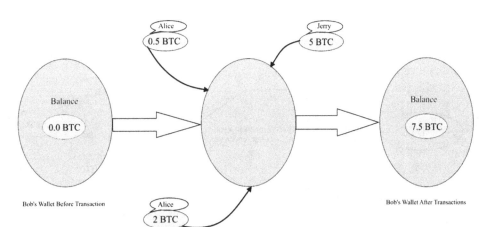

Two people sent amount to addresses held by Bob's Bitcoin wallet

if one virtually peeks into the wallet he would not see the amount as any of the above two cases, but the amount would be grouped as per their original transactions as 0.5, 5 and 2 BTC.

The amount received by a transaction does not mix up with the amount present in the wallet Figure 3. Amount of every transaction remains separate in the wallet and is used separately for other transactions. As shown in figure of example the three amounts are present separately, these amounts are said to be the outputs of their originating transactions. These outputs are always disconnected, independent and distinct in the bitcoin wallet.

An *output* is an amount that is sent to a bitcoin address. The amount is encrypted using some encryption rules. The amount along with these set of rules are sent to the address so that the amount can be unlocked at receiver's side. This output amount in the language of bitcoin parlance is a called as "unspent transaction output" or *UTXO*.

A standard transaction output which is sent by the sender and received by the receiver is unlocked using private key associated with the receiving address. We have not yet discussed the public/private key pairs which may be discussed in the same or next paper. For now, we are concerned with the output amount only.

Let's consider an example to understand how a bitcoin transaction works.

Consider a scenario where Bob wants to transfer 1.2 BTC to Alice. Actually, Bob has to transfer the amount to the address created by Alice. As already discussed above, the amount would be grouped as per the original transactions in the wallet. We cannot select 1.2 BTC from the undifferentiated pool of 7.5BTC to transfer the amount to Alice's address. Instead, the wallet selects one of the outputs sufficient for the amount of transaction required. The amount is selected as a whole without dividing it, so here,

Figure 3. How Bitcoins are in wallet

Content of Bitcoin Wallet

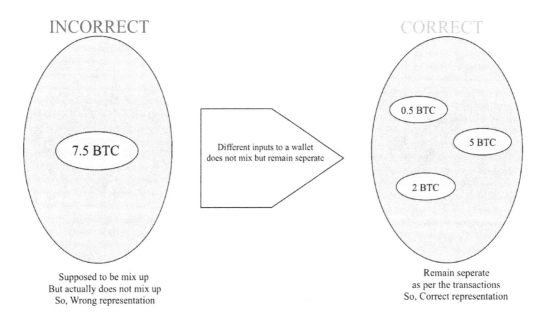

Figure 4. Inputs and outputs of a Bitcoin transaction

Bitcoin transaction Input and Output

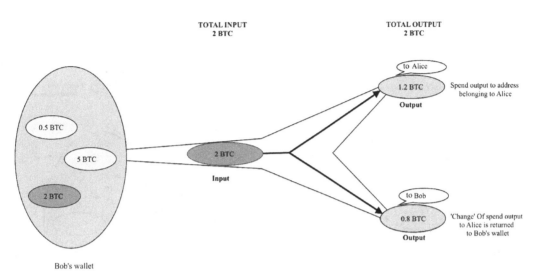

in this case, the 2 BTC output is selected. The 2 output is unlocked by the wallet and the amount of 2 BTC as a whole is used as an input to the new transaction for 1.2 BTC. Thus 2 BTC is the output which is said to be "spent" in the process. The actual amount which needs to be transferred to the Alice is only 1.2 BTC. This is controlled by the spend transaction created by the sender's wallet.

Out of the 2 BTC, spend transactions sends 1.2 BTC to Alice's address- these will remain in Alice's wallet as output to be spent on his wallet for some other transaction. The remaining amount 0.8 BTC is called the change. The change is sent back by the transaction to the sender's wallet through a newly created address. Thus 0.8BTC are sent back to Bob's wallet which appears as a new output of 0.8 in your wallet ready to spend in some new transaction. So the new outputs in the wallet will appear as shown in Figure 5.

All the three outputs which are "waiting to be spent", are secure in the wallet of the bitcoin account holder until they are selected for next transaction which we are going to spend as input. One or more than one outputs are chosen as input(s) to the new spend transaction. To select the output(s) as input for the next spent transaction, different wallets use different methods or rules. So selecting UTXOs as inputs to new spend transactions are based on the logic applied to the wallet client. Most of the coin selection wallet policies use the older UTXOs first, but different algorithms are followed by different approaches depending on conditions and factors. A merchant might get a number of small incoming payments and then makes a single or few outgoing payments, whereas in case of a mobile wallet agent the incoming payment may be single and the outgoing payment may be many in number. The process of UTXOs selection from the wallet is not of much concern here but still, it is briefly discussed ahead in this paper. The objective of the subtopic is that the amount received by the wallet remains separate and distinct and is spent separately unlike the physical wallet.

Briefly discussing how bitcoin transactions work, a number of different transactions received by a user remain separately in the wallet of the user unlike they do in a physical wallet. While creating the spend transaction these separate received amounts (UTXO's) are used individually or in combination to

Figure 5. Consuming and creating new UTOXs

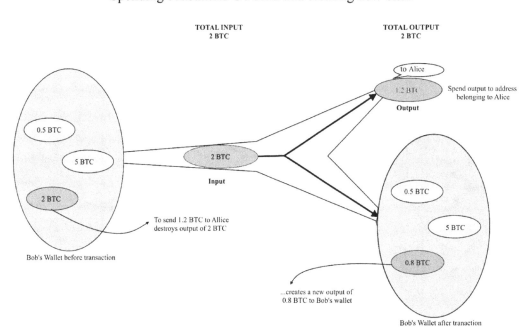

make the amount sufficient to satisfy the amount we want to send to the other address. Since the amount selected as input is always large than we actually need to transfer. In the network, the input is broken down into two outputs: One for the receiver and one as the change which the sender receives back into his wallet. The change which the sender receives back becomes the net UTXO in his wallet, and the amount sent to the receiver becomes another UTXO to the receiver's address. The original UTXO which was sent by the sender is spent in the transaction and destroyed forever (Figure 5).

As the UTXO is chosen for payment, it needs the private key correlated with the address that accepted it. This private key acknowledged by the UTXO and admit it to become an input in a new spend transaction. This mechanism in which the former transactions outputs are again used by spend transactions as new inputs is the basic principle to the bitcoin protocol Figure 6 function as defined by the creator Nakamoto Satoshi in Satoshi's design.

In bitcoin networks, a transaction is a process that enables the transmission of bitcoin amounts from one bitcoin account to another Bitcoin account. This process works on peer to peer basis. The recipient account holder can use these bitcoins for some new transaction that authorizes the transfer of possession to some other account. Every time a transaction consists of one or more than one inputs which show the debt against a bitcoin account. These inputs are converted to one or more outputs during the transaction process by the network which shows the credit added to a bitcoin account.

The sum of inputs and the outputs of any transaction are not always same, the reason being a small amount of the bitcoins is contributed to the miner as a transaction fee. The fee is very small and the miner's account is credited by that as processing fee and hence the sum of inputs is slightly larger than the sum of outputs in a transaction.

Figure 6. Flow of bitcoin transaction("Bitcoin")

How a bitcoin transaction works

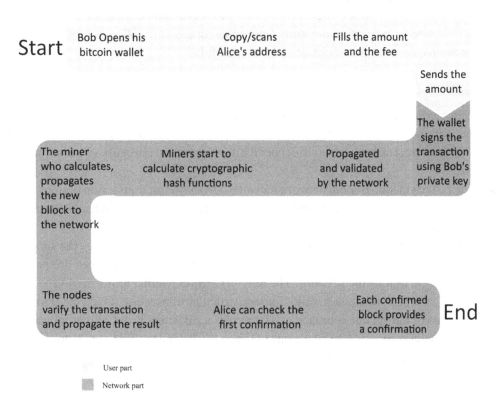

Bitcoin Payments

In case of online transactions, the exchange of services and goods and money occurs simultaneously, hence immediate transaction verification is required. Once the payment is verified the goods or services are dispatched or provided at the same time, e.g., in case of fast credit cards. Otherwise, the goods and services are provided or dispatched only after the payment by the receiver is processed. These two scenarios in transactions are called as slow payments and fast payments. Bitcoin transactions use both fast payment and slow payment scenarios. In this section, how bitcoin transactions are processed in these two scenarios are briefly discussed below. Assume a system in which a vendor V and set of customer's C in a bitcoin P2P network.

"Slow Payments": Transaction Confirmation

This type of payment is the most conventional and secure for vendor V where the vendor waits for the confirmation of the payment of the customer C by any of the blocks prior to provide services to C. The transaction is verified by the network and after confirmation, it is added to the blockchain as confirmed. Only then the vendor initiates the services to the customer. Since the client or customer C can intimate the vendor V about the transaction confirmation, so there are negligible chances for a malicious client A in tricking V to accept false or double-spent transactions. Confirmed transactions on the bitcoin network are accepted by the legitimate peers only.

Transaction confirmation time is the time which the transaction takes to be confirmed in the network. On an average, it takes 10 minutes to generate a new block but can be more or less depending on the hash power of the bitcoin network. Sometimes more than one confirmation is required usually, 3 to 6 confirmations are required for a transaction to be successful.

Fast Payments: Transaction Reception

In this fast technological era, it is obvious that more transaction confirmation time hinders the progress of many organizations that are symbolized by fast services. So, vendors such as Vending machines, stores, supermarkets etc. cannot have confidence in bitcoin payments because of more transaction confirmation time.

To facilitate fast payments, Bitcoin network networks also have fast transaction options to the vendors to provide services without waiting for confirmation of the transaction, only when the transaction is not of much amount (Rieke, 2013).

As such, for low-cost transactions with zero confirmation, the vendor provides the services or goods once the transaction amount has been sent to one of its addresses. The services are provided before confirmation of transaction by the network. The only verification at that moment of time by the vendor is that the vendor can check in client's wallet for the particular transaction. Once the transaction by the client to the address of the vendor is broadcasted provides a sufficient proof of that transaction. It takes few seconds only for the transaction to propagate between sender and the receiver through the transaction amount takes some time to be in the receiver's wallet- which supports the "zero-confirmation transactions" and fast transactions and payments.

Blockchain

Till now, we briefly defined blockchain and defined it as a distributed ledger. This is correct but there is something more about it to spot. It is time to take a closer look at to the structure and functionality of the blockchain. Rather we will say the question is how bitcoin keep these blocks in order and comes to a system-wide consistent consensus.

The blockchain is the technology that makes it possible to move digital currency or bitcoins from one account to another account in a bitcoin network, in the network. The ownership of the coin is determined by the order of the blocks and for this reason, a pointer is in the blocks pointing to the last validated block in the blockchain. This is shown in Figure 7 (Tschorsch, 2015). This pointer is implemented using the hash of the previous block and this makes the structure of the blockchain linked list type. The block height of the chain is defined as the number of blocks from beginning of the list to the end of the list. The block in the chain confirms that this transaction has prevailed at the time when added to the blockchain. Bitcoin implements a distributed variant of a time-stamping service along the lines of Haber (1991).

The miners mining the bitcoins are also increasing the blockchain constantly. Also due to the popularity of the Bitcoin, the number of transactions in the network chain is increasing tremendously. As a result, it increases the block size and so the blockchain. The increase in the number of transactions itself increases the efforts to validate a particular transaction. To make this transaction cost and time reasonable

Figure 7. Blockchain diagram (Tschorsch, 2015)

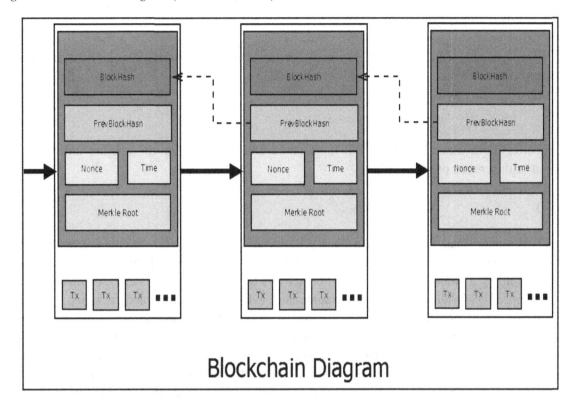

bitcoin network uses Si on Simplified Payment verification (SPV) (Nakamoto, 2008) based on Merkle tree (Becker, 2008; Merkle, 1987). This adds new transactions as the leaves and builds a tree with hash value as the root of the tree. The hash tree facilitates the confirmation without the need for all transactions. Branches or new nodes can be loaded from un-trusted sources but the root is secured during the mining process. If the calculated hash value does not match the original hash, then the transaction is detected as tempered or illegal and is discarded. If the hash values match, then the transaction is considered as legitimate by the network and is then added to the blockchain as confirmed.

So, in theory, we can consider blockchain as an unchangeable database or ledger. In the application, the forks and the mathematical rules that control the blockchain are capable to alter it. These are like ledgers for keeping records of bitcoin transactions and are maintained by the network nodes that run bitcoin software. The transaction between the sender and the receiver is broadcasted for the nodes running the bitcoin software. Once the transaction is validated it is stored in their blockchain ledger or database.

The blockchain works by these three steps:

- When the transaction is forwarded by the sender, the miner creates a block with all the transactions stored before it and is validated by Markle root hash tree (Becker, 2008; Merkle, 1987).
- The miner works on the block and once it is found that a given amount of work is done on that block. It uses some mathematical formulas and cryptographically finds the hash that satisfies the legitimacy of the transaction.

- As the hash matches, the block is broadcasted and also stored in the blockchain by the miner as the leading block of the chain.

The cryptographic security in the Hash lies in that there are no same hash values for two transactions, this is termed a collision.

Units

The bitcoin is represented by BTC, XBT. Its standard unit is bitcoin and the smallest unit is Satoshi names after the creator of the bitcoin.

Mining

The bitcoin miners (Paul, 2014) in the network use special software to solve the complex mathematical problems and also provide a service of maintaining the blocks in the blockchain. Since it repeatedly verifies the newly forwarded transactions in the network so, maintains consistency, completeness and makes the records unalterable. The cryptographic hash value of the former block is stored by the new block. It uses SHA-a256 hash Algorithm. The newly added block to the network should satisfy the condition to be accepted by the network. It means that the miner should be able to find a number which is used for hashing of the block content. The result after the hashing should be less than the networks difficult target. The number used is called a nonce. The proof is easy to verify but very much difficult to generate for a node, which is the reason behind the strength of the hash algorithm for cryptographic use.

Wallet

Bitcoin wallets are cryptocurrency digital wallets. The Bitcoin wallet is a software application where bitcoins are stored, received from other wallets and send to addresses created by other wallets. It is like a bank account but controlled by none, unlike banks. Bitcoin uses the public key cryptography for its transactions and wallet is supposed to store one of the public/private keys at least. There are various types of wallets, well known among them are:

Software Wallets

Software wallet application or client software that needs to be downloaded, create and use the wallet Software wallets. They are available for both mobiles and computers. Further the applications are available for different platforms like Android, Windows, MAC etc. One should also keep this in mind that these wallets are as secure as the devices which they are used on.

Online Wallets

It cannot be denied that online wallets are the easiest wallets to use for all the bitcoin wallets. Creating a Bitcoin wallet is as easy as creating an account on any website. One can create and use this wallet using any device like the phone, computer, tablet etc. connected to the internet. The security threat, in this case, is that the user's credentials are stored on some other server which can be compromised. This type of wallet should be used only for the small day to day transactions.

Hardware Wallets

Hardware wallets are hardware devices that can be plugged into the computer for making transactions. These are the devices like flash drives, USB shaped devices potable to carry with you. These are most secure wallets and also secure from computer malware threats. This is because the device remains offline so the credentials generated are more secure. They are also easy to use because they don't need to understand any complex technical details. The hardware devices can be made safer by securing the wallet device with password protection. If the client is a regular user and deals in big transactions, then he should definitely use hardware wallets like TREZOR or Ledger wallet.

Paper Wallets

it is also an offline mode of wallet and is more secure than the counterpart online wallets and software wallets. In this type, the credentials are printed on a paper. But one should keep in mind that the paper can be stolen, damaged or torn so, it is important to keep the paper in safer places and with multiple copies.

SECURITY ISSUES WITH BITCOIN TRANSACTIONS

Like threats computers and computer network there is the number of security issues (Pozzolo et al.,2014) with the bitcoin transaction processing systems. Some of the major issues are as bellow:

Threats to the Wallet Software

Wallet applications (Rieke et al.,2013) and website are prone to denial of service attacks. Sometimes the credentials of the wallets can be compromised. The security of the wallet can be manipulated in many ways (Sharma et al.,2012). For example, Impersonation- in which the attacker steals the credentials of the user and act as the legitimate user to perform the fraudulent transactions. There are other ways like malware attacks, the man in the middle attack and phishing etc. Although, some countermeasures are also available for such type of threats (Halvaiee, 2014; Aggarwal, 2007; Haber, 1991).

Time Jacking Attack

The attacker manipulates the bitcoin network by announcing the wrong time stamps. The attacker deceives the node by altering the network time counter of the node due to which it may accept an alternate blockchain. It leads to the wastage of computational resources of the network and can also make it easy for the attacker to carry out double-spending attacks.

>50% Attack

This attack is also called as 51% attack and is considered as one of the major threats to the bitcoin transaction processing system. It occurs when a user or group of user get more than 50% computational power in the mining process and have an intent of perturbing the network. What they can do is determine which transactions to include or not to include. They can perform denial of service in the network. They can prevent commerce from happening. If they have a substantial network power they can roll back the transactions, could prevent new blocks from being added and can reverse the prior confirmations that are already in place by powering the legitimate minors with their illicit mining. But they cannot alter transactions, cannot adjust people's balances and cannot misrepresent transactions.

Double Spending Attack

Double spending is a type of attack in which the same bitcoin is used for two different transactions by the sender. Here the sender is the attacker and invalidates the actual transaction. This issue occurs mostly in fast transaction modes where the receiver provides the services before the transaction is confirmed (Pinz & Rocha, 2012; Kadam, 2015).

The double spending attack works as: Suppose the attacker A wants services from vendor V. A creates two transactions, one for V and another for himself. A forwards the transaction to V (A to V) and starts secretly mining the transaction to himself (A to A) using powerful miners. The vendor gives services to A without transaction confirmation. The fraudulent high power miners make the chain of blocks longer in less time than the legitimate one. So the fraudulent transaction is confirmed by the network and the actual one is rejected. This is called the double-spending attack (see Figure 8).

Selfish Mining

In selfish attack, the miner mines the block but does not propagate the blocks to the network. The miner may be a miner or a pool of miners. This allows It allows the attacker to extend the leads of blocks with less hashing power and is also considered as the shortcut of 51% attack. The selfish mining allows the miner to take advantage of not publishing the mined blocks in order to gain a slight edge on the other miners.

CYBER LEGALITY AND ETHICS

The Information Technology Act passed in 2000 to deal with cybercrimes (Upadhyaya et al., 2016) and the e-commerce offenses against the law. The major amendment to the law was made in 2008 came into force on 29 Oct 2009. List of offenses and corresponding punishments as per the Information Technology (Amendment) Act 2008 are shown in Table 1.

IPC cyber-crime sections along with offenses are also shown in Table 2.

The IT Act and IPC section of cyber-crimes include cyber terrorism, bullying, cyber stalking, forgery, illegitimacy, dishonesty, cheating or fraudulent, unauthorized computer usage or data tempering etc. (Shrivastava, 2017). IPC sections also have some special law against the defamation, intimidation, extortion by sending messages or emails. It also has special laws against copyright acts under piracy as shown in Table 2.

Figure 8. Double spending attack

Double Spending Attack

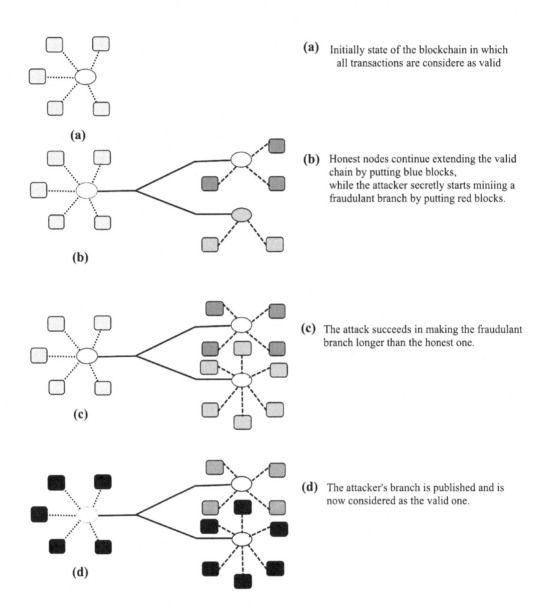

(a) Initially state of the blockchain in which all transactions are considere as valid

(b) Honest nodes continue extending the valid chain by putting blue blocks, while the attacker secretly starts miniing a fraudulant branch by putting red blocks.

(c) The attack succeeds in making the fraudulant branch longer than the honest one.

(d) The attacker's branch is published and is now considered as the valid one.

CONCLUSION

In this paper, the bitcoin and its nature and characteristics are mentioned. It also includes concepts on which the bitcoin network is based. The process of the transaction of bitcoin from one wallet to another is shown. Decentralized nature of the network and the threats to the networks are also included. The

Table 1. Important sections related to cyber-crimes

No	Section/ Sub-section	Offence	Penalty
1	65	Tempering with computer source documents	Up to 3years' custody and/or up to 2 lakh fine
2	66	Hacking with computer system	Up to 3years' custody and/or up to 5 lakh fine
3	66B	Receiving stolen computer or communication device	Up to 3years' custody and/or up to 1 lakh fine
4	66C	Using password of another person	Up to 3years' custody and/or up to 1 lakh fine
5	66D	Cheating using computer resources	Up to 3years' custody and/or up to 2 lakh fine
6	66E	Publishing private images of others	Up to 3years' custody and/or up to 2 lakh fine
7	66F	Acts of cyber terrorism	Lifetime imprisonment
8	67	Publishing offensive information in electronic form	Up to 5 years' custody and/or up to 10 lakh fine
9	67A	Publishing images containing sexual acts	Up to 7 years' custody and/or up to 10 lakh fine
10	67B	Publishing child porn or predating children online	On1st conviction Up to 3years' custody and/or up to 10 lakh fine On 2nd convection Up to 7 years' custody and/or up to 10 lakh fine
11	67C	Failure to maintain records	Up to 3years' custody and/or some fine also
12	68	Failure/Refusal to comply with orders	Up to 3years' custody and/or up to 2 lakh fine
13	69	Failure/Refusal to decrypt data	Up to 7 years' custody and/or possible fine
14	70	Securing access or attempting to secure access to a protected system	Up to 7 years' custody and/or possible fine.
15	71	Misrepresentation	Up to 3years' custody and/or up to 1 lakh fine
16	72	Rupture of confidentiality and privacy	Up to 3years' custody and/or up to 1 lakh fine
17	72A	Breaking legal contract by leaking information	Up to 5 years' custody and/or up to 5 lakh fine
18	73	distributing the false signature electronically	Up to 2 years' custody and/or up to 1 lakh fine
19	74	Spreading fake information in public or illicit purpose	Term of 2 years and/or fine.
20	84C	Endeavour to achieve illegal act	Longest term of jail term and/or fine

Table 2. Offences or crimes which come under IPC and special laws

Sections of Cyber Crime	Genre	Offences
51 IPC	Piracy	Breach or violation of copyright
63 IPC	Piracy	Unlawfully copying a computer programme
63B IPC	Piracy copyright act	Violating the rules of copyright act
292 IPC	Obscenity	Sale of indecent or offensive in form of books, videos etc.
293 IPC	Obscenity	Sale of indecent, offensive or immoral content to minors
294 IPC	Obscenity	Indecent or offensive representation of female clan
378,379 IPC	Thievery	Thieving of computer hardware
383 IPC	Blackmail/ Shakedown	Blackmailing anyone to upload anything vulgar or illicit online
420 IPC	Cyber frauds	Creation of foul websites
463 IPC	Forgery or dummy	Using false emails for forgery of computer documents
499 IPC	Ruthless defamation	Sending defaming messages by email
500,509 IPC	Email abuse or online disparage	Defaming a person or any harmful play act to women
503 IPC	Threat	Sending email which threatens a person
506,507 IPC	Criminal alarm	Offence of criminal menace

cyber-crimes and their punishments are also well compared. Bitcoin network is increasing day by day. Days are not away when the market of e-commerce will be controlled by the bitcoins worldwide because it is not restricted by the boundaries of nations.

REFERENCES

Aggarwal, D., Singhal, P., Kaur, S., & Bhatnagar, V. (2007, November). PDOD: Tree-Based Algorithm For Outlier Detection. *Proceedings of Int'l Conference on Computer Vision and Information Technology.*

Barber, S., Boyen, X., Shi, E., & Uzun, E. (2012, February). Bitter to better—how to make bitcoin a better currency. In *International Conference on Financial Cryptography and Data Security* (pp. 399-414). Springer. 10.1007/978-3-642-32946-3_29

Becker, G. (2008). *Merkle signature schemes, merkle trees and their cryptanalysis.* Ruhr-University Bochum, Tech. Rep.

Clark, J. B. A. M. J., Edward, A. N. J. A. K., & Felten, W. (2015). *Research Perspectives and Challenges for Bitcoin and Cryptocurrencies.* Academic Press.

Dal Pozzolo, A., Caelen, O., Le Borgne, Y. A., Waterschoot, S., & Bontempi, G. (2014). Learned lessons in credit card fraud detection from a practitioner perspective. *Expert Systems with Applications, 41*(10), 4915–4928. doi:10.1016/j.eswa.2014.02.026

Haber, S., & Stornetta, W. S. (1990, August). How to time-stamp a digital document. In *Conference on the Theory and application of Cryptography* (pp. 437-455). Springer.

Halvaiee, N. S., & Akbari, M. K. (2014). A novel model for credit card fraud detection using Artificial Immune Systems. *Applied Soft Computing, 24*, 40–49. doi:10.1016/j.asoc.2014.06.042

Kadam, M., Jha, P., & Jaiswal, S. (2015). Double spending prevention in bitcoins network. *International Journal of Computer Engineering and Applications, 9.*

Khaosan, V. (2014). *How Bitcoin Transaction Works.* Retrieved from https://www.cryptocoinsnews.com/bitcoin-transaction-really-works/

Ladd, W. (2012). *Blind signatures for bitcoin transaction anonymity.* Retrieved from http://wbl.github.io/bitcoinanon.pdf

Maxwell, J. C. (1892). *A treatise on electricity and magnetism* (3rd ed.; Vol. 2). Clarendon Press.

Meiklejohn, S., Pomarole, M., Jordan, G., Levchenko, K., McCoy, D., Voelker, G. M., & Savage, S. (2013, October). A fistful of bitcoins: characterizing payments among men with no names. In *Proceedings of the 2013 conference on Internet measurement conference* (pp. 127-140). ACM. 10.1145/2504730.2504747

Merkle, R. C. (1987, August). A digital signature based on a conventional encryption function. In *Conference on the Theory and Application of Cryptographic Techniques* (pp. 369-378). Springer.

Moore, T., & Christin, N. (2013, April). Beware the middleman: Empirical analysis of Bitcoin-exchange risk. In *International Conference on Financial Cryptography and Data Security* (pp. 25-33). Springer. 10.1007/978-3-642-39884-1_3

Nakamoto, S. (2008). *Bitcoin: A Peer-to Peer Electronic Cash System.* Retrieved from https://bitcoin.org/bitcoin.pdf

Paul, G., Sarkar, P., & Mukherjee, S. (2014, December). Towards a more democratic mining in bitcoins. In *International Conference on Information Systems Security* (pp. 185-203). Springer. 10.1007/978-3-319-13841-1_11

Pinzón, C., & Rocha, C. (2016). Double-spend Attack Models with Time Advantange for Bitcoin. *Electronic Notes in Theoretical Computer Science, 329*, 79–103. doi:10.1016/j.entcs.2016.12.006

Rieke, R., Zhdanova, M., Repp, J., Giot, R., & Gaber, C. (2013, September). Fraud detection in mobile payments utilizing process behavior analysis. In *Availability, Reliability and Security (ARES), 2013 Eighth International Conference on* (pp. 662-669). IEEE. 10.1109/ARES.2013.87

Sharma, K., Shrivastava, G., & Singh, D. (2012). Risk Impact of Electronics-Commerce Mining: A Technical Overview. *Risk (Concord, NH), 29.*

Shrivastava, G. (2017). Approaches of network forensic model for investigation. *International Journal of Forensic Engineering, 3*(3), 195–215. doi:10.1504/IJFE.2017.082977

Stack Exchange. (2017). *What does a Bitcoin transaction consist of?* Retrieved on October 30, 2017 from https://bitcoin.stackexchange.com/questions/4838/what-does-a-bitcoin-transaction-consist-of

Tschorsch, F., & Scheuermann, B. (2016). Bitcoin and beyond: A technical survey on decentralized digital currencies. *IEEE Communications Surveys and Tutorials, 18*(3), 2084–2123.

Upadhyaya, R., & Jain, A. (2016, April). Cyber ethics and cyber crime: A deep dwelved study into legality, ransomware, underground web and bitcoin wallet. In *Computing, Communication and Automation (ICCCA), 2016 International Conference on* (pp. 143-148). IEEE. 10.1109/CCAA.2016.7813706

What is Bitcoin? (n.d.). Retrieved from http://www.coindesk.com/information/what-is-bitcoin/

Chapter 22
A Robust Biometrics System Using Finger Knuckle Print

Ravinder Kumar
HMR Institute of Technology and Management, India

ABSTRACT

Among various biometric indicators, hand-based biometrics has been widely used and deployed for last two decades. Hand-based biometrics are very popular because of their higher acceptance among the population because of their ease of use, high performance, less expensive, etc. This chapter presents a new hand-based biometric known as finger-knuckle-print (FKP) for a person authentication system. FKP are the images obtained from the one's fingers phalangeal joints and are characterized by internal skin pattern. Like other biometrics discrimination ability, FKP also has the capability of high discrimination. The proposed system consists of four modules: image acquisition, extraction of ROI, selection and extraction of features, and their matching. New features based on information theory are proposed for matching. The performance of the proposed system is evaluated using experiment performed on a database of 7920 images from 660 different fingers. The efficacy of the proposed system is evaluated in terms of matching rate and compromising results are obtained.

INTRODUCTION

Biometrics deals with the automated system for authentication and authorization of individuals based on the characteristics possessed by him or her. Various biometrics modalities proposed in the latest research literature are: fingerprints (Maltoni et al., 2009; Kumar et al., 2012a, 2012b, 2012c; Kumar et al., 2013a, 2013b, 2013c; Kumar et al., 2014a, 2014b; Kumar et al., 2016; Jain et al., 2004), face (Jain & Li, 2011; Alling et al., 2016), retinal scan (Seto, 2015), hand geometry (Kumar et al., 2017), speech (Rabiner & Juang, 1993), iris (Huang et al., 2002), hand vein (Kumar & Prathyusha, 2009), and voiceprint (Wang et al., 2004) etc. With the advancement of technology, biometric-based personal verification and identification solutions have become the necessity of our highly secured networked society. The need for a secure biometric authentication system for individual identification and authentication is becoming apparent as the fraud and security breaches increases.

DOI: 10.4018/978-1-5225-4100-4.ch022

To provide the security and privacy of electronic and financial transactions, personal data and to restrict access, biometric-based security solutions are highly desirable. The need for such biometrics had been observed in almost all domains like governments, military, and other commercial applications. The recent advancements of biometrics technologies had also contributed to the other domains of the society such as organizational secure network infrastructures, enforcement of law and order, online transactions, access to health and social services, government identification services (Like Aadhar in India).

The latest research combines fingerprints with other biometrics indicators in order to have better results and to enhance acceptability among the large population. Various biometrics fusions can be performed like fingerprint and face, lip movement and voice, speech and face, hand geometry and fingerprint, fingerprint speech and face, fingerprint and palm print, fingerprint, palm print and hand geometry to get multimodal biometrics with improved matching performance. This fusion of multibiometric traits can happen at various levels like image level, features level, rank level, and decision level etc.

As our society is becoming more and more mobile and electronically connected the traditional systems of passwords (for access control over e-resources) and ID cards (used in commercial and financial transactions) no longer remain reliable for access to the highly restricted systems. Therefore, breaches of the security in such systems become very easy as cards may be lost or stolen, PIN or password can be guessed by an impostor. Further, complex passwords are difficult to be remembered or recall by the legitimate users and very simple passwords can easily be guessed by an impostor. The problem of recognition of a person or providing access to the security infrastructure had been addressed by the emergence of biometrics-based authentication system over the verification methods.

Biometrics is the Greek term, where bios means life and metron means measurement is the tool used for automatic authentication of a person using the physiological and behavioral properties possess by a person (see Figure 1). By using biometrics, it becomes easy to associate an identity to an individual by asking question like "who you are," not by "what you possess" (e.g. Physical Identity card) or "what you remember" (e.g. code or password). Currently deployed biometric authentication systems are based on face, retina, fingerprints, iris, facial thermograms, hand geometry, palm print, gait, signature, and voiceprint to establish an identity with an individual. In unimodal biometrics systems, various biometrics indicators in alone are used, whereas in multimodal biometrics system two or more biometrics indicators are fused together at different level like: at feature extraction level, at score computation level or at rank or matching level to increase the performance. Biometric systems may also have certain limitations, but these can be overlooked while comparing with traditional method of secure access. Besides empowering the security, user convenience, the need of design and remembering passwords are also alleviated by the used of biometrics systems. Biometrics systems are also deployed for negative authentication in which it determines whether this is the person, who he or she denies to be.

Biometric systems operate in two modes i.e. verification (one to one matching) mode and identification (one to many matching) mode. In identification mode, the identity of an individual is established, whereas in verification mode, the user is identified against the identity claimed by him or her. The applications of biometrics systems are uncountable where access control or security is desired e.g. ATMs, computer logins, driver's licenses, airport kiosks, grocery stores etc. The large number of biometrics applications or uses did not implied that it is a fully solved and researched problem, still the scope of improvement of design of new devices or biometrics indicators are always there.

A biometric authentication system can be described as a pattern recognition system which, consists of sensors to capture biometrics data, feature extractor module to extract features from captured data, template generation module to represent extracted features, and recognition module which match the captured features against previously stored features in database to take decision based on the matching result, A block diagram of typical biometric authentication system is shown in figure 1.

Training a biometrics authentication system means to make the system capable of extract the salient features from the captured biometrics data (generally images). The acceptance of any biometrics system lies with extraction of most translational and rotational invariant features under different diverging conditions. Template generation is a very crucial task as this is to take care of various design issues of biometrics system like accuracy, computational speed, system cost, exception handling security and privacy etc. During testing phase, extracted features template from unknown test images are compared with the templates already stored in database for identification, and with claimed template IDs for verification purpose. From the above discussion, it is very clear that the whole process of biometrics authentication system lies in the domain of pattern recognition problem. Final matching result of this pattern matching process helps to make decision of accept or reject the person identity or to give access to secured resources.

OVERVIEW OF BIOMETRICS MODALITIES

Presently, various biometrics modalities are used in various domains of secure systems in practice. During past many years exhaustive research on Biometric modalities have been done by many researches and has proved that many modalities like Face, Iris, Retina, Ear, Tongue print, Palm print, Fingerprint, Hand vein, Hand Geometry, Finger vein, Finger surface, Inner Knuckle Print, Voice, Signature and Gait are unique among population and can be utilized as biometric indicator in biometric-based authentication system. Various biometrics indicators are shown in Figure 2.

There are several characteristics which can determine the suitability of a physical or behavioral (Jain *et al.*, 2004) traits, which can be used as a Biometric Indicator or modality, including:

- **Universality:** Each and every person should have the underlying trait.
- **Uniqueness:** With respect to the given population, a person should be uniquely distinguished on the basis of underlying trait i.e. the minimal chance of similar characteristic posses by any two-individual.

Figure 1. A typical biometrics recognition system

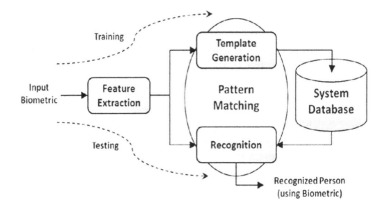

Figure 2. Different kinds of biometric indicators

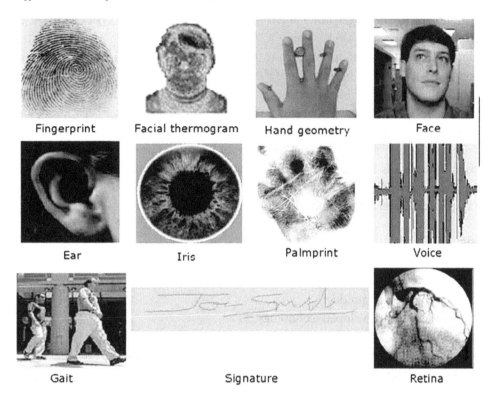

- **Permanence:** The trait should be permanent and invariant over the years.
- **Measurability:** The characteristic should be quantitatively measurable.
- **Performance:** Measures the speed, accuracy, and robustness of used matching technology.
- **Acceptability:** Determines up to what extend some particular biometrics is accepted among the population.

It has been shown in the literature that none of the Biometric Indicators possess all these listed characteristics. The selection of biometric indicators lies in the fact that for which application domain it has to be used. This implies that no biometrics can be called as perfect, these are application specific only. The suitability of any specific biometric modality with an application is determined by the purpose and characteristics of the modalities to be used. Different biometrics indicators are discussed one by one in the following section:

Fingerprint

Fingerprint identification had been used from ancient time for establishing the identity for criminal and financial investigations and is most popular among all biometrics indicators nowadays also. Because of their characteristics like distinctiveness and consistency over the years advocated it utilities over the years. Other properties like easy to capture, measurability, availability, universality, and performance also contributed towards its popularity over other biometrics for automated biometric recognition system. Figure 3 illustrates the use of fingerprints in car ignition and door locking systems (Zhou et al., 2000; Kumar, 2018).

Fingerprint is assumed as a pattern of furrows and ridges on the finger-tips of individuals. The characteristics points like ending and bifurcation of ridges are referred as minutia points and are designated as key points for the purpose of identification and verification. Another Image-based approach uses various key descriptors like this pattern of ridges and furrows can be analyzed at various scales exhibit various types of features as: level 1 (global Level) at this level the singular points like core, loop, and delta points are consider for first level indexing. At level 2, minutia points are used for discrimination. At level 3, very fine details like width, shape, curvature, edge contours of ridges are considered for discrimination among subjects. As fingerprint offer various features at various levels for biometrics recognition system, and thus offers many advantages as follows:

Advantages

1. Fingerprints have high accuracy.
2. Cost effective biometrics products.
3. Highly researched and developed technology.
4. Easy to capture or acquire.
5. Fingerprint template needs less storage as the size of fingerprint images are small.
6. Many standards are available like NIST, FVC etc.

Disadvantages

1. It is very intrusive because is still related to criminal identification.
2. The system will not perform well in case of dry and wet images.
3. To capture good quality images more memory is required for databases. Many systems require 500 dpi, 8 bits per pixel for the effective performance of the system.

Figure 3. Fingerprints based biometric systems (a) physical access control system using fingerprints (b) The fingerprint-based identification system for car ignition by its owner or authorized person

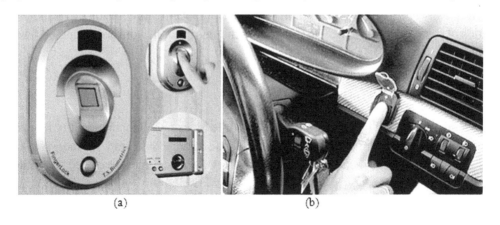

(a)   (b)

Facial Recognition

A facial recognition system is inspired from natural way of human recognition based on facial structure and certain key points. With the advancement of computing technology and network technology the need of automated facial recognition arises for identifying or authenticating an individual from an image or captured video frame from sensing sources. As wide varieties of acquisition devices are available for capturing facial images, naturally there are wide variations among captured images. The National Institute of standards and Technology (NIST) have proposed guidelines by for facial image acquisition. Major face recognition approaches presented in the research literature are mainly classified into two classes as: *face appearance* and *face geometry*. Facial biometrics based systems are generally installed on checkpoints and it was first used by China at entrance security checks during Olympic opening ceremony as shown in Figure 4.

Various face recognition approaches have been proposed in the literature over a decade. Eigen face approach had popularized among many other approaches as it can deal very well with lighting variation and large size of face images. Key feature based approaches are based on automatics detection of certain feature from the face images using local appearance model. Indeed, many hybrid approaches have also been used by many researchers, which are based on global model of human faces. Although lots of techniques for human identification using face images exists, still this field is not matured as fingerprints due to some challenges discussed below:

Challenges

1. Frequent changes in facial appearance over a time.
2. Image acquisition geometry is not rotation and translation invariant.

Figure 4. A face recognition system installed at entrances of National Stadium for audience's identification checks on August 8, 2008

3. The facial based recognition system is a very costly affair.
4. High storage space is required as image size is very large as compared to other biometrics traits, and compression using JPEG and MPEG degrade the image quality.

Speech Recognition

Speech is the only biometrics which can be captures over telephonic conversation to identify the person. In this technology spoken words are translated into text. Training of some speech recognition system is performed for individual speaker by translating into text when the speaker reads sections of text. In this system, the voice print of the individual voice is analyzed to enhance the matching accuracy of the system. Those systems which don't require training are refereed as "Speaker Independent" whereas those systems which need training are known as "Speaker Dependent" systems.

Advantages

1. Highly accepted by society.
2. Very less recognition time.
3. Cost effective solution.

Disadvantages

1. Affected by the state of an individual like cold, stress and emotional.
2. Recognition accuracy is not up to the mark.
3. Voiceprint might be mimicked by extraordinary skilled individuals.

Signature Recognition

The way an individual sign his name can also be accepted as biometrics for individual identification. Signature-based recognition had been in use for a long time in government, commercial, and legal transactions.

Advantages

1. No cost technology.
2. Verification time is very less.
3. Non-intrusive.

Disadvantages

1. Behavioral characteristics change over a time and also depend on the individual state of emotional and physical condition of the speaker.
2. Variation in signs of signatories, even successive signature varies a lot for the same signatory.
3. May also be forged by the skilled person.

DNA

DNA is considered as the ultimate biometrics as DNA sequence is found in each cells of the body in digital form. DNA based authentication is based on the comparison of alleles of DNA sequences found in nucleus of each cell of the body.

Advantages

1. Perfect accuracy.
2. The standardized method of identification in medical sciences.
3. Very less possibility of errors.

Disadvantages

1. Identical twins will have the same DNA.
2. Very complex and expensive operation to compare two DNE sequences.

Retinal Scanning

Retinal scanning is used for the comparison of images of the blood-vessels in the back lit of the eye. Retinal scanning in also very expensive process, because image acquisition can only be done in near infer red, to which retina is transparent.

Advantages

1. The permanent structure, not affected by anything.
2. Almost impossible to construct fake retina.
3. Very good accuracy

Disadvantages

1. The acquisition is not many users friendly.
2. The imaging device is the very costly affair.
3. Can only be applicable to living human beings.

Iris Recognition

Iris is the colored part of the human eye, which is rich in textural information. Iris recognition uses complex pattern recognition mathematical techniques to analyze the video images of iris of an individual in designing an automated biometric system for human identification. The iris capturing device is a distance image capturing device that will capture iris image without contact and at a fixed distance from the lens of the imaging system as shown in Figure 5.

Figure 5. Different types of iris capturing systems

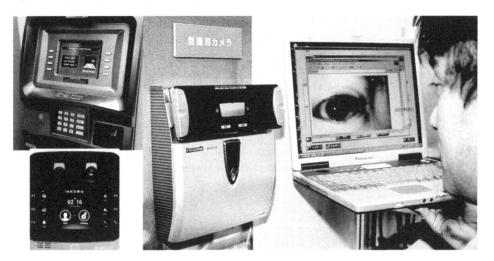

Advantages

1. Highly accurate biometrics if, captured images have high resolution.
2. Very fast processing system.

Disadvantages

1. The imaging system is highly expensive.
2. More storage is required for processing.
3. The processing system is very costly.
4. The whole process is not too user-friendly.

Hand Geometry

The characteristics of the human hand are not very peculiar, but relatively invariant (length of fingers) for a human being. During enrollment phase user cooperation is needed in placing the hand over the scanner to capture frontal and side view images as shown in Figure 6. A Hand Geometry has very few distinctive features to be extracted from hand images e.g. finger lengths, widths, distances etc. the template size is very small, hence resulted in very fast matching process. Because of very limited distinctiveness, hand image based authentication can only be used for verification not very well suited for identification.

Advantages

1. Very fast processing.
2. Preferably used in authorization systems due to the compact size.
3. Can easily be used in smartcards due to the small size and fast matching.

Figure 6. The outlook of hand geometry system

Disadvantages

1. Capturing device is highly sophisticated and costly.
2. Accuracy is very less.
3. Limited use only.

FINGER KNUCKLE SURFACE AS BIOMETRIC IDENTIFIER

With the advancement in the field of information technology and a very rapid growth in online transactions in our daily life needs a very reliable user authentication system for a very effective and highly secured access control. From the above discussion, it is very well understood that none of the biometrics indicators fully satisfy the requirements of the ultimate biometric identifier. In comparison with other biometric indicators hand based biometrics has gained popularity in recent time because of their distinctive inherent features and high acceptance rate amongst users. The touchless and peg-free environment of the capturing process also made hand-based biometric systems more convenient and user-friendly. The latest research has focused on hand-based biometrics indicator to further explore the additional features for the application of hand image based authentication method for various person authentication using hand images. This chapter focused on the development of automated recognition system to extract knuckle print texture and other hand geometry based features extracted from the back side surface of the finger and to evaluate their performance to be a potential biometric indicator.

Personal identification has gained popularity among institutions and industries because of its use in variety of domains including access control to resources, financial and commercial transactions and law enforcement, etc. Biometric characteristics of an individual can be used to establish the identity of individuals and are accepted in the networked society and also in the justice of court as a proof of the identity. With the fast development in the software and hardware technology in the domain of computational techniques, many researchers have pay their focus on the application of new biometric characteristics, like fingerprint, hand vein, retina, hand geometry, palm print, iris, face, inner knuckle print, signature, voice, gait, ear, finger surface, etc. during past three decades. Some of the biometric systems are not fully exploited in terms of research and development, while some of these have been used at large scale in government, banking and other authentication domains; for example, since 2004 the government of Hong Kong has deployed a fingerprint-based authentication system in its automated passenger clearance system. It has seen that hand-based biometrics has attracted a considerable focus in comparison to other kinds of biometric identifiers. In literature, it has observed that hand based biometrics like the palm print, hand geometry, fingerprint, inner knuckle print, and hand vein are well studies and utilizes in biometric systems deployed in industries, governments, and institutions. The major reason for the popularity of hand-based biometrics is attributed to higher accuracy, ease of use, and user acceptance. In recent year, it has been found that the image pattern of knuckle surface is unique among the population and can be identified as a unique biometric trait. First time 3-D features from finger surface were extracted by Woodward et al. (2005), band setup 3-D hand databases of knuckle surfaces with the Minolta 900/910 sensor to establish a person's identity. The solution provided by them did not use as feasible as this not enough efficient for acceptance as a recognition system using only finger outer surface characteristics. The practical difficulty in implementing finger outer surface biometrics features are like: sensor capability cost, size and weight of acquisition device. This process is also very time- consuming for the acquisition of 3-D data and processing to be deployed in real applications. Figure 7 shows the set-up of knuckle print acquisition system and obtained image using Minolta 900/910 sensor.

In later years, more approaches to individual identification using two-dimensional finger-knuckle surface print was proposed by Kumar and Ravikanth, (2009). They have captured hand back images by a device developed by them and then after preprocessing the captured hand back images they have extracted a finger knuckle area. Kumar and Ravikanth have used sub-space analysis approach Like ICA, LDA and PCA and their combination to extract the feature for performing matching. An image of extracted knuckle print is shown in Figure 8.

Figure 7. (a) An acquired image (b) Acquisition set up using Minolta 900/910 sensor

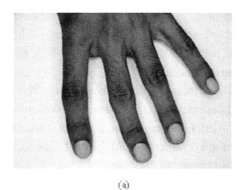 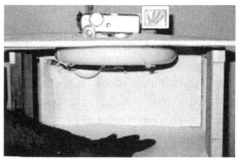

(a)   (b)

Figure 8. Extracted finger knuckle print

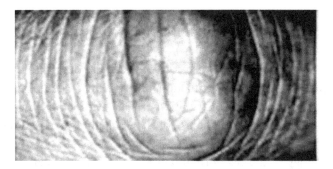

KNUCKLES

The studies of biometric, in particularly the hand anatomy of an individual, are related to the branch of medical science and biology and are considered as very complicated. The back-surface area of fingers also referred as dorsum of the hand and is highly useful in the design of biometrics system for personal identification. This area is still under investigation and attracted a lot of attention from researchers recently. Knuckle print is the image pattern formed at the bending point of fingers and is highly unique and distinctive. On the other hand, geometrical features can also be captured for the same finger during the acquisition process and are integrated with knuckle print matching system to enhance the matching accuracy of the system. The imaging environment without hand fixation for image acquisition makes this system of matching most convenient to the users. These FKP images can also be acquired by online means, which are also used to extract invariant finger knuckle features for individual identification.

LITERATURE REVIEW

Recently a new hand based biometrics has been proposed in the literature referred as Finger Knuckle Print (FKP), which has the wide scope of application because of its easiness in acquire and use and also possesses unique texture features. To add to its advantage, it is an uphill task to spoof the FKP. Knuckles being on the dorsal part of the hand are not subject to cuts and bruises, unlike fingerprints. Hence, they are safer and more reliable. The ground breaking work of Zhang and his coworkers (Zhang et al., 2009, 2010, 2011) has made the knuckles prominent biometric modality. The following section presents a brief literature survey on FKPs and their use in the authentication.

Their acquisition system device captures FKP pattern when the texture is clear on bending of finger and has to be placed properly, so that unique FKP features can be extracted. The local direction map is used to align the image and an ROI is cropped. The Gabor filter which combines magnitude and orientation information is used for the feature extraction. In Kumar and Zhou, (2009) have extracted the local orientation using a coding scheme and then global features are captured using the application of Fourier transform on local features. They have compared two FKPs by using their angular distances calculating along with the code maps.

Two feature subsets of the extracted features are combined, which were extracted from Gabor transform and statistics then there score are fused together to give good identification results. The Local Gabor

Binary Patterns (LGBP) has been successfully implemented for the recognition of faces motivated to use LGBP for FKPs identification as presented by Xiong et al., (2011). To reduce the dimensionality of the large size Gabor features Orthogonal Linear Discriminant Analysis (OLDA) is used to reduce the dimension of FKP by Usha & Ezhilarasan, (2016).

The SURF algorithm in Le-Qing, (2011) uses different feature descriptors and key-point detectors. This algorithm uses the Hessian matrix approximation for key-point detection and it reduces computation complexity by using integral images. The distribution of Haar-wavelet response in the neighborhood to the point of interest describes descriptors. The use of SURF features is based on the sign of the Laplacian to enhance the matching speed and robustness.

In order to enhance the image, a 2D Gabor filter is used and then processed using Orientation enhanced SIFT (OE-SIFT) descriptors (Morales *et al.,* 2011). Kumar and Zhang (2005) proposed a technique, which uses features combination computed from the gradients of the Finger Knuckle Print. This technique employs the orientation (gradient field direction) and also improves the averaged gradient to the vectors of local gradient which helps in extract the position of the phalangeal joint in the Finger-Knuckle.

Zhang et al., (2009) proposed to use a technique in which the features and similarity are evaluated using coefficients of Fourier transform of the image using the band-limited phase-only correlation (BLPOC) technique between the sets of Fourier transform coefficients.

RieszCompCode for feature extraction contains six bit-planes, where the image responses of 2nd-order Riesz transforms forms the first three planes and the next three are derived from the classical CompCode scheme. This technique is advantageous in local image features characterizing by using Riesz transform and CompCode and is implemented in Grover and Hanmandlu, (2017).

Monogenic Code examines pixel to implicitly extract the local orientation and local phase at that point. This is an isotropic 2-D extension of the 1-D analytic signal (Zhang et al., 2010b).

The angle and distances between data vectors of an image are proposed to evaluate the similarities. Both of these parameters are combined using the parallel fused strategy, and then to extract the low-dimensional features, complex locality preserving projections (CLPP) are used, which preserve the manifold structure of the input data set. The redundant information among features is removed by extended CLPP known as OCLPP (Orthogonal Complex Locality Preserving Projections) to produce orthogonal functions (Jing et al., 2011; Matallah et al., 2017; Yang et al., 2018).

Woodard & Flynn, (2005a) extracted the hand knuckle surface information comprise of texture, color, finger length measurements, and crease patterns using the 3D range image information. Ravikanth and Kumar, (2007) implemented a subspace analysis technique for extraction of features using 2D finger knuckle surface images.

Gabor wavelets are used for extracting the fusion code for both the finger knuckles and the palm prints and then the Hamming distance is employed to generate the scores in order to fuse both the modalities at the decision level (Zhang et al., 2009).

FKP RECOGNITION SYSTEM

Schematic Diagram of Imaging System of FKP

The structure of typical FKP biometric identification system is depicted in Figure 9. The proposed authentication system mainly comprises of two modules: data processing module and data capturing

Figure 9. Typical processing diagram of the person authentication system using FKP

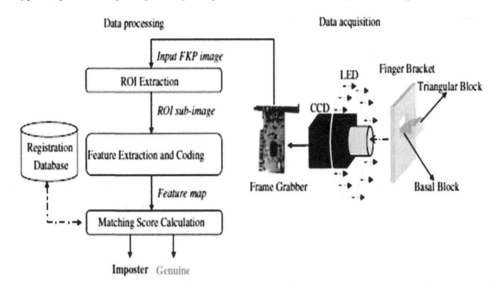

module. This data capturing module further contains various components like finger bracket, a CCD camera, frame grabber and a LED light source. The processing module mainly consists of three steps: ROI extraction, extraction and representation of features and finally a matching stage. Figure 6 shows the flow diagram of FKP image acquisition device having dimensions as $160 \times 125 \times 100$mm. The objective and requirement of the data acquisition are to provide a constant environment in which data collection is consistent and stable. This consistency helps to reduce the variation between images collected from the same finger i.e. intraclass variations. In the similar fashion, the data processing and data acquisition algorithms complexity can effectively be reduced by stability in image acquisition process and thus recognition accuracy is enhanced. To make the acquisition system more user-friendly, other constraints must also be removed or minimized. In order to enhance the consistency, the stability of and friendliness of data acquisition, a special capturing environment is created in our system. For constant illumination and fixed capturing, the CCD camera and LED light source are enclosed in a box. Most difficult part of this system is that how a user can place their finger on the basal block such the variation should be minimum. To handle this situation a fixed finger bracket is constructed to support the placement of the finger to the system. As shown in Figure 1, the user has to fix the position of their finger joint on the specially designed basal block and the triangular block of the device. For acquisition of FKP images, the device with above arrangement, the basal block is used to put the finger and the two slops of the blocks are used to put the proximal phalanx and the middle phalanx. This design will efficiently reduce the variations inserted during data capture. To maintain a constant angle between the proximal phalanx and the middle phalanx this triangular block can be used, and this way the knuckle surfaces line features can be imaged effectively. Once the clear images are captured, they need to be processed by various processing blocks like pre-processing, extraction of features and matching. The FKP images so acquired have a size of 768×576 with 400 dpi of resolution. The sample images thus captured using the above-developed device is shown in Figure 3. Each row shows the images captured from the same figure. The images captured from the same finger are collected at various times or session at least at an interval of 56 days. This developed image capturing device has an advantage of very less intraclass variations even the images captured from the same finger at the different session. On the other hand, the system has a very large inter class variations in which images from different finger are very much different from, and this property of less intraclass variation and high inter-class variation make the FKP a good biometric indicator for person authentication.

(PolyU) Finger-Knuckle-Print Database

Hand based biometrics has gained popularity among various other biometric identifiers, in the recent years. Around the phalangeal joint of the finger, an inherent pattern of the outer surface is referred to as Finger-knuckle-print, and it is established that it has high discriminative and distinctive characteristics.

The FKP capturing device has been developed by Hong Kong Polytechnic University in its Biometric Research Centre and also constructed a standard FKP database. This dataset helps in the advancement of research and to provide the standard dataset to test their results in the area of FKP recognition. The effectiveness of various FKP recognition algorithms developed by the different researcher is tested using the constructed FKP database by making it available for free of charge for academic, non-commercial uses.

PolyU FKP Database Description

FKP database images are taken from 125 males and 40 female's volunteers out of these 143 subjects were in the age group ranging from 20~30 years and remaining were in the age group ranging from 30 to 50 years. Different sessions were organized to collect samples from individuals. Four fingers (except thumb) of each hand were considered for data collection and taken 6images of each finger for each user.

Figure 10. Sample FKP images. (a), (b) are from the same finger captures at a gap of 56 days while (c) and (d) are taken from different fingers

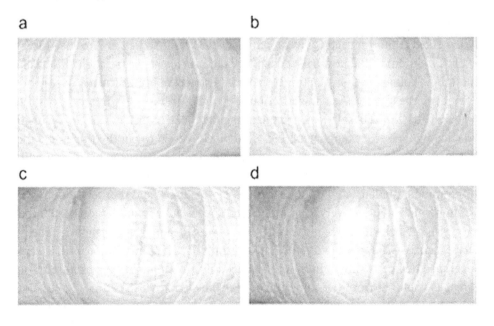

In total, 48 images from each subject were collected at the rate of six images for 8 fingers. PolyU FKP database finally contain165 × 48 = 7,920 images from 1320 different fingers. The sessions for data collection were organized at an average interval of 25 days.

The captured data was stored in folders named as "nnn_fingertype". "nnn" to identify the individuals. Finally, this database all the original FKP images collected during two different sessions are saved as "FKP Database.zip". The Hong Kong Polytechnic University also extracted ROI using the extraction algorithm described to provide the ROI images, and saved them with the filename "FKP ROI.zip".

ROI Extraction

Because of the wide variation in finger knuckle print image collection in term of size and intensity illumination, extraction of the region of interest has become a mandatory step. It is also obvious that the images collected for the same finger during various sessions also vary a lot, due to the variation in placement (spatial locations) of the finger on the capturing device. Therefore, for extraction of meaningful and relevant feature from the image area, it is crucial and mandatory to align the images with respect to a local coordinate system. Rather than aligning and processing the whole image, it is advisable to consider only the area of interest where most of the discriminatory information available, this region is referred as the region of interest (ROI). This section presents a method for extraction of reliable ROI. While extracting ROI we considered the fact that finger is always placed flatly on the capturing surface, it is observed that the bottom boundary of the image always remains stable and that is considered as X-axis. Initially, the Y-axis is taken in the center of the phalangeal joints as it is assumed that most of the relevant features are contained in within ROI. It can be found that line drawn along both the sides of the phalangeal joint will have varied convex directions. By considering this fact it is proposed that convex directions of code line pixels help in the determination of Y-axis. These steps of determination of coordinates and extraction of ROI are illustrated in Figure 11. Above discussed steps are listed below:

1. Down-sample the image
2. Determine the X-axis coordinate of the system
3. Extract ROI by cropping an image
4. Apply Canny edge detector
5. Determine convex direction to locate the Y-axis of the system

Mode of Operation of Biometrics

Biometric recognition system generally operates in two different modes: identification or verification. Verification confirms the claim of the identity of a person. In this system user provides the PIN or username and propose an identity, the biometric system captures the characteristics from the user, generate a template and verify it against the stored templates to find the match / non-match decision. This type of operation is also called as one–one (1: 1) matching. On the other hand, in an identification process, the user need not provide any claim of the identity, rather system captures the biometrics data of the user, process it and generate a template. Then this template is matched against the entire stored template to find the match. If the match is found that identity is associated with that user. This type of matching is also referred as one–many (1: M) matching and the questions like "who am I" can be answered using

Figure 11. Steps of determination of coordinates and extraction of ROI.(a) An image obtained after a Gaussian smoothing and down-sampling operation (lD)(b) Determination of X-axis of the system (c) obtained ROI image (IS) (d) image (IE) obtained after application of Canny edge detector on (Is) (e) apply the convex direction coding scheme to (IE)to obtained (ICD) image (f)A plot of convexity magnitude on X–axis of FKP image(g)obtain a line X=xo' and (h) obtain a coordinate system, here rectangle shows an area of the extracted ROI.

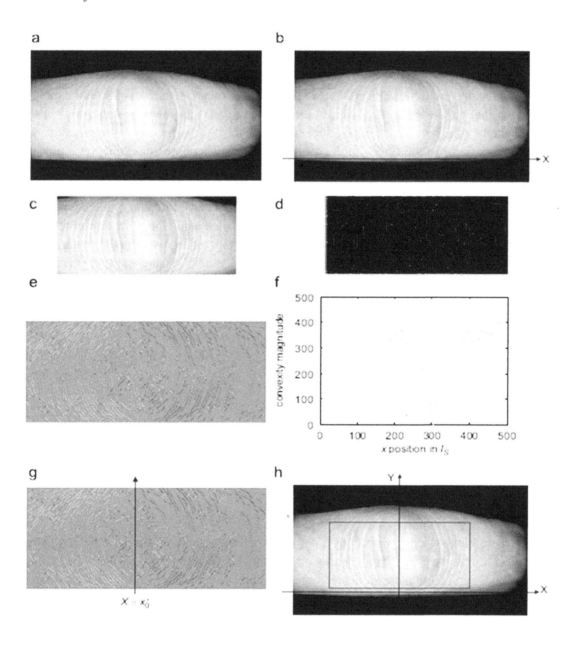

identification mode of operation of any biometrics system. The process of identification is computationally very expensive in case of large databases as compared to the verification process. This issue can be tackled by indexing the databases at the time of enrollment template.

FEATURE EXTRACTION AND FEATURE SELECTION

Extraction of Features

Feature selection and extraction process play a major role in the success of any biometrics system. Features extraction is the process of selection and enhancement of the key points in the biometric sample. A set of algorithms are used to extract and enhance these features. Research on biometrics thus, focusing on design and development of reliable algorithms for features extraction, selection, enhancement, representation and matching in a computationally efficient way. These algorithms are varying depending on deployed for which types of biometrics authentication system. Sometimes it also required reducing the dimensionality from D-dimensional to d dimensional (d < D) to minimize the space and time requirements.

The typical block diagram of an FKP acquisition system is depicted in figure 9, which provides easy access to the user where an individual can easily place his/her hand on the basal block by adjusting fingers in such a way that the middle phalanx and the proximal phalanx are touching both the slopes of the triangular block. The capturing device was designed in such a way that the spatial variation in placement of finger can be minimized during the different capturing session. The specially design triangular block helps in maintain the constant angle between the middle phalanx and the proximal phalanx to have a fixed magnitude for clear capturing of FKP surfaces ridge features. The captured raw image is further pre-processed for feature extraction, template representation, and matching. The device captured an FKP image of size 768×576 with a resolution of 400 dpi. The captured four sample images are shown in Figure 10, in which first two images in row one are taken for the same finger at varied sessions at 56 days interval and second-row images are taken from the different finger. The non-variation of FKP sample from the same finger over a time advocates the acceptance of FKP as a biometric indicator in biometric authentication systems. Figure 12 shows a typical image acquisition device.

Figure 12. (a) FKP image acquisition device

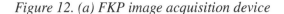
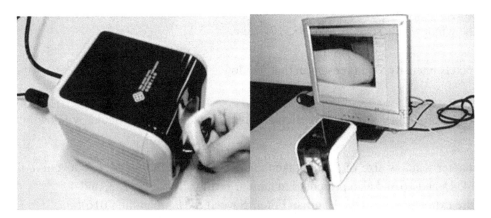

Feature extraction process used for different biometrics indicators:

- Typical features extracted for a fingerprint are ending and bifurcation of ridges.
- Removal of noises of certain frequencies and pattern in voice recording system.
- Removal of certain artifact from the digital images of ears, cheekbones, forehead, and nose.
- The encoding of mapping of striations and furrows in the iris.

All pattern recognition problems involve the automatics matching / retrieving of images from a large collection of image databases on the basis of the content of the query image. This area of pattern recognition is referred as CBIR (Content-Based Image Retrieval), and which have gained an intensive attention amongst research community of image information retrieval. Generally, the algorithms used in such pattern recognition problems are commonly performed following three tasks:

- Feature extraction
- Feature selection, and
- Feature classification

Feature extraction, highly important and crucial task in pattern recognition problems and is defined as a process of creating feature templates, which is to be used in the classification and selection tasks. To improve the processing time size of the feature set is to be reduced considerably without the loss of key feature. In this way, feature selection process will assist in selecting the only discriminative feature from the feature set and are used in the classification task. Finally, the selected features known as the feature vector of the template are provided to the classification or matching module to take a decision on match or non-match.

In this proposed chapter, process of feature extraction is applied on the finger print database comprising of 7960 images of around 165 users with a minimum of 12 samples each of right_index, left_index, right_middle and left_middle. Few functions that are applied for feature extraction are discussed below:

The Hanman_Anirban entropy Function is (Hanmandlu, 2011):

$$\sum_{1}^{k} h(k) * g(k) * e^{-\left(g(k)/n^{\wedge}3\right)} \tag{1}$$

where n is the window size such as 3×3, 5×5, 7×7 etc.

$g(k)$ is the pixels intensity value present in that window.

$h(k)$ is the count of number of times a particular intensity occurs in a particular window

In this chapter window size of 5×5 is taken and the result in the form of ROC curve is shown in Figure 13, 14, 15 and 16 and also presented in tabular form in Tables 1, 2, 3, and 4

The feature extraction using the Hanman Filter (Sayeed & Hanmandlu, 2016):

Table 1. Performance of knuckle

Modality	Recognition Rate (%)
left_index	91%
right_index	92%
left_middle	91%
right_middle	86%

Figure 13. ROC of (a) left_index (b) right_middle (c) right_index (d) left_middle

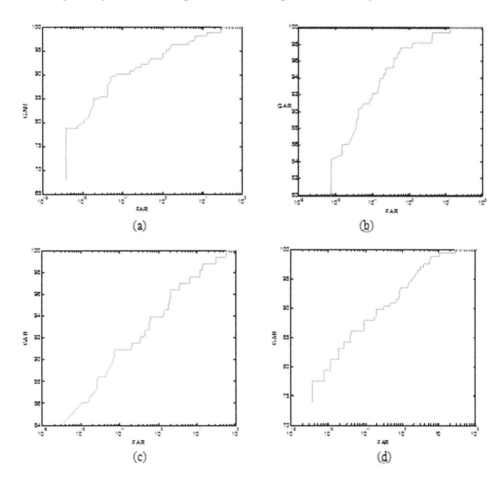

$$f\left(x\right) = \mu_{ij} * I\left(i, j\right) * \cos\left(2\pi / v\right) \tag{2}$$

$$\mu_{ij}\left(s\right) = e^{-\left[\frac{I(i,j) - I_{avg}}{s * f_{ref}}\right]^{a}} \tag{3}$$

Table 2. Performance of knuckle

Modality	Recognition Rate (%)
left_index	87%
right_index	85%
left_middle	90.5%
right_middle	87%

Figure 14. ROC curve of (a) left_index_ (b) left_middle (c) right_middle (d) right_index

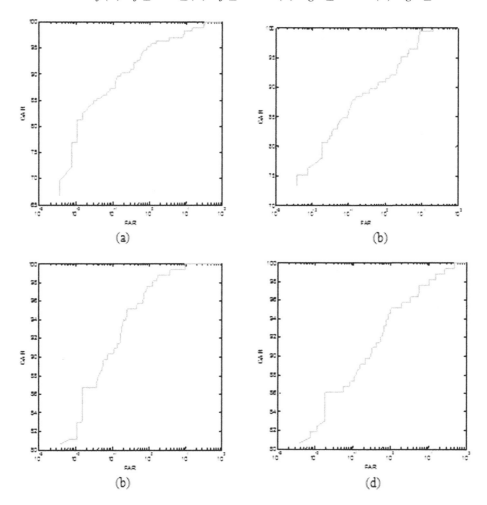

u=1, 2, 3

s=0.4, 0.6, 0.8, 1.0

v=1, 2, 3, 4

Another variation of feature extraction using Hanman filter is shown as (Sayeed & Hanmandlu, 2016):

$$f\left(x\right) = \mu_{ij} * I\left(i, j\right) * \cos\left(\frac{2\pi}{v}\right) * f_{ij}\left(s, u\right) \tag{4}$$

$$\mu_{ij}\left(s\right) = e^{-\left[\frac{I(i,j)-I_{avg}}{s*f_{ref}}\right]^2} \tag{5}$$

$$f_{i,j}\left(s, u\right) = f_u^{\left[\left(I(i,j)-I_{avg}\right)/2^{s}\right]} \tag{6}$$

$$f_u = \frac{f_{max}}{2^{u/2}} \tag{7}$$

$$u = 1, 2, 3$$

$$s = 0.4, 0.6, 0.8, 1.$$

The Hanman-Anirban entropy Function for feature extraction (Hanmandlu, 2011):

$$\sum_1^k g\left(k\right) * e^{-\left[\left(\frac{g(k)}{n^3}\right)*h(k)\right]} \tag{8}$$

Extraction of Feature Using SURF Algorithm

Speeded-Up Robust Features (SURF) (Le-Qing, 2011), an improvement of SIFT(Scale Invariant Feature Transform), which are widely accepted and adopted in the domain of object recognition technique and

Table 3. Performance of knuckle

Modality	Recognition Rate (%)
left_index	86%
right_index	86%
left_middle	83.5%
right_middle	87.5%

Figure 15. ROC curve of (a) right_index (b) right_middle (c) left_middle (d) left_index.

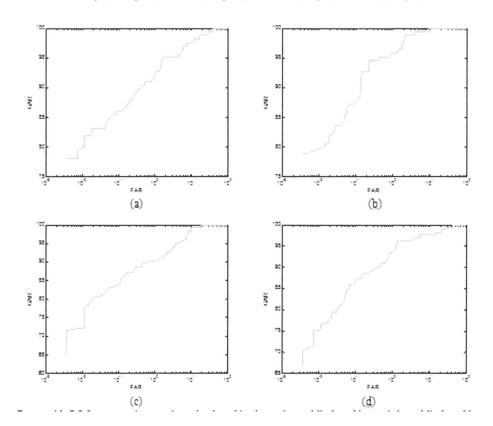

is also applied very efficiently to the problem of fingerprint and face recognition. SIFT and SURF algorithm is different in term of the key point they detect and deleted the way the feature is described and used. These key point detectors are based on the Hessian matrix approximation, and they make uses of integral images for the reduction in computation time, therefore they are also called the 'Fast-Hessian' descriptor (Badrinath et al., 2011; Gupta et al., 2013). On other parts of it, Haar-wavelet response in the neighborhood of the point of interest is represented by its descriptors. The use of integral images also enhances the computational efficiency. These uses of indexing step not only increase invariance of the descriptor but also improve the matching speed by using the sign of the Laplacian by SURF. At a location $x = (x,y)$ .the value of integral image $I\Sigma(x)$ .is represented by the region generated by the point x .of an input image I . by the mean of sum of pixels around the origin in rectangular form. This cal-

Table 4. Knuckle performance

Modality	Recognition Rate (%)
left_index	56%
right_index	64%
left_middle	58%
right_middle	66%

Figure 16. ROC curve of (a) left_index (b) left_middle c) right_index (d) right_middle

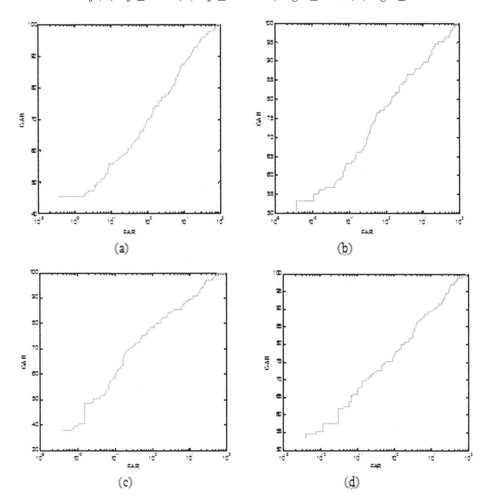

(a)

(b)

(c)

(d)

culation of $I\Sigma(x)$ .only takes four steps of additions and this is the sum of intensities over the image. The matching accuracy of only 20% is achieved for left middle knuckle modality.

Selection of Features

Selection of features is equally important as feature extraction and is the process of choosing most useful or relevant features from the feature set based on certain correlation, information, selection criteria and mutual information to filter out the unimportant and redundant features. Specialized classifiers like embedded or wrapper methods can be used to achieve feature selection and classify the dataset. Feature reduction or selection also reduces the feature dimensionality by selecting the subset of original variables. For feature selection, variable subset selection or attribute selection for building robust learning methods machine learning and statistical methods have been widely used in the literature. These feature selection techniques have also been used in the domain of biology and the process is referred as discriminative gene selection. Only influential genes based on DNA microarray experiments are detected by this selection. The performance of learning models has been improved by removing the most redundant and irrelevant features by:

1. Removing the curse of dimensionality effect.
2. Enhancement of capability generalization.
3. Improving speed of the learning process.
4. Improving model interpreting capability.

The use of supervised learning in designing of biometric-based recognition system requires feature selection and reduction. Existing research in the domain of biometrics-based person authentication systems does not evaluate the importance of features that are proposed in the literature. The process of feature subset selection helps to locate as well as remove the presence of redundant and irrelevant features. A minor reduction in dimensionality of the feature set further helps in reduction of the hypothesis, which is most crucial for the success of deployment of person recognition system. It has been shown in the literature that classification performance is adversely affected by the presence of irrelevant and redundant training features. This is the motivation behind the performance of experiments for selection of features subset and combination of various biometric modalities.

ROC

The ROC (Receiver Operating Curve) is used to represents matching or classification results in a graphical form. ROC is a graph of Genuine Acceptance Rate (GAR) and False Acceptance Rate (FAR) at various threshold values (η) as shown:

$$ROC\left(\eta\right) = \left(FAR\left(\eta\right), GAR\left(\eta\right)\right) \tag{9}$$

ROC is the common way of presenting the performance of any personal identification system.

The Genuine accept rate (GAR) is $1-$ False Rejection Rate$\left(FRR\right)$. FRR is the probability that the legitimate users are accepted by the biometric recognition system. Both the FRR and FAR are referred as error rate and the function of the threshold value $\left(\eta\right)$.

These error rates are explained using hypothesis as

H_0 : $I \neq T$, Template and verification features are not from the same finger

H_1 : $I = T$, Template and verification features are from the same finger

The decisions associated with each hypothesis are given as:

D_1 match

and, D_0. non-match

The hypothesis H_0 .is also referred to the null hypothesis and results in non-match as the input image (I . features do not match with template image (T) .features. In this null hypothesis, the similarity score $S(I, T)$ .is below the threshold value (η . then we decide D_0 .(rejection) otherwise D_1 . (acceptance) decision has to be taken. The matching process in biometrics-based recognition system is prone to two types of error based on hypothesis testing formulation as:

$$Type1 : False\,match\left(if\,H_0\,is\,true\,then\,D_0\,is\,decided\right).$$

$$Type2 : False\,non-match\left(if\,H_1\,is\,true\,then\,D_1\,is\,decided\right).$$

Therefore, from the above errors, as the probability of type 1 error is depicted by the FAR (false accept rate) (i.e. accepting H_0 .n imposter user), and the probability of type 2 error is depicted by the FRR (false rejection rate) (i.e. rejecting the H_0 .n genuine user). The third type of error is also commonly used in presenting ROC is Equal Error Rate (EER) and defined as the value of $\left(\eta\right)$ .at which both error rates (FRR = FAR) are equal.

EXPERIMENTAL RESULTS AND CONCLUSION

Experimental Results

Experiments were performed on Intel core i5 with MATLAB version 7.12 and Windows 7. The matching is performed by comparing the features extracted for each image with the features of all other images in the dataset, $660\left(165 \times 4\right)$ .different classes were used in our experiment and 3960 (660×6) images are there in the database for computing FAR and FRR. We observed total numbers of true matches and false matches as 23,760 and 8,28,920 respectively. Choice of the value of matching threshold $\left(\eta\right)$. will control the matching rate. A plot of false accept rate (FAR) and genuine accept rate (GAR) for all possible values of the threshold is drawn for each finger and is referred as receiver operating characteristic (ROC) curve. This ROC plot indicates the performance of the biometric recognition system. The detailed results of recognition rate for different modalities using different feature extraction functions are shown in Table 5.

CONCLUSION

Authentication system based on Finger Knuckle Print (FKP) introduces a new biometric trait for authentication. These features have the capability to acquire the market of the fingerprint based authentication system as it has the advantages of ease of use, small template size, good recognition accuracy etc. An experimental result obtained in this chapter indicates that FKP can have the strength of becoming future

Table 5. Feature functions with their respective matching accuracies

Feature Function	Modality	Matching Rate
$\sum_{1}^{k} h(k) \times g(k) \times e^{-(g(k)/n^{\wedge}3)}$	Left_index	91%
	Right_index	92%
	Left_middle	91%
	Right_middle	86%
$f(x) = \mu_{ij} \times I(i, j) \times \cos\left(\dfrac{2\pi}{v}\right) \times f_{ij}(s, u)$	Left_index	87%
	Right_index	85%
	Left_middle	90.5%
	Right_middle	87%
$f(x) = \mu_{ij} \times I(i, j) \times \cos\left(\dfrac{2\pi}{v}\right) \times f_{ij}(s, u)$	Left_index	86%
	Right_index	86%
	Left_middle	83.5%
	Right_middle	87.5%
$\sum_{1}^{k} g(k) \times e^{-\left|\left[\frac{g(k)}{n^{3}}\right]*h(k)\right|}$	Left_index	56%
	Right_index	64%
	Left_middle	58%
	Right_middle	66%

biometrics with high accuracy and efficiency. Information theory based features extraction functions are used to transform rich contents of the image into feature extraction. Most discriminatory features were selected and thus, created a feature vector to be used in classification task to enhance matching accuracy and improve the time complexity. The experiments were performed on FKP dataset designed and created by Hong Kong Polytechnic University containing 7960 images captured by the device designed by them. Out of four functions for feature extraction is most discriminatory and performs better. Other features might also be exploited in order to enhance the matching accuracy and finger knuckle print as some prominent biometrics for person authentication.

REFERENCES

Alling, A., Powers, N. R., & Soyata, T. (2016). Face recognition: A tutorial on computational aspects. In *Emerging Research Surrounding Power Consumption and Performance Issues in Utility Computing* (pp. 405–425). IGI Global. doi:10.4018/978-1-4666-8853-7.ch020

Badrinath, G. S., Nigam, A., & Gupta, P. (2011, November). An efficient finger-knuckle-print based recognition system fusing sift and surf matching scores. In *International Conference on Information and Communications Security* (pp. 374-387). Springer. 10.1007/978-3-642-25243-3_30

Bharadi, V. A. (2012). Texture Feature Extraction for Biometric Authentication using Partitioned Complex Planes in Transform Domain. *Proceedings of the International Conference & Workshop on Emerging Trends in Technology.*

Borgen, H., Bours, P., & Wolthusen, S. D. (2008, August). Visible-spectrum biometric retina recognition. In *Intelligent Information Hiding and Multimedia Signal Processing, 2008. IIHMSP'08 International Conference on* (pp. 1056-1062). IEEE. 10.1109/IIH-MSP.2008.345

Ferrer, M. A., Travieso, C. M., & Alonso, J. B. (2006). Using hand knuckle texture for biometric identification. *IEEE Aerospace and Electronic Systems Magazine, 21*(6), 23–27. doi:10.1109/MAES.2006.1662005

Grover, J., & Hanmandlu, M. (2017). Personal identification using the rank level fusion of finger-knuckle-prints. *Pattern Recognition and Image Analysis, 27*(1), 82–93. doi:10.1134/S1054661817010059

Gupta, J. P., Singh, N., Dixit, P., Semwal, V. B., & Dubey, S. R. (2013). Human activity recognition using gait pattern. *International Journal of Computer Vision and Image Processing, 3*(3), 31–53. doi:10.4018/ijcvip.2013070103

Hanmandlu, M. (2011). Information sets and information processing. *Defence Science Journal, 61*(5), 405. doi:10.14429/dsj.61.1192

Huang, Y. P., Luo, S. W., & Chen, E. Y. (2002). An efficient iris recognition system. In *Machine Learning and Cybernetics, 2002. Proceedings. 2002 International Conference on* (Vol. 1, pp. 450-454). IEEE.

Jain, A. K., & Li, S. Z. (2011). *Handbook of face recognition*. New York: Springer.

Jain, A. K., Ross, A., & Prabhakar, S. (2004). An introduction to biometric recognition. *IEEE Transactions on Circuits and Systems for Video Technology, 14*(1), 4–20. doi:10.1109/TCSVT.2003.818349

Jing, X., Li, W., Lan, C., Yao, Y., Cheng, X., & Han, L. (2011, November). Orthogonal complex locality preserving projections based on image space metric for finger-knuckle-print recognition. In *Hand-Based Biometrics (ICHB), 2011 International Conference on* (pp. 1-6). IEEE.

Kumar, A., & Prathyusha, K. V. (2009). Personal authentication using hand vein triangulation and knuckle shape. *IEEE Transactions on Image Processing, 18*(9), 2127–2136. doi:10.1109/TIP.2009.2023153 PMID:19447728

Kumar, A., & Ravikanth, C. (2009). Personal authentication using finger knuckle surface. *IEEE Transactions on Information Forensics and Security, 4*(1), 98–110. doi:10.1109/TIFS.2008.2011089

Kumar, A., & Zhang, D. (2005, July). Biometric recognition using feature selection and combination. In *International Conference on Audio-and Video-Based Biometric Person Authentication* (pp. 813-822). Springer Berlin Heidelberg. 10.1007/11527923_85

Kumar, A., & Zhou, Y. (2009). Personal identification using finger knuckle orientation features. *Electronics Letters, 45*(20), 1023–1025. doi:10.1049/el.2009.1435

Kumar, A., & Zhou, Y. (2009, September). Human identification using knuckle codes. In *Biometrics: Theory, Applications, and Systems, 2009. BTAS'09. IEEE 3rd International Conference on* (pp. 1-6). IEEE.

Kumar, R. (2017). Fingerprint matching using rotational invariant orientation local binary pattern descriptor and machine learning techniques. *International Journal of Computer Vision and Image Processing, 7*(4), 51–67. doi:10.4018/IJCVIP.2017100105

Kumar, R. (2017). Hand Image Biometric Based Personal Authentication System. In *Intelligent Techniques in Signal Processing for Multimedia Security* (pp. 201–226). Springer International Publishing. doi:10.1007/978-3-319-44790-2_10

Kumar, R., Chandra, P., & Hanmandlu, M. (2012a). Fingerprint matching based on orientation feature. *Advanced Materials Research*, *403*, 888–894.

Kumar, R., Chandra, P., & Hanmandlu, M. (2012c). Statistical descriptors for fingerprint matching. *International Journal of Computers and Applications*, *59*(16).

Kumar, R., Chandra, P., & Hanmandlu, M. (2013a). *Fingerprint matching based on texture feature. In Mobile communication and power engineering* (pp. 86–91). Berlin: Springer. doi:10.1007/978-3-642-35864-7_12

Kumar, R., Chandra, P., & Hanmandlu, M. (2013b, December). Fingerprint matching using rotational invariant image based descriptor and machine learning techniques. In *Emerging Trends in Engineering and Technology (ICETET), 2013 6th International Conference on* (pp. 13-18). IEEE.

Kumar, R., Chandra, P., & Hanmandlu, M. (2013c, December). Local directional pattern (LDP) based fingerprint matching using SLFNN. In *Image Information Processing (ICIIP), 2013 IEEE Second International Conference on* (pp. 493-498). IEEE.

Kumar, R., Chandra, P., & Hanmandlu, M. (2014a). Rotational invariant fingerprint matching using local directional descriptors. *International Journal of Computational Intelligence Studies*, *3*(4), 292–319. doi:10.1504/IJCISTUDIES.2014.067032

Kumar, R., Chandra, P., & Hanmandlu, M. (2016). A Robust Fingerprint Matching System Using Orientation Features. *Journal of Information Processing Systems*, *12*(1), 83-99.

Kumar, R., Chandra, P., & Hanmandlu, M. (2012b). Fingerprint singular point detection using orientation field reliability. *Advanced Materials Research*, *403*, 4499–4506.

Kumar, R., Hanmandlu, M., & Chandra, P. (2014b). An empirical evaluation of rotation invariance of LDP feature for fingerprint matching using neural networks. *International Journal of Computational Vision and Robotics*, *4*(4), 330–348. doi:10.1504/IJCVR.2014.065569

Le-Qing, Z. (2011, July). Finger knuckle print recognition based on SURF algorithm. In *Fuzzy Systems and Knowledge Discovery (FSKD), 2011 Eighth International Conference on* (*Vol. 3*, pp. 1879-1883). IEEE.

Maltoni, D., Maio, D., Jain, A., & Prabhakar, S. (2009). *Handbook of fingerprint recognition.* Springer Science & Business Media. doi:10.1007/978-1-84882-254-2

Matallah, H., Belalem, G., & Bouamrane, K. (2017). Towards a New Model of Storage and Access to Data in Big Data and Cloud Computing. *International Journal of Ambient Computing and Intelligence*, *8*(4), 31–44. doi:10.4018/IJACI.2017100103

Morales, A., Travieso, C. M., Ferrer, M. A., & Alonso, J. B. (2011). Improved finger-knuckle-print authentication based on orientation enhancement. *Electronics Letters*, *47*(6), 380–381. doi:10.1049/el.2011.0156

Rabiner, L. R., & Juang, B. H. (1993). *Fundamentals of speech recognition*. Academic Press.

Ravikanth, C., & Kumar, A. (2007, June). Biometric authentication using finger-back surface. In *Computer Vision and Pattern Recognition, 2007. CVPR'07. IEEE Conference on* (pp. 1-6). IEEE.

Seto, Y. (2015). Retina recognition. Encyclopedia of biometrics, 1321-1323. doi:10.1007/978-1-4899-7488-4_132

Shariatmadar, Z. S., & Faez, K. (2011, November). An efficient method for finger-knuckle-print recognition by using the information fusion at different levels. In *Hand-Based Biometrics (ICHB), 2011 International Conference on* (pp. 1-6). IEEE.

Usha, K., & Ezhilarasan, M. (2016). Personal recognition using finger knuckle shape oriented features and texture analysis. *Journal of King Saud University-Computer and Information Sciences*, *28*(4), 416–431. doi:10.1016/j.jksuci.2015.02.004

Wang, Y., Wang, Y., & Tan, T. (2004). Combining fingerprint and voiceprint biometrics for identity verification: an experimental comparison. *Biometric Authentication*, 289-294.

Woodard, D. L., & Flynn, P. J. (2005). Finger surface as a biometric identifier. *Computer Vision and Image Understanding*, *100*(3), 357–384.

Sayeed, F., & Hanmandlu, M. (2016). Three information set-based feature types for the recognition of faces. *Signal, Image and Video Processing*, *10*(2), 327–334.

Xiong, M., Yang, W., & Sun, C. (2011, May). Finger-knuckle-print recognition using LGBP. In *International Symposium on Neural Networks* (pp. 270-277). Springer Berlin Heidelberg.

Yang, W., Sun, C., & Sun, Z. (2011, July). Finger-knuckle-print recognition using gabor feature and olda. *In Control Conference (CCC), 2011 30th Chinese* (pp. 2975-2978). IEEE.

Yang, W., Wang, X., Song, X., Yang, Y., & Patnaik, S. (2018). Design of Intelligent Transportation System Supported by New Generation Wireless Communication Technology. [IJACI]. *International Journal of Ambient Computing and Intelligence*, *9*(1), 78–94. doi:10.4018/IJACI.2018010105

Zhang, L., Zhang, L., & Zhang, D. (2009). Finger-knuckle-print verification based on band-limited phase-only correlation. In Computer analysis of images and patterns (pp. 141-148). Springer Berlin/Heidelberg.

Zhang, L., Zhang, L., & Zhang, D. (2009, November). Finger-knuckle-print: a new biometric identifier. In *Image Processing (ICIP), 2009 16th IEEE International Conference on* (pp. 1981-1984). IEEE.

Zhang, L., Zhang, L., & Zhang, D. (2010, August). Monogeniccode: A novel fast feature coding algorithm with applications to finger-knuckle-print recognition. In *Emerging Techniques and Challenges for Hand-Based Biometrics (ETCHB), 2010 International Workshop on* (pp. 1-4). IEEE.

Zhang, L., Zhang, L., Zhang, D., & Zhu, H. (2010). Online finger-knuckle-print verification for personal authentication. *Pattern Recognition*, *43*(7), 2560–2571. doi:10.1016/j.patcog.2010.01.020

Zhang, L., Zhang, L., Zhang, D., & Zhu, H. (2011). Ensemble of local and global information for finger–knuckle-print recognition. *Pattern Recognition*, *44*(9), 1990–1998. doi:10.1016/j.patcog.2010.06.007

Zhou, X. S., Cohen, I., Tian, Q., & Huang, T. S. (2000). Feature extraction and selection for image retrieval. *Urbana (Caracas, Venezuela)*, *51*, 61801.

Compilation of References

Abbasi, A., Zhang, Z., Zimbra, D., Chen, H., & Nunamaker, J. F. Jr. (2010). Detecting fake websites: The contribution of statistical learning theory. *Management Information Systems Quarterly, 34*(3), 435–461. doi:10.2307/25750686

Abd-Eldayem. (2013). A proposed security technique based on watermarking and encryption for digital imaging and communications in medicine. *Egyptian Informatics Journal, 14*, 1–13. doi:10.1016/j.eij.2012.11.002

Abdullah, M. T., Mahmod, R., Ghani, A., Azim, A., Abdullah, M. Z., Sultan, M., & Bakar, A. (2008). Advances in computer forensics. *International Journal of Computer Science and Network Security, 8*(2), 215–219.

Ablon, L., Libicki, M. C., & Golay, A. A. (2014). *Markets for cybercrime tools and stolen data: Hackers' bazaar*. Rand Corporation.

Adya, M. (2007). *Audio watermark resistant to mp3 compression* (Doctoral dissertation). Department of Computer Science and Engineering Indian Institute of Technology Kharagpur, India.

Aggarwal, D., Singhal, P., Kaur, S., & Bhatnagar, V. (2007, November). PDOD: Tree-Based Algorithm For Outlier Detection. *Proceedings of Int'l Conference on Computer Vision and Information Technology*.

Agrawal, R., Kiernan, J., Srikant, R., & Xu, Y. (2004). Order-preserving encryption for numeric data. *Proceedings of SIGMOD '04*, 563 – 574. 10.1145/1007568.1007632

Ahmed, A. S., Kumaran, T. S., Syed, S. S. A., & Subburam, S. (2015). Cross-layer design approach for power control in mobile ad hoc networks. *Egyptian Informatics Journal, 16*(1), 1–7. doi:10.1016/j.eij.2014.11.001

Ahuja, Y., & Yadav, S. K. (2013). Statistical Approach to Support Vector Machine. [IJEAT]. *International Journal of Engineering and Advanced Technology, 2*(3), 556–559.

Airehrour, D., & Gutierrez, J. A. (2015). An analysis of secure MANET routing features to maintain confidentiality and integrity in IoT routing. In CONF-IRM (p. 17).

Alamulla, S., Iraqi, Y., & Jones, A. (2013). A Distributed Snapshot Framework for Digital Forensics Evidence Extraction and Event Reconstruction from Cloud Environment. *Proceedings of IEEE International Conference on Cloud Computing Technology and Science*, 699-704. 10.1109/CloudCom.2013.114

Alejandre, F. V., Cortés, N. C., & Anaya, E. A. (2017, February). Feature selection to detect botnets using machine learning algorithms. In *Proceedings of the International Conference on Electronics, Communications and Computers (CONIELECOMP)*. 10.1109/CONIELECOMP.2017.7891834

Alexa. (2017) Retrieved March 1, 2017, from https://www.alexa.com/topsites

Al-Hamadi, H., & Chen, I. R. (2015). Integrated intrusion detection and tolerance in homogeneous clustered sensor networks. *ACM Transactions on Sensor Networks, 11*(3), 47. doi:10.1145/2700830

Alheeti, K. M. A., Gruebler, A., & McDonald-Maier, K. D. (2015). An intrusion detection system against malicious attacks on the communication network of driverless cars. In *Proceedings of the 2015 12th Annual IEEE Consumer Communications and Networking Conference (CCNC)*, Las Vegas, NV (pp. 916-921). IEEE. 10.1109/CCNC.2015.7158098

Ali, A., & Huiqiang, W. (2012, March). Node centric load balancing routing protocol for mobile ad hoc networks. In *Proceeding of International MultiConference of Enginners Computer Scientists.*

Alieyan, K., ALmomani, A., Manasrah, A., & Kadhum, M. M. (2017). A survey of botnet detection based on DNS. *Neural Computing & Applications*, *28*(7), 1541–1558. doi:10.100700521-015-2128-0

Al-Jarrah, O. Y., Alhussein, O., Yoo, P. D., Muhaidat, S., Taha, K., & Kim, K. (2016). Data randomization and cluster-based partitioning for botnet intrusion detection. *IEEE Transactions on Cybernetics*, *46*(8), 1796–1806. doi:10.1109/TCYB.2015.2490802 PMID:26540724

Alling, A., Powers, N. R., & Soyata, T. (2016). Face recognition: A tutorial on computational aspects. In *Emerging Research Surrounding Power Consumption and Performance Issues in Utility Computing* (pp. 405–425). IGI Global. doi:10.4018/978-1-4666-8853-7.ch020

Al-Nahari, A., Mohamad, M. M., & Al-Sharaeh, S. (2013, December). Receiver-based AODV routing protocol for MANETs. In *Proceedings of the 2013 13th International Conference on Intelligent Systems Design and Applications (ISDA)* (pp. 126-130). IEEE. 10.1109/ISDA.2013.6920721

Alpaydin, E. (2004). *Introduction to Machine Learning*. MIT Press.

Al-Rafee, S., & Cronan, T. P. (2006). Digital piracy: Factors that influence attitude toward behavior. *Journal of Business Ethics*, *63*(3), 237–259. doi:10.100710551-005-1902-9

Al-Sultan, S., Al-Doori, M. M., Al-Bayatti, A. H., & Zedan, H. (2014). A comprehensive survey on vehicular Ad Hoc network. *Journal of Network and Computer Applications*, *37*, 380–392. doi:10.1016/j.jnca.2013.02.036

Anandakumar, H., & Umamaheswari, K. (2017b). An Efficient Optimized Handover in Cognitive Radio Networks using Cooperative Spectrum Sensing. *Intelligent Automation & Soft Computing*, 1–8. doi:10.1080/10798587.2017.1364931

Anandakumar, H., & Umamaheswari, K. (2017a). Supervised machine learning techniques in cognitive radio networks during cooperative spectrum handovers. *Cluster Computing*, *20*(2), 1505–1515. doi:10.100710586-017-0798-3

Anandakumar, H., & Umamaheswari, K. (2017c). A bio-inspired swarm intelligence technique for social aware cognitive radio handovers. *Computers & Electrical Engineering*. doi:10.1016/j.compeleceng.2017.09.016

Ananthakumar, A., Ganediwal, T., & Kunte, A. (2015). Intrusion detection system in wireless sensor networks: A review. *International Journal of Advanced Computer Science and Applications*, *6*(12), 131–139. doi:10.14569/IJACSA.2015.061218

Andress, J., & Winterfeld, S. (2013). *Cyber warfare: techniques, tactics, and tools for security practitioners*. Elsevier.

Andriole, K. P. (2014). Security of Electronic Medical Information and Patient Privacy: What You Need to Know. *Journal of the American College of Radiology*, *11*(12), 1212–1216. doi:10.1016/j.jacr.2014.09.011 PMID:25467897

Apisdorf, J., Claffy, K., Thompson, K., & Wilder, R. (1996). OC3MON: Flexible, affordable, high-performance statistics collection. In *Proceedings of the 10th USENIX conference on System administration* (pp. 97-112). Chicago, IL: USENIX Association.

Appelbaum, D. (2016). Securing Big Data Provenance for Auditors: The Big Data Provenance Black Box as Reliable Evidence. *Journal of Emerging Technologies in Accounting*, *13*(1), 17–36. doi:10.2308/jeta-51473

Arora, V. K., Sharma, V., & Sachdeva, M. (2016). A survey on LEACH and other's routing protocols in wireless sensor network. *Optik-International Journal for Light and Electron Optics, 127*(16), 6590–6600. doi:10.1016/j.ijleo.2016.04.041

Arshad, S., Abbaspour, M., Kharrazi, M., & Sanatkar, H. (2011). An anomaly based botnet detection approach for identifying stealthy botnets. in *Proceedings of the IEEE International Conference on Computer Applications and Industrial Electronics*, Penang, Malaysia (pp. 564–569).

Arulmurugan, R., Sabarmathi, K. R., & Anandakumar, H. (2017). Classification of sentence level sentiment analysis using cloud machine learning techniques. *Cluster Computing.* doi:10.100710586-017-1200-1

Aswale, S., & Ghorpade, V. R. (2015). Survey of QoS routing protocols in wireless multimedia sensor networks. *Journal of Computer Networks and communications*, 7.

Atzori, L., Iera, A., & Morabito, G. (2010). The internet of things: A survey. *Computer Networks, 54*(15), 2787–2805. doi:10.1016/j.comnet.2010.05.010

Atzori, L., Iera, A., & Morabito, G. (2011). Siot: Giving a social structure to the internet of things. *IEEE Communications Letters, 15*(11), 1193–1195. doi:10.1109/LCOMM.2011.090911.111340

Atzori, L., Iera, A., & Morabito, G. (2014). From" smart objects" to" social objects": The next evolutionary step of the internet of things. *IEEE Communications Magazine, 52*(1), 97–105. doi:10.1109/MCOM.2014.6710070

Atzori, L., Iera, A., Morabito, G., & Nitti, M. (2012). The social internet of things (siot)–when social networks meet the internet of things: Concept, architecture and network characterization. *Computer Networks, 56*(16), 3594–3608. doi:10.1016/j.comnet.2012.07.010

Ayala, L. (2016). Cyber Standards. In *Cybersecurity Lexicon* (pp. 199–200). Apress. doi:10.1007/978-1-4842-2068-9_28

Babu, K. S., & Sekharaiah, K. C. (2014). CLDASR: Cross Layer Based Detection and Authentication in Secure Routing in MANET. *International Journal of Computer Networks and Wireless Communications.*

Badrinath, G. S., Nigam, A., & Gupta, P. (2011, November). An efficient finger-knuckle-print based recognition system fusing sift and surf matching scores. In *International Conference on Information and Communications Security* (pp. 374-387). Springer. 10.1007/978-3-642-25243-3_30

Baggili, I., & Breitinger, F. (2015). Data Sources for advancing cyber forensics: What the social world has to offer. *Proceedings of AAAI Spring Symposium*, 6-9.www.aaai.org/docs

Baggili, I., & Breitinger, F. (2015). Data Sources for Advancing Cyber Forensics: What the Social World Has to Offer. In *Proceedings of the 2015 AAAI Spring Symposium.*

Bakare, A., & Argiddi, R. (2017). To Study, Analyze and predict the Diseases using Big Data. *International Journal of Computers and Applications, 165*(7), 17–19. doi:10.5120/ijca2017913917

Balkanli, E., Alves, J., & Zincir-Heywood, A. N. (2014). Supervised learning to detect DDoS attacks. In *Proceedings of the 2014 IEEE Symposium on Computational Intelligence in Cyber Security (CICS)*, Orlando, FL. IEEE. 10.1109/CICYBS.2014.7013367

Balogh, E. P., Miller, B. T., & Ball, J. R. (Eds.). (2015). *Committee on Diagnostic Error in Health Care; Board on Health Care Services; Institute of Medicine; The National Academies of Sciences, Engineering, and Medicine. Improving Diagnosis in Health Care*. Washington, DC: The National Academies Press.

Bamasag, O., & Toumi, K. Y. (2016). Efficient multicast authentication in internet of things. In *Proceedings of International Conference on Information and Communication Technology Convergence (ICTC)* (pp. 429-435). Jeju, South Korea: Academic Press. 10.1109/ICTC.2016.7763512

Banks, A., Vincent, J., & Anyakoha, C. (2007). A review of particle swarm optimization. Part I: Background and development. *Natural Computing*, 6(4), 467–484. doi:10.100711047-007-9049-5

Barati, M., Abdullah, A., Udzir, N. I., Mahmod, R., & Mustapha, N. (2014). Distributed Denial of Service detection using hybrid machine learning technique. In *Proceedings of the 2014 International Symposium on Biometrics and Security Technologies (ISBAST)* (pp. 268-273). IEEE. 10.1109/ISBAST.2014.7013133

Barber, S., Boyen, X., Shi, E., & Uzun, E. (2012, February). Bitter to better—how to make bitcoin a better currency. In *International Conference on Financial Cryptography and Data Security* (pp. 399-414). Springer. 10.1007/978-3-642-32946-3_29

Bassia, P., Pitas, I., & Nikolaidis, N. (2001). Robust audio watermarking in the time domain. *IEEE Transactions on Multimedia*, 3(2), 232–241. doi:10.1109/6046.923822

Basurra, S. S., De Vos, M., Padget, J., Ji, Y., Lewis, T., & Armour, S. (2015). Energy efficient zone based routing protocol for MANETs. *Ad Hoc Networks*, 25, 16–37. doi:10.1016/j.adhoc.2014.09.010

Batarseh, F., Yang, R., & Deng, L. (2017). A comprehensive model for management and validation of federal big data analytical systems. *Big Data Analytics*, 2(1), 2. doi:10.118641044-016-0017-x

Batashvili, D. (2017). EUobserver - Russia's cyber war: past, present, and future. *EUobserver*. Retrieved from https://euobserver.com/opinion/136909

Bates, A., Tian, D., & Butler, K. R. B. (2016). Trustworthy Whole-System Provenance for the Linux Kernel. *Proceedings of 24th USENIX Security Symposium*, 319-334.

Bayles, W. J. (2001). The Ethics of Computer Network Attack. *Information Warfare Site*. Retrieved from http://www.iwar.org.uk/iwar/resources/ethics-of-cna/bayles.htm

BBNT Patent. (2005). *Systems and methods for network performance measurement using packet signature collection*. Patent 6978223, Issued 20 December 2005 to BBNT Solutions LLC (Cambridge, MA). Retrieved July 11, 2017, from http://www.patentgenius.com/patent/6978223.html

Becker, G. (2008). *Merkle signature schemes, merkle trees and their cryptanalysis*. Ruhr-University Bochum, Tech. Rep.

Belenky, A., & Ansari, N. (2003a). IP traceback with deterministic packet marking. *IEEE Communications Letters*, 7(4), 162–164. doi:10.1109/LCOMM.2003.811200

Belenky, A., & Ansari, N. (2003b). On IP traceback. *IEEE Communications Magazine*, 41(7), 142–153. doi:10.1109/MCOM.2003.1215651

Bellavista, P., Cardone, G., Corradi, A., & Foschini, L. (2013). Convergence of MANET and WSN in IoT urban scenarios. *IEEE Sensors Journal*, 13(10), 3558–3567. doi:10.1109/JSEN.2013.2272099

Bellovin, S. M., Leech, M., & Taylor, T. (2003). *ICMP traceback messages*. Marina del Ray, CA: Internet Engineering Task Force; doi:10.7916/D8FF406R

Benaicha, S. E., Saoudi, L., Guermeche, S. E. B., & Lounis, O. (2014). Intrusion detection system using genetic algorithm. In *Proceedings of the Science and Information Conference (SAI)*, London, UK (pp. 564-568). IEEE.

Bennett, D. W. (2011). *The Challenges Facing Computer Forensics Investigators in Obtaining Information from Mobile Devices for Use in Criminal Investigations*. Retrieved from http://articles.forensicfocus.com

Beqiri, E. (2009). Neural networks for intrusion detection systems. In *Global Security, Safety, and Sustainability* (pp. 156-165).

Berbecaru, D. (2004). MBS-OCSP: an OCSP based certificate revocation system for wireless environments. In *Proceedings of the Fourth IEEE International Symposium on Signal Processing and Information Technology (ISSPIT 2004)* (pp. 267-272). Rome, Italy: IEEE. 10.1109/ISSPIT.2004.1433737

Berbecaru, D., & Albertalli, L. (2008). On the Performance and Use of a Space-Efficient Merkle Tree Traversal Algorithm in Real-Time Applications for Wireless and Sensor Networks. In *Proceedings of IEEE International Conference on Wireless and Mobile Computing, Networking and Communications (WIMOB 2008)* (pp. 234-240). Avignon, France: IEEE. 10.1109/WiMob.2008.14

Berbecaru, D., Albertalli, L., & Lioy, A. (2010). The ForwardDiffSig Scheme for Multicast Authentication. *IEEE/ACM Transactions on Networking*, *18*(6), 1855–1868. doi:10.1109/TNET.2010.2052927

Berman, P., Karpinski, M., & Nekrich, Y. (2004). *Optimal Trade-Off for Merkle Tree Traversal*. Report No. 49, Electronic Colloquium on Computational Complexity. Retrieved July 13, 2017, from http://preprints.ihes.fr/2004/M/M-04-29.pdf

Berman, P., Karpinski, M., & Nekrich, Y. (2007). Optimal Trade-Off for Merkle Tree Traversal. *Theoretical Computer Science. Elsevier Science Publishers.*, *372*(1), 26–36. doi:10.1016/j.tcs.2006.11.029

Beyer, M. (2011). *Gartner Says Solving 'Big Data' Challenge Involves More Than Just Managing Volumes of Data*. Gartner.

Bhabad, M. A., & Bagade, S. T. (2015). Internet of things: Architecture, security issues and countermeasures. *International Journal of Computers and Applications*, *125*(14).

Bhagwath, S., & Mallikarjun Math, D. (2016). Distributed Systems and Recent Innovations: Challenges Benefits and Security Issues in Distributed Systems. *Bonfring International Journal Of Software Engineering And Soft Computing*, *6*(Special Issue), 37–42. doi:10.9756/BIJSESC.8239

Bharadi, V. A. (2012). Texture Feature Extraction for Biometric Authentication using Partitioned Complex Planes in Transform Domain. *Proceedings of the International Conference & Workshop on Emerging Trends in Technology*.

Bharti, A. K., & Chaudhary, M. (2013). Prevention of Session Hijacking and Ip spoofing with Sensor Nodes and Cryptographic Approach. *International Journal of Computers and Applications*, *76*(9).

Bhatsangave, S. P., & Chirchi, V. R. (2012). OAODV routing algorithm for improving energy efficiency in MANET. *International Journal of Computers and Applications*, *51*(21).

Bhatt, C. M., Dey, N., & Ashour, A. (2017). Internet of Things and Big Data Technologies for Next Generation Healthcare (Vol. 23).

Bhatt, C., Dey, N., & Ashour, A. S. (2017). Internet of Things and Big Data Technologies for Next Generation Healthcare. In *Studies in Big Data*. Springer International Publishing.

Bhopal, M. P., & MP, I. B. (2012). A Review of Computer forensic & Logging System. *International Journal (Toronto, Ont.)*, *2*(1).

Bhushan, M., Gupta, A., & Yadav, S. K. (2016). Big Data Suite for Market Prediction and Reducing Complexity Using Bloom Filter. *The Human Element of Big Data: Issues, Analytics, and Performance*, 281.

Bhushan, M., & Yadav, S. K. (2014). Cost based Model for Big Data Processing with Hadoop Architecture. *Global Journal of Computer Science and Technology*, *14*(2-C), 13.

Big Data Analytics for Security Intelligence. (2013). Retrieved from www.cloudsecurityalliance.org/research/big-data

Big Data and Privacy principles under pressure in the age of Big Data analytics. (2014). Retrieved from https://dzlp.mk/en/node/2736

Bilge, L., Strufe, T., Balzarotti, D., & Kirda, E. (2009, April). All your contacts belong to us: automated identity theft attacks on social networks. In *Proceedings of the 18th international conference on World wide web* (pp. 551-560). ACM. Retrieved from http://www.eurecom.fr/en/publication/2782/detail/all-your-contacts-are-belong-to-us-automated-identity-theft-attacks-on-social-networks

Binh, H. T. T., Hanh, N. T., & Dey, N. (2016). Improved Cuckoo Search and Chaotic Flower Pollination optimization algorithm for maximizing area coverage in Wireless Sensor Networks. *Neural Computing & Applications*.

Boneh, D., & Waters, B. (2007). Conjunctive, subset, and range queries on encrypted data. *Theory of Cryptography Conference (TCC '07)*, 535–554. 10.1007/978-3-540-70936-7_29

Boneh, D., Di Crescenzo, G., Ostrovsky, R., & Persiano, G. (2004). Public key encryption with keyword search. Advances in Cryptology – EUROCRYPT '04, 506–522.

Borgen, H., Bours, P., & Wolthusen, S. D. (2008, August). Visible-spectrum biometric retina recognition. In *Intelligent Information Hiding and Multimedia Signal Processing, 2008. IIHMSP'08 International Conference on* (pp. 1056-1062). IEEE. 10.1109/IIH-MSP.2008.345

Boroumand, M., & Fridrich, J. (2016). Boosting Steganalysis with Explicit Feature Maps. *Proceedings of 4th ACM Workshop on Information Hiding and Multimedia Security*. doi: 10.1145/2909827.2930803

Borthakur, D. (2008). HDFS architecture guide. *Hadoop Apache Project*, 53.

Bossler, A. M., & Holt, T. J. (2009). On-line activities, guardianship, and malware infection: An examination of routine activities theory. *International Journal of Cyber Criminology*, *3*(1), 400.

Bradley, P. (2013). Implications of Big Data Analytics on Population Health Management. *Big Data*, *1*(3), 152–159. doi:10.1089/big.2013.0019 PMID:27442197

Brakerski, Z., Gentry, C., & Vaikuntanathan, V. (2011). Fully Homomorphic Encryption without Bootstrapping. *Cryptology ePrint Archive Report*.

Brakerski, Z., & Vaikuntanathan, V. (2011). Efficient Fully Homomorphic Encryption, LWE. *Proceedings of FOCS*.

Breene, K. (2016). World Economic Forum - Who are the cyberwar superpowers? *WEForum*. Retrieved from https://www.weforum.org/agenda/2016/05/who-are-the-cyberwar-superpowers/

Bridges, C. P., & Vladimirova, T. (2013). Towards an agent computing platform for distributed computing on satellites. *IEEE Transactions on Aerospace and Electronic Systems*, *49*(3), 1824–1838. doi:10.1109/TAES.2013.6558023

Brightman, H. J. (2011). *Today's White Collar Crime: Legal, Investigative, and Theoretical Perspectives*. Routledge.

Brindha, C. K., Nivetha, S. K., & Asokan, R. (2014, February). Energy efficient multi-metric QoS routing using genetic algorithm in MANET. In *Proceedings of the 2014 International Conference on Electronics and Communication Systems (ICECS)*. IEEE. 10.1109/ECS.2014.6892695

Britz, M. T. (2009). *Computer Forensics and Cyber Crime: An Introduction, 2/E*. Pearson Education India.

Buchanan, B. (2004). Money laundering—a global obstacle. *Research in International Business and Finance, 18*(1), 115–127. doi:10.1016/j.ribaf.2004.02.001

Buchmann, J., Dahmen, E., & Schneider, M. (2008). Merkle Tree Traversal Revisited. In *Post-Quantum Cryptography: Proceedings of PQCrypto 2008 (LNCS)* (*vol. 5299*, pp. 63-78). Berlin, Germany: Springer. doi: 10.1007/978-3-540-88403-3_5

Butun, I., Morgera, S. D., & Sankar, R. (2014). A survey of intrusion detection systems in wireless sensor networks. *IEEE Communications Surveys and Tutorials, 16*(1), 266–282. doi:10.1109/SURV.2013.050113.00191

Campbell, R., Al-Muhtadi, J., Naldurg, P., Sampemane, G., Mickunas, M.D. (2003). Towards Security and Privacy for Pervasive Computing, Springer-Verlag Berlin Heidelberg. 1–15

Carl, G., Kesidis, G., Brooks, R. R., & Rai, S. (2006). Denial-of-service attack-detection techniques. *IEEE Internet Computing, 10*(1), 82–89. doi:10.1109/MIC.2006.5

Casey, E. (Ed.). (2001). *Handbook of computer crime investigation: forensic tools and technology*. Academic Press.

Cashell, B., Jackson, W. D., Jickling, M., & Webel, B. (2004). The economic impact of cyber-attacks. *Congressional Research Service Document,* Retrieved from http://www.au.af.mil/au/awc/awcgate/crs/rl32331.pdf

Cekerevac, Z., Dvorak, Z., Prigoda, L., & Cekerevac, P. (2017). Internet of things and the man-in-the-middle attacks–security and economic risks. *Journal MESTE, 5*(2), 15–25.

Chandramouli, R., & Memon, N. (2001). Analysis of LSB based image steganography techniques. *Proceedings of ICIP 2001*. 10.1109/ICIP.2001.958299

Chang, Y. C., & Mitzenmacher, M. (2005). Privacy preserving keyword searches on remote encrypted data. *ACNS 05, 3531*, 442–455.

Chanu, Singh, & Tuithung. (2012). Image Steganography and Steganalysis: A Survey. *International Journal of Computer Applications, 52*(2), 1-11.

Chen, L., Xu, L., Yuan, X., & Shashidhar, N. (2015, February). Digital forensics in social networks and the cloud: Process, approaches, methods, tools, and challenges. In *Computing, Networking and Communications (ICNC), 2015 International Conference on* (pp. 1132-1136). IEEE.

Chen, B., Zhao, J., & Wang, D. (2008, May). An Adaptive Watermarking Algorithm for MP3 Compressed Audio Signals. In *Instrumentation and Measurement Technology Conference Proceedings, 2008. IMTC 2008. IEEE* (pp. 1057-1060). IEEE. 10.1109/IMTC.2008.4547194

Cheng, H., & Ma, L. (2009). White collar crime and the criminal justice system: Government response to bank fraud and corruption in China. *Journal of Financial Crime, 16*(2), 166–179. doi:10.1108/13590790910951849

Cheng, H., Rong, C., Hwang, K., Wang, W., & Li, Y. (2015). Secure big data storage and sharing scheme for cloud tenants. *China Communications, 12*(6), 106–115. doi:10.1109/CC.2015.7122469

Chen, R., Bao, F., & Guo, J. (2016). Trust-based service management for social internet of things systems. *IEEE Transactions on Dependable and Secure Computing, 13*(6), 684–696. doi:10.1109/TDSC.2015.2420552

Chen, X., Gao, G., Liu, D., & Xia, Z. (2016). Steganalysis of LSB Matching Using Characteristic Function Moment of Pixel Differences. Image Detection and Analysis Technique. *China Communications, 13*(7), 66–73. doi:10.1109/CC.2016.7559077

Cheon, Coron, Kim, Lee, Lepoint, Tibouchi, & Yun. (2013). Batch fully homomorphic encryption over the integers. *EUROCRYPT,* 315-335.

Chibelushi, C., Eardley, A., & Arabo, A. (2013). Identity management in the internet of things: The role of manets for healthcare applications. *Computer Science and Information Technology, 1*(2), 73–81.

Choi, K. H., & Dai, H. K. (2004, May). A marking scheme using Huffman codes for IP traceback. In *Parallel Architectures, Algorithms and Networks, 2004. Proceedings. 7th International Symposium on* (pp. 421-428). IEEE. 10.1109/ISPAN.2004.1300516

Choi, Y. S., Kim, I. K., Oh, J. T., & Jang, J. S. (2012). Aigg threshold based http get flooding attack detection. *Information Security Applications*, 270-284.

Choi, H., Lee, H., Lee, H., & Kim, H. (2007, October). Botnet detection by monitoring group activities in DNS traffic. In *Proceedings of the 7th IEEE International Conference on Computer and Information Technology* (pp. 715-720). 10.1109/CIT.2007.90

Choras, M., Kozik, R., Torres Bruna, M. P., Yautsiukhin, A., Churchill, A., Maciejewska, I., & Jomni, A. (2015). Comprehensive approach to increase cyber security and resilience. In *Proceedings of ARES (International Conference on Availability, Reliability and Security)*, Touluse (pp. 686-692). 10.1109/ARES.2015.30

Chou, B. H., & Tatara, K. (2009). A Secure Virtualized logging scheme for digital Forensic in comparison with Kernel Module approach. *Proceedings of the international conference of ISA.*

Choudhury, D. R., Ragha, L., & Marathe, N. (2015). Implementing and improving the performance of AODV by receive reply method and securing it from Black hole attack. *Procedia Computer Science, 45*, 564–570. doi:10.1016/j.procs.2015.03.109

Chowdhuri, S., Dey, N., Chakraborty, S., & Baneerjee, P. K. (2015). Analysis of Performance of MIMO Ad Hoc Network in Terms of Information Efficiency. In *Advances in Intelligent Systems and Computing* (pp. 43–50). Springer International Publishing; . doi:10.1007/978-3-319-13731-5_6

Chowdhuri, S., Dey, N., Chakraborty, S., & Baneerjee, P. K. (2015). Analysis of Performance of MIMO Ad Hoc Network in Terms of Information Efficiency. In *Proceedings of the Emerging ICT for Bridging the Future-Proceedings of the 49th Annual Convention of the Computer Society of India CSI* (Vol. 2, pp. 43–50). Cham: Springer; doi:10.1007/978-3-319-13731-5_6.

Chowdhuri, S., Roy, P., Goswami, S., Azar, A. T., & Dey, N. (2014). Rough set based ad hoc network: A review. *International Journal of Service Science, Management, Engineering, and Technology, 5*(4), 66–76. doi:10.4018/ijssmet.2014100105

Chowdhury, A. (2016, October). Recent Cyber Security Attacks and Their Mitigation Approaches–An Overview. In Proceedings of the International Conference on Applications and Techniques in Information Security (pp. 54-65). Springer Singapore. doi:10.1007/978-981-10-2741-3_5

Cisco. (n.d.). IOS NetFlow. Retrieved March 1, 2017 from http://www.cisco.com/en/US/products/ps6601/products_ios_protocol_group_home.html

Clark, J. B. A. M. J., Edward, A. N. J. A. K., & Felten, W. (2015). *Research Perspectives and Challenges for Bitcoin and Cryptocurrencies.* Academic Press.

Cogranne, R., Denemark, T., & Fridrich, J. (2014). Theoretical model of the FLD ensemble classifier based on hypothesis testing theory. *IEEE International Workshop on Information Forensics and Security (WIFS)*, 167–172. 10.1109/WIFS.2014.7084322

Cogranne, R., & Fridrich, J. (2015). Modeling and extending the ensemble classifier for steganalysis of digital images using hypothesis testing theory. *IEEE Transactions on Information Forensics and Security, Volume, 10*(12), 2627–2642. doi:10.1109/TIFS.2015.2470220

Cogranne, R., Sedighi, V., Pevný, T., & Fridrich, J. (2015). Is Ensemble Classifier Needed for Steganalysis in High-Dimensional Feature Spaces? *IEEE International Workshop on Information Forensics and Security.* 10.1109/WIFS.2015.7368597

Coleman, K. (2008). Hezbollah's Cyber Warfare Program. DefenseTech. Retrieved from https://www.defensetech.org/2008/06/02/hezbollahs-cyber-warfare-program/

Collin, B. C. (2013). The Future of CyberTerrorism. In *Proceedings of the 11th Annual International Symposium on Criminal Justice Issues.* Retrieved from http://www.crime-research.org/library/Cyberter.htm

Collins, T., Hopkins, D., Langford, S., & Sabin, M. (1997). *Public Key Cryptographic Apparatus and Method.* US Patent #5,848,159.

Cooke, E., Jahanian, F., & McPherson, D. (2005). The Zombie Roundup: Understanding, Detecting, and Disrupting Botnets. *SRUTI, 5,* 6.

Coron, J. S., Lepoint, T., & Tibouchi, M. (2014). Scale-invariant Fully Homomorphic Encryption over the Integers. *PKC 2014, 8383,* 311–328.

Coron, Naccache, & Tibouchi. (2012). Public key compression and modulus switching for fully homomorphic encryption over the integers. EUROCRYPT 2012, 446-464.

Corriero, N., Covino, E., & Mottola, A. (2011). An approach to use FB-AODV with Android. *Procedia Computer Science, 5,* 336–343. doi:10.1016/j.procs.2011.07.044

Cosmo (1765).From the movie Sneakers, from http://quotegeek.com/quotes-from-movies/sneakers/1765/

Couchot, J.-F., Couturier, R., Guyeux, C., & Salomon, M. (2016). *Steganalysis via a Convolutional Neural Networks using Large Convolution Filters for embedding process with same stego key.* Cornell University Library.

Cox, O. (2013). Citadel's defences breached. *Symantec.* Rederived March 13, 2017, from http://www.symantec.com/connect/blogs/citadel-s-defenses-breached

Criscuolo, P. J. (2000). *Distributed denial of service: Trin00, tribe flood network, tribe flood network 2000, and stacheldraht (No. CIAC-2319).* California Univ. Livermore radiation lab. doi:10.2172/792253

Curphey, M., & Arawo, R. (2006). Web application security assessment tools. *IEEE Security and Privacy, 4*(4), 32–41. doi:10.1109/MSP.2006.108

Cvejic, N. (2004). Algorithms for audio watermarking and steganography. Oulun yliopisto.

Cvejic, N., & Seppanen, T. (2003, September). Robust audio watermarking in wavelet domain using frequency hopping and patchwork method. In *Image and Signal Processing and Analysis, 2003. ISPA 2003. Proceedings of the 3rd International Symposium on* (Vol. 1, pp. 251-255). IEEE. 10.1109/ISPA.2003.1296903

Cvejic, N. (Ed.). (2007). *Digital audio watermarking techniques and technologies: applications and benchmarks: applications and benchmarks.* IGI Global.

Da Silva, E., Dos Santos, A. L., Albini, L. C. P., & Lima, M. N. (2008). Identity-based key management in mobile ad hoc networks: Techniques and applications. *IEEE Wireless Communications, 15*(5), 46–52. doi:10.1109/MWC.2008.4653131

Daeinabi, A., & Rahbar, A. G. (2013). Detection of malicious vehicles (DMV) through monitoring in Vehicular Ad-Hoc Networks. *Multimedia Tools and Applications*, *66*(2), 325–338. doi:10.100711042-011-0789-y

Dal Pozzolo, A., Caelen, O., Le Borgne, Y. A., Waterschoot, S., & Bontempi, G. (2014). Learned lessons in credit card fraud detection from a practitioner perspective. *Expert Systems with Applications*, *41*(10), 4915–4928. doi:10.1016/j. eswa.2014.02.026

Damon, E., Dale, J., Laron, E., Mache, J., Land, N., & Weiss, R. (2012, October). Hands-on denial of service lab exercises using slowloris and rudy. In Proceedings of the 2012 information security curriculum development conference, 21-29. doi:10.1145/2390317.2390321

Danchev, D. (2010). Study finds the average price for renting a botnet. *Zdnet.com*. Retrieved from http://www.zdnet. com/article/study-finds-the-average-price-for-renting-a-botnet/

Das, S., & Nayak, T. (2013). Impact of cyber crime: Issues and challenges. *International Journal of Engineering Sciences & Emerging Technologies*, *6*(2), 142–153.

David. (2012). Open DNS Security Talk: The Role of DNS in Botnet Command & Control. *Open DNS Inc*. Rederived March 13, 2017, from info.opendns.com/rs/opendns/images/WB-Security-Talk-Role-Of-DNS-Slides.pdf

Davidson, Bergman, & Bartlett. (2005). An artificial neural network for wavelet steganalysis. *Proceedings of SPIE- The International Society for Optical Engineering, Mathematical method in Pattern and Image Analysis, 5916*, 1-10.

De Rango, F., Veltri, F., & Fazio, P. (2011). Interference aware-based ad-hoc on demand distance vector (IA-AODV) ultra wideband system routing protocol. *Computer Communications*, *34*(12), 1475–1483. doi:10.1016/j.comcom.2010.09.011

Dean, D., Franklin, M., & Stubblefield, A. (2001). An algebraic approach to IP traceback. In *Proceedings of Network and Distributed System Security Symposium (NDSS 2001)* (pp. 3-12). Retrieved July 13, 2017, from http://www.csl.sri. com/users/ddean/papers/ndss2001a.pdf

Dean, J., & Ghemawat, S. (2008). MapReduce: Simplified data processing on large clusters. *Communications of the ACM*, *51*(1), 107–113. doi:10.1145/1327452.1327492

Deepa, S., & Uma Rani, R. (2016). Steganalysis on images based on the classification of image feature sets using SVM classifier. *International Journal on Computer Science and Engineering*, *5*(5), 15–24.

Delic, K. A. (2016). On Resilience of IoT Systems: The Internet of Things (Ubiquity symposium). *Ubiquity*, *2016*(February), 1.

Deloitte. (2017). About Deloitte. Retrieved from https://www2.deloitte.com/us/en/pages/about-deloitte/articles/about-deloitte.html

Denning, D. E. (1987). An intrusion-detection model. *IEEE Transactions on Software Engineering*, *13*(2), 222–232. doi:10.1109/TSE.1987.232894

Dennis, M. A. (1998). Cybercrime. *Encyclopedia Britannica*. Retrieved from https://www.britannica.com/topic/cybercrime

Desai, M., Patel, S., Somaiya, P., & Vishwanathan, V. (2016). Prevention of Distributed Denial of Service Attack using Web Referrals: A Review. *International Research Journal of Engineering and Technology*, *3*(4), 1994–1996.

Dey, N., Ashour, A. S., & Bhatt, C. (2017). Internet of Things Driven Connected Healthcare. In Internet of Things and Big Data Technologies for Next Generation Healthcare (pp. 3-12). doi:10.1007/978-3-319-49736-5_1

Dey, N., Maji, P., Das, P., Biswas, S., Das, A., & Chaudhuri, S. S. (2013, January). An edge based blind watermarking technique of medical images without devalorizing diagnostic parameters. In *Advances in Technology and Engineering (ICATE), 2013 International Conference on* (pp. 1-5). IEEE. 10.1109/ICAdTE.2013.6524732

Dhar, V. (2014). Big Data and Predictive Analytics in Health Care. *Big Data*, 2(3), 113–116. doi:10.1089/big.2014.1525 PMID:27442491

Dhawan, H., & Waraich, S. (2014). A comparative study on LEACH routing protocol and its variants in wireless sensor networks: a survey. *International Journal of Computers and Applications*, 95(8).

Diesner, J. (2015). Small decisions with big impact on data analytics. *Big Data & Society*, 2(2), 205395171561718. doi:10.1177/2053951715617185

Dietzel, C., Feldmann, A., & King, T. (2016, March). Blackholing at ixps: On the effectiveness of ddos mitigation in the wild. In *Proceedings of the International Conference on Passive and Active Network Measurement* (pp. 319-332). 10.1007/978-3-319-30505-9_24

Differential Privacy for Everyone. (2012). Retrieved from http://download.microsoft.com/Differential_Privacy_for_Everyone.pdf

Ding, F., Wang, X., Shen, Y., Lu, Y., & Hu, J. (2012, June). Non-embedded audio watermark based on wavelet transform. In *Software Engineering and Service Science (ICSESS), 2012 IEEE 3rd International Conference on* (pp. 8-11). IEEE. 10.1109/ICSESS.2012.6269393

Doeppner, T., Klein, P., & Koyfman, A. (2000). Using router stamping to identify the source of IP packets. In *Proceedings of the 7th ACM conference on Computer and communications security* (CCS) (pp. 184-189). Athens, Greece: ACM. 10.1145/352600.352627

Dolk, V. S., Tesi, P., De Persis, C., & Heemels, W. P. M. H. (2017). Event-triggered control systems under denial-of-service attacks. *IEEE Transactions on Control of Network Systems*, 4(1), 93–105. doi:10.1109/TCNS.2016.2613445

Donnelly, S. F. (2002). *High Precision Timing in Passive Measurements of Data Networks* (Ph.D. Thesis). University of Waikato, Hamilton, New Zealand. Retrieved July 14, 2017 from https://wand.net.nz/pubs/1/pdf/stephen-thesis.pdf

Dos Santos, C. R. P., Bezerra, R. S., Ceron, J. M., Granville, L. Z., & Tarouco, L. M. (2011, October). Identifying botnet communications using a mashup-based approach. In *Network Operations and Management Symposium (LANOMS), 2011 7th Latin American* (pp. 1-6). IEEE. 10.1109/LANOMS.2011.6102273

Douligeris, C., & Mitrokotsa, A. (2004). DDoS attacks and defense mechanisms: Classification and state-of-the-art. *Computer Networks*, 44(5), 643–666. doi:10.1016/j.comnet.2003.10.003

Duhart, B. A. M., & Hernández-Gress, N. (2016, December). Review of the Principal Indicators and Data Science Techniques Used for the Detection of Financial Fraud and Money Laundering. In *Proceedings of the 2016 International Conference on Computational Science and Computational Intelligence (CSCI)* (pp. 1397-1398). IEEE. 10.1109/CSCI.2016.0267

Durai, M. K. N., & Priyadharsini, K. (2014). A Survey on Security Properties and Web Application Scanner. *International journal of computer science and mobile computing*, 3(10). 10.4018/978-1-59904-280-0.ch001

Ehrenkranz, T., & Li, J. (2009). On the state of IP spoofing defense. *ACM Transactions on Internet Technology*, 9(2), 6. doi:10.1145/1516539.1516541

Eldefrawy, M. H., Khan, M. K., Alghathbar, K., & Cho, E. (2010). Broadcast Authentication for Wireless Sensor Networks Using Nested Hashing and the Chinese Remainder Theorem. *Sensors (Basel)*, 10(9), 8683–8695. doi:10.3390100908683 PMID:22163679

Elhayatmy, G., Dey, N., & Ashour, A. S. (2018). Internet of Things Based Wireless Body Area Network in Healthcare. In Internet of Things and Big Data Analytics Toward Next-Generation Intelligence (pp. 3-20). doi:10.1007/978-3-319-60435-0_1

Elhayatmy, G., Dey, N., & Ashour, A. S. (2017). Internet of Things Based Wireless Body Area Network in Healthcare. In *Studies in Big Data* (pp. 3–20). Springer International Publishing; .

Ellison, L., & Akdeniz, Y. (1998). Cyber-stalking: The Regulation of Harassment on the Internet. *Criminal Law Review (London, England)*, *29*, 29–48.

Elshazly, A. R., Nasr, M. E., Fuad, M. M., & El-Samie, F. A. (2016, May). Synchronized double watermark audio watermarking scheme based on a transform domain for stereo signals. In *Electronics, Communications and Computers (JEC-ECC), 2016 Fourth International Japan-Egypt Conference on* (pp. 52-57). IEEE. 10.1109/JEC-ECC.2016.7518966

Endace, D. A. G. (2015). *Endace Ltd. Datasheet: Endace DAG 7.5G4 network monitoring card.* Retrieved September 26, 2017 from https://www.endace.com/dag-7.5g4-datasheet.pdf

Endace. (2017). *Endace Delivers High Performance, Reliability and Affordability with new 1/10/40 Gbps Packet Capture Card.* Endace.

Engler, D. R., & Kaashoek, M. F. (1996). DPF: Fast, flexible message demultiplexing using dynamic code generation. In *Proceedings of ACM SIGCOMM '96 conference on Applications, technologies, architectures, and protocols for computer communication* (pp. 53-59). Palo Alto, CA: ACM. 10.1145/248156.248162

Eslahi, M., Rohmad, M., Nilsaz, H., Naseri, M., Tahir, N., & Hashim, H. (2015). Periodicity classification of http traffic to detect http botnets. In *Proceedings of the IEEE Symposium on Computer Applications Industrial Electronics*, Langkawi, Malaysia (pp. 119–123). 10.1109/ISCAIE.2015.7298339

Everett, C. (2015). Big data – the future of cyber-security or its latest threat? *Computer Fraud & Security*, *2015*(9), 14–17. doi:10.1016/S1361-3723(15)30085-3

Farash, M. S., Turkanović, M., Kumari, S., & Hölbl, M. (2016). An efficient user authentication and key agreement scheme for heterogeneous wireless sensor network tailored for the Internet of Things environment. *Ad Hoc Networks*, *36*, 152–176. doi:10.1016/j.adhoc.2015.05.014

Farid, H. (2002) Detecting hidden messages using higher-order statistical models. *Proceedings of IEEE International Conference Image Processing*, *2*, 905–908. 10.1109/ICIP.2002.1040098

Farsi, H., & Shahi, A. (2014). Steganalysis of images based on spatial domain and two-dimensional JPEG array. *Journal of the Chinese Institute of EngineersVolume*, *37*(8), 1055–1063. doi:10.1080/02533839.2014.929711

Fatima, H., Satpathy, S., Mahapatra, S., Dash, G. N., & Pradhan, S. K. (2017). Data fusion & visualization application for network forensic investigation - a case study. In *Proceedings of the 2nd International Conference on Anti-Cyber Crimes (ICACC)* (pp. 252-256), Abha, Saudi Arabia: ICACC. 10.1109/Anti-Cybercrime.2017.7905301

Fei, H. (2016). Robust cyber-physical systems: Concept, models, and implementation. *Future Generation Computer Systems*, 449–475.

Feinstein, L., Schnackenberg, D., Balupari, R., & Kindred, D. (2003, April). Statistical approaches to DDoS attack detection and response. In DARPA Information Survivability Conference and Exposition (pp. 303-314). doi:10.1109/DISCEX.2003.1194894

Ferrer, M. A., Travieso, C. M., & Alonso, J. B. (2006). Using hand knuckle texture for biometric identifications. *IEEE Aerospace and Electronic Systems Magazine*, *21*(6), 23–27. doi:10.1109/MAES.2006.1662005

Fidelie, L. W. (2009). Internet Gambling: Innocent Activity or Cybercrime? *International Journal of Cyber Criminology*, *3*(1), 476.

Filler, T., & Fridrich, J. (2010). Gibbs Construction in Steganography. *IEEE Transactions on Information Forensics and Security, Volume, 5*(4), 705–720. doi:10.1109/TIFS.2010.2077629

Fjäder, C. O. (2016). National Security in a Hyper-connected World. In Exploring the Security Landscape: Non-Traditional Security Challenges (pp. 31-58). Springer International Publishing. doi:10.1007/978-3-319-27914-5_3

Fokuoh Ampratwum, E. (2009). Advance fee fraud "419" and investor confidence in the economies of sub-Saharan African (SSA). *Journal of Financial Crime*, *16*(1), 67–79. doi:10.1108/13590790910924975

Foo, S. W. (2008). *Audio-watermarking with stereo signals*. Academic Press.

Forouzan, B. A., & Mosharraf, F. (2012). *Computer networks: a top-down approach* (p. 931). McGraw-Hill.

Fraleigh, C., Diot, C., Lyles, B., Moon, S. B., Owezarski, P., Papagiannaki, D., & Tobagi, F. A. (2001). Design and deployment of a passive monitoring infrastructure. In *Evolutionary Trends of the Internet (LNCS)* (Vol. 2170, pp. 556–575). Berlin, Germany: Springer; doi:10.1007/3-540-45400-4_36

Fridrich, J., Kodovský, J., Goljan, M., & Holub, V. (2011). Breaking HUGO – the process discovery. *Information Hiding, 13th International Workshop*, *6958*, 85–101.

Fridrich, J., Kodovský, J., Goljan, M., & Holub, V. (2011). Steganalysis of content-adaptive steganography in spatial domain. *Information Hiding, 13th International Workshop*, 6958, 102–117. 10.1007/978-3-642-24178-9_8

Fridrich, J., Pevný, T., & Kodovský, J. (2007). Statistically Undetectable JPEG Steganography: Dead Ends, Challenges, and Opportunities. *Proceedings of the 9th ACM Multimedia & Security Workshop*, 3–14.

Fridrich, J., & Goljan, M. (2006). On estimation of secret message length in LSB steganography in spatial domain. In Proceedings of Security, steganography, and watermarking of multimedia Contents VI. *Proceedings of the Society for Photo-Instrumentation Engineers*, *5306*, 23–34. doi:10.1117/12.521350

Fridrich, J., Goljan, M., & Du, R. (2001). Detecting LSB steganography in color and gray-scale images. *IEEE MultiMedia*, *8*(4), 22–28. doi:10.1109/93.959097

Fridrich, J., & Kodovský, J. (2012). Rich models for steganalysis of digital images. *IEEE Transactions on Information Forensics and Security*, *7*(3), 868–882. doi:10.1109/TIFS.2012.2190402

Furnelb, S. M., & Warren, M. J. (1999). Computer Hacking and Cyber Terrorism: The Real Threats in the New Millennium. *Computers & Security*, *18*(1), 28–34. doi:10.1016/S0167-4048(99)80006-6

Gandomi, A., & Haider, M. (2015). Beyond the hype: Big data concepts, methods, and analytics. *International Journal of Information Management*, *35*(2), 137–144. doi:10.1016/j.ijinfomgt.2014.10.007

Garcia, L. M. (2008). Programming with libpcap: Sniffing the network from our own application. *Hakin9, 3*(2), 38-46. Retrieved September 28, 2017 from http://recursos.aldabaknocking.com/libpcapHakin9LuisMartinGarcia.pdf

García, S., Grill, M., Stiborek, J., & Zunino, A. (2014). An empirical comparison of botnet detection methods. *Computer Security Journal*, *45*, 100–123. doi:10.1016/j.cose.2014.05.011

Garfinkel, S., & Spafford, G. (2002). *Web security, privacy & commerce*. O'Reilly Media, Inc.

Garg, S., & Sharma, R. M. (2017). Classification Based Network Layer Botnet Detection. In *Advanced Informatics for Computing Research* (pp. 332–342). Singapore: Springer. doi:10.1007/978-981-10-5780-9_30

Gartner warns of big data security problems. (2014). *Network Security, 20*(6). doi:10.10161353-4858(14)70062-5

Gaub, F. (2017). Trends in terrorism, European Union Institute for Security Studies (EUISS). doi:Retrieved from https://www.iss.europa.eu/sites/default/files/EUISSFiles/Alert_4_Terrorism_in_Europe_0.pdf. 10.2815/66788

Geeksforgeeks.org. RSA. (n.d.). Algorithm in Cryptography. Retrieved May 25, 2017 from http://www.geeksforgeeks.org/rsa-algorithm-cryptography

Geetha, S. (2016). Social internet of things. *World Scientific News, 41*, 76.

Gentry, Halevi, & Nigel. (2015). *Homomorphic evaluation of the AES circuit* (Updated Implementation).

Gentry, C. (2009). Fully homomorphic encryption using ideal lattices. *Symposium on the Theory of Computing (STOC)*, 169-176.

Gheyas, I., & Abdallah, A. (2016). Detection and prediction of insider threats to cyber security: A systematic literature review and meta-analysis. *Big Data Analytics, 1*(1), 6. doi:10.118641044-016-0006-0

Ghiglieri, M., & Waidner, M. (2016). HbbTV Security and Privacy: Issues and Challenges. *IEEE Security and Privacy, 14*(3), 61–67. doi:10.1109/MSP.2016.54

Giroire, F., Chandrashekar, J., Taft, N., Schooler, E., & Papagiannaki, D. (2009) Exploiting Temporal Persistence to Detect Covert Botnet Channels. In: E. Kirda, S. Jha, & D. Balzarotti (Eds.), *International Workshop on Recent Advances in Intrusion Detection: Recent Advances in Intrusion Detection*, LNCS (Vol. 5758, pp. 326-345). Springer, Berlin, Heidelberg 10.1007/978-3-642-04342-0_17

Global Financial Integrity (GFI). (n.d.). Money laundering. Retrieved from http://www.gfintegrity.org/issue/money-laundering/

Goh, E. J. (2003). Secure indexes. *Cryptology ePrint Archive*. Retrieved from https://eprint.iacr.org/2003/216.pdf

Golle, P., & Modadugu, N. (2001). Authenticating Streamed Data in the Presence of Random Packet Loss. In *Proceedings of Network and Distributed System Security Symposium (NDSS 2001)* (pp. 13–22). San Diego, CA: Internet Society.

Gong, C., & Sarac, K. (2008). A more practical approach for single-packet IP traceback using packet logging and marking. *IEEE Transactions on Parallel and Distributed Systems, 19*(10), 1310–1324. doi:10.1109/TPDS.2007.70817

Goodman, S. E. (2007). Cyberterrorism and Security Measures, Science and Technology to Counter Terrorism. In *Proceedings of an Indo-U.S. Workshop*. Retrieved from https://www.nap.edu/read/11848/chapter/6

Goodrich, M. T. (2002). Efficient packet marking for large-scale IP traceback. In *Proceedings of the 9th ACM conference on Computer and communications security* (pp. 117–126). Washington, DC, USA: CCS. doi:10.1145/586110.586128

Goodrich, M. T. (2008). Probabilistic packet marking for large-scale IP traceback. *IEEE/ACM Transactions on Networking, 16*(1), 15–24. doi:10.1109/TNET.2007.910594

Gordy, J. D., & Bruton, L. T. (2000). Performance evaluation of digital audio watermarking algorithms. In *Circuits and Systems, 2000. Proceedings of the 43rd IEEE Midwest Symposium on* (Vol. 1, pp. 456-459). IEEE.

Goswami, S., Roy, P., Dey, N., & Chakraborty, S. (2016). Wireless body area networks combined with mobile cloud computing in healthcare: a survey. *Classification and Clustering in Biomedical Signal Processing, 388.*

Goswami, S., Roy, P., Dey, N., & Chakraborty, S. (2017). Wireless Body Area Networks Combined with Mobile Cloud Computing in Healthcare. In *Classification and Clustering in Biomedical Signal Processing* (pp. 388–402). IGI Global.

Gottschalk, P. (2010). *Policing Cyber Crime*. Bookboon.

Green, M. A. (2015). China's Growing Cyberwar Capabilities. *The Diplomat*. Retrieved from https://thediplomat.com/2015/04/chinas-growing-cyberwar-capabilities/

Grover, J., Gaur, M. S., & Laxmi, V. (2010). A novel defense mechanism against sybil attacks in VANET. In *Proceedings of the 3rd international conference on Security of information and networks* (pp. 249-255). ACM. 10.1145/1854099.1854150

Grover, J., & Hanmandlu, M. (2017). Personal identification using the rank level fusion of finger-knuckle-prints. *Pattern Recognition and Image Analysis*, 27(1), 82–93. doi:10.1134/S1054661817010059

Gu, G., Perdisci, R., Zhang, J., & Lee, W. (2008, July). BotMiner: Clustering Analysis of Network Traffic for Protocol-and Structure-Independent Botnet Detection. In USENIX security symposium (Vol. 5, No. 2, pp. 139-154). Academic Press.

Gu, G., Zhang, J., & Lee, W. (2008, February). BotSniffer: Detecting Botnet Command and Control Channels in Network Traffic. In NDSS (Vol. 8, pp. 1-18). Academic Press.

Guan, Y. (2003). Evidence and Collection Analyses Tools. Retrieved October 30, 2003, from home.eng.iastate.edu/~guan/course/backup/CprE-592-YG-Fall.../Lecture15.pdf

Gu, G., Perdisci, R., Zhang, J., & Lee, W. (2008). BotMiner: clustering analysisof network traffic for protocol- and structure- independent botnet detection. In *Proceedings of the 17th conference on Security symposium,* San Jose, CA (pp. 139-154).

Gu, G., Perdisci, R., Zhang, J., & Lee, W. (2008, July). BotMiner: Clustering Analysis of Network Traffic for Protocol- and Structure-Independent Botnet Detection. *USENIX Security Symposium*, 5(2), 139-154.

Gu, G., Porras, P., Yegneswaran, V., & Fong, M. (2007). BotHunter: Detecting malware infection through IDS-driven dialogcorrelation. In *Proceedings of 16th USENIX Security Symposium on USENIX Security Symposium*, Boston, MA (pp. 167–182).

Gu, G., Zhang, J., & Lee, W. (2008). BotSniffer: Detecting botnet command and control channels in network traffic. In *Proceedings of the Network and Distributed System Security Symposium*, San Diego, CA.

Gu, G., Zhang, J., & Lee, W. (2008). BotSniffer: Detecting botnet commandand control channels in network traffic. In *Proceedings of the Network and Distributed System Security Symposium*, San Diego, CA.

Guntuku, S. C., Hota, C., Singh, K., & Thakur, A. (2014). Big data analytics framework for peer-to-peer botnet detection using random forests. *Information Sciences*, 278, 488–497. doi:10.1016/j.ins.2014.03.066

Guo, H., Jin, B., & Huang, D. (2010). Research and review on computer forensics. In *Proceedings of the International Conference on Forensics in Telecommunications, Information, and Multimedia* (pp. 224-233). Springer Berlin Heidelberg.

Guo, Ni, & Shi. (2014). Uniform Embedding for Efficient JPEG Steganography. *IEEE Transactions on Information Forensics and Security, 9*(5), 814–825. 10.1109/TIFS.2014.2312817

Guo, L., Ni, J., & Shi, Y.-Q. (2012). An Efficient JPEG Steganographic Scheme Using Uniform Embedding. *Proceedings of Fourth IEEE International Workshop on Information Forensics and Security*. 10.1109/WIFS.2012.6412644

Guoming, C., Qiang, C., Dong, Z., & Weighing, Z. (2012). *Particle swarm optimization feature selection for image steganalysis*. IEEE Computer Society.

Gupta, B. B., Joshi, R. C., Misra, M., Meena, D. L., Shrivastava, G., & Sharma, K. (2010). Detecting a Wide Range of Flooding DDoS Attacks using Linear Prediction Model. In Proceedings of the 2nd IEEE International Conference on Information and Multimedia Technology (ICIMT 2010) (Vol. 2, pp. 535-539).

Gupta, B. B., Joshi, R. C., Misra, M., Meena, D. L., Shrivastava, G., & Sharma, K. (2010). Detecting a Wide Range of Flooding DDoS Attacks using Linear Prediction Model. In Proceedings of the IEEE 2nd International Conference on Information and Multimedia Technology (ICIMT 2010) (pp. 535-539).

Gupta, M., Shrivastava, G., Gupta, S., Gupta, R. (2017). Role of Cyber Security in Today's Scenario. *Detecting and Mitigating Robotic Cyber Security Risks*, 177.

Gupta, P., Singh, J., Arora, A. K., & Mahajan, S. (2011). Digital forensics: A technological revolution in forensic sciences.

Gupta, B. B., Joshi, R. C., Misra, M., Meena, D. L., Shrivastava, G., & Sharma, K. (2010). Detecting a Wide Range of Flooding DDoS Attacks using Linear Prediction Model. In *2nd International Conference on Information and Multimedia Technology* (pp. 535-539). IEEE.

Gupta, B. B., Joshi, R. C., Misra, M., Meena, D. L., Shrivastava, G., & Sharma, K. (2010). Detecting a Wide Range of Flooding DDoS Attacks using Linear Prediction Model. In *Proceedings of the 2nd International Conference on Information and Multimedia Technology (ICIMT 2010)* (Vol. 2, pp. 535-539).

Gupta, J. P., Singh, N., Dixit, P., Semwal, V. B., & Dubey, S. R. (2013). Human activity recognition using gait pattern. *International Journal of Computer Vision and Image Processing*, *3*(3), 31–53. doi:10.4018/ijcvip.2013070103

Gupta, S. (2012). Buffer Overflow Attack. *IOSR Journal of Computer Engineering*, *1*(1), 10–23. doi:10.9790/0661-0111023

Haber, S., & Stornetta, W. S. (1990, August). How to time-stamp a digital document. In *Conference on the Theory and application of Cryptography* (pp. 437-455). Springer.

Hachem, N., Mustapha, Y. B., Granadillo, G. G., & Debar, H. (2011, May). Botnets: lifecycle and taxonomy. In *Network and Information Systems Security (SAR-SSI), 2011 Conference on* (pp. 1-8). IEEE. 10.1109/SAR-SSI.2011.5931395

Haddadi, F., Phan, D. T., & Zincir-Heywood, A. N. (2016). How to choose from different botnet detection systems? In *Proceedings of the IEEE/IFIP Network Operations and Management Symposium,* Istanbul, Turkey (pp. 1079–1084). 10.1109/NOMS.2016.7502964

Hagen, J. M., Sivertsen, T. K., & Rong, C. (2008). Protection against unauthorized access and computer crime in Norwegian enterprises. *Journal of Computer Security*, *16*(3), 341–366. doi:10.3233/JCS-2008-16305

Hajdarbegovic, N. (2017). Are we creating an insecure internet of things (iot)? security challenges and concerns. *Toptotal. Accessed Feb, 1.*

Halder, T. K., Chowdhury, C., & Neogy, S. (2014, August). Power aware AODV routing protocol for MANET. In *Proceedings of the 2014 Fourth International Conference on Advances in Computing and Communications (ICACC)* (pp. 331-334). IEEE. 10.1109/ICACC.2014.84

Halvaiee, N. S., & Akbari, M. K. (2014). A novel model for credit card fraud detection using Artificial Immune Systems. *Applied Soft Computing*, *24*, 40–49. doi:10.1016/j.asoc.2014.06.042

Hanmandlu, M. (2011). Information sets and information processing. *Defence Science Journal*, *61*(5), 405. doi:10.14429/dsj.61.1192

Hansen, L. L. (2009). Corporate financial crime: Social diagnosis and treatment. *Journal of Financial Crime*, *16*(1), 28–40. doi:10.1108/13590790910924948

Hao, Y., Cheng, Y., Zhou, C., & Song, W. (2011). A distributed key management framework with cooperative message authentication in VANETs. *IEEE Journal on Selected Areas in Communications*, *29*(3), 616–629. doi:10.1109/JSAC.2011.110311

Harbawi, M., & Varol, A. (2016, April). The role of digital forensics in combating cybercrimes. In *Proceedings of the 2016 4th International Symposium on Digital Forensic and Security (ISDFS)* (pp. 138-142). IEEE. 10.1109/ISDFS.2016.7473532

Harichandran, V. S., Breitinger, F., Baggili, I., & Marrington, A. (2016). A cyber forensics needs analysis survey: Revisiting the domain's needs a decade later. *Computers & Security*, *57*, 1–13. doi:10.1016/j.cose.2015.10.007

Harishankar, S., Woungang, I., Dhurandher, S. K., Traore, I., & Kaleel, S. B. (2015, March). E-MAnt Net: An ACO-Based Energy Efficient Routing Protocol for Mobile Ad Hoc Networks. In *Proceedings of the 2015 IEEE 29th International Conference on Advanced Information Networking and Applications (AINA)* (pp. 29-36). IEEE.

Hasbullah, H., & Soomro, I. A. (2010). Denial of service (DOS) attack and its possible solutions in VANET. *International Journal of Electrical, Computer, Energetic, Electronic and Communication Engineering*, *4*(5), 813–817.

Hashem, I. A. T., Yaqoob, I., Anuar, N. B., Mokhtar, S., Gani, A., & Khan, S. U. (2015). The rise of "big data" on cloud computing: Review and open research issues. *Information Systems*, *47*, 98–115. doi:10.1016/j.is.2014.07.006

Hashmi, M. J., Saxena, M., & Saini, R. (2012). Classification of DDoS attacks and their defense techniques using intrusion prevention system. *International Journal of Computer Science and Communication Networks*, *2*(5), 607–614.

Hastie, T., Tibshirani, R., Friedman, J., & Franklin, J. (2009). *The elements of statistical learning: data mining, inference and prediction* (2nd ed.). Springer. doi:10.1007/978-0-387-84858-7

Heady, R., Luger, G., Maccabe, A., & Sevilla, M. (1990, August). The architecture of a network level intrusion detection system (technical report). University of New Mexico.

Helplinelaw.com. (2000), *Helplinelaw.com is one of the pioneers of the online legal Services*. Retrieved from http://www.helplinelaw.com/docs/indian%20law/aboutus.shtml

Henning, J. (2009). Perspectives on financial crimes in Roman-Dutch law: Bribery, fraud and the general crime of falsity (falsiteyt). *Journal of Financial Crime*, *16*(4), 295–304. doi:10.1108/13590790910993771

Herland, M., Khoshgoftaar, T., & Wald, R. (2014). A review of data mining using big data in health informatics. *Journal Of Big Data*, *1*(1), 2. doi:10.1186/2196-1115-1-2

Hetzl, S., & Mutzel, P. (2005). A Graph-Theoretic Approach to Steganography. *Communications and Multimedia Security, 9th IFIP TC-6 TC-11 International Conference, CMS 2005*, 119–128. 10.1007/11552055_12

Hidarimanesh, S. N., & Esfahani, M. S. (2016). Bank fraud. *Recht & Psychiatrie*, *724*(2247), 518–525.

Holotyak, T., Fridrich, J., & Voloshynovskiy, S. (2005). Blind statistical steganalysis of additive steganography using wavelet higher order statistics. *Proceedings of 9th IFIP Conference on Communication and Multimedia Security, LNCS 3677*, 273–274. 10.1007/11552055_31

Holub, V., & Fridrich, J. (2015). Phase-Aware Projection Model for Steganalysis of JPEG Images. *Proceedings of SPIE, Electronic Imaging, Media Watermarking, Security, and Forensics 2015, 9409*, 1–11.

Holub, V., & Fridrich, J. (2015). Low-Complexity Features for JPEG Steganalysis Using Undecimated DCT. *IEEE Transactions on Information Forensics and Security*, *10*(2), 219–228. doi:10.1109/TIFS.2014.2364918

Holub, V., Fridrich, J., & Denemark, T. (2014). *Universal distortion function for steganography in an arbitrary domain*. EURASIP Journal on Information Security.

Honeynet Project and Research Alliance. (2008). *Know your enemy: Tracking Botnets*. Retrieved October 8, 2008, from http:// www. honeynet. org/papers/bots

Hoque, M. S., Mukit, M., Bikas, M., & Naser, A. (2012). An implementation of intrusion detection system using genetic algorithm. *International Journal of Network Security & Its Applications*, *4*(2), 109–120. doi:10.5121/ijnsa.2012.4208

Horowitz, B., & Lucero, D. (2016). System-aware cyber security: A systems engineering approach for enhancing cyber security. *Insight (American Society of Ophthalmic Registered Nurses)*, *19*(2), 39–42. doi:10.1002/inst.12087

Hoskins, M. (2014). Common Big Data Challenges and How to Overcome Them. *Big Data*, *2*(3), 142–143. doi:10.1089/big.2014.0030 PMID:27442494

Hoßfeld, T., Lehrieder, F., Hock, D., Oechsner, S., Despotovic, Z., Kellerer, W., & Michel, M. (2011). Characterization of BitTorrent swarms and their distribution in the Internet. *Computer Networks*, *55*(5), 1197–1215. doi:10.1016/j.comnet.2010.11.011

Ho, T. K. (1995). Random decision forests. *Proceedings of International Conference on Document Analysis and Recognition*, 278–282.

Hou, X., Zhang, T., & Xu, C. (2016). New framework for unsupervised universal steganalysis via SRISP-aided outlier detection. *Image Communication*, *47C*, 72–85.

Huang, Y. P., Luo, S. W., & Chen, E. Y. (2002). An efficient iris recognition system. In *Machine Learning and Cybernetics, 2002. Proceedings. 2002 International Conference on* (Vol. 1, pp. 450-454). IEEE.

Huang, Z., Yamamoto, R., & Tanaka, Y. (2014, February). A multipath energy-efficient probability routing protocol in ad hoc networks. In *Proceedings of the 2014 16th International Conference on Advanced Communication Technology (ICACT)* (pp. 244-250). IEEE. 10.1109/ICACT.2014.6778932

Huang, C. T., & Sakib, M. N. (2016). Using anomaly detection based techniques to detect HTTP-based botnet C&C traffic. In *Proceedings of the IEEE International Conference on Communications*, Kuala Lumpur, Malaysia.

Huang, Y. M., Yeh, C. H., Wang, T. I., & Chao, H. C. (2007). Constructing secure group communication over wireless ad hoc networks based on a virtual subnet model. *IEEE Wireless Communications*, *14*(5), 70–75. doi:10.1109/MWC.2007.4396945

Hua, Z., Fei, G., Qiaoyan, W., & Zhengping, J. (2011). A Password-Based Secure Communication Scheme in Battlefields for Internet of Things. *China Communications*, *8*(1), 72–78.

Huberman, B. A. (2016). Ensuring Trust and Security in the Industrial IoT: The Internet of Things (Ubiquity symposium). *Ubiquity*, *2016*(January), 2. doi:10.1145/2822883

Hu, F. (2016). *Security and Privacy in Internet of Things (IoTs): Models, Algorithms, and Implementations*. CRC Press. doi:10.1201/b19516

Hui, L. C., Chow, K. P., & Yiu, S. M. (2007). Tools and technology for computer forensics: research and development in Hong Kong. In *Proceedings of the International Conference on Information Security Practice and Experience* (pp. 11-19). Springer Berlin Heidelberg

Hu, L., Zhang, X., Wang, F., Wang, W., & Zhao, K. (2012). Research on the Architecture Model of Volatile Data Forensics. *Procedia Engineering*, *29*, 4254–4258. doi:10.1016/j.proeng.2012.01.653

Hussain, N. I., & Saikia, P. (2014). *Big Data ppt*. Retrieved from http://www.slideshare.net/nasrinhussain1/big-data-ppt-31616290

Hussain, A., & Roy, A. (2016). The emerging era of Big Data Analytics. *Big Data Analytics*, *1*(1), 4. doi:10.118641044-016-0004-2

ICERT - Indian Computer Emergency Response Team. (2017). Ministry of Electronics & Information Technology, Government of India. Retrieved from http://meity.gov.in/content/icert

IEEE Internet Initiative. (2015). Towards a definition of the Internet of Things (IoT) (Revision-1). Retrieved from http://iot.ieee.org/images/files/pdf/IEEE_IoT_Towards_Definition_Internet_of_Things_Revision1_27MAY15.pdf

Ierace, N., Urrutia, C., & Bassett, R. (2005). Intrusion prevention systems. *Ubiquity*, *2005*(June), 2–2. doi:10.1145/1071916.1071927

Ikeda, M., Kulla, E., Hiyama, M., Barolli, L., Miho, R., & Takizawa, M. (2012, July). Congestion control for multi-flow traffic in wireless mobile ad-hoc networks. In *Proceedings of the 2012 Sixth International Conference on Complex, Intelligent and Software Intensive Systems (CISIS)* (pp. 290-297). IEEE. 10.1109/CISIS.2012.83

Internet Live Stats. (n.d.). Retrieved from www.internetlivestats.com

Interpol. (n.d.). *INTERPOL is the world's largest international police organization, with 190 member countries*. Retrieved from www.interpol.int/public/FinancialCrime/Default.asp

Investopedia. (2017). Identity theft. Retrieved from www.investopedia.com/terms/i/identitytheft.asp

Jabeen, K. (2016). *Scalability Study of Hadoop MapReduce and Hive in Big Data Analytics*. International Journal Of Engineering And Computer Science; doi:10.18535/ijecs/v5i11.11

Jain, Gyanchandani, & Khare. (2016). Big data privacy: A Technological Perspective and Review. *Journal of Big Data*, *3*(25).

Jain, H. R., & Sharma, S. K. (2014, August). Improved energy efficient secure multipath AODV routing protocol for MANET. In *Proceedings of the 2014 International Conference on Advances in Engineering and Technology Research (ICAETR)*. IEEE. 10.1109/ICAETR.2014.7012847

Jain, A. K., & Li, S. Z. (2011). *Handbook of face recognition*. New York: Springer.

Jain, A. K., Ross, A., & Prabhakar, S. (2004). An introduction to biometric recognition. *IEEE Transactions on Circuits and Systems for Video Technology*, *14*(1), 4–20. doi:10.1109/TCSVT.2003.818349

Jain, A., & Bhatnagar, V. (2017). Concoction of Ambient Intelligence and Big Data for Better Patient Ministration Services. *International Journal of Ambient Computing and Intelligence*, *8*(4), 19–30. doi:10.4018/IJACI.2017100102

Jakobsson, M., Leighton, T., Micali, S., & Szydlo, M. (2003). Fractal Merkle Tree Representation and Traversal. In *Proceedings of Topics in Cryptology - CT-RSA 2003: The Cryptographers' Track at the RSA Conference 2003 (LNCS)* (vol. 2612, pp. 314-326). Berlin, Germany: Springer. 10.1007/3-540-36563-X_21

Jayakumar, G., & Gopinath, G. (2007). Ad hoc mobile wireless networks routing protocols–a review. *Journal of Computational Science*, *3*(8), 574–582. doi:10.3844/jcssp.2007.574.582

Jewkes, Y. (Ed.). (2013). *Crime online*. Routledge.

Jiang, Y.-G., & Wang, J. (2016). Partial Copy Detection in Videos: A Benchmark and an Evaluation of Popular Methods. *IEEE Transactions on Big Data*, *2*(1), 32–42. doi:10.1109/TBDATA.2016.2530714

Jin, S., & Yeung, D. S. (2004, June). A covariance analysis model for DDoS attack detection. In *Proceedings of the IEEE International Conference on Communications* (Vol. 4, pp. 1882-1886).

Jing, X., Li, W., Lan, C., Yao, Y., Cheng, X., & Han, L. (2011, November). Orthogonal complex locality preserving projections based on image space metric for finger-knuckle-print recognition. In *Hand-Based Biometrics (ICHB), 2011 International Conference on* (pp. 1-6). IEEE.

Jing, Q., Vasilakos, A. V., Wan, J., Lu, J., & Qiu, D. (2014). Security of the internet of things: Perspectives and challenges. *Wireless Networks*, *20*(8), 2481–2501. doi:10.100711276-014-0761-7

Jongsuebsuk, P., Wattanapongsakorn, N., & Charnsripinyo, C. (2013, January). Network intrusion detection with Fuzzy Genetic Algorithm for unknown attacks. In *Proceedings of the 2013 International Conference on Information Networking (ICOIN)*. IEEE. 10.1109/ICOIN.2013.6496342

Jonson, J., & Kaliski, B. (2003). *Public-Key Cryptography Standards (PKCS) #1: RSA Cryptography Specifications Version 2.1*. IETF, RFC-3447. Retrieved July 12, 2017, from https://tools.ietf.org/html/rfc3447

Joseph, A. (2013a). *Enhanced Resource Management on cloud systems using Distributed Policy and Rule Engines* (Master's Thesis). VTU Bangalore, India.

Joseph, A. (2012). Cloud Computing with Advanced Resource Management. *International Journal of Advanced Technology and Engineering Research*, *4*, 21–25.

Joseph, A. (2013b). Enhanced Resource Management using Distributed Policy and Rule Engines. *Proceedings of International Conference on Advanced Computing and Information Technology*.

Joseph, A. (2017). Provenance of Digital Assets-Blockchains and Bitmarks. *IEEE ComSocNwesletter*, *1*, 5.

Joseph, A., & Singh, K. J. (2016). The latest Trends and challenges in cyber forensics. *Proceedings of International Conference ICMCECE*, 107.

Juneja, P., & Kashyap, R. (2016). Energy based Methods for Medical Image Segmentation. *International Journal of Computers and Applications*, *146*(6).

Juneja, P., & Kashyap, R. (2016). Optimal Approach For CT Image Segmentation Using Improved Energy Based Method. *International Journal of Control Theory and Applications*, *9*(41), 599–608.

Juzenaite, R. (2015). Infosec Institute - The Most Hacker-Active Countries. Retrieved from http://resources.infosecinstitute.com/the-most-hacker-active-countries-part-i/#gref

Kabir, M. H. (2013). Research issues on vehicular ad hoc network. *International Journal of Engineering Trends and Technology*, *6*(4), 174–179.

Kadam, M., Jha, P., & Jaiswal, S. (2015). Double spending prevention in bitcoins network. *International Journal of Computer Engineering and Applications, 9*.

Kalra, S., & Sekhri, B. (2016). Security threats in big data. *Far East Journal of Electronics and Communications*, 623-633. 10.17654/ecsv3pii16623

Kamal, S., Ripon, S. H., Dey, N., Ashour, A. S., & Santhi, V. (2016). A MapReduce approach to diminish imbalance parameters for big deoxyribonucleic acid dataset. *Computer Methods and Programs in Biomedicine*, *131*, 191–206. doi:10.1016/j.cmpb.2016.04.005 PMID:27265059

Kang, J., & Zhang, J. Y. (2009, May). Application entropy theory to detect new peer-to-peer botnet with multi-chart CUSUM. In *Proceedings of the Second International Symposium on Electronic Commerce and Security* (Vol. 1, pp. 470-474). 10.1109/ISECS.2009.61

Kaseb, S. A., Mohan, A., Koh, Y., & Lu, Y.-H. (2017). Cloud Resource Management for Analyzing Big Real-Time Visual Data from Network Cameras. *IEEE Transactions on Cloud Computing*, 1–1. doi:10.1109/tcc.2017.2720665

Kashyap, R., & Gautam, P. (2015, November). Modified region based segmentation of medical images. In *Communication Networks (ICCN), 2015 International Conference on* (pp. 209-216). IEEE. 10.1109/ICCN.2015.41

Kashyap, R., & Gautam, P. (2017). Fast Medical Image Segmentation Using Energy-Based Method. *Pattern and Data Analysis in Healthcare Settings*, 35-60.

Kashyap, R., & Gautam, P. (2013). Microarray Image Segmentation using Improved GOGAC Method. *Science and Engineering*, 2(4), 67–74.

Kashyap, R., & Gautam, P. (2016, August). Fast Level Set Method for Segmentation of Medical Images. In *Proceedings of the International Conference on Informatics and Analytics* (p. 20). ACM. 10.1145/2980258.2980302

Kashyap, R., & Tiwari, V. (2017). Energy-based active contour method for image segmentation. *International Journal of Electronic Healthcare*, 9(2-3), 210–225. doi:10.1504/IJEH.2017.083165

Ker, A. K. (2006). Fourth-order structural steganalysis and analysis of cover assumptions. Proceedings of SPIE 6072, Security, Steganography, and Watermarking of Multimedia Contents VIII, 6072, 1–14. doi:10.1117/12.642920

Kesharwani, R. (2016, August). Enhancing Information Security in Big Data. *International Journal of Advanced Research in Computer and Communication Engineering*, 5(8).

Khan, A. R., Rakesh, N., Bansal, A., & Chaudhary, D. K. (2015, December). Comparative study of WSN Protocols (LEACH, PEGASIS, and TEEN). In *Proceedings of the 2015 Third International Conference on Image Information Processing (ICIIP)* (pp. 422-427). IEEE.

KhanS. (n.d.). Retrieved from C# from www.programmersheaven.com

Khanse, A. (2014). Cyber Attacks – Definition, Types, Prevention, The Windows Club. Retrieved from http://www.thewindowsclub.com/cyber-attacks-definition-types-prevention

Khaosan, V. (2014). *How Bitcoin Transaction Works*. Retrieved from https://www.cryptocoinsnews.com/bitcoin-transaction-really-works/

Khari, M., Shrivastava, G., Gupta, S., Gupta, R. (2017). Role of Cyber Security in Today's Scenario. *Detecting and Mitigating Robotic Cyber Security Risks*, 177.

Khari, M., Shrivastava, G., Gupta, S., Gupta, R. (2017). Role of Cyber Security in Today's Scenario. In *Detecting and Mitigating Robotic Cyber Security Risks* (pp. 177).

Khari, M., & Karar, A. (2013). Preventing SQL-Based Attacks Using Intrusion Detection System. *International Journal of Science and Engineering Applications*, 2(6), 145–150. doi:10.7753/IJSEA0206.1006

Khari, M., & Kumar, M. (2016). Comprehensive study of web application attacks and classification. In *3rd International Conference on Computing for Sustainable Global Development*, New Delhi, India (pp. 2159-2164).

Khari, M., & Kumar, N. (2013). User Authentication Method against SQL Injection Attack. *International Journal of Scientific & Engineering Research.*, 4(6), 1649–1653.

Khari, M., & Sangwan, P. (2016). Web-application attacks: A survey. In *Proceedings of the 3rd International Conference on Computing for Sustainable Global Development*, New Delhi, India (pp. 2187-2191).

Kim, J. E., Maron, A., & Mosse, D. (2015, June). Socialite: A flexible framework for social internet of things. In *Proceedings of the 2015 16th IEEE International Conference on Mobile Data Management (MDM)* (Vol. 1, pp. 94-103). IEEE. 10.1109/MDM.2015.50

Kimbahune, V. V., Deshpande, A. V., & Mahalle, P. N. (2017, January). Lightweight Key Management for Adaptive Addressing in next Generation Internet. *International Journal of Ambient Computing and Intelligence, 8*(1), 50–69. doi:10.4018/IJACI.2017010103

Kim, H. S., & Kim, H. K. (2011). Network Forensic Evidence Acquisition (NFEA) with Packet Marking. In *Proceedings of the 9th IEEE International Symposium on Parallel and Distributed Processing with Applications Workshops* (pp. 388-393). Busan, Korea: IEEE. 10.1109/ISPAW.2011.27

Kirubavathi, G., & Anitha, R. (2016). Botnet detection via mining of traffic flow characteristics. *Computers & Electrical Engineering, 50*, 91–101. doi:10.1016/j.compeleceng.2016.01.012

Kishor, A. (2008, December 11). Scan your network for security vulnerabilities using GFI languard. *Helpdeskgeek.* Retrieved on August 25, 2017 from http://helpdeskgeek.com/product-reviews/scan-your-network-for-security-vulnerabilities-using-gfi-languard/

Kizza, J. M. (2017). Cyber Crimes and hackers. In *Guide to Computer Network Security* (pp. 105–131). Springer International Publishing. doi:10.1007/978-3-319-55606-2_5

Kleinberg, J. (2008). The convergence of social and technological networks. *Communications of the ACM, 51*(11), 66–72. doi:10.1145/1400214.1400232

Kocher, P. C. (1998). On certificate revocation and validation. In R. Hirchfeld (Ed.), *Financial Cryptography: Proceedings of Financial Cryptography 1998 (LNCS)* (Vol. 1465, pp. 172–177). Berlin, Germany: Springer; doi:10.1007/BFb0055481

Kodovský, J., & Fridrich, J. (2012). Steganalysis of JPEG Images Using Rich Models. *Proceedings SPIE, Electronic Imaging, Media Watermarking, Security, and Forensics 2012, 8303.* 10.1117/12.907495

Kodovský, J., & Fridrich, J. (2011). Steganalysis in high dimensions: Fusing classifiers built on random subspaces. *Proceedings SPIE, Electronic Imaging, Media Watermarking, Security and Forensics of Multimedia XIII, 7880*, 1–13.

Kodovský, J., Fridrich, J., & Holub, V. (2012). Ensemble classifiers for steganalysis of digital media. *IEEE Transactions on Information Forensics and Security, 7*(2), 432–444. doi:10.1109/TIFS.2011.2175919

Kolias, C., Kambourakis, G., & Maragoudakis, M. (2011). Swarm intelligence in intrusion detection: A survey. *Computers & Security, 30*(8), 625–642. doi:10.1016/j.cose.2011.08.009

Krizhevsky, A., Sutskever, I., & Hinton, G. (2012). Imagenet classification with deep convolutional neural networks. Proceedings of Communications of the ACM, 60(6), 84-90.

Kshetri, N. (2014). The emerging role of Big Data in key development issues: Opportunities, challenges, and concerns. *Big Data & Society, 1*(2). doi:10.1177/2053951714564227

Kumar, A., & Zhang, D. (2005, July). Biometric recognition using feature selection and combination. In *International Conference on Audio-and Video-Based Biometric Person Authentication* (pp. 813-822). Springer Berlin Heidelberg. 10.1007/11527923_85

Kumar, A., & Zhou, Y. (2009, September). Human identification using knuckle codes. In *Biometrics: Theory, Applications, and Systems, 2009. BTAS'09. IEEE 3rd International Conference on* (pp. 1-6). IEEE.

Kumar, R., Chandra, P., & Hanmandlu, M. (2013b, December). Fingerprint matching using rotational invariant image based descriptor and machine learning techniques. In *Emerging Trends in Engineering and Technology (ICETET), 2013 6th International Conference on* (pp. 13-18). IEEE.

Kumar, R., Chandra, P., & Hanmandlu, M. (2013c, December). Local directional pattern (LDP) based fingerprint matching using SLFNN. In *Image Information Processing (ICIIP), 2013 IEEE Second International Conference on* (pp. 493-498). IEEE.

Kumar, R., Chandra, P., & Hanmandlu, M. (2016). A Robust Fingerprint Matching System Using Orientation Features. *Journal of Information Processing Systems*, *12*(1), 83-99.

Kumar, A., & Prathyusha, K. V. (2009). Personal authentication using hand vein triangulation and knuckle shape. *IEEE Transactions on Image Processing*, *18*(9), 2127–2136. doi:10.1109/TIP.2009.2023153 PMID:19447728

Kumar, A., & Ravikanth, C. (2009). Personal authentication using finger knuckle surface. *IEEE Transactions on Information Forensics and Security*, *4*(1), 98–110. doi:10.1109/TIFS.2008.2011089

Kumar, A., & Zhou, Y. (2009). Personal identification using finger knuckle orientation features. *Electronics Letters*, *45*(20), 1023–1025. doi:10.1049/el.2009.1435

Kumar, P., Kumar, R., Kumar, S., & Kumar, R. D. (2010). Improved modified reverse AODV protocol. *International Journal of Computers and Applications*, *12*(4), 22–26. doi:10.5120/1665-2242

Kumar, R. (2017). Fingerprint matching using rotational invariant orientation local binary pattern descriptor and machine learning techniques. *International Journal of Computer Vision and Image Processing*, *7*(4), 51–67. doi:10.4018/IJCVIP.2017100105

Kumar, R. (2017). Hand Image Biometric Based Personal Authentication System. In *Intelligent Techniques in Signal Processing for Multimedia Security* (pp. 201–226). Springer International Publishing. doi:10.1007/978-3-319-44790-2_10

Kumar, R., Arun, P., & Selvakumar, S. (2009, March). Distributed denial-of-service (ddos) threat in collaborative environment-a survey on ddos attack tools and traceback mechanisms. In *Proceedings of the IEEE International Advance Computing Conference* (pp. 1275-1280).

Kumar, R., Chandra, P., & Hanmandlu, M. (2012a). Fingerprint matching based on orientation feature. *Advanced Materials Research*, *403*, 888–894.

Kumar, R., Chandra, P., & Hanmandlu, M. (2012b). Fingerprint singular point detection using orientation field reliability. *Advanced Materials Research*, *403*, 4499–4506.

Kumar, R., Chandra, P., & Hanmandlu, M. (2012c). Statistical descriptors for fingerprint matching. *International Journal of Computers and Applications*, *59*(16).

Kumar, R., Chandra, P., & Hanmandlu, M. (2013a). *Fingerprint matching based on texture feature. In Mobile communication and power engineering* (pp. 86–91). Berlin: Springer. doi:10.1007/978-3-642-35864-7_12

Kumar, R., Chandra, P., & Hanmandlu, M. (2014a). Rotational invariant fingerprint matching using local directional descriptors. *International Journal of Computational Intelligence Studies*, *3*(4), 292–319. doi:10.1504/IJCISTUDIES.2014.067032

Kumar, R., Hanmandlu, M., & Chandra, P. (2014b). An empirical evaluation of rotation invariance of LDP feature for fingerprint matching using neural networks. *International Journal of Computational Vision and Robotics*, *4*(4), 330–348. doi:10.1504/IJCVR.2014.065569

Kushner, D. (2013). The Real Story of Stuxnet. Retrieved from http://www.nytimes.com/2012/06/04/technology/cyberweapon-warning-from-kaspersky-a-computer-security-expert.html?pagewanted=all

Kuwatly, I., Sraj, M., Al Masri, Z., & Artail, H. (2004, July). A dynamic honeypot design for intrusion detection. In *Proceedings of the IEEE/ACS International Conference on Pervasive Services ICPS '04* (pp. 95-104). IEEE.

Kuyoro Shade, O., Frank, I., Awodele, O., & Okolie Samuel, O. (2012). Security issues in web services. *International Journal of Computer Science and Network Security, 12*(1).

Ladd, W. (2012). *Blind signatures for bitcoin transaction anonymity*. Retrieved from http://wbl.github.io/bitcoinanon.pdf

Lafferty & Ahmed. (2004). Texture based steganalysis: results for color images. *Proceedings of SPIE, Mathematics of Data/Image Coding, compression and encryption VII with applications, 5561*, 145-151.

Lafuente, G. (2015). The big data security challenge. *Network Security, 2015*(1), 12–14. doi:10.1016/S1353-4858(15)70009-7

Larbi, S. D., & Jaïdane-Saïdane, M. (2005). Audio watermarking: A way to stationnarize audio signals. *IEEE Transactions on Signal Processing, 53*(2), 816–823. doi:10.1109/TSP.2004.839899

Larsson, P. (2006). Developments in the regulation of economic crime in Norway. *Journal of Financial Crime, 13*(1), 65–76. doi:10.1108/13590790610641242

Laudon, K. C., & Laudon, J. P. (2004). Management information systems: Managing the digital firm.

Lauter, Naehrig, & Vaikuntanathan. (2011). Can homomorphic encryption be practical? ACM-CCSW, 113–124.

Lecuyer, M., Spahn, R., Geambasu, R., Huang, T.-K., & Sen, S. (2017). Pyramid: Enhancing Selectivity in Big Data Protection with Count Featurization. *2017 IEEE Symposium on Security and Privacy (SP)*. 10.1109/SP.2017.60

Lee, D. W. (2016). A Study on Actual Cases & Meanings for Internet of Things. *International Journal of Software Engineering and Its Applications, 10*(1), 287–294. doi:10.14257/ijseia.2016.10.1.28

Legal Dictionary. (n.d.). Bank Fraud. Retrieved from https://legaldictionary.net/bank-fraud/

Lemon, J. (2002, February). Resisting SYN Flood DoS Attacks with a SYN Cache. In *BSDCon* (pp. 89-97).

Le-Qing, Z. (2011, July). Finger knuckle print recognition based on SURF algorithm. In *Fuzzy Systems and Knowledge Discovery (FSKD), 2011 Eighth International Conference on (Vol. 3*, pp. 1879-1883). IEEE.

Lerch-Hostalot, D., & Megías, D. (2013). LSB matching steganalysis based on patterns of pixel differences and random embedding. *Computers & Security, 32*, 192–206. doi:10.1016/j.cose.2012.11.005

Lerch-Hostalot, D., & Megías, D. (2016) Unsupervised steganalysis based on artificial training sets. *Proceedings of EngApplArtifIntell, 50*, 45–59. 10.1016/j.engappai.2015.12.013

Lewis, J. (2003). Cyber Terror: Missing in Action. *Knowledge, Technology & Policy, 16*(2), 34–41. doi:10.100712130-003-1024-6

Li, B., Liu, Y., & Chu, G. (2010, August). Improved AODV routing protocol for vehicular Ad hoc networks. In *Proceedings of the 2010 3rd International Conference on Advanced Computer Theory and Engineering (ICACTE) (Vol. 4*, pp. V4-337). IEEE.

Li, N. (2007). t-Closeness: privacy beyond k-anonymity and L-diversity. *IEEE 23rd international conference on Data engineering (ICDE)*.

Li, X., & Xue, Y. (2011). A survey on web application security. Vanderbuilt University, Nashville, TN.

Li, Y., & Hu, W. (2010, September). Optimization strategy for mobile ad hoc network based on AODV routing protocol. In *Proceedings of the 2010 6th International Conference on Wireless Communications Networking and Mobile Computing (WiCOM)*. IEEE. 10.1109/WICOM.2010.5601193

Lim, K. (2015). Big Data and Strategic Intelligence. *Intelligence and National Security*, *31*(4), 619–635. doi:10.1080/02684527.2015.1062321

Lindsay, J. R. (2013). Stuxnet and the Limits of Cyber Warfare. *Security Studies*, *22*(3), 365–404. doi:10.1080/09636412.2013.816122

Lipson, H. F. (2002). Tracking and tracing cyber-attacks: Technical challenges and global policy issues. Retrieved from https://resources.sei.cmu.edu/library/asset-view.cfm?assetid=5831

Li, T., Tang, J., & Xu, J. (2016). Performance Modeling and Predictive Scheduling for Distributed Stream Data Processing. *IEEE Transactions on Big Data*, *2*(4), 353–364. doi:10.1109/TBDATA.2016.2616148

Liu, H. (2010, October). A new form of DOS attack in a cloud and its avoidance mechanism. In *Proceedings of the 2010 ACM workshop on Cloud computing security workshop* (pp. 65-76). 10.1145/1866835.1866849

Liu, J., Xiao, Y., Ghaboosi, K., Deng, H., & Zhang, J. (2009, December). Botnet: Classification, attacks, detection, tracing, and preventive measures. *EURASIP Journal on Wireless Communications and Networking*, *2009*(1), 1184–1187. doi:10.1155/2009/692654

Liu, L., Zhu, L., Lin, L., & Wu, Q. (2012). Improvement of AODV routing protocol with QoS support in wireless mesh networks. *Physics Procedia*, *25*, 1133–1140. doi:10.1016/j.phpro.2012.03.210

Liu, Q., Sung, A. H., Qiao, M., Chen, Z., & Ribeiro, B. (2010). An improved approach to steganalysis of JPEG images. *Information Sciences*, *180*(9), 1643–1655. doi:10.1016/j.ins.2010.01.001

Liu, S. (2011). Exploring the future of computing. *IT Professional*, *15*(1), 2–3. doi:10.1109/MITP.2012.120

Liu, S., Yao, H., & Wen, G. (2003). Neural Network based steganalysis in Still Images. *Proceedings of IEEE International Conference on Multimedia and Expo (ICME)*, 509-512. doi:10.1109/ICME.2003.1221665

Liu, W., & Yu, M. (2014). AASR: Authenticated anonymous secure routing for MANETs in adversarial environments. *IEEE Transactions on Vehicular Technology*, *63*(9), 4585–4593. doi:10.1109/TVT.2014.2313180

Li, W., Xue, X., & Lu, P. (2006). Localized audio watermarking technique robust against time-scale modification. *IEEE Transactions on Multimedia*, *8*(1), 60–69. doi:10.1109/TMM.2005.861291

Li, X., Liang, X., Lu, R., Shen, X., Lin, X., & Zhu, H. (2012). Securing smart grid: Cyber attacks, countermeasures, and challenges. *IEEE Communications Magazine*, *50*(8), 38–45. doi:10.1109/MCOM.2012.6257525

Long, N., & Thomas, R. (2001). Trends in denial of service attack technology. *CERT Coordination Center*. Retrieved from https://resources.sei.cmu.edu/library/asset-view.cfm?assetid=52490

Lyu, S., & Farid, H. (2004). Steganalysis using color wavelet statistics and one-class vector support Machines. Proceedings of SPIE security, steganography and watermarking of multimedia contents, 5306, 35–45. doi:10.1117/12.526012

Machanavajjhala, A., Gehrkc, J., Kifer, D., & Venkitasubramaniam, M. (2006). L-diversity: privacy beyond k-anonymity. *Proceedings of 22nd International Conference Data Engineering (ICDE)*. 10.1109/ICDE.2006.1

MadhanMohan, R., & Selvakumar, K. (2012). Power controlled routing in wireless ad hoc networks using cross layer approach. *Egyptian Informatics Journal, 13*(2), 95–101. doi:10.1016/j.eij.2012.05.001

Makhoul, A., Guyeux, C., Hakem, M., & Bahi, J. M. (2016). Using an epidemiological approach to maximize data survival in the Internet of Things. *ACM Transactions on Internet Technology, 16*(1), 5. doi:10.1145/2812810

Malan, G. R., & Jahanian, F. (1998). An extensible probe architecture for network protocol performance measurement, In *Proceedings of ACM SIGCOMM '98 conference on Applications, technologies, architectures, and protocols for computer communication* (pp. 215-227). Vancouver, Canada: ACM. 10.1145/285237.285284

Malek, A. G., Chunlin, L. I., Zhiyong, Y., Hasan, A. N., & Xiaoqing, Z. (2012). Improved the energy of ad hoc on-demand distance vector routing protocol. *IERI Procedia, 2*, 355–361. doi:10.1016/j.ieri.2012.06.101

Malliga, S., & Tamilarasi, A. (2010). A hybrid scheme using packet marking and logging for IP traceback. *International Journal of Internet Protocol Technology, 5*(1-2), 81–91. doi:10.1504/IJIPT.2010.032617

Mall, R. (2009). *Real-time systems: theory and practice.* Pearson Education India.

Maltoni, D., Maio, D., Jain, A., & Prabhakar, S. (2009). *Handbook of fingerprint recognition.* Springer Science & Business Media. doi:10.1007/978-1-84882-254-2

Manikandakumar, M., Mano Sharmi, K., & Shanthini Devi, S. (2015). Analyzing Spam Messages and Detecting the Zombies Using Spam Count and Percentage Based Detection Algorithm. *International Journal of Applied Engineering Research, 10*(55), 1284–1289.

Manikandakumar, M., & Shanthini Devi, S., & VengaLakshmi, S. (2015). A Survey on Data Warehousing and Data Mining Technology for Business Intelligence. *International Journal of Applied Engineering Research, 10*(77), 352–356.

Marin, G. A. (2005). Network security basics. *IEEE Security and Privacy, 3*(6), 68–72. doi:10.1109/MSP.2005.153

Matallah, H., Belalem, G., & Bouamrane, K. (2017, October). Towards a new model of storage and access to data in Big Data and Cloud Computing. *International Journal of Ambient Computing and Intelligence, 8*(4), 31–44. doi:10.4018/IJACI.2017100103

Mate, M. H., & Kapse, S. R. (2015). Network Forensic Tool -- Concept and Architecture. In *Proceedings of the Fifth International Conference on Communication Systems and Network Technologies (CSNT)* (pp. 711-713), Gwalior, India: Academic Press. doi: 10.1109/CSNT.2015.204

Mathews, M. L., Joshi, A., & Finin, T. (2016, February). Detecting botnets using a collaborative situational-aware idps. In *Proceedings of the Second International Conference on Information Systems Security and Privacy* (Vol. 1, pp. 290-298). 10.5220/0005684902900298

Ma, X., & Wu, D. (2014). Research on Information Security Issues Facing the Era of Big Data. *Applied Mechanics and Materials, 651-653*, 1913–1916. . doi:10.4028/www.scientific.net/AMM.651-653.1913

Ma, X., Zhang, J., Li, Z., Li, J., Tao, J., Guan, X., ... Towsley, D. (2015). Accurate DNS query characteristics estimation via active probing. *Journal of Network and Computer Applications, 47*, 72–84. doi:10.1016/j.jnca.2014.09.016

Maxwell, J. C. (1892). *A treatise on electricity and magnetism* (3rd ed.; Vol. 2). Clarendon Press.

McKinsey Global Institute. (2011). *Big data: The next frontier for innovation, competition, and productivity.* Author.

Mehmood, Natgunanathan, Xiang, Hua, & Guo. (2016). Protection of Big Data Privacy. *IEEE Access on Special Section on Theoretical Foundations for Big data Applications: Challenges and Opportunities,* 1821 – 1834.

Mehmood, A., Natgunanathan, I., Xiang, Y., Hua, G., & Guo, S. (2016). *Protection of big data privacy*. IEEE Translations and Content Mining.

Meiklejohn, S., Pomarole, M., Jordan, G., Levchenko, K., McCoy, D., Voelker, G. M., & Savage, S. (2013, October). A fistful of bitcoins: characterizing payments among men with no names. In *Proceedings of the 2013 conference on Internet measurement conference* (pp. 127-140). ACM. 10.1145/2504730.2504747

Mejri, M. N., & Ben-Othman, J. (2017). GDVAN: A New Greedy Behavior Attack Detection Algorithm for VANETs. *IEEE Transactions on Mobile Computing, 16*(3), 759–771. doi:10.1109/TMC.2016.2577035

Merkle, R. C. (1988). A digital signature based on a conventional encryption function. In Proceedings of Advances in Cryptology - CRYPTO '87 (LNCS) (vol. 293, pp. 369-378). Springer Berlin Heidelberg. doi:10.1007/3-540-48184-2_32

Merkle, R. C. (1982). *Secrecy, Authentication and Public Key Systems*. UMI Research Press.

Merkle, R. C. (1987, August). A digital signature based on a conventional encryption function. In *Conference on the Theory and Application of Cryptographic Techniques* (pp. 369-378). Springer.

Messai, M. L. (2014). Classification of Attacks in Wireless Sensor Networks. arXiv:1406.4516

Meyerson, A., & Williams, R. (2004). On the complexity of optimal k-anonymity. *Proceedings of the ACM Symposium on Principles of Database Systems*.

Miciuła, I., & Miciuła, K. (2015). The key trends for business building in the industry of big data. *Zeszyty Naukowe Uniwersytetu Szczecińskiego. Studia Informatica, 36*, 51–63. doi:10.18276i.2015.36-04

Miessler, D. (2015). *A tcpdump Tutorial and Primer with Examples*. Retrieved September 28, 2017, from https://danielmiessler.com/study/tcpdump/

Miglani, A., Bhatia, T., Sharma, G., & Shrivastava, G. (2017). An energy efficient and trust aware framework for secure routing in LEACH for wireless sensor networks. scalable computing. *Practice and Experience, 18*(3), 207–218.

Miglani, A., Bhatia, T., Sharma, G., & Shrivastava, G. (2017). An Energy Efficient and Trust Aware Framework for Secure Routing in LEACH for Wireless Sensor Networks. Scalable Computing. *Practice and Experience, 18*(3), 207–218.

Milne, G. R. (2003). How well do consumers protect themselves from identity theft? *The Journal of Consumer Affairs, 37*(2), 388–402. doi:10.1111/j.1745-6606.2003.tb00459.x

Miner, S., & Staddon, J. (2001). Graph-based authentication of digital streams. In *Proceedings of IEEE Symposium on Security and Privacy (S&P)* (pp. 232–246). Oakland, CA: IEEE. doi: 10.1109/SECPRI.2001.924301

Miorandi, D., Sicari, S., De Pellegrini, F., & Chlamtac, I. (2012). Internet of things: Vision, applications and research challenges. *Ad Hoc Networks, 10*(7), 1497–1516. doi:10.1016/j.adhoc.2012.02.016

Mirkovic, J., & Reiher, P. (2004). A taxonomy of DDoS attack and DDoS defense mechanisms. *Computer Communication Review, 34*(2), 39–53. doi:10.1145/997150.997156

Mishra, A., Nadkarni, K., & Patcha, A. (2004). Intrusion detection in wireless ad hoc networks. *IEEE Wireless Communications, 11*(1), 48–60. doi:10.1109/MWC.2004.1269717

Mishra, Y., Singhadia, A., & Pandey, R. (2014). Energy Level Based Stable Election Protocol in Wireless Sensor Network. *International Journal of Engineering Trends and Technology, 17*(1), 32–38. doi:10.14445/22315381/IJETT-V17P206

Moore, T., & Christin, N. (2013, April). Beware the middleman: Empirical analysis of Bitcoin-exchange risk. In *International Conference on Financial Cryptography and Data Security* (pp. 25-33). Springer. 10.1007/978-3-642-39884-1_3

Morales, A., Travieso, C. M., Ferrer, M. A., & Alonso, J. B. (2011). Improved finger-knuckle-print authentication based on orientation enhancement. *Electronics Letters*, *47*(6), 380–381. doi:10.1049/el.2011.0156

Morris, J., Smalley, S., & Kroah-Hartman, G. (2002, August). Linux security modules: General security support for the Linux kernel. *USENIX Security Symposium*.

Muhaimin, H., Danudirdjo, D., Suksmono, A. B., & Shin, D. H. (2015, August). An efficient audio watermark by autocorrelation methods. In *Electrical Engineering and Informatics (ICEEI), 2015 International Conference on* (pp. 606-611). IEEE. 10.1109/ICEEI.2015.7352571

Mukherjee, A., Dey, N., Kausar, N., Ashour, A. S., Taiar, R., & Hassanien, A. E. (2016). A disaster management specific mobility model for flying ad-hoc network. *International Journal of Rough Sets and Data Analysis*, *3*(3), 72–103. doi:10.4018/IJRSDA.2016070106

Mythili, K., & Anandakumar, H. (2013). Trust management approach for secure and privacy data access in cloud computing. In *2013 International Conference on Green Computing, Communication and Conservation of Energy (ICGCE)*. IEEE.

Nadeem, A., & Howarth, M. P. (2013). A survey of MANET intrusion detection & prevention approaches for network layer attacks. *IEEE Communications Surveys and Tutorials*, *15*(4), 2027–2045. doi:10.1109/SURV.2013.030713.00201

Nakamoto, S. (2008). *Bitcoin: A Peer-to Peer Electronic Cash System*. Retrieved from https://bitcoin.org/bitcoin.pdf

Nakhaee, A., Harounabadi, A., & Mirabedini, J. (2011, October). A novel communication model to improve Mobile Ad hoc Network routing reliability. In *Proceedings of the 2011 5th International Conference on Application of Information and Communication Technologies (AICT)*. IEEE. 10.1109/ICAICT.2011.6110971

Naor, D., Shenhav, A., & Wool, A. (2006). One-Time Signatures Revisited: Practical Fast Signatures Using Fractal Merkle Tree Traversal. In *Proceedings of the 24th Convention of Electrical & Electronics Engineers in Israel* (pp. 255-259). Eilat, Israel: Academic Press. doi: 10.1109/EEEI.2006.321066

Neela, K., & Kavitha, V. (2017). Enhancement of data confidentiality and secure data transaction in cloud storage environment. *Cluster Computing*. doi:10.100710586-017-0959-4

Neha, J.A. (2015). Social Networking and Securing the IoT. *International Journal of Science and Research*.

NfDump. (2017). Retrieved March 1, 2017 from http://nfdump.sourceforge.net/

Ning, H., & Wang, Z. (2011). Future internet of things architecture: Like mankind neural system or social organization framework? *IEEE Communications Letters*, *15*(4), 461–463. doi:10.1109/LCOMM.2011.022411.110120

Nishanthini, C., Rajkumar, G., & Jayabhavani, G. N. (2013, January). Enhanced performance of AODV with power boosted alternate path. In *Proceedings of the 2013 International Conference on Computer Communication and Informatics (ICCCI)*. IEEE. 10.1109/ICCCI.2013.6466148

Nitti, M., Girau, R., Atzori, L., Iera, A., & Morabito, G. (2012, September). A subjective model for trustworthiness evaluation in the social internet of things. In *Proceedings of the 2012 IEEE 23rd International Symposium on Personal Indoor and Mobile Radio Communications (PIMRC)* (pp. 18-23). IEEE. 10.1109/PIMRC.2012.6362662

Northeastern University. (1898) Northeastern. Retrieved from www.northeastern.edu/neuhome/academics/departments-programs.html

Nykodym, N., Ariss, S., & Kurtz, K. (2008). Computer addiction and cyber-crime. *Journal of Leadership, Accountability and Ethics*, *35*, 55–59.

Ogilvie, E. (2000, December). The Internet and cyberstalking. In *Proceedings of Criminal Justice Responses Conference*, Sydney.

Ollmann, G. (2009). Botnet communication topologies. *Retrieved from* http://www.technicalinfo.net/papers/PDF/WP_Botnet_Communications_Primer_(2009-06-04).pdf

OpenSSL library. (2016). *Welcome to OpenSSL!* Retrieved from http://www.openssl.org/

Osanaiye, O., Choo, K. K. R., & Dlodlo, M. (2016). Distributed denial of service (DDoS) resilience in cloud: Review and conceptual cloud DDoS mitigation framework. *Journal of Network and Computer Applications, 67*, 147–165. doi:10.1016/j.jnca.2016.01.001

Ozsoyoglu, Singer, & Chung. (2003). Anti-tamper databases: Querying encrypted databases. *Proceedings of the 17th Annual IFIP WG 11.3 Working Conference on Database and Applications Security.*

Padmavathi, S., & Ramanujam, E. (2015). Naïve Bayes classifier for ecg abnormalities using multivariate maximal time series Motif. *Procedia Computer Science, 47*, 222–228. doi:10.1016/j.procs.2015.03.201

Panda, J., & Kumar, M. (2011, October). Application of energy efficient watermark on audio signal for authentication. In *Computational Intelligence and Communication Networks (CICN), 2011 International Conference on* (pp. 202-206). IEEE. 10.1109/CICN.2011.40

Panja, B., Ogunyanwo, O., & Meharia, P. (2014, June). Training of intelligent intrusion detection system using neuro fuzzy. In *Proceedings of the 2014 15th IEEE/ACIS International Conference on Software Engineering, Artificial Intelligence, Networking and Parallel/Distributed Computing (SNPD).* IEEE. 10.1109/SNPD.2014.6888688

Paramasivan, B., Prakash, M. J. V., & Kaliappan, M. (2015). Development of a secure routing protocol using game theory model in mobile ad hoc networks. *Journal of Communications and Networks (Seoul), 17*(1), 75–83. doi:10.1109/JCN.2015.000012

Park, G., Chung, L., Khan, L., & Park, S. (2017). A modeling framework for business process reengineering using big data analytics and a goal-orientation. *2017 11th International Conference on Research Challenges in Information Science (RCIS).* doi:10.1109/rcis.2017.7956514

Park, K., & Lee, H. (2001, August). On the effectiveness of route-based packet filtering for distributed DoS attack prevention in power-law internets. *Computer Communication Review, 31*(4), 15–26. doi:10.1145/964723.383061

Parry, J., Hunter, D., Radke, K., & Fidge, C. (2016). A network forensics tool for precise data packet capture and replay in cyber-physical systems. In *Proceedings of the Australasian Computer Science Week Multiconference (ACSW)* (pp. 1-10). Canberra, Australia: Academic Press. 10.1145/2843043.2843047

Pathak & Selvakumar. (2014). Blind image steganalysis of JPEG images using feature extraction through the process of dilation. *Digital Investigation, 11*, 97–77.

Patil, V. P. (2012). Efficient AODV Routing Protocol for MANET with enhanced packet delivery ratio and minimized end to end delay. *International journal of scientific and Research Publications, 2*(8).

Pattanayak, B. K., & Rath, M. (2014). A mobile agent based intrusion detection system architecture for mobile ad hoc networks. *Journal of Computational Science, 10*(6), 970–975. doi:10.3844/jcssp.2014.970.975

Paul, G., Sarkar, P., & Mukherjee, S. (2014, December). Towards a more democratic mining in bitcoins. In *International Conference on Information Systems Security* (pp. 185-203). Springer. 10.1007/978-3-319-13841-1_11

Pease, S. G., Phillips, I. W., & Guan, L. (2016). Adaptive intelligent middleware architecture for mobile real-time communications. *IEEE Transactions on Mobile Computing*, *15*(3), 572–585. doi:10.1109/TMC.2015.2412932

Peisert, S., Bishop, M., Karin, S., & Marzullo, K. (2005). Principles-Driven Forensic Analysis. In *Proceedings of the 2005 New Security Paradigms Workshop (NSPW)* (pp. 85-93). Lake Arrowhead, CA: Academic Press. 10.1145/1146269.1146291

Peltier, T. R. (2016). *Information Security Policies, Procedures, and Standards: guidelines for effective information security management*. CRC Press.

Peng, J., & Sikdar, B. (2003, December). A multicast congestion control scheme for mobile ad-hoc networks. In *Proceedings of the Global Telecommunications Conference GLOBECOM'03* (Vol. 5, pp. 2860-2864). IEEE.

Pérez, M. G., Celdrán, A. H., Ippoliti, F., Giardina, P. G., Bernini, G., Alaez, R. M., ... Carrozzo, G. (2017). Dynamic Reconfiguration in 5G Mobile Networks to Proactively Detect and Mitigate Botnets. *IEEE Internet Computing*, *21*(5), 28–36. doi:10.1109/MIC.2017.3481345

Perrig, A., Song, D., Canetti, R., Tygar, J. D., & Briscoe, B. (2005). *Timed Efficient Stream Loss-Tolerant Authentication (TESLA): Multicast source authentication transform introduction*. IETF, RFC-4082. Retrieved July 14, 2017 from https://tools.ietf.org/html/rfc3447

Perrig, A., Tygar, J., Song, D., & Canetti, R. Efficient. (2000). Authentication and Signing of Multicast Streams over Lossy Channels. In *Proceeding 2000 IEEE Symposium on Security and Privacy* (pp. 56–63). Berkeley, CA: IEEE. 10.1109/SECPRI.2000.848446

Petroni, M. J. (n.d.). The Social Network of Things. *CauseIT*. Retrieved June 05, 2017, from http://www.causeit.org/the-social-network-of-things/

Pevný, T., Filler, T., & Bas, P. (2010). Using high-dimensional image models to perform highly undetectable steganography. In *Information Hiding, 12th International Workshop, Lecture Notes in Computer Science*. Springer-Verlag. 10.1007/978-3-642-16435-4_13

Pevny, T., Fridrich, J., & Ker, A. D. (2012). From blind to quantitative Steganalysis. *IEEE Transactions on Information Forensics and Security*, *7*(2), 445–454. doi:10.1109/TIFS.2011.2175918

Pibre, L., Pasquet, J., Ienco, D., & Chaumont, M. (2016). Deep learning is a good steganalysis tool when embedding key is reused for different images, even if there is a cover source-mismatch. *Proceedings of SPIE, IS&T International Symposium on Electronic Imaging, Media Watermarking, Security, and Forensics*. 10.2352/ISSN.2470-1173.2016.8.MWSF-078

Picard, M. (2009). Financial services in trouble: The electronic dimension. *Journal of Financial Crime*, *16*(2), 180–192. doi:10.1108/13590790910951858

Pickett, K. S., & Pickett, J. M. (2002). *Financial crime investigation and control*. John Wiley & Sons.

Pinzón, C., & Rocha, C. (2016). Double-spend Attack Models with Time Advantange for Bitcoin. *Electronic Notes in Theoretical Computer Science*, *329*, 79–103. doi:10.1016/j.entcs.2016.12.006

Pohly, D., McLaughlin, S., McDaniel, P., & Butler, K. (2012). Hi-Fi: Collecting High-Fidelity Whole-System Provenance. *Proceedings of Annual Computer Security Applications Conference*.

Pontell, H. N., Geis, G., & Brown, G. C. (2007). Offshore internet gambling and the World Trade Organization: Is it criminal behavior or a commodity? *International Journal of Cyber Criminology*, *1*(1), 119–136.

Popa, R. A., Zeldovich, N., & Balakrishnan. (2011). *CryptDB: A practical encrypted relational DBMS*. Technical MITCSAIL-TR-2011-005, MIT Computer Science and Artificial Intelligence Laboratory, Cambridge, MA.

Porambage, P., Ylianttila, M., Schmitt, C., Kumar, P., Gurtov, A., & Vasilakos, A. V. (2016). The quest for privacy in the Internet of Things. *IEEE Cloud Computing*, *3*(2), 36–45. doi:10.1109/MCC.2016.28

Poturalski, M., Flury, M., Papadimitratos, P., Hubaux, J. P., & Le Boudec, J. Y. (2010, September). The cicada attack: degradation and denial of service in IR ranging. In *Proceedings of the IEEE International Conference on Ultra-Wideband* (Vol. 2). 10.1109/ICUWB.2010.5616900

Prasad, K. M., Reddy, A. R. M., & Rao, K. V. (2014). *DoS and DDoS attacks: defense, detection and traceback mechanisms-a survey*. Global Journal of Computer Science and Technology.

Promrit, N., & Mingkhwan, A. (2015). Traffic Flow Classification and Visualization for Network Forensic Analysis. In *Proceedings of 29th International Conference on Advanced Information Networking and Applications* (pp. 358-364). Gwangiu, South Korea: Academic Press. 10.1109/AINA.2015.207

Provos, N., & Holz, T. (2007). *Virtual honeypots: from botnet tracking to intrusion detection*. Pearson Education database.

Provos, N. (2001). Defending Against Statistical Steganalysis. *Proceedings of 10th USENIX Security Symposium*, 323–335.

Qian, Y., Dong, J., Wang, W., & Tan, T. (2016). Learning and transferring representations for image steganalysis using convolutional neural network. *IEEE International Conference on Image Processing*, 2752–2756. DOI:10.1109/ICIP.2016.7532860

Qiankun, Z., Tingxue, X., Hongqing, Z., Chunying, Y., & Tingjun, L. (2011). A Mobile Ad Hoc Networks Algorithm Improved AODV Protocol. *Procedia Engineering*, *23*, 229–234. doi:10.1016/j.proeng.2011.11.2494

Qian, Y., Dong, J., Wang, W., & Tan, T. (2015). Deep learning for steganalysis via convolutional neural networks. In *Proceeding of SPIE 9409*. Media Watermarking, Security, and Forensics. doi:10.1117/12.2083479

Qin, Z., Denker, G., Giannelli, C., Bellavista, P., & Venkatasubramanian, N. (2014, May). A software defined networking architecture for the internet-of-things. In *Proceedings of the 2014 Network Operations and Management Symposium (NOMS)*. IEEE. 10.1109/NOMS.2014.6838365

Rabiner, L. R., & Juang, B. H. (1993). *Fundamentals of speech recognition*. Academic Press.

Rafique, S., Humayun, M., Gul, Z., Abbas, A., & Javed, H. (2015). Systematic Review of Web Application Security Vulnerabilities Detection Methods. *Journal of Computer and Communications*, *3*(09), 28–40. doi:10.4236/jcc.2015.39004

Rafizadeh, M. (2016). Al Arabiya - Iran's asymmetrical warfare: The cyberattack capabilities. Retrieved from http://english.alarabiya.net/en/views/news/middle-east/2016/04/02/Iran-s-asymmetrical-warfare-The-cyberattack-capabilities.html

Ragesh, G., & Baskaran, K. (2016). Cryptographically Enforced Data Access Control in Personal Health Record Systems. *Procedia Technology*, *25*, 473–480. doi:10.1016/j.protcy.2016.08.134

Ramanujam, T. (2009). Intrusion Detection System Using Advanced Honeypots. *International Journal of Computer Science & Information Security*, *2*(1).

Ramanujam, E., & Padmavathi, S. (2016). Multi-objective genetic motif discovery technique for time series classification. *International Journal of Business Intelligence and Data Mining*, *11*(4), 318–337. doi:10.1504/IJBIDM.2016.082214

Ramirez, E. (2015). *Privacy and the IoT: Navigating policy issues*. US FTC.

Ranum, M. J., Landfield, K., Stolarchuk, M., Sienkiewicz, M., Lambeth, A., & Wall, E. (1997). Implementing a generalized tool for network monitoring. In *Proceedings of the 11th Conference on Systems Administration* (pp. 1-8). Berkeley, CA: USENIX Association.

Rashidi, R., Jamali, M. A. J., Salmasi, A., & Tati, R. (2009, October). Trust routing protocol based on congestion control in MANET. In *Proceedings of the International Conference on Application of Information and Communication Technologies AICT '09*. IEEE. 10.1109/ICAICT.2009.5372623

Rath, M., & Panda, M. R. (2016, December). MAQ system development in mobile ad-hoc networks using mobile agents. In *Proceedings of the 2016 2nd International Conference on Contemporary Computing and Informatics (IC3I)* (pp. 794-798). IEEE. 10.1109/IC3I.2016.7918791

Rath, M., Pati, B., & Pattanayak, B. K. (2017, January). Cross layer based QoS platform for multimedia transmission in MANET. In *Proceedings of the 2017 11th International Conference on Intelligent Systems and Control (ISCO)* (pp. 402-407). IEEE. 10.1109/ISCO.2017.7856026

Rath, M., Pattanayak, B. K., & Pati, B. (2016). QoS Satisfaction in MANET Based Real Time Applications. *International Journal of Control Theory and Applications*, *9*(7), 3069-3083.

Rath, M., Pattanayak, B. K., & Pati, B. (2016, March). Inter-layer communication based QoS platform for real time multimedia applications in MANET. In *Proceedings of the International Conference on Wireless Communications, Signal Processing and Networking (WiSPNET)* (pp. 591-595). IEEE. 10.1109/WiSPNET.2016.7566203

Rath, M., Pattanayak, B., & Pati, B. (2016). Comparative analysis of AODV routing protocols based on network performance parameters in Mobile Adhoc Networks. In *Foundations and Frontiers in Computer, Communication and Electrical Engineering* (pp. 461-466).

Rathee, A., Singh, R., & Nandini, A. (2016). Wireless Sensor Network-Challenges and Possibilities. *International Journal of Computers and Applications*, *140*(2).

Rath, M., Pati, B., Pattanayak, B. K., Panigrahi, C. R., & Sarkar, J. L. (2017). Load balanced routing scheme for MANETs with power and delay optimisation. *International Journal of Communication Networks and Distributed Systems*, *19*(4), 394–405. doi:10.1504/IJCNDS.2017.087386

Rath, M., & Pattanayak, B. K. (2017). MAQ: A Mobile Agent Based Quality of Service Platform for MANETs. *International Journal of Business Data Communications and Networking*, *13*(1). doi:10.4018/IJBDCN.2017010101

Rath, M., Pattanayak, B. K., & Pati, B. (2015). Energy Competent Routing Protocol Design in MANET with Real Time Application Provision. *International Journal of Business Data Communications and Networking*, *11*(1), 50–60. doi:10.4018/IJBDCN.2015010105

Rath, M., Pattanayak, B. K., & Pati, B. (2016). Energy Efficient MANET Protocol Using Cross Layer Design for Military Applications. *Defence Science Journal*, *66*(2), 146–150. doi:10.14429/dsj.66.9705

Rath, M., Pattanayak, B. K., & Pati, B. (2016). Resource Reservation and Improved QoS for Real Time Applications in MANET. *Indian Journal of Science and Technology*, *9*(36). doi:10.17485/ijst/2016/v9i36/100910

Rath, M., Pattanayak, B. K., & Pati, B. (2017). Energetic Routing Protocol Design for Real-time Transmission in Mobile Ad hoc Network. In *Computing and Network Sustainability* (pp. 187–199). Singapore: Springer. doi:10.1007/978-981-10-3935-5_20

Rath, M., Pattanayak, B., & Pati, B. (2016). A Contemporary Survey and Analysis of Delay and Power Based Routing Protocols in MANET. *Journal of Engineering and Applied Sciences (Asian Research Publishing Network)*, *11*(1).

Rath, M., Rout, U. P., Pujari, N., Nanda, S. K., & Panda, S. P. (2017). Congestion Control Mechanism for Real Time Traffic in Mobile Adhoc Networks. In *Computer Communication, Networking and Internet Security* (pp. 149–156). Singapore: Springer. doi:10.1007/978-981-10-3226-4_14

Ravikanth, C., & Kumar, A. (2007, June). Biometric authentication using finger-back surface. In *Computer Vision and Pattern Recognition, 2007. CVPR'07. IEEE Conference on* (pp. 1-6). IEEE.

Raw, R. S., Kumar, M., & Singh, N. (2013). Security challenges, issues and their solutions for VANET. *International Journal of Network Security & Its Applications*, *5*(5), 95–105. doi:10.5121/ijnsa.2013.5508

Reina, D. G., Toral, S. L., Barrero, F., Bessis, N., & Asimakopoulou, E. (2013). The role of ad hoc networks in the internet of things: A case scenario for smart environments. In *Internet of Things and Inter-Cooperative Computational Technologies for Collective Intelligence* (pp. 89–113). Springer Berlin Heidelberg. doi:10.1007/978-3-642-34952-2_4

Reuters, T. (2010). *Web of Science*. Retrieved from https://clarivate.com/products/web-of-science/

Rieke, R., Zhdanova, M., Repp, J., Giot, R., & Gaber, C. (2013, September). Fraud detection in mobile payments utilizing process behavior analysis. In *Availability, Reliability and Security (ARES), 2013 Eighth International Conference on* (pp. 662-669). IEEE. 10.1109/ARES.2013.87

Rivest, R. L., & Shamir, A. (1997). PayWord and MicroMint: Two simple micropayment schemes. In M. Lomas (Ed.), *Security Protocols: Proceedings of Security Protocols 1996. (LNCS)* (Vol. 1189, pp. 69–87). Berlin, Germany: Springer; doi:10.1007/3-540-62494-5_6

Rivest, R., Shamir, A., & Adleman, L. (1978). A method for obtaining digital signatures and public-key cryptosystems. *Communications of the ACM*, *21*(2), 120–126. doi:10.1145/359340.359342

Roesch, M. (1999). Snort—Lightweight intrusion detection for networks. In *Proceedings of the 13th USENIX conference on System administration*, Seattle, WA (pp. 229-238).

Romdhani, I. (2017). Security Concerns in Social IoT. In Securing the Internet of Things (pp. 131–132). Cambridge, MA: Syngress. Retrieved May 08, 2017. doi:10.1016/B978-0-12-804458-2.00008-1

Rose, K., Eldridge, S., & Chapin, L. (2015). The internet of things: An overview. *The Internet Society (ISOC)*.

Ruiz, M., Sutter, G., López-Buedo, S., & de Vergara, J. E. L. (2016). FPGA-based encrypted network traffic identification at 100 Gbit/s. In *Proceedings of International Conference on ReConFigurable Computing and FPGAs (ReConFig)* (pp. 1-6). Cancun, Mexico: Academic Press. 10.1109/ReConFig.2016.7857172

Russakovsky, O., Deng, J., Su, H., Krause, J., Satheesh, S., Ma, S., ... Li, F.-F. (2015). ImageNet large scale visual recognition challenge. *International Journal of Computer Vision*, *115*(3), 211–252. doi:10.100711263-015-0816-y

Saad, S., Traore, I., Ghorbani, A., Sayed, B., Zhao, D., & Lu, W. et al. (2011). Detecting P2P botnets through network behavior analysis and machine learning. In Proceedings of ninth annual international conference on privacy, security and trust, Montreal, Canada (pp. 174–80).

Sabeti, V., Samavi, S., Mahdavi, M., & Shirani, S. (2010). Steganalysis and payload estimation of embedding in pixel differences using neural networks. *Pattern Recognition*, *43*(1), 405–415. doi:10.1016/j.patcog.2009.06.006

Safa, H., Karam, M., & Moussa, B. (2014). PHAODV: Power aware heterogeneous routing protocol for MANETs. *Journal of Network and Computer Applications*, *46*, 60–71. doi:10.1016/j.jnca.2014.07.035

Saha, S., Nandi, S., Verma, R., Sengupta, S., Singh, K., Sinha, V., & Das, S. K. (2016). Design of efficient lightweight strategies to combat DoS attack in delay tolerant network routing. *Wireless Networks*.

Saied, A., Overill, R. E., & Radzik, T. (2016). Detection of known and unknown DDoS attacks using Artificial Neural Networks. *Neurocomputing*, *172*, 385–393. doi:10.1016/j.neucom.2015.04.101

Saini, R., & Khari, M. (2011). An Algorithm to detect attacks in mobile ad hoc network. In *International Conference on Software Engineering and Computer Systems* (pp. 336-341). Springer, Berlin, Heidelberg 10.1007/978-3-642-22203-0_30

Saini, R., & Khari, M. (2011). Defining malicious behaviour of a node and its defensive methods in ad hoc network. *International Journal of Computers and Applications*, *20*(4), 18–21. doi:10.5120/2422-3251

Sajedi, H. (2016). Steganalysis based on steganography pattern discovery. *Journal of Information Security and Applications*, *30*, 3–14. doi:10.1016/j.jisa.2016.04.001

Sajjadi, S. M. S., & Pour, B. T. (2013). Study of SQL Injection Attacks and Countermeasures. *International Journal of Computer and Communication Engineering*, *2*(5), 539–542. doi:10.7763/IJCCE.2013.V2.244

Sallee, P. (2005). Model-Based Methods for Steganography and Steganalysis. *International Journal of Image and Graphics*, *5*(1), 167–190. doi:10.1142/S0219467805001719

Samarati, P., & Sweeney, L. (1998). *Protecting privacy when disclosing information: k-anonymity and its enforcement through generalization and suppression.* Technical Report SRI-CSL-98-04, SRI Computer Science Laboratory.

Sammons, J. (2012). *The basics of digital forensics: the primer for getting started in digital forensics.* Elsevier.

Sammons, J. (2015). *The Basics of Digital Forensics - The Primer for Getting Started in Digital Forensics. 2nded.* Syngress Publications.

Sanders, C. (2010). Understanding Man-in-The-Middle Attacks-Part 2 DNS spoofing. *Windows Security.com.*

Sanders, C. (2010, June). Understanding Man-In-The-Middle Attacks-Part 4: SSL Hijacking.

Sanders, C. (2010, March). Understanding Man-in-the-Middle Attacks - ARP Cache Poisoning (Part 1).

Sanders, C. (2010, May). Understanding Man-In-The-Middle Attacks - Part 3: Session Hijacking.

Sandhya, G., & Julian, A. (2014, May). Intrusion detection in wireless sensor network using genetic K-means algorithm. In *Proceedings of the 2014 International Conference on Advanced Communication Control and Computing Technologies (ICACCCT)* (pp. 1791-1794). IEEE.

Sankaranarayanan, V. (2010, September). Early detection congestion and control routing in MANET. In *Proceedings of the 2010 Seventh International Conference on Wireless And Optical Communications Networks (WOCN).* IEEE.

Sarmah, A. (2001). Intrusion detection systems; definition, need and challenges. Retrieved March 2017 from https://www.sans.org/reading-room/whitepapers/detection/intrusion-detection-systems-definition-challenges-343

Savage, S., Wetherall, D., Karlin, A., & Anderson, T. (2000). Practical network support for IP traceback. In *Proceedings of the 2000 SIGCOMM conference on Applications, Technologies, Architectures, and Protocols for Computer Communication* (pp. 295-306). Stockholm, Sweden: ACM. doi: 10.1145/347059.347560

Savage, S., Wetherall, D., Karlin, A., & Anderson, T. (2000, August). Practical network support for IP traceback. *Computer Communication Review*, *30*(4), 295–306. doi:10.1145/347057.347560

Saxena, A., Shrivastava, G., & Sharma, K. (2012). Forensic investigation in cloud computing environment. *The International Journal of forensic computer science*, *2*, 64-74.

Saxena, A., Shrivastava, G., & Sharma, K. (2012). Forensic investigation in cloud computing environment. *The International Journal of Forensic Computer Science, 2*, 64-74.

Sayeed, F., & Hanmandlu, M. (2016). Three information set-based feature types for the recognition of faces. *Signal, Image and Video Processing*, *10*(2), 327–334.

Schmidt, D., Chen, W.-C., Matheson, M. A., & Ostrouchov, G. (2017). Programming with BIG Data in R: Scaling Analytics from One to Thousands of Nodes. *Big Data Research, 8*, 1–11. doi:10.1016/j.bdr.2016.10.002

Schweitzer, N., Stulman, A., Shabtai, A., & Margalit, R. D. (2016). Mitigating denial of service attacks in OLSR protocol using fictitious nodes. *IEEE Transactions on Mobile Computing, 15*(1), 163–172. doi:10.1109/TMC.2015.2409877

Scientific Working Group on Digital Evidence (SWGDE). (2015). Retrieved from http://www.swgde.org

Sciolino, E. (2004). Bombing in Madrid: The Attack. *New York Times*. Retrieved from http://www.nytimes.com/2004/03/12/world/bombings-in-madrid-the-attack-10-bombs-shatter-trains-in-madrid-killing-192.html

Sectools.org. (2011), SecTools.Org: Top 125 Network Security Tools. Retrieved from http://sectools.org/

Sedayao, J., & Bhardwaj, R. (2014). Making Big Data, Privacy, and Anonymization work together in the enterprise: Experiences and Issues. *Big Data Congress*. 10.1109/BigData.Congress.2014.92

Sedighi, V., & Fridrich, J. (2017). Histogram Layer, Moving Convolutional Neural Networks Towards Feature Based Steganalysis. *Proceedings of IS&T, Electronic Imaging, Media Watermarking, Security, and Forensics.*

Selim, S., Hashem, M., & Nazmy, T. M. (2011). Hybrid multi-level intrusion detection system. *International Journal of Computer Science and Information Security, 9*(5), 23–29.

Sen, J. (2011). Secure Routing in Wireless Mesh Networks. In Wireless Mesh Networks. InTech. doi:10.5772/13468

Sen, N., Sen, R., & Chattopadhyay, M. (2014). An effective back propagation neural network architecture for the development of an efficient anomaly based intrusion detection system. In *Proceedings of the 2014 International Conference on Computational Intelligence and Communication Networks (CICN)*, Bhopal, India (pp. 1052-1056). IEEE. 10.1109/CICN.2014.221

Senie, D., & Ferguson, P. (1998). Network ingress filtering: Defeating denial of service attacks which employ IP source address spoofing. *Network. Retrieved from* https://buildbot.tools.ietf.org/html/rfc2267

Sethi, P., & Sarangi, S. R. (2017). Internet of Things: Architectures, Protocols, and Applications. *Journal of Electrical and Computer Engineering.*

Seto, Y. (2015). Retina recognition. Encyclopedia of biometrics, 1321-1323. doi:10.1007/978-1-4899-7488-4_132

Shakshuki, E. M., Kang, N., & Sheltami, T. R. (2013). EAACK—a secure intrusion-detection system for MANETs. *IEEE Transactions on Industrial Electronics, 60*(3), 1089–1098. doi:10.1109/TIE.2012.2196010

Shamoto, H., Shirahata, K., Drozd, A., Sato, H., & Matsuoka, S. (2016). GPU-Accelerated Large-Scale Distributed Sorting Coping with Device Memory Capacity. *IEEE Transactions on Big Data, 2*(1), 57–69. doi:10.1109/TBDATA.2015.2511001

Shankar & Upadhyay. (2016). Performance analysis of various feature sets in calibrated blind steganalysis. *International Journal of Computer Science and Network Security, 16*(8), 29-34.

Shanmugavadivu, R., & Nagarajan, N. (2011). Network intrusion detection system using fuzzy logic. *Indian Journal of Computer Science and Engineering, 2*(1), 101–111.

Shariatmadar, Z. S., & Faez, K. (2011, November). An efficient method for finger-knuckle-print recognition by using the information fusion at different levels. In *Hand-Based Biometrics (ICHB), 2011 International Conference on* (pp. 1-6). IEEE.

Sharma, K., Shrivastava, G., & Singh, D. (2012). Risk Impact of Electronics-Commerce Mining: A Technical Overview. In *Proceedings of the International Conference on Computing Communication and Information Technology 2012* (pp. 93-96).

Sharma, S., & Patheja, P. S. (2012). Improving AODV routing protocol with priority and power efficiency in mobile ad hoc WiMAX network. *International journal of computer technology and electronics engineering*, *2*(1), 87-93.

Sharma, K., Bala, S., Bansal, H., & Shrivastava, G. (2017). Introduction to the special issue on secure solutions for network in scalable computing. *Scalable Computing, Practice and Experience*, *18*(3), iii–iv.

Sharma, K., Bala, S., Bansal, H., & Shrivastava, G. (2017). Introduction to the Special Issue on Secure Solutions for Network in Scalable Computing. Scalable Computing. *Practice and Experience*, *18*(3), iii–iv.

Sharma, K., & Gupta, B. B. (2016). Multi-layer defense against malware attacks on smartphone wi-fi access channel. *Procedia Computer Science*, *78*, 19–25. doi:10.1016/j.procs.2016.02.005

Sharma, K., & Shrivastava, G. (2011). Public Key Infrastructure and Trust of Web Based Knowledge Discovery. *International Journal of Engineering, Sciences and Management*, *4*(1), 56–60.

Sharma, K., Shrivastava, G., & Singh, D. (2012). Risk Impact of Electronics-Commerce Mining: A Technical Overview. *Risk (Concord, NH)*, 29.

Sharma, S., Sethi, D., & Bhattacharya, P. P. (2015). *Wireless Sensor Network Structural Design and Protocols: A Survey*. Communications on Applied Electronics.

Shi, T., Wan, J., Cheng, S., Cai, Z., Li, Y., & Li, J. (2015, October). Time-bounded positive influence in social networks. In *Proceedings of the 2015 International Conference on Identification, Information, and Knowledge in the Internet of Things (IIKI)* (pp. 134-139). IEEE. 10.1109/IIKI.2015.37

Shi, Y. Q., Sutthiwan, P., & Chen, L. (2012). Textural features for steganalysis. In *Information Hiding. 14th International Conference, IH 2012*. Springer.

Shinder, D. (2010). *Profiling and Categorizing Cyber Criminals*. Retrieved October 2016, from www.TechRepublic.com/blog/it-security

Shipley, A. J. (2013). Security in the internet of things, lessons from the past for the connected future. *Security Solutions, Wind River, White Paper*.

Shirey, R. (2003). RFC 2828–Internet security glossary. Retrieved from http://www.faqs.org/rfcs/rfc2828.html

Shirudkar & Motwani. (2015). Big-Data Security. *International Journal of Advanced Research in Computer Science and Software Engineering*, *5*(3).

Shrestha, R., Han, K. H., Choi, D. Y., & Han, S. J. (2010, April). A novel cross layer intrusion detection system in MANET. In *Proceedings of the 2010 24th IEEE International Conference on Advanced Information Networking and Applications (AINA)* (pp. 647-654). IEEE. 10.1109/AINA.2010.52

Shrivastava, G. (2016, March). Network forensics: Methodical literature review. In *Computing for Sustainable Global Development (INDIACom), 2016 3rd International Conference on* (pp. 2203-2208). IEEE.

Shrivastava, G. (2016, March). Network forensics: Methodical literature review. In *Proceedings of the 2016 3rd International Conference on Computing for Sustainable Global Development (INDIACom)* (pp. 2203-2208). IEEE.

Shrivastava, G., & Gupta, B. B. (2014, October). An encapsulated approach of forensic model for digital investigation. In *Consumer Electronics (GCCE), 2014 IEEE 3rd Global Conference on* (pp. 280-284). IEEE.

Shrivastava, G., & Gupta, B. B. (2014, October). An encapsulated approach of forensic model for digital investigation. In *Proceedings of the 2014 IEEE 3rd Global Conference on Consumer Electronics (GCCE)* (pp. 280-284). IEEE. 10.1109/GCCE.2014.7031241

Shrivastava, G., Sharma, K., & Bawankan, A. (2012, May). A new framework semantic web technology based e-learning. In *Proceedings of the 2012 11th International Conference on Environment and Electrical Engineering (EEEIC)* (pp. 1017-1021). IEEE. 10.1109/EEEIC.2012.6221527

Shrivastava, G., Sharma, K., & Kumari, R. (2016, March). Network forensics: Today and tomorrow. In *Computing for Sustainable Global Development (INDIACom), 2016 3rd International Conference on* (pp. 2234-2238). IEEE.

Shrivastava, G., Sharma, K., & Kumari, R. (2016, March). Network forensics: Today and tomorrow. In *Proceedings of the 2016 3rd International Conference on Computing for Sustainable Global Development (INDIACom)* (pp. 2234-2238). IEEE.

Shrivastava, G., Sharma, K., & Rai, S. (2010, December). The Detection & Defense of DoS & DDoS Attack: A Technical Overview. In *Proceeding of ICC* (*Vol. 27*, p. 28). Academic Press.

Shrivastava, G. (2017). Approaches of network forensic model for investigation. *International Journal of Forensic Engineering*, *3*(3), 195–215. doi:10.1504/IJFE.2017.082977

Shrivastava, G., & Bhatnagar, V. (2011). Secure Association Rule Mining for Distributed Level Hierarchy in Web. *International Journal on Computer Science and Engineering*, *3*(6), 2240–2244.

Shrivastava, G., & Kumar, P. (2017). Privacy Analysis of Android Applications: State-of-art and Literary Assessment. Scalable Computing. *Practice and Experience*, *18*(3), 243–252.

Shrivastava, G., Pandey, A., & Sharma, K. (2013). Steganography and its technique: Technical overview. In *Proceedings of the Third International Conference on Trends in Information, Telecommunication and Computing* (pp. 615-620). Springer. 10.1007/978-1-4614-3363-7_74

Shrivastava, G., Sharma, K., & Dwivedi, A. (2012). Forensic computing models: Technical overview. CCSEA, SEA, CLOUD, DKMP. *CS & IT*, *5*, 207–216.

Shrivastava, G., Sharma, K., & Rai, S. (2010, December). The Detection & Defense of DoS & DDoS Attack: A Technical Overview. In *Proceeding of ICC* (Vol. 27, p. 28).

Shrivastava, S. (2013). Rushing Attack and its Prevention Techniques. *International Journal of Application or Innovation in Engineering & Management*, *2*(4), 453–456.

Shuang, H. Z., & Hong, B. Z. (2007). Blind steganalysis using wavelet statistics and ANOVA. *Proceedings - International Conference on Machine Learning and Cybernetics*, *5*, 2515–2519.

Sichitiu, M. L. (2005, May). Wireless mesh networks: opportunities and challenges. In *Proceedings of World Wireless Congress* (Vol. 2).

Silva, R., Silva, J. S., & Boavida, F. (2015, April). A symbiotic resources sharing IoT platform in the smart cities context. In *Proceedings of the 2015 IEEE Tenth International Conference on Intelligent Sensors, Sensor Networks and Information Processing (ISSNIP)*. IEEE. 10.1109/ISSNIP.2015.7106922

Simpson, S. (2009). *White Collar Crime: An Opportunity Perspective. Criminology and Justice Studies*. Taylor & Francis. doi:10.1007/978-0-387-09502-8

Singer, A. P. (2004). U.S. Patent No. 6,724,894. Washington, DC: U.S. Patent and Trademark Office.

Singh, N., Dua, R., & Mathur, V. (2012). Wireless sensor networks: Architecture, protocols, simulator tool. *International Journal (Toronto, Ont.)*, *2*(5), 229–233.

Singh, S. K., Kumar, P., & Singh, J. P. (2017). Localization in Wireless Sensor Networks Using Soft Computing Approach. *International Journal of Information Security and Privacy, 11*(3), 42–53. doi:10.4018/IJISP.2017070104

Singh, S. K., Singh, M. P., & Singh, D. K. (2010). A survey of energy-efficient hierarchical cluster-based routing in wireless sensor networks. *International Journal of Advanced Networking and Application, 2*(02), 570–580.

Sinha, A., & Kumar, P. (2016). A Novel Framework for Social Internet of Things. *Indian Journal of Science and Technology, 9*(36). doi:10.17485/ijst/2016/v9i36/102162

Sinha, A., Kumar, P., Rana, N. P., Islam, R., & Dwivedi, Y. K. (2017). Impact of internet of things (IoT) in disaster management: A task-technology fit perspective. *Annals of Operations Research.*

Smaha, S. E. (1988, December). Haystack: An intrusion detection system. In *Proceedings of the Fourth Aerospace Computer Security Applications Conference* (pp. 37-44). IEEE.

Smith, R., Grabosky, P., & Urbas, G. (2004). Cyber criminals on trial. *Criminal Justice Matters, 58*(1), 22–23. doi:10.1080/09627250408553240

Snoeren, A. C., Partridge, C., Sanchez, L. A., Jones, C. E., Tchakountio, F., Kent, S., & Strayer, W. T. (2001). Hash-based IP traceback. In *Proceedings of the 2001 SIGCOMM conference on Applications, Technologies, Architectures, and Protocols for Computer Communications* (pp. 3-14). San Diego, CA: ACM.

Snort I. D. S. (2009). *Snort IDS.* Retrieved January 5, 2009, from http://www.snort.org

Snyder, H., & Crescenzi, A. (2009). Intellectual capital and economic espionage: New crimes and new protections. *Journal of Financial Crime, 16*(3), 245–254. doi:10.1108/13590790910973089

Softflowd. (n.d.). Retrieved March 1, 2017 from http://www.mindrot.org/projects/softflowd/

Sokolova, M., & Matwin, S. (2015). *Personal privacy protection in time of Big Data.* Berlin: Springer.

Somani, G., Gaur, M. S., Sanghi, D., Conti, M., & Buyya, R. (2017). Service resizing for quick DDoS mitigation in cloud computing environment. *Annales des Télécommunications, 72*(5-6), 237–252. doi:10.100712243-016-0552-5

Song, X., Liu, F., Yang, C., Luo, X., & Zhang, Y. (2015). Steganalysis of Adaptive JPEG Steganography Using 2D Gabor Filters. *The 3rd ACM Workshop on Information Hiding and Multimedia Security (IH&MMSec '15).*

Song, D. X., Wagner, D., & Perrig, A. (2000). Practical techniques for searches on encrypted data. *Proceedings of IEEE Symposium on Security and Privacy*, 44–55.

Song, D., & Perrig, A. (2001). Advanced and authenticated marking schemes for IP traceback. In *Proceedings of IEEE INFOCOM 2001 Conference* (pp. 878–886). Anchorage, AK: IEEE.

Sorina, D., Xiaolin, W., & Zhe, W. (2003). Detection of LSB steganography via sample pair analysis. *IEEE Transactions on Signal Processing, 51*(7), 1995–2007. doi:10.1109/TSP.2003.812753

Springer reference. (2014). *DNS based botnet detection.* Retrieved July 15, 2014, from http://www.springerreference.com/docs/html/chapterdbid/317753.html

Sreenivas, B. C., Prakash, G. B., & Ramakrishnan, K. V. (2013, February). L2DB-TCP: An adaptive congestion control technique for MANET based on link layer measurements. In *Proceedings of the 2013 IEEE 3rd International Advance Computing Conference (IACC)* (pp. 1086-1093). IEEE.

Sridhar, S., Baskaran, R., & Chandrasekar, P. (2013). Energy supported AODV (EN-AODV) for QoS routing in MANET. *Procedia: Social and Behavioral Sciences, 73*, 294–301. doi:10.1016/j.sbspro.2013.02.055

Stack Exchange. (2017). *What does a Bitcoin transaction consist of?* Retrieved on October 30, 2017 from https://bitcoin.stackexchange.com/questions/4838/what-does-a-bitcoin-transaction-consist-of

Stohl, M. (2007). Cyber terrorism: a clear and present danger, the sum of all fears, breaking point or patriot games? In *Crime Law and Social Change*. Springer Science + Business Media B.V. doi:10.1007/s10611-007-9061-9

Strayer, W. T., Lapsely, D., Walsh, R., & Livadas, C. (2008). Botnet Detection Based on Network Behavior. In W. Lee, C. Wang, & D. Dagon (Eds.), *Botnet Detection. Advances in Information Security* (Vol. 36, pp. 1–24). Boston, MA: Springer. doi:10.1007/978-0-387-68768-1_1

Studymode Research. (2010), *Computer Crime and its Effects*. Retrieved May 30, 2010, form www.studymode.com/essays/Computer-Crime-And-Its-Effects-63666883.html

Su, Z., & Xu, Q. (2017). Security-Aware Resource Allocation for Mobile Social Big Data: A Matching-Coalitional Game Solution. *IEEE Transactions on Big Data*, 1-1. 10.1109/tbdata.2017.2700318

Suganya, M., & Anandakumar, H. (2013). Handover based spectrum allocation in cognitive radio networks. *2013 International Conference on Green Computing, Communication and Conservation of Energy (ICGCE)*. 10.1109/ICGCE.2013.6823431

Sun, E., Zhang, X., & Li, Z. (2012). The internet of things (IOT) and cloud computing (CC) based tailings dam monitoring and pre-alarm system in mines. *Safety Science*, *50*(4), 811–815. doi:10.1016/j.ssci.2011.08.028

Sun, Y., Bai, J., Zhang, H., Sun, R., & Phillips, C. (2015). A Mobility-Based Routing Protocol for CR Enabled Mobile Ad Hoc Networks. *International Journal of Wireless Networks and Broadband Technologies*, *4*(1), 81–104. doi:10.4018/ijwnbt.2015010106

Supriya, K. M. (2012). Mobile Ad Hoc Netwoks Security Attacks and Secured Routing Protocols: A Survey. In N. Meghanathan, N. Chaki, & D. Nagamalai (Eds.), *Advances in Computer Science and Information Technology, Networks and Communications* (Vol. 84, pp. 119–124). Berlin, Heidelberg: Springer. doi:10.1007/978-3-642-27299-8_14

Swan, M. (2013). The quantified self: Fundamental disruption in big data science and biological discovery. *Big Data*, *1*(2), 85–99. doi:10.1089/big.2012.0002 PMID:27442063

Szegedy, Liu, Jia, Sermanet, Reed, Anguelov, … Rabinovich. (2015). Going deeper with convolutions. *Proceedings of IEEE International Conference on Computer Vision and Pattern Recognition (CVPR)*, 1–9.

Szydlo, M. (2004). Merkle Tree Traversal in Log Space and Time. In C. Cachin & J. L. Camenisch (Eds.), *Advances in Cryptology - EUROCRYPT 2004: Proceedings of Eurocrypt 2004 (LNCS)* (Vol. 3027, pp. 541–554). Berlin, Germany: Springer; doi:10.1007/978-3-540-24676-3_32

Tabash, I. K., Ahmad, N., & Beg, S. (2011, October). A congestion window control mechanism based on fuzzy logic to improve tcp performance in manets. In *Proceedings of the 2011 International Conference on Computational Intelligence and Communication Networks (CICN)* (pp. 21-26). IEEE. 10.1109/CICN.2011.5

Taboona, A. (2017) Top 20 Free Digital Forensic Investigation Tools for SysAdmins. Retrieved from https://techtalk.gfi.com/top-20-free-digital-forensic-investigation-tools-for-sysadmins/

Tajbakhsh, A., Rahmati, M., & Mirzaei, A. (2009). Intrusion detection using fuzzy association rules. *Applied Soft Computing*, *9*(2), 462–469. doi:10.1016/j.asoc.2008.06.001

Tan, S., & Li, B. (2014). Stacked convolutional auto-encoders for steganalysis of digital images. *Signal and Information Processing Association Annual Summit and Conference (APSIPA)*. 10.1109/APSIPA.2014.7041565

Tang, K., Obraczka, K., Lee, S. J., & Geria, M. (2002, October). A reliable, congestion-control led multicast transport protocol in multimedia multi-hop networks. In *Proceedings of the 5th International Symposium on Wireless Personal Multimedia Communications* (Vol. 1, pp. 252-256). IEEE. 10.1109/WPMC.2002.1088171

Tan, S., Li, X., & Dong, Q. (2015). Trust based routing mechanism for securing OSLR-based MANET. *Ad Hoc Networks*, *30*, 84–98. doi:10.1016/j.adhoc.2015.03.004

Tao, Z., & Xijian, P. (2003). Reliable detection of LSB steganography based on the difference image histogram. *Proceedings of. IEEE International Conference on Acoustics, Speech, and Signal Processing*, 545–548.

Tarekegn, G. B., & Munaye, Y. Y. (2016). Big Data: Security Issues, Challenges and Future Scope. *International Journal of Computer Engineering & Technology*, *7*(4), 12–24.

Tartary, C., Wang, H., & Ling, H. (2011). Authentication of Digital Streams. *IEEE Transactions on Information Theory*, *57*(9), 6285–6303. doi:10.1109/TIT.2011.2161960

Tayal, D. K., & Yadav, S. K. (2016). Fast retrieval approach of sentimental analysis with implementation of bloom filter on Hadoop. In *Proceedings of the 2016 International Conference on Computational Techniques in Information and Communication Technologies (ICCTICT)* (pp. 14-18). IEEE. 10.1109/ICCTICT.2016.7514544

Tayal, D. K., & Yadav, S. K. (2017). Sentiment analysis on social campaign "Swachh Bharat Abhiyan" using unigram method. *AI & Society*, *32*(4), 633–645. doi:10.100700146-016-0672-5

TechPayments. (2016). *20 Eye-Opening Cybercrime Statistics*. Retrieved from http://www.fitech.com/news/20-eye-opening-cybercrime-statistics/

Tegeler, F., Fu, X., Vigna, G., & Kruegel, C. (2012, December). Botfinder: Finding bots in network traffic without deep packet inspection. In *Proceedings of the 8th international conference on Emerging networking experiments and technologies* (pp. 349-360). ACM. 10.1145/2413176.2413217

Tennakoon, H. (2016). *The need for a comprehensive methodology for profiling cyber-criminals*. Retrieved on November 2016, from http://www.newsecuritylearning.com

Thai, T. H., Cogranne, R., & Retraint, F. (2014). Optimal Detection of OutGuess using an Accurate Model of DCT Coefficients. *Sixth IEEE International Workshop on Information Forensics and Security*. 10.1109/WIFS.2014.7084324

Thai, T., Cogranne, R., & Retraint, F. (2014). Statistical Model of Quantized DCT Coefficients: Application in the Steganalysis of Jsteg Algorithm. *IEEE Transactions on Image Processing*, *23*(5), 1–14. doi:10.1109/TIP.2014.2310126 PMID:24710399

Thamilarasu, G., Balasubramanian, A., Mishra, S., & Sridhar, R. (2005, November). A cross-layer based intrusion detection approach for wireless ad hoc networks. In *Proceedings of the IEEE International Conference on Mobile Adhoc and Sensor Systems Conference*. IEEE. 10.1109/MAHSS.2005.1542882

The Cisco Network Simulator. (n.d.). Router Simulator & Switch Simulator. Retrieved June 6, 2017 from http://www.boson.com/netsim-cisco-network-simulator

The Economist Intelligence Unit Ltd. (2012). *Big Data: Lessons from the Leaders*. Retrieved from http://www.bdvc.nl/images/Rapporten/SAS-Big-data-lessons-from-the-leaders.pdf

The Government of the Hong Kong Special Administrative Region (n.d.). InfoSec website is produced and managed by the Office of the Government Chief Information Officer of the Government, from https://www.infosec.gov.hk/english/crime/what_crc_1.html

The National Fraud Intelligence Bureau (NFIB). (n.d.). Advance Fee Fraud. Retrieved from www.actionfraud.police. uk/fraud-az-advance-fee-fraud

Thuraisingham, B. (2003, November). Security issues for the semantic web. In Proceedings of the 27th Annual International Computer Software and Applications Conference COMPSAC '03 (pp. 633-638). IEEE.

Top Ten Security Big Data Security and Privacy Challenges. (2013). Retrieved from http://www.cloudsecurityalliance.org

Tromp, E., Pechenizkiy, M., & Gaber, M. (2017). Expressive modeling for trusted big data analytics: Techniques and applications in sentiment analysis. *Big Data Analytics*, 2(1), 5. doi:10.118641044-016-0018-9

Tschorsch, F., & Scheuermann, B. (2016). Bitcoin and beyond: A technical survey on decentralized digital currencies. *IEEE Communications Surveys and Tutorials*, 18(3), 2084–2123.

Tsikoudis, N., Papadogiannakis, A., & Markatos, E. P. (2016). LEoNIDS: A low-latency and energy-efficient network-level intrusion detection system. *IEEE Transactions on Emerging Topics in Computing*, 4(1), 142–155.

Ullah, I., Khan, N., & Aboalsamh, H. A. (2013, April). Survey on botnet: Its architecture, detection, prevention and mitigation. In *Proceedings of the 10th IEEE International Conference on Networking, Sensing and Control (ICNSC)* (pp. 660-665). 10.1109/ICNSC.2013.6548817

Umamaheswari, S., & Radhamani, G. (2015). Enhanced antsec framework with cluster based cooperative caching in mobile ad hoc networks. *Journal of Communications and Networks (Seoul)*, 17(1), 40–46. doi:10.1109/JCN.2015.000008

Unit, E. I. (2007). *World investment prospects to 2011: Foreign direct investment and the challenge of political risk.* Academic Press.

Upadhyaya, R., & Jain, A. (2016, April). Cyber ethics and cyber crime: A deep dwelved study into legality, ransomware, underground web and bitcoin wallet. In *Computing, Communication and Automation (ICCCA), 2016 International Conference on* (pp. 143-148). IEEE. 10.1109/CCAA.2016.7813706

Upham, D. (n.d.). *Steganographic algorithm JSteg.* Retrieved from http://zooid.org/ paul/crypto/jsteg

Uplap, P., & Sharma, P. (2014, May). Review of heterogeneous/homogeneous wireless sensor networks and intrusion detection system techniques. In *Proceedings of Fifth International Conference on Recent Trends in Information, Telecommunication and Computing* (pp. 22-29).

Usha, K., & Ezhilarasan, M. (2016). Personal recognition using finger knuckle shape oriented features and texture analysis. *Journal of King Saud University-Computer and Information Sciences*, 28(4), 416–431. doi:10.1016/j.jksuci.2015.02.004

Vacca, J. R. (2012). *Computer and information security handbook.* Newnes.

Vaidya, H., Mirza, S., & Mali, N. (2016). Intrusion Detection System. *International Journal of Advanced Research in Engineering, Science & Technology*, 3.

Valikannu, R., George, A., & Srivatsa, S. K. (2015, February). A novel energy consumption model using Residual Energy Based Mobile Agent selection scheme (REMA) in MANETs. In *Proceedings of the 2015 2nd International Conference on Signal Processing and Integrated Networks (SPIN)* (pp. 334-339). IEEE.

Veerasamy, N. (2010). Motivation for cyberterrorism. In *Proceedings of ISSA.* Retrieved from http://icsa.cs.up.ac.za/ issa/2010/Proceedings/Research/02_paper.pdf

Walker, R. (2004). *Audio watermarking, R&D White Paper WHP 057.* British Broadcasting Corporation.

Walker, J. (1999). How big is global money laundering? *Journal of Money Laundering Control, 3*(1), 25–37. doi:10.1108/eb027208

Wall, D. (Ed.). (2003). *Crime and the Internet.* Routledge.

Walters, R. (2014). Cyber attacks on US companies in 2014. *Heritage Foundation Issue Brief, 4289.*

Wang, C., & Bo, G. (2014). A novel approach to generate and extract audio watermark. *International Journal of High Performance Systems Architecture, 5*(1), 33-38.

Wang, W. (2010, December). A new average quantized watermark for audio signal. In *Information Science and Engineering (ICISE), 2010 2nd International Conference on* (pp. 1728-1731). IEEE.

Wang, X., Wong, J. S., Stanley, F., & Basu, S. (2009, July). Cross-layer based anomaly detection in wireless mesh networks. In *Proceedings of the Ninth Annual International Symposium on Applications and the Internet SAINT'09* (pp. 9-15). IEEE. 10.1109/SAINT.2009.11

Wang, Y., Wang, Y., & Tan, T. (2004). Combining fingerprint and voiceprint biometrics for identity verification: an experimental comparison. *Biometric Authentication*, 289-294.

Wang, J., Crawl, D., Altintas, I., & Li, W. (2014). Big Data Applications Using Workflows for Data Parallel Computing. *Computing in Science & Engineering, 16*(4), 11–21. doi:10.1109/MCSE.2014.50

Wang, L., Tasoulis, S., Roos, T., & Kangasharju, J. (2016). Kvasir: Scalable Provision of Semantically Relevant Web Content on Big Data Framework. *IEEE Transactions On Big Data, 2*(3), 219–233. doi:10.1109/TBDATA.2016.2557348

Wang, P., Sparks, S., & Zou, C. C. (2010). An advanced hybrid peer-to-peer botnet. *IEEE Transactions on Dependable and Secure Computing, 7*(2), 113–127. doi:10.1109/TDSC.2008.35

Wang, X., Qi, W., & Niu, P. (2007). A new adaptive digital audio watermarking based on support vector regression. *IEEE Transactions on Audio, Speech, and Language Processing, 15*(8), 2270–2277. doi:10.1109/TASL.2007.906192 PMID:20428476

Wang, Y. (2016). Big Opportunities and Big Concerns of Big Data in Education. *TechTrends, 60*(4), 381–384. doi:10.100711528-016-0072-1

Wang, Y., Wang, J., & Chen, X. (2016, December). Secure Searchable Encryption: A survey. *Journal of Communications and Information Networks., 1*(4), 52–65. doi:10.1007/BF03391580

Watson. (2013). *ExtremeXOS Operating System.* Technical Specification Report. The University of Cambridge.

Weebly. (n.d.). Cyber Crime. Retrieved from http://cybercrimeproject.weebly.com/sources.html

Weiler, N. (2002). Honeypots for distributed denial-of-service attacks. In *Proceedings of the Eleventh IEEE International Workshops on Enabling Technologies: Infrastructure for Collaborative Enterprises* (pp. 109-114).

Weimann, G. (2005). The Sum of All Fears. *Studies in Conflict & Terrorism, Taylor & Francis., 28*(2), 129–149. doi:10.1080/10576100590905110

Weis, B. (2006). *The Use of RSA/SHA-1 Signatures within Encapsulating Security Payload (ESP) and Authentication Header (AH).* IETF, RFC-4359. Retrieved July 14, 2017, from https://www.ietf.org/rfc/rfc4359.txt

Wei, W., Zhang, J., Wang, W., Zhao, J., Li, J., Shen, P., ... Hu, J. (2013). Analysis and Research of the RSA Algorithm. *Information Technology Journal, 12*(9), 1818–1824. doi:10.3923/itj.2013.1818.1824

Westfeld, A. (2001). High Capacity Despite Better Steganalysis (F5 – A Steganographic Algorithm). In *Information Hiding, 4th International Workshop* (Vol. 2137, pp. 289-302). Springer-Verlag.

What is Bitcoin? (n.d.). Retrieved from http://www.coindesk.com/information/what-is-bitcoin/

White, T. (2012). *Hadoop: The definitive guide.* O'Reilly Media, Inc.

Wiener, M. (1990, May). Cryptanalysis of Short RSA Secret Exponents. *IEEE Transactions on Information Theory*, *36*(3), 553–558. doi:10.1109/18.54902

Wigley, A., Sutton, M., Wheelwright, S., Burbidge, R., & Mcloud, R. (2002). *Microsoft. net compact framework: Core reference.* Microsoft Press.

Wikipedia. (n.d.). Mobile ad hoc network. Retrieved May 2017 from https://en.wikipedia.org/wiki/Mobile_ad_hoc_network

Win, T., Tianfield, H., & Mair, Q. (2017). Big Data Based Security Analytics for Protecting Virtualized Infrastructures in Cloud Computing. *IEEE Transactions on Big Data*, 1-1. 10.1109/tbdata.2017.2715335

Winter, J. (2015). Algorithmic discrimination: Big data analytics and the future of the internet. In *The future internet* (pp. 125–140). Springer International Publishing. doi:10.1007/978-3-319-22994-2_8

Wong, C. K., & Lam, S. S. (1999). Digital Signatures for Flows and Multicasts. *IEEE/ACM Transactions on Networking*, *7*(4), 502–513. doi:10.1109/90.793005

Woodard, D. L., & Flynn, P. J. (2005). Finger surface as a biometric identifier. *Computer Vision and Image Understanding*, *100*(3), 357–384.

Wright, C., Cowan, C., Morris, J., Smalley, S., & Kroah-Hartman, G. (2002, June). Linux security module framework. In *Ottawa Linux Symposium* (*Vol. 8032*, pp. 6-16). Academic Press.

Wurzinger, P., Bilge, L., Holz, T., Goebel, J., Kruegel, C., & Kirda, E. (2009) Automatically Generating Models for Botnet Detection. In M. Backes & P. Ning (Eds.), *Computer Security – European Symposium on Research in Computer Security, LNCS* (Vol 5789, pp. 232-249). Springer, Berlin, Heidelberg 10.1007/978-3-642-04444-1_15

Wu, S., Zhong, S., & Liu, Y. (2017). Deep residual learning for image steganalysis. *Multimedia Tools and Applications*, 1–17.

Wu, X., Zhu, X., Wu, G., & Ding, W. (2014). Data mining with big data. *IEEE Transactions on Knowledge and Data Engineering*, *26*(1), 97–107. doi:10.1109/TKDE.2013.109

Wu, Z., & Chin, O. (2014). From Big Data to Data Science: A Multi-disciplinary Perspective. *Big Data Research*, *1*, 1. doi:10.1016/j.bdr.2014.08.002

Xia, F., Liu, H., Lee, I., & Cao, L. (2016). Scientific Article Recommendation: Exploiting Common Author Relations and Historical Preferences. *IEEE Transactions on Big Data*, *2*(2), 101–112. doi:10.1109/TBDATA.2016.2555318

Xiang, Y., & Zhang, W. H. (2012). Effective steganalysis of YASS based on statistical moments of wavelet characteristic function and Markov process. *Proceedings of International conference on computer science and electronics engineering*, 606–610. 10.1109/ICCSEE.2012.218

Xiangyang, L., Fenlin, L., Shiguo, L., Chunfang, Y., & Stefanos, G. (2011). On the typical statistic features for image blind steganalysis. *IEEE Journal on Selected Areas in Communications*, *29*(7), 1404–1422. doi:10.1109/JSAC.2011.110807

Xiao, H., Sidhu, N., & Christianson, B. (2015, August). Guarantor and reputation based trust model for social internet of things. In *Proceedings of the Wireless Communications and Mobile Computing Conference (IWCMC), 2015 International* (pp. 600-605). IEEE. 10.1109/IWCMC.2015.7289151

Xia, Z., Wang, X., Sun, X., Liu, Q., & Xiong, N. (2016). Steganalysis of LSB matching using differences between non-adjacent pixels. *Multimedia Tools and Applications, 75*(4), 1947–1962. doi:10.100711042-014-2381-8

Xiong, M., Yang, W., & Sun, C. (2011, May). Finger-knuckle-print recognition using LGBP. In *International Symposium on Neural Networks* (pp. 270-277). Springer Berlin Heidelberg.

Xiong, G., Ping, X., Zhang, T., & Hou, X. (2012). XiaodanHou. (2012). Image textural features for steganalysis of spatial domain steganography. *Journal of Electronic Imaging, 21*(3), 033015-1. doi:10.1117/1.JEI.21.3.033015

Xu, G. (2017). Deep Convolutional Neural Network to Detect J-UNIWARD. *Proceedings of 5th ACM Workshop Information Hiding Multimedia Security. (IH &MMSec).* 10.1145/3082031.3083236

Xu, G., Wu, H.-Z., & Shi, Y.-Q. (2016). Ensemble of CNNs for steganalysis: An empirical study. *Proceeding of 4th ACM Workshop on Information Hiding and Multimedia Security (IH&MMSec '16)*, 103–107. DOI: 10.1145/2909827.2930798

Xuan, G. R., Shi, Y. Q., & Gao, J. J. (2005). Steganalysis based on multiple features formed by statistical moments of wavelet characteristic functions. *Proc. 7th International Information Hiding Workshop, LNCS 3727*, 262–277. 10.1007/11558859_20

Xu, G., Wu, H.-Z., & Shi, Y.-Q. (2016, May). Structural design of convolutional neural networks for steganalysis. *IEEE Signal Processing Letters, 23*(5), 708–712. doi:10.1109/LSP.2016.2548421

Yaar, A., Perrig, A., & Song, D. (2006). StackPi: New packet marking and filtering mechanisms for DDoS and IP spoofing defense. *IEEE Journal on Selected Areas in Communications, 24*(10), 1853–1863. doi:10.1109/JSAC.2006.877138

Yachir, A., Amirat, Y., Chibani, A., & Badache, N. (2016). Event-aware framework for dynamic services discovery and selection in the context of ambient intelligence and Internet of Things. *IEEE Transactions on Automation Science and Engineering, 13*(1), 85–102. doi:10.1109/TASE.2015.2499792

Yadav, P., Sharma, S., Tiwari, P., Dey, N., Ashour, A. S., & Nguyen, G. N. (2018). A Modified Hybrid Structure for Next Generation Super High Speed Communication Using TDLTE and Wi-Max. In Internet of Things and Big Data Analytics Toward Next-Generation Intelligence (pp. 525-549). doi:10.1007/978-3-319-60435-0_21

Yamin, M., & Sen, A. A. A. (2018). Improving Privacy and Security of User Data in Location Based Services. *International Journal of Ambient Computing and Intelligence, 9*(1), 19–42. doi:10.4018/IJACI.2018010102

Yang, J., & Yecies, B. (2016). Mining Chinese social media UGC: A big-data framework for analyzing Douban movie reviews. *Journal of Big Data, 3*(1), 3. doi:10.118640537-015-0037-9

Yang, M. H., & Yang, M. C. (2012). RIHT: A novel hybrid IP traceback scheme. *IEEE Transactions on Information Forensics and Security, 7*(2), 789–797. doi:10.1109/TIFS.2011.2169960

Yang, W., Sun, C., & Sun, Z. (2011, July). Finger-knuckle-print recognition using gabor feature and olda. *In Control Conference (CCC), 2011 30th Chinese* (pp. 2975-2978). IEEE.

Yang, W., Wang, X., Song, X., Yang, Y., & Patnaik, S. (2018). Design of Intelligent Transportation System Supported by New Generation Wireless Communication Technology. *International Journal of Ambient Computing and Intelligence, 9*(1), 78–94. doi:10.4018/IJACI.2018010105

Yang, Y., Xu, H. Q., Gao, L., Yuan, Y. B., McLaughlin, K., & Sezer, S. (2017). Multidimensional Intrusion Detection System for IEC 61850-Based SCADA Networks. *IEEE Transactions on Power Delivery, 32*(2), 1068–1078. doi:10.1109/TPWRD.2016.2603339

Yerajana, R., & Sarje, A. K. (2009, March). A timestamp based multipath source routing protocol for congestion control in MANET. In *Proceedings of the IEEE International Advance Computing Conference IACC '09* (pp. 32-34). IEEE. 10.1109/IADCC.2009.4808975

Yick, J., Mukherjee, B., & Ghosal, D. (2008). Wireless sensor network survey. *Computer Networks, 52*(12), 2292–2330. doi:10.1016/j.comnet.2008.04.002

Yi, Z., & Dohi, T. (2015). Toward Highly Dependable Power-Aware Mobile Ad Hoc Network–Survivability Evaluation Framework. *IEEE Access: Practical Innovations, Open Solutions, 3*, 2665–2676. doi:10.1109/ACCESS.2015.2507201

Yogesh, Simmhan, Plale, & Gannon. (n.d.). *A Survey of Data Provenance Techniques.* Technical Report IUB-CS-TR618.

Yoon, C. (2011). Theory of planned behavior and ethics theory in digital piracy: An integrated model. *Journal of Business Ethics, 100*(3), 405–417. doi:10.100710551-010-0687-7

Yu, F., Xie, Y., & Ke, Q. (2010, February). Sbotminer: large scale search bot detection. In *Proceedings of the third ACM international conference on Web search and data mining* (pp. 421-430). 10.1145/1718487.1718540

Yuhara, M., Bershad, B. N., Maeda, C., & Moss, J. E. B. (1994). Efficient packet demultiplexing for multiple endpoints and large messages. In *Proceedings of the Winter 1994 USENIX Technical Conference* (pp. 13-13). San Francisco, CA: USENIX Association.

Yu, M., Zhou, M., & Su, W. (2009). A secure routing protocol against byzantine attacks for MANETs in adversarial environments. *IEEE Transactions on Vehicular Technology, 58*(1), 449–460. doi:10.1109/TVT.2008.923683

Yusuf, I. I., Thomas, I. E., Spichkova, M., & Schmidt, H. W. (2017). Chiminey: Connecting Scientists to HPC, Cloud and Big Data. *Big Data Research, 8*, 39–49. doi:10.1016/j.bdr.2017.01.004

Zeidanloo, H. R., Manaf, A. B., Vahdani, P., Tabatabaei, F., & Zamani, M. (2010). Botnet detection based on traffic monitoring. In *Proceedings of the International Conference on Networking and Information Technology*, Manila, Philippines (pp. 97-101).

Zeidanloo, H. R., & Rouhani, S. (2012). *Botnet detection by monitoring common network behaviors.* Lambert Academic Publishing.

Zeltser, L. (2000). The evolution of malicious agents. Retrieved Oct 12, 2006 from http://www.zeltser.com/malicious-agents

Zeng, J., Tan, S., Li, B., & Huang, J. (2017). *Large-scale JPEG image steganalysis using hybrid deep-learning framework.* arXiv: 1611.03233v2

Zhang, C., Shang, W., Lin, W., Li, Y., & Tan, R. (2017). Opportunities and challenges of TV media in the big data era. *2017 IEEE/ACIS 16th International Conference on Computer and Information Science (ICIS).* doi:10.1109/icis.2017.7960053

Zhang, J., & Zulkernine, M. (2005). Network intrusion detection using random forests. In *Proceedings of the Third Annual Conference on Privacy, Security and Trust,* St. Andrews, Canada (pp. 53–61).

Zhang, L., & Guan, Y. (2006, August). TOPO: A topology-aware single packet attack traceback scheme. In Securecomm and Workshops, 2006 (pp. 1-10). IEEE. doi:10.1109/SECCOMW.2006.359556

Zhang, L., & He, D. (2009, January). A novel robust audio watermark algorithm based on stochastic resonance. In *Micro-electronics & Electronics, 2009. PrimeAsia 2009. Asia Pacific Conference on Postgraduate Research in* (pp. 185-188). IEEE. 10.1109/PRIMEASIA.2009.5397415

Zhang, L., Zhang, L., & Zhang, D. (2009). Finger-knuckle-print verification based on band-limited phase-only correlation. In Computer analysis of images and patterns (pp. 141-148). Springer Berlin/Heidelberg.

Zhang, L., Zhang, L., & Zhang, D. (2009, November). Finger-knuckle-print: a new biometric identifier. In *Image Processing (ICIP), 2009 16th IEEE International Conference on* (pp. 1981-1984). IEEE.

Zhang, L., Zhang, L., & Zhang, D. (2010, August). Monogeniccode: A novel fast feature coding algorithm with applications to finger-knuckle-print recognition. In *Emerging Techniques and Challenges for Hand-Based Biometrics (ETCHB), 2010 International Workshop on* (pp. 1-4). IEEE.

Zhang, H., Cheng, P., Shi, L., & Chen, J. (2016). Optimal DoS attack scheduling in wireless networked control system. *IEEE Transactions on Control Systems Technology, 24*(3), 843–852. doi:10.1109/TCST.2015.2462741

Zhang, L. J. (2007). Challenges and opportunities for web services research. In *Modern Technologies in Web Services Research*. Hershey, PA: IGI Global.

Zhang, L., Zhang, L., Zhang, D., & Zhu, H. (2010). Online finger-knuckle-print verification for personal authentication. *Pattern Recognition, 43*(7), 2560–2571. doi:10.1016/j.patcog.2010.01.020

Zhang, L., Zhang, L., Zhang, D., & Zhu, H. (2011). Ensemble of local and global information for finger–knuckle-print recognition. *Pattern Recognition, 44*(9), 1990–1998. doi:10.1016/j.patcog.2010.06.007

Zhang, S., Meng, X., & Wang, L. (2016). An Adaptive Approach for Linux Memory Anaysis based on Kernel Code Reconstruction. *Eurasip Journal of Information Security, 14*, 13.

Zhang, T., Li, W., Zhnag, Y., Zheng, E., & Ping, X. (2010). Steganalysis of LSB matching based on statistical modeling of pixel difference distributions. *Information Sciences, 180*(23), 4685–4694. doi:10.1016/j.ins.2010.07.037

Zhang, T., & Ping, X. (2003). A Fast and Effective Steganalytic Technique AgainstJsteg-like Algorithms. *Proceedings of the ACM Symposium on Applied Computing*, 307–311.

Zhang, Y., & Lee, W. (2000, August). Intrusion detection in wireless ad-hoc networks. In *Proceedings of the 6th annual international conference on Mobile computing and networking* (pp. 275-283). ACM.

Zhang, Y., Lee, W., & Huang, Y. A. (2003). Intrusion detection techniques for mobile wireless networks. *Wireless Networks, 9*(5), 545–556. doi:10.1023/A:1024600519144

Zhao, D., Traore, I., Ghorbani, A., Sayed, B., Saad, S., & Lu, W. (2012). Peer to Peer Botnet Detection Based on Flow Intervals. In D. Gritzalis, S. Furnell, & M. Theoharidou (Eds.), *Information Security and Privacy Research: IFIP Advances in Information and Communication Technology* (Vol. 376, pp. 87–102). Berlin, Heidelberg: Springer. doi:10.1007/978-3-642-30436-1_8

Zhou, T., Choudhury, R. R., Ning, P., & Chakrabarty, K. (2007). Privacy-preserving detection of sybil attacks in vehicular ad hoc networks. In *Proceedings of the Fourth Annual International Conference on Mobile and Ubiquitous Systems: Networking & Services MobiQuitous '07*, Philadelphia, PA. IEEE. 10.1109/MOBIQ.2007.4451013

Zhou, X. S., Cohen, I., Tian, Q., & Huang, T. S. (2000). Feature extraction and selection for image retrieval. *Urbana (Caracas, Venezuela), 51*, 61801.

Zhu, B., Joseph, A., & Sastry, S. (2011, October). A taxonomy of cyber attacks on SCADA systems. In *Proceedings of the 2011 international conference on Internet of things (iThings/CPSCom) and 4th international conference on cyber, physical and social computing* (pp. 380-388). IEEE. 10.1109/iThings/CPSCom.2011.34

Zong, Z., Ge, R., & Gu, Q. (2017). Marcher: A Heterogeneous System Supporting Energy-Aware High Performance Computing and Big Data Analytics. *Big Data Research*, *8*, 27–38. doi:10.1016/j.bdr.2017.01.003

Zuech, R., Khoshgoftaar, T. M., & Wald, R. (2015). Intrusion detection and big heterogeneous data: A survey. *Journal of Big Data*, *2*(1), 3. doi:10.118640537-015-0013-4

About the Contributors

Gulshan Shrivastava received Bachelor's of Engineering (B.E.) in Computer Science & Engineering from the Maharishi Dayanand University, India. He also earned his Master of Technology (M.Tech.) in Information Security from GGSIPU Delhi, India and MBA degree in Information Technology & Finance from Punjab Technical University, India and pursuing Ph.D. degree in Computer Science & Engineering from the National Institute of Technology Patna, India. He earned certification of SCJP from Sun Microsystem. He has co-editor of more than 3 books, author of more than 6 book chapters, 30 articles in International Journals and Conferences of high repute including IEEE, Elsevier, ACM, Springer, Inderscience, IGI Global, Bentham Science etc. He is also serving as Associate Editor of Journal Global Information Management (JGIM), IGI Global and Section Editor of Scalable Computing (SCPE). He is also serving many journals as editorial board member and as member, international advisory board of several national and international journals. Moreover, he has also delivered expert talk, guest lecturers in International Conference and serving as reviewer for Journals of IEEE, Springer, Inderscience, IGI Global etc. He is Publicity Chair in ICACCE-2018, SICBS-2017. He also served as Organizing Chair of Special Session in ICRTCSE in 2017 in Malaysia, in Springer Third IC3T, 10th INDIACom; 3rd IEEE ICCSSGD, ACM 2nd ICICTCS in 2016 in India. He has also served as founder and organizing chair of International Workshop on Recent Trends in Security and Forensic Investigation ICT in conjunction with IEEE 4th International Conference on Advanced in Computing & Communication Engineering (ICACCE-2018), Paris, France in June 2018. He is currently actively working on a project for risk monitoring and android behavior analysis. He has also served as Technical program committee (TPC) member of International conferences worldwide. He is member of IEEE, CSI, ACM, SIGCOMM, and many professional bodies. He was also visiting researcher with Datec Ltd., Papua New Guinea (PNG) in 2010. At present, He is working as research scholar in the Department of Computer Science & Engineering, National Institute of Technology Patna (Institute of National Importance), India. He has an ardent inclination towards field of Analytics. His research interest includes Information Security, Android, Data Analytics, Cyber Security & Forensic, Mobile Computing, Intrusion Detection and Computer Networks.

Prabhat Kumar is currently the Head of Computer Science and Engineering Department at National Institute of Technology Patna, India. He is also the Professor-In-charge of the IT Services of the institute and has experience of more than eight years in Network Planning & Management. He is, currently, the State Student Coordinator of Bihar, India for Computer Society of India (CSI). He holds a Ph.D. in Computer Science and M. Tech. in Information Technology. He has over 50 publications in various International/National Journals & Conferences (viz. IEEE, ACM, Springer and Elsevier). He is also the reviewer of several reputed journals indexed in SCI, SCIE and Scopus. He has chaired sessions at several international conferences held in India and abroad. He is also in the Program Committee of various National/International Conferences. He is an associate member of IEEE, professional member of ACM, life member of CSI, International Association of Engineers (IAENG) and global member of Internet Society. He has delivered expert talks and guest lectures at various prestigious institutes. His research area includes Wireless Sensor Networks, Internet of Things, Social Networks, Operating Systems, Software Engineering, E-governance, etc.

B. B. Gupta received PhD degree from Indian Institute of Technology Roorkee, India in the area of Information and Cyber Security. In 2009, he was selected for Canadian Commonwealth Scholarship and awarded by Government of Canada Award ($10,000). He spent more than six months in University of Saskatchewan (UofS), Canada. He has published more than 90 research papers (including 01 book and 14 chapters) in International Journals and Conferences of high repute including IEEE, Elsevier, ACM, Springer, Inderscience, etc. He has visited several countries, i.e. Canada, Japan, China, Malaysia, Hong-Kong, etc to present his research work. His biography was selected and publishes in the 30th Edition of Marquis Who's Who in the World, 2012. Dr Gupta received International travel grant award from various organizations i.e. Microsoft Research (MSR) India, ACM Special Interest Group on Data Communication (SIGCOMM) ($525), DST, Govt. of India (Young Scientist travel grant award) (2-times), CSIR, IITR-heritage fund to attend various conferences and present his research work worldwide. He is also serving as Editor-in-Chief of International Journal of Cloud Applications and Computing (IJCAC) (IGI Global), US, Associate Editor of IEEE Access journal and IJICS, Inderscience and Executive Editor of IJITCA, Inderscience. He is also serving many journals as editorial board member and as member, international advisory board. Moreover, he is serving as reviewer for Journals of IEEE, Springer, Wiley, Taylor & Francis, etc. Currently he is guiding 11 students for their Master's and Doctoral research work in the area of Information and Cyber Security. He also served as Organizing Chair of Special Session on Recent Advancements in Cyber Security (SS-CBS) in IEEE Global Conference on Consumer Electronics (GCCE), in 2014, and 2015 in Japan. In addition, Dr Gupta received Best Poster presentation award and People choice award for Poster presentation in CSPC-2014, Aug., 2014, Malaysia. He served as Jury in All IEEE-R10 Young Engineers' Humanitarian Challenge (AIYEHUM-2014), 2014. He has also served as founder and organizing chair of International Workshop on Future Information Security, Privacy and Forensics for Complex Systems (FISP-2015, 2016, 2017, 2018) in conjunction with ACM International Conference on Computing Frontiers (CF-2015). He has also served as Technical program committee (TPC) member of more than 20 International conferences worldwide. Dr Gupta is member of IEEE, ACM, SIGCOMM, The Society of Digital Information and Wireless Communications (SDIWC), Internet Society, Institute of Nanotechnology, Life Member, International Association of Engineers (IAENG), Life Member, International Association of Computer Science and Information Technology (IACSIT). He also worked as a post doctoral research fellow in UNB, Canada. He was also visiting researcher with Yamaguchi University, Japan in 2015 and with Guangzhou University, China in 2016, respectively. At present, Dr. Gupta is working as Assistant Professor in the Department of Computer Engineering, National Institute of Technology Kurukshetra (Institute of National Importance), India. His research interest includes Information security, Cyber Security, Mobile/Smartphone, Cloud Computing, Web security, Intrusion detection, Computer networks and Phishing.

Suman Bala received Ph.D. and M.E. degree in Computer Science & Engineering from Thapar University, India. She received B.Tech. degree from Punjab Technical University, India. She worked as a research engineer at Orange Labs, France. During this assignment, she worked on LoRA-WAN technology and submitted a patent for an efficient communication strategy among client, network server and application server. She has published more than 30 peer-reviewed articles in international journals, conference proceedings and books. She is serving as a reviewer for various journals such as IJCS (Wiley Press), SCN (Springer), Encyclopedia of Information Systems and Technology (Taylor and Francis), Journal of Theoretical Physics and Cryptography. Additionally, she has served on the programme committee's member of the conferences ICCCA-17, ICCCA-16, ICCCA-15, ISS-16 Thailand, SPIN-16, Confluence-16, ICIBET-13, Beijing, China. She is currently working as a freelance security consultant. Her area of interest includes key management in Wireless Sensor Networks and IoT.

Nilanjan Dey is an Assistant Professor at the Department of Information Technology, Techno India College of Technology, Kolkata, W.B., India. He holds an honorary position of Visiting Scientist at Global Biomedical Technologies Inc., CA, USA and Research Scientist of Laboratory of Applied Mathematical Modeling in Human Physiology, Territorial Organization of- Scientific and Engineering Unions, BULGARIA. He is an Associate Researcher of Laboratoire RIADI, University of Manouba, TUNISIA. His research topic is Medical Imaging, Soft computing, Data mining, Machine learning, Rough set, Computer Aided Diagnosis, Atherosclerosis. He has 20 books and 300 international conferences and journal papers. He is the Editor-in-Chief of International Journal of Ambient Computing and Intelligence (IGI Global), US, International Journal of Rough Sets and Data Analysis (IGI Global), US, the International Journal of Synthetic Emotions (IJSE), IGI Global, US, and International Journal of Natural Computing Research (IGI Global), US. Series Editor of Advances in Geospatial Technologies (AGT) Book Series, (IGI Global), US, Executive Editor of International Journal of Image Mining (IJIM), Inderscience, and Associated Editor of IEEE Access journal and the International Journal of Service Science, Management, Engineering and Technology, IGI Global. He is a life member of IE, UACEE, and ISOC.

* * *

Prachi Ahlwat has eight years of teaching experience at both postgraduate and undergraduate level. She has completed her Ph.D. thesis in the area of Wireless Sensor Network at Banasthali University, Rajasthan. She has done her M.Tech in Computer Science and Engineering from Banasthali University, Rajasthan in the year 2009 with honors. She has done her industrial training with ST Microelectronics, Greater Noida and completed three live projects for partial fulfillment of her M.Tech degree. She has completed her B.E. in Computer Science and Engineering from M.D. University, Rohtak in the year 2007. She specializes in Computer Network and Programming courses. She had guided 5 M.Tech Thesis and 8 B.Tech Projects. Her area of research interest includes Wireless Sensor Networks and Security Issues in Wireless Sensor Networks. She is author of 30 refereed articles in these areas, 17 in peer reviewed, reputed international journal indexed in international databases and 13 in IEEE/ Springer indexed International Conferences. She is a member of team responsible for setting up of CISCO Academy. Dr. Prachi is departmental coordinator for National Board of Accreditation. Further, she is certified in Usable Security and Software Security from University of Maryland. Dr. Prachi is also working as Editorial Board member of International Journal of Computer Network & Applications and program committee member of many IEEE Conferences. She is UGC-NET/JRF Qualified.

Rohit Anand is working as an Assistant Professor in G.B. Pant Engineering College, New Delhi, India. He received Bachelor of Engineering degree in Electronics and Communication Engineering from M.D. University, Rohtak, India in 2001. He received Master of Technology degree in Electronics and Communication Engineering from Punjab Technical University, Punjab, India in 2008. He is currently pursuing Ph.D. in Antenna from from Punjab Technical University, Punjab, India. He is a Life Member of Indian society for Technical Education. He has published more than 40 papers in National and International Conferences and Journals. His main interests include Antenna, Wireless Communication, Security and Image Processing.

Mannat Aneja obtained bachelor degree from Visvesvaraya Technological University in 2012 and master's degree from Thapar University in 2016 in Information Security discipline. His area of interest are wireless networks and network security.

Arushi Arora is a research scholar and is passionate about finding new approaches to solve various challenges in the field of computer networks and data communication security and privacy. She is highly motivated and is currently working on the applications of Blockchains to secure and authenticate a network. These include VANETs and AANETs and protocols like ADS-B. She is open to new ideas and is enthusiastic and willing to learn new skills and technologies.

Diana Gratiela Berbecaru is a Senior Research Assistant in the Department of Automatics and Informatics at Politecnico di Torino. She holds a Ph.D in Computer Science from Politecnico di Torino and a MSc from University of Craiova, Romania. Her research interests lie in the area of public key infrastructures, advanced formats for digital signatures and multicast authentication protocols. In the past years she has been also involved in several European projects in the area of federated digital identity management.

Abhishek Bhardwaj is currently doing B.Tech. (ECE) from G.B.Pant Engineering College, New Delhi, India. His areas of interests include Network Security, Antenna, Wireless Communication, etc.

Tarunpreet Bhatia is currently working as lecturer in the department of Computer Science and Engineering at Thapar University, Patiala. She received her M.E. degree with university medal from Thapar University and B. Tech with Honors from Kurukshetra University, both in area of computer science. She has published over 20 papers in referred journals and conferences. Her research interests include wireless networks, information security, machine learning and cloud computing.

Mohamed Salim Bouhlel is a full professor at Sfax University, Tunisia. He is the Head of the Research Group: Sciences and Technologies of Image and Communication since 2003. He was the director of the Higher Institute of Electronics and Communications of Sfax-TUNISIA (ISECS) 2008-2011 He received the golden medal with the special appreciation of the jury in 1999 on the occasion of the first International Meeting of Invention, Innovation and Technology (Dubai, UAE). He was the vice president and founder member of the Tunisian Association of the Specialists in Electronics and the Tunisian Association of the Experts in Imagery. He is the president and founder of the Tunisian association on Human-Machine Interaction since 2013. He is the Editor in Chief of the international Journal "Human-Machine Interaction" and a dozen of special issues of international journals. He is the Chairman of many international conferences and member of the program committee of numerous international conferences. His research interests are Image processing, Telecommunication and Human-Machine Interaction in which he has obtained more than 20 patents so far. More than 500 articles were published in international journals, conferences and books. Moreover, he has been the principal investigator and the project manager for several research projects dealing with several topics concerned with his research interests mentioned above.

Chellappan C. is Former professor in the Department of Computer Science and Engineering at Anna University, Chennai, India. Dr. C. Chellappan is currently Principal of GKM College of Engineering & Technology, Chennai, India. He received his B.Sc. degree in Applied Sciences and M.Sc in Applied Science–Applied Mathematics from PSG College of Technology, Coimbatore, affiliated to the University of Madras, in 1972 and 1977. He received his M.E and Ph.D degrees in Computer Science and Engineering from Anna University in 1982 and 1987. He is currently the Dean of the College of Engineering, Guindy, Anna University, Chennai. He was the Director of Ramanujan Computing Centre (RCC) for 3 years at Anna University (2002–2005). He has published more than 70 papers in reputed International Journals and Conferences. His research areas are computer networks, Distributed /mobile computing and soft computing, software agent, object oriented design and network security.

Ezhilmaran D. was born in Puduppalayam, Tamilnadu, India, in 1976. He received the B.Sc. degree in Mathematics from the University of Madras, Chennai, India, in 1997, and the M. Sc. degrees in Mathematics from the Bharathidasan University, Tiruchirappalli, India, in 1999. The M. Sc. degree in Information Technology and Ph.D. degrees in Mathematics from the Alagappa University, Karaikudi, India, in 2003 and 2011, respectively. In 1999, he joined the Department of Mathematics, Arunai Engineering College, as a Lecturer, and in 2005 became a Senior Lecture. Since June 2007, he has been with the Department of Mathematics, KSR College of Technology, Tiruchengode, where he was an Assistant Professor, became an Associate Professor in 2011. At present he has been with the Department of Mathematics, Vellore Institute of Technology, India. He has eighteen plus years of experience in teaching and more than ten years of experience in research. His current research interests include Fuzzy Algebra, Fuzzy Image Processing, Data Mining and Cryptography. Dr. Ezhilmaran is a Fellow of the Indian Academy of Science; the National Academy of Science, India; He is a Life Member of the Indian Society for Technical Education (ISTE). He has published more than sixty research article in peer-reviewed international journals. He also presented more than thirty paper presented in national and international conferences. He has guided five Ph. D Scholar and five Ph. D Scholar were working the same domain. He has received Best Faculty Award and Best Researcher Award in every year in VIT University, Vellore, India.

Sachin Dube has completed M.Tech. from Delhi University in 2011. He has worked as Assistant Professor in Galgotias University, Uttar Pradesh, for four years. Currently he is pursuing Ph.D from Malviya National Institute of Technology, Jaipur, India. His research areas include, Image processing, Deep learning, Security & Privacy etc.

Ramanujam Elangovan received the Masters degree in Computer Science and Engineering and pursuing research degree at Anna University, chennai. He is currently an Assistant Professor with the department of Information Technology, Thiagarajar College of Engineering, Madurai, India. His research interest includes Data Analytics and time-series data mining.

Anandakumar Haldorai Assistant Professor (SG), Department of Computer Science and Engineering, Akshaya College of Engineering and Technology, Coimbatore, Tamil Nadu, India has completed his Master's in Software Engineering from PSG College of Technology, Coimbatore. Currently he is pursuing his PhD in Information and Communication Engineering from PSG College of Technology under, Anna University, Chennai. He has published more than 35 papers in international journals. His research areas include Cognitive Radio Networks, BigData, Mobile Communications and Networking Protocols.

Hemalatha Jeyaprakash received the B.E and ME degree in Computer Science and Engineering under Anna University Chennai in 2007 and 2013. She is currently pursuing the Ph.D. degree in Information and Communication Engineering with Anna University, Chennai, India. In July 2013, she joined the Department of Computer Science and Engineering at P.S.R Engineering College, Sivakasi. India. Her research interests include Digital steganography, Steganalysis, Machine Learning and Image Processing. She has published more papers in reputed International Conferences and Journals.

Asha Joseph received the B.Tech degree in Computer Science and Engineering from National Institute of Technology formerly known as Regional Engineering College, Calicut, India, in 1997, Professionally Certified Engineer on Network and Security from CompTIA, Texas, USA, in 2003. She received M.Tech degree in Software Engineering from Visvesvaraya Technological University, India. This author is a Member (M) of IEEE and Member of ACM. Currently, she is pursuing Ph.D in the field of digital forensics at VIT University, Vellore and working as Associate Professor at Bangalore Technological Institute, Bangalore. Her Research interests include Cyber Forensics, Operating Systems, Cloud and Network Security, Information Security and Operations Research. She has published a many papers on cloud computing and Information security.

Ramgopal Kashyap's areas of interest are image processing, pattern recognition and machine learning. He has published more than 20 research papers, and book chapters in international journals and conferences like Springer, Inderscience, Elsevier, ACM and IGI-Global indexed by Science Citation Index (SCI) and Scopus (Elsevier).He has Reviewed Research Papers in the Science Citation Index Expanded, Springer Journals and Editorial Board Member and conferences programme committee member of the IEEE, Springer international conferences and journals held in countries: Czech Republic, Switzerland, UAE, Australia, Hungary, Poland, Taiwan, Denmark, India, USA, UK, Austria, and Turkey. He has written many book chapters published by IGI Global, USA.

Manju Khari an Assistant Professor in Ambedkar Institute of advanced communication technology and research, Under Govt. Of NCT Delhi affiliated with Guru Gobind Singh Indraprastha University, Delhi, India. She is also the Professor- In-charge of the IT Services of the Institute and has experience of more than twelve years in Network Planning & Management. She received Ph.D. in Computer Science & Engineering from National Institute Of Technology Patna and She also received her master's degree in Information Security from Ambedkar Institute technology of advanced communication technology and research, formally this institute is known as Ambedkar Institute Of Technology affiliated with Guru Gobind Singh Indraprastha University, Delhi, India. Her research interests are software testing, software quality, software metrics, information security and nature-inspired algorithm. She has 60 published papers in refereed National/International Journals & Conferences (viz. IEEE, ACM, Springer, Inderscience, and Elsevier), 06 book chapters in a springer. She is also co-author of two books published by NCERT.

Prashant Kumar has published number of research papers in International Journals and Conferences of high repute. He also served as Organizing Chair of many Session in India. At present, He is working as an Assistant Professor in GCET, Greater Noida, India. His research interest includes Computer Network, Information security, Cyber Security & Forensic, Mobile/Smartphone security & forensic.

Ravinder Kumar received Ph.D. in IT from GGSIP University, Delhi in 2013 and M. Tech. degree in Computer Science & Engineering in 1998 from GJ University of Science and Technology, Hisar, India. Since 1999, he has been with the University School of ICT, GGSIP University, Delhi. Currently, he is Professor and Head, Department of CSE with HMR Institute of Technology and Management Delhi, India. His research interest is in the image processing and biometrics.

Reema Kumari received her M.Tech. degree in Computer Engineering from Galgotias University, India. She is currently working in software industry, India. She also holds experience of academic where she has worked in various domains such as Information Security and Internet of Things. Her main research areas include Internet of Things, Adhoc Networks, Security and Privacy, etc.

Kavisankar Leelasankar is currently working as Associate Professor, School of Computing Sciences, Department of Computer Science and Engineering, Hindustan Institute of Technology & Science. He was working as Associate Professor, Department of Information Technology, Sree Vidyanikethan Engineering College, A. Rangampet,Tirupati, Andhra Pradesh. He worked as Assistant Professor in SRM University, kattankulathur, Chennai. Dr. L. Kavisankar was a Research Associate in the Research project "Collaborated Directed Basic Research- Smart and Secure Environment" (CDBR-SSE). The Smart and Secure Environment Research Consortium was funded by National Technical Research Organization (NTRO), Government of India, New Delhi which is used to connect the eight institutions across Tamilnadu, India namely IIT Madras, NIT Trichirapalli, College of Engineering-Guindy - Anna University, Pondicherry University Pondicherry, PSG College of Technology Coimbatore, Thiyagaraja College of Engineering-Madurai, Madurai Kamaraj University-Madurai, and Alagappa University-Karaikudi through MPLS-VPN network. The worth of the project is nearly 9 cores which were for the duration of 5 years (2007-2012) covering major vulnerabilities with respect to cyber security. His research work is under the "Intrusion Detection & Prevention" and his title of research is "An Efficient Mitigation Framework to Detect and Defend Against Multi-Vector DDOS Attacks" which he has done under the guidance of Dr. C. Chellappan, Former Dean, CEG, Anna University, Chennai. He has published 11 papers in reputed International Journals and Conferences. He has also published book chapter. He has Citation indices with Citations 31, h-index 3, i10-index 1. His current research is on IOT, Cyber security, Computer Forensics and Network security. He is a member of many professional bodies like IET, Indian Science Congress. He has won many awards like "Public Servicing Awards-2014" (Technology Category), Working Journalists Union of TamilNadu, 2014 and Won gold medal in the Research day function at SRM University, Kattankulatur, 2016. He is technical committee member for ncetta17 National Conference in Tindivanam, TamilNadu.

Kavitha Devi M. K. received her Under Graduate and Graduate Degree in Computer Science and Engineering, and her Ph.D. Degree in Information and Communication Engineering in 1994, 2004 and 2011 respectively. Her research focuses on Recommender Systems, Information Security & Hiding, Cloud Computing, and Big data. She has received the Best Computer Science Faculty Award in

2014 from Association of Scientists, Developers and Faculties (ASDF). She has published more than 20 refereed Journal and International Conference papers in these areas. She is the reviewer in referred Journals including IEEE Intelligent Systems and Springer - Journal of The Institution of Engineers (India): Series B. She organized Faculty Development Programs, Workshops and Conference. Under her guidance, 10 Ph.D scholars from Anna University, Chennai are working in her area. Currently, she is an Associate Professor at the Department of Computer Science and Engineering, Thiagarajar College of Engineering, Madurai, India.

M. Manikandakumar received the Masters degree in Computer Science and Engineering and pursuing research degree at Anna University, Chennai. He is currently an Assistant Professor with the department of Information Technology, Thiagarajar College of Engineering, Madurai, India. His research interest includes Security, Internet of Things and Big Data.

Sivasankar P. is an Assistant Professor in the Department of Electrical and Electronics and communication Engineering, National Institute of Technical Teachers Training and Research, Government of India, Ministry of Human Resource Development, Chennai, India. He received his BE in Electronics and Communication Engineering from the University of Madras in 2001. He obtained his ME in Applied Electronics from the Anna University in 2005. He received his PhD in Computer Science from the Anna University in 2013. He has published more than 20 papers in reputed international journals and conferences. His research areas are mobile adhoc networks and wireless sensor networks.

Bibudhendu Pati is currently working as an Associate Professor and Head in the Department of Computer Science and Engineering at C.V. Raman College of Engineering, Bhubaneswar, India. He received his PhD from IIT Kharagpur, India. His current research interests include Big Data, Internet of things, Cloud Computing, and Wireless Sensor Networks. He has over 19 years of teaching, research, and industry experience. He is a life member of Computer Society of India (CSI), Indian Society for Technical Education (ISTE), and member of IEEE. He is the author of several scholarly research papers.

Binod Kumar Pattanayak completed his M. S. in Computer Engineering from Kharkov Polytechnic Institute, Kharkov, Ukraine in the year 1992 and Ph. D. in Computer Science and Engineering from Siksha 'O' Anusandhan University, Bhubaneswar, Odisha, India in the year 2011. He has a teaching experience of 17 years in undergraduate, post graduate and Ph. D. Levels in computer science and engineering. There are more than 50 research publications to his credit in reputed international journals and conferences. He has successfully guided 1 Ph. D. Scholar and more than 13 M. Tech. Level students. He is currently placed as an Associate Professor in the department of computer science and engineering in Institute of Technical Education and Research (ITER), the faculty of Engineering of Siksha 'O' Anusandhan University, India. His research areas include Ad-hoc Networks, Software Engineering, Artificial Intelligence and Compiler Design.

Sheng-Lung Peng is a full Professor of the Department of Computer Science and Information Engineering at National Dong Hwa University, Taiwan. He received the BS degree in Mathematics from National Tsing Hua University, and the MS and PhD degrees in Computer Science and Information Engineering from the National Chung Cheng University and National Tsing Hua University, Taiwan, respectively. His research interests are in designing and analyzing algorithms for Combinatorics, Bioinformatics, and Networks.Dr. Peng has edited several special issues at journals, such as Soft Computing, Journal of Internet Technology, Journal of Computers and MDPI Algorithms. He is also a reviewer for more than 10 journals such as IEEE Transactions on Emerging Topics in Computing, Theoretical Computer Science, Journal of Computer and System Sciences, Journal of Combinatorial Optimization, Journal of Modelling in Management, Soft Computing, Information Processing Letters, Discrete Mathematics, Discrete Applied Mathematics, Discussiones Mathematicae Graph Theory, and so on. He has about 100 international conferences and journal papers.Dr. Peng is now the director of the Library and Information Center of NDHU and an honorary Professor of Beijing Information Science and Technology University of China. He is a secretary general of Institute of Information and Computing Machinery (IICM) in Taiwan. He is also a director of the ACM-ICPC Contest Council for Taiwan. Recently, he is elected as a supervisor of Chinese Information Literacy Association and of Association of Algorithms and Computation Theory (AACT). He has been serving as a secretary general of Taiwan Association of Cloud Computing (TACC) from 2011 to 2015 and of AACT from 2013 to 2016. He was also a convener of the East Region of Service Science Society of Taiwan from 2014 to 2016.

Albert D. Piersson is an Assistant lecturer at the University of Cape Coast, Department of Imaging Technology and Sonography, Cape Coast, Ghana. He teaches 2 cohort undergraduate students pursuing Bachelor of Science in Diagnostic Imaging Technology, and Diagnostic Medical Sonography. He has extensive clinical experience in general radiography, computed tomography, fluoroscopy, magnetic resonance imaging, and ultrasound over a decade. He holds MSc in Magnetic Resonance Imaging from the Anglia Ruskin University, UK. He has published in Elsevier journals, and has presented scientific studies both locally and internationally. His research interests include MRI, Ultrasound, Pica, Geophagia, Brain, Maternal, and Child Health.

Aarthee R. under graduated in Mathematics from University of Madras, India, and post graduated in mathematics from Thiruvallur University, India. Currently, she works as a Research Associate of Mathematics department (School of Advanced Sciences), at Vellore Institute of Technology, India. Her research interest in Mathematical Modelling, Machine Learning, and Digital Forensics. She is working in the area of research in probabilistic models for analyzing and predicting the digital forensic crimes.

Kasarapu Ramani, Ph.D., is Professor at Department of Information Technology, Sree Vidyanikethan Engineering College (Autonomous), Tirupati with over 19 years of experience. She teaches Information technology courses to under graduate and post graduate students of Engineering. She is guiding 06 Ph. D scholars in the areas of Data Mining, Cloud Computing, Software Engineering, Image and Video Processing. She is the principal investigator for the UGC Minor project titled Fast Content -based Search, Navigation and Retrieval System for e-Learning. Reviewer for International Research Journal of Electrical and Electronics Engineering, and many International IEEE, and Springer conferences. She also published more than 15 research papers in Journals and Conferences.

Arulmurugan Ramu received his PhD. degrees in Information and Communication Engineering from Anna University, Chennai, Tamil Nadu, India. He is currently working as Assistant Professor in the Department of Information Technology, Bannari Amman Institute of Technology, Sathyamangalam, Tamil Nadu. His research interests include Digital Image Processing, Biomedical Image Processing Computer vision, pattern recognition, and machine learning.

Mamata Rath received her Ph.D (Comp.Sc) from Siksha 'O' Anusandhan University, India. She has completed her M.Tech in Computer Science from Biju Patnaik University of Technology, Odisha, India.She has been working as Assistant Professor at C.V.Raman College of Engineering (Dept. of I.T), Bhubaneswar,India and her research interests include Mobile Adhoc Networks Internet of Things and Computer Security.

Geetha S. received the B.E., and M.E., degrees in Computer Science and Engineering in 2000 and 2004,respectively, from the Madurai Kamaraj University and Anna University of Chennai, India. She obtained her Ph.D. Degree from Anna University in 2011. She has rich teaching and research experience of 15+ years. She has published more than 60 papers in reputed International Conferences and refereed Journals. She joins the review committee for IEEE Transactions on Information Forensics and Security and IEEE Transactions on Image Processing. Her research interests include steganography, steganalysis, multimedia security, intrusion detection systems, machine learning paradigms and information forensics. She is a recipient of University Rank and Academic Topper Award in B.E. and M.E. in 2000 and 2004 respectively. She is also the proud recipient of ASDF Best Academic Researcher Award 2013.

Gaurav Sharma is currently working as a postdoc researcher at Université libre de Bruxelles. He received his Ph.D and M.E degree in Computer Science & Engineering from Thapar University, Patiala, India. He had received M.Sc. as well as B.Sc. Degree from CCS University, Meerut, India. His area of interests is routing and security in Ad hoc networks.

Kavita Sharma is a PhD Scholar in the Department of Computer Engineering at National Institute of Technology, Kurukshetra, (Institution of National Importance) India. Her research area is Mobile Device/Smartphone Security under the Supervision of Dr. B. B. Gupta. In addition, she is also awarded Fellowship from Ministry of Electronics and Information Technology, government of India to carry her Doctoral research work. Previous to joining PhD, she has worked as an Assistant Professor in Dronacharya College of Engineering, Greater Noida, India and Lecturer in Northern India Engineering College, Delhi, India. She received the Master of Technology (M. Tech.) in Information Security from Ambedkar Institute technology of advanced communication technology and research, formally this institute is known as Ambedkar Institute of Technology affiliated with Guru Gobind Singh Indraprastha University, Delhi, India. She has completed her Bachelor of Technology (B. Tech.) in Information Technology from the I.M.S. Engineering College, Ghaziabad, India. She has published more than 25 research papers in International Journals and Conferences of high repute. She is member of IEEE, CSI-Life Member, The Society of Digital Information and Wireless Communications (SDIWC), Internet Society, Institute of Nanotechnology-Life Member, International Association of Engineers (IAENG)-Life Member, International Association of Computer Science and Information Technology (IACSIT), Computer Science Teachers Association (CSTA), International Association of Online Engineering (IAOE). She has actively participated in different faculty development programs. She has participated in different National & International Workshop. Her area of interest includes Information and Cyber Security, Mobile Computing, Android, Web Mining, Data Analytics and Machine Learning.

Nidhi Sindhwani is working as an Assistant Professor in Amity School of Engineering and Technology, New Delhi, India. She received B.Tech degree in Electronics and Communication from MDU Rohtak in 2004 and M.Tech in Signal Processing from MDU Rohtak in 2008. She has more than 11 years of teaching experience at the level of UG level at different institutes. She is currently pursuing the PhD degree in Wireless Communication at Punjabi university, Patiala, India.She is author/co-author of more than 20 scientific papers of the refereed Journals and International Conferences. Her research focuses on signal processing and wireless communication including MIMO OFDM, multiuser MIMO communications.

K. John Singh received Ph.D degree in the Faculty of Information and Communication Engineering from Anna University, Chennai, India in 2013. He received M.S degree in Information Technology from Manonmaniam Sundaranar University, Tirunelveli, India in 2002 and M.Tech degree in Computer and Information Technology from Center for Information Technology and Engineering, Manonmaniam Sundaranar University, Tirunelveli, India in 2004. Currently, he is working as Associate Professor in the School of Information Technology and Engineering, VIT University, Vellore, India. His research interests include Network and Information Security, Cloud Security and Image Processing. He has published several papers in journals and conferences.

Akash Sinha received his M.Tech. degree in Computer Engineering from National Institute of Technology Kurukshetra, India. He is currently pursuing his PhD from National Institute of Technology Patna, India. He also holds experience of Telecom Industry where he has worked in various domains such as 3G, LTE and Internet of Things. His main research areas include Internet of Things, Peer to Peer Networks, Adhoc Networks, Software Engineering, etc.

Sonam has completed her M.Tech in Information Security from Ambedkar Institute of Advance Communication Technology & Research (AIACTR), GGSIPU. She has completed her B. Tech in CSE from IMS Engineering College, UPTU. Her area of interest are wireless sensor networks, information security, web-attacks, operating system. She has published two research papers.

Aswin Sreeraj is currently doing B.Tech. (ECE) from G.B.Pant Engineering College, New Delhi, India. His areas of interests include Cyber Security, Network Forensics, Wireless Communication, Antenna, Biomedical Engineering, etc.

Saurabh Ranjan Srivastava completed his graduation in Computer Engineering stream from University of Rajasthan, Jaipur in year 2006 and M.Tech in Computer Engineering from Malviya National Institute of Technology, Jaipur in year 2013. With a teaching experience of 11 years at Swami Keshvanand Institute of Technology, Jaipur, currently he is pursuing Ph.D from Malviya National Institute of Technology, Jaipur. His research interests include cybersecurity, information retrieval, data mining and machine learning.

Jhum Swain is Ph.D Scholar at Siksha 'O' Anusandhan University, India. Her research interests include Mobile Adhoc Networks, Internet of Things and Computer Security. Her special interest lies in routing issues in Mobile Adhoc Networks.

Feroz Ahmad Tantray is pursuing his M.Tech from Galgotias University. His research interest includes Computer Network, Information Security and Mobile computing.

Sumit Kumar Yadav is currently a Research Scholar in Computer Science Department, USET, GSIPU Delhi, India. He received his BTech (CSE) and MS-InfoSec from Indian Institute of Information Technology-Allahabad, Uttar Pradesh, India. His research area includes data mining, sentiment analysis and opinion mining, fuzzy logic, network security, information security, soft computing. He has published more than twenty research papers in international journals and conferences.

Syeda Erfana Zohora received her B.E. degree in Computer Science and Engineering from Mysore University, Karnataka, India and M.S. in Software Systems from BITS Pilani, Rajasthan, India. She is pursuing her Ph.D Degree in the Dept. of Electronics from Mangalore University, Karnataka, India. She is currently working in the College of Information Systems, Taif University, Taif, Saudi Arabia. She is the member of the Editorial Review Board of International Journal of Ambient Computing and Intelligence (IGI Global), U.S., member of the Editorial Review Board of International Journal of Synthetic Emotions(IGI Global),U.S., Ad hoc member in Neural Computing and Applications(NCAA), Microscopic and Research Techniques-Wiley Online Library, Electrical Engineering, Springer Journal and International Journal in Global Information Systems(IJIM). Her research interest includes Network Forensic and Analysis Techniques, Synthetic Emotional Intelligence, Soft Computing Techniques, Artificial Neural Networks, Support Vector Machine, Fuzzy Logic, Image Processing, Artificial Intelligence and Machine Learning.

Index

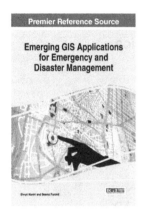
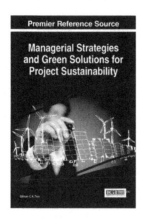

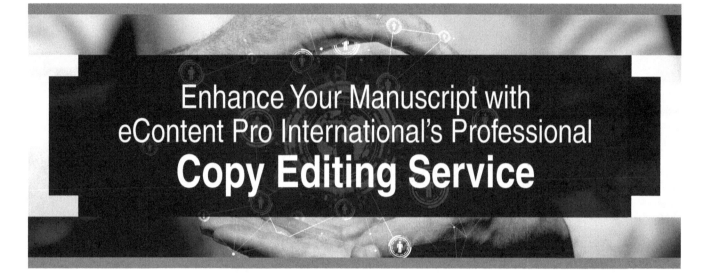

Printed in the United States
By Bookmasters